EMBATTLED

ECUMENISM

THE NATIONAL COUNCIL OF CHURCHES,
THE VIETNAM WAR,
AND THE TRIALS OF THE
PROTESTANT LEFT

JILL K. GILL

NIU PRESS / DeKalb

© 2011 by Northern Illinois University Press

Published by the Northern Illinois University Press, DeKalb, Illinois 60115

Manufactured in the United States using postconsumer-recycled, acid-free paper.

All Rights Reserved

Design by Julia Fauci

Library of Congress Cataloging-in-Publication Data

Gill, Jill K.

Embattled ecumenism : the National Council of Churches, the Vietnam War, and the trials of the Protestant left / Jill K. Gill.

   p.   cm.

Includes bibliographical references (p.   ) and index.

ISBN 978-0-87580-443-9 (clothbound : alk. paper)

1. National Council of the Churches of Christ in the United States of America—

History—20th century. 2. Vietnam War, 1961–1975—Religious aspects—Christianity.

3. United States—Church history—20th century. I. Title.

BX6.N2G55 2011

277.3'08206—dc22

2011014780

Frontispiece courtesy of CALC Records, Swarthmore College Peace Collection,

Swarthmore, PA

CONTENTS

ACKNOWLEDGMENTS

My immense gratitude extends to many who helped bring this twenty-year project to fruition. Foremost thanks go to those connected with the ecumenical enterprise who granted extended and multiple interviews, oftentimes opening their offices, guest rooms, and dinner tables to this former graduate student. The selfless generosity that I experienced time and again from this group moved me deeply. This list includes Ed Espy, Dean Kelley, Robert S. Bilheimer, Robert E. Bilheimer, Allan Parrent, Jim Hamilton, Alan Geyer, Gerhard Elston, Richard Fernandez, David Hunter, William P. Thompson, Herman Will, John McCullough, Robert Edgar, Paul Crow, and Ronald Stenning. The same gracious gift of time and information was also extended by former Secretary of State Dean Rusk. My special thanks also go to Sarah Vilankulu, the NCC's longtime communications expert, who helped me numerous times and from the very beginning to access materials and better understand the institutional ecumenical world. I am grateful as well for Philip Jenks's aid in securing photos and permissions. For their patient help and research assistance, I wish to thank staffs of the following archives: the Presbyterian Historical Society, the United Methodist General Commission on Archives and History, the Swarthmore College Peace Collection, Union Theological Seminary's Burke Library, the National Archives II, and the American Friends Service Committee Library, as well as staff at the National Council of Churches in New York and at its Washington office. For financial assistance, I thank the Louisville Institute, Boise State University (both the history department and dean's office of the College of Social Sciences and Public Affairs), the University of Findlay, the University of Pennsylvania's American Civilization Department, and the trust of L. Presley Gill.

A special thanks also to professional colleagues who lent their insights, expertise, and support to improving the manuscript and advising the author, including James Findlay, Darren Dochuk, Mitchell Hall, Patrick Henry, Nancy Ammerman, Rick Nutt, Michael Friedland, Judy Austin, Todd Shallat, Barbara Brown Zikmund, Mark Toulouse, David Settje, Gerald Sittser, Martin Marty, Chip Berlet, Melvyn Hammarberg, Don Yoder, Murray Murphey, and 2003 Louisville Institute Summer Stipend Fellows. For their patience and expertise in honing this work into publishable form, I am indebted to Mary Lincoln, Amy Farranto, Julia Fauci, and Susan Bean at Northern Illinois University Press, as well as to Sharon Matthies, whose keen editorial skills polished the manuscript and improved it in every way. I'm grateful as well to the editors of the *Journal of Presbyterian History*, *Religion and American Culture*, *Peace and Change: A Journal of Peace Research*, and *Methodist History* for kindly allowing me to publish here parts of articles that appeared within their covers. Friends lent invaluable support and insights through the years too, including Kathy Lee, Jim Hunt, Cindy Beal, Val Cerra, Mary Bear, Kate Crandall, Betty Beck, colleagues and students in Boise State's history department, and members of Boise's interfaith and human rights communities.

A most special thanks goes to my family, whose love, support, laughter, and hugs have sustained me, including Evelyn and Fred Maurmann, Vera and L. Presley Gill, Sharon Matthies, Evelyn and Bunk Troxell, and Larry Gill. To these, I owe all that I am.

ABBREVIATIONS USED IN TEXT

ACCC	American Council of Christian Churches
ADA	Americans for Democratic Action
AFSC	American Friends Service Committee
AIM	American Indian Movement
BIA	Bureau of Indian Affairs
CALCAV	Clergy and Laymen Concerned About Vietnam
CCIA	Commission of the Churches on International Affairs
CCUN	Church Center for the United Nations
CIA	Central Intelligence Agency
COs	conscientious objectors
COCU	Consultation on Church Union
CRS	Catholic Relief Services
CWS	Church World Service
DCLM	Division of Christian Life and Mission
DCS	Division of Church and Society
DOM	Division of Overseas Ministries
EACC	East Asia Christian Conference
FBI	Federal Bureau of Investigation
FCC	Federal Council of Churches
FCNL	Friends Committee on National Legislation
FOR	Fellowship of Reconciliation
GVN	Government of Vietnam
HUAC	House Un-American Activities Committee
IAC	International Affairs Commission
IRD	Institute on Religion and Democracy
IRS	Internal Revenue Service

IVS	International Voluntary Services
MOBE	National Mobilization Committee to End the War in Vietnam
NAE	National Association of Evangelicals
NCC	National Council of Churches
NGO	nongovernmental organizations
NLF	National Liberation Front
NSCF	National Student Christian Federation
POW	prisoners of war
PRC	People's Republic of China
PRG	Provisional Revolutionary Government
RCA	Reformed Church in America
SACSSAWR	Staff Advisory Committee on Selective Service and War Resistance
SACVN	Special Advisory Committee on Vietnam
SADIA	Staff Associates of Departments of International Affairs
SANE	Committee for a Sane Nuclear Policy
SCM	Student Christian Movement
UAW	United Auto Workers
UCC	United Church of Christ
UCM	University Christian Movement
UN	United Nations
USAID	United States Agency for International Development
UTS	Union Theological Seminary
VC	Vietcong
VEP	Vietnam Education Project
VNCS	Vietnam Christian Service
WCC	World Council of Churches
WSCF	World Student Christian Federation

EMBATTLED
ECUMENISM

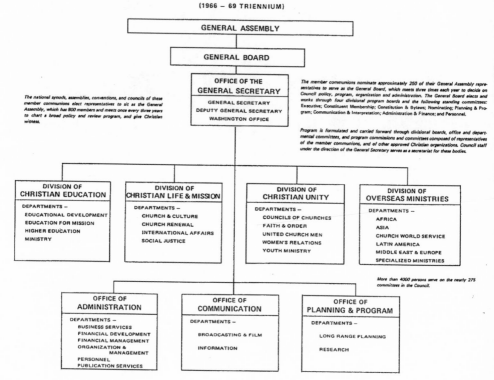

— Administrative Organization of —

NATIONAL COUNCIL OF THE CHURCHES OF CHRIST IN THE UNITED STATES OF AMERICA

(1966 — 69 TRIENNIUM)

GENERAL ASSEMBLY

GENERAL BOARD

OFFICE OF THE GENERAL SECRETARY
GENERAL SECRETARY
DEPUTY GENERAL SECRETARY
WASHINGTON OFFICE

The national synods, assemblies, conventions, and councils of these member communions elect representatives to sit as the General Assembly, which has 800 members and meets once every three years to chart a broad policy and review program, and give Christian witness.

The member communions nominate approximately 250 of their General Assembly representatives to serve as the General Board, which meets three times each year to decide on Council policy, program, organization and administration. The General Board elects and works through four divisional program boards and the following standing committees: Executive; Constituent Membership; Constitution & Bylaws; Nominating; Planning & Program; Communication & Interpretation; Administration & Finance; and Personnel.

Program is formulated and carried forward through divisional boards, office and departmental committees, and program commissions and committees composed of representatives of the member communions, and of other approved Christian organizations. Council staff under the direction of the General Secretary serves as a secretariat for these bodies.

DIVISION OF CHRISTIAN EDUCATION
DEPARTMENTS —
EDUCATIONAL DEVELOPMENT
EDUCATION FOR MISSION
HIGHER EDUCATION
MINISTRY

DIVISION OF CHRISTIAN LIFE & MISSION
DEPARTMENTS —
CHURCH & CULTURE
CHURCH RENEWAL
INTERNATIONAL AFFAIRS
SOCIAL JUSTICE

DIVISION OF CHRISTIAN UNITY
DEPARTMENTS —
COUNCILS OF CHURCHES
FAITH & ORDER
UNITED CHURCH MEN
WOMEN'S RELATIONS
YOUTH MINISTRY

DIVISION OF OVERSEAS MINISTRIES
DEPARTMENTS —
AFRICA
ASIA
CHURCH WORLD SERVICE
LATIN AMERICA
MIDDLE EAST & EUROPE
SPECIALIZED MINISTRIES

More than 4000 persons serve on the nearly 275 committees in the Council.

OFFICE OF ADMINISTRATION
DEPARTMENTS —
BUSINESS SERVICES
FINANCIAL DEVELOPMENT
FINANCIAL MANAGEMENT
ORGANIZATION & MANAGEMENT
PERSONNEL
PUBLICATION SERVICES

OFFICE OF COMMUNICATION
DEPARTMENTS —
BROADCASTING & FILM
INFORMATION

OFFICE OF PLANNING & PROGRAM
DEPARTMENTS —
LONG RANGE PLANNING
RESEARCH

NCC Organizational Chart, 1966–1969. (NCC Records, Presbyterian Historical Society, Presbyterian Church [USA], Philadelphia, PA)

Ecumenism and the Vietnam War

The fire will test what sort of work each has done.
—I Corinthians 12:13

The Christian Bible speaks of tests or trials by fire.[1] Ordeals test character, priorities, and perseverance. Fire can burn away surfaces, revealing the strengths and weaknesses of the core. The Vietnam War and the era that encompassed it were the most divisive since the Civil War, tearing Americans apart and violently unleashing their frustrations. For the National Council of the Churches of Christ in the USA (NCC), which was motivated by its ecumenical Christian vision to oppose that war and unify people, Vietnam and its convulsive era became the fire that challenged, splintered, and changed it.[2] The Council's efforts on the war exposed its strengths and imploded its weaknesses in ways instructive for religious institutions that bring their faith into politics. This book explores the ecumenical vision, anti–Vietnam War efforts, and consequent legacy of the NCC, serving as a window into mainline Protestants' manner of engaging political issues at a unique time of national crisis and religious transformation. It also strives to illuminate an ecumenical institution, a vision, and a movement that have been largely misrepresented by the religious right, dismissed by the secular left, misunderstood by laity, and ignored by scholars outside of ecumenical circles.

THE TURNING POINT, 1965

As 1965 dawned, the kum-ba-ya spirit of the early 1960s was wearing off. But the nation didn't yet know it. The civil rights movement was achieving major legislative victories, to which the NCC contributed.[3] With expansive optimism, President Lyndon Johnson promised to help create a Great Society that would eliminate poverty in America. Big government was in vogue; bureaucracies were tributes to modern managerial methods of problem-solving. The liberal establishment had reached its peak of cultural and political power. So too had the liberal mainline churches and their premier ecumenical organization, the National Council of Churches. The NCC represented over thirty Protestant and Orthodox denominations comprising more than forty million members, almost half of America's voters.[4] In service to the broader ecumenical movement, which fostered Christian unity, the NCC developed cooperative Christian responses to important social issues and personified the bureaucratic ideal. It also enjoyed a close working relationship with the White House on several measures and could get audiences with presidential administrations upon request. In fact, for decades, top politicians had recognized the Council as an influential organization to court. Republican President Dwight D. Eisenhower traveled to New York City to lay the cornerstone of the NCC's new headquarters, the Interchurch Center, in 1958. Going back at least to Franklin Roosevelt's administration, the NCC and its predecessor, the Federal Council of Churches, enjoyed presidential meetings, cabinet-level visits, and an intimate working relationship with those in the rising liberal establishment on a range of issues from labor unions to the United Nations, and from nuclear test ban treaties to civil rights.

This study ushers one into the prestigious "God Box," nickname for the Interchurch Center, where the NCC and several other church organizations generalled their operations. The location, 475 Riverside Drive in upper Manhattan, New York City, sat at the center of liberal religious power in America. Across the street stood the cathedral-like Riverside Church built by John D. Rockefeller. Its podium became a platform for such prominent liberal clergy as the Reverends Harry Emerson Fosdick, William Sloane Coffin Jr., and James Forbes. Other notables including Martin Luther King Jr. utilized it to make important speeches. Across the intersection, and kitty-corner to the NCC, cutting-edge theologians such as Reinhold Niebuhr, Paul Tillich, and John Bennett trained young ministers at Union

Theological Seminary. In the 1950s and 1960s, its reputation was among the finest, and most activist, in the nation. The influential Protestant journal *Christianity and Crisis* was published there.[5] Across the street from Union beamed another bastion of liberal thought, the Jewish Theological Seminary, which boasted a cadre of activist leaders including the esteemed Rabbi Abraham Heschel. In 1965 that two-block square of real estate was home to some of the most powerful religious entities in the nation.

As the year began, the Council felt muscular, motivated, and idealistic about its position and mission when, under President Johnson, Vietnam's civil war became America's military responsibility to win. The United States had been engaged in a troubled nation-building experiment there since the mid-1950s, but this drew only sporadic public attention until U.S. combat troops were first deployed later that spring and summer. Therefore, 1965 was a turning point. With it came the disastrous war in Vietnam, escalating protests at home, and the beginning of forty years in the wilderness for the Protestant left in America. Akin to the liberal political establishment, the NCC's leadership saw few clues to foreshadow the rapid loss of identity, clout, and resources that would plague the Protestant mainline by the time troops left Vietnam in 1973.[6]

Like most of the American public, mainline churches had largely ignored the Vietnam conflict until 1965. The NCC and its denominational members supported America's resistance to communism, but factions within the ecumenical community's leadership had already begun questioning the government's presuppositions underlying Cold War foreign policy. When the Vietnam conflict became America's latest military bulwark against communism, these factions pushed the NCC to take the prophetic lead by organizing church responses to the war. The NCC was the logical organization to do so, and its ecumenical vision compelled it to address this ambiguous war in a particular way.

Ecumenism is a complex, confusing concept. And this was part of the NCC's problem in the 1960s. On the one hand, ecumenism embodies a compelling ancient vision about the inherent unity and interdependence, not only of Christians but humanity.[7] It emphasizes community over self-interest, peaceful discussion over violence, collaboration over competition, universalism over exclusivity, the prophetic role of the church to "speak truth to power" over affirming an oppressive status quo, benevolence over individual acquisition, preaching social justice over mere personal piety, and the separation of church and state. Specifically within the Christian community (or "body of Christ"), groups sought to manifest their unity by forging common theological ground, understandings of mission, and biblically derived positions on social issues. On the other hand, in the mid-twentieth century, ecumenism came to be equated specifically with structural manifestations of unity. This included merging two or more denominations institutionally into one, or creating organizations such as the NCC that operated almost like a United Nations for American churches; it brought denominations together to debate, find consensus, collaborate on issues of common concern, and eventually pioneer productive relationships with other faiths. The NCC became a bloated bureaucracy of divisions, departments, committees, and task forces, all doing ecumenical work on behalf of the churches.

While the ecumenical *vision* motivated and shaped the NCC's response to Vietnam, few outside of its leadership circles understood what ecumenism was beyond its *structural* roles. Few also understood the specific feedback-loop process by which ecumenists believed that theological unity, social action, and church renewal should be wedded. ("Renewal" refers to the church's constant transformation process as it seeks to self-reflect, repent from past short-sightedness, and become more whole.) The NCC's international affairs staff saw the Vietnam War as a potential tool for teaching the ecumenical vision and transforming national worldviews. It also saw the war as a vehicle for strengthening the international ecumenical movement and renewing the American one. However, with the exception of expanding basic interdenominational and interfaith relationships, the NCC's international affairs director, Robert S. Bilheimer, feared that real ecumenism was actually lost during the Vietnam period. He felt that a combination of factors contributed to this, divesting ecumenism of its theological grounding, its interconnected process, and its full depth of meaning.

American ecumenical leaders spent too little time teaching ecumenism to both clergy and laity.[8] As a result, many parishioners assumed that ecumenism simply referred to cooperation or socialization between different religious groups. Interchurch collaboration can serve as one important baby step in the ecumenical process; but this does not encompass ecumenism by itself and may indeed occur totally apart from advancing full ecumenism. For example, conservative evangelical groups within the National Association of Evangelicals (NAE) have long cooperated with each other while at the same time opposing the ecumenical movement and vision.

Throughout the twentieth century, American ecumenical leaders have contributed to this general confusion by lacking unity themselves around the subject. In fact, I argue, the Vietnam War exposed and exacerbated factionalism within ecumenism. Leadership emphasized different aspects of ecumenism, divided internally over its meaning, and disagreed over how best to put it into practice. Splits widened between traditional ecumenists and activists called "new breeders," relief and social justice personnel, NCC staff and denominational secretaries, and more broadly, church leaders and laity. This was a major source of the NCC's problems in the Vietnam era and a catalyst for its subsequent structural transformations. In addition, the bureaucratic, top-down, corporate style of mid-twentieth-century ecumenism came under sharp attack from the left and right in the 1960s when Americans began to question authority, including the liberal establishment of which the NCC had been a part. When people lost faith in elite white-male-dominated institutions, subsequently rebelling against them, and when ecumenists became obsessed with restructuring them amid steep declines in resources, the full ecumenical vision that had once animated the NCC became a displaced, sometimes forgotten or discredited casualty in church circles. The internal divisions within ecumenism, and the winners and losers among them, contributed to this. Unceasing attacks by conservatives took their toll, too. This was especially true when conservative Republican and religious visions rose politically in the wake of the war, becoming largely hegemonic, while their champions replaced both liberal political and religious groups as the establishment's new power brokers. In fact, the NCC has lived its entire life in the crosshairs of conservatives eager not only to criticize it but to destroy it and the ecumenical movement it advocates.

My main point here is that ecumenism is a critical component to understanding how and why the mainline Protestant churches responded to the Vietnam War, and their successes and failures in doing so. The NCC's particular ecumenical identity and motivations made it different from most antiwar groups. Additionally, internal struggles within ecumenical circles help explain difficulties experienced by the NCC, and more broadly the Protestant left. Books about 1960s-era transformations within mainline religion have often skirted lightly across the surface of ecumenism, while histories of the anti–Vietnam War movement have often neglected the role of official church institutions.[9] This study helps address both subjects through its examination of the National Council of Churches.

In addition, several texts exist on the ecumenical movement, but the vast majority were written by seminary-trained insiders for other insiders, or by conservatives seeking to vilify it.[10] Rather, I approach this subject as an interested outsider, as a U.S. history professor seeking to integrate discussions of ecumenism into discourses of American religious history, post–World War II U.S. history, and specifically the anti–Vietnam War movement, for it has been an important player within those fields. More broadly, the ecumenical vision and the NCC's specific history wrestling with the U.S. government, conservatives, and itself over foreign policy are relevant today for those engaged in the interplay of religion and politics.

My focus hones tightly in on the NCC, not the entirety of the American ecumenical movement. Nevertheless, since that organization operated as the movement's flag-bearer and operational center on national issues, it serves as a useful window into the movement's worldview, priorities, actions, and problems. It's an eastern elite view to be sure, much like a peek within the Pentagon or White House would be of military or political action on Vietnam. Yet, such a look is worthwhile given the NCC's once central, generously resourced, and politically connected place within American mainline Protestantism.

In 1965, three influences shaped the NCC's initial agenda with respect to the Vietnam War. First, its own history and that of the ecumenical movement created precedents in terms of what it felt it should and could do. A half century of ongoing ecumenical developments in worldview via theological discussions, and volumes of positions amassed on sociopolitical issues, created a directional vector for the NCC when approaching Vietnam. So, too, did its own experiences—and that of its predecessor, the Federal Council of Churches—as they tackled particular events such as World War I, the labor movement, the Great Depression, World War II, the Cold War, McCarthyism, and civil rights. The Federal and National Councils' perceived successes in advocating legislatively for and mobilizing laity around the creation of the United Nations and civil rights laws created high expectations within leadership circles for what the NCC might be able to accomplish on the Vietnam War. These also affected how some people thought it should approach that work.

Second, its ecumenical vision affected how it responded to the war. Ecumenism stresses transcending cultural biases through listening to others; creating a church witness that speaks its truth to power; remaining separate from government, political parties, and cultural bandwagons in order to preserve its voice and identity as the church, yet engaging secular forces to advance sought-after results; educating others through open dialogue; serving those hurt by unjust policies; directly opposing those policies through action; and renewing the church constantly via self-criticism, repentance, and transformation while being "salt" and "light" to the broader world. These elements within the NCC's vision led it to take the following kinds of actions on the war. It listened to a wide variety of perspectives when processing the Vietnam conflict, including those of government officials, military commanders, journalists, church leaders, and civilian experts from the United States, North and South Vietnam, other Asian nations, and Europe. Based upon this gathered information, ecumenical leaders debated, crafted, and updated positions that were then communicated to laity and pressed before policy makers. The NCC's international affairs director employed tactics he hoped would influence the White House to change course in Vietnam, but he assiduously resisted ones that might compromise its ecumenical identity as a voice of the church. NCC leaders also collaborated with other church and secular organizations on antiwar efforts that fit within the Council's policy mandate. Its staff worked with them to oppose specific war-related policies considered immoral or unjust. Simultaneously, and in tandem with its denominations, the NCC pursued a vigorous "debate and action" educational program designed to motivate laity to discuss and take action on the war. Meanwhile, the Council created and participated in programs designed to meet the needs of persons put in jeopardy by the war, in both the United States and Vietnam. Finally, it viewed its own work and structure with a self-critical eye. It remained open to others' criticism and transformed itself where its leaders believed they heard God's challenge to change. In these ways, the NCC's actions on Vietnam reflected its ecumenical vision.

Third, the Council's structure limited what it could do to implement its vision with respect to Vietnam. The NCC's denominational member churches, not parishioners, were its direct clients. Therefore, the leaders of those denominations largely funded and made NCC policy. They also tended to be more liberal than the majority of laity. They wanted the NCC to serve as the denominations' "snowplow" on controversial issues, stepping out ahead to blunt icy winds and clear a path for them on stormy topics. In addition, the mandates that came from the NCC's General Board and General Assembly restricted what the Council's staff could do. Denominational leaders served on these, so their votes birthed those mandates. Thus, the NCC's prophetic mission came from the denominations.

The NCC could only create programs and implement actions in line with policy directives. Therefore, consensus among the leaders within its thirty-plus denominations had to be developed on the war before it could act. The NCC provided a unique forum in which diverse church executives could debate and persuade each other on difficult issues, then create joint plans for action. Yet, when consensus emerged, it was usually more liberal than (and emerged far in advance of) lay opinion. This frequently put the NCC on a collision course with an increasingly vocal and angry lay population—one from which it was already bureaucratically distanced.

As time passed, circumstances changed, and ecumenical leaders learned new information about the war; therefore, the NCC continually altered and updated its positions, actions, and strategies. It discovered quickly that Vietnam was a tougher and murkier issue, both politically and morally, than civil rights. On Vietnam, the NCC faced a hostile White House, had its patriotism questioned, and found it harder to access information. Also, whereas the liberal Christian moral position on civil rights appeared singular and clear (at least in 1965), the Christian community struggled to navigate two competing moral arguments made about the war.[11] For example, some Christians asserted that communism was evil; therefore America's struggle in Vietnam was justified to support the freedom of South Vietnamese citizens against communist aggression. Others charged America with acting like an imperial power, forcing its will upon a people who rejected its interference in their struggle for independence from foreign control. From this vantage point, America's unilateral military effort in Vietnam failed to fit Christian "just war" criteria, and potentially courted World War III.[12] A third group of ecumenical leaders tried to juxtapose truths they found in both positions.

Complicating matters further, the NCC was responding to the war amid a swirl of cultural change, polarization, political upheaval, and a crisis within mainline Protestantism that saw sharp drops in resources, morale, authority, and clout. At times it was an accomplice mired in problems that needed attention; in other instances it offered a courageous, open, and savvy example of how to manage religious-political challenges in the Vietnam era. All of the above make the Vietnam War a particularly revelatory case study for observing the escalating tribulations that confounded American ecumenism as well as ecumenism's underappreciated strengths. The legacies and lessons of both are relevant to the current religious-political scene, and to those seeking to affect it, whether from the left or right.

SOURCES AND METHODOLOGY

This study focuses fairly exclusively on the ecumenical work of the NCC itself. It does not claim or attempt to represent the independent efforts of the Council's thirty-plus denominations on Vietnam. I have limited my research to the NCC's programs and projects, which of course required denominational resources, staff, input, and approval. Therefore, the majority of my sources come from the NCC's own massive repository of records. However, since the powerful Methodist and Presbyterian Churches were among those most widely involved in the Vietnam work, I explored their denominational journals and materials, too. I sought particularly to gauge the perspectives of their leaders and local clergy with respect to the Council and the war. In addition, I accessed supplementary materials at other sites and conducted interviews with people who provided a variety of denominational and ecumenical vantage points. They infused flesh and blood into the story and offered invaluable insights into the feelings, stress points, relationships, and priorities of these volatile years. To gain a broader ecumenical perspective on the war, I reviewed the movement's two main independent journals, the *Christian Century* and *Christianity and Crisis*, and selectively perused publications from various mainstream and religious media.

ORGANIZATION

The NCC's story unfolds chronologically to capture the chaotic cause-and-effect escalation of events as its staff experienced them. This approach aims to unveil the cumulative nature of how the Council's understanding of the war developed and official positions came into being. It also conveys a sense of how church organizations functioned in real time. The goal is to supply readers with what cultural anthropologists call emic and etic perspectives. "Emic" refers to understanding a culture from within, as an insider might; "etic" refers to an outsider's scholastic analysis. The narrative approach aims to blend the two in order to enhance both historical and ethnographic understanding.

In addition to an introduction, epilogue, and appendix, this book contains five major sections that demark important trends, eras, or shifts in strategy for the Council. Part One provides background on ecumenism and the NCC, setting the stage for major narrative threads in the book. It introduces Robert S. Bilheimer and Gerhard Elston, two of the NCC's main players with respect to the Vietnam War. Particular experiences, events, and theological ideas shaped their understanding of ecumenism, the relationship between church and state, and the role of the church in the world. These experiences typified those of the generation that helped birth and govern the World and National Councils of Churches. This section also highlights precedent-setting historical moments for the Federal and National Councils, with an emphasis upon U.S. foreign policy from 1908 to 1963. It describes the influence the Councils enjoyed both with government and the grass roots during those years, as well as their active engagement with political issues, their top-down style of leadership, their positions on issues of war, peace, dissent, and communism, the nature of right-wing attacks against them, their image battles, and the rising activism of new breed clergy on civil rights. The section concludes with brief background on the Vietnam conflict before 1963.

Part Two covers the period from 1964 to 1965 when the ecumenical community struggled to evaluate Lyndon Johnson on foreign policy as he moved the nation from an advisory to a combat role in Vietnam. It also chronicles the NCC's cautious initial reactions to the war spearheaded by its longtime International Affairs director, Ken Maxwell. A coalition of forces merged, questioning Maxwell's close relationship with the State Department and his ability to lead prophetically on Vietnam, forcing him out of office and pushing the NCC toward its first major critical statement on the war.

Part Three covers 1966 to 1968 when the NCC's new International Affairs director, Robert Bilheimer, worked to develop a broad ecumenical witness on the war. His team tried reasoned arguments, detailed data, and peer appeals to persuade the Johnson administration to change its policy. Bilheimer and Secretary of State Dean Rusk each attempted to woo the other into questioning their respective assumptions about the war. When these efforts failed, the NCC's clout with the White House faded. The Council also began cooperating with antiwar groups and struggled to stimulate local Christians to debate and act upon the war. It made contacts with church councils in other nations, utilized data from international sources, and grew aware of how its connections with the U.S. government threatened its ecumenical image overseas. The NCC also engaged in election-year politics during 1968. Tensions within the ecumenical community produced internal rifts while the laity's anti-authoritarian rebellion against church leadership exploded.

Part Four covers 1969, the most chaotic and disruptive year for the NCC during the war. Early months inspired hope. The war seemed to be winding down and the new president, Richard Nixon, appeared interested in NCC input. But hope proved illusory as Nixon escalated the war and dismissed the NCC's carefully crafted recommendations for facilitating peace with a contemptuousness that stunned Council leaders. The Nixon administration became the target of a rejuvenated antiwar movement in which the NCC participated with more energy, critical bite, and breadth than ever before. However, the Council also found itself under siege from secular and religious groups on the left and right. Disgruntled impatient young activists and conservative laity both withdrew support from organized ecumenism. Nixon's appeals for a resurgence of power for America's "silent majority" paralleled similar sentiments within the churches. Major Protestant denominations, such as the Methodist and Presbyterian Churches, were splitting along conservative and liberal fault lines manifested by the culture wars, making denominational identities often less definitive or important than ideological ones. Within the NCC, all of these reactions stimulated considerable frustration, critical introspection, and questions about the organization's future. Morale among church leaders plummeted amid the chaos and infighting even as the denominations were largely united in opposition to the war, and as the Council stepped further to the left to address social justice and peace issues.

Part Five covers the period from 1970 to 1973 that inspired a new NCC strategy. The Council abandoned its practical, advisory, White House appeals in order to organize a massive moral indictment against the war. It sought to generate a worldwide religious censure that would strip Nixon of his moral authority and dash assumptions that God blessed America's battles in Vietnam. In doing so, the Council tried to transform America's failure there into a redemptive opportunity for the nation. It hoped the disaster in Vietnam might awaken U.S. citizens to their nation's ability to sin, as well as to America's need for repentance, reflection, and growth with respect to its identity and role in the world. The Council also refocused its appeals onto Congress, hoping the legislative branch might stop the executive's ability to continue the war. Meanwhile, the rapid decline of mainline Protestant finances, members, and goodwill distressed those within NCC and denominational headquarters. The denominations retrenched, forcing the Council to trim programs, lay off staff, and restructure. As the Paris Peace Accords ended U.S. military involvement in Vietnam, and as Nixon reeled under Watergate allegations, several of the NCC's leaders on Vietnam departed the Council feeling tired, bitter, and defeated. Bilheimer believed that, in the Vietnam era, the NCC had abandoned its understanding of real ecumenism and, hence, had lost sight of itself just as had the nation.

A detailed epilogue traces Vietnam-era themes through the NCC's tribulations and transformations from 1973 to 2010. In the appendix that follows, I use the NCC's history to assess its Vietnam-related work, explore explanations for its ensuing difficulties, address common critiques of the Council, and offer reflections relevant to the contemporary political-religious scene.

A BRIEF PROLOGUE—AMERICAN CHRISTIANITY SPLITS INTO "LEFT" AND "RIGHT"

What gave rise to the modern "liberal" and "conservative" factions within American Christianity that stir the nation's culture wars? Most religion scholars trace them back to the Modernist-Fundamentalist controversy of the early twentieth century.[13] For those unfamiliar with this history, it is worth a brief overview, for the NCC was born from Christianity's liberal wing. Understanding its birth and characteristics helps frame the larger story.

From the late nineteenth century through the 1920s, the Modernist-Fundamentalist controversy engulfed many of America's Protestant churches. Momentous changes in academic knowledge and modern culture split the Christian community. Most significantly, Darwinist theories in biology along with discoveries in new academic fields such as anthropology, archeology, comparative religion, and linguistics raised questions about the historical and scientific validity of information in the Bible. Panic set in among Christians who feared that doubting the inerrancy of scripture might doom their religion. Others feared for Christianity's future if it failed to account for and adapt its understanding of the Bible to incorporate modern knowledge.

Conservatives clung to professions of biblical inerrancy and asserted that true believers must interpret the Bible literally or forfeit their claim to the religion. Liberals chose to amend their understanding of the Bible, seeing it as a book of faith rather than history or science. In other words, it contained God's enduring spiritual truths but also human errors, allegorical stories, and cultural biases. As such, it should be read in a manner that gleaned spiritual principles from the text while taking account of its cultural, historical, and political contexts and the human factors within them. Along with scripture, liberals also utilized reason, personal experience, and church traditions to help them interpret the divine will. They felt they were holding truer to the Bible's actual design and intent than conservatives who tried sometimes to drive liberals out of their pulpits through heresy trials. After five decades of struggle, liberals dominated most of the leadership positions within mainline Protestant denominations, colleges, and seminaries. In turn, some conservatives began building Bible schools, colleges, and denominations of their own, while others stayed within the mainline fold to continue the fight there. Fundamentalists took their name from the fact that they strove to boil down the Christian belief system to rock-solid fundamentals.[14] Anyone who did not adhere to their set of doctrines could not rightly call themselves Christian. Fundamentalists also promoted separation from those who did not profess their version of the faith. The more moderate and less separatist of them would eventually create the neo-evangelical movement.

Another issue dividing Christian conservatives and liberals was the church's proper response to modern culture, which had grown more secular and influential in people's lives. Adhering to the biblical directive to be "in the world, but not of it," conservatives remained suspicious of secular culture and politics. These seemed full of worldly temptations that threatened to corrupt the purity they sought to maintain. Conversely, liberals saw God as operating through and within modern culture; therefore they advocated that Christians engage it and American political life with the hope of doing God's work in the world. Liberals were often called "modernists" because of their positive view of modern culture.

The famous Scopes Trial (1925)—in which John Scopes was convicted for breaking Tennessee's ban on teaching evolution in its public schools—further polarized religious conservatives and liberals. In the 1920s, the U.S. population became more urban than rural. When Scopes appeared to win the support of most urban Americans, who also seemed more "secular," many conservative religious leaders took this as confirmation of America's moral downfall. They urged their flocks to focus on saving souls while preparing for Jesus' impending return, thus leaving politics to the more tainted, worldly, religious liberals.[15] (Many conservatives also believed that converting souls would reform society as a by-product.) Conversely, religious liberals embraced interaction with modern culture and politics. Many claimed the label "progressive," which denoted their confidence in human progress and their sense that people could transform the world, through practical Christian-motivated reforms, into the kingdom of God. They also spread a "social gospel" that addressed systemic social sins, such as human exploitation by institutional powers, rather than merely individual immoralities; for individual conversions had often failed to change systemic oppression. Christians were called to love their neighbors by helping them secure a decent existence in this life as well as the next. The "social gospelers," often called "praying progressives," were part of the broader Progressive movement advocating measures such as child labor laws, government reforms, and anti-trust legislation. To them, the shift from an individual-focused faith to a social Christianity where human needs trumped human greed helped Christianity rediscover its original spirit.

Shortly before mid-century a group of evangelicals—who held fast to their belief in an inerrant Bible and the core doctrines of fundamentalist Christianity—left their more strident, separatist colleagues to form a neo-evangelical movement. While asserting their primary mission of saving souls, they shed the fundamentalists' harsher tones. Like liberals, they also felt called to work through the culture, using it to spread the gospel and do Christian good works, but they remained critical of secular culture and the ecumenical actions and beliefs of liberal Christians, which seemed too worldly.[16]

The development of different civil religions also distinguished the Protestant right and left in the twentieth century. A "civil religion" encompasses the general religious terms, expectations, understandings, and visions that citizens apply to their nation. It reflects a religious-toned nationalism that often engenders patriotism and unity. America's earliest civil religion stemmed from the notion that God harbored a special purpose for America: to be a leader for, an example to, and even a redeemer of other nations, religiously, politically, and economically. According to this, America was special in God's eyes and existed to serve God's purposes on Earth. It became God's right arm in fulfilling the divine plan for humankind. America was special because, to many conservatives, it was and had always been a Christian nation, decreed so by its founders, whom they almost deified. Most American Protestants in the nineteenth century adhered to this patriotic-religious vision. So too did most Christians who supported the Vietnam War. However, according to sociologist Robert Wuthnow, Christian liberals helped shape a second, alternative, civil religion in the twentieth century. They infused it with the ecumenical spirit. Their religious vision for the nation rested upon expectations that America, with its many blessings, should indeed be a world leader, but by serving humanity rather than trying to dominate it politically, militarily, or economically. In fact, this vision emphasized God's love for humanity over any sense that America was uniquely chosen of God. It also stressed that America was part of a community of nations; it had the responsibility to help ease human problems and facilitate justice, both because of its blessings and because at times it had contributed to others' suffering through imperialist acts to build power rather than peace. This civil religion lifted up biblical prophets as examples, along with people such as Gandhi and Mother Teresa, who spoke truth to power and called for justice as a sign of obedience to God. This alternative version echoed through the positions of Christians who opposed U.S. military policy in Vietnam.[17]

The Federal and National Councils of Churches stand within the liberal Christian tradition. While the NCC's Orthodox and historically African American churches might exempt themselves, given their own distinctive paths, most of its Protestant denominations positioned their organizations within the liberal wing of Protestant Christianity. Indeed the creation of the FCC and NCC were intended, in part, to bring their cooperative good works to bear upon modern culture and life. Christian liberals and conservatives often tempered their positions as events and new ideas challenged them. Many liberals, for example, became more "realistic" and less optimistic about human culture with the advent of the Great Depression, World War II, and neo-orthodox theology. Nevertheless, the social gospel tradition also retained a strong hold on them. As the political liberal establishment rose to power with Franklin Roosevelt, liberal religious organizations also grew in prominence, often collaborating with that political establishment on issues of mutual concern.

My use of the terms "Protestant left" and "Christian liberal" refer to Christians who fell theologically toward the modernist side of the modernist-fundamentalist split, and whose political beliefs often reflected a moderate-to-liberal progressive agenda. This included a belief that government (and the church, for that matter) should help ensure justice for the most vulnerable Americans, that *unregulated* capitalism threatened both democracy and Christian values, and that peace and world order should be pursued through international organizations, international law, and diplomacy rather than military means whenever possible. Many in the Protestant left also clung to the liberal belief that reason and good data could educate people into changing behavior as well as persuade leaders to make policy changes.

It is important to note that the leadership ranks of the FCC and NCC contained both life-long Democrats and Republicans. For example, Arthur Flemming, the NCC's president during the heat of America's escalation in Vietnam, was a devoted Republican. However, since Jerry Falwell's Moral Majority helped inspire religious conservatives to engage public politics en masse behind a Republican presidential candidate in 1979, the Republican Party moved to the right and made Christian conservatives one of its key voter bases. While a vocal minority of liberal-leaning evangelical Christians exists, several past NCC leaders mourned the fact that the once sizeable body of progressive Christian Republicans, from which the NCC formerly drew many staffers, no longer thrives in America.[18]

Now, to weave ecumenism into this story: by 1900, Christianity possessed a long, fractious, violent history that had splintered the faith into hundreds of competing denominations. This inspired the creation of the ecumenical movement around the dawn of the twentieth century, and it blossomed in the years between the Great Depression and the Vietnam War. It emerged from the desire that Christians should rediscover their inherent God-given unity with one another as the living "body of Christ" in the world. The term "ecumenical" comes from the Greek word "oikoumene," which means "the whole inhabited earth." Therefore, Christian unity and the movement's work include the entire world. Protestant liberals embraced this movement most strongly, for they sought theological dialogue and practical cooperation on projects with members of other Protestant churches. Indeed, two prominent branches of early ecumenism were called the "Faith and Order" movement, which nurtured unity through theological and doctrinal discussions, and the "Life and Work" movement, which emphasized joint work in the world, often for social justice and peace.[19]

Christian conservatives, who guarded their spiritual purity through separation from the wayward, were not drawn to this ecumenical vision. Instead, fundamentalists and evangelicals each created their own umbrella organizations to bring their churches together for fellowship and cooperation. These include the fundamentalist American Council of Christian Churches (ACCC) and the National Association of Evangelicals (NAE). But these have defined themselves intentionally as associations or fellowships of churches, not as a movement with an ecumenical vision. In fact, while the NAE recognizes the unity of the body of Christ (that is, fellow believers of its accepted doctrines), historically it has not used the word "ecumenical" to describe its vision or mission.[20] Therefore, I employ this word exclusively to refer to the mainline Protestant ecumenical movement as embodied by the Federal, National, and World Councils of Churches.[21]

The ecumenical vision ignited the imaginations of future NCC leaders such as Robert Bilheimer and Gerhard Elston in the 1930s and 1940s while the Nazis stormed across Europe. At that time, churches sought to play a unifying, peacemaking, justice-facilitating global role that governments seemed incapable of alone. Bilheimer's and Elston's exposure to, conception of, and professional paths within ecumenism typified those of many traditional ecumenists working within the major ecumenical councils. Therefore, a detailed look at their journeys sheds light upon the worldview and events that motivated later actions and tensions on Vietnam.

PART ONE

AMERICAN

ECUMENISM AND

INTERNATIONAL AFFAIRS,

1908–1963

CHAPTER ONE

The Roots of Ecumania

For just as the body is one and has many members, and all the members of the
body, though many, are one body, so it is with Christ. . . . Now you are the body of
Christ and individually members of it.

—1 Corinthians 12:12, 27

As autumn leaves floated downward on Yale's campus in 1936, Robert Bilheimer was ecumenically reborn. The sophomore had been complaining
vehemently about the church. His friend Fay Campbell sought clarifica-
tion. "What do you mean by the church?" asked the Student Christian
Movement (SCM) secretary. "These local churches and their denominations," Bilheimer retorted. Campbell countered with a different definition. "The church is the Body of Christ," the people of God. Bilheimer
fell silent, for that view of church hadn't resonated with him before. Now
it transformed his understanding of the Christian faith and, for the first
time, ignited real passion for it within him. "That concept . . . burned its
way into my mind and soul," he explained. "That new vision produced a
wholly new seriousness about 'church,' 'ministry,' and the Christian faith
itself. I no longer saw these as optional or peripheral. . . . I had had, quite
unwittingly, a classic SCM experience."[1]

Bilheimer began exploring the ecumenical way of being Christian.
He learned to see the church not simply as bricks and mortar or divided

denominations but rather as a worldwide "people amidst peoples" called to transcend individualism, nationalism, and culture.[2] Ecumenists believed that God had already given *spiritual* unity to the church; the interconnected body of Christ existed in God's eyes despite its schismatic divisions. Like the scattered pieces of a mosaic that discover their fullest shape only when joined together, ecumenists believed that each Christian faction needed the gifts of the others in order to be the church as God intended. When they transcended their cultures and truly listened to each other, ecumenists trusted that Christians globally could find some theological unity, some consensus, on the interconnected issues affecting humankind. They strove therefore to communicate to the world with one voice while holding their ecclesiastical differences in creative tension. These ideas resonated with Bilheimer, and spreading this form of Christian good news became his life's mission.

He joined the budding ecumenical movement, which was reconceptualizing the meaning of church and its relationship to society. The movement merged two formerly independent but interconnected branches. The "Faith and Order" movement challenged Christians to discuss their doctrinal differences, seeking unity there; the "Life and Work" movement joined Christians together to do the good works commanded by Christ, making their faith relevant to people's daily lives.[3] Both were central to the church's identity and power. Ecumenists saw good works as a tangible expression of theological beliefs, giving them life. These beliefs in turn gave reason, meaning, and motive to the church's actions. Therefore, the ecumenical vision asserted that theological discussions, public witness, service actions, and church renewal were all interdependent and mutually reinforcing.

In the mid-1930s, enthusiastic ecumenical leaders across the globe were formalizing their movement by creating an organized international body, a process that eventually flowered in the 1948 dedication of the World Council of Churches (WCC). The young Bilheimer played a critical role in the WCC's formation, as it did in his. Shortly thereafter, in 1950, American ecumenists revamped their own overly stretched ecumenical body, the Federal Council of Churches, by merging it with other service and mission organizations to establish the National Council of the Churches of Christ in the United States of America (NCC). Bilheimer worked successively for both organizations, and throughout his career, he promoted the World Council's traditional vision of ecumenism described above. In fact, when

Bilheimer directed the NCC's International Affairs Commission during the Vietnam War, he put together a team so devoted to this vision that they were playfully, and sometimes pejoratively, called "ecumaniacs."[4]

Born in 1917 to Gus Bilheimer, a secretary of the Young Men's Christian Association (YMCA), Robert was first exposed to ecumenical activities in his childhood home. John R. Mott visited frequently. The inspirational YMCA leader had birthed three worldwide ecumenical organizations, including the World Student Christian Federation (WSCF) in which Bilheimer truly learned what the ecumenical perspective meant to Christian faith.[5] The SCM connected Bilheimer with a generation of serious young Christians in the 1930s who felt moved to apply their faith to a world scarred by the Great Depression, New Deal controversies, one world war, and the threat of another. They did so with students from other SCM groups around the world, free from outside ecclesiastical control.

The Student Christian Movement was a seedbed and training ground for many of ecumenism's foremost leaders after World War II. There they gained a deep appreciation for ecclesiastical, ethnic, and cultural diversity within the global body of Christ. As Bilheimer wrote, "we received an enlarged view of the church as not merely institution . . . but as movement combined with institution. Either side without the other suffered."[6] Several who shared the SCM experience ultimately found vocations administering those institutions.

Bilheimer's life wove through the crystallizing events of ecumenism's institutional formation. These influences refined his ideas about ecumenism and how it should do its work. His career path also typified that of many ecumenical leaders of the 1960s. This included student movement involvement, seminary or graduate training at one of the nation's preeminent liberal, urban, theological or professional schools, experience working overseas, and commitment to a bureaucratic rather than a ministerial career track.[7]

Bilheimer's journey to the NCC included each of these. At Yale (1935–1939), he served as president of its SCM. As a Yale divinity student (1941–1945), he became a graduate secretary of the Interseminary Movement, the "SCM" for theological schools, while studying under H. Richard Niebuhr. Bilheimer called Niebuhr "my great professor," one who "exercised more influence on my thinking in life than any other." Bilheimer absorbed Niebuhr's lesson that the church's real power resided in asserting its mission as the divinely inspired transcender and transformer of culture.

This required church resistance to cultural accommodation while recognizing Christ's ability to change the culture through the church's active engagement in it.[8]

After ordination in the Presbyterian Church in the United States of America in 1945, Bilheimer sought employment within ecumenical organizations, partly because this freed him from the confines of denominational isolation.[9] To his delight, the national Interseminary Movement, then chaired by Henry Pitney Van Dusen, appointed him executive secretary (1945–1948).[10] Impressed by his intellect and skill at coordinating large student movement conferences, Van Dusen recommended to W.A. Visser 't Hooft (general secretary of the World Council's Provisional Committee) that he hire Bilheimer to plan the visitors' program for the WCC's founding assembly in Geneva, Switzerland. Visser 't Hooft described the young man as a gifted "ecumenical engineer," and Bilheimer agreed that what he desired "more than anything else [was] to help make the 'ecumenical' happen."[11] The WCC's birth in 1948 generated worldwide excitement and received front page attention in the New York Times. The organizational conference pattern that Bilheimer helped establish in Geneva became the prototype used for over thirty years.[12]

International conferences were ecumenism's primary tool for inducing the communication, study, and planning necessary for its organizational growth. Major conferences occurred every few years, and Bilheimer attended each one between 1945 and 1966 before joining the NCC.[13] He thrived in them. They drew together prominent church leaders to debate and determine the theological groundings of an ecumenical witness on key issues. Participants then recommended actions consonant with that witness. Generally, they communicated their conclusions through formal mimeographed statements, filled with cerebral language, which they distributed through denominational channels to local churches. While this top-down method of discernment, decision-making, and communication would become problematic in the anti-authoritarian 1960s, one cannot overstate the importance of such meetings to furthering church work. For religious leaders who operated in an oral and idea-based culture, these gatherings helped hone their thinking about issues and create effective coalitions.[14]

After the World Council's founding, Bilheimer stayed on staff until 1963. He served first as program director in New York City from 1948 to 1953 while pastoring a largely black congregation in Jamaica, New York, on weekends. The WCC then promoted him to associate general secretary in Geneva.[15] Bilheimer admired the early "ecumenical giants," as he called them, who created and administered both the World and National Councils of Churches in their infancies; Visser 't Hooft and Van Dusen became models and mentors. He relished the thrill of establishing this worldwide movement in the volatile postwar era.

The WCC's birth catalyzed those involved because it demonstrated the reality of these ecumenists' deepest ideals: that people could put aside their differences, move beyond parochial selfishness, and unite to benefit the universal "brotherhood of man."[16] The intention was not to create a single super church, as detractors have claimed but, rather, to respect ecclesiastical and cultural differences while recognizing "the universalism of their faith." Bilheimer wrote that, for many ecumenists living in war-torn Europe, the international crises of the 1930s and 1940s disillusioned them about nationalism and the culture-bound church while enhancing their appreciation for each other's membership in the peoplehood of God. "A new perception of the universalism of God-in-Christ produced among these Christians a self-transcendence that has become a chief animating force in ecumenical development."[17] Bilheimer called the period "terribly exciting; terrific!"[18] The newly formed United Nations, which the ecumenical movement helped birth, was also trying to facilitate unity on a political level. Therefore, the traditional idea of ecumenism emerged from this sober yet heady moment in history when world wars and economic depression had made international cooperation a source of hope and victory over the destructive path of militaristic nationalism.

Bilheimer's Geneva years were the most fulfilling of his professional life. Although the WCC's headquarters was small then, he experienced the ecumenical church as a force that could challenge principalities and powers. A personal high point occurred in 1960. Shortly after the massacre of anti-apartheid protesters in Sharpeville, South Africa, and against all odds, Bilheimer convened an ecumenical conference in Cottlesloe, South Africa, at which he united black and white church leaders in a ringing declaration against apartheid. In retaliation, the Afrikaner government forced nearly every Afrikaner minister to retract their signatures. Only the prestigious white pastor, C. F. Beyers Naude, refused, becoming one of the most courageous voices against apartheid for the next several decades. Bilheimer secured funding from the Ford Foundation to help Naude start his famous justice-seeking Christian Institute of Southern Africa.[19] To Bilheimer, this exemplified prophetic ecumenism at its best.

His collaboration with the early ecumenical giants in giving shape and direction to the WCC influenced his vision and style when he was charged later with directing the NCC's response to the Vietnam War. It also brought him into eventual conflict with American-trained, American-oriented church leaders whom he felt lacked the broader Geneva perspective on the meaning and mission of ecumenism. It was difficult, he would learn, to help American Christians see their own subconscious captivity to culture—whether they be so-called new breed activists, who focused more on political demonstrations than theology, or conservatives so vested in America's original civil religion that their fusion of patriotism and Protestantism prevented them from truly standing, weeping, and acting with the world's church community.

Consciousness-raising of this sort proved especially challenging when the United States went to war unilaterally in Vietnam. In this effort, Bilheimer gained assistance from Gerhard Elston, a German-born Lutheran refugee whom he hired in 1967 from the National Student Christian Federation to be his director of Vietnam Affairs within the NCC's International Affairs Commission. The gregarious impish immigrant brought a non-institutional style to the commission that contrasted with Bilheimer's more strait-laced, driven, corporate approach. Elston would become Bilheimer's entrée to youthful and secular "new left" antiwar groups that the clean-cut bureaucrat could not have accessed similarly. Yet the same ecumenical vision blazed inside them; their mutual devotion to and innate understanding of it stemmed from firsthand experiences in the 1930s and 1940s.

GERHARD ELSTON AND THE CONFESSING CHURCH MODEL

Like Bilheimer, Gerhard Elston gained his ecumenical training in the Student Christian Movement. However, he learned the meaning of ecumenism in Nazi Germany when a small group of churches openly opposed Hitler's plans for them. This church struggle became another educational catalyst for ecumenically minded Christians worldwide, but particularly in the United States. It shocked American ecumenists, who loved and trusted their own government, into a renewed understanding of why their nation's founders had separated church from state.

Gerhard Edelstein (later changed to Elston) was one of Berlin's native sons. Born in 1924, he witnessed Hitler's rise to power in 1933. The Nazis dubbed his family ethnically Jewish, although they had been Lutheran for generations, making them vulnerable to new exclusionary rules about the place of Jews in churches. The Nazis legitimated these by teaching that Jesus was a Galilean born to Mary and a Roman centurion, making him Aryan, not Jewish. They asserted that Jews had killed this Aryan savior, thus ostensibly justifying Jewish persecution. Educators and pastors who failed to teach such revisionism drew swift punishment. One of Elston's favorite teachers who refused to comply was shuttled to a reeducation camp and blackballed from teaching.[20] Every German Christian had to make a choice between supporting the Nazis, and what many viewed as their paganized church, or adhering to a biblical faith and risking Nazi wrath.

In May 1934 Germany's churches split over Nazism's interference with the church and its doctrine. Hitler skillfully wooed most Protestant and Catholic leaders into his corner with gestures of respect and promises of worldly power and protection. Many German clergy also proactively pushed to align church doctrine and practices with Nazism to court Hitler's favor. Laity dutifully followed. Those few churches that opposed nazification formed what they called the "Confessing Church," because they would confess their true biblical faith and autonomy in the face of state pressure. Gathering at a conference in Barmen, and inspired by the well-known pastor and World War I U-boat commander Martin Niemoeller, the Confessing Church gave birth to its movement in the Barmen Declaration. Three years later, the Gestapo captured Niemoeller, imprisoning him until U.S. troops arrived in 1945.[21]

It took courage to live one's true faith in Germany. From Geneva, New York, and elsewhere, ecumenical leaders watched with awe and fascination. Visser 't Hooft called the Confessing Church the "great ecumenical event of our time" for it modeled the sort of transcendence, autonomy, devotion to theological truth, and willingness to act upon it that were core to the ecumenical mission.[22] At the World Council's founding assembly in 1948, Bilheimer recalled that "speech after speech was made about how Niemoeller defied Hitler" and how the Confessing Church aided the fuehrer's downfall. As a result, attending Americans felt connected to those German Christians.[23] They were doing what the nations seemingly could not do: cooperating to focus on the universal good of humankind. Both the Confessing Church and the creation of the WCC fueled a triumphal vision of the church as a world force that could transform cultures and affect history. The confessing movement illustrated also that the church must remain vigilant, fight to preserve its autonomy as the church, and resist identifying itself with any one nation's way of life or political agenda.[24]

Elston felt the Confessing Church's impact firsthand. As a youth, when he began the long Lutheran confirmation process, fellow students recognized him as one of "Niemoeller's boys," which they were also, and invited him to join their confirmation group. The boys knew that including the non-Aryan would violate Nazi policy, yet they voted unanimously to do so. It was a brave and principled act that made an indelible impression on Elston.[25] So too did his pastor who, after baptizing him, was interrogated by the Nazis for anointing a Jewish child. His classmates and pastor had recognized him as part of the body of Christ and put their loyalty to that body before obedience to nation, civil religion, or culture. Years later, Elston would aim to emulate this act on behalf of the Vietnamese and dissenters from U.S. Vietnam policy.

During 1937 and 1938, as the Nazi government increased pressure on Jews and dissidents, Elston was forced to live "underground." While the family struggled to secure visas to get out of Germany, he spent every night in a different safe house. In December 1938, visas arrived for him and his younger brother. In February 1939 they left their parents and headed for England. Elston was nearly fifteen years old.

Two aspects of these early experiences influenced Elston's faith, worldview, and perspective of church-state relationships. First, the church struggle in Germany inspired him "to take on the Vietnam War and the church struggle in this country," to "remain separate from the U.S. State Department," and to be "critical of government actions." He knew firsthand the dangerous repercussions and high price paid when the church allowed itself to be co-opted and corrupted by a nation-state. He also understood the value of an independent church witness, especially during wartime. Unlike most Americans of the pre-Watergate era, Elston never invested blind faith in the innate goodness of any government.

Second, his primary identity was that of a refugee. He said, "My thinking is refugee-thinking. You bunk with people. You support people. You're not at home anywhere. You don't believe in a safe place." He felt he belonged to no country and was captive to no particular national myths. This refugee mentality grounded Elston's primary loyalty in the worldwide church and would help him cultivate the trust of the Indochinese as well as that of young antiwar radicals who were generally suspicious of anyone connected with the establishment.

Elston's parents made it to the United States. He joined them there on April 12, 1945, shortly before his twenty-first birthday. He found America distasteful at first, saying, "I wouldn't have come if my parents weren't here." The racism and ethnocentrism within the U.S. Army, well publicized in England, were not topics Elston wished to face. Yet, within days of arriving, the law required him to register for that army.[26]

Since he was not called up to serve immediately, he continued his education at New York University and then the University of Chicago, where he ran its Lutheran student affairs office. A brief tour in the U.S. military, which interrupted his studies, ironically launched his education in U.S. Asia policy. While stationed for a year in Manila, Elston got a close look at Western imperialism in Asia. From his base, "it became clear that the U.S. was supporting the return of the Dutch to their colonies." It horrified him to discover that the United States stood against those fighting for independence in Indonesia.

Then in 1954, he began a two-year stint working for the Lutheran World Federation in Geneva. Indochina's political future was the talk of the town, and Elston immersed himself in it. The Geneva Convention, the international conference that drafted terms to end the Vietnamese-French War and temporarily divided Vietnam into northern and southern sections, occurred in 1954. Elston had befriended several Vietnamese through student conferences, and together they followed events in Vietnam via the French news. This included America's violation of the Geneva Accords as it began a nation-building project in the anticommunist southern section of the country. When he returned stateside he "realized the falsification of everything" in America's perceptions of Vietnam. Elston remarked that he "became a bit of an expert on the stuff" and later brought that knowledge to the NCC's Vietnam Affairs program. In 1967 he was the only NCC international affairs staff member who knew any Vietnamese personally. He had also cultivated important Buddhist contacts, which would provide the Council with an independent source of information during the war.

While in Geneva, Elston briefly became reacquainted with Bilheimer, whom he had known from his student movement days. During this period, the two of them also separately met Kurtis Naylor, a sharp young Brethren pacifist who was working in Geneva organizing the Brethren relief effort in Germany for Church World Service. In 1966, when hired to direct the NCC's international affairs programs, Bilheimer would recruit Naylor to serve as associate director. And Naylor would recommend hiring Elston for his Vietnam expertise.

After a brief position with Church World Service (1956–1957), Elston joined the National Student Christian Federation's staff. As a student movement leader, Elston often rubbed elbows with the NCC until officially joining its ranks in January 1967.

Bilheimer and Elston, along with fellow NCC staff members, tried to generate a prophetic witness on U.S. foreign policy from the Council's International Affairs Commission (IAC). The style, precedents, image, and reputation established by the American ecumenical movement in its first decades reverberated through the NCC later during the Vietnam era, informing Council decisions and affecting its public perception. To appreciate the challenges, direction, and repercussions of its efforts, one must first understand the historical context from which these sprung.

ECUMENISM IN AMERICA, 1908-1950

Several separate organizations drove the ecumenical vision prior to the NCC's formation in 1950. Among the most prominent stood the student movements and the Federal Council of Churches, which represented roughly thirty denominations, including most considered mainline. Organized in Philadelphia in 1908, the FCC reflected the social gospel slant of its creators.[27] Amid modernization and the federal government's expanding power, churches saw their old cultural domains dwindle. As secular organizations assumed cultural roles previously left to churches, the Council hoped to counter this by "secure[ing] a larger combined influence for the churches of Christ in all matters affecting the moral and social condition of the people."[28] Its focus on social needs quickly became dominant, for it filled a service void little addressed by other large organizations, and its leaders and rich benefactors willed it so.[29] But in its first two decades, the Federal Council's radical-seeming, perfection-seeking social gospel platform was one that most member denominations avoided. Not until the 1940s did they feel served enough, and safe enough, to contribute much financially to the Council's continuance. Prior to that time, the FCC drew most of its donations from liberal elites such as John D. Rockefeller, while its member denominations kept the socialist-seeming Council at arm's length.[30]

As religious historian Sydney Ahlstrom has noted, social gospel groups such as the Federal Council helped "to convert the self-oriented Christian consciousness into one that was neighbor-oriented."[31] In essence, the FCC prodded Christians to address systemic social injustices along with personal behavioral sins. However, it also provoked the ire of conservative Protestants devoted to laissez-faire economics, social Darwinism, and a more individualistic, soul-saving, moralistic religion. The social gospel's modernist theology was challenged from within ecumenical ranks after World War I and toned down further in the late 1930s when denominational unity seemed vital; but the neighbor-oriented emphasis always remained central to the ecumenical worldview.

Disillusionment over the meaning and results of World War I, followed by frustration with capitalist excesses and the social pains of the Great Depression, jarred several ecumenical leaders away from their modernist faith in inevitable progress and the innate goodness of human culture. These events illustrated the relative powerlessness, selfishness, and destructive capacities of human beings. Meanwhile, the Federal Council's structure continued to grow as it stretched to meet human needs and lobby for social justice reforms. While not uncritical of the New Deal, the FCC comfortably allied with an active government to alleviate human suffering. The New Deal's controversial protection of labor's bargaining rights drew the Council's loudest applause. In recognition of their shared concerns, Roosevelt addressed its twenty-fifth anniversary ceremony in December 1933, where he directly "equated the ideals of the church and the government."[32]

However, the social gospel approach was always more popular with clergy than laity. Many grassroots Protestants, with no personal ties to their denomination's leadership or FCC representatives, felt quite differently about labor, the New Deal, Roosevelt, and the proper role of the church. Upset by the Federal Council's seemingly radical, unrepresentative stands, some parishioners punished it both verbally and financially through withdrawn funds.[33] This foreshadowed a pattern that would accelerate in the 1960s. Its endorsement of labor first sparked charges that the Council was a communist-friendly organization. When the polarizing issues of labor and prohibition dissipated in the 1930s and 1940s, the FCC's image moderated—briefly. A change in leadership contributed as well.

The interwar period spawned a vital time of ecumenical theology, transformation, and growth. Leaders wrestled not only with the disillusioning issues mentioned above but also with new theological ideas like neo-orthodoxy emerging from Europe and America as the Nazi menace rose in Germany. As just noted, young Protestant theologians, affected by the destabilizing effects of World War I, largely rejected the progressive, culture-embracing aspects of social gospel theology popular with the previous generation. Led by people with ecumenical roots in student Christian movements, they spoke strongly against the racism and nationalism that they felt fostered international conflict. As they assumed leadership positions in the Protestant establishment, they criticized the naïveté about human nature that underpinned earlier modernist views of culture. In the late 1920s, Reinhold Niebuhr, Van Dusen, and Francis Miller started articulating the need for a less optimistic, less symbiotic relationship between "the church and the world."[34] Studying the European neo-orthodox theologies of Karl Barth and Emil Brunner further accelerated their move away from modernism toward Christian realism.[35] The neo-orthodox tended to emphasize the corruption of human culture, sinfulness of human beings, and transcendence of God. They combined this, however, with a steadfast liberal approach to scripture that rejected biblical inerrancy and used critical methods to interpret the Bible. They were highly intellectual and often disdained emotional forms of religious expression. Neo-orthodoxy became quite popular in American seminaries and church bureaucracies, touching local churches to a lesser extent.

Fascism's rise stimulated a drive for international ecumenical unity. The Nazi threat motivated American theologians to set aside their differences and hone in on shared priorities. It also inspired Christians to get their hands dirty in the corrupted world of power politics to forestall what they judged to be the greater of two evils: a Nazi victory. From the beginning of Hitler's ascent, ecumenical leaders in Europe and America kept abreast of his activities through their contacts in the student movements and Federal Council; therefore they knew the extent of his atrocities.[36] This made the courageous voice of Germany's Confessing Church particularly impressive. Motivated by that example, many ecumenists felt it was time to free American Protestantism from its captivity to culture and empower it to lead as an independent Christocentric agent in the world.

Beginning in 1934, a group of about twenty-five theologians convened biannually to study, discuss, and reach some consensus on the hot theological questions raised by world events, neo-orthodoxy, and political realism. Dubbed the Theological Discussion Group, it boasted such notable figures as Van Dusen, the Niebuhr brothers, John Bennett, Paul Tillich, Walter Horton, Georgia Harkness, Wilhelm Pauck, John MacKay, and Samuel McCrea Cavert.[37] While these theologians grew critical of modernist liberalism and moved toward Christian realism, not all advanced neo-orthodoxy. The Niebuhr brothers did articulate a brand of neo-orthodoxy in America. However, several of their discussion group colleagues, such as Bennett, Van Dusen, Harkness, and Henry Sloane Coffin, are often classified as neo-liberals. Since there was considerable cross-over between this group and the FCC, it is important to note that the Federal (and later National) Council of Churches always included a wide range of theological perspectives that cut across denominational lines, including social gospel, orthodox, neo-liberal, neo-orthodox, reformed, and evangelical.[38] Further, some ecumenists, such as Bilheimer, winced at any label applied to themselves other than ecumenist; for transcending narrow denominational and theological schools of thought was part of the ecumenical mission.

Nevertheless, a more transcendent Christian realism was the talk of the day. Paul Tillich and H. Richard Niebuhr condemned the cultural captivity of churches and urged they be freed for action as Christocentric "confessing" moral agents in society. To do so, they encouraged the church to remember that it was tied to a personal and transcendent—not a culturally bound—God.[39]

Reinhold Niebuhr added the other important corollary, and one that Americans, wrapped in national narratives of innocence, divine mission, and moral rectitude, were loathe to face in their collective selves: sin. Reinhold's concept of sin was particularly powerful because he lifted it beyond the individual's moralistic list of naughty no-no's, which is what "sin" meant to most people. Rather, he depicted sin broadly as the common condition of humanity, and especially institutions. Niebuhr reminded people that—even though sinful individuals could occasionally with God's grace act altruistically in ways motivated by love—institutions, organizations, and nations never could. But at least society could require them to be just.[40] Appeals to morality and love would fail to press them toward justice, however. Since self-interest and power moved such entities, Niebuhr urged local people to create pressure groups, like social action organizations, to curb the power of oppressors. This directly challenged the old social gospel idealism that sought to create the Kingdom of God on Earth simply by infusing institutions with Christian ethics and motivations. It also helped keep justice anchored to the forefront of the ecumenical agenda. And it led to the realistic strategy of engaging leaders in detailed policy analysis in order to affect change rather than making moral appeals from behind stained-glass windows. But recognizing and addressing systemic sin through social change was anathema to many conservative white evangelicals who clung to sin as an individual matter only. Systemic explanations were seen as dodges of personal responsibility or excuses to advance a statist society.[41]

Like their progressive predecessors, Christian realists encouraged the church to be active in the world, promoting peace with justice. They wanted to create awareness of the collective suffering that self-interested groups imposed on other human beings. However, the realists did not expect society to be perfected in the process, and Niebuhr cautioned against hubris. He summoned America and its churches to admit and take responsibility for rectifying the injustices caused by their corporate sin. The United States, Niebuhr said, would be freed and redeemed only when it learned to weep with the world, share others' suffering, admit its culpability, accept responsibility as part of an interdependent world, and work powerfully for justice for *all* of humankind.

For these reasons, Niebuhr and others in the Theological Discussion Group campaigned hard against the pacifism and neutralism dominating American Protestantism, including the Federal Council, in the 1930s. Prior to Japan's attack on Pearl Harbor, they urged the United States to aid the allies against Hitler. Niebuhr helped found the influential journal *Christianity and Crisis* in February 1941 to articulate these perspectives.[42]

Young ecumenical leaders widely embraced Christian realism; it shaped the perspective from which they would decipher the church's role in social and political crises well into the early 1970s. And their experiences and insights from the interwar years seeded some of the disconnect seen later between church leaders and laity. The international ecumenical movement's major conferences drew American leaders beyond their denominations and national biases into an exciting, globally diverse Christian community. There they spoke of unity, world mission, and justice for people in an expansive context uncommon to most Americans. These exchanges also gave them a larger, more sophisticated perspective of foreign affairs than most Christians. It is important to realize the theological awakenings discussed thus far were experienced most fully by an elite group of denominational and ecumenical leaders worldwide who had rich access to such opportunities. Many local clergy (except seminarians) and most American laypersons lived in religious circles far removed from the transformational ecumenical discussions taking place. Therefore, the gap between executive-level clergy and laity solidified well before the 1960s.[43]

The international Life and Work Conference in Oxford, England, in 1937 shaped ecumenical understanding significantly. Facing threatening world crises, it repeated a key refrain: "Let the church be the church." And this duty to be a confessing church must be lived through passionate engagement with the world. According to Bilheimer, this conference produced an ecumenical impact similar to that of a papal encyclical for Catholics. It drew American church leaders into international dialogue, transformed their theological consciousness, and helped them develop a more cosmopolitan worldview than most parishioners. As Bilheimer said, they were exposed "to a vision of Christianity as a world force that they hadn't known before."[44]

Other church leaders—who lacked much international ecumenical involvement, or were overly influenced by Cold War ideology, or were simply unable to transcend their own Americanism or nationalism—never truly grasped what ecumenism meant to its early institutional founders, what it meant for the church to be the body of Christ in the *world*. Anticommunism's divisive influence also took a toll on the ecumenical movement and people's understanding of it.

WAR, PEACE, AND AMERICAN ECUMENISM

Cold War fears soon compromised the cooperative international spirit of World War II, the United Nations' early unity, and its drafting of a Universal Declaration of Human Rights in 1948. These anxieties also energized a virulent Christian nationalism that made ecumenism's work suspect.[45] The considerable influence of anticommunism upon American Protestantism becomes starker if one first surveys American ecumenical responses to World War II and its international repercussions. The influence of that war on the Federal Council of Churches provides the historical context that helped shape Bilheimer's approach and goals related to Vietnam.

As Hitler's ambitions grew apparent, and after Japan bombed Pearl Harbor, most American mainline denominations abandoned pacifism to embrace a "just war" theory compatible with Christian realism.[46] However, ecumenists were anxious to ensure that this world war, unlike the first, resulted in a "just and durable peace." They did not trust secular agencies alone to make this happen. The ecumenical community knew, even as war raged, that many competing visions for global order were vying to shape the postwar world. It mobilized supporters quickly in order to place its vision prominently before world leaders, and it established an influential role for itself. In December 1940 the Federal Council created the Commission on Just and Durable Peace to study the bases of such a peace, as well as discern the church's role in nurturing it.[47] John Foster Dulles, a well-known Christian layperson and future secretary of state, chaired this commission. He had become a powerful force in the Federal Council's international affairs division and had been deeply involved in Oxford's 1937 Life and Work Conference.

In 1942 the Federal Council sponsored a "National Study Conference on the Churches and a Just and Durable Peace." Using the earlier commission's research, it generated "Guiding Principles," which resulted in the formulation of "Six Pillars of Peace." These helped lay the groundwork for the United Nations. In addition to emphasizing human brotherhood as the basic moral concept to which all institutions should adhere, they recognized that economic and political security were equally important in maintaining a just peace. The principles questioned unlimited national sovereignty rights, emphasizing that national self-interest must be subordinated to the general welfare and that military establishments be made subject to international law and control. The churches, meanwhile, were directed to continue nurturing a worldwide Christian community that could model a transcendence of "nation, race and class" they hoped countries might emulate.[48] As mentioned earlier, they did not expect perfection or even a Christianized society. As John Bennett said, "American churches never went in heavily for world government, because of the influence of [realists] Reinhold Niebuhr and John Foster Dulles."[49] Genuine peace through global justice was the goal, not eliminating national self-interest or creating the Kingdom of God on Earth.

In 1943 the Federal Council launched another study on war. Eighteen Theological Discussion Group members joined seven other scholars as part of a new FCC commission to report on "The Relation of the Church to the War in the Light of the Christian Faith." They tackled a contentious topic: the proper role of churches during wartime. The resulting 1944 report echoed the Guiding Principles' emphases. But it also urged humility for anyone attempting a Christocentric interpretation of war. As Niebuhr had noted, all people were sinful, all were fallible, and even the best Christian scholars were likely to err when extrapolating church direction from their versions of revealed truth. The report concluded that war was often preventable if nations better understood one another and could grasp how justice might be advanced for various groups. The church should work prophetically for similar ends but remain free to serve as both "critic and supporter" of the state. It must remind governments constantly that they do not possess absolute sovereignty—rather, God does—and summon them continually into international community. This FCC report was perceived as "an important landmark in American ecumenical theology."[50] It would echo through decades of debates over the church's role during wartime.

The struggle of ecumenical leaders to deal with domestic and international crises from World War I through the end of World War II had spawned in them a humanity-encompassing worldview. By 1945 their ecumenical model was, in some secular respect, being writ large in the United Nations (UN). In fact, ecumenists played a role in helping shape the UN Charter and then selling the idea to the public through their churches. At a time when many Christians perceived the postwar world as being full of both promise and threat, the UN seemed one means of advancing mutual understanding and disarming conflict before it became nuclear.[51]

Two men deeply involved in international ecumenism, and both experts on foreign affairs, directed church efforts to influence the UN's formation. John Foster Dulles helped draft the UN Charter and ensured that its moral purpose—preserving human rights and justice—was integrated clearly into that document.[52] O. Frederick Nolde virtually authored Article 18 of the Universal Declaration of Human Rights, which protected religious liberty. Ecumenical leaders championed the declaration because it provided a global ethos of common values that seemed consonant with Christianity—and a good basis for world order. A year after the UN's birth, Nolde and Dulles created the Commission of the Churches on International Affairs (CCIA), which became the international affairs agency of the World Council of Churches.[53]

While Dulles and Nolde exerted influence at the UN's founding conference, ecumenical and denominational leaders played a significant public relations role by rallying grassroots support for the UN in 1945. Church people penned over one million letters to Congress supporting ratification of its charter.[54] Writing to Dulles in early November, President Harry Truman confirmed, "If today we Americans have a clearer understanding of our place in [the] world community—as I believe we have—it is due, in no small part, to the churches' advanced position in international thinking taken by the Federal Council."[55] Because of these initial ties and expectations, most ecumenists felt especially invested in the UN's mission. This remained strong in succeeding decades.[56] For their work in seeking a just merciful peace, for helping craft and promote the UN, and for emphasizing concern for humanity worldwide after the war, religion scholar Edward Long Jr. credited ecumenists with "creating one of the most positive thrusts in international public policy in America's history. But the Cold War," he noted, "would shortly take its toll of such gains."[57] Less than five years after the UN's inauguration, the Cold War began, virtually paralyzing its Security Council, weakening its overall authority, and fueling doubts about the ecumenical vision itself.

Following World War II, everything changed. Stalin dropped his "iron curtain" around Eastern Europe, and the Cold War between communist and democratic nations heated quickly. People began seeing the world not as an interconnected international community but as two fiefdoms, one communist, controlled in Moscow, and the other democratic, commanded in Washington. Both competed for advantage as they stockpiled nuclear weapons and stood ready to fight nearly anywhere on the globe to maintain their balance of power. In this environment, international incidents were construed in light of larger bipolar power plays. Complex cultural conflicts around the globe were reduced, twisted, and drawn into ideological competition by the two superpowers, and persons living in the sphere of one or the other were encouraged to think nationalistically rather than situationally when interpreting international events. It became difficult for Americans to maintain a transcendent, human-community perspective.

Exchanging a multinational, multicultural worldview for a bipolar, nationalistic, anticommunist one proved tempting for American Christians since the Communist Party formally tied itself to atheism and tried to suppress the church where it reigned. Missionizing in communist areas often drew a violent response. For many Christians, therefore, the battle between "democratic Christian America" and "godless communistic Russia" was more than a political, economic, or ideological war. It embodied a spiritual struggle between good and evil, between God and Satan. Conservatives became particularly vitriolic because they tended to extrapolate the Cold War to this level and reflected this perspective from pulpits and periodicals. As a result, passionate anticommunism became a potent uniter of right-leaning Christians.[58]

Ecumenical leaders struggled with their nation's embrace of a bipolar worldview. Most roundly criticized communism and its suppression of the church, though many could also understand its appeal to poor and oppressed peoples. Showing unique insight, the First Assembly of the World Council in 1948 suggested that Christians "should recognize the hand of God in the revolt of multitudes against injustice that gives Communism much of its strength," for its attraction emanated largely from "a vision of human equality and universal brotherhood for which they [the multitudes] were prepared by Christian influences." It also regretted that, in the name of this vision, communism perpetuated new injustices and totalitarianism.[59]

The World Council developed a vision of a "Responsible Society" built around a concept of justice that stood in contrast to oppressions observed in both capitalist and communist countries. The WCC therefore encouraged resistance to aspects in *any* society that oppressed others and denied victims a way of voicing their distress. This concept guided ecumenists throughout the Cold War period. As Bilheimer described, "When it criticized both the West and the East, the Responsible Society offered a penultimate witness to the transcendence of God-in-Christ; when it gave guidance to action for freedom and justice, it offered a penultimate witness to the immanence of God-in-Christ. In it the voice of the church did not echo the voice of the world."[60]

However, the WCC's vision was not reflected throughout the American ecumenical community. In fact, several of its most prominent leaders became fervent cold warriors. John Foster Dulles's stunning shift from global ecumenist to nationalistic cold warrior provided the most shocking example. His ecumenical colleagues were particularly puzzled by his address at the World Council's 1948 assembly when he "espoused a clear Western Christian viewpoint . . . in the idiom of his own culture, against communism."[61] When the WCC politely rejected his Westernized interpretation, Dulles mourned the wrongheadedness of his church friends.[62]

Dulles was not alone. American religious leaders generally viewed communism as a menacing threat. After the war, the Federal Council and several mainline denominational officials advised caution in dealing with the dangers of communism.[63] As the iron curtain fell across Eastern

Europe, and as Stalin's own purging atrocities and bellicose behavior became clear, many viewed him as potentially another Hitler. Bennett saw Stalin as another totalitarian force of evil, declaring U.S. efforts against him justified. Reinhold Niebuhr also became a staunch cold warrior and served on an advisory committee of the State Department's policy planning staff chaired by containment architect George Kennan.[64] Biographer Richard Wightman Fox described Niebuhr as the "establishment theologian," respected and sought by men in power, and Patrick Lloyd Hacker correctly dubbed him "the moral philosopher" for postwar internationalist officials seeking to rationalize the conscience-twinging repercussions of their containment policies. Like other liberal churchmen with social gospel roots and a socialist-flirting past, Niebuhr demonstrated his patriotism through ardent anticommunism.[65]

Not only did Stalin's government seem evil and worth forceful resistance, but World War II had left Americans feeling morally superior by comparison. The image of America as a force for good meshed easily with national folklore that saw the United States as God's chosen nation, his "city upon a hill," a moral example of liberty for the world. As a result, when the Cold War arose, Elston noted that "it was hard to get the country to disabuse itself [of the notion] that we were the good guys, the communists were the bad guys, and therefore anything we do to fight communism is good."[66] As Reinhold Niebuhr had argued, Americans' pervading sense of innocence often impeded their ability to empathize with people in other lands. Whenever the American way of life was equated with God's will, its adherents developed a certain tunnel vision—seeing only through narrow cultural channels, captive to their defining walls. Dulles exemplified this. The fresh postwar sense of American righteousness, combined with rising fears of a conquest-bent communist movement, drew many American Christians, to varying degrees, back into captive allegiance to their culture's nationalism.

In 1949, the same year Russia acquired its first nuclear weapons, Mao Zedong brought China under communist rule. Mao expelled Christian missionaries and began to "reeducate" his people. This "fall" of China fueled anticommunist fervor within churches perhaps more than any other single incident. It may be difficult to understand today what China meant to millions of American Christians who supported missionary work there during the first half of the twentieth century. For them, China was the primary, most coveted, and idealized missionary target around which Christians spun moving stories about bringing the heathen to

Jesus. Many knew of and helped missionaries who served there.[67] Their emotional attachment to China and their correlating hatred of Mao was truly significant.

Some American missionaries in China understood the reasons behind Chinese anger at the West and how the missionaries' paternalism fed anti-imperialistic sentiment. However, Elston surmised that most were furious at the communists for taking China and intending to destroy its churches.[68] This anger later fueled distrust of Ho Chi Minh and North Vietnam's communists as well, whom many Americans assumed were supported, and even controlled, by communist China. American antipathy toward China greatly influenced people's feelings about the Vietnam conflict and U.S. intervention in it.

In 1950 three more events fueled anticommunist fervor in the United States. First, the Korean War began, with China clearly supporting the communist North. Eventually, China would join the war and drive General Douglas MacArthur's troops deep into the South.

Second, the United States assumed primary financial and advisory responsibility for assisting the French in their war against Vietnam's nationalist-communist Vietminh. The French wanted to re-take control of their former colony, an objective that many Americans, including President Roosevelt, had criticized five years prior. By 1950, however, general perceptions had changed. Americans no longer perceived the French as imperialists trying to reassert control over a former colony desiring independence; rather, they saw the French as democratic freedom fighters trying to save Vietnam from communist takeover. At this time, Americans commonly believed that communism was a monolithic conquest-bent force led by Moscow and Peking. Therefore, many were inclined to support any noncommunist government willing to battle a communist foe, even if that ally was undemocratic or imperialist.

Third, a publicity-seeking senator named Joseph McCarthy claimed to know of over two hundred communists employed by the State Department. With this specious charge, McCarthy initiated a domestic witch hunt to root out suspected communists from American society and fostered an atmosphere of suspicion and hyper-Americanism that long outlived him. As a result of McCarthy's accusations and America's hatred of Red China, three of the State Department's true Asia experts, who had predicted Mao's takeover, were dismissed as suspected communists. This impaired the quality of information it received on Indochina.[69]

Each of these events fed the dominant anticommunist worldview of the early 1950s. They also affected American ecumenical perspectives of international affairs, not to mention church membership and the views of Protestants in the pews. In the 1950s, church membership rose in most denominations along with finances. While some interpreted this church boom as another great awakening of spiritual interest, others called it a repercussion of the materialistic Cold War mentality that equated patriotism with church involvement, and God's blessings with the free enterprise system. Recent scholarship indicates that both interpretations were true. A subset of laity did grapple seriously with personal theological questions, especially notions of original sin and grace, to help them navigate the uncertainties of the early Cold War era, while churches provided a social badge, family center, and comfort station to Christians generally. The common thread is that faith spun primarily around personal individual needs, whether theological or sociocultural. With President Eisenhower's considerable encouragement, popular faith expressions also hewed closely to America's traditional, patriotic, civil religion. Though individuals were sinful and in need of salvation, the nation as a whole was perceived as the world's protective redeemer, as God's right arm against the communist foe. Reinhold Niebuhr's McCarthy-era warnings about the myth of national innocence failed to resonate as he had hoped. So, too, the growing ecumenical emphases upon systemic institutional sins, worldwide community, pluralism, and peace through plowshares instead of swords were falling out of step with much of white, mainstream, 1950s America.[70]

The era's most popular preacher, Billy Graham, helped fuse patriotism with Protestantism by claiming that God and America were battling the united forces of Satan and communism in the world. Throughout the 1950s his sermons hammered this theme as he called on God-fearing Americans to help combat communist infiltration. "If you would be a true patriot," he stressed, "then become a Christian. If you would be a loyal American, then become a loyal Christian."[71] The popular Presbyterian G-man and head of the Federal Bureau of Investigation (FBI), J. Edgar Hoover, also summoned Christians to view their faith as a motivating force for fighting communist infiltration in America. In 1953 Hoover declared, "Communism is secularism on the march. It is a moral foe of Christianity. . . . The two cannot live side by side."[72] Even Truman and Eisenhower urged Americans to marshal spiritual forces against the reds.[73] As patriotism and Protestantism blended, religion morphed into a societal shield, and Americans learned that a publicly paraded Christianity helped inoculate one against accusations of disloyalty.[74]

The cultural climate of the early Cold War era made adhering to, articulating, and acting upon an ecumenical worldview especially challenging. The combination of seminary, student movement, and international experiences that shaped ecumenical leaders' faiths helped provide an anchor point during these strange times. But there is no easy way to explain why some people's worldviews were utterly transformed by anticommunism while others' were not. Suffice it to say that nearly every church leader in the 1950s claimed to be anticommunist. Pressure to prove one's anticommunism time and again was relentless, particularly for those who had flirted with socialism or expressed pacifist sentiments before the war.[75] Religious leaders who attempted to keep anticommunism in ecumenical perspective received considerable scrutiny from those they viewed as culture-driven Christians.[76]

CHAPTER TWO

The NCC and the American Way of Life

ECUMENICAL PATRIOTISM

On November 28, 1950, the Federal Council and several other ecumenical agencies merged to form the National Council of the Churches of Christ in the United States of America. Twenty-five Protestant and four Orthodox denominations joined as initial members, with more added later.[1] This religious conglomerate created an immense bureaucracy that reflected popular corporate business models. Born in the heyday of McCarthyism, this new and improved Council tried to demonstrate its Americanism while proclaiming its ecumenical membership in the larger body of Christ. Delegates at its founding ceremony sat in red, white, and blue chairs gazing at a ten-foot-tall banner proclaiming "This Nation Under God." Symbolizing the global nature of ecumenism, flags from every nation surrounded a central altar that held an open Bible. Only a raging snowstorm prevented President Truman and Secretary of State Dean Acheson from addressing the attendees.[2] Church leaders found the juxtaposition of ecumenism and patriotism difficult to sell to the broader public, much of which still perceived ecumenism in shades of pink.[3] Nevertheless, the NCC saw the two symbiotically, especially in the early 1950s, and tried to explain how ecumenism complemented and reflected American values.

In its founding message "To the People of the Nation," the NCC embraced ecumenism's goals of unity, peace, and justice as well as American principles of freedom, liberty, and inalienable human rights. Leaders composed this carefully in order to balance the NCC on that precarious fence between a sensible anticommunism and the irrational, freedom-suppressing fear generated by McCarthy. The Council also declared itself a shaper rather than a reflector of American society—a hopeful catalyst for a new era of human relations. "The Church is not the religious phase of the civilization in which it finds itself," it claimed. Rather, "it is the living center out of which lasting civilizations take life and form. In this sense the Council will be an organ through which the will of God may become effective as an animating, creative and unifying force within our national society."[4] The NCC compared its mission to that of the United Nations, anticipating that it "could do for religion what it was hoped the UN would do for the world."[5] Yet, despite this carefully crafted Americanism and triumphal Christian spirit, the NCC immediately faced charges of disloyalty and inherited old FCC stereotypes.[6]

Some of the sharpest criticism came from the American Council of Christian Churches. Created in 1941, the ACCC comprised several tiny anti-ecumenical, fundamentalist, splinter denominations under the leadership of Carl McIntire, a Presbyterian minister. Fearing Christianity's erosion and where pluralist messages might lead, he made it his life's mission to attack modernism in the churches. The Federal/National and World Councils became his prime targets. Thus, for decades, he appeared regularly at their meetings, toting protest signs, and often organizing opposing conferences designed to rebut FCC/NCC positions. Contrary to some fundamentalist jeremiads against worldly political involvement, he plunged his voice into political commentary, especially on the virtues of free-market capitalism and crushing communism. His ACCC created a political lobbying arm funded by business interests. NCC leaders viewed him as a colorful pest rather than a substantial threat. But this media master knew how to get attention and stir up trouble for the Councils.[7]

Shortly after the NCC's birth, the ACCC distributed a pamphlet entitled *How Red Is the National* (with the word "Federal" superimposed over "National") *Council of Churches?* It implied that the Federal Council just "went underground" by becoming part of the NCC, where its original commie-friendly agenda and leadership remained intact. Inside, the pamphlet named names of supposed "Federal Council Leaders Who

Have Helped Communist Organizations," listed titles of "Some of the Red Groups They Have Aided," and implied that the NCC wanted to scrap free-enterprise capitalism for socialism.[8]

Even though McIntire and his small organization were not widely respected as credible sources, their punch had more power than size might suggest. Council leaders understood how damaging such accusations could be to their young organization's image in that incriminating McCarthyite atmosphere. So the NCC published a corrective pamphlet, *Plain Facts about the National Council of the Churches of Christ in the U.S.A.*, to discredit the ACCC's accusations. *Plain Facts* even reproduced a letter from FBI director J. Edgar Hoover confirming that he had never made "any statements criticizing the Federal Council of Churches or the National Council of Churches." The pamphlet lamented that the ACCC's leaders seemed "unable to distinguish between Communism and support of constructive measures of social advance prompted by the Christian conscience" and scolded them for "scatter[ing] the adjective 'Red' as indiscriminately as a shotgun blast against all who do not share their own pet ideas."[9] Rather, the pamphlet promoted patriotism that encouraged loyalty to Christian conscience and love of neighbor over knee-jerk allegiance to simplistic ideological concepts. The NCC would echo such sentiments repeatedly throughout the century whenever conservative groups painted its positions "pink."

The fundamentalist ACCC was minor league compared to the National Association of Evangelicals, the NCC's most significant competitor. Founded in 1942, the NAE had thirty-two institutional members representing 1.5 million parishioners by 1960. This more polite, culturally active, and respect-seeking organization defined its agenda as evangelical rather than ecumenical (or soul-saving before society-saving) while emphasizing unity among doctrinally sound groups.[10] Its members preached an individualistic morality that targeted personal rather than systemic sin and praised an antistatist view of government. Billy Graham was its poster boy, and it was not sparing in criticism of the Federal and National Councils' so-called liberal, secularized, political agendas. Yet in 1943, the NAE established a Washington office to strategize advocacy of its own pet political issues and relief work with the State Department; in 1950 it promoted "participation by Christians in political affairs and training of Christian young people for government." Communism's threat to mission work and the free market made evangelicals passionate opponents of the "red menace." (Capitalism's defense of private property rights also came in handy for any Christian seeking a God-and-country argument for resisting integrationist fair housing laws.) Additionally, conservative evangelicals eyed the UN suspiciously as a prideful secular "tower of Babel" destined to facilitate Armageddon rather than peace; the NCC's support of it bore witness to ecumenists' human-worshipping apostasies. Only God could save the world. Besides, to many anticommunist evangelicals, defense of spiritual truth and American freedom should always trump the perceived liberal agenda of peace at any price. Ironically, the NAE and NCC each saw the other as overly culture-bound.[11]

Issues and attitudes throughout the 1950s challenged the NCC to defend the delicate balance between loyalty to American values and commitment to an international, justice-focused, ecumenical worldview. Several Protestant businessmen led by the conservative Presbyterian oilman J. Howard Pew, for whom laissez-faire economics was one of those values, worked tirelessly to steer the NCC toward championing the American way of life.[12] But being a religious rubber stamp for American mores was not its mission. Rather, it intended to serve the nation as both supporter and critic, depending upon the dictates of its Christian faith. Once Pew realized that the NCC would not sell control of its message or politics to his deep pockets, he proclaimed the NCC "the most subversive force in the United States" and publicly condemned churches that let political, social, or economic issues sidetrack evangelism.[13] When the Council occasionally did witness against some aspect of U.S. culture, policy, or law, it drew rebuke from nearly all quadrants for questioning the notion that God and America automatically operated as one unified moral force for good.

Being ecumenical was hard work. Dissenting from majority opinions proved difficult in the 1950s. So did probing past one's own inbred biases in order to consult the broader Christian conscience. The World Council's cultural diversity and pluralism of perspectives helped keep that organization in ecumenical check. Alternately, Americans dominated discussions within the NCC. To keep ecumenically oriented amid the pressures and prejudices of one's cultural breeding was more than many could do consistently.

One of the liberal biases stemming from the FCC's days involved an inherent faith in big government. Unlike Germany's Confessing Church and certain WCC members, most in the NCC still had confidence in the decency of government to mediate social ills and enforce justice, and they believed church and state should cooperate toward these ends. So, throughout the 1950s, the NCC maintained close ties with government officials. In fact, many Council leaders crossed in and out of high government posts. These included John Foster Dulles, chair of several Federal Council international affairs committees who became Eisenhower's secretary of state; Arthur Flemming, Eisenhower's secretary of Health, Education, and Welfare who also served as an NCC vice president 1950–1954 and 1963–1966, and then as NCC president 1966–1969; and Ernest Gross, Truman's assistant secretary of state, legal adviser to the State Department, and ambassador delegate to the UN, who also chaired the NCC's International Affairs Commission from the mid-1950s through the Vietnam period. The NCC positioned itself strategically for intimate involvement with government and other power brokers by maintaining a headquarters in Manhattan, home of the UN and Wall Street, along with an office on Capitol Hill in Washington, D.C.

Government, likewise, saw benefits in cultivating ties with the NCC. At the time, religious publications enjoyed a larger circulation than the nation's daily newspapers.[14] Therefore, it made political sense for elected officials from both parties to nurture mutually affirming relationships with the NCC; they perceived mainline Protestant leaders to be important shapers of grassroots opinion. Politicians spoke regularly at NCC events to explain their policies and court that constituency.[15] The fact that several ecumenical leaders had government ties and were in many respects peers to those serving in government encouraged their desire to trust and cooperate with government throughout the Vietnam era.

Incidents did arise in the 1950s, however, that inspired the Council to speak from an independent Christian conscience. The involvement of the NCC in the World Council, and the fact that the WCC hosted its second assembly purposefully in the United States (in 1954, Evanston, Illinois), helped the American movement stay attentive to perspectives throughout the broader body of Christ. WCC general secretary W. A. Visser 't Hooft understood that America's divisive Cold War culture provided poor soil for ecumenism, so he tried to fertilize the terrain whenever possible. World Council executives hoped that strong ecumenical bonds would keep the NCC separate enough from U.S. culture to speak prophetically on crisis issues raised by the Cold War. When the NCC did so, it usually incurred the wrath of conservative Christians as well as the misunderstanding of laypersons. It also created a precedent for a future ecumenical witness against U.S. Vietnam policy and relationship problems with parishioners.

The NCC confronted McCarthyism head-on when Congress subpoenaed one of its own. The Council proudly claimed to be one of the first major institutions to do so and "at a time," general secretary Roy Ross recalled, "when most of Capitol Hill was either afraid, confused or both."[16] As touched upon earlier, the Cold War and rise in anticommunist sentiment provided conservatives with a perfect platform from which to attack liberals. In this atmosphere, several leaders active in the Federal, World, and National Councils of Churches contended regularly with charges of communism, as did the organizations themselves. The popular outspoken Methodist bishop G. Bromley Oxnam, for decades highly positioned in all three Councils, was one of those frequently queried about his patriotism.[17]

In 1953, a chief investigator for the House Un-American Activities Committee (HUAC), publicly declared that at least seven thousand Protestant clergymen in America supported the Communist Party as "fellow-travelers, espionage agents, party-line adherents, and unwitting dupes."[18] With no substantiating proof, he maintained nevertheless that the earlier social gospel theology had poisoned certain seminaries with a bleeding-heart liberalism that weakened the clergy's resolve to fight communism's insidious advance. The warning was clear: curb one's focus on social justice or be tagged a pinko traitor. HUAC then targeted Oxnam as a public example. McCarthy did so also in a Senate speech that conservative minister and radio personality Billy James Hargis researched and ghostwrote.[19] HUAC's action was part of a broader conservative attempt to crush the liberal wing of American Protestantism by toppling one of its prominent pillars.[20]

Communist implications against Oxnam peppered the press. Consequently, in July 1953, Oxnam demanded the right to "face his accusers" and rebut HUAC's charges. He did so deftly, tearing apart the charges with a rapier so sharp that the issue of communist infiltration into America's churches appeared ridiculous to many discerning government officials. Oxnam accused HUAC of irresponsible undemocratic practices that violated the rights and integrity of upstanding citizens. In fact, he asserted, "the churches have done and are doing far more to destroy the Communist threat to faith and to freedom than all investigating committees put together."[21] By confronting HUAC, Oxnam declared that American ecumenism would not buckle under cultural pressures to exchange its Christian principles for Billy Graham's, Carl McIntire's, or J. Howard Pew's. The ecumenical vision did blur at times when clouded by nationalistic rhetoric. But it did not lose sight of itself—yet.

Joseph McCarthy and the sport of commie-hunting fell into disrepute in 1954. Nevertheless, the attacks took their toll on liberal Protestantism by chilling some of its moral fervor to lead on social justice issues.[22] Other factors did, too, such as the NCC's initial dependence on donations from rich conservative businessmen for sufficient operating funds and its sensitivity to the anticommunist, laissez-faire attitudes of most lay church members in the 1950s. However, as the denominations assumed primary responsibility for the NCC's financial needs, as the country's mood shifted, and as younger, more bureaucratic, and differently educated persons moved into Council leadership roles, its social justice statements grew bolder.[23] Activism followed in the next decade, with the civil rights movement as catalyst for both domestic and foreign policy.

While the Council largely avoided direct action on justice issues during the 1950s, neither was it motionless. By generating resolutions and policy statements against injustices such as segregation and the erosion of civil liberties, the NCC helped prepare its churches to assume greater moral leadership in the 1960s.[24] This was also true with foreign affairs. Throughout the 1950s, the Council questioned the growing globalism and triumphalism apparent in U.S. policy, particularly related to Asia. As the nuclear threat expanded, the NCC challenged America's reliance on military means for preserving security. Finally, as it began to see differences between communist nations, it also raised doubts about the wisdom of the containment policy itself.

In 1953 when Stalin died, so did the rigidity of some church leaders' Cold War attitudes.[25] For example, Reinhold Niebuhr began sensing a clear danger in America's tendency to interpret "its responsibility for world order" as "a responsibility to impose an American order on the world."[26] Niebuhr, Bennett, and other ecumenists contrasted the latter impulse called "globalism" with true "internationalism" promoted through the UN. To them, globalism was a dangerous form of isolationism—another way to avoid interfacing responsibly and respectfully with the world's diverse peoples. It was also oppressive and selfish, two things Niebuhr hoped Christian realism would help restrain.

John Bennett, likewise, grew wary of the tilt of Cold War thinking in policy circles. Reflecting upon the globalist attitudes of policy architects, he once remarked, "They had too-rigid views of the early Cold War conflict, and they were too one-sided in the values to which they were sincerely devoted." This included Dulles, who was "too sure of his goals and moral standards, of how they should be applied, and of the location of moral evil." Bennett also criticized Dean Acheson's unmitigated goal of creating and preserving free societies (that is, nation building) via military means. This aim "became the idol." Bolstered by the arms race, American power emerged as an end in itself, and this, combined with an anticommunist globalist foreign policy, posed a "threat to humanity."[27]

There is no question that NCC leaders remained staunchly anticommunist; but they fell far shy of making a cult out of it, which disturbed those who did.[28] A cooling of Cold War temper within the Council worried their former International Justice and Goodwill chairman, John Foster Dulles, who left that position in 1952 when he became secretary of state. What really alarmed Dulles and frayed his ties with the NCC was its increasingly flexible position on China. In turn, the Council grew dismayed by Dulles's abandonment of his ecumenical worldview in favor of a combative, bipolar, nationalistic one once he entered the State Department. Most important, the growing separation between Dulles and the Council, between the State Department's presuppositions about issues unfolding in the Far East and the NCC's understanding of those events, foreshadowed their future church-state division over Vietnam.

What provoked the shift in Dulles's perspective? Religious historian Mark Toulouse cites a number of factors, among the most significant being Soviet intransigence at postwar conferences, the Korean War, America's resolve to deter "dominoes," and Dulles's duties at State, which drew him out of the churches and onto Eisenhower's team.[29] The constant for Dulles, says Toulouse, was his belief that international policy should reflect the spirit of the "moral law." After 1946 Dulles's understanding of the moral law (or highest good) metamorphosed from "the welfare of humankind," an ecumenical definition, into "the American Way of Life," a globalistic view. When he merged the "purpose of the church" with "the purpose of the nation," America suddenly shone as "God's redemptive agent in the world."[30]

After accepting the cabinet position in 1952, Dulles resigned from all NCC board and committee responsibilities, promising to convey the ecumenical vision to the State Department. "You can be confident that I shall continue to carry in my mind and heart the purposes to which we have been dedicated together," he assured.[31] Dulles never seemed to realize how far askew his positions had shifted from the ecumenical plumb line. His church colleagues certainly noticed his drift, one common for

Americans at the time, but they didn't realize then the extent to which it would divide them over the next few years.

Initially, NCC leaders were thrilled to have one of their own shaping foreign policy, not to mention excited about the government access that Dulles could provide them. Elston mentioned that the churches enjoyed being "cozy with the State Department during [that] period."[32] But shortly after Dulles assumed his new post, ecumenical confidence in him faded.

Church leaders looked beneath Dulles's Christian language, beyond his former ecumenical reputation, and examined his rhetoric and actions as secretary of state. Therein his militaristic globalism grew clearer, and several ecumenists felt that Dulles frequently "opened his mouth to change feet."[33] Shortly after becoming secretary, Dulles stretched a cooperative hand toward the Council as it planned its Fourth World Order Study Conference, saying, "Please let me know if there is any assistance the Department of State can give you."[34] This would be the first without Dulles's involvement.

The conference assembled in October 1953 with the theme "Christian Faith and International Responsibility." Coming a few months after Oxnam's biting testimony before the House Un-American Activities Committee, the conference addressed the grave "threat to civil liberty" from McCarthyism. It stated, "There is a serious danger that in an anxious quest for security in an insecure world, our people shall fail to distinguish between a legitimate security from espionage and a bogus security from dissent . . . [T]he demagoguery which, in the name of 'Americanism,' seeks to exploit fears, foment suspicion, bypass due process of law, and stifle differences of opinion, is a most grievous type of un-Americanism."[35] Defending the right to dissent was becoming a staple within ecumenical circles and would be articulated fervently again after the Fifth World Order Study Conference's recommendations on U.S. China policy in 1958. In 1953, however, China's engagement in the Korean War quieted the fourth conference on the China issue. It simply advocated flexibility, suggesting that the United States keep policy adaptable to changing conditions. The conference then encouraged the Council to research the China question for later discussions.[36]

In the immediate years that followed, the Council took sparse interest in Indochina while that region's political future was being manipulated by native and international forces in subversion of the 1954 Geneva Accords. The NCC blandly supported creation of the Southeast Asia Treaty Organization (SEATO), seeing it uncritically as an Asian version of NATO

(North Atlantic Treaty Organization), and favored Eisenhower's plan to dispense foreign aid specifically to Asia's "free" nations.[37] With respect to foreign affairs, the Council's attention focused upon preaching restraint and negotiations in the Formosa Strait crisis in 1955, utilizing the UN during the Middle East and Hungarian crises in 1956, and preventing government from slashing foreign and technical aid programs in 1957.[38]

China became a focus for the Fifth World Order Study Conference in November 1958. And this stage hosted the NCC's major showdown with Dulles. The Council invited Dulles to address his old colleagues and present the State Department's foreign policy philosophy, especially as it related to the Far East. A few months earlier the State Department had reaffirmed its containment policy by isolating the People's Republic of China (PRC). Perceiving a monolithic communist conspiracy in pursuit of world domination, the department warned that "the Soviet bloc, of which Communist China is an important part, is engaged in a long-range struggle to destroy the way of life of the free countries. . . . East Asia is particularly vulnerable." It emphasized "deter[ring] Communist aggression" as critical in this region, and denying China legitimacy by withholding U.S. recognition and UN membership.[39]

Dulles hoped to rally church leaders, as well as the conference's listening public, to the State's position through his radio broadcast address. He laced it with religious appeals to halt the godless communist menace from spreading its influence through the developing world. Asserting that America and the UN must not give quarter to the PRC, he reminded his audience that "International Communists do not share the [UN] Charter's concepts either with respect to the non-use of force, or as to justice and international law. . . . And both the Soviet Union and the Chinese Communists have repeatedly invoked force to achieve their ends."[40] Therefore, communist China must be refused UN membership because it did not abide by the UN's principles. Likewise, the United States should continue denying China recognition, not only for moral reasons but to demonstrate that its policies stemmed from unwavering convictions. Dulles aimed each point to rebut arguments raised by the ecumenical community.

Bishop Oxnam, then vice president of the NCC's Division of Christian Life and Work, which handled international affairs, had addressed the conference earlier that day and espoused an entirely different worldview upon which to base foreign policy. In the face of communist aggression, Oxnam stated, "We became fearful" and decided to counter it by "mass[ing] greater force than man had known." Americans forgot that Christian faith and American values were the basis of our security, Oxnam said; thus they played the same "materialistic" game as the communists, perpetuating a deadly arms race while ignoring people's basic needs, to which communists often spoke. Foreshadowing insights the Council would make later about Vietnam, he said, "True, we have held certain lines, but we have lost vast areas. We have failed to get through to the minds and hearts of the people. Once our proclamations reached the peoples of the world. We talked of life, liberty, and the pursuit of happiness."[41]

Prescient observations continued as Oxnam analyzed the U.S. government's regressive security aims and secretive methods. For him these were diametrical to America's values of openness, freedom, and liberty, as well as contrary to the ecumenical value of unity. He chastised government for breeding suspicion and suppressing information the public ought to have. "Let us strike down the secrecy psychology," he pleaded. "Would it not be worth the effort to use a few billion to open doors, throw up the windows, and let people and light come i[n?] Let the Russians visit us by the tens of thousands. I think this dear land will stand the scrutiny and prove to be the best answer to Soviet propaganda. . . . Let us try the hand-clasp instead of the finger-print." Oxnam emphasized that American values had little meaning apart from real impact on human lives; therefore, U.S. policy should focus on the human equation as it responded to world events. Regarding China, again Oxnam asserted that reconciliation remained impossible if parties were left out of discussions; Christians must be willing to face political realities and extend themselves in the name of peace.[42] This was a gutsy statement to make before an audience that still mourned the loss of its Chinese missions. Yet many old China hands, such as the Council's own Wallace Merwin from the Division of Foreign Missions, believed that political acceptance of and communication with China would be prerequisites to renewing church ties there.[43]

In conclusion, Oxnam called Christians to lead a prophetic "move from fear to faith" when responding to world events. "Too much of our policy," he explained, "is based upon fear of communism rather than faith in freedom. . . . Let the hysterical stay under the beds as they search for the communists. Let the Americans of faith march into the light, by way of altar, library and laboratory to solve our problems in the interest of the common good, removing the real dangers to freedom that lie in segregation, exploitation, and discrimination."[44]

Oxnam's progressive faith in the power of education, scientific ingenuity, and religious values to battle society's ills was apparent. He hit Dulles's arguments head-on and summoned the assembly to take the higher road of faith over fear, peace over belligerency, and ecumenism over Christian nationalism. This debate over China in the late 1950s between the Council and the State Department bears remarkable similarity to that which emerged over Vietnam in the late 1960s between Bilheimer and Secretary of State Dean Rusk. Echoes appeared again in the early twenty-first century when the NCC criticized the globalism, materialism, unilateralism, and erosion of civil liberties in the international and domestic policies of President George W. Bush.

The contrast between Dulles's and Oxnam's perspectives was clear. The Fifth World Order Conference repudiated the State Department's position, becoming one of the first large American mainstream bodies to appeal for a change in China policy. The specific wording of the conference message is important, as it was often misrepresented and misconstrued: "*Christians should urge reconsideration* by our government of its policy in regard to the People's Republic of China. While the rights of the people of Taiwan and of Korea should be safeguarded, steps should be taken toward the inclusion of the People's Republic of China in the United Nations and for its recognition by our government. Such recognition does *not* imply moral approval [italics added]." The conference defended its recommendation on practical grounds; isolating China hurt the United States as much as it did Peking.[45] Reopening China's churches was part of the Council's motivation. Nevertheless, the general public, government, and many evangelical Protestants were livid at its supposed disloyalty and stirred up a flurry of attacks. In the *Christian Century*, Robert Smylie noted that the "China statement evoked a storm of criticism which threatened to engulf the NCC" and gave extreme conservatives the fuel they needed to publicly discredit American ecumenism.[46]

All World Order Study Conferences, although sponsored by the Council, spoke independently from it. The conferences usually drew between three and five hundred delegates who were appointed by the NCC's member denominations; they included clergy as well as laity from government, business, and academia. Conference messages generally were referred back to the Council and denominations for possible study, comment, dissemination, and policy adoption. The fifth conference's message was so controversial that the NCC merely passed the report to its International

Affairs Commission without taking action on it. Nevertheless, most critics were not savvy to the independent nature of the conference or to the
Council's official silence on the matter, nor were they discriminating about
the message's specific appeal for *reconsideration* of policy rather than for
change itself.[47] Consequently, they attacked the Council for advocating the
recognition and UN membership of "Red China." Charges of communist
infiltration among the clergy ran rampant again. The NCC's leftist image
gained new life among churchgoers, and public perception of the Council's
China position remained problematic throughout the Vietnam War.

The level of vitriol startled the NCC. Most worrisome, though, was the
large outcry raised against the churches' right to comment on sociopolitical issues, not to mention the still widespread tendency to label dissenting
voices as un-American. In response, the Council issued a policy statement
called the Hartford Appeal (February 1959). It defended both the right
and *duty* of churches to comment upon all aspects of life, including social
issues, economics, foreign policy, and politics. It also attacked the automatic association of dissent with disloyalty. Reaffirming that democracy's
health hinged upon protecting freedom of speech, belief, and conscience
the NCC declared, "Such a right is especially vital to the Church, which
owes a duty to lead and to inform, so that its members may be aided in
reaching morally valid judgments in the light of their common faith."[48]
Fearing the attacks might intimidate church groups into squelching discussion of controversial issues, so vital to the ecumenical discernment process,
the Council asked members to encourage frank discussion of them. The
Hartford Appeal, along with the World Order Study Conference's approach
to the China issue, established another precedent for the NCC when it
struggled later not only with America's Vietnam policy but also with the
castigation of antiwar activists as un-American.

The Council's prominent split with Dulles demonstrated that, in the
darkness of McCarthy's shadow and under great pressure to echo the
Christian nationalism prevalent at the time, America's ecumenical leaders could separate themselves enough from the dominant culture and
their own establishment ties to speak their perceived truth to power on
a controversial foreign policy issue. It also illustrated how far apart the
NCC and government officials had grown here. The Cold War consensus
among establishment liberals was cracking. Dulles felt wounded by the
NCC's repudiation of his positions. Recounting Dulles's last year, his sister Eleanor mentioned how hurt, disappointed, and suspicious he was of

possible organized betrayal by certain church leaders. Dulles died shortly after the conference. In their remembrances, Council members selectively honored his earlier ecumenical work.[49]

In January 1960 the U.S. Air Force surprised the Council with fresh communist accusations. The Air Force printed a training manual warning of widespread communist infiltration into America's churches.[50] Citing controversial ecumenical stands such as the recent one on China, NCC projects such as the Revised Standard Version of the Bible, and comments from right-wing religious propaganda as evidence, the manual urged vigilance against traitors by suspecting Christians who questioned American values, policies, or structures.[51] It specifically named the NCC and its liberal associations.[52] Both the Federal and National Councils had long advocated keeping the military on a short civilian leash; therefore concerns about one another were old and mutual.[53]

Gerhard Elston recalled wryly that "this Air Force Manual was the nicest thing that happened" to boost the Council's public relations campaign against its conservative critics. Comparing it to the opportune public mistakes made by southern state officials during civil rights demonstrations, against which activists could publicize the justness and reasonableness of their own cause, Elston said the Air Force's printing of bogus material gave the Council a spotlight in which to defend itself.[54] NCC Associate General Secretary James Wine raised the issue directly with Secretary of Defense Thomas Gates Jr. Wine accused the Air Force of violating the first amendment's separation of church and state and blasted its reliance on erroneous, libelous sources generated by the NCC's most extreme right-wing critics. He then demanded that the manual and all distributed copies be withdrawn.[55]

This issue received nationwide press, and the Air Force, thoroughly embarrassed, promptly withdrew the manual. Wine was invited to the Pentagon for a personal apology. Gates, along with some congressional committees, also ordered an investigation of military publication procedures and, as Wine reported, instituted tougher reviews to ensure that all manuals "meet high standards of accuracy, good taste and common sense."[56] The House Un-American Activities Committee took the opposite approach. It affirmed that "Communists have duped large numbers of the clergy, as well as lay leaders of the churches, into supporting Communist fronts and causes which masquerade behind deceitful facades of humanitarianism" and maintained that it (HUAC) found in the Council "over 100 persons in leadership capacity with either Communist-front records or records of service to Communist causes." HUAC then summoned Secretary of the Air Force Dudley Sharp to badger him about withdrawing the manual and apologizing to the NCC.[57]

James Wine was pleased with the military's response to the manual's objectionable text. Yet he raised a broader concern that he felt lay "beyond the proper indignation of the churches." It was the "totalitarian" "un-American" message and manner in which this manual, among others, attempted to indoctrinate military personnel. Specifically, the NCC warned against government efforts to "induce or coerce regimentation of expression" in such a way as to create loyalty tests of thought or belief. These included attempts to equate social justice concerns with "infidelity to the American ideal."[58] By addressing these issues publicly and at the highest levels of government, Wine felt, the Council "has truly and in fact voiced the conscience of America."[59] In response to the Air Force manual affair, the American ecumenical movement had, once again, publicly challenged the suppression of critical thought occurring under the guise of national security. It would do so repeatedly in the next decade.

The manual controversy also stirred up the familiar modernist-fundamentalist debate in the churches, which crescendoed again from 1960 through the end of the Vietnam War.[60] The NCC not only faced the usual conservative attacks on its sociopolitical stands; it also found itself under investigation by its own member denominations' local churches, for many were divided internally between conservative and liberal sentiments. The Council received considerable correspondence from congregations critical of its sociopolitical pronouncements. Influenced perhaps by the frequent publicized attacks, some began questioning the NCC's patriotism. Others felt it should focus more intently upon traditional church duties such as mission work and spiritual nurture. Still others felt the NCC was stepping too far beyond the sentiments of laity in its pronouncements, chastised it for not representing parishioners, and protested the presumption that the Council reflected the opinions of the more than forty million Christians within its member denominations.

The NCC simply reaffirmed its right and duty to address crucial issues facing humankind from a moral, Christian perspective. The young presidential candidate John F. Kennedy concurred. "The most unfortunate aspect of the Air Force Manual fiasco," he said, "is that it plays into the hands of those who want to silence the views of the National Council—

because they do not share those views. They are not communistic views." Kennedy added that "however controversial" the nation's current socio-economic issues were, "they involved ethical considerations—and I would expect many church leaders and organizations to feel they have an obligation to speak out on them."[61] Kennedy validated the Council's belief that it must challenge Christians to engage issues and take positions based upon reason and religious values.

But were people filling the churches to be challenged or comforted? Did they want to be confronted with sociopolitical issues or confirmed in their ways of living and believing?[62] What were people seeking from their church and pastors? It is important to consider also what clergy wanted and expected from their pastorates. The answers to these questions no doubt varied by many factors. However, research conducted by sociologists such as Rodney Stark, Charles Glock, and Jeffrey Hadden have made clear that many clerics, particularly those in mainline denominations, were moving in a different direction from their flocks.[63] A "new theology," less doctrinally oriented and more socially focused, was sweeping through urban seminaries, Christian journals, and the leadership of religious organizations. Traditionally, church leaders had believed that God's will moved first through the church and then out to the world. Churches thus filtered, interpreted, and then articulated God's agenda to the fallen world. The new theology that blossomed in the 1960s, however, saw the order differently; to its practitioners, God's will moved from God directly into the world. It was the church's job to discover where God was moving and then join that divine force. This implied that Christians must leave their sanctuaries to encounter God where God was working in the streets. It also meant churches were called to listen and serve rather than just pontificate.

This activist-oriented theology, and the new breed clergy that practiced it, fed in to some areas of the ecumenical movement's elite ranks. At the local level, however, Christian expectations often were devotionally based and personal. Many of the faithful did not appreciate what seemed like the growing secularization of their faith. Those laypersons who did become more liberal and socially focused in the 1960s, such as youth, often disengaged from the church, which seemed antiquated, establishment-tied, and bureaucratically slow. To many laity who stayed, mainline churches felt increasingly sterile, irrelevant to their core of meaning, and ineffective at giving them spiritually and socially what they wanted. Pulpits were becoming, what sounded to some, like political platforms. A gap between clergy and laity—between mainline Protestantism's leadership and parish-ioners—was emerging. Issues such as civil rights and the Vietnam War would expose this gap and wrench it into a chasm.

Complicating matters, denominations carefully guarded their direct relationship with church members. Generally, they did not want the NCC jumping over their heads to get immediate access to the people. At the same time, ecumenical leaders were focused more on forwarding their collective agenda through education, statements, and political influence than on responding to the needs, perspectives, and desires of laity. There was a general sense that laity were naïve, ill-informed, culture-driven, and parochial on most issues.

The Council did consider itself a representative body, however. Its denominations selected representatives proportionate to their populations to serve on the NCC's General Board and Assembly. The General Board, which met three or four times a year, and the General Assembly, which met triennially, were the only NCC bodies empowered to make policy or pass resolutions. Therefore Council actions were always tied to denominational opinion, albeit mostly at the executive level. Yet the NCC did not speak directly for the denominations and, in certain instances, stepped ahead of them on controversial issues—at their behest. Council staff observed denominational representatives voting more prophetically on tough issues within the Council than they did within their own communions. Thus, NCC staff sensed that denomination heads expected the Council to lead on contentious issues, thereby taking the flak to spare the denominations from direct parishioners' attacks. One staffer likened the NCC to a snow-plow used to blaze paths through stormy subjects so member churches could advance more easily in desired directions.[64]

Ecumenists' genuine passion for peace, justice, and the Christian faith were potent motivators for prophetic impulses. These also revealed a confidence that their vision of God's will for America and the church was clearer and more correct than contrary ones from those in government, in non-mainline, non-ecumenical communions, and at the grass roots. While theoretically supportive of the body-of-Christ idea of Christian unity, they nevertheless had their own litmus tests for which part of the body lay closest to the mind and heart of God. Of course, religious con-servatives who sought to discredit and even destroy the NCC did, too; for many who championed the narrative that America was God's chosen nation, questioning America became akin to doubting God.

So the NCC functioned officially as a representative body of its denominations' forty million members, but not necessarily a reflective one. Just as the nation's forefathers empowered representatives to speak independently in what they deemed the people's best interests, so the Council attempted to represent, in this classic sense, the American Christian conscience. And just as commoners resented the elitism of the early U.S. Congress, so too did many laypeople resent the NCC's apparent disregard of their opinions.

PEACE AND CIVIL RIGHTS

Between 1960 and 1963, peace and civil rights became the primary foci of the NCC's Division of Christian Life and Work (later renamed the Division of Christian Life and Mission, or DCLM), which dealt with foreign policy and social justice. These remained so throughout the 1960s. The Council's efforts on both issues during the Kennedy administration again laid important groundwork for how it responded to the Vietnam War.

Like most Americans, the Council sought peace amid the ever-lurking threat of nuclear war. To some extent, ecumenists saw nuclear proliferation as a spiritual test, challenging Christians to get busy as peacemakers or face divine wrath when humans annihilated God's creation with an array of mushroom clouds. The Council helped build a Church Center for the United Nations (CCUN) across the street from the UN itself, to heighten Christians' involvement in foreign affairs. Funded by Methodist women, the twelve-story center aimed to foster two-way communication between churches and the UN, as well as promote education about global issues within the churches.[65] The NCC's International Affairs Commission assumed responsibility for coordinating all CCUN programs. Indicative of the CCUN's perceived significance, its September 1963 dedication ceremony drew such distinguished speakers as Secretary of State Dean Rusk, and the presence of UN Ambassador Adlai Stevenson and UN Secretary General U Thant.[66]

The Council also produced significant pronouncements and programs on peace. In June 1960, it issued a defining statement called "Toward a Family of Nations Under God: Agenda of Action for Peace." Its peace plan was typical ecumenical fare and would vary little over the next decade. While asking Christians to get involved generally in international affairs, it encouraged them specifically to appeal for a diplomatic end to the arms race, as well as for nations to use multinational means of adjudicating international disputes.[67] Open communication to advance reconciliation in a polarized world should not be viewed as weakness or appeasement. At this time the Council was fighting the proposed Connally Amendment, which would have allowed the United States to exempt itself from World Court rulings on cases involving America.[68] Emphasizing the oneness of all people, the NCC's pronouncement also clarified that improving people's standards of living was a moral privilege. Helping others was self-benefiting, too, for America's national welfare was connected with theirs. Reminding Christians that promoting human rights and freedom was a central part of Christ-like living, the statement connected America's domestic injustices to the nation's credibility in the world community. "Full respect for the United States rests upon our own respect for the dignity and equality of all our citizens before the law."[69]

Harry Seamans, the State Department's liaison to nongovernmental organizations (NGOs), encouraged the NCC's aspirations to play a significant role in fostering world peace. As he told its International Affairs Commission (IAC) in 1960, "the National Council of Churches represents the largest single constituency of any organization in the United States. With a common concern for world's mankind rooted in the Christian religion, you can be the most effective instrument for world peace in America." Affirming the triumphal spirit already within the NCC, he added, "I'm convinced that the churches are in a unique position to influence the international scene as no other private organization."[70] Seamans recognized the churches' growing "sophistication and realism in world affairs" and noted the substantial international and governmental expertise of several Council leaders. To his mind, this combination of realism, acumen in foreign affairs, large constituency, and ecumenical worldview empowered the NCC to serve as a successful advocate for world peace.

In May 1960, the IAC launched a five-year peace education and action program. This extended project grew out of a successful one-year program that a Council report said had "'penetrated' to the churches more than any other yet sponsored by the N.C.C."[71] As one practical effort within it, the NCC and WCC met with President Kennedy, Secretary of State Rusk, and Undersecretary of State Averell Harriman to discuss the nuclear test ban treaty.[72] Like the earlier peace pronouncement "Toward a Family of Nations," this NCC program emphasized that the churches were blessed with "unique resources" and "crucial responsibilities" at a time of "world crisis" containing both "peril and promise." Therefore, domestic and international peace hinged upon achieving justice for people, and justice would follow if America truly lived its democratic and spiritual values.

Although the Council had long opposed segregation and racism in its official pronouncements and education, it took Martin Luther King Jr.'s "Letter from a Birmingham Jail" (April 1963), John F. Kennedy's subsequent speech supporting civil rights legislation (June 1963), and King's March on Washington (August 1963) to inspire the NCC to demonstrate these convictions with others in the streets, in the South, and before Congress. Civil rights was such a clear moral issue of right versus wrong for most ecumenists that they felt compelled to lead their predominantly white constituencies into the arena of social and political activism with King.[73] The civil rights movement provided the context for perhaps the Council's greatest contribution toward watershed legislative victories: the Civil Rights Act of 1964 and Voting Rights Act of 1965. Civil rights and the Vietnam War dominated the NCC's attention during the 1960s, with civil rights deemed the more pressing, compelling, and morally obvious one. Yet, they were in many ways two interrelated parts of the Council's ecumenical witness throughout this period. The rollercoaster rise and fall of mainline American ecumenism from 1960 to 1975 cannot be understood without taking full account of both.

The Council's participation in the civil rights movement impacted its later efforts on Vietnam in three significant ways. First, it propelled the Council into social activism that went beyond education and pronouncements to physical demonstrations of conscience in the streets and in the halls of government. It also motivated the NCC, as did the earlier UN effort, to organize massive grassroots outreach and a "national lobbying effort," which Hubert Humphrey praised as a difference-maker in getting civil rights legislation passed. The Council was so heartened by its perceived civil rights successes that it felt competent to serve as a prophetic voice leading Americans through its "peace with justice" agenda.[74] Certain ecumenical leaders wanted the NCC's actions on civil rights to be used as models for constructing its witness on the Vietnam War. Discussions around this fueled a debate over the nature of a true ecumenical witness. Not only were civil rights approaches adapted for an antiwar witness, several white church leaders utilized their civil rights networks to help raise an initial voice against U.S. Vietnam policy.

Second, civil rights drew the Council back into a closer relationship with the White House. Both Kennedy and Johnson met with NCC leaders to discuss civil rights and involved them at top levels in their executive efforts. This high-profile, victorious collaboration with government not only reaffirmed the sense among Council leaders that church and government should join forces to protect the general welfare; it also reconfirmed that mainline Protestantism was still an important part of the establishment.[75] After the bitter McCarthy period, civil rights sweetened ecumenical leaders' faith in government as they forged mutually beneficial ties about which some Council leaders grew protective. The fact that the White House was seen clearly as friend, not foe, of the ecumenical vision regarding civil rights made opposing the sensitive Johnson administration on Vietnam difficult for both personal and professional reasons. The Council's establishment image, bolstered by its White House connections on civil rights, also enhanced anti-establishment groups' suspicions that the NCC might be a lackey of the liberals in power.

Finally, the Council's engagement in civil rights deepened its awareness of institutionalized racism in America. This also alerted the NCC to racism in U.S. foreign policy, especially with regard to Latin America, South Africa, and Asia. Within the World Council of Churches, members from non-white nations vented anger over their experiences with Western imperialism, and American ecumenical leaders expanded their understanding of ties between U.S. imperialism and racism. These leaders also began soliciting non-white, non-American perspectives when assessing domestic and foreign policy.[76] As U.S. combat troops engaged the Vietnamese, Council leaders recognized the racism inherent in America's Cold War rhetoric and understood Stokely Carmichael's rage that Vietnam was essentially about "white people sending black people to make war on yellow people in order to defend the land they stole from red people."[77] When the war began draining precious funds from Johnson's poverty-fighting Great Society programs, the NCC again joined voices with civil rights workers to cry "foul."

Overall, the Council's budding activism on civil rights sensitized its leaders to the racism protruding from U.S. Vietnam policy. It also awakened them to the hypocrisy imbedded in America's altruistic rhetoric about saving a people whose nation and culture its war policy was tearing apart. Just as ecumenists had learned from both world wars, the NCC observed again that racism, combined with nationalism and globalism, sowed the seeds of martial conflict. They saw this manifested in America's domestic riots as well as overseas in Indochina.

A TIME OF VIOLENCE AND CHANGE

On November 22, 1963, Lee Harvey Oswald assassinated President John F. Kennedy in Dallas. Kennedy was scheduled to address the NCC's triennial General Assembly in Philadelphia days later.[78] As the assembly met that first week of December, its delegates felt viscerally the press of violence and change upon the world. In its "Message to the Churches," the Sixth General Assembly wrote, "With the loss of our President we suddenly looked into the full depth of our crisis. We see here the disclosure of mounting hatreds in the nation which threaten our very structure as a democracy. Yet even before the sudden tragedy came it was clear that in the United States too the most salient mark of our time is change accelerated, radical, often irreversible." Facing changes and acts of violence that seemed difficult to comprehend, the Council affirmed its belief that God moves through world events. In what they described as a divisive revolutionary time, delegates focused again on justice as the cry of humanity and called Christians to a new oneness in advancing it worldwide. Justice was the basis for true peace. And, in pursuing it, one encountered God.[79]

From 1964 through 1965, as the Council began struggling with U.S. Vietnam policy, it also faced more keenly than perhaps ever before the message's challenge to "think as servants of the eternal Kingdom and not merely as members of a nation state."[80] Earlier, when the Federal and National Councils spoke out for labor, for aiding the allies in World War II, against McCarthyism, and on behalf of civil rights, they had support in powerful places. Conversely, when the NCC protested U.S. Vietnam policy, it would not only lack the support of most Americans but also stand in opposition to the U.S. government. While still celebrating legislative civil rights victories it helped procure, the Council tried to act with similar triumphal force on Vietnam. But foreign policy proved to be a stickier wicket than domestic policy, and Vietnam a more ambiguous issue morally than seeking civil rights legislation. Competing moral arguments on the war captured widespread support and muddied Christian dialogue.[81] Additionally, many critics continued to believe churches should stick to saving souls and not meddle in foreign policy. Just as with China policy, the Council's interference was excoriated. But, because young Americans were actually fighting and dying for freedom in Vietnam, the intensity of the attacks became magnified and permanently scarring. It was tough for a largely mainline Protestant establishment with long ties to government and deep roots in middle America to speak against a war after U.S. troops were engaged, especially one that government and middle America initially supported. This got even tougher when the establishment of which the Council's churches were part, and through which they operated, found itself torn by chaotic forces of change motivated by the very justice issues that the NCC advocated.

CHAPTER THREE

A Brief Interlude on Vietnam, to 1963

Most Americans knew little about Vietnam, or America's involvement with it, prior to the deployment of U.S. combat troops.[1] This left the American people especially vulnerable to believing uncritically the government's spin of events once U.S. soldiers were engaged. The NCC had also paid scant attention to Vietnam, having ignored it in official resolutions and pronouncements prior to 1965. Therefore, its leaders experienced a steep learning curve beginning in late 1964 as they struggled to make sense of events and separate fact from fiction. To appreciate this, and evaluate NCC understanding of the war as it unfolded, one must have an advantage that most NCC leaders and U.S. citizens did not cultivate before 1965: a general knowledge of the historical dynamics underlying the conflict.

For millennia, the Vietnamese fought against invading armies seeking domination and resources. Chinese war lords colonized them for about a thousand years before the Vietnamese finally drove them out. The Vietnamese reared their children on stories about peasant heroes who fought the Chinese. Therefore, a proud nationalist spirit ran deep within their culture. A tradition of local village self-government enhanced Vietnamese desire for self-determination and suspicion of outside manipulation.

Vietnamese sovereignty was challenged by a new invader in the 1860s, as France entered on the heels of Catholic missionaries. Taking control in 1883, it ruled the largely Buddhist nation with a heavy hand. The French saw the Vietnamese as inferiors, tried to suppress their native cultures, and used them as economic pawns. Except for a minority of elites who collaborated with the imperialists, the Vietnamese never accepted French domination as legitimate.

Raised in a strongly nationalist village, Ho Chi Minh left Vietnam at the age of twenty-one to see the world and quickly became an advocate for Vietnamese independence. In 1919 while in France, he appealed for self-determination at the Versailles peace talks which ended World War I. When Woodrow Wilson and other Western leaders rebuffed him, Ho sought allies among the communists. He returned to Indochina and organized what later became the Indochinese Communist Party. This attracted noncommunist nationalists as well because it positioned itself as the strongest nationalist force in Vietnam.

When Germany occupied France in 1940, France lost its hold on Indochina, so the opportunistic Japanese essentially took Vietnam from the French.[2] Ho Chi Minh launched a popular resistance movement against the newest occupiers. He helped create a broad coalition known as the Vietminh, which drew support well beyond communist circles because of its nationalist aims. As a fellow victim of Japanese expansion, China supported the Vietminh; and since the United States was aiding China financially and fighting the Japanese, the United States also ended up arming Ho's rebels.[3] Franklin Roosevelt supported Vietnam's goal of self-determination and wanted colonialism ended there after the war. Since America had once freed itself from colonial rule, the United States and Vietnam seemed like natural allies against imperialism.

The Japanese forfeited Vietnam in August 1945, after Japan's defeat in the broader world war. The new Democratic Republic of Vietnam celebrated its long-sought independence in September at a national rally. U.S. military officers stood with Ho Chi Minh as a band played the "Star Spangled Banner." The people listened to Ho read Vietnam's Declaration of Independence, modeled upon America's, which began with the familiar words, "All men are created equal. They are endowed by their Creator with certain unalienable Rights; among these are Life, Liberty, and the pursuit of Happiness." This document also reminded the United States and its allies of their stated support for self-determination in the UN charter. It closed with a warning and a promise: the Vietnamese were willing to make all necessary sacrifices to defend their independence should any nation plan to subvert it.[4]

The French were indeed entertaining such plans, and the British backed them. This put the United States in a bind between its wartime rhetoric and its evolving postwar political and economic interests. While Britain, France, and Vietnam were all U.S. war allies, America clearly needed the postwar help of its European compatriots to achieve its geopolitical goals, especially with respect to checking Russian power. Besides, the United States had commercial designs for Asia, centered around its reconstruction of Japan, which U.S. policy makers felt could best be achieved through a French-controlled Vietnam. So the United States not only consented to but aided France's reentry into Vietnam. The Vietminh, under Ho Chi Minh's leadership, responded exactly as promised. After negotiation attempts failed, they fomented a military resistance.[5] Thus, in 1946, France and Vietnam plunged into war. The Vietnamese effort was one of many anticolonial wars that emerged in the wake of World War II, initiated by peoples of color in Asia, Africa, and Latin America who resented foreign dominance. Many black civil rights leaders in the United States identified with this worldwide plea for freedom and liberation from oppression.

Meanwhile, the emerging Cold War transformed perceptions of the French-Vietnamese conflict. In 1946, Americans knew Vietnamese resistance to French control was inspired by anti-colonial desires. But by 1950, they saw the war solidly in communist/anticommunist terms—as a struggle between the communist-led Vietminh and the democratic free French.

When the American colonies were battling the British in the 1770s, Americans correlated "freedom" with "self-determination." Ho Chi Minh had petitioned for U.S. support in part because of that history. However, in the late 1940s, "anticommunism" took precedence for American officials as freedom's closest synonym. Since communism was seen as the antithesis of freedom, anticommunist forces of any kind were treated as freedom's bulwark. And since Americans assumed that communism only spread through force and intimidation, communism was also viewed as incongruous with true nationalism and self-determination. This led the U.S. government to discount nationalism as a legitimate force within revolutionary movements that contained communist leadership elements. It was a serious oversight. Assuming Ho Chi Minh was a tool of the Soviets or Chairman Mao, the United States began bankrolling France's war against the Vietminh; by 1950, America had committed to providing hundreds of millions in aid, arms, aircraft, ships, and even fertilizer.

Yet by 1954, despite U.S. backing, the French had all but lost. To avoid surrender, France appealed to have the war settled diplomatically by the five permanent UN Security Council nations, along with Indochinese representatives. They met in Geneva. Although able to win on the battlefield, under Chinese pressure the Vietminh agreed to the talks because a diplomatic solution might earn them U.S. recognition and forestall the American impulse to replace French forces with their own. The United States participated in the talks, but not happily.

The Geneva Accords of 1954 created a settlement that is critical for understanding the grievances that raged throughout the subsequent United States–Vietnam War. The accords temporarily divided Vietnam into two cease-fire zones at the 17th parallel. The French were then to extricate themselves and turn control of the southern zone over to local leadership. The Vietminh retained control of the northern zone. In no way was this cease-fire division meant to be permanent or denote the creation of separate nations. Within two years, both zones were supposed to take part in nationwide elections to be monitored by an International Control Commission that included Canada, India, and Poland. The winners would then create a government to reunify the country. Other nations were to desist from military or political interference in Vietnam.

The United States was not thrilled with the accords. While it did not sign, it agreed to abide by them. It soon broke this promise, however. Ho Chi Minh planned to run in the upcoming elections, for the nation's two-time liberator enjoyed considerable popularity. The Americans hoped to build up a viable anticommunist government in the South that could rival Ho's favor with the people. Championed by high-ranking U.S. officials and many influential U.S. Catholics, the anticommunist Vietnamese nationalist, Ngo Dinh Diem, was appointed prime minister of southern Vietnam after the French relinquished control. With clandestine support from the CIA and a hefty dose of U.S. funds, Diem tried to create a government and power base of support from which to rule.

When the question of reunifying elections was broached, Diem refused to accede to them, preferring instead to decree the creation of "South Vietnam" and have himself elected president there via a corrupted process. Recognizing that Ho Chi Minh would emerge victorious from a monitored election process, the United States backed Diem's move. This again proved that America valued an anticommunist definition of freedom over one rooted in self-determination. Even if communism advanced by free election rather than force, U.S. officials argued that its spread would still infect the region and threaten global security.

Meanwhile, in an effort to contain communism in Southeast Asia while providing support to Diem's government, Dulles quickly created the regional defense group SEATO in 1954. He considered Indochina under its protective jurisdiction. In what eventually came back to bite the United States, SEATO inevitably tied U.S. credibility to the defense of a "nation," South Vietnam, that was not a free-standing, popularly supported, legitimate entity. In reality, the United States was engaged in a nation-building experiment there.

All of this defied the Geneva Accords. The North Vietnamese did not accept the nation's division and treated South Vietnam as a fiction born in the minds of the Americans. They remained furious at the subversion of Vietnam's promised nationwide elections. America's interference proved to them that the United States was another imperialist power seeking to impose its will. Therefore, Ho Chi Minh sought and received assistance from the Chinese and Soviets, playing them deftly one off the other to preserve his country's independence from their overt control as well. He built a centralized communist government in the North and readied his people for another revolution against a paternalistic foreign power.

Meanwhile, America's nation-building experiment faltered as Diem rejected democratic principles. Preferring autocracy and nepotism, he appointed his brothers to key leadership positions and allowed his tactless flamboyant sister-in-law to operate much like a "first lady." A Catholic from the mandarin class, Diem belittled the Buddhists who comprised the majority of Vietnam's population. South Vietnamese citizens grew restless under Diem's oppressive rule. The United States poured vast sums and adviser assistance into South Vietnam, trying to create a democratic anticommunist nation as well as a military there that could defend itself. To the chagrin of U.S. officials, however, corruption infected the government and its armed forces. Diem alienated the people by violating village self-rule, putting heavy-handed family members in power, attacking Buddhists and their holy sites, and persecuting dissenters. Political prisoners were often tortured and killed.

By 1960, the South was engulfed in civil war. Some southerners resented Diem's dictatorial American-sponsored rule and sought national reunification under Ho Chi Minh's leadership; others wanted the South to have an opportunity to determine its own path apart from Ho, Diem, and the Americans; a third group, tied to Diem, wanted to preserve the new U.S.-backed power base. Students and Buddhist monks took to the streets to protest Diem's repression and U.S. ties. An indigenous guerilla force emerged in the South that aimed to overthrow Diem and rid themselves of U.S. interference. Some members were communists; some were not. Nationalism united them. Dubbed the Vietcong (VC) by Diem, these farmers by day and fighters by night received assistance from Ho's government and the North Vietnamese Army (NVA), a trained and battle-hardened force. The VC created a political wing of their southern resistance movement called the National Liberation Front (NLF).

Like Diem's forces, the VC and the NVA used brutal tactics to punish those resisting their will. With the North assisting the VC, the United States stepped up its support of a faltering Diem. President Kennedy increased the number of American advisers working to train Diem's forces from eight hundred to about sixteen thousand. But this did not improve Diem's situation. Weeks before Kennedy's assassination, Diem was murdered in a South Vietnamese military coup. Those who masterminded the coup felt they had received the go-ahead from U.S. officials who believed Diem had grown so incompetent they needed new leadership in the South. But following Diem's demise, the government fell to a sequence of leaders who were no better. In fact, Secretary of Defense Robert McNamara later described Diem as the best of a bad lot.

With Kennedy's assassination, Johnson inherited a mess in Vietnam. The nation-building experiment was in dire straits. Democracies require two critical foundations to flourish: skilled leadership that values democratic principles and the consent of the governed. South Vietnam had neither throughout the entire span of its existence. This virtually ensured the defeat of America's goals there from the outset. The military mission for South Vietnam's army and its U.S. advisers was to stop the VC uprising and contain the NVA north of the 17th parallel. Military efforts were designed to support the larger political goal of building a free-standing democratic nation in the South by quelling the rebellion. The United States hoped the South's army could accomplish this, but its military was riddled with VC, corruption, and a questionable will to win. When U.S. troops later adopted this military mission as their own, they would be trying to aid a government that could never stand by itself. And, as the latest unwanted outside invader, they would be fighting against forces that had considerable village support.

When Johnson assumed the problem in Vietnam, he saw four main options: keep relying upon U.S. advisers and the South Vietnamese military, hoping they might eventually turn the tide; withdraw from Vietnam, letting the South's government collapse, and blame it on Diem's intransigence; try to negotiate a political settlement, which would create a coalition government in the South that included communists; or Americanize the war by assigning U.S. combat soldiers to do the job that South Vietnamese forces either couldn't or wouldn't.

Johnson and Kennedy before him had perpetuated the false impression that South Vietnam was indeed a viable democratic government that enjoyed popular support. American officials had painted Diem as an anticommunist hero, a skilled leader, and a loyal ally. They characterized the VC as stooges of the aggressive communist North, which they deemed a pawn of the Chinese and Soviets. They told the American people that South Vietnam was a strategic beachhead of freedom, which the United States could not let fall without dire consequences for the entire region and ultimately for U.S. security and power. These were erroneous images that drew many unknowing patriotic Americans into supporting their nation's efforts there.

Until the end of 1963, the Federal and National Councils had largely ignored Vietnam. They had passed no resolutions or policy statements that spoke to the Vietnamese push for independence, the French-Vietnamese War, the Geneva Accords, the Diem regime and its repression, or even Buddhist resistance to Diem, which included Buddhist self-immolation—all topics that from human rights, race, international order, and religious freedom standpoints might have attracted ecumenical interest. Their attention in Asia was focused instead on China and Taiwan. Vietnam would hold the NCC's gaze only when it did the rest of the nation's. The war's divisive capacity would become apparent during the 1964 U.S. campaign season. Fissures within the ecumenical community that had remained hidden, unrecognized, or minor in nature would be exacerbated by the presidential election and then split wide open as the NCC developed gradual yet firm stands against America's military involvement in Indochina.

PART
TWO

MUSTERING THE

PEACE FORCES,

1964-1965

CHAPTER FOUR

Awakening a Loyal Opposition, 1964–July 1965

HIGH STAKES IN THE 1964 ELECTION

Nothing seemed more crucial than the Civil Rights Bill being filibustered in Congress—at least not for the NCC's staff during the first seven months of 1964. The Council channeled considerable effort and treasure into mobilizing church-based support for its passage. The Johnson administration praised the NCC's effectiveness. Ecumenists appreciated Johnson's leadership and legislative skill on civil rights as well. Here was a president with whom they could partner on issues of mutual concern. His Great Society agenda and the ecumenical vision of the Responsible Society shared several domestic objectives, including racial and economic justice.

The new president's approach to international affairs was still unknown, however. Even though Johnson assured the UN that he would seek an end to the Cold War, church leaders remained uncertain.[1] In March, the old cold warrior Reinhold Niebuhr revealed his skepticism. "Everyone seems to agree that the new President's exploitation of the Kennedy legacy in civil rights has been brilliant. . . . President Johnson's foreign policy, on the other hand, is much less than brilliant. Aspects of it threaten to be catastrophic." Niebuhr fretted about Johnson's attempt to be more hawkish than the Republicans on Cuba in order to avoid accusations of being "soft on Castro." Niebuhr also questioned his uncoordinated handling of political instability in South Vietnam and the dearth of White House information, which left citizens ignorant and dependent upon blind trust in their government.[2]

Niebuhr had identified a precipitous reality that foreshadowed Johnson's handling of the war. Unbeknownst to many beyond Johnson's innermost circle, his administration was already avoiding negotiations and bending toward Americanizing and militarizing the conflict. To Johnson, negotiating with communists was a weak and unmanly option. He and his closest advisers were trying to protect their political credibility via their Vietnam policies. Throughout 1964 and into early 1965, Niebuhr and a handful of other realists pressed their critiques into print. These gadflies included journalist Walter Lippman, political scientist Hans Morgenthau, and senators William Fulbright, Hubert Humphrey, and Mike Mansfield. But they were too few, and ultimately, too quiet. So, also, were the vast majority of U.S. allies overseas, who saw America's escalation in Vietnam as folly. Like many domestic leaders, they shied away from confronting the mercurial president for fear of losing his support on other matters of concern. With the exceptions of Niebuhr, Bennett, and a few others, most church leaders (including those within the NCC) knew little about the Vietnam situation. In this they reflected the general ignorance of most Americans. Church leaders' growing uncertainty about Johnson inspired them to pay more attention as the election year proceeded, but their learning curve lagged too far behind Johnson's steps toward escalation to have much influence on events.[3]

A month earlier, in February 1964, the Chinese and Russian communist parties feuded bitterly when China accused the Soviets of betraying true communism. This taught attentive church people a lesson about communist diversity.[4] They saw that communism did not operate as a monolithic bloc, that race and economic differentiations between communist nations mattered, and that communism's appeal in developing nations hinged upon economic deprivation and nationalist desires. As a result, the *Christian Century* and *Christianity and Crisis* appealed for a policy that treated communist governments situationally and individually. To many ecumenists, outdated Cold War attitudes were precipitating policies out of proportion to real security dangers and fostering unnecessary ill will within both political and ecumenical communities. Church leaders wondered what Johnson would do as the presidential campaign escalated. "Will the Administration be driven to take 'know-nothing' positions in order to avoid the suspicion that it is soft on communism?" Bennett queried.[5]

As it turned out, Johnson tried to distinguish himself from his Republican rival, Barry Goldwater, by becoming the moderate voice of reason. Compared to Goldwater, who wore Cold War extremism as a badge of honor, Johnson could easily paint himself as the peace candidate while adhering to a traditional containment policy. This attracted the NCC, given that its International Affairs Commission was directing a nationwide lay education effort on peace sponsored by its denominational members. This program came in response to a State Department estimate that "nine out of ten Americans are 'uninformed and unconcerned' in international affairs."[6] Johnson seemed to be the most compatible candidate with this emphasis. He even endorsed the NCC's peace project as one "of great importance."[7]

Ecumenists were also growing more sensitive to non-Western perspectives of foreign policy and heeding them as never before. They challenged America's religious bureaucrats to take a broader worldview. In May 1964, church leaders gathered at Duke University to discuss "Christianity and Social Revolution in Newly Developing Nations," focusing especially on Africa, Asia, and Latin America. White ecumenists admitted there that American missionaries often operated as mediums of Western imperialism, inciting resentment. Several even recommended that Christians address Third World financial needs by cooperating with economic changes championed by communists. They felt God was working on the front lines of people's needs rather than in respectable white churches where reactionary rhetoric often rang.[8]

The NCC's educational peace program inspired its increased attention to developments in Vietnam. The Council also began receiving information from nongovernmental sources that challenged official accounts. A group of Japanese Christian pacifists, called the Japan Christian Council for Peace in Vietnam, approached the NCC out of concern about U.S. Asia policy and the silence of America's churches. Through the NCC, they met with U.S. church leaders to discuss and pray about the Vietnam crisis. They viewed it as a threat not only to Asia but possibly to humankind.[9]

These contacts helped enhance the NCC's understanding of the conflict. So too did a confidential government briefing secured by the NCC. Amiya Chakravarty, a Boston University professor, had just returned from South

Vietnam. His analysis of the war clearly clashed with the Johnson administration's. Chakravarty had seen a deteriorating situation in the South, and he called U.S. policies both morally wrong and self-defeating. For example, U.S. military tactics were contributing to the loss of Vietnamese hearts and minds. The Vietcong also had momentum on their side. Therefore he recommended the United States commence negotiations with both North Vietnam and China, which would address all of Southeast Asia, and end its unilateral involvement by including the UN.[10]

Chakravarty sensed that the administration leaned toward escalation in the summer of 1964. Nevertheless, the coming presidential election inspired Johnson to speak of peace and assure Americans that "We are not going to send American boys nine or ten thousand miles away from home to do what Asian boys ought to be doing for themselves."[11] Behind the scenes, Johnson skirted North Vietnamese invitations to negotiate, because the United States was in a poor bargaining position, and sent additional advisers to the South.[12] By playing tough with North Vietnam, Johnson tried to disprove Goldwater's accusations that he was soft on communism. While some ecumenical leaders cringed at Johnson's rigid adherence to the domino theory and containment policy, most welcomed his assurance that America would not deploy combat troops. Goldwater, on the other hand, stood willing to unleash America's fire power onto North Vietnam, including possibly nuclear weapons.[13] Due to Goldwater's bellicosity and his states' rights stance against civil rights legislation, both the *Christian Century* and *Christianity and Crisis*, for the first time in their histories, felt morally compelled to oppose a political candidate. With respect to the 1964 election and U.S. Vietnam policy, these two journals played catalyst roles within ecumenical circles by raising critical questions for debate, exemplifying a prophetic posture on foreign policy, and challenging cautious organizations such as the NCC to do likewise.

In July the *Century*'s lead editorial proclaimed "Goldwater? No!" This piece put its tax exempt status in jeopardy for what its editors considered reasons of conscience and responsible citizenship. The journal worked to defeat Goldwater, for "his election would . . . jeopardize the position of the United States in the world, would inflame the cold war and sap the confidence of our allies. . . . We can see no gain to come from his election."[14] When Goldwater won the Republican nomination (a party to which the *Century* had often been favorably disposed), the journal attacked Goldwater's philosophy that "Extremism in the defense of liberty is no vice." It tried to expose his anticommunist fear tactics as regressively dangerous and asked readers to let their better reason win out. "His main hope of winning the election is to frighten the nation into a stampede for 'security,'" it declared. "He cannot win if the nation maintains its nerve, insists on doing justice and loving mercy, [and] persists in facing on their merits the real issues of domestic and foreign policy."[15]

The possibility that Goldwater's crusader rhetoric would appeal to Christians, just as Billy Graham's had a decade earlier, concerned ecumenists. Believing the church responsible for helping foster informed and morally conscious public opinion, the *Century* wrote that "churchmen and other persons of religious faith must ask themselves how religion can help people under stress fight fear with faith, panic with confidence, terror with courage. Misapplied and mistaken religion is one of four roots of extremism."[16] The *Christian Century* spoke for many ecumenists when it warned of the divisive, warlike potential of Goldwater's leadership.

Christianity and Crisis opposed his candidacy for similar reasons. As John Bennett explained, Goldwater took contrary positions on nearly "everything for which America's three faiths stand in respect to international relations, civil rights and economic policy." He added that the 1964 campaign was aggravating a painful fracture between various denominations' headquarters and the grass roots, as well as between parish clergy and laity, over social and international issues. Bennett worried especially about ministers in the Midwest, South, and Southwest, for "in church after church there is likely to be strong support among the laity for Goldwater. . . . It often sounds as though Goldwater regards himself as the prophet of true religion and of true morality against the many false prophets who differ from him on most issues." Fearing religious polarization and pastoral difficulties, Bennett stressed, "We dread this campaign more than we can say." Divisions would worsen with the war.[17]

On August 2 and 3 the Johnson administration received reports of North Vietnamese torpedo attacks on U.S. destroyers in the Gulf of Tonkin, which had been assisting covert South Vietnamese assaults on the North. The North struck at one of the destroyers and was repelled. Johnson did nothing. Reports of a second attack inspired his retaliation, however, even after the ship's captain declared them dubious. Johnson railed against North Vietnamese aggression and rallied congressional support for the Tonkin Gulf Resolution. Passed on August 7, this gave the president authority to take "all necessary steps" to defend the freedom of any SEATO nation that came under communist attack. In effect, this resolution gave Johnson the power to wage a war in Vietnam without asking Congress for an official declaration. With the presidential election just three months away, both parties wanted to appear stalwart in their commitment to stand down aggression.[18]

Johnson affirmed the moral rightness of America's duty to defend smaller nations against communist assaults.[19] He refused to be the next Democratic president to lose an Asian nation to communism and determined not to give Republicans such fodder again. On top of this, Johnson held traditional views of the Cold War, which included belief in the domino theory and the necessity of containment.[20] Therefore, while needing to convince the public he was a man of moderation and reason, Johnson nevertheless sent a clear message to his administration: "win the war!"[21] Defense Secretary Robert McNamara also recalled that South Vietnam's shaky political situation, and consequently America's weak bargaining position with the North, allowed negotiation to become equated with surrender in the minds of the administration.

Ecumenical leaders knew little about the extent of Johnson's hardening heart on Vietnam policy. Like the rest of America, they viewed him as a champion of civil rights, a masterful legislative consensus builder, and compared to Goldwater, the more sensible voice on foreign affairs. While the Christian Century felt Johnson overreacted to the Tonkin Gulf incident, criticized the subsequent resolution, and suspected that right-wing pressures motivated his increased belligerency, it still backed him in a piece entitled "Johnson? Yes!"[22]

The editorial board reminded readers that, not only did Goldwater denounce positions taken by ecumenical churches on critical issues facing humankind, his most vocal right-wing Christian supporters were among those who had tried repeatedly to destroy "the World Council of Churches, the National Council of Churches, [and] the social concerns divisions of the major denominations." Knowingly sacrificing its valuable tax exempt status, the Century's editors then made clear they were ready to endorse Johnson.[23] While candid about their reservations, the critical difference to them was Johnson's seeming ability to "coexist" in three ways that Goldwater could not. These included coexistence with communist China and the Soviet Union, coexistence between the races, and coexistence with a plurality of views and interest groups thriving in the nation. Because the Century believed all these were essential to peace, it chose to risk backing

Johnson for president. Not only did this move upset some readers, who felt the journal stepped out of bounds and sacrificed objectivity, but its tax exempt status was indeed revoked for several years.[24]

Other religion editors rejected Goldwater privately, but many refused to go public for, as the *Century* said, they "are aware of the strength of WASPism . . . in the backwoods and badlands of Protestantism and do not choose to counter it."[25] Those at *Christianity and Crisis* were not among them. The October 5 issue led with the editorial, "We Oppose Senator Goldwater."[26] Like the *Century*, this was the first time *Christianity and Crisis* had allied itself with a political candidate, and it did so for similar reasons. It clarified that its objection to Goldwater "comes not from pacifism, which we have consistently criticized, but from a belief that America must *both* maintain strong military power *and* exercise that power with moral and judicious restraint. We exalt wisdom over 'winning.'" In the subsequent issue, its editorial board endorsed "The Johnson-Humphrey Team." The president's strong legislative record on behalf of civil rights and his continuance of Roosevelt's legacy on economic issues won their support. The board also ventured a vote of confidence in his future foreign policy performance. Since he had mastered wheeling and dealing legislation into law, the journal predicted that Johnson would be practical and flexible enough to pursue better relations with communist nations. "Leaders whose strength is in the making of a consensus," it affirmed, "will necessarily move with the times. They will not symbolize great moral convictions or be known for their single-minded devotion to principles or causes. But without their help the prophets would see few of their concerns enacted into law."[27] Thus, ecumenical leaders hoped Johnson would be a president whom they could influence to rally legislative support on key issues. Certainly on civil rights they had shared an effective partnership. They assumed that Johnson could extrapolate their mutual understanding about the need for economic, social, and political justice on the home front into a similar agenda for the world.

In October, a month before the election, three events occurred that eventually impacted U.S. Vietnam policy and the antiwar movement. Martin Luther King Jr. received the Nobel Peace Prize, an honor that he felt compelled him to lead on world peace and not just racial justice; Leonid Brezhnev and Alexi Kosygin ousted Nikita Khrushchev from power in the Soviet Union, intensifying the Cold War; and, perhaps most significant, China detonated its first nuclear bomb, making it the fifth nation to enter the "nuclear club." This last event solidified most ecumenical leaders behind Johnson's candidacy. As the *Century* described it, China's nuclear ascendancy made it "A Time for Cool Heads and Steady Hands."[28]

Cooler heads did prevail in the voting booths. Assisted by Goldwater's poor campaign strategy, Johnson won a landslide victory. Both the *Christian Century* and *Christianity and Crisis* heaved a sigh of relief while taking a wait-and-see attitude regarding Johnson. With campaign pressures eliminated, would he consider a fresh flexible approach to the Cold War? Bennett kept urging ecumenists to press their vision with Johnson. It was time for prophets to point the way toward a better future so the president could lead people down that path.[29]

But Johnson was not the open-minded blank slate on international matters that ecumenists had hoped for. He was a mature politician whose Cold War commitment had been intensified by McCarthyite attacks on his party. Because of this, his eyes always searched the past for lessons on how to outmaneuver his right-wing challengers on foreign policy. His habit of looking backward for guidance prevented him from understanding and responding effectively to the revolutionary changes taking place worldwide. Ecumenical leaders had gambled that Johnson's advocacy of justice for people of color, the poor, and the disadvantaged in this country would engender sensitivity to the same worldwide, leading to foreign policies they could support. However, the bipolar worldview that dominated American culture and Goldwater's positions also drove Johnson's perceptions of international affairs.

Additionally, ecumenical organizations suffered repercussions from the 1964 presidential campaign. As predicted, it exacerbated tensions between clergy and laity; on the eve of full-scale U.S. combat in Vietnam, these stresses helped set the stage for greater antagonism between church officials and parishioners on foreign policy. Back in April, during the fight for the Civil Rights Bill, a *Christian Century* article noticed that seminarians expressed more sensitivity than parishioners on social issues, especially civil rights. The author, a faculty member at Vanderbilt's divinity school, described the catch-22 this created for young clergy and the problems it sowed for mainline denominations in the years ahead. "[O]ur faculty has been forced to note with pain and regret that whenever its students and graduates have actually preached the gospel they had been taught, they have risked deepening the chasm between them and their white laymen." Then, foreshadowing what statistics would later reveal on Vietnam, he observed, "Under the circumstances the minister, far from raising the educational and ethical standards of his congregations, very often finds himself pulled down to its level. . . . It is no wonder that the churches have lagged behind in witness to social concerns. We have failed to prepare the laity, and thus to take seriously the priesthood of all believers."[30] The last point was particularly important. Since the 1930s ecumenists had experienced a theological education and awakening of social and world consciousness that few laity shared. One-year educational programs, such as the NCC's on peace in 1964, were a start; but these seemed too little, and too late, to counter generations of fusion between nationalism and Protestantism that the Cold War exacerbated.

Once past the election, both the *Christian Century* and *Christianity and Crisis* returned to their usual nonpartisan positions, but they also continued to defend the church's moral duty to voice its conscience on key issues. As the *Century* reminded readers, the Founding Fathers' intent in the First Amendment was not to remove religion from politics but rather to free it to serve the nation as an independent moral agent. Those Christian voices who spoke against Goldwater's extremism, it said, helped head off a national, and potentially international, tragedy. While the *Century* had felt compelled to back Johnson in 1964, it defended the separation of church and state in politics. "The churches and their agencies should not become the fawning lackeys of parties and factions, for they are the servants of a Lord who does not countenance this kind of shared allegiance."[31]

Nevertheless, the journal reiterated that the body of Christ had a responsibility both to minister to people's interior lives and to work for justice and reconciliation in the world. "The churches should be in the thick of this venture," it insisted, adding that the church "more than any other institution must help the nation rediscover its soul and its purpose." Robert Bilheimer would echo this exact redemptive mission during the Vietnam War.

This ecumenical stance ran counter to the predominant evangelical belief that a Christian's primary duty was to save souls, and thus the nation, via conversions. An editorial in November highlighted the severity of this dispute between clergy and their more evangelical laity over the role of the church in society. "Among the laity in several quarters there has been a growing discontent about the 'church's'—that is, the clergy's—involvement in some of the social issues of our time. Any minister who deals with laity in planning and programming activities has discovered that there exists a great gap of communication, almost as if two different languages were being spoken." To the writer it signaled "a new reformation," which could not be dismissed as simply the repercussion of temporary political passions.[32] The fact that many professional ecumenists felt compelled in subsequent years to witness against U.S. Vietnam policy, whether the laity agreed or understood, ultimately created many politically (and some might add religiously) impotent "generals without armies."[33]

Reinhold Niebuhr provided an incisive post-election analysis of the clergy-laity gap exposed by the campaign. He argued that Goldwater had tapped into four lurking strains of Protestant individualism still present among middle-class laity but roundly rejected by more liberal clergy. These included a "Social Darwinist" complacent individualism, a nonpolitical pietism, a rigid perfectionist morality, and nativism. These anchored a worldview that condoned a nationalistic, militaristic foreign policy and the original civil-religion narrative that saw America as the vehicle of God's will.[34] It did not help when John Stormer published the popular book *None Dare Call It Treason* in 1964, which repeated empty accusations that the NCC functioned as a communist front and its churches were riddled with traitors. Thus, as ecumenists began to discuss the Vietnam conflict, they confronted a communication gap with both the U.S. government and many churchgoers, which grew from divergent worldviews.

WAIT, WATCH, AND WORRY, JANUARY-JULY 1965

By the end of 1964, South Vietnam's political situation had degenerated into chaos and corruption. The Vietcong controlled much of the countryside, and neither the South Vietnamese army nor its government engendered confidence among their people. Frustrated, Johnson knew his administration was nearing a crossroads. His advisers presented him with three options: continue the present Vietnam policy and face ultimate defeat, concentrate heavy bombing on North Vietnam to force favorable negotiations, or begin a graduated bombing campaign to encourage negotiations while minimizing the risk of widening the war. Disengagement, of course, remained a fourth option, but Johnson was not willing to risk losing Vietnam to the communists. He could not accept defeat and believed the American people would not either. The election also had illustrated that most Americans disapproved of tactics that risked nuclear war. Therefore, limited escalation appeared to be the lesser of the evils. According to McNamara, between January 28 and July 28, 1965, Johnson "made the fateful choices" that committed the United States to war in Vietnam, a move that "ultimately destroyed his presidency and polarized America like nothing since the Civil War."[35]

The polarization had not yet begun. At the time, most Americans could not identify Vietnam on a map and were paying little attention to the conflict. Yet, the seeds of antiwar dissent were being sown in the student, pacifist, and intellectual communities. In 1965 these started sprouting into an antiwar movement. Organized protests increased in frequency and size, even though liberals, radicals, pacifists, and "just war" proponents fought bitterly over strategies, values, and goals. Throughout the year, Protestant, Catholic, and Jewish leaders studied the developing Vietnam situation and spoke out to varying degrees as their organizations and consciences guided them. Most of the earliest Vietnam War critics were also among Johnson's greatest domestic policy supporters. This fence proved awkward to walk yet difficult for many to abandon. They still needed his backing, especially on civil rights. Besides, many liberals expected the war to end quickly and did not wish to alienate themselves from their loyalty-loving president.[36] People also felt uninformed about what was really happening in Vietnam, and why the United States was engaged there militarily. To help address this vacuum in public knowledge, students held campus teach-ins about the war. The ecumenical journals began covering the war in greater detail, utilizing their overseas contacts as sources of information to go beyond that dispensed by government. The NCC's staff, however, waited, watched, and worried. As a bureaucratic organization, the Council had no consensus, governing board authority, or direction yet with which to work. But the two major ecumenical journals would help force its hand.

Prior to the presidential election, the editorial board of *Christianity and Crisis* had dedicated an entire issue to the Vietnam conflict. It contained articles representing three different perspectives, which the board hoped would spark discussion about America's choices.[37] In the preface, the editors stated that their "optimum objective" was "a free and stable Vietnam (South Vietnam, in the foreseeable future) at peace with its neighbors and requiring no extraordinary measures of American military and economic participation." This was not significantly different from the aim of the Johnson administration. However, they doubted that military means could be used to stabilize, democratize, and popularize the South Vietnamese regime. Therefore, the editors asked readers to consider what results short of the ideal would be worth the potential costs inherent in waging war with communist powers.

Wayne Morse—a senator from Oregon and one of two dissenters opposing the Tonkin Gulf Resolution—wrote the first article favoring withdrawal from Vietnam. It represented the general stance of liberal intellectuals and pacifists who opposed U.S. policy. The premise of this position held that America was illegally and unwisely interfering in Vietnam for imperialistic ends. Morse accused the United States of hypocrisy in violating the Geneva Accords, subverting the UN Charter at the nation's convenience, and putting its interest in containment and world prestige over the wishes and independence of the Vietnamese people.[38] Since this created a no-win situation for the United States, he advocated a UN–negotiated settlement and a return to the anticolonialist agenda of Roosevelt in 1944. Obviously, Morse felt America was less interested in Vietnamese self-determination than in keeping the area anticommunist, and free of Chinese influence, at all cost. Therefore, he not only criticized the military means used to enforce U.S. policy; he also questioned the myopic anticommunist-driven policy itself, as well as the manner in which the United States imposed its agenda upon Vietnam. His position in 1964 foreshadowed the direction in which the NCC would move after Bilheimer joined its staff in 1966.

The second article, penned by Frank Trager, professor of international affairs at New York University, essentially defended Johnson's policy and methods as necessary. Trager discounted the withdrawal option as an abandonment of a "weak friend to the Communist enemy who has been pressing in on him all these years."[39] Such action would "dishonor its [America's] moral commitment" made personally to the South Vietnamese and officially through SEATO. He also supported the limited use of military strikes, both offensively and defensively, to halt communist advancement in South Vietnam. Herein, Trager outlined the alternative moral and political argument that compelled many Christians such as the Presbyterian secretary of state, Dean Rusk, to support U.S. military actions in Vietnam.

Alan Geyer, a political science teacher at Mary Baldwin College, crafted the third article. It represented the general sentiment of the NCC's International Affairs Commission then led by Ken Maxwell.[40] When Bilheimer assumed that role in 1966, Geyer was administering the international affairs efforts of the United Church of Christ (UCC), eventually becoming one of the most influential denominational secretaries in the NCC's Vietnam-related work.[41] In this 1964 article, Geyer criticized America's unilateral military involvement in Vietnam's political struggles. But he did not criticize the U.S. policy's aims of helping South Vietnam create a viable, popular, anticommunist government. He simply urged using multilateral diplomatic means.[42]

At the time, the ecumenical community knew relatively little about Vietnamese perspectives on the issue, the historical complexities of the conflict, or the ramifications of U.S. policy in the region. Therefore, ecumenists found it difficult and uncomfortable to assess the policy. But they were fairly united in their distaste for military responses to political problems, especially when unilateral. To their mind, the United States did not have the authority or the wisdom to police the world. No nation did. The United Nations existed to serve as an international mediator. It distressed them greatly when the major powers, including the United States, tended to short-circuit that institution whenever their own interests were involved.

In the study guide created to accompany the NCC's yearlong "Nationwide Program of Education and Action for Peace," Maxwell encouraged Christians to be aware of their personal biases and go beyond convenient media and political sources for information on controversial issues. He urged them to read popularly disseminated information critically, to "see the slants of all that comes to us, and to keep in mind that most of it is not thought out from a specifically Christian viewpoint."[43] With respect to Vietnam, the Council was beginning to follow its own advice by inviting the perspectives of people living in the region.

In January 1965, the International Affairs Commission received the confidential notes of U Kyaw Than on Vietnam. Than was associate general secretary of the East Asia Christian Conference (EACC)—the ecumenical body for East Asia and a fellow member of the World Council.[44] The EACC became the NCC's invaluable teacher on Asian perspectives of the war, significantly influencing the Council's comprehension of the conflict and region. Than explained how America's Vietnam policy was misguided and counterproductive. The Vietnamese wanted their nation reunited and would not accept the 17th parallel cease-fire line as demarcating two countries. It was unrealistic to think that a foreign power could assert its will over the indigenous desires of the people.

In addition, the EACC believed, like it or not, that communist China would be involved in Southeast Asian affairs simply by virtue of its proximity and power. Therefore, Southeast Asian nations could not formulate their policies only in terms of a "negative approach to Communism," something the United States often demanded. The region had bigger needs and priorities. South Vietnam's approval of U.S. policy in the region meant nothing to Asians for, as Than explained, "it is not yet clear whom that government represents," and according to most observers, "it simply represents those in whose hands military power at the moment resides." The only way to prevent communist influence in Vietnam, Than continued, would be for the United States to occupy and claim the South as a colonial dependency, which the United States seemed to be doing at present. But this situation was unsustainable. The Vietnamese wanted freedom from foreign domination more than anything else and would resist any occupying power. Than reminded his fellow ecumenists that Asians considered Ho Chi Minh a hero because of his strong nationalist leadership. Since Vietnam's wish for independence also traditionally included freedom from Chinese influence, Than blamed U.S. policy for driving the North Vietnamese into the hands of Chinese communists. Many in the region also thought the U.S. military was eagerly "testing out their new weapons on Asian soil," and they were asking, "Is human life in Asia cheap?"

America's image in Southeast Asia had suffered because of these miscues, Than asserted. U.S. officials often defended their Vietnam policy by arguing that, if America neglected its SEATO obligations, its reputation as a reliable defender of its allies would suffer. But Than explained that U.S. methods already produced negative results. How, he asked, "can the countries of Asia which look to the U.S. for economic aid as well as political stability really depend on the U.S. if it creates the impression that in the last analysis it will use its overwhelming military power to protect what are primarily its own immediate interests?"

America's poor reputation in Asia was an albatross for its churches, because Asians often associated the two. Historically, U.S. church missions had functioned as handmaidens for American economic and cultural imperialism in Asia. Ecumenists wanted to sever this church-state association in Asian minds. Even the EACC worried that its own efforts to help the Mennonite Central Committee provide relief assistance in Vietnam "might be seen as assisting the U.S. 'to get out of a fix.'" The fact that Western church agencies had for years dispensed U.S. government–provided aid and cultural biases in Asia meant that every church-related agency with connections to the West might be perceived as assisting the U.S. government's "hearts and minds" efforts in the war. Indeed, Church World Service, the relief arm of the NCC, had such a government relationship. (Problems with this will be discussed below.) Most important, the EACC's candid assessments helped awaken the NCC, and its more reluctant General Board members, to the importance of independent international sources of information and alerted them to underlying problems within America's Vietnam policy.[45]

Only 105 of 705 religious leaders polled in January 1965 were willing to sign a petition asking the Johnson administration to pursue a cease-fire and negotiated settlement in Vietnam. Their apprehension derived in part from the assumption that they lacked competence in foreign affairs and therefore should trust the president's advisers in this touchy area.[46] It also derived from the fact that few parishioners were comfortable hearing their religious leaders critique political issues, particularly international ones, when they were supposed to specialize in matters of the soul. As E. Raymond Wilson, of the Friends Committee on National Legislation (FCNL), wrote, "The view seems to be that while God can be expected to shed his light on missionary activities in Cambodia, or the Congo, it would be 'unchurchly' for his light to be shed on Congress, whose members are often in the dark in regard to the concerns of most of Christendom." This partially explains why the NCC wanted to study Vietnam quietly and thoroughly, from all angles, before venturing out publicly with an official opinion. The NCC had the personnel and funding to pursue such studies, while, as Wilson pointed out, its member denominations were sparsely staffed with social action or international affairs experts. Only ten of its thirty-one members had agencies with at least one full-time staffperson in social education and action; six had voluntary staff. This, Wilson felt, left the denominations in a woefully inadequate position to lead responsibly on current crises requiring church witness.[47] So the NCC became the logical choice to spearhead Vietnam-related action on behalf of the mainline denominations, just as it had done earlier on civil rights.

Meanwhile, the ecumenical journals took the religious lead in speaking out on Vietnam and against America's inflexible China policy.[48] Several pacifist groups and individual clergy did as well. In February, Reinhold Niebuhr voiced doubts about South Vietnam's desire and ability to become a viable nation, declared its political situation "insoluble," and said that while Americans "cannot criticize the Administration for failing to solve an impossible problem," they should protest its lack of candor.[49] Certain church leaders suspected America's involvement was less about Vietnam than China. Therefore, they assumed, if Americans could break free from their demonizing fear of China and rigid containment policies, they might also learn to see the Vietnam situation more clearly, perhaps even accepting a "live and let live" policy with its nationalist communists.[50] The Council's international affairs staff had received enough antagonistic feedback to be well aware that many American Christians opposed softening U.S. policy toward China. The NCC still stung from the spanking it had received in 1958 over China; therefore it remained wary of stirring that issue.[51]

Ernest Gross, chair of the NCC's International Affairs Commission, concurred that U.S. military forces could not solve Vietnam's political problems. Gross had held Dulles's old NCC position since the 1950s, and as a former UN deputy ambassador, his assessments carried weight. "The needs of North and South Viet Nam are the product of a painful, protracted liquidation of empire," he clarified. Therefore, Gross urged the church to bring its unique moral leadership to the unresolved justice issues that forestalled real peace.[52]

On February 7, 1965, after the Vietcong attacked Pleiku, killing nine Americans, Johnson ordered retaliatory bombing of North Vietnam.[53] The following day the president received a telegram from several leaders of the Methodist General Board of Christian Social Concerns urging "respectfully" that he explore "every possible means of ending the conflict through United Nations action" before ordering unilateral military responses.[54] Dudley Ward, the general secretary of that board, would become one of the most tenacious proponents within the NCC for bold challenges to U.S. Vietnam policy. On February 12, UN General Secretary U Thant, a Burmese long familiar with Vietnam, also asserted that U.S. military actions would fail to bring a settlement; diplomacy and political negotiations were the region's only hope for peace. He admitted as well that, while the UN might not be the most effective mediator of this conflict since only half of the parties involved were members, multilateral assistance like a reconvened Geneva conference should be used.[55]

The Council concurred. NCC President Reuben Mueller sent Johnson a gingerly worded letter applauding his restraint and earnest desire to secure a peaceful resolution while urging that "continuing efforts be made to create conditions for honorable and effective negotiations."[56] Thus NCC staff, still lacking focus on Vietnam and still trusting the president's intentions, at least expressed its convictions to the extent that these were formed. Little did they know that Johnson had already ordered "Rolling Thunder," an extended bombing campaign against North Vietnam, to begin March 2. It would continue for three years. Johnson kept the order quiet, to prevent public distraction from his Great Society programs and avert a rise in hawkish right-wing pressure.[57]

The UN's ability to help was questionable. In early 1965 it was hamstrung by debt, paralysis in the Security Council, and hostility from developing nations who thought it a tool of the West.[58] Yet, the ecumenical movement's historic bond with the UN, combined with its desire to see the UN empowered to serve humankind as originally intended, encouraged the Council to lean in its direction. U Thant was receptive to NCC invitations to discuss Vietnam, and the NCC respected his leadership efforts. The State Department did not. Rusk complained that U Thant's independent attempts to arrange talks between Hanoi and the United States the previous autumn had bred stressful communication gaps between U Thant, Hanoi, and UN ambassador Adlai Stevenson. As a result, the United States did not respond to Thant's latest initiative for five months. Finally, on February 24, U Thant's frustration boiled over at a press conference. He charged the Johnson administration with being uninterested in peace and unwilling to extend itself to prevent bloodshed. From this point on, Rusk considered Thant a liar and resented him for damaging American prestige, exacerbating rumors of a "credibility gap," and straining relations between Rusk and Stevenson.[59] This may partially explain the administration's reluctance to use the UN.

On February 25, the NCC's General Board passed its first resolution on Vietnam.[60] Worded carefully, it gently criticized the military means used but not the ultimate objectives of U.S. policy. It also affirmed Johnson's assertions that the United States must fulfill its responsibilities to the South Vietnamese people dependent upon U.S. aid. The board pressed the U.S. government for a cease-fire, negotiations via the UN, and a Mekong Delta development program for Vietnam. Beyond putting in a good Christian word for peace and nonviolent cooperation, this statement contained little of a profound or challenging nature.

Bennett, now president of Union Theological Seminary, unleashed a barrage of queries about Vietnam that were designed to drive the NCC deeper—not only into the moral issue of "means" but also into an investigation of the policy itself. In *Christianity and Crisis*, he probed the government's policy influences and questioned its understanding of Vietnam's culture and history with China. He inquired about military limits regarding the extent of escalation, targets, and risks. He asked about America's underlying intentions and whether its actions reflected the altruistic, humanitarian values in its rhetoric. Finally, he scrutinized the logic of using South Vietnam as a base for defending anticommunism in the region as well as the degree of real danger posed by North Vietnamese communism. While still supportive of nurturing democracy in Asia in order to balance China's influence there, Bennett doubted the wisdom of "defending" South Vietnam. To make his point, he quoted an *Observer* editorial: "To make South Vietnam the symbol of America's ability to sustain the confidence of the neighboring states is to rest the whole structure of US policy in Southeast Asia on a swamp."[61]

Bennett soon gained company. In March and April, the *Christian Century*, the World Council's Commission of the Churches on International Affairs, and the Friends Committee on National Legislation voiced similar concerns.[62] Two pacifist denominations also issued statements on Vietnam similar to the NCC's.[63] The Clergymen's Emergency Committee on Vietnam of the Fellowship of Reconciliation (FOR) launched a "Vietnam Project," which sponsored mass mailings and newspaper ads appealing for negotiations. NCC staffers helped. Nevertheless, civil rights still commanded the Council's energy and priorities; it had just helped promote the voting rights march from Selma to Montgomery. Therefore, according to NCC President Reuben Mueller, most staffers were willing to give Johnson, temporarily, the benefit of the doubt on Vietnam in order "to keep the matter on an even keel."[64] But ecumenical interest in Vietnam was growing with the war itself. Several prominent sociopolitical figures among the Johnson faithful had begun critiquing his Vietnam actions; so too had some religious organizations—albeit tentatively.

Along with domestic calls for negotiation, seventeen nonaligned nations also echoed that appeal "without preconditions."[65] Therefore, on April 7, only three weeks after Johnson had delighted liberals with perhaps his greatest congressional speech supporting voting rights legislation, Johnson responded to liberals' war concerns in a major address at Johns Hopkins University. Speaking favorably of many positions raised by the NCC and other liberal critics, he proclaimed his readiness "for unconditional discussions."[66] He echoed their preference for using aid, technological development, and cooperation over military measures to expand freedom in other nations. But Johnson also reiterated that the United States must be the protector-defender of small independent nations such as South Vietnam whose freedom was threatened by communist aggression. He described America's military presence there in terms reminiscent of a selfless Boy Scout mission about which Americans could be proud. In this effort, he assured his listeners, the United States was driven not by imperial interests but by an altruistic belief in freedom. The nation was motivated as well by duty to uphold its commitments and help preserve world security. Johnson promised to proceed with restraint but also tenacity in deterring commu-nist influence in South Vietnam. With the stick unveiled, Johnson also pro-duced a carrot: a billion-dollar "TVA-styled" Mekong River development project for North Vietnam should it come to the peace table. The NCC had suggested something similar in its February resolution.[67]

To Council staff, Johnson's speech illustrated that its lobbying had worked. Hubert Humphrey's letter to Quaker leader and NCC participant E. Raymond Wilson confirmed this assumption. "In his [Johnson's] mov-ing appeal for collaboration under the leadership of the United Nations for economic and social development of this beleaguered area, the Presi-dent surely supplied some of the 'vital ingredients' which you felt were missing from American policy."[68] But Johnson often feigned listening as a political tool to quiet dissent.[69] He used the speech to mollify and assure liberals that he was still the steady hand at the controls, doing only what was necessary to deter aggression while preferring a negotiated peace. He also tried to assuage conservatives that he would not appease communist advancement. In essence, he was willing to soften his means, provided the enemy would as well, but remained convinced of the rightness of his policy's objectives and rationale.

The speech seriously obscured many facts of the situation in Vietnam and America's relationship with it. It made the tottering, undemocratic, unpopular South Vietnamese government sound viable and free. In saying that America sought only to protect South Vietnam's right to self-deter-mination, Johnson ignored that the United States had already restricted what it would allow South Vietnam to "self-determine" (that is, no com-munism, even by free election). He spoke of South Vietnam as if it were an independent nation invaded aggressively by another, which was dubious on two counts. First, the whole country had never been split officially into two separate nations, and second, the southern section of the country was enveloped in a civil war sparked by America's backing of despotic rulers there. The Vietnamese fought primarily for real self-determination, not communism, even though the mix of people resisting U.S. involvement included both communists and noncommunists. Therefore, the president's speech was misleading but also persuasive to the majority of unknowing patriotic citizens for whom this served as their first introduction to the "why's" of America's escalating presence in Vietnam.

The speech thrilled Ken Maxwell, the Council's international affairs director, since it contained a portion of what the NCC wanted.[70] He declared this a victory, a sign that the Council exercised real influence with the president. Thus Johnson achieved his goal of appeasing some liberal critics. The speech temporarily salved the worries of several moderate doves who wanted to see the best in their government.[71] With White House ears now apparently receptive, Maxwell declared the NCC no longer needed to exert public pressure on the administration through further statements and actions—at least not in the near future. The speech confirmed for him that "we have open channels to the working parties in the White House and at the Department of State for our responsible approaches and a readiness to listen to what we may have to say."[72] Maxwell now had what he wanted for the churches on Vietnam: a variety of reliable information sources, a communication conduit to the White House, and apparently a decently motivated president. This had been the winning formula for cooperative victories on civil rights. Besides, Maxwell felt that other foreign affairs issues needed his attention, too. He was glad to sideline Vietnam for a while.

The fact that Maxwell was so easily assuaged upset some. During his ten-year tenure directing the IAC, he developed a close relationship with the State Department, especially via his NGO activities, and trusted its basic motives, expertise, and mechanisms. The State Department, in turn, viewed him as a valuable ally in disseminating foreign policy information. By 1965, however, Maxwell's friendship with the State Department began to hurt him with those who wanted the NCC to think more incisively about Vietnam.[73]

Hanoi denounced the Johns Hopkins speech and responded with its own Four Point Plan for peace, the fourth point of which demanded that the South Vietnamese be left to settle their own internal affairs in accordance with the National Liberation Front's agenda.[74] Since this implied a communist government, Johnson saw no room to negotiate. The White House then quietly approved the U.S. military's request for an offensive role against the Vietcong and sent in twenty thousand more marines. The day before Easter, Students for a Democratic Society (SDS), which called Johnson's speech deceitful, sponsored an antiwar demonstration in Washington, D.C., that attracted about twenty thousand participants, the largest to date. It drew media attention to the growing student antiwar movement.[75]

Shortly thereafter, Johnson began sending troops into the Dominican Republic to stem the rise of what he feared might be another Castro-type government. While most Americans supported the president's action and thin justifications, the invasion alienated his once staunch supporter William Fulbright. As chair of the Senate Foreign Relations Committee, Fulbright had engineered the swift and nearly unanimous passage of the Tonkin Gulf Resolution through the Senate, giving Johnson the authority to pursue military actions in Vietnam. Doubts began to haunt Fulbright shortly thereafter, and with time he felt as though Johnson had used and betrayed him. Like Bennett and others, Fulbright questioned the wisdom of an inflexible containment policy. He viewed Johnson's invasion of the Dominican Republic and his military escalation in Vietnam as symptoms of "the arrogance of power."[76] For many liberal foreign policy critics, Johnson's tendency to say one thing and do another in the Dominican Republic invasion foreshadowed the credibility gap they suspected might also exist between his Vietnam-related rhetoric and his actions. Besides, if the U.S. military could perpetrate secret atrocities in Santo Domingo, some wondered, was it perhaps also doing the same in Southeast Asia?[77]

The NCC had not yet made this leap, and it was still working to cultivate positive relations with the Johnson administration. In May, Ernest Gross invited the president to address its upcoming Sixth World Order Study Conference with flattering words. "I have cherished the expectation that you would be our main speaker. It is quite natural for us to turn in your direction, because of the continuous and close relationship which our Commission always maintains—and has over the years—with the presidential office and our friends in the Department of State."[78] Unbeknownst to Gross, the conference would catapult the NCC to a new level of critical thinking about Vietnam.

In May, antiwar activity expanded on several levels. After the Johns Hopkins speech, antiwar liberals perceived Vietnam policy as being open to their influence. Campus teach-ins increased, some of which were televised. Moderate doves in public office offered their advice.[79] On May

4–6, fourteen religious organizations, including the NCC, sponsored a "Washington Visitation by Religious Representatives on Vietnam." Over sixty Jewish and Christian leaders visited legislators and administration representatives "to express their concern about the war" and press for a negotiated end to the suffering.[80] A week later, an Interreligious Committee on Vietnam conducted a silent vigil at the Pentagon to reinforce shared concerns. Vigil committee members included NCC staff, denominational executives, Jewish leaders, Catholic priests, and Martin Luther King Jr., whom the *Christian Century* described as "some of the most highly and widely respected churchmen in the nation."[81]

Again, these actions did not imply that the NCC was protesting Johnson's Vietnam policy; the Council was merely suggesting that military means would not achieve political objectives as effectively or humanely as would negotiations. And as individuals, NCC leaders and representatives were not of a single mind on Vietnam. Behind the scenes, some pushed for a total rejection of U.S. Vietnam policy. However, NCC President Mueller clung to his basic support of Johnson. In response to a private letter criticizing his backing of the government's Vietnam and Dominican policies, Mueller defended his faith in Johnson. "I may be 'naïve' as you state in your letter" he retorted, "but I will take second place to no one (not even you) in my opposition to war. I believe you will find that the men who have been presidents, of both political parties, do not oppose the administration's overseas policies. So you follow your 'loyal opposition' policy and I'll stick to the Eisenhower-Truman idea of supporting the President of the United States. We will see who turns out to be the most 'naïve.'"[82]

On May 26, a *Christian Century* editorial cleverly titled "Nothing Personal, Mr. President" tracked the rising desertion rate from Johnson's former cadre of loyalists. While still praising his domestic agenda, it noted that his foreign policy in one week "was sharply condemned by such columnists as Walter Lippmann and Emmett John Hughes; by university, college and seminary professors in New England; . . . by the *New York Times*, *The Nation*, the *New Republic*, the *Progressive*; by clergymen and other churchmen of all faiths demonstrating at the Pentagon; by influential members of the President's own party—to mention a few." Ironically, while Johnson's old friends were losing confidence, his Vietnam policy drew new supporters from Goldwater's camp. The editorial clarified, however, that concerned liberals still hoped they might be able "to make a great President out of a half-great one."[83]

Behind White House doors, the policy train steamed unabated toward greater military entanglement. On June 7, General Westmoreland requested a massive troop increase in two installments, eventually totaling 175,000, and with no assurance this would suffice.[84] Knowing that Westmoreland's request meant committing the United States to an extensive, potentially lengthy, land war, Johnson spent June and July consulting his closest advisers, former President Eisenhower, certain congressional leaders, a prestigious group of past and present foreign policy makers tagged the "Wise Men," and public opinion polls. He also explored potential negotiation leads. The advice he received overwhelmingly favored escalation, the negotiation leads were deemed fruitless, and opinion polls indicated most people would tolerate a troop increase. Therefore, on July 27, Johnson approved Westmoreland's request.

Meanwhile *Christianity and Crisis* and the *Christian Century* became more derogatory about the presuppositions underlying what they considered a flawed Vietnam policy. Their frustration with the NCC also grew. Its reluctance to confront Johnson at the policy level and its lack of real prophetic leadership on behalf of the churches regarding Vietnam smacked of dereliction of duty. Both journals swung into high gear using words as billy clubs to force the NCC to move. To incite more analysis, *Christianity and Crisis's* editors published a signed statement outlining underlying weaknesses of U.S. policy in Vietnam. These included Johnson's inappropriate application of the Munich analogy as a rationale for using military means, the irrational self-defeating nature of U.S. China policy, the fallacy that its containment policy would preserve the trust of noncommunist Asians, the erroneous belief that South Vietnam's communist insurgency was not indigenous and therefore could be settled by U.S. military interference, the discrepancy between inviting unconditional negotiations while declaring South Vietnamese independence non-negotiable, and excluding the Vietcong from any role in South Vietnam's political future.[85]

Two days later, *Century* editor Kyle Haselden chastised the NCC's General Board for erring again on the side of caution. Vietnam was absent from its June meeting agenda. But someone introduced a surprise amendment on Vietnam from the floor. Several members opposed it on the grounds that they lacked sufficient knowledge to advise Johnson. Therefore, its language was "modified and softened" to reflect the board's earlier statements, rendering it largely innocuous. The new "Resolution on Vietnam" did include a more emphatic request that government "reappraise the relationship between the military and the political aspects of the conflict in Vietnam." But, as Haselden wrote, "For the most representative church body in the nation to ask of the government anything less than a reappraisal of its Vietnam policy at a time when that policy is under sharp questioning by numerous informed and responsible citizens would be a most serious default of that church body's duty. The General Board said the least that it could say with honor."[86]

Christianity and Crisis followed with another editorial highlighting the credibility gap between the administration's words and deeds, and the growing frustration of those who sought facts but were losing trust in government sources.[87] While NCC General Board members shied away from advising Johnson because they felt poorly informed, the article's author warned of a president who seemed eager to obscure the information released.

Finally, on July 7, 1965, the two friendly rivals, *Christianity and Crisis* and the *Christian Century*, joined forces to give the NCC a sharp rap on the knuckles. Their boards published a joint editorial "On Foreign Policy" criticizing the IAC's lack of ecumenical leadership.[88] The editors were disappointed with the International Affairs Commission for failing to provide churches with independent, bold direction on recent Cold War crises such as the Vietnam War. They contrasted the IAC's passivity on Vietnam with the "imagination and drive" of the NCC's Commission on Religion and Race in its work for civil rights. The editors expressed dismay, even embarrassment, that the academic community was out front sparking public debates about foreign policy, while the NCC did little more than meet with government officials. They feared that the IAC's staff was too enamored with its governmental connections to speak truth to power and came away from those meetings more influenced than influential. As the editors observed, "influence can flow in either direction through such contacts, and it would be unfortunate if [meeting with government officials] led to the silencing of the Council's criticism of national policy." The editors urged the NCC to start stimulating ecumenical dialogue within the denominations so they could find consensus and then begin to impact the nation with a united witness.

This rare joint editorial from America's two leading ecumenical journals was a clarion cry for prophetic leadership from the NCC on foreign affairs, especially Vietnam. It was also a clear indictment of Ken Maxwell's performance, even though it never mentioned his name. These two journals wielded larger megaphones in the 1960s than in subsequent years, and they were using them. According to Elston, this editorial, combined with results of the Sixth World Order Study Conference later in October, led to Maxwell's resignation and a significant shift in NCC action on Vietnam.[89]

Ironically, like President Johnson, while fending off expected attacks from the far right, the NCC found itself blindsided by liberal criticism from within its own circle urging it to live and lead from its values. It would not be the last time. Yet, while a minority of church people wanted the NCC to step out as it had on civil rights, a great many more saw too much ambiguity and national security danger in the Vietnam issue to justify giving supposedly unqualified clergy much of an authoritative voice. The latter also wanted to prevent churches from becoming another political lobby.[90] As Clifford Earle, the United Presbyterian Church's secretary of international affairs, explained to the IAC, "Truth is—that the thinking of many of the churches leaders—who now speak out in strong protest against U.S. policy in Vietnam and the Caribbean, is not the by-and-large thinking of our 'churches'—even our 'churchmen' (meaning, mainly, our ministers)."[91]

Throughout July, however, the Council received further encouragement from overseas church communities to focus on Vietnam. The East Asia Christian Conference kept apprising the NCC of Asian perspectives of U.S. policy, the war, and steps they viewed as imperative for negotiations. They pressed the NCC and British Council of Churches to share this information with their governments and appeal for a policy change.[92] Likewise, the Japanese Peace Team met with NCC and other church leaders as part of its American tour. It warned Council staff about the skewed and dangerous anticommunist, anti-China foundation of fear that undergirded U.S. foreign policy in Asia. A thick wall existed between Americans and Asians in their separate understandings of the Vietnam conflict, and the EACC made clear to the Council that Americans did not comprehend the Asian mind on issues surrounding the war. Nor, it asserted, did they understand the facts of the conflict because their fear and presuppositions about Asia blinded them to alternative viewpoints. So too did their allegiance to a nationalistic expression of Christianity and "their too-self-justifying understanding of liberty and democracy."[93]

American Protestant leaders were not used to listening to Asian Christians on issues of U.S. foreign policy or faith. Even for ecumenists with social justice orientations, this was a relatively new experience and not entirely comfortable.[94] But the complexities of the Vietnam War daunted, confused, and concerned NCC staff. Therefore, Asians were invited to minister to and enlighten their American brethren. By doing so, they helped transform not only the Council's understanding of U.S. Vietnam policy but also its conception of itself in relation to government and Third World Christians overseas. Through the Japanese Peace Mission and the Council's contacts with the EACC, it became clear that this perceived misunderstanding of Asian perspectives fueled tensions not only between the United States and non-Western nations but also between American Christians and those in developing countries. For church leaders who had marched recently with Martin Luther King Jr., and who were witnessing the growing influence of non-Western voices in the World Council of Churches, this charge of American ignorance of nonwhite perspectives, and hence of deeper truths, struck a chord. After talking with the Japanese, Norman Baugher, general secretary of the Church of the Brethren and an NCC vice president, urged a more forthright, independent, ecumenical lead on Vietnam. Writing to NCC General Secretary R. H. Edwin Espy, he said, "It seems imperative to me that the Christian Church speak as prophetically regarding the international situation generally and war specifically as it did with regard to the civil rights situation in the United States. From our discussions in the meeting with the Japanese delegation, I must say that I am distressed with the strong pressures to make the church simply a supportive influence of USA foreign policy."[95]

Since government sources of information were inadequate, Baugher wanted the Council to send a team to Vietnam to collect firsthand data, establish contacts, listen, survey needs, and communicate their ecumenical vision. FOR's Clergymen's Emergency Committee for Vietnam ended up doing so instead. The group, which included NCC-connected personnel, returned highly critical of U.S. Vietnam policy and the misery it perpetuated. Meanwhile, leaders of the Methodist Division of Peace and World Order pushed for an immediate consultation of church leaders and international affairs experts to evaluate U.S. policy and "propose a future strategy for the churches."[96]

Finally, when Espy asked for Bob Spike's advice, the activist director of the NCC's Commission on Religion and Race said, "I am more and more persuaded this is a crisis [Vietnam] that ought to trouble the conscience of the leadership of Protestantism in the same way the racial issue has." His well-respected voice added weight to the pleas of Methodists and ecumenical periodicals for creation of a special Vietnam study committee to make recommendations to the NCC. Asians' perspectives should be treated very seriously too, Spike concurred, and the NCC must become more engaged with the global ecumenical community on Vietnam. As he affirmed, "I just believe that the churches in the Council and the Council itself are altogether too detached and removed from the deep crisis that confronts us internationally to make any impact at all. We have got to get more involved, and the involvement has to include the world church."[97]

Agreeing, Espy finally summoned a special ad hoc meeting of thirty-three top NCC staff and denominational leaders "for advice and counsel" on Vietnam for July 27. Coincidentally, this occurred the same day that Johnson approved Westmoreland's massive troop buildup, committing America to a protracted land war in Asia. The president announced this on July 28, but he did so in a manner meant to minimize the momentous decision. Fearing right-wing pressure to expand the war even further, as well as the financial gutting of his beloved social programs, he elected to hide the Vietnam mess under the rug for as long as possible while praying for a speedy resolution.[98] Council staff were beginning to realize that more than prayers would be needed to help resolve the military mire spreading in Vietnam. The "Asians' war" was becoming America's.

CHAPTER FIVE

Taking a Stand

A Message on Vietnam to the Churches, July–December 1965

Over the previous six months, the NCC had received a crash course on Vietnam and the secretive hawkish nature of U.S. foreign policy driven by its civil rights partner in the Oval Office. The Council's instructors included the U.S. government, the *Christian Century* and *Christianity and Crisis*, American visitors to Vietnam, and Asians themselves. To date, the mild-mannered curious student had been cautious and, at times, reluctant to apply its learning. With the two ecumenical journals, Methodist leadership, and pacifist groups holding its feet to the fire, however, the NCC finally jumped into action just as Johnson escalated his troop buildup in Vietnam.

On July 27, Ed Espy assembled thirty-three staff and denominational leaders from across the NCC's constituency for a summit meeting. It was the first time the NCC had truly focused on Vietnam. Maxwell was not among them, but his associate Leonard Kramer attended. Espy asked those gathered for advice and counsel regarding a suitable course of action.[1]

American churches' past ties with imperialistic foreign policy bred Asian mistrust, and this problem now hounded the NCC. For decades, religious groups had administered U.S. government relief efforts overseas because the government had goods and funds to give while religious groups possessed the structures, missionary relationships, and relief focus necessary to dispense them. During the Vietnam War, the government purposefully relied upon religious-sponsored relief work to help win the hearts and minds of the Vietnamese.[2]

The NCC's connection came through Church World Service, a branch of the NCC's Division of Overseas Ministries (DOM) and one of its most strongly funded, grassroots-supported entities. Church World Service, Inc., a nonprofit corporation, was registered with the State Department's Advisory Committee on Voluntary Foreign Aid. Since the 1950s, CWS had become a major distributor of government-supplied aid around the world. In fact, it helped draft Public Law 480 in 1954, which made surplus food available for voluntary agencies to distribute in overseas relief efforts.[3] It then partnered directly with the State Department's Agency for International Development (USAID) in its "Food for Peace" program (also called "Food for Freedom"), which, according to CWS director James MacCracken, aimed "to utilize current United States harvests in overseas nation-building efforts."[4] CWS also accepted government funds and logistical support to conduct its relief work.

CWS leaders valued their government sources and relationships. However, participants at the July 27 meeting worried that, if the Vietnamese viewed the NCC's relief activities as part of the government's hearts-and-minds agenda, NCC credibility would plummet, both within and outside of Vietnam. Asian Christians wondered if the bond between America's church and state was stronger than that cohering the Christian community globally. Norman Baugher explained that a prophetic verbal witness on Vietnam would hold little weight with the rest of the world if the American church's image was still tied to U.S. foreign policy, and especially if it seemed a mere government lackey in nation-building efforts. Recalling the words of the Japanese Peace Team he said, "it must be imperative for the Christian Church of the West to have an image in Southeast Asia other than that which is represented by U.S.A. foreign policy and the presence of military personnel in that area of the world. If we cannot manifest a different image, the Christian Church is simply irrelevant to the people of that area."[5]

Willem Visser 't Hooft, of the World Council, also lamented this growing rift between Asian and American Christians as well as its negative repercussions for world ecumenism.[6] Angry ecumenical representatives from the developing world had gained influence within the WCC, and the NCC began to pay heed. The NCC's sense of its constituency, as well as to whom the credibility of its image was tied, was broadening from the American white mainline population and government to include politicized persons of color, both domestically and overseas. Liberal denominational executives, who channeled funds to the NCC, encouraged this shift.

Participants at the July 27 summit also debated several issues related to U.S. Vietnam policy, the proper role of the UN in it, and Johnson's part in the escalation. While attendees ideally favored UN involvement, the UN's internal problems, combined with the fact that China and North Vietnam were not members, led several to doubt its ability to mediate the situation. Some supported the idea of a reconvened Geneva Convention to do so.[7] But all agreed to appeal for the involvement of a multilateral force to help end the fighting and settle the conflict through negotiations. The unilateral audacity of the United States to involve itself militarily in an Asian nation when its security interests were not directly threatened appalled church leaders. They worried that such actions would, at minimum, damage America's image overseas and, at maximum, tempt the outbreak of regional or nuclear war.

Meeting members floated uncertain guesses about what Johnson's real role in the escalation might be. To what extent could he still be influenced? Was he "a tool of the Pentagon," as one member believed, just needing to be rescued by a strong clear moral force?[8] Or was Johnson himself actually driving a policy that seemed to become more Goldwateresque every week? Should an NCC delegation try to meet with him now, or should they wait until they had a clear new message to deliver? Within inner circles, Methodist leaders were pushing the NCC hard toward bold action. For example, Dudley Ward, the Methodist social concerns secretary, advocated a presidential visit to emphasize the Council's position, efforts to rally constituent interest, and cooperation with "dove" legislators on the Hill.[9] He agreed with the two ecumenical periodicals: the International Affairs Commission was being overly cautious. Along with Robert Spike, Ward urged Espy to create a committee to study the Vietnam situation in detail, outline possible strategies, and recommend actions to the General Board.

Espy concurred. The following day, he asked President Mueller to appoint a special presidential panel to do just that. Arthur Flemming, an NCC vice president soon to be elected president, was named chair of the new Special Advisory Committee on Viet-Nam (SACVN).[10]

At the time, no consensus or coordination existed among member denominations or their General Board representatives regarding Vietnam.[11] With few exceptions, the denominations lacked good information, leadership, and grassroots interest on the subject and were lying low, avoiding controversy. The Greek Orthodox Church, an NCC member, opposed even mild criticism of America's Vietnam policy and argued that the church should refrain from political involvement. SACVN's members knew that one of their objectives must be to help the NCC establish some interdenominational consensus on Vietnam. They also knew SACVN must first answer important questions raised by the July 27 meeting, especially regarding the UN's viability as a potential mediator. Finally, the committee had to figure out how the NCC could extend an ecumenical witness through traditional relief and reconciliation ministries in Vietnam without being viewed or used as part of the government's war effort.[12]

On August 5, SACVN met for the first time. So many perspectives bubbled forth that Espy predicted it would take considerable time to resolve member differences. At least critics could not accuse the NCC of "loading" the panel with "pre-determined conclusions," Mueller mused.[13] SACVN agreed to raise its questions with top administrative officials before formulating recommendations.[14] Therefore, before the next meeting, members talked with UN Ambassador Goldberg, Secretary of State Rusk, Secretary of Defense McNamara, and Chester Cooper of the National Security Council. The committee concluded that Johnson wanted to keep the conflict and U.S. objectives in Vietnam limited. They also surmised that he sought negotiations but could not marshal enough government support for what many perceived as a dovish approach. So SACVN discerned a mission for the NCC: help generate media and constituency support for negotiations.[15]

SACVN knew as well that it needed more information from Asian contacts. Therefore, on its recommendation, Espy and Mueller agreed to send an NCC delegation to meet with EACC representatives in Bangkok, Thailand. This would occur simultaneously with the NCC's December General Board meeting. In the meantime, SACVN further studied the Japanese Peace Team's earlier report. Although dismissed by some who felt the Peace Team's pacifism compromised its objectivity, most panelists respected its Christian perspectives. The Peace Team's distress at the silence of American churches on Vietnam added more volume to the chorus of groups pressing the NCC toward a leadership role.

At an August 20 staff meeting, attendees learned that "most church people are not ready to criticize U.S. foreign policy," yet they widely favored negotiations and UN involvement.[16] The NCC's stands on Vietnam therefore reflected what many sitting in the pews considered palatable. The

Century's editorial board expected more from the Council than simply mirroring misinformed parishioners. Rather, it encouraged SACVN to seek the will of God and then lead the churches from that prophetic place. "If [SACVN] is true to its reason for being and to its declared purpose the panel will not poll Christians in search for the greatest common denominator on Vietnam but . . . will seek to throw the vast and relevant wisdom of Christian thought on the war" into its recommendations.[17] The International Affairs Commission would still need a push in the prophetic direction, however, and this would come from the Sixth World Order Study Conference in October.

Before the conference, SACVN met for a second time to hear Harold Row's eye-popping report on Vietnam. The executive secretary of the Brethren Service Commission had just returned from a fact-finding relationship-building mission there for his denomination. Row had been to Vietnam previously and had studiously nurtured a longtime interest in Southeast Asia. The NCC had cosponsored Row's trip so he could serve as its eyes and ears and offer a Christian witness on its behalf as well. His grim message minced no words.[18]

America had "blundered miserably in its judgments and policy actions on Vietnam," Row asserted. It had consistently "bet on the wrong horses" there, and the repercussions were exactly what America had tried to avoid: a loss of international respect, the disdain of most Asians, compounded human misery, and the prevention of a people's right to self-determination. America's real goal in South Vietnam, Row stated flatly, was to prevent a communist government from arising. His words described the United States as "prostitut[ing]" the South Vietnamese in its ideological "holy crusade" against "international communism." U.S. involvement had little to do with Vietnam's welfare or helping the Vietnamese people, and Asians knew this, he exclaimed. The hypocritical discrepancies between U.S. words and actions were blasphemous to Asians. For example, Operation Toy Drop was designed to display America's compassionate heart. The U.S. military used bombers to drop loads of toys and propaganda fliers expressing U.S. concern for Vietnamese children over Vietnam. But, as Row described, "They saw us one day dropping bombs that killed children, then the next day showering them with toys, with messages of love, then the following days again dropping the killing bombs." To Vietnamese, Row said, "Americans were making sport of child slaughter." Americans proved time and again that they misunderstood the Vietnamese mind, culture, and situation. Because of this, Row implored the NCC to help generate a bold ecumenical Christian witness in Vietnam.[19]

In addition to stemming the suffering, Row also provided self-serving reasons for such a witness. The war was definitely damaging ecumenical relationships between Asian and American churches and souring them more broadly between those in developing nations and the West, he confirmed. The link between American relief activities and the U.S. military agenda in Vietnam had already marred the reputation of U.S. churches abroad. Earning Asians' trust would require a radical church stand against the immorality perpetrated by U.S. involvement in Vietnam, followed by a call to American Christians to live a code of justice, not simplistic anticommunism. Therefore, Row urged the NCC to create a visible service program in Vietnam to help alleviate human suffering and provide a positive counter image. For the greatest damage would flow from abdicating responsibility, letting the fusion of U.S. policy and humanitarian relief go unchallenged, and allowing the U.S. military to be the sole face of Americans to the Vietnamese.[20]

Since service and relief programs were a traditional part of church activity and always popular with local Christians, SACVN made this issue high priority. The daunting challenge at hand, however, was determining how they might circumvent U.S. government regulations, dispel the need for logistical military support in a war zone, and prevent government influence upon such an independent service program. Further, convincing Christian sponsors to fund an aid structure not necessarily controlled by Americans, while convincing Asians that the program was separate from the government's hearts and minds effort, would be tricky for the NCC's Division of Overseas Ministries.[21] Although still without answers, SACVN was identifying some key hurdles. The Sixth World Order Study Conference would soon add its own judgment.

In the meantime, SACVN counseled the NCC to refrain from making immediate statements and, when crafting future ones, to retain its soft touch. Wanting the Council to exude civility, compassion, and respect, SACVN urged words of sympathy for the Johnson administration during such trying times. Additionally, statements should avoid implying that the United States was completely at fault in Vietnam, or that it had no defensible reason for involvement. Along with encouraging further study of Vietnam, SACVN also felt the NCC should begin an in-depth examination into the use of power as preparation for a policy statement on that controversial subject. Within the next few years, the NCC would do so; the question of how to exercise power morally underpinned much of its evolving witness on Vietnam.[22]

As autumn commenced, so did antiwar protests focused on the draft. In October the "International Days of Protest" drew one hundred thousand demonstrators and included the first public draft-card burning in response to a stricter conscription law. Dissenters also resisted what they viewed as an almost fascist-like pressure to remain uncritically nationalistic. They condemned the public's retreat from a principle asserted in the Nuremburg trials following World War II—namely, when the state orders individuals to commit an immoral or illegal act, they must obey their consciences and resist or be held culpable. Angry counter demonstrators clashed with antiwar protesters in the streets as public expressions of support for Johnson's war policy rippled through every region, even on college campuses. Popular magazines such as *Time* and *Life* painted the protesters as extremists. *Time* called them "Vietniks," connoting a bond with communist insurgents.[23]

The antiwar movement was by no means a united entity. While its radical fringe demanded immediate U.S. withdrawal from Vietnam, the movement also contained a more moderate liberal element. Like the NCC, most antiwar liberals wanted to see multilateral-sponsored negotiations replace unilateral militarism and sought a revision of America's inflexible Cold War policies. They had argued these points for well over a year.[24] This liberal wing was internally divided, however. One camp included those who still favored a strong anticommunist emphasis in foreign policy and preferred mainly to "advise the administration" on how to be more effective. The other contained those who viewed anticommunist containment as outmoded and potentially dangerous; they felt the times called for an outright critique of Johnson's entire Vietnam approach.[25] The American ecumenical community contained both schools of thought, with few willing to challenge Johnson head-on.[26]

The editorial boards of *Christianity and Crisis* and the *Christian Century* were among those itching to confront Johnson and push the churches into prophetic action. Rev. William Sloane Coffin Jr. felt similarly. The Yale chaplain had helped spearhead white religious activism on civil rights; therefore he used his civil rights contacts to unite a body of religious-affiliated liberals around the educational goal of inspiring people to reevaluate U.S. Asia policy.[27] He enlisted John Bennett and David Hunter, Espy's deputy, to serve on his "Americans for Reappraisal of Far Eastern Policy Committee" along with several others, including Christian socialist Norman Thomas.

Another veteran peace activist, A. J. Muste, was equally disturbed by the church's inertia on Vietnam. Writing to Bennett, he complained that the NCC and other church organizations "are not saying or doing anything of real significance in relation to the problem. I have the feeling they are simply marking time and so contribute to the attitude of 'going along' with the Johnson Administration, which is so widespread and, in my view, so dangerous." Like others, he pointed out the "great contrast to what happened among church people in relation to the race situation during the past half dozen years or so."[28] If moderates remained quiet while radicals protested, peace activists feared Johnson's policies would gain tacit support from citizens who, though privately concerned about the war, stayed silent to avoid being associated with the radical fringe. Clerical collars at antiwar rallies could also help legitimate humanistic arguments against the war's immoralities, as well as offset the moral authority hawkish anticommunists drew from conservative ministers. Coffin, Bennett, Thomas, and Muste knew that it was vital for clean-cut, upright, law-abiding, religious liberals to become public activists for peace in Southeast Asia. If they were prominent church leaders so much the better.

In "A Theology of Demonstration" published in the *Century* that October, ethics and society professor Gibson Winter pinpointed one of the primary road blocks to church activism. Like Martin Luther King Jr., he recognized that most white Christians associated Christian love with harmony, or "absence of conflict." On the other hand, they viewed direct action as inciting discord. For white clergy, King's nonviolent civil rights activism had helped clarify the difference between superficial social order and real Christian justice. In fact, pastors began to recognize that advancing the latter often depended upon purposeful disordering of an unfair status quo. Yet activism—even the lawful kind—still unnerved many, and most laity remained appalled by clergy who stirred up trouble through public protests.[29]

The Student Christian Movement did not fear creative conflict on behalf of justice. While Maxwell's IAC prepared position papers to guide delegates at the upcoming Sixth World Order Study Conference, SCM delegates strategized to push it toward positions far beyond what the IAC was willing to advocate.[30] Unbeknownst to the planners, the conference would provide the stage for a clash between the two liberal factions and precipitate a changing of the guard in the IAC.

Gerhard Elston, then a student movement leader, helped prepare the National Student Christian Federation (NSCF) delegates for the conference.[31] Long before, America's support of South Africa's apartheid government had helped awaken student leaders to some of the ignoble factors driving U.S. foreign policy after World War II. One of these, Leonard Clough, described himself and his peers as "a prophetic generation that does not hesitate to challenge time-honored ways of doing things or measuring value." The SCM delegates longed to inspire an ecumenical church consensus that would speak to the unmet justice needs embedded in revolutions erupting internationally. They sought to use the conference to help advance this goal, which was gaining sporadic support within denominational hierarchies. On a practical note, they also wanted the NCC to understand that it could no longer maintain cozy relations with the State Department and remain credible overseas. They wanted to communicate that U.S. military involvement in Vietnam had little to do with protecting Vietnamese self-determination, America's vital interests, or advancing justice, peace, or security. Rather, they accused the United States of imposing governmental styles, ideologies, and values comfortable to Americans upon other people regardless of the detrimental repercussions unleashed. To these students, U.S. foreign policy was driven by blind militant anticommunism, the thirst to expand U.S. power, and greed.[32]

The NSCF devoted its own summer conference to planning how its delegates might shake things up at the Sixth World Order Study Conference. The students labored for months, writing resolutions for presentation, positioning its representatives strategically within the conference's working groups, and preparing them to raise key questions for discussion. Elston helped engineer and manage their strategy.[33] They would be pleasantly surprised to learn they were not alone in their quest to push the NCC's position on U.S. Asia policy to a new level.

The sixth conference met in St. Louis from October 20 to 23, 1965. Having endured public venom over the fifth's statements on China in 1958, which incited years of McCarthyite attacks both from right-wing critics and from congregations within its member denominations, the Council publicized its official independence well ahead of time. The conference spoke for itself only, and its conclusions were submitted to the NCC merely as recommendations, not directives.[34] In those three days, the meeting's five hundred delegates were barraged by what Kyle Haselden described as a "ludicrous" amount of world order topics; key among them were issues related to U.S. policy on China, Vietnam, Latin America, and communism.

Maxwell's staff had drafted background and position papers for consideration by conference working groups. Tradition dictated that such papers were usually discussed and rubber-stamped with minor changes as the conference's recommendations to the NCC. Not so at the sixth. Delegates asserted their own minds and, after spirited debate, roundly rejected many of the IAC's papers, including one penned by its avidly anticommunist vice chair Kenneth Thompson.[35] They also exercised their right to draft prescriptive recommendations rather than just descriptive reports. Efforts by a few to subvert tough questions on China left over from the fifth conference were "overwhelmingly voted down."[36] Delegates were more sympathetic to the students' positions than to those articulated in the IAC's prepared papers, which some described as being of poor quality. The students' impact was impressive and significant, especially in light of their relatively small number. Attendees noted that a general concern for humanity, justice, and peace pervaded the gathering. This provided an outlet for a growing consensus of ecumenists who rejected strict Cold War liberalism and assertions that churches should protect their high government connections.[37] While conference recommendations moved beyond those in IAC position papers, they still seemed moderate to a group of delegates surveyed afterward by the *Century*'s editor. Regarding China, the sixth conference reiterated recommendations similar to those of the fifth, favoring cultural exchanges and UN admission. But it endorsed these with an ease that would have shocked those who met in 1958. This illustrated the degree to which church leaders' opinions had changed on China in seven years.[38] In conjunction, the sixth conference asked Americans to rethink their containment policy and the simple notion of communism upon which it was based. A more accurate understanding of dynamics in developing nations was vital to world peace. And those gathered warned of grave danger if Americans continued "to confuse the magnitude of our military power with its relevance," especially in Asia.[39]

U.S. government positions were well represented in the sessions.[40] Yet, regarding Vietnam, the conference exposed substantial dissatisfaction with Johnson's war policy. Elston entered into a floor debate with a congressman who put forth a motion that church people needed to unify in support of their government.[41] In response, Elston asked if he would have implored Germany's churches to support the Nazi government in 1934. The motion failed. But so also did more radical efforts to include "serious judgment of the war" in conference reports.[42]

The conference's recommendations formed the backbone of what would become the NCC's first major stand on the Vietnam War.[43] Delegates urged the NCC to press the U.S. government to initiate a bombing pause over North Vietnam, seek UN assistance for a cease-fire and negotiations, proclaim America's interest in a phased troop withdrawal, and offer generous development assistance. They also favored securing complete self-determination for the South Vietnamese to select any governmental option, even one distasteful to America's cold warriors.[44] In response to Johnson's denigration of antiwar protesters, delegates defended the right of dissent, the government's responsibility to respect and protect it, and the church's duty to speak on controversial moral issues facing humankind. These recommendations generally mirrored those articulated by other liberal antiwar groups. While not innovative, they were significant for the ecumenical community. The sixth conference uncovered, nurtured, and released a current of consensus among church leaders that favored a more confrontational revisionist perspective on international issues than that held by the IAC. The gathering's rejection of IAC positions signaled the beginning of the end for Maxwell and his team at the NCC.[45]

As conference reports hit the press, the massive Battle of Ia Drang unfolded on television before a largely government-supportive audience. In the first two weeks of November, two Americans—one Quaker and one Catholic—immolated themselves before the Pentagon and the UN. Imitating Vietnamese Buddhist monks who had self-immolated in 1963 as acts of protest, these two men did it to express their deep spiritual anguish over human suffering caused by the war. Toward the end of November, the National Committee for a Sane Nuclear Policy (SANE) drew 35,000 citizens to protest "respectfully" before the White House while President Johnson listened to military arguments for increasing troop levels from 120,000 to 400,000 by the end of the following year. As 1965 moved toward closure, the tragedy and expanse of the war was coming home in a burgeoning way.[46]

A POLICY STATEMENT ON VIETNAM

The IAC used the sixth conference's results to draft statements on the Vietnam War for the General Board to consider in December.[47] It also discussed the challenges of providing relief services in Vietnam. While I will not delve deeply into the service, relief, and missions aspect of the NCC's response to

Vietnam, the Council's entanglements in the U.S. government's pacification program certainly complicated its ecumenical efforts on the war.

Back in October 1965, the Council's Division of Overseas Ministries formed a new service program eventually called Vietnam Christian Service (VNCS). Church World Service and the Mennonite Central Committee (MCC) jointly administered it. A historic peace church, the Mennonites already had an established relief program in Vietnam and a history of cooperating with the U.S. military while insisting upon maintaining an independent identity. CWS likewise had collaborated with the U.S. government for years, as had its newly hired director, James MacCracken.

A word about CWS and James MacCracken is needed, for he led CWS and its VNCS program until 1974 when he was forced to resign over the church-state issue.[48] Whereas the Council's social justice wing, the DCLM, was the most publicly unpopular, highly criticized branch of the Council because of its supposed radicalism and activism, CWS was the more richly funded darling of the grass roots. Many a parishioner who found the social justice side of the Council suspect, distasteful, and perhaps a little "pink" continued to support the NCC because, by the mid-1960s, overseas missions and relief was receiving over 50 percent of the Council's annual budget compared to the small amount dedicated to social issues.[49] Within the NCC's structure, CWS enjoyed the unique privilege of being able to solicit funds directly from parishioners, which it did with great success. Its two best fund-raisers, the "CROP Walk" and "One Great Hour of Sharing," attracted generous donations from individuals representing a broad spectrum of theological beliefs. Most important, fund-raising tied its awareness to grassroots opinion in a way not shared by other Council departments that received budgeted money from denominational bureaucracies rather than directly from individuals.[50] Some social action people within the NCC resented these private donations, arguing that they simply gave local Christians an easy "out" or a conscience-salving excuse not to deal with the root causes of suffering.[51] CWS attributed such criticism to jealousy of its considerable financial resources and public goodwill.

Over the first few years of the war, the Council's international affairs team helped lead the NCC firmly onto the antiwar side of the Vietnam debate while CWS approached war-induced problems using traditional, less critical, U.S. government–supported strategies. This reflected MacCracken's disposition against politicizing relief work in ways that bit the government hands that fed it.[52] His supporters argued articulately that there was no other effective way to distribute life-saving relief in a politically polarized world.[53] It was also true, however, that MacCracken used this argument to obscure his own ideological biases and dodge having to admit how purportedly apolitical work with governments facilitated the political agendas of those government partners.

Prior to becoming CWS's director in 1965, MacCracken had bundled his many years of relief efforts routinely with America's Cold War objectives. For example, he had managed the Tolstoy Foundation, which combined humanitarianism and anticommunism. Then, in his first major assignment with CWS, he had organized "Flights for Freedom," which shuttled Cubans out of Castro's country in the early 1960s entirely on the U.S. government's dollar.[54] In November 1965, Hugh Farley, another CWS staffer with a similar slant, praised the symbiotic relief relationship between the U.S. government and church agencies after returning from a government-sponsored trip to investigate U.S. management of the Vietnamese refugee situation. Along with his CWS role, Farley served as associate secretary for the DOM and as chair of the American Council of Voluntary Agencies for Foreign Service. His report bubbled with accolades for the government's refugee program as he stressed how close collaboration between government and voluntary agencies produced positive results.[55]

Conversely, Harold Row had urged the churches to create an independent relief program that could make an effective counter witness to the activities of the U.S. military. But Farley deemed this impractical. The American churches were not yet able to surface enough volunteers for this, he explained to SACVN, whereas the government could easily round up aid workers. Farley also noted "all the private agencies together are handling only about 10% of the refugee problem." The government was managing the other 90 percent. On top of this, it usually required all aid agencies to use government logistics support in-country. Starting in 1965, the State Department made mandatory a coordinated link between all Food for Peace relief efforts in South Vietnam and the government's pacification program, which aimed to win the support and trust of South Vietnamese civilians.[56] The Food for Peace program distributed relief only to noncommunist nations. VNCS joined this in January 1966, exacerbating the NCC's difficulty of creating a counter image. Nevertheless, SACVN decided to keep investigating this church-state relief conundrum. Years later, in a scathing 1974 article titled "The Politics of Charity," Farley's 1965 assessments were cited as examples of the uncritical "simple acceptance of U.S. military and political strategy and a willingness to work within this framework" that co-opted church agencies into serving the government's war agenda.[57]

Although Council leaders became aware of the problematic dichotomy between the NCC's growing criticism of the war and CWS's government-tied work in Vietnam, they were cautious and slow to address it. This was likely due to the fact that few options existed for providing massively needed aid to the suffering in Vietnam, and CWS enjoyed widespread grassroots support. Besides, CWS also came in handy as an image booster whenever the NCC drew attacks for focusing too heavily on liberal political causes rather than on what many laypersons considered real church work. The Council's executive staff could point to CWS and its generous share of the budget as proof that conservative critics overexaggerated NCC political activities.[58] While the NCC saw CWS as a benefit to its image at least with laity (and used it as such), CWS experienced the NCC's social justice wing as a detriment to its reputation, particularly as the Council became more critical of the war and as America's political power base grew more conservative in succeeding decades. Over time, the Vietnam War would split the Division of Overseas Ministries' staff between those who preferred apolitical silence in order to preserve government resources and goodwill and those who saw a need to critique root problems fed by government policies in order to get beyond band-aiding the symptoms.[59]

In November 1965, NCC staff prepared for two major policy-shaping gatherings: a consultation on Vietnam between the NCC and the East Asia Christian Conference in Bangkok, Thailand, and the next General Board meeting where Vietnam led the agenda. Both events were set to run concurrently from December 1 through 3, 1965.[60] The considerable overlap of personnel among the various groups feeding recommendations to the board (that is, the sixth conference, SACVN, the IAC, and the DCLM) promoted continuity and moderation in the materials placed before it. Flemming and Maxwell urged the board to acknowledge President Johnson's good intentions and show awareness of right-wing pressures upon him to expand the war. SACVN wanted the churches to generate more "dove" pressure for negotiations. It also felt that the churches must try to move their constituencies toward a more ecumenical and moral view of the war. Denominational leaders Dudley Ward (Methodist) and John Coventry Smith (Presbyterian) both pushed the idea of a personal meeting with Johnson to underscore the importance of White House accountability to positions in the Johns Hopkins speech. They, along with Espy, saw Johnson as a Christian man who could be wooed and reasoned with from a faith perspective.[61] SACVN members did puzzle briefly over why the United States was in Vietnam. But most NCC staffers in late 1965 agreed with their colleagues cited above— that Johnson was a well-intentioned, peace-seeking president who was hamstrung politically by Cold War hawks.

On the eve of the General Board meeting, seven NCC representatives left for Bangkok.[62] They aimed to listen genuinely to Asian Christians on the Vietnam conflict, clarify the NCC's and its denominations' positions related to Asia, and seek an ecumenical consensus regarding how Christians should respond to the war. The EACC delegation sent to confer with the NCC admitted that it did not reflect a balanced regional perspective, for most of its membership came from Indonesia, the Southeast Asian nation perhaps most critical of U.S. involvement in Vietnam.[63] The EACC also told the NCC delegation there was no single Asian mind regarding Vietnam. In fact, South Korean, Taiwanese, and Filipino Christians often supported U.S. policy, but then again, so too did their governments, which received military and financial assistance from the United States.[64] Yet, despite this, the NCC delegation discovered similar strains of thought, culture, and need among Asians. These included a "common antipathy" to Western imperialism and an overwhelming support of nationalism as the medium through which Asians hoped to create a brighter future. Several NCC delegation members made side trips to other Asian nations before and after the EACC meeting in order to glean as many perspectives as possible.

These Asian opinions served as a vital counterbalance for American ecumenists. The NCC deduced several common denominators.[65] Overwhelmingly, Asians felt that Vietnam's civil war was not America's business and should be left to the Vietnamese. They saw the Vietcong as nationalists continuing the fight for liberation from foreign intrusion they had begun against the French. To Asians, the United States had sabotaged the Geneva Accords of 1954, first by not signing and then by preventing the reunification elections in 1956 through which they would have been fulfilled. Fueling additional resentment, the United States, in fearful hatred of communism, picked Vietnam as the place to halt the communist advance without regard to its people's wishes, which might very well lean toward a nationalist-styled communism different and fiercely independent from China's or Russia's. American activity in Asia also seemed motivated predominantly by self-interest, and only cursorily intended to benefit Asian lives. And Americans were so blindly "obsessed" with being anticommunist that Asians doubted Americans' ability to understand their region's openness to communism's potential ability to help people meet their basic needs. Of course, Asians also feared the Vietnam conflict might escalate. U.S. involvement was drawing China and potentially Russia into the picture, thereby imperiling more Asian lives and the peace of the world. Thus, Asians roundly called for an end to American isolation of China and supported its entry into the United Nations. From a diplomatic perspective, they confirmed that U.S. involvement in Latin America and Vietnam had severely wounded its moral stature in the East. When speaking of Vietnam, nothing was more important than self-determination. While connoting the right of a people to choose their own form of government, Americans must accept that this did not always imply use of a Western model. To the Vietnamese, the "Will of Heaven" reflected the will of the community and was not necessarily determined by popular vote.[66] Altogether, this provided a stunning earful for the NCC.

The Council's delegation failed to get consensus from the EACC representatives about specific facts of the Vietnam conflict.[67] This opacity contributed to the delegation's anxiety over U.S. involvement in a situation where "right" and "wrong" fluctuated upon a myriad of perceptions. The delegation also returned convinced that America's attitude toward communism required serious reexamination, for it seemed to be the root of troubling repercussions in U.S. relations with other countries. These included U.S. actions overseas that contradicted democratic values and inadvertently strengthened China's position in Southeast Asia, as the Japanese Peace Team had observed, by driving North Vietnam toward Chinese assistance against the Americans. The one female member of the NCC group, Edna Sinclair, noted Asians' rising resentment against a white nation that treated Asian lives cheaply. She intimated that America's advances on the race issue at home were mocked by its activities abroad.[68] But while the delegation regretted U.S. involvement in Vietnam, it also advised against immediate withdrawal prior to a cease-fire and negotiations. This illustrated its cautious realism and differentiated it from more radical New Left and pacifist groups.

A few NCC delegates made a side trip to Saigon to investigate service programs for the growing numbers of refugees. They saw the magnitude of deprivation yet could discern no clear way for churches to separate their relief services from the U.S. military. Therefore, favoring what they saw as the greater Christian imperative, the delegation supported expanding CWS's new Vietnam Christian Service while continuing to wrestle with the inherent church-state and image problems. The importance of nurturing communication between East Asian and American Christians was also clear. The Bangkok meeting revealed Americans' strong subconscious proclivity to reflect their nation's biases in international matters. NCC delegates caught this in themselves. Seeing it as a wake-up call, they advised fellow Christians to work tirelessly toward developing a personal international vision grounded in the gospel and body of Christ.[69]

The insights gleaned in Bangkok certainly helped NCC leaders find better footing for a confessing church stance on Vietnam. At minimum, they had identified their cultural biases and further revised their understanding of Cold War politics. By processing data not easily surfaced outside of Asia, they had also begun to grasp the general Asian perspective on international affairs and especially on U.S. activities in Vietnam. As John Coventry Smith said later before the WCC's Central Committee, "the time has come when none of us in a single country will know what it is that God would have us say to our own nation until we have listened to what the rest of the Body of Christ is saying to us."[70] These insights helped Council staff better interpret the materials on Vietnam already at their disposal. They also exposed them to causes of the conflict that lay beneath the polarizing rhetoric on both sides. David Hunter, a Bangkok delegate, confirmed that those lessons motivated the General Board toward greater action on Vietnam. It proved much more difficult to inspire church action on an issue of corporate morality, like the nation's war in Vietnam, he noted, than on one many Christians saw rooted in personal morality, such as racial prejudice that inhibited support for civil rights. Yet, once the denominations' national boards were activated on Vietnam, they became very outspoken, even though member churches remained divided within themselves.[71]

With the Bangkok meeting underway, the NCC's General Board met to discuss several issues, none more pressing than Vietnam. In fact its six-hour debate on the war bumped other topics off the agenda.[72] After much amending of proposals, the board passed its first policy statement on Vietnam by a vote of ninety-three to ten. The NCC had passed resolutions on Vietnam previously. However, policy statements carried greater weight, for they actually established Council policy and provided the governing authority upon which staffs could build an active witness.[73] And herein lay one of the NCC's main functions: to help facilitate national policy statements so churches had official mandates under which they could act.

Without a policy mandate, individuals could act on their own, but church organizations, programmatically, could not. The NCC's first Vietnam policy statement was mild and reflected the consensus already generated by the sixth conference, the IAC, and SACVN. Nonetheless, it was one of the first such statements by a large, national, mainstream American institution against the war. Arising at a time when the impulse to rally around the flag ran high, it caught the attention of the White House and edged the NCC into the antiwar movement.[74]

While recognizing divided church sentiments and praising Johnson's peacemaking gestures, the Council's statement reiterated its critique of the government's unilateral military methods and stressed real self-determination for South Vietnam as the objective of a settlement. It also authorized the Council to establish a more focused peace program, which would launch the Council's active witness on the war. While the statement did not receive much coverage by the secular press, one aspect did garner headline attention: the NCC's suggestion of a bombing halt over North Vietnam to help create a better climate for negotiations.[75]

A written "Message to the Churches" accompanied the policy statement, which, when distributed by the denominations to their congregations, served as a cover letter.[76] In it, one sees the Council's effort to address not just the war but the worldviews that shaped public opinion. For example, it emphasized keeping loyalty to God and awareness of the human factor in war uppermost in mind. It encouraged multinational Christian communication in order to break through national biases and nurture bonds within the body of Christ. It also reminded Christians to act as reconcilers by supporting international efforts that fostered peace. After commending the policy statement to the churches for study, the message then asked Christians "to do more." It urged them to resist the spread of a warmonger mentality that dehumanized the enemy, numbed citizens to human suffering, and threatened world peace. This included loving and praying for those labeled "enemy"; seeing the racism involved in a white nation's military destruction of Asian lives, while understanding the resulting "distrust and hatred" this cultivated overseas; and encouraging utilization of multinational means for preserving peace. Essentially, Christians should frame their consideration of the war within an ecumenical worldview.

Espy hoped that the message, policy statement, and Bangkok report would "bring the Vietnam problem into better perspective in the consciousness of the churches."[77] *Christianity and Crisis* published the statement in full, introducing it as "one of the most significant statements to appear on the subject," and added that it "provides an admirable basis for discussion in Church Councils and local churches."[78] Ironically, editors now perceived the cautious Council as ahead of most other large institutions within the liberal establishment on the war, and this at a time when most of the media and populace still supported Johnson's policy.

No one disliked the NCC's Vietnam position more than white American southerners who already discredited the Council for its civil rights activities and supposed communist proclivities. According to Harold Davis, a white southern Presbyterian leader, the aversion lay deeper than differences on race. "The basic issue," he explained, "is the nature of the church and its mission. I am convinced that many thoughtful laymen are opposed to the NCC, not because of its involvement in the racial revolution, but because they think the church is a 'spiritual' body which should take no part in 'secular' affairs."[79] This was a common and convenient way to rationalize white church avoidance of the moral dilemma of race.[80] Nevertheless, Davis, who worried about "the deteriorating image of the Council in this area of the country," explained that a severe gap existed between southern laypeople, particularly wealthier professionals, and clergy with respect to the NCC. For example, laypeople within the Memphis Presbytery of the Presbyterian Church U.S. nearly voted in an overture to the 1966 PCUS General Assembly to withdraw from the Council. This was barely defeated by ministers who felt southern protests could be expressed best by retaining membership. Nearly all denominations in the South were experiencing similar internal battles over the NCC's sociopolitical pronouncements and actions.[81] The rector of St. John's Episcopal Church in Hampton, Virginia, echoed Davis's concerns, saying, "Parishes and churches are being split wide open over the National Council."[82]

Davis also told Hunter that the NCC's seeming contempt for white southern church people fed the antipathy. He wondered if the Council had written off southern white churches as "beyond redemption" by stonewalling their representatives and dismissing them as if unworthy of serious consideration. He wanted the NCC to reconsider its behavior and work to reconcile with them. Another factor further straining this relationship was the militarism and nationalism within southern culture, heightened particularly during a time of war.

Southern white Christians were not the only ones suspicious of the NCC's social and political stands. To many of America's millions of Protestants, the NCC's Vietnam pronouncement put it in suspect company. In fact, its position was not far removed from that of certain Jewish and Catholic leaders who had recently published their own stands on the war. In November, the Union of American Hebrew Congregations mourned "the growing violence and mounting loss of life" in Vietnam and, like the NCC, asked Johnson to consider a cease-fire and bombing halt as prelude to UN-mediated, inclusively attended, negotiations. It also supported the idea of offering development aid to Vietnam. The Synagogue Council of America offered a similar policy statement in January.[83]

Official Catholic bodies were more cautious. The Roman Catholic Ecumenical Council's Constitution on "The Church in the Modern World" never mentioned Vietnam by name, choosing to speak more generally against relying on military methods to deal with world conflicts.[84] Specifically, it decried nondefensive military actions that sought "the subjugation of other nations." It warned against the moral and physical horrors of modern war and expressed conviction that the arms race theory of deterrence led to faulty, dangerous methods of trying to preserve a real peace. Pope Paul VI, likewise, when speaking before the UN General Assembly in October, avoided mention of Vietnam, yet he condemned the hubris that led to war.[85] Explaining, he said, "Men cannot be brothers if they are not humble. It is pride, no matter how legitimate it may seem to be, that provokes tension and struggles for prestige, for predominance, colonialism, egoism; that is, pride disrupts brotherhood." American Catholics often sympathized with the anticommunist Catholic minority population in South Vietnam, once led by the Catholic Diem. Therefore, the official Catholic voice against U.S. policy started slowly then grew steadily along with that of the American public.[86] Alternately, American Jewish antiwar sentiment flashed early and compatibly with the NCC's but would stifle significantly after the Six Day War in the Middle East in 1967.

Overseas, the NCC's statement received mixed reactions. Communist governments applauded it. The Moscow Domestic Service called it "one of the most important events of the past week. . . . For the first time in history," it emphasized, "this very large church organization came forward with an energetic protest against the official policy of the U.S. Government." The Russian press was delighted that the antiwar movement contained more than fringe elements. Based upon the NCC's stand, it surmised a bit prematurely that "a mass popular movement is rapidly growing in the United States for an immediate end to the criminal adventure of American imperialism in Vietnam."[87]

Conversely, the National Christian Council in Japan was disappointed by the NCC's statement. While acknowledging its sincerity, the Japanese recoiled at its American bias and mourned their brethren's continued misunderstanding of the war's nature. Noting several "points of inadequacy" and expressing "dissatisfaction with the concrete proposals you put forward," the Japanese pinpointed "common defects" shared by Johnson's fourteen points for peace and the NCC's recommendations that impeded positive replies from "the communist side."[88] For example, like Johnson, the NCC failed to recognize that the conflict in the South was a civil war precipitated by a Vietcong rebellion against the southern government; therefore a North Vietnamese invasion did not start the war. While commending the NCC for recommending a bombing halt over North Vietnam, the Japanese also deemed this insufficient, urging that all U.S. bombing be terminated and troops withdrawn prior to negotiations. The Japanese were particularly saddened by the statement's lack of reference to the Geneva Accords, the violation of which had sparked the current quagmire. To them, the only road to peace lay with a return to those accords. They placed little hope in UN assistance because of its lack of universal membership.

Whether the NCC's first policy statement on Vietnam was significant or insufficient, it put an end to the Council's "marking time" on Vietnam, and gave it marching orders. This became its launching point for generating ecumenical consensus on Vietnam. It also signaled the end of Ken Maxwell's ten-year reign as director of the IAC.[89] Maxwell had earned respect for his integrity, kindness, good intentions, and management. Sometime near the end of 1965 he departed, followed months later by his associate Leonard Kramer, and eventually by the head of the NCC's Washington office, Vernon Ferwerda.[90] The tasks then remaining before the Council, aside from filling these men's shoes, were to draw the divided denominations into ecumenical dialogue and consensus on Vietnam and attempt to mobilize grassroots opinion. These challenges would fall soon to Robert Bilheimer and Gerhard Elston.

In that period of personnel flux, antiwar activities culminated around a U.S. Christmas bombing pause—a dovish gesture of receptivity to the negotiations the NCC had called for in its policy statement. As the new year dawned, the Council began to take its place within the antiwar movement.

Banners announce the names of founding churches as delegates gather for the National Council of Churches' constituting convention in Cleveland, Ohio, November 28– December 1, 1950. (NCC Records, Presbyterian Historical Society, Presbyterian Church (USA), Philadelphia, PA)

President Dwight D. Eisenhower in New York City in 1958 lays the cornerstone of the Interchurch Center, home of the NCC and offices for the World Council of Churches, as well as for several denominations and religious organizations. (Religious News Service Photo, NCC Records, Presbyterian Historical Society, Presbyterian Church (USA), Philadelphia, PA)

Rising nineteen stories, the newly minted and majestic "God Box," as the Interchurch Center was called, exuded the ecumenical movement's triumphal spirit and hopes of facilitating Christian unity. Photograph circa 1959. (Records of the Construction of the Interchurch Center Collection, 1955–1961, Interchurch Center, New York, NY)

Secretary of State John Foster Dulles (left), NCC President Rev. Dr. Edwin T. Dahlberg (center), and chair of the NCC's International Affairs Commission Ernest Gross (right) chat informally at the Fifth World Order Study Conference, Cleveland, 1958. (Rebman Photo Service, Cleveland, OH, NCC Records, Presbyterian Historical Society, Presbyterian Church (USA), Philadelphia, PA)

Ken Maxwell and Dean Rusk dedicate the John Foster Dulles Library and Research Center in New York City, along with other ecumenists and government leaders, May 1962. From left to right: Former NCC Associate General Secretary Rev. Dr. Roswell P. Barnes, CCIA Director Rev. Dr. O. Frederick Nolde (WCC), Dean Rusk, former CIA Director Allen Dulles, Rev. Dr. Kenneth Maxwell, Rev. Dr. Henry Pitney Van Dusen, Bishop G. Bromley Oxnam, and publisher Henry Luce. (NCC Records, Presbyterian Historical Society, Presbyterian Church (USA), Philadelphia, PA)

Secretary of State Dean Rusk chats with UN Secretary General U Thant after speaking at the dedication of the Church Center for the United Nations, September 1963. From left to right: Methodist Bishop F. Gerald Ensley, NCC President J. Irwin Miller, Dean Rusk, UN Ambassador Adlai E. Stevenson, and U Thant. (NCC Records, Presbyterian Historical Society, Presbyterian Church (USA), Philadelphia, PA)

NCC Seal, circa 1965. (NCC Records, Presbyterian Historical Society, Presbyterian Church (USA), Philadelphia, PA)

NCC President Bishop Reuben H. Mueller conducts Easter services for men of the USS *Krishna*, a naval supply ship off the coast of South Vietnam, mid-1960s. Mueller spent a week in the war zone. (Religious News Service Photo, NCC Records, Presbyterian Historical Society, Presbyterian Church (USA), Philadelphia, PA)

Rev. Dr. Robert Sperry Bilheimer (above) and Gerhard Albert Elston (below), circa 1966, joined the National Council of Churches to lead its ecumenical peace effort in response to the Vietnam War. (Bilheimer photo: RG414, Presbyterian Historical Society, Presbyterian Church (USA), Philadelphia, PA; Elston photo: Elston Papers, Swarthmore College Peace Collection, Swarthmore, PA)

Evangelist Billy Graham (third from left) attends the Laity Luncheon at the NCC's General Assembly, 1966, along with (left to right) the popular advocate of positive thinking Rev. Dr. Norman Vincent Peale, outgoing NCC President Reuben H. Mueller, and incoming NCC President Dr. Arthur Flemming. (NCC Records, Presbyterian Historical Society, Presbyterian Church (USA), Philadelphia, PA)

PART THREE

DEBATE, ACTION,

AND DIVISION,

DECEMBER 1965-

NOVEMBER 1968

CHAPTER SIX

Building an Ecumenical Peace Witness, 1966

It took weeks of debate before President Johnson authorized a short bombing pause over North Vietnam, to begin Christmas Eve 1965. Antiwar liberals had lobbied hard for it, and Secretary of Defense McNamara tried to convince him to extend it indefinitely. Privately, McNamara had lost confidence in the prospect of a swift military victory. With 184,000 American troops engaged and more on the way, he foresaw a protracted war that did not promise to result in America's objectives. Therefore, he persuaded Johnson to combine diplomatic efforts with an extended pause aimed at precipitating talks.[1]

The NCC entered the holiday season with prayerful anticipation. Its support for a bombing pause and all-out push for negotiations had finally found a willing White House. Council President Mueller wired Johnson to praise his statesmanship in taking this risk for peace.[2] Convinced that the halt endangered U.S. troops, however, the Joint Chiefs pressured Johnson throughout to resume bombing. So antiwar forces, including churches, rallied voices behind sustaining it.

This led to the birth of perhaps the most prominent antiwar organization for religiously motivated people: Clergy and Laymen Concerned About Vietnam (CALCAV).[3] In a small NCC office, a group gathered to mobilize quick church support for the pause. They generated lists of clergy across the United States, many known from shared civil rights efforts, and used seminary volunteers to contact them about planning grassroots activities urging negotiations. A few weeks of nightly phone calls produced about 165 budding local committees, which put pressure on Washington in a variety of ways.[4] A notable feat, given that many clergy feared the condemnation such action might draw from their congregations. The NCC provided CALCAV's physical and financial launching pad and would sustain it for years. CAL-CAV gave religious people who opposed the war a separate and independent organization through which to express their sentiments freely outside of their more restrictive religious structures. It could carry out interfaith projects at will through local chapters and at the national level. Conversely, the NCC could not act without approval from its governing bodies. And unlike CALCAV, the Council lacked direct access to the grass roots because its structural design permitted communication with denominational boards, not parishioners. Yet, the NCC could mobilize denominational consensus against the war, which CALCAV was powerless to do. Therefore, while frustration sometimes erupted between the two organizations, their varied roles, access, and abilities complemented each other.

CALCAV's founders originally named their group the National Emergency Committee of Clergy Concerned About Vietnam (CCAV). This connoted what they thought would be a short-term emergency action to rally clergy behind extending the bombing pause, resistance to future escalation, and negotiations.[5] They also aimed to generate a different image of the dissenter. The *Christian Century* had high hopes. "This program . . . may seem modest; but once it is under way it can achieve that massiveness and momentum which enabled the clergy to help turn the tide in the civil rights struggle."[6]

Since CCAV's objectives fell within the NCC's recent policy mandate, Associate General Secretary David Hunter persuaded the Council to provide its organizers with an office and a phone line.[7] It also agreed to cover CCAV expenses until it could reimburse the Council, and process donations on its behalf so it could benefit from the NCC's tax exempt status. This financial arrangement spawned future tensions.[8] Still the Council provided CCAV/CALCAV with a safety net for years.

Toward the end of January, President Johnson grew frustrated with Hanoi's unresponsiveness. An NCC delegation met with Secretary of State Rusk to urge patience and perseverance.[9] But their plea proved fruitless. Johnson resumed bombing. A poll released the day of his decision showed that most Americans would support increases in bombing and troop deployments up to five hundred thousand.[10] The failed diplomatic effort embittered the president, making him resistant to future suggestions for bombing halts and causing McNamara to lose clout inside the Oval Office. While the administration's attempts to spark negotiations may have been genuine, its diplomatic ineptitude became a saboteur. To the *Century*, renewed bombing made a mockery of Johnson's simultaneous request for UN help in opening negotiations and embarrassed Security Council members.[11] CCAV added that the administration's ban on Vietcong diplomatic representation, combined with its erroneous understanding of the war's causes, also hindered future talks.

While CCAV built its base, NCC leaders reshaped the Council's infrastructure for long-range activity on international affairs.[12] Several wanted to move the Council beyond statements to programmatic action and make it as effective in that arena as it was on civil rights.[13] They hoped the Council's new Priority Program for Peace, under design for General Board consideration, would fit this bill. And herein lies a pattern. Church leaders active in civil rights struggles pushed hardest for the NCC to tackle the war by mimicking its race program. They extended their sense of accomplishment in moving laity and government on civil rights into similar high expectations for the churches on Vietnam. Their desire for a direct action program on the war stemmed from their belief that this had worked on civil rights. They even drew expertise from veterans of the race issue to help craft the NCC's peace program. But this transfer of expectations would prove naïve, as the astute J. Irwin Miller predicted. The former NCC president had proposed the peace program idea. Yet he saw in the student movement's efforts the difficulties inherent in tackling this war. "The race crisis was pretty clear," he observed. The students "could see where the right was and how to fight for it. The peace crisis is different. They see how confused it is, and their own action is confused and confusing."[14] Throughout 1966 the NCC saw firsthand how this perplexing, morally obtuse war divided Christians and complicated the task of Christian unity. Power, turf, and image issues would do so as well.

Despite the murkiness of international affairs, ecumenists felt compelled to be peacemakers, as Jesus commanded. So they laid out a theological foundation for the now nicknamed "Peace Priority Program." The church's task, they explained, involved not only enhancing justice in tangible ways but also encouraging conversions away from globalism toward embracing a pluralistic international community—in effect, creating a secular embodiment of ecumenism.[15] Therefore, this peace program was, from its inception and prior to Bilheimer's arrival, focused upon more than simply stopping the war. The Council also hoped to coordinate its divisions and denominations in ways to provide effective means of advancing "peace with justice." Such an education process must start with the church's own laity, for "the movement can bear real fruit only when the laity are trained for their participation in this witness." Thus, the clergy-laity gap over the church's proper role in the world must be addressed.

The General Board approved the Priority Program for Peace as February's cold thawed. It was grand and expensive, costing between $200,000 and $300,000 per year. Since the plan stated that "The Council must relate all its activities to 'the things that make for peace,'" all Council units were summoned to assist its success.[16] This included redistributing funds from smaller programs. The NCC also received an anonymous gift of $150,000 specifically for the peace program to use over a four-year period—a sum the Council asked denominations to supplement through increased donations.[17]

The Vietnam conflict would command center stage in the peace program's work. Yet, U.S. Vietnam policy was seen as one repercussion of deeper maladies on which the program must focus. Again, the NCC's Vietnam effort was intended to be much more than an antiwar cry to "bring the boys home"; it was to be a pro-justice witness on a worldwide scale. This distinguished the Council's goals from those of many other antiwar groups.

As initial guidance, the board directed the Peace Priority Program toward several key tasks that would encompass its mission for years.[18] For example, it should articulate the theological bases for the church's involvement in international affairs and peace. It must delve into related policy and economic issues. It needed to better educate and involve laity. It should relate NCC peace efforts with those underway in member denominations, Catholic and Jewish communities, the World Council, other religious groups such as CALCAV, and the secular community. It must discern the proper relationship between churches and government, and "bring a dimension which diplomacy cannot encompass no matter how expert it is."[19] Finally it needed to ascertain which issues were priorities, how the NCC would explore them, and then how it should respond. These "goals and objectives" were refined over subsequent months, but they reflected an immediate emphasis on theology, education, networking, discernment, cooperative action, and prophetic speech, which marked a traditional ecumenical approach.[20]

The broad agenda and councilwide nature of the Peace Priority Program mandated selection of a staff officer who could administer it effectively and report directly to the general secretary.[21] Maxwell's resignation left the post of IAC director open as well. Since the two positions were closely related, the Council decided to hire one person to do both. President Mueller appointed a new Advisory Committee on Peace to replace SACVN and assist this director.[22] The new hire would have to be an ecumenical veteran experienced in international affairs and committed to the belief that the American ecumenical community must act as the living body of Christ in the world, not as another rubber-stamp for the U.S. establishment. Within two months, Espy recruited his old friend from student movement days, Robert S. Bilheimer, for the role. Administering the program would prove far harder than planning it. For when Bilheimer tried to hew closely to the board's initial directives, others attempted to dilute certain aspects, such as exploring theological bases and determining the appropriate relationship to government.

Along with authorizing the Peace Priority Program, the board tied off two other threads left dangling by the Sixth World Order Study Conference and December board meeting. Following up on the conference's defense of dissent, the board unanimously passed a policy statement urging Christians to "resist any effort to curtail freedom of speech, assembly, and petition, especially in this time of international crisis and domestic conflict."[23] The NCC's history of battling McCarthyite accusations made it rather fearless on this issue. Of course Protestants had fought to preserve freedom of conscience for centuries; these rights were critical to protecting faith expressions. The NCC's statement decried the government's use of patriotic appeals to suppress protest. Human beings' first loyalty must be to God and their consciences, for in this very "freedom and responsibility under God" lies "the essential dignity of man." Dissent was both a divine and an American right and, when motivated by the common good, was also patriotic.

The board also finally passed a "Policy Statement on China" basically adopting the recommendations of its Fifth World Order Study Conference in 1958. These included UN membership for China and a reevaluation of U.S. China policy with the hope of future diplomatic recognition.[24] Contrary to popular belief and the accusations of its right-wing critics, this 1966 statement was the first time the NCC officially made such a stand.

The fact that it happened quietly, sparking little furor, illustrates how much the Dulles-like Cold War consensus on communism had dissipated over the intervening years.

Ecumenists knew the Vietnam War was more complex than ideological politics. Like other civil rights activists, Robert Spike emphasized to the board the relationship between race and Vietnam.[25] The Vietnam conflict would puzzle Americans until they faced the root causes of the "civil rights rebellion," he said, for both shared a common thrust for justice. "Men are rebelling everywhere against injustice, against privilege, against gross poverty in a world of abundance, against being less than the men they have been called upon to be," Spike described. "Moreover, both the war in Viet Nam and the civil rights rebellion are partly a revolution of color." America's racial prejudices were being played out on a world stage. Asian, African, and Latin American nations noticed that America's diplomacy-based foreign policy with white governments contrasted sharply with the crushing militancy used against developing nations. The United States sprayed Vietnam with napalm, burned villages, and killed civilians with little demonstrable concern, actions that developing countries doubted would be unleashed upon white peoples, even Russians. Linking America's racial bias to growing non-Western appeals for communism, Spike explained that "some of our policies in Viet Nam make it appear to many persons in Africa and Asia that the alternative of communism might be less destructive than the price of having America 'protect' them from tyranny."[26]

That February, *Christianity and Crisis* celebrated its twenty-fifth anniversary. Born to condemn Christian pacifism and urge U.S. military engagement against Hitler, it subsequently took a tough anticommunist line against Stalin. Now, surprising many, it condemned U.S. military involvement in Vietnam. In its anniversary edition, Reinhold Niebuhr and John Bennett explained why, as Christian realists, they opposed U.S. Vietnam policy.[27] Both differentiated between Nazism, Stalinism, and the diverse forms of communism that existed in the 1960s. Both discussed how the nuclear age changed international relations and methods of exercising power. Bennett clarified why the oft-cited "Munich analogy" lesson from 1938, about never appeasing aggressors, was inapplicable to Vietnam. This again signaled that liberal Protestant leaders had broken with Cold War policies trumpeted by many a decade earlier. So too did the cool reception given Vice President Hubert Humphrey at the journal's anniversary banquet. A longtime hero and friend of church leaders, Humphrey was invited to deliver the main address. But his loyalty to Johnson's war policies made the evening awkward. Bennett and his wife, Anne, sat with Humphrey at the head table. Anne had pinned to her dress a large white dove easily seen from across the room.[28] The vice president's attempt to convince this audience of the wisdom of U.S. actions in Vietnam was "disenchanting" for both speaker and audience.[29]

The journal's anniversary issue featured a piece by Eugene Carson Blake, Visser 't Hooft's new replacement as general secretary of the World Council. Blake's election elevated the first American to that global role. He was an interesting choice, given that many quietly questioned whether American churchmen truly understood the ecumenical vision. But the WCC was in the early stages of a tremendous demographic shift as representatives from developing nations, bitter about Western imperialism, swelled its membership. Blake had earned worldwide prestige when, as Stated Clerk of the United Presbyterian Church, his arrest during a civil rights protest drew considerable publicity. Many saw it as a calculated move on Blake's part, inspired as much by his desire for fame as it was to mobilize church support for civil rights. Nevertheless, his championing of racial justice earned favor with the WCC's people of color. Blake had charisma, a considerable sense of self-importance, and a triumphal belief in the church's global responsibilities. He was a known figurehead, too, which perhaps the WCC desired.[30] His ecumenical acumen would be questioned years later by those who linked the WCC's diminishing power to Blake's tenure. Nevertheless, at the time, his installation empowered the American ecumenical movement. His criticism of U.S. Vietnam policy was also well-known, giving the NCC an important partner when coordinating ecumenical support on this issue.

Just prior to joining the WCC, Blake identified five external threats to the church's ecumenical witness. These included the propensity to see "war as the instrument of national policy" and to connect patriotism and Protestantism too symbiotically.[31] The latest wave of anti-NCC sentiment from its southern members reinforced the difficulty of questioning such conceptions.[32] Fellow Presbyterian Robert Bilheimer agreed with Blake. The challenge of raising an ecumenical witness within American church communities would convince Bilheimer to fill Maxwell's shoes at the NCC's International Affairs Commission and to direct the new Peace Priority Program.

THE BILHEIMER ERA BEGINS

In mid-March, Espy began prodding Bilheimer to take the position and asked Visser 't Hooft to add his encouragement.[33] Back in 1963, Bilheimer left the WCC to become minister of Central Presbyterian Church in Rochester, New York. He had been second-in-command to Visser 't Hooft at the World Council and, as his eldest son recalled, "was deeply and profoundly hoping that he would be named General Secretary" upon Visser 't Hooft's departure. Bilheimer believed wholeheartedly in the WCC and coveted its top position. Being passed over and then watching Blake, another white American Presbyterian, get his dream job was a crushing disappointment that his family thought "marked him . . . for the rest of his life." Perhaps the WCC hadn't wanted to promote an insider like Bilheimer. Besides, Blake was flashier and better known while Bilheimer had the reputation of being "a tough guy." Both could be arrogant. Adding to the tension, Blake and Bilheimer were close friends. All three of Bilheimer's sons loved "Uncle Gene," who played with the boys and hosted campouts. After Blake's installation, he and Bilheimer remained friends. But, without the WCC, Bilheimer felt professionally adrift.[34]

Central Presbyterian Church attracted wealthy professionals who appreciated Bilheimer's past work. There he delivered the kind of challenging sermons that had signified his preaching in the 1950s when he pastored a black church in Jamaica, New York.[35] By early 1966, however, he had grown frustrated at his inability to convince this elite white congregation "that democracy and the Kingdom of God weren't the same thing."[36] Laity, he realized, tended to "go to church for an individual belief, a one-to-one belief to get through the day and to answer the big questions."[37] He wanted to stretch their understanding of Christianity beyond their own individualism, nationalism, and simple missions work based upon proselytizing. He saw the work of the church as much "bigger than converting the heathen and snatching souls" and likened the ecumenical movement's mission to "a kind of second reformation." "The function of the ecumenical enterprise," he clarified, "was to revive the reality of the body of Christ in the world," and for him this was imperative in America.[38] He felt he was on the verge of a breakthrough with his parishioners when Espy contacted him about the NCC job.

Bilheimer saw in it the underlying ecumenical challenge that drove his spirit. The Vietnam War was raising catalytic questions that potentially could shake the foundations of America's sense of identity, just as World War II and anticolonial revolutions had done among Christians internationally. Therefore, Bilheimer viewed the war as a vehicle through which to expand not only America's understanding of itself but also the role of the church in the world. Wrestling with the underlying issues raised by the war could force the churches to see themselves within a global framework as a body of Christ that must sometimes stand apart from nations and cultures in moral witness. Likewise, if the NCC could help generate a true ecumenical witness on Vietnam, it might help Americans look critically at themselves in the mirror of U.S. foreign policy.[39] Bilheimer wanted people to consider what this policy revealed about people's understanding of what it meant to be an American, for he believed that "A basic task of the church is to help people discover who they are." He saw the NCC's role as "a continuation of the best that I was doing in the World Council of Churches, but now on the U.S. scene: to fight the American imperium. We had fought the British imperium," he added. But now America was "doing in Vietnam what Britain had done in India."[40]

Bilheimer admitted that he was not really "an anti–Vietnam War guy," in the sense of being focused simply upon stopping the war. Rather, he was more interested in using the war to ecumenize the churches and then, through a public witness, to challenge the presuppositions that led to wars like the one in Vietnam.[41] His first priority was always the ecumenical movement; for him, participation in antiwar activities was one expression of the church's ecumenical witness, not an end in itself. Therefore, church involvement in any other movements, be they antiwar or civil rights, should always be done in a manner that embodied rather than sidelined the full ecumenical vision and process. Regardless of whether the church's efforts succeeded in sparking desired social transformations, he felt an ecumenical witness had to be made. As his early experiences had taught him, the church must always stand up and be the church. If he shirked this challenge, then, he felt, he "had no business being a Christian."[42] He jumped at the job.[43]

Bilheimer's appointment as director of the Peace Priority Program and the IAC was not cheered by some denominations' international affairs secretaries.[44] Bilheimer assumed they viewed him suspiciously for being part of the WCC's "brain trust," not the mover and shaker they hoped would spearhead an activist church wing of the antiwar movement modeled on the NCC's Commission on Religion and Race. They were right. Bilheimer was not an activist poised to lead church protests for an end to the war. Rather, he was an ecumenist who felt compelled to raise a confessing church witness against the presuppositions underlying U.S. foreign policy, the repercussions of which were being unleashed in Vietnam. This difference mattered to Bilheimer. He thought the American ecumenical movement was straying from its foundations, so its leadership had to wage a constant battle to keep it as free from cultural biases and bandwagons as possible. The limited degree to which this was possible always compromised its witness somewhat. But Bilheimer also said that the "perennial American problem was the question of the nature and reality of the Church." He perceived many Christian activists as lost ecumenical sheep who wanted to rise onto soapboxes and organize cooperative actions around single-shot issues without developing the theological underpinnings of their witness.[45] To him, this was not real ecumenism. The activists allowed themselves to become captives of issues rather than transcendent leaders of them, sacrificing the church's unifying theological grounding in the process.[46]

By no means did Bilheimer oppose action. Rather, he insisted on it as part of a real Christian witness. But he understood that the 1960s ushered in an approach that measured church work solely by its relevance to addressing human needs and social justice. Being the hands of Jesus in the world became more important to many than explaining the work of those hands theologically. This wrongly pitted action against the discursive theological process that fostered Christian unity and developed its witness, favoring one ecumenical function over another when all were mutually reinforcing. Doing so damaged—even gutted—ecumenism, according to Bilheimer. He also rejected the false dichotomy between appealing to the individual soul and challenging the social system, which often divided conservatives and liberals. Again, he stressed that each of these elements was essential to ecumenical work based upon transcendence, unity, witness, service, and renewal. He agreed strongly with activists' emphasis upon bringing justice to fruition in the world. The IAC supported groups taking direct action against what Bilheimer viewed as an imperialistic war. He simply opposed skipping steps that made this witness an ecumenical one. He also demanded that people think theologically, and that this thinking be rigorous and clear. A leader who jumped into prophetic action without cultivating theological understanding and ecumenical consensus (often judging these irrelevant or too time-consuming) gutted the church's power by becoming another issue-based activist "screaming in the wind."[47]

To Bilheimer, many denominational leaders never grasped the fact that cooperative interdenominational activism on single-shot issues did not qualify as ecumenism. After a weeklong trip to the United States, Visser 't Hooft reached the same conclusion. He noticed that American church people frequently misused the word *ecumenism*, saying sarcastically that, "every time a couple of Methodists and Baptists get together for a tea party, it's the ecumenical movement."[48] Elston later agreed, noting that many faith leaders were very dedicated yet "didn't have the vision." They "conceived of [ecumenism] as successful interchurch activity," but "there is a difference between an ecumenical movement and an interchurch one."[49]

Bilheimer also stressed that the church must preserve some distance from both government and secular activists in terms of vision and motivation. It must generate a theologically grounded, consensus-driven analysis that connected the myriad of soapbox issues driving people's concerns and then communicate its message to those in power.[50] When the church stood up in this way, Bilheimer believed, it helped create opportunities for the Holy Spirit to transform people's worldviews and reinforced its unique identity as the church.[51] Because Bilheimer worried that the NCC's Vietnam thrust was not sufficiently grounded in theological understanding, he deemed it his mission to draw denominational secretaries out of isolation and into fruitful conversation about *why* Christian belief mandated a stand against U.S. Vietnam policy—a task he felt Maxwell had not understood. In fact, he said the basic function of the IAC "should be . . . creating a truly ecumenical, prophetic consensus of Christian conviction on international affairs. It should be concerned with issues, not primarily with program projects."[52] Circumnavigating denominational leaders' egos, given their own strong ideas about what the NCC's peace program should do, also posed a challenge for the new man at the helm.[53] Several deemed the problem mutual.

Many of the denominations' own secretaries for international affairs and social concerns had marched for racial justice and were now ready for real action on Vietnam. The Methodists and United Presbyterians had been pushing the NCC to get off the "consensus seat" on Vietnam since the summer of 1965.[54] The United Church of Christ, as well as pacifist communions such as the Quakers and Brethren, had the luxury of constituent support to push for stronger stances.[55] Several of these communions already had long-established peace programs, often staffed by people with more experience on the American scene and in running such programs than Bilheimer. This fueled tension between him and certain denominational officers.

These officers appreciated Bilheimer's readiness to lead the Council in a prophetic witness and were eager to cooperate on antiwar efforts. However, they sometimes resented his attempts to give orders and subsume their work under an NCC umbrella. They did not want the good things being done in their own mature programs, nor the resources dedicated to them, to be sapped by the NCC.[56] Attempting to explain the complaints of his colleagues, Alan Geyer (UCC international affairs director) noted that, while Bilheimer was extremely bright, competent, and kind, he could also behave like a "steamroller," or a "bull in a china shop," coming off as abrasive, bossy, and aggressive. He used a top-down, authoritative style, sometimes pushing for a program without first seeking input from denominational staffs. Bilheimer's faith identity and professional experiences were clearly anchored in ecumenism, but not in any particular denominational tradition; thus, he often struggled to understand and work with leaders devoted to their own denominational identities, organizations, and cultures. Geyer noticed, as well, that Bilheimer sometimes appeared oblivious to the need for church programs to work with and listen to laity.[57] Perhaps this reflected the fact that Bilheimer came to the NCC already frustrated by the Christian nationalism imbedded in lay beliefs. It might have also simply resulted from his responsibilities at the NCC, which centered upon interactions with government and the denominations, not with laity. Then again, the denominations may have used this as an excuse to retain control over programs; for laity did not give their executives high marks for listening to them either during this period.

Bilheimer, in turn, saw the secretaries as eager to preserve their own denominational turfs and bragging rights rather than fold their work into an ecumenical package. He saw them as clinging to their power structures while resisting his pleas to operate as a body of Christ on Vietnam.[58] One Presbyterian executive admitted that the denominations often used the NCC as a place to discuss problems, then they "hived off" to work on their own, parsing out tasks to the Council that fell along the periphery of their interests or abilities to act. Thus, they tried to keep the most desirable work within their own bureaucracies.[59]

Often, as well, only a few denominations were willing to give funds to particular NCC programs. The method used to finance the NCC contributed to these turf problems. Cognate funding, as it was called, meant that the largest denominations with the biggest programs often ended up funding and donating staff to help run similar ones at the NCC. For example, the Methodists' sizeable Division of Peace and World Order, run by Herman Will, was tapped for resources to fuel Bilheimer's program. Will resisted but was overridden by his boss, Dudley Ward.[60] Cognate funding also fed the expectation that the larger denominations would receive considerable influence in shaping NCC programs. As a result, smaller communions felt ignored in decision-making, and the biggest sometimes exerted a degree of leverage that challenged and weakened NCC staff authority.[61]

Since denominational leaders generally did not differentiate between interdenominational cooperation and true ecumenism, Bilheimer felt that he was hired, in part, to muscle the NCC's members back toward real ecumenism. (Years later, certain colleagues described him as a WCC-trained missionary seeking to spread the ecumenical gospel within NCC circles.) Therefore, regardless of his program's funding sources, Bilheimer's desire to unite the churches in a true ecumenical witness inspired his assertive top-down leadership style, resulting in some mutual resentment. The turf, style, and resource issues exhibited here caused friction that escalated in the 1960s as lay support shrank in supply.

Bilheimer also had to deal with members who held conservative theological and political sentiments, such as the Greek Orthodox Church, which supported U.S. Vietnam policy. The NCC comprised over thirty denominations and could not take official positions without General Board approval. Several more liberal denominations, therefore, pursued their own independent peace actions and did what they could to encourage the NCC and their fellow churches to move forward. The Methodist Board of Christian Social Concerns, led by Dudley Ward, worked tirelessly to build a political wave of grassroots pressure on President Johnson.[62] The Methodists also joined with other church organizations to coordinate "Wednesdays in Washington," when Christians visited congressional offices to express opinions on Vietnam.[63] A few weeks later the UCC created its own Peace Priority Program that Geyer administered.[64] The Friends Committee on National Legislation (FCNL) and American Friends Service Committee (AFSC) also worked in Washington on war-related issues. Denominations such as these were ready to campaign hard on Vietnam.

So was the Emergency Committee of Clergy Concerned About Vietnam. In April it declared its permanence by renaming itself Clergy and Laymen

Concerned About Vietnam and hiring Rev. Richard Fernandez as executive director.[65] Fernandez, an army veteran, was a seasoned civil rights activist who, like his mentor Robert Spike, believed that people had "to act themselves into thinking instead of think themselves into acting."[66] Fernandez epitomized the new breed approach that urged clergy to prioritize action ahead of theological dialogues, for God was already moving in the streets. To such individuals, therefore, Bilheimer seemed strong on the issues but overly academic, systematic, and cautious in the witness.[67] The differences in definition, method, and style between Bilheimer's traditional ecumenism and that of the new breeders would chafe against both throughout the Vietnam era. In fact, they caused rifts within both the World and National Councils that reverberated for decades.[68]

Other ecumenical bodies added their voices to the Vietnam debate during this period. The WCC released a firm statement that paralleled the NCC's.[69] In March the National Inter-Religious Conference on Peace— uniting over four hundred Catholic, Jewish, and Protestant participants (including NCC members)—also issued a similar statement and pleaded for religious groups to "intensify their work for peace."[70] Aspects of this meeting aired on ABC television.

The first nine months of 1966, therefore, were chaotic formative ones for the NCC's international affairs wing. Coming on board in mid-1966, Bilheimer spent much of the summer and fall assembling a staff.[71] Most of his recruits shared his Geneva background and understanding of ecumenism. In one of his first official acts, he appointed Kurtis Naylor to be associate director.[72] Bilheimer had first met him in Geneva, where the pacifist Brethren had administered relief efforts. Elston described Naylor as an open-minded, genuine individual with a sly sense of humor and an incisive mind. Naylor could debate with the best but knew how to hide this skill behind a laid-back country-boy image.[73] Bilheimer called him a "godsend."

To serve as Vietnam secretary, Naylor urged Bilheimer to hire Gerhard Elston, who was still with the student movement that had offices located conveniently in the Interchurch Center. The three had met briefly in Geneva in the 1950s when Elston worked with Church World Service's Hungarian relief program. Elston shared their grounding in a strong, confessing church view of ecumenism. But his personal style was so different from Bilheimer's that it would take them time to learn how to blend their complementary strengths. Elston's passionate, somewhat avant garde, unbureaucratic, yet system-respecting style was unique in the Council's halls. His full beard caused a minor crisis among clean-cut churchmen because they feared it made him look too much like a hippie. Since Elston's job would include interfacing with secular peace groups (including students suspicious of "the system"), his uncorporate manner meant he could serve the Council in ways perhaps no other staff member could. Bilheimer called Elston "invaluable" and "my answer to the left wing." He also had an easy way with people. Another NCC staffer described him as an excellent catalyst man who left people feeling differently after talking with him. Bilheimer said, "you could never get mad at him and you couldn't write him off. He was sincere" and had "a whale of a brain."[74]

Like Bilheimer, Elston believed his faith mandated his ecumenical witness on Vietnam. To Elston, Christ gave his life on the cross for every person, not because anybody deserved it but because God loved them. Therefore, the corollary to this, he said, was that "whenever I look at another person, for the sake of my own salvation, I must see them as me; I can't tolerate injustice for them. If I quibble about justice for them, I am blasphemous." Elston did not feel driven to "save the world." Rather, he felt called "to be a sister or brother to the person who is suffering." Associating this concept with his experience in Nazi Germany, it meant "one must be willing to go to the ovens for someone else, which is tough to do." Relating this to Vietnam, he explained, "We must feel the death of any child in Vietnam as the death of 'my baby.'"[75] To this former refugee, Vietnamese suffering struck a personal chord.

Elston joined Bilheimer's team as 1967 was dawning. Shortly thereafter, Bilheimer hired Allan Parrent to be the IAC's conduit in the Council's Washington office. The seminary-trained graduate student from Virginia came highly recommended for his knowledge of Capitol Hill politics and issues. Bilheimer described Parrent as the personification of the Virginia gentleman—except that, unlike many southerners, he strongly opposed America's military involvement in Vietnam. He would serve the team by keeping track of Congress on Vietnam-related issues and articulating Council opinions on the Hill.[76]

Bilheimer recruited one other man at the request of the Methodist Church, which had bankrolled the Church Center for the United Nations. Paul Dietterich was hired to direct the CCUN's programs related to international affairs. While officially part of the IAC team, he was not significantly connected to the Vietnam work of the other members.

These five comprised the NCC's new international affairs staff and spearheaded the Council's efforts on Vietnam for the next seven years.[77] While the team was still in formation, however, the broader church community kept responding to the growing war.

Like gadflies, the two ecumenical journals raised questions that irritated and edged Christian leaders toward deeper analysis of the war. By March, *Christianity and Crisis*'s editorial board was fed up with the mixed signals coming from the White House regarding U.S. objectives in Vietnam. So it published another signed declaration, entitled, "We Protest the National Policy in Vietnam." What was really going on, and why? Even giving the government's explanations full benefit of the doubt, the editors still tagged eight aspects of its policy as self-defeating and dangerous. They complained of a "stubborn vanity," a lack of "willingness to look at realities," and a deficiency of "moral imagination to seek better methods than the present contradictory mixture of peaceful rhetoric and stubborn policy." The editors implored their readers "to challenge dogmatisms that imperil ourselves and our world." And they introduced their appeal with an apt quotation from Herbert Butterfield's *Christianity and History*: "The hardest strokes of heaven fall in history upon those who imagine that they can control things in a sovereign manner, as though they were kings of the earth, playing Providence . . . and gambling on a lot of risky calculations in which there must never be a mistake."[78] If pride comes before a fall, the editors feared impending repercussions in a tense nuclear world.

A piece in the *Christian Century* condemned the churches' weak spines in dealing with conscientious objection. Since churches played a pivotal role in shaping the convictions that inspired many conscientious objectors (COs), why were they now shrinking from this cause? Were they more protective of their patriotic images than the rights of their young men? The article complained that churches covered their mouths while the secular American Civil Liberties Union (ACLU) defended the sanctity of men's consciences. Thus, it called for compassion and responsibility, reminding Christians that "the conscientious objectors—those who oppose all wars and those who oppose this one—are the church's own whether they admit it or not."[79] As the war escalated, the NCC and its member communions eventually embraced this controversial issue. In fact, the Council's new Advisory Committee on Peace discussed a proposed resolution on selective objectors for presentation at its next General Board meeting.[80]

Perhaps the most challenging aspect of the Peace Priority Program involved educating and motivating the grass roots in international affairs. Because the Council's members were denominations, not individuals, the NCC had to depend upon the communions to disseminate information and rally their people.[81] So, in June, President Mueller asked the heads of all member denominations to encourage local pastors to mobilize parishioners around U Thant's recent Vietnam proposal for negotiations.[82]

The NCC received a stunningly weak response. Part of the problem resided in transmission issues. Church leaders with congregants who were more open to NCC positions generally forwarded Council materials more effectively than others.[83] Those who didn't were often stymied by the fact that they lacked a similar authorizing statement on the war within their denominations. NCC policy was not binding upon the churches. Therefore, even though the NCC's December 1965 policy gave it a mandate to rally people against the war, the heads of churches that lacked such a statement could not do likewise.

For example, Mueller's request placed Franklin Clark Fry, president of the Lutheran Church of America, in this awkward position. Writing back, Fry explained that, while he personally agreed with the NCC on Vietnam, his denomination had not yet made that leap.[84] "[I]f we mean sincerely— and I do—that actions of the various organs of the NCCCUSA do not become actions of the member communions except as the communions themselves explicitly endorse them, I regret to say that I fail to see how a man in my position can appeal to the pastors and communicants of the Lutheran Church in America to do what you request."[85] Hence, the NCC had to build consensus on Vietnam among the denominations if it hoped to rally the grass roots. As consensus grew, and denominations passed similar statements on Vietnam, clergy who had stifled their own personal criticisms of the war finally received the necessary, protective, bureaucratic cover to speak their minds and encourage others to do the same. The NCC enhanced the consensus-building process by creating opportunities where church leaders could debate the issues and learn from one another. It was a slow yet vital process that the NCC could facilitate well.

Another problem resulted from the fact that, when a denomination's governing bodies finally passed an official statement authorizing and encouraging congregational study of the war, laity frequently resisted and clergy balked. (This will be discussed later.) Suffice it to say that even denominations most energetic in transmitting discussion materials still often received a stiff arm from their local churches. The Methodist Church is a prime example. By 1965 its Board of Christian Social Concerns was publishing challenging articles on the war in church periodicals that targeted both clergy and laity. It publicized NCC and denominational statements on the war in those journals and encouraged their use as study documents. The United Presbyterians did similarly.[86] Yet, they received disparaging letters with respect to their Vietnam positions, and many clergy seemed reluctant to stimulate congregational debate. Problems using these modes of communication, combined with a top-down leadership style, multiplied in the 1960s when questioning authority became the era's mantra.

FORGING A PEACE PRIORITY STRATEGY

As the war worsened, churches used its sheer destructiveness to make a case for peace. In late June 1966, the United States bombed North Vietnamese petroleum plants abutting two key cities, Hanoi and Haiphong. In response, North Vietnam threatened to try captured U.S. airmen as war criminals. China and the USSR also became more involved in supplying the North. China allowed the North Vietnamese to operate within its borders and, along with Russia, shuttled them weaponry. The U.S. military, in turn, escalated its manpower and firepower, as the American people continued to back Johnson's efforts to force Hanoi's hand through intensified bombing.[87] The NCC and several member denominations, along with Christian councils around the world, publicly condemned the escalation. The *New York Times* published the NCC's position alongside a contrary statement by the Greek Orthodox Church, which gave "whole-hearted support of the United States' stand against all aggression particularly in Vietnam."[88]

Several denominational and Council staffers were restless for a stronger NCC witness against the summer buildup.[89] But what approach would yield the best results? Bilheimer hoped a meeting with Dean Rusk would render clues. He wanted the church's strategy to be tied "to what the real intent, the real dilemma of the administration is."[90] On July 28, Rusk told a visiting NCC delegation that the administration was "hearing a great deal more from the hawks than they were from the doves." Arthur Flemming therefore extrapolated that Rusk wanted the churches to spearhead a global opinion-shaping effort that would "pressure . . . all parties to the conflict to move from the battlefield to the conference table."[91]

Council leaders also left stunned by Rusk's outmoded Cold War views. Espy was troubled by Rusk's narrow vision of U.S. foreign policy and particularly its relationship to developing nations. Elston described Rusk as an intelligent man with a small flow of perception deriving directly from Munich.[92] Since Rusk had served in the State Department under Truman when it "lost" China, Geyer surmised that traumatic accusations of softness on communism may have inspired him to harden himself excessively in response.[93] Regardless, like Flemming, Bilheimer focused on the fact that Rusk seemed to be hinting for heightened pressure from doves to balance that felt from hawks, giving the administration greater public mandate to flex its policy. Bilheimer got the impression that timing was important—that if dove pressure were applied soon, a breakthrough for negotiations might occur. As a result, the NCC's best strategy seemed clear: mount an all-out campaign for negotiations, help turn the public mood, and thereby give leverage to the supposedly stifled doves within the administration.[94]

The international aspect of this effort naturally included the World Council of Churches. In late July, it hosted its first Conference on Church and Society since 1937. The WCC's changing demographic contributed to emboldened criticism of U.S. Vietnam policy. *Time* magazine noticed the shift in personnel and tone. "With the gradual admission of many new churches from Africa, Asia and Latin America, and the Russian Orthodox Church in 1961. . . . the conference offered a platform for Africans and Asians to express their differences with the affluent Christians of the West, particularly of the U.S."[95] Two hundred fifty attendees demonstrated in Geneva's streets, waving banners reading "World Peace or the World in Pieces" and "An Impatient World Challenges a Complacent Church." According to *Time*, the seventy-three American delegates were swept up by "the radical tide" and telegrammed Johnson about their distress over Vietnam. Perturbed by the conference's anti-American tone, the editor of *Christianity and Crisis* called it "the most radical event in the life of the World Council."[96]

Throughout the summer the NCC received copies of statements from church councils globally protesting U.S. Vietnam policy. While a few American allies such as the British, Australian, and Japanese governments publicly supported U.S. military involvement, their ecumenical communities lined up against it.[97] Therefore, Bilheimer spent summer and fall talking with their leadership. He hoped the British Council, in particular, might generate grassroots pressure on its government to condemn America's escalation and appeal for negotiations. But British ecumenists explained that they lacked the resources, citizen interest, and Christian consensus to support a witness to their government. Feeling powerless, they asked instead for the NCC's help.[98]

Bilheimer then sought assistance in Asia. On September 20, he began a forty-day trip to consult with Asian leaders about their perceptions of U.S. policy on Vietnam. He did not enter Vietnam but visited Japan, Korea, Indonesia, India, Thailand, and the Philippines.[99] Although the Japanese Christian population was quite critical of U.S. military involvement in Vietnam, it was too small to influence its government, which benefited economically from the U.S. military. Indonesians felt similarly and stressed the deep desire of Vietnamese for independence from imperialism, which far surpassed their interest in communism. As Indonesians explained, developing countries needed assistance; but since the United States tied it tightly to imperialistic agendas, these nations opted instead for communist aid. For those in Asia, Indonesians told Bilheimer, "Freedom is our dignity." And regarding Vietnam, they said, the United States "has committed an offense against Asian dignity." They drew comparisons with their own battle against the Dutch. Why, they inquired, did the United States distrust other peoples so greatly that it felt compelled to intrude?[100] Bilheimer wrote to Naylor: "How greatly we are paying for the Dulles policies!" The Koreans felt differently, however. It shattered Bilheimer to discover they apparently "didn't give a damn" about Vietnam and seemed more interested in what they might get from the Americans. Just as the NCC's Bangkok delegation had discerned earlier, Asian opinion was divided on Vietnam. But unity prevailed on certain subjects such as race. "I have heard more outspokenly than before the protest against white superiority!" Bilheimer told Naylor. "Race is a key issue in Asia."[101]

As church bodies around the world grew more skeptical of U.S. policy, they also faulted American churches' Vietnam statements for recognizing South Vietnam as a separate nation with the option to remain so, for this violated the 1954 Geneva Accords.[102] The Protestant Federation of France emphasized this particular point to Bilheimer.[103] As a result of its discussions with the East Asia Christian Conference, the World Council had revised its statement to reflect that Vietnam was one entity—not two nations—that must decide its future as a whole.[104] The NCC had not. This illustrated that many within the NCC and its denominations were anti-communists who cringed at the thought of communism spreading south.

On the American front, the U.S. population gave Johnson a vote of confidence to pursue a heightened military course. With a few denominational exceptions, local Christians reflected the sentiments of the population.[105] According to Geyer, division trumped consensus on Vietnam at all levels of the church, and this was both hampering the NCC's consensus-building efforts and poisoning personal relationships. Caught in what he termed "a moral crossfire," Geyer agonized over these strains as well as his own personal quandary. "This is not simply an academic observation," he wrote. "It is an existential cry of pain from one who freely confesses to being a muddled moderate in the middle on most of the issues of this war, a posture which led one indignant pastor to denounce me in print as 'a castrated neutralist.'"[106]

Geyer concurred with those who saw disagreements arising in part from the confusing moral complexities of war issues, which were largely absent from the civil rights movement. On civil rights, he explained, church leaders enjoyed a unique luxury—"a virtual unanimity concerning an obvious and massive injustice on one side of the conflict." Therefore, the "full power of moral indignation could be unleashed because of this unanimity." Because the black freedom struggle had seemed clearly cut into good and evil sides, he felt it had led to an absolutist sense of right and wrong. To Geyer, this attitude caused problems when people transferred it to the ambiguous foreign policy questions raised by the Vietnam War. Simply put, "the line up of 'good guys' and 'bad guys'" that church people recognized in the civil rights struggle "is just not very easy to match in Viet-Nam." He wanted church leaders to treat Vietnam, and one another's opinions on it, with the sensitivity and open mindedness he felt they deserved.[107]

Bilheimer's intention to use dialogue to build consensus created stress because certain denominational leaders wanted to jump immediately into organizing action programs that would mobilize people politically against the war.[108] Bilheimer circulated a draft paper for critical comment titled "Christian Witness in International Affairs." It described his consultation-type approach and suggested priorities for the Council's peace program. He hoped to revise it for presentation at the NCC's triennial General Assembly in December, but the Methodists did not like it. They intimated they might withhold their substantial financial contribution to the peace program unless they were guaranteed that it would focus on education and action. Therefore, both David Hunter and Ed Espy urged Bilheimer to alter the paper's language so as not to "give Tracey [Jones] and Dudley [Ward] the impression they fear." The head of the Division of Christian Life and Mission, Jon Regier, agreed and suggested Bilheimer include a section in his paper "that borders on describing the National Council of Churches as being involved in lobbying. As you know, even using the word isn't too strong for me."[109] The Methodists demanded it, and they were not alone.[110] Robert Fangmeier, director of Christian Citizenship for the Disciples of Christ, also worried that Bilheimer's paper focused too little on "mobilizing people who are already committed." He felt that "Education is not complete unless it includes action also."[111] Clearly, several denominations and staff colleagues were seeking a more utilitarian approach to the war. With his arm twisted, Bilheimer integrated these aims into his peace program agenda. The thrust now included both debate and action on Vietnam.

As divisions between church leaders grew more visible, the chasm between them and the grass roots remained difficult to bridge. Many local clergy felt trapped between church hierarchies critical of Vietnam and parishioners with sons fighting and dying there. For example, Naylor received a pastor's letter about sharing the NCC's Vietnam statement with twenty-five fellow ministers; only one in his group completely concurred with it.[112] It was difficult for clergy with families of deployed soldiers in their congregations to say anything when those families expressed 100 percent commitment to U.S. policy. Wounded vets in the pews often saluted likewise. Additionally, the pastor described a television message aired before every program stating, "Think American, act American, be American," making it suspect for clergy to dissent. This environment—combined with people's tendencies to trust their government and believe that U.S. soldiers were always ambassadors of righteous goodwill—mitigated against openness to the Council's positions. Naylor admitted how divisive the Vietnam issue was even within the NCC: "[Whenever] we suggest an alternative or a program of action we bifurcate and splinter into so many groups that almost no consensus seems at this time possible."[113]

Robert Bulkley, secretary of the Office of Church and Society for the United Presbyterian Church, warned Dudley Ward against moving too far ahead of church policy and parishioners despite having a morally defensible position. Doing so, he said, severely reduced the effectiveness of the church's witness, for without broad backing, protest simply became an "academic" act rather than an influential representative one. Bulkley also cited the lack of consensus within the NCC's membership: "I see no evidence that the church really knows its mind on this subject. The National Council statements are pretty innocuous. . . . And most of the denominations I know anything about—and I certainly have to include the United Presbyterians here—haven't even gone as far as the National Council. . . . [W]hat my personal convictions are and the position the church is prepared to take are quite a long way apart. And I would have to be guided in this sort of program by the position of the church—which isn't much."[114]

Walking the tightrope between witnessing prophetically from one's own position and being a practical, administratively responsible church leader challenged almost every bureaucrat allied with the Council. The NCC recognized that its job, on one hand, was to step ahead of the denominations on tough issues in order to clear a path for them.[115] On the other hand, its mission was to build ecumenical unity and a church witness in the world. By unity, the NCC meant generating similar denominational position statements on Vietnam that would empower church organizations to work together on the war issue. This was the kind of unity the NCC could realistically produce, and with time, it would. But widening tensions between church administrators and laity ensured that its witness remained prophetic rather than reflective of the congregations. This would affect the nature of its power within the nation.

Frustrated by the slow pace of consensus-building and the tepid nature of statements on Vietnam, church leaders often acted more boldly as private individuals through organizations such as CALCAV and the Fellowship of Reconciliation.[116] Driven by an "act first, think later" philosophy of social activism, CALCAV also budgeted using a "spend first, raise funds later" method. This allowed it to expand rapidly. But it could do so only because the NCC paid what it could of CALCAV's sizeable bills from its own peace program resources, thus buying CALCAV time to fund-raise and then reimburse the NCC.[117]

On November 8, 1966, ALCAV held its first religious "mobilization" against the Vietnam War in the hope of influencing midterm congressional elections.[118] However, as the *Christian Century* sadly observed, the war "apparently had little influence on voters."[119] Nevertheless, CALCAV and the FCNL continued training clergy of all faiths to lobby Congress.[120] The NCC endorsed this while focusing upon its upcoming General Assembly in Miami.

Unlike the General Board, the General Assembly met once every three years and was the NCC's largest, most representative, governing body. The last assembly had gathered in 1963, shortly after Kennedy's assassination. Much had transpired since. The assembly needed to provide the Council with a new set of officers and an official direction for the next three years. With regard to international affairs, Bilheimer presented a proposal designed to enforce an ecumenical method while drawing member denominations together on Vietnam.

He suggested specific steps to accomplish this. Listening came first. The churches must seek God's will through a listening ministry of Christians from around the world. He felt that Americans in general, and American Christians in particular, practiced this art poorly. Yet it was essential in order to help them see beyond their own assumptions: "the insight of . . . Christians throughout the world must be allowed to inform ours," he said, "to the end that our witness be made in the light of the mind (so far as we can secure it) of the whole."[121]

The second consensus-building step required discerning, as best one could, the will of God with respect to the church's witness on specific issues facing humankind. The church must tie what it hears from people globally to directives from the gospel. To Bilheimer, this required vigorous theological work rooted in "dialogue between those of different perspectives." And the NCC must facilitate this with an eye toward reaching consensus. Once it emerged, the task then became "articulat[ing] our common witness" and developing the means to educate Christians broadly about international affairs while drawing laity into the process. Bilheimer's consensus-building method therefore was a top-down procedure that started with global discussion among church elites followed by grassroots education. Public action came next. The NCC should help provide ways to present church conclusions influentially to those in power. Bilheimer emphasized that the witness be made strongly, yet humbly, with full awareness that "our self-interest, culture and tradition powerfully determine even our thought as Christians."[122]

The NCC's staff proposed two large umbrella themes for the new triennium: "Reconciliation and Mission in a Secular Age" and "Peace and Justice in a Divided World." To fit the IAC's work within this plan, Bilheimer pressed for a focus on economic justice, race, the Vietnam War, and peace and change within the global community. His recommended action steps were largely discursive, such as reviewing and developing church policies, creating educational programs, providing ways to involve churchgoers in international affairs, and nurturing ecumenical relationships, especially by hosting consultations. None of his suggestions was radical or illegal, and all were things usually done dressed in one's Sunday best. The NCC's General Assembly easily approved them.[123]

The next day, after much debate, the assembly passed "An Appeal to the Churches Concerning Vietnam." Recognizing divided opinion among Christians, it nevertheless promoted use of the United Nations, asked for honest communication from the White House, urged a bombing halt over North Vietnam, and launched the Peace Priority Program for sparking study, debate, and action among the churches. The more liberal delegates complained that it said nothing new and might even be weaker than the board's December (1965) statement.[124] Frustrated *Century* editor Kyle Haselden agreed, calling the assembly a "holding operation" where delegates "reaffirmed" the old rather than forging ahead. He even detected hints of conservatism similar to that which had permeated the nation's recent congressional elections and swirled outside the assembly's Miami conference hall. He saw it as well in the assembly's effusive welcome of evangelist Billy Graham, who addressed the delegates. And Haselden heard it in Hubert Humphrey's speech, which admonished attendees "to be peacemakers" not protesters.[125]

Haselden's disappointment compounded when the assembly thinned the substance of its proposed Vietnam resolution during debate. It reduced the resolution's status to that of an appeal in order to give it a gentler character. Then, the assembly voted overwhelmingly to delete the portion that included a statement of Christian repentance for the war. Repentance was a critical step within the ecumenical process of church renewal. Haselden and Bennett felt this omitted section was perhaps the most truly Christian aspect of the entire document. Yet, delegates seemed to go out of their way to protect the conception that America was motivated by innocent goodwill in Vietnam, and that it somehow became swept up by destructive forces beyond its control. This reflected again how divided and cautious the churches remained on Vietnam in late 1966.

Bennett focused on the bright side. When the NCC's larger and more representative General Assembly affirmed the General Board's December position, it solidified the NCC's footing within a deeper constituent base. This victory deserved a cheer. So, too, did the *New York Times*'s decision to print the lengthy appeal in full. Like Bilheimer, Bennett valued the fact that the appeal was getting churchgoers talking about U.S. policy. It was inspiring people reared on Christianized Cold War doctrines to question them. The appeal was one more step in a consciousness-raising marathon. As he explained to Haselden, "If each local church and each denomination would begin a process of thinking and speaking that starts with this document it would soon become plain that there is an irreconcilable conflict between the assumptions of our government . . . [and] the convictions which have emerged wherever these issues are faced in the context of the [worldwide] Church."[126] Bilheimer agreed, adding that the assembly accomplished "a kind of coalescence of purpose and conviction" that was crucial for peace program effectiveness. Its call for churches to "mount a major effort to expand their study, debate and action" on Vietnam empowered Bilheimer and Elston to move forward.[127]

A top priority for the IAC was creating an educational multimedia tool for local churches to help ignite congregational discussion. It wanted local church folk to become involved quickly in the kinds of debates happening within church hierarchies in order to help close the clergy-laity gap in worldview and applied faith. For example, while Haselden complained about the assembly's conservatism, the demographic profile of that governing body was still a far cry from Christians on "Mainstreet, USA." *Christianity Today* highlighted these discrepancies in an article based upon the NCC's own survey figures, which showed that assembly delegates were older and far more liberal, modern, educated, wealthy, white, and cosmopolitan than parishioners. These demographics correlated with a large difference in worldview and opinion. For example, on civil rights, 67 percent of assembly delegates thought change was proceeding too slowly, whereas 70 percent of average Americans thought it was going too fast. On Vietnam, 52 percent of delegates favored consideration of U.S. troop withdrawal compared with only 18 percent of citizens. In fact, 55 percent of the U.S. population advocated increased attacks on Vietnam, while only 13 percent of assembly delegates did so.[128] Most polls also revealed that regular churchgoing Protestants were more conservative on issues than Americans who did not attend church consistently. Since the NCC's December 1965 Vietnam statement, more letters about Vietnam filled its mailbox. As of December 1966, the IAC was receiving approximately fifty per month (far more than on civil rights at that time), evenly split between those offering support and those condemning its positions.[129]

Four other assembly actions affected the Council's Vietnam work. It passed a "Resolution on Military Conscription," which promoted a voluntary system over consistent use of the draft. In conjunction, it crafted a "Policy Statement on Compulsory National Service," extending the above suggestion to noncombat forms of national service.[130] On a different yet significant subject, the assembly approved formation of the University Christian Movement (UCM) as a related aspect of the Council. The UCM replaced the former National Student Christian Federation and included Roman Catholic and Orthodox components for the first time.[131] With this move, activist-minded Christian students who were chafing within their churches' bureaucratic structures sought and received more leadership control, greater flexibility for direct action, and broader ecumenicity than under the old SCM structure. However, idealism would not sustain this experiment for long, and its demise in three years would remove a vital ecumenical training ground from successive generations.[132]

Lastly, the assembly elected new officers to lead the Council through the next chaotic triennium. Arthur Flemming, a Methodist layperson, civil rights champion, and political scientist with high-profile government experience, replaced Mueller as NCC president.[133] The Reverend Tracey K. Jones Jr., a Methodist, became chair of the Advisory Committee on Peace. This gave the Methodists two key positions from which to voice their concerns regarding NCC Vietnam activities. The pace would certainly pick up with the start of the new triennium.

Shortly after the General Assembly, President Johnson made an apparent step toward negotiations, which inspired another flurry of telegrams from Council staff requesting church support. UN Ambassador Goldberg asked U Thant to "take whatever steps you consider necessary to bring about the necessary discussions which could lead to a cease-fire" in Vietnam.[134] According to media reports, Johnson was backing the UN's initiative despite criticism from certain advisers and the military brass.[135] Goldberg specifically called for massive church encouragement of his diplomatic efforts. Pleased to assist, Flemming and Espy telegrammed all denomination heads plus an additional 500 church leaders; Bilheimer followed with a letter to 590 local church council leaders and a press release, and Blake read Flemming's telegram on the television news show *Face the Nation*.[136] All these dispatches encouraged Christians who agreed with the effort to make an extra Christmas gesture for peace by voicing their support to the president. Responsiveness to these appeals varied; overall, it seemed stronger than earlier ones, but using a top-down approach to motivate action on something as controversial as Vietnam remained problematic.[137]

Hope for a negotiated peace heightened during a holiday cease-fire. However, a widened bombing campaign that struck near Hanoi, causing many civilian deaths, short-circuited Goldberg's efforts.[138] Interestingly, a few months later, Alan Geyer and Herman Will met a baffled North Vietnamese ambassador in Prague who asked if they knew why that had happened, for his government had been ready to start talks. Later, through two unsolicited, separate contacts, Geyer received troubling information from government insiders that Rusk had urged the bombing attack that sank Goldberg's initiative.[139] Was Rusk as eager for a negotiated peace as he presented himself to be? Church leaders wondered. By the end of 1966, over 385,000 U.S. military personnel were fighting in Vietnam, and the escalation continued.

CHAPTER SEVEN

Sparking Debate and Action, 1967

SWAYING LAITY

Launching a widespread "debate and action" campaign topped Bilheimer's to-do list. About a hundred church leaders gathered at the Council to brainstorm ways of igniting discussion on Vietnam through all levels of the church. They hoped Christians might help shape "a 'political will' within the nation" for a diplomatic solution.[1] Harold Row described the meeting as "frustrating and glorious," clearly "one of the most representative and intense" on Vietnam that he had attended. The NCC offered to provide coordination and cooperation opportunities, but it stressed that denominations and local church councils must each "grab the ball and run with it," driving local actions. Administering the Council's effort fell mainly to Gerhard Elston.[2]

One initial piece of the debate and action program involved using the NCC's "Appeal to the Churches on Vietnam" as a springboard for local church discussions. The appeal was lengthy—ten pages in pamphlet form—and textbook-like in tone. It was not something an average churchgoer was apt to pick up from an information table and read on their own. Instead of revising it to enhance accessibility and interest, however, the Council simply surrounded it with study aids. The appeal became the centerpiece of a multimedia packet that could be purchased cheaply and used as a ready-made tool to lead study groups on the war.

To accompany the appeal, the Council produced a twenty-minute audio recording on a vinyl record album to stimulate group discussions. On one side, Bilheimer's voice summarized the appeal's five main points, drawing attention to key aspects for debate. The other side contained suggestions for congregational action. In addition to the album and ten copies of the appeal, each packet included a study guide with questions, a short history on Vietnam, a bibliography, and tips for working with local media. At two dollars each, the denominations purchased so many sets the NCC had to run a second edition of the album.[3]

"VIETNAM" was emblazoned in red letters across the original jacket cover. In one of Elston's first acts as Vietnam director, he changed the color to a neutral gold. Surely the Council did not want to reinforce the hawks' contention that the war was essentially about communism. Flaming red letters symbolically conjoined the two and might have prejudiced discussions. He also fine-tuned the study guide's history section and sharpened the questions.[4] From the beginning, Elston's value to the IAC was clear.

His tasks as Vietnam secretary were threefold: stimulate debate and action efforts in the churches, stay abreast of unfolding events in Vietnam and nurture contacts there, and keep tabs on the entire spectrum of groups active on the war—prowar to antiwar, religious to secular.[5] To accomplish the third, he not only placed himself on mailing lists of every Vietnam-related group possible; he also joined their boards and attended their meetings. On the secular front, for example, he kept in touch with Students for a Democratic Society (SDS) and the Mobilization ("Mobe").[6] On the religious front, he joined CALCAV, becoming the Council's main link to it.

Elston took an active role in a new NCC-affiliated group called Staff Associates of Departments of International Affairs (SADIA). It brought the denominations' international affairs secretaries together for "sharing, joint planning for action, intellectual stimulation, spiritual enrichment, professional growth, and testing of ideas" relative to the church's witness on international issues.[7] Bilheimer created the group in order to help draw denominations with active international affairs programs into a more ecumenical environment under NCC guidance. His motivation reflected his gut feeling that the initial coolness he felt from these secretaries sprang from their lack of ecumenical understanding. The secretaries found the forums useful, especially for discussing independently sponsored, interreligious actions, like CALCAV's vigils and lobbying sessions.

The NCC also launched an informal Vietnam strategy group, which united its international affairs staff with that of various Jewish organizations. Rabbi Henry Siegman, executive vice president of the Synagogue Council of America, and Rabbi Balfour Brickner represented the Jewish community. The group eventually enlisted Catholic participation, too.[8] Both SADIA and this interreligious group developed communication and cooperation among religious bodies in their responses to the war.

While Elston drove the debate and action program and maintained links with other groups, Bilheimer worked on the consultation, policy, and strategic level. This included keeping in contact with the U.S. government. And Secretary of State Dean Rusk had requested a meeting.

Rusk was a devout Presbyterian who took church positions seriously, kept up on them, and respected the responsibility of religious groups to take stands on moral issues. He was convinced, however, that the NCC was wrong about U.S. Vietnam policy and diagnosed insufficient information as the cause. Therefore, he urged the NCC to conduct another study on the organization of a "just and durable peace," similar to the one done by the Federal Council during World War II. Perhaps such a project might lead the Council toward more realistic conclusions about the components of global security amid a Cold War, he thought. Rusk also wanted to discuss the NCC's triennium thrust on international affairs, especially the connection between "peace-keeping" and "Vietnam."

On January 9, Rusk met for over an hour with Robert Bilheimer, Kenneth Thompson, and Ernest Gross. He laid out how U.S. Vietnam policy fit into the larger context of international peace-keeping. Then he asked, "Are the churches and the N.C.C. placing sufficient weight upon the total context of the organization of peace in which the Vietnam War is being fought?" Obviously, Rusk felt that church leaders had lost sight of the big Cold War picture. Conversely, Bilheimer and Gross noticed again how Dulles-like presuppositions, a bipolar worldview, and misapplication of the Munich analogy framed Rusk's perceptions.[9]

Bilheimer described this meeting as "unquestionably one of the most thought-provoking discussions" of the last few months, and it shaped his strategy in dealing with government. Rusk seemed genuinely interested in and respectful of church policy, open to frank discussion, and philosophically thoughtful.[10] Perhaps he might be persuadable. However, Bilheimer also realized that, because the basic presuppositions guiding Rusk's and Johnson's perspectives about world order were so different from those of the ecumenical community, the two politicians were likely to deem church statements misguided and dismiss them out of hand. Without a common foundational understanding of international affairs, discussion of specific issues became futile.[11] Therefore, Bilheimer believed that Council statements would also have to trace church stands back to their conceptual roots in order to inspire men like Rusk to question their own interpretations of recent history and current events.[12]

For the rest of Johnson's presidential term, the NCC worked from a two-pronged strategy: strengthen the hand of doves in government by increasing public antiwar efforts, and transform the worldviews of local laity and government by challenging their basic assumptions of world order.[13] Bilheimer began making more explicit the ecumenical suppositions underlying the NCC's concept of security. This was important since previous statements left these unsaid, as if they were common sense. Within the next few months, Bilheimer began drafting a policy statement to lay them out clearly. He would later regard the resulting document the most significant that his IAC ever produced.

When spring arrived, Vietnam-related activities gained energy nationwide. Debate in Congress rose. Martin Luther King Jr. grew impatient to voice his displeasure about the war and was seeking the right forum. Meanwhile, discussions about selective conscientious objection began to swirl within church circles. Current law granted conscientious objector status only to persons from pacifist churches who could demonstrate long-term religious belief against all wars. Many Christians desiring CO status were denied. At its February meeting, the NCC's General Board passed a policy statement favoring the rights of COs of particular wars; it also advocated extending CO status to nonreligious persons who felt compelled by conscience to seek it.[14] An individual's right to act on conscience was a traditional Protestant value. The related issues of selective conscientious objection and the draft system became rallying points for debate and protest throughout 1967, and the NCC inserted itself into them, even testifying at Congress's Selective Service Hearings.

The Council also endorsed a new moderate antiwar group of policy realists called Negotiations Now! A collection of clerics and professors, including Reinhold Niebuhr, Episcopal bishop George Barrett, and economist John Kenneth Galbraith, launched it to broaden the base of the peace movement. Negotiations Now! spoke to middle America from a moderate center that was critical both of Johnson's militaristic policy and radical calls for unconditional withdrawal. The group gave strong anticommunists a place within the movement and attracted some high-ranking Catholic leaders for the first time. Specifically, it sought to collect a million signatures on a petition for a bombing halt over North Vietnam. Its goals of generating public pressure for negotiations and rallying support for U Thant's efforts as well as doves in Congress fit well within the NCC's mandate.[15] In fact, providing strong leadership from the center was what several ecumenists desired from the Council.[16] Therefore, many were thrilled about the group; Elston and Geyer even joined its guiding committee.[17] Enthusiasm would wane over the next year, however, as suspicions emerged about its motives.

Meanwhile, certain denominations were taking up the NCC's challenge to "grab the ball and run with it" in terms of stimulating their congregations to debate and act upon the war. The Methodist and United Presbyterian Churches had already been using their own publications to transmit information and church positions to their judicatories (that is, regional offices), clergy, and laity. After the NCC's meeting, however, the Methodist Church intensified its efforts by creating an "emergency program of education and action" called Vietnam Emphasis. This aimed to get parishioners talking about Vietnam by pressuring regional church staff and local clergy to create discussion opportunities for parishioners, while the national offices provided resources.[18]

Vietnam Emphasis was a top-down affair with a trickle-down strategy. Methodist executives tried to light a fire under judicatory leaders and give them enough tinder so that they might carry the flame to local clergy and then into the congregations. They channeled their efforts into places where local and regional church leaders gathered, such as annual conferences, schools of Christian mission, assemblies, institutes, and regional strategy conferences. They specifically targeted Methodist conferences (which are regional judicatory areas), hoping they might produce their own statements on the war. In order to stimulate this, the national church encouraged each local district office to form a committee on Vietnam.[19] This committee's task was to get every congregation within its district doing something related to the war. To assist, the national office published bulletins to keep church leaders informed of relevant Methodist, NCC, and related church activities. It listed all of the available educational resources and where one could order them. It provided ideas for speaking out on the war. It included updates on other denominations' positions on U.S.

Vietnam policy. In addition, Vietnam Emphasis sent judicatory leaders free samples of the NCC's album and study packet. It ran leadership training sessions, created a speakers bureau for Vietnam-related events, and even drafted a special war-related litany for worship services that included two prayers.[20] All told, the program was an ambitious good-faith effort to generate debate and action that ultimately hit a bottleneck of resistance at the congregational level.

While Methodists and United Presbyterians succeeded occasionally in mobilizing congregations, and clergy and laity sometimes got involved in antiwar efforts as individuals, clergy often balked at pressing their congregations very hard and laity often resisted what pressure there was. Several factors accounted for this, including rising tensions between laity and church executives. The disconnect was worsening, and local clergy found themselves in an uncomfortable middle position that defied easy negotiation. No doubt, parishioners chatted privately about the war during church fellowship hours and in adult Sunday school sessions. Their strong personal opinions often gained expression in letters to denominational magazines and national staff. However, mainline churches traditionally contained such a wide range of theological and political views in the pews that planned discussions on controversial issues became potentially divisive. And divisions could threaten congregational health. Thus, despite strong lay opinions, relatively few local congregations created organized discussion sessions or united to speak out on the war in the manner that national staffs did.[21]

Elston encountered similar problems with the NCC's debate and action program. From spring through fall 1967, Elston and Naylor visited with denominational and local church council leaders, helping to organize Vietnam consultations in nine major U.S. cities.[22] Elston attended nearly every one. While most participants appeared uneasy about the war, they remained reluctant to discuss it and even more resistant to doing anything about it. He recited six common reasons:

(1) It is confusing

(2) We don't know enough and Washington knows more

(3) Questions of loyalty and patriotism

(4) Resentment of protesters and unwillingness to be identified with them

(5) Fear of intimidation or reprisals

(6) Fear of causing dissension within church, family, etc.[23]

Thus, Elston noted that "in the churches there has been less discussion than at any other level in the country."[24] Vietnam's divisiveness was indeed a major deterrent, as many equated conflict avoidance with proper, neighborly, Christian behavior. The fact that some Christian activists sought revolution rather than reconciliation—and stirred up division without a spirit of grace—fueled others' desire to resist controversy.[25] Mainline Protestants also generally preferred mild-mannered civic involvement to loud public protests. The latter were not their style.[26] It did not help that regular Protestant church attendance often correlated with conservative attitudes on foreign affairs. Elston knew the government deterred debate, too, by accusing doubters of aiding the enemy while compromising the welfare of U.S. troops. Lingering accusations of communist tendencies exacerbated the Council's difficulty with grassroots communication.[27]

The assumption that churches could educate laity quickly on Vietnam likely stemmed from the NCC's sense that they had done so for the civil and voting rights acts. But by 1964, the southern civil rights movement had been buzzing for ten years, and Christians had had time to process it as a moral issue. Conversely, Vietnam was barely a year old in the minds of most. Thus, expectations may have outpaced the possible. Then again, from Bilheimer's perspective, Vietnam created a teachable moment on issues that both included and went beyond the war. To ponder and speak about it as a church community was critical to him regardless of results.

The NCC's more conservative General Board members, especially southerners, were particularly frustrated by the poor rapport between laypeople and the NCC. They blamed the NCC for the sour relationship. Ed Grant, a lay board member from the Presbyterian Church U.S—the "southern Presbyterians"—expressed this discontent to Espy. His letter is worth quoting at length, for his message was common and fundamental: the NCC was out of touch with the concerns of local churches and pursued controversial tangents while ignoring their real needs.

> I have a very definite feeling, growing out of observation only, that the membership of the General Board represents only a minority of our church constituencies in its point of view. How much longer a minority of leadership may speak for a dissenting majority is problematic. . . .

It is getting harder and harder in my own case, for example, to get our denominational representatives to attend the General Board meeting. . . . There is a feeling of "what's the use. They are not interested in anything but controversial issues, and some of these are not even the Church's primary concerns." . . .

As over against this, our denomination and our Boards are being plagued with problems about which it might appear the General Board has little or no concern and no contribution to offer. For example, we are facing a situation of decreasing church memberships in proportion to population rise . . . slackening of interest in youth organizations in the church, the rise of behavior problems in "respectable" families, youth sex problems, spiritual ministry to the poor and disinherited, much talk about ecumenicity on a world scale with little or nothing ecumenical in local churches, and so on. The widening of the gulf between local churches and their denominational boards is a problem all to itself, and the losing of confidence in denominational leadership is something the National Council is in a unique position to do something about. Yet these are barely mentioned before the General Board and some I have never heard referred to at all.[28]

After again experiencing the familiar sense of General Board futility, even Grant was "losing . . . enthusiasm." His letter foreshadowed hard times. The NCC was being summoned in many directions and criticized from both left and right.

Espy insisted that denomination heads shared the blame. Denominational leaders' own liberalism often fluctuated depending upon the audience, he noticed, and this contributed to the NCC's alienation from local churches. For example, church executives would push the NCC to the left when speaking and voting in Council meetings. However, they conveniently muted such sentiments and took a more conservative posture when operating within their own structures. This gave laity the impression that the Council was an impudent organization. Explaining this to Grant, Espy added, "I do not like to see the National Council having to take the rap for that kind of thing. I have a feeling that sometimes the NCC is being taken for a ride by some who take advantage of the platform the National Council provides."[29] In the competitive religious marketplace, denominations were tied to pleasing their constituencies while the NCC was bound to do the bidding of the denominations' headquarters that provided its funding. This put the Council in a damned-if-you-do, damned-if-you-don't position at times. Denomination heads wanted the NCC to cast its line ahead of the churches, identifying snags and rocks so they could float in safely behind. If the masses rebelled, however, these church executives could cut bait and leave the Council dangling alone in unfriendly waters.

The day Grant wrote his letter, Bilheimer attended a consultation, sponsored by the United Presbyterian social and evangelism office, at which several attendees urged the Peace Priority Program to become more involved on the political front lines of the Vietnam War. Bilheimer certainly hoped Christians would see their faith in broader terms than mere "parish maintenance functions" and "personal decency."[30] But political lobbying in its usual form did not fit his understanding of the church's role. He differentiated between lobbying and making an ecumenical witness. Lobbying was aimed at influencing policy to get a desired result from the state. An ecumenical witness's goal was invested in the process of generating that witness, and then in being publicly prophetic, whether the government actually listened or not.

Political scientists sometimes distinguish between the "winning" and "witnessing" models of religious lobbying.[31] Bilheimer clearly embraced the latter. This is not to say that he devalued changing U.S. policy, for he expended considerable effort in numerous attempts to do just that. But compromising the witness for a possible win was unacceptable. Bilheimer measured success by whether the church was being the church in word and deed, not by whether the government responded. As he described, "The church is servant, leavening agent, a minority force everywhere; this is theologically and practically significant. Practically speaking, we're kidding ourselves about the power of American Protestantism, despite all the people on the rolls. The theological point is even more important. It isn't the role of the church to lobby, but to be certain it is heard in the right ways in the right places in reference to crucial issues." In fact, he believed that, "In a sense the church's task fundamentally is done when it is certain it is heard." Reinhold Niebuhr asserted that power for social change must come through grassroots pressure groups, but Bilheimer clarified that the church's real power was not political; it resided in its prophetic voice. Thus, the church had a distinct role and type of power to offer. "I still have a basic conviction that truth in the Biblical sense is ultimate power. Truth is more powerful than organized power. The man with power needs to have his mind opened to truth, through questions raised by the church."[32] Bilheimer's view reflected the Quaker notion that church people must speak truth to power, trusting that spiritual truth *was* power, even if the church itself lacked worldly influence. The church must speak on sociopolitical issues in order to affirm its identity and be true to its ecumenical mission.

Denominational leaders insisted the church speak out within America's democratic society for very practical reasons, too. They argued vociferously with parishioners who preferred church silence on political matters, stating how vital it was for the body of Christ to be included in the chorus of debate, despite internal discordance. Its prioritization of spiritual, moral, and ethical values and its consideration of global humanity over nation added balance to policy discussions that generally preferenced national power over questions of love or justice. As a result, ecumenical voices might serve as a tempering influence on policies. They might also help Americans remember the humanity of those called "enemy" and ponder the ethical concerns embedded in global repercussions of their actions.[33]

Additionally, church executives challenged the common argument that church folk lacked sufficient competence and therefore should defer to the "experts" on public policy. Presbyterian Dieter Hessel and Methodist Herman Will both reminded constituents that political and military leaders were not simply objective experts making the smartest, most-informed decisions within a vacuum. Rather, they were human beings who operated on hunches, were influenced by cultural biases, and played politics with the information they received. Their views were affected by non-expert public opinion polls as well as by interest groups with narrow self-serving motives. Besides, government officials often received their offices via appointment and may not have been the most competent people in a given area. Government and military leaders also often made decisions within a bubble of like-minded colleagues who provided affirmations rather than challenging options. Subordinates seeking promotion might keep their concerns quiet. In addition, the value placed upon loyalty within government and military circles helped quell internal dissent. And the momentum of a given policy direction, regardless of its effectiveness, created its own rationale for staying the course.[34] Finally, Will and other church leaders knew that government experts disagreed over Vietnam, meaning perhaps that public opinion might be the wild card that moved policy to change. Given this entire situation, church people had better get their voices into this mix, ecumenists insisted, lest the motives that drove Christian concerns be drowned out by less savory, and potentially damaging, interests.[35]

Many congregants resented that their church executives' positions on the war might be perceived as speaking for them. While Herman Will and others recognized that laity were divided over the war, they also knew many national church agencies had reached consensus. Why, then, should these agencies stifle that consensus? Was it necessary for them to remain quiet just because laity did not yet know their own minds, or felt uncomfortable making a public witness, or held a different position? Mainline churches had always contained a variety of theological and political views and valued their ability to hold such differences in creative tension. But doing so had never required silence; indeed Will reminded fellow Methodists that the "Wesleyan tradition is one of grappling with tough social issues."[36] Yet Will's position distressed many churchgoers, who expressed their disagreement in a variety of ways. Ultimately, this dissent did compromise whatever practical political power the ecumenical community had leveraged prior to the war.

Bilheimer was correct. The NCC lacked lobbying strength on Vietnam, especially given weak, divided, grassroots support for its stands. Rusk knew it too, for even though the Council had influenced parishioners on past issues, he saw the growing gap between the Council and laity over the war. "We [the administration] did not accept them [NCC leaders] as spokesmen of the grass roots," Rusk said. "We gave attention to the pronouncements of the NCC as the statement of the officials who put it together but not necessarily of the congregations that made up the National Council."[37] Rusk continued to take Council leaders seriously, though, hoping they might be convinced to change positions and be useful to government again.

Bilheimer and Rusk had two more opportunities to bend each other's ears. On March 16, Rusk invited about thirty-five religious leaders, including Bilheimer, to brainstorm collaboration ideas for what he called "our common objective" for a "durable peace." Rusk valued contacts with religious leaders, telling them he "realize[d] full well that they contribute importantly to a vigorous and informed public opinion that is so important to your government in shaping both domestic and foreign policies."[38] He also expected several things from the churches. For example, he hoped they would back nonviolent means of negotiating disagreements over the Geneva Accords, encourage debates over Vietnam to be grounded in contextual discussions of the international "organization of peace," support the administration's desire to prevent dangerously inflamed public opinion, be attentive to Hanoi's responsibilities and role, and include more practical factual information on the war in discussions of its moral dimensions.[39] Rusk's and Bilheimer's mutual attempts to influence each other continued throughout the summer—and especially via a trip that Bilheimer led to Vietnam in July.

In the meantime, Martin Luther King Jr. found a suitable forum to make his growing antiwar views public. On April 4, exactly a year before his assassination, King gave his most famous antiwar speech at Riverside Church.[40] It was timed to buffer his upcoming keynote address at the large Spring Mobilization antiwar rally eleven days later. Most Mobe leaders were radicals, some had communist affiliations, and King's friends feared that his association with the Mobe might undercut his effectiveness on civil rights. King decided to do it anyway but wished to present his antiwar views beforehand in a more widely respected arena. Riverside Church seemed the perfect site. King expected his first significant antiwar speech to create controversy, thus requiring careful planning.[41] The CALCAV member asked for its aid, and received it aplenty. Gathering in Bennett's home, Andrew Young and Al Lowenstein helped draft the speech, and Richard Fernandez helped edit it. King made the final revisions.[42] To shield King from critics, his friends flanked him with three indisputably credible speakers: Bennett, Heschel, and historian Henry Steele Commager. Being attacked amid such company was not a liability.

The four delivered powerful speeches to a packed house of over three thousand people and droves of media. King connected his civil rights work with his stand against U.S. Vietnam policy. In one of the speech's hallmark lines, he said, "I knew that I could never again raise my voice against the violence of the oppressed in the ghettos without having first spoken clearly to the greatest purveyor of violence in the world today—my own government."[43] He also tied his motivation explicitly to his Christian faith. King's speech provided the antiwar movement with more respectability and moral legitimacy. Ecumenical leaders were ecstatic to have the Nobel Peace Prize winner publicly with them. However, many of his fellow civil rights leaders, such as Ralph Bunche, Roy Wilkins, Whitney Young, and the NAACP's board, resented his antiwar plank. For one, King's speech alienated Johnson, the president who had done more to facilitate civil rights legislation than perhaps any other elected official. For another, many feared that fusing the civil rights and antiwar movements would siphon energy away from their primary cause. The news media also pilloried King. Accusations flew that he was an unpatriotic traitor who supported communist revolution.[44] The breadth and severity of criticism stunned him.

The subsequent Mobilization, held simultaneously in San Francisco and New York City, was a diverse and impressive antiwar event drawing several hundred thousand people into public demonstration. Most liberal religious-based organizations such as CALCAV, FOR, SANE, and the NCC did not officially endorse it. However, staff members participated as unaffiliated individuals.[45]

These organizations did endorse a new debate and action project called Vietnam Summer. Fernandez served as codirector. Martin Luther King Jr. and Dr. Benjamin Spock announced it to the media. Taking another page out of the civil rights playbook, it was a "teach-out" modeled on the Mississippi Freedom Summer program in 1964 that registered black voters. It sent thousands of student volunteers into communities to educate, to provide draft counseling, and to mobilize people against the war prior to the 1968 elections.[46] Since it complemented the NCC's own summer convocation efforts, Elston jumped on board. He thought the program might draw Americans with doubts about the war into collaboration with moderate peace groups and raise electoral pressure for negotiations.[47] Fernandez also hoped it might move more local churches to action, for their widespread apathy disappointed him. While national church organizations had condemned the war more strongly than perhaps any other major American institution, "local congregations seem more intent upon maintaining either an indifferent or totally passive position," he noticed, not electing to view it "as a substantially ethical-political issue" of Christian concern.[48] Vietnam Summer drew about four thousand volunteers; congregations helped recruit and house them.[49] It accomplished creative work via seven hundred local projects. However, ideological bickering among sponsoring factions and the flightiness of volunteers undercut its potential.[50]

In fact, divisiveness marked the entire antiwar movement, making cooperative endeavors challenging. When the NCC launched its Peace Priority Program, it called all parts of the Council to participate. From early on, however, the Division of Overseas Ministries and particularly Church World Service felt that Bilheimer's team slighted their contributions.[51] To an outsider, the work of CWS and the IAC seemed complementary—one dealt with the war's effects through meeting the practical needs of those hurt by the war, and the other addressed its causes by working to change U.S. policy. An ecumenical witness required both. However, their divergent postures toward government, funding sources, understandings of the war, and philosophies about the church's proper focus created considerable tension between the Council's service and social justice wings.[52] Nevertheless, Bilheimer's team tried to be sensitive to the DOM's desire for inclusion and recognition. In the spring, Howard Schomer, of the DOM's Special Ministries program, became its liaison staff officer with the Peace Priority Program.[53]

Schomer was a Harvard graduate, a member of the United Church of Christ, and president of the University of Chicago's Divinity School. His pacifism led him to seek conscientious objector status during World War II.[54] He spoke flawless French, had taught in France for years, and had forged contacts within its Vietnamese community. He had also visited South Vietnam with FOR's delegation in 1965. Over the remaining years of the war, the peace program repeatedly utilized Schomer's facility with the French language and his connections with influential Vietnamese. (In April, Schomer personally shared the NCC's Appeal on Vietnam with Mai Van Bo, North Vietnam's chief representative in Europe.)[55] But his vocal anticommunism and irascible personality did not endear him to certain members of Bilheimer's team. He and Elston barely managed to stay on speaking terms.[56]

Elston felt that many in the Council's service wing were too enamored of government and American culture to embody a confessing church stance on Vietnam.[57] As an example, he cited CWS's blueprint for the churches' role in postwar Vietnam. As part of the mission wing's contribution to the peace program, CWS launched a "Commission on Tomorrow's Vietnam," to plan how churches would help rebuild Vietnam after the war.[58] It was clear to the IAC staffers, who were invited onto the commission, that CWS shared certain government assumptions and was willing to cooperate with it in an unquestioning fashion. For example, CWS assumed that the United States would eventually have its way in Vietnam, that North Vietnam would collapse under U.S. punishment, and that America and its churches would then be invited in to help pick up the pieces just as they had done in damaged nations after World War II. Frank Hutchison, of CWS, predicted that its Vietnam Christian Service program "would be working with—and almost part of—the United States Government reconstruction effort." This, he assumed, might include loaning staff to the U.S. program while helping recruit and train government workers.[59] Clearly, CWS did not view the separation of church and state in the same manner as did Bilheimer's staff, nor did CWS perceive the same inherent ecumenical problems in its partnership with the State Department. Of course, cooperation with government had always been essential to CWS's work overseas. CWS saw itself as forced to work within limits set by the U.S. government if food was to get into war-ravaged areas.[60]

Elston was asked to critique CWS's first draft of its reconstruction planning program. He concluded quickly that CWS's assumptions about the war's end and aftermath naïvely mirrored the Johnson administration's. He also called CWS's projections about a future church role presumptive. The international affairs team questioned whether the United States could achieve military victory and if the Vietnamese would automatically welcome the postwar interference of U.S. institutions in their country.[61] Additionally, if American churches were invited to assist with Vietnam's postwar relief, they should work through worldwide ecumenical or indigenous organizations, not via the U.S. government. They should ask the Vietnamese if their assistance was desired, and in what forms. Bilheimer categorized CWS's approach to postwar planning under James MacCracken as "humanitarian imperialism," adding that it gave him "the cold chills."[62] However, CWS's planning for "Tomorrow's Vietnam" evolved over the next few years and received considerable input. As a result of these critiques, events, and internal pressures, it gradually morphed from being a typical World War II–styled, American-driven program into one that was willing to let indigenous groups direct rebuilding efforts.[63]

While CWS planned its postwar role, the war showed no sign of slowing down. In fact, according to Clark Clifford, a Johnson adviser soon to replace McNamara as defense secretary, the administration felt better than ever about the war. Positive reports came from many sources. In April, General William Westmoreland, the U.S. commander in Vietnam, confirmed an inevitable victory before a cheering Congress.[64] But as the stakes increased, so did the questions. In May the Chinese premier Chou En-lai threatened to engage his military if the United States invaded North Vietnam. Also that month McNamara shared his growing doubts in a controversial memo that soon led to his resignation. In direct opposition to Westmoreland's and the Joint Chiefs' requests to escalate further, McNamara urged the administration to seek negotiations and begin planning withdrawal.[65] Instead, Johnson heeded the military's advice and introduced fifty-five thousand more troops into Vietnam. The air war also intensified.

Official denominational consensus against the war continued to strengthen. In May, the United Presbyterian Church's 179th General Assembly approved the "Confession of 1967." It was the first real overhaul of the Presbyterian statement of faith since the 1647 Westminster Confession. Focused on reconciliation, the new confession influenced passage of the church's "Declaration of Conscience" on Vietnam, which was read from Presbyterian pulpits June 11. The declaration voiced distress over Johnson's reliance upon unilateral military escalation and lack of "moral courage" to pursue multilateral paths to peace.[66] It also advocated opening relations with China and expanding conscientious objection qualifications. This was an important step by one of the Council's most influential members. Inspired, Presbyterians also asked the NCC to rally members behind an interdenominational day of prayer for peace in Vietnam, which it did.[67]

On June 1–2, the NCC's General Board took several more steps to address the war. It passed another "Resolution on Vietnam," which sharply criticized the bombing of North Vietnam as an impediment to negotiations and warned of America's growing moral isolation.[68] The board endorsed a "Resolution on Counseling Men Eligible for Military Service," which urged churches to offer draft counseling that would provide men with spiritual support and instruction about their rights and choices.[69] Finally, since his last meeting with Rusk, Bilheimer had labored on a paper critiquing the presuppositions undergirding U.S. Vietnam policy. He used the June meetings to circulate a draft for review. Since the policy reflected the worldview of many Americans, ecumenists faced a considerable challenge arguing against it.[70] Bilheimer continued revising through November, when it would be honed into a landmark policy statement for 1968.

Then on June 5, 1967, another war grabbed headlines. Tensions in the Middle East boiled over, and Israel attacked Egypt. Six days later Israel emerged the resounding victor over its Muslim neighbors and in possession of new territory. Prior to this point, American Jewish leaders had stood as steady allies with Protestant ecumenists in opposing U.S. Vietnam policy. Now, needing support from the U.S. government for Israel's war efforts, many Jewish voices quieted on Vietnam. To criticize the government on one war while trying to encourage support for another proved too awkward. Adding tension to the mix was the appeal of many Protestant leaders for equanimity in dealing with both Palestinians and Israelis.[71] Some Protestants even criticized Israel's bloody military aggression. After the Six Day War, the joint Jewish-Protestant witness against U.S. Vietnam policy cooled. Around the same time, however, cooperation between Protestant and Catholic leaders slowly grew with respect to international affairs.[72]

ESCALATION, ENTRENCHMENT, AND DIVISION, SUMMER-FALL 1967

On June 9, Bilheimer flew to Asia with Dean Rusk's blessing. Back in early April, Bilheimer, Kenneth Thompson, and Ernest Gross had met with Rusk for the third time. The encounter revealed how leaders within church and state sought to influence each other on the war, and why. Bilheimer wished to visit South Vietnam with an NCC team to get a firsthand look at the situation there. Rusk agreed, thinking that an on-site experience might awaken ecumenists to the hard geopolitical, balance-of-power realities that church leaders like Dulles had understood and show them what the United States was really up against in Asia. He offered State Department help in securing the transportation and interviews that NCC representatives desired.[73] Bilheimer made clear to Rusk that, while the Council would appreciate such help, it did not want the trip to turn into a government-packaged promotional tour. The NCC wanted to arrange its own itinerary. The State Department respectfully complied. Rusk gave Bilheimer's team a letter directing the U.S. embassy to assist as needed but also to honor its independent wishes.[74]

Bilheimer then told Rusk that the team also wanted to visit North Vietnam and meet with the National Liberation Front. After a pregnant pause, Rusk asked, "That's a curious thing for the church to do, isn't it?"[75] Bilheimer replied that the Bible contained teachings about the enemy, and church leaders felt called to conduct a mission of concern to the North as well.[76] He convinced Rusk that the Council's purpose was not political but, rather, theological and ecumenical. With this, Rusk agreed to support the NCC's application for visas from North Vietnam, but he warned that it usually granted them only to those who would serve its propaganda needs. Nevertheless, Bilheimer felt the Council had to try. After all, Martin Niemoeller, the German pastor imprisoned by the Nazis during World War II, had traveled into North Vietnam back in January as a World Council president. During that visit, he met Ho Chi Minh himself.[77] Regardless of whether visas came through, Bilheimer considered it a coup to have the secretary of state understand and respect the autonomous role of the churches enough to help facilitate an independent, church-sponsored investigation of U.S. involvement in Vietnam.

Rusk had his own reasons for approving the trip and aiding its logistics. U.S. policy restricted citizens' travel to North Vietnam. However, the State Department could authorize passports on an ad hoc basis if it thought the travel "would serve the national interest. In the case of North Viet-Nam," the State Department ruled, "we could consider an applicant's travel to be in the national interest if the applicant's position made his views of the restricted area a matter of importance to the Government, the Congress, or the public in the United States." Rusk felt the NCC's visit would meet this requirement. First, the NCC's respectable image would reflect well upon the United States in Vietnam. The State Department described the Council as a "large, influential body" represented by church officials who "can be expected to conduct themselves in North Vietnam responsibly and in such a manner as to convey to the North Vietnamese people . . . that our quarrel is not with them. The public effect, here and abroad, would reinforce our posture of reasonableness and moderation." Second, the State Department felt that if the NCC visited the South first, its perceptions of the war would be "more balanced . . . than many recent visitors to North Vietnam." The government knew the NCC leaders to be a rational, studious, moderate group. It saw value in encouraging North Vietnam to admit such visitors, "who they cannot be sure will share their view of the war and who may correct their misconceptions about the extent and practical effect of dissent in this country." Third, the State Department hoped the NCC visitors might inquire about American POWs while there and perhaps be permitted a visit.[78] Thus, while Rusk hoped the trip would both correct Council perspectives and reflect positively upon the U.S. government's image in Vietnam, Bilheimer planned it with an eye toward influencing Rusk upon their return.

The NCC's Mission of Concern, as it was called, ran from June 9 to July 5.[79] Elston arranged the interviews, and true to Rusk's promise, the U.S. government provided transportation wherever the group desired to go.[80] Bilheimer assembled a delegation of church executives to accompany him that he felt Rusk would listen to and respect. For example, he selected William P. Thompson, the Stated Clerk of the United Presbyterian Church, not only because Rusk was Presbyterian but because Thompson had served as an assistant prosecutor during Japan's war crimes trials following World War II. With a reserved statesmanlike manner, Thompson approached subjects judiciously and possessed an incisive mind. Bilheimer knew that no one, including Rusk, could discount him as some naïve, dovish left-winger.[81] Bilheimer also chose Episcopal Bishop George Barrett for his status, respectability, and cautious objectivity. Such an establishment man, Bilheimer thought, would not be discredited easily. The fourth member of the team, Dr. Tracey K. Jones Jr., chaired the NCC's Advisory Commission on Peace. Jones had grown up in China, the child of Methodist missionaries, and retained his long-standing interest in Asia. Of the four, he was also the most activist on peace and represented that faction of the NCC. As the Methodists were the most populous and financially powerful denomination in NCC, their representation was important.

Bilheimer did not want the group painted as another radical antiwar contingent with preconceived agendas. Rather, he wanted to highlight its composition of credible, centrist, fair-minded Christians who visited Vietnam to share concern for all who suffered and to investigate the actual conduct of the war. Bilheimer particularly sought a firsthand glimpse of the repercussions stemming from the government's presuppositions about foreign policy for his written critique, which he hoped would become the NCC's next major policy statement. He and Elston wanted local churches, as well as Rusk, to see that the Council approached the war responsibly, and to trust that its statements were based upon gathered facts, not hyperbole or hearsay.[82]

Schomer and Naylor both met with Mai Van Bo in Paris to appeal for the team's entry into North Vietnam. Final word about the visas would arrive during the trip. Naylor thought the possibility looked good.[83] Bilheimer asked his team to keep the potential visit to the North secret, fearing publicity might jeopardize their chances.[84] But he also asked Naylor and Espy to grease the wheels for a large post-visit media spread, hopefully in the *New York Times*, which he felt had neglected recent NCC actions.[85] Bo warned Naylor that North Vietnam could not guarantee the safety or comfort of the NCC team.[86] So Bilheimer took out $50,000 life insurance policies for each traveler. He had heard American church leaders made good targets.[87]

Bilheimer's group traveled to South Vietnam, Thailand, and Cambodia. It conducted interviews with high-ranking persons representing a wide array of interests, including almost all of the major South Vietnamese presidential candidates campaigning for the September elections, along with many local religious and cultural leaders. It met with Prime Minister Nguyen Cao Ky and General Nguyen Van Thieu, General Westmoreland, General Edward Landsdale, and Ambassador Ellsworth Bunker.[88] Through a Quaker contact the team talked with Cambodian Prince Sihanouk, Thailand's Princess Poon, and the president of the World Buddhist Federation.[89]

While several ecumenical leaders preferred that South Vietnam remain separate and anticommunist, current U.S. support for a regime that forced loyalty through intimidation disturbed them. Therefore, South Vietnam's upcoming elections concerned the mission team. If fair and democratic, its unrepresentative political structure could be legitimized through popularly chosen leaders that the people might back in a bid for peace. Ky and Thieu both assured the team that elections would be fair, and they invited international observers.[90] While in South Vietnam, the team also visited a showcase government pacification area and some church-run refugee camps. There they chatted with Vietnam Christian Service workers who resented the U.S. government's use of voluntary agencies to further its military objectives, including USAID's tactics.[91] James MacCracken quickly quelled such grumbling in hope of preserving smooth relations with Johnson's administration.[92]

Unfortunately, on June 29, the team learned that North Vietnam had denied their visas. Bilheimer was deeply disappointed. As their Quaker contact, Paul Johnson in Phnom Penh, explained, "North Vietnam is very tough just now about admitting anyone who does not support their line and policy completely." Apparently it had even refused Quakers who wished to set up a medical facility. Rusk also surmised that the timing was poor.[93] Elston attributed the cause elsewhere: to Schomer's strong anticommunism. While in Paris, a North Vietnamese contact asked Elston directly how he could work for the same organization as someone with Schomer's views. Elston heard through the grapevine that Mai Van Bo may have advised against the visas because the NCC's staff included such unwavering anticommunists.[94] Bilheimer never discovered why the North denied the visas. He retained hope that American ecumenists might visit in the future.[95]

The delegation returned to the States seriously questioning the effectiveness and viability of U.S. efforts in Vietnam. Nevertheless, its report was as cautious and balanced as were the people involved. Writing the report proved challenging, since consensus between delegation members did not emerge easily. When they presented it verbally, each added their own perceptions of the war. Bishop Barrett's awkward passivity during the trip disappointed Bilheimer, who viewed his contribution as less than expected.[96] In his journal, Barrett admitted that the trip left him "with few fixed opinions" and that his "Anglican establishmentarian background sometimes shows" in his reluctance to criticize the government.[97] Thompson's contribution pleased Bilheimer more. Ever the careful lawyer, he often posed the keenest questions to those interviewed. Bilheimer appreciated Thompson's intelligence, leadership, precision, and integrity.[98] Tracey Jones kept his eye on the revolutionary nature of the war, asking his colleagues to consider "who rules at night?"[99]

The mission team's report raised questions about the government's perceptions of the enemy and America's approach to communism. Specifically, it said that the United States could not impose peace, freedom, justice, or order upon Vietnam because "these goals must be achieved by the Vietnamese themselves," and heavy-handed military solutions might be counterproductive. The report also questioned the government's assumption that Peking controlled Hanoi and suggested that negotiation possibilities might exist if North Vietnam was preserving its independence from China. Surmising as well that elements within the Vietcong's National Liberation Front (NLF) might be more nationalist than communist, team members wondered whether nationalist elements could be "separated from its communist" ones. They pointed out problems in America's pacification program, upon which officials placed so much importance. And, as Bilheimer had hoped, they raised concerns about basic U.S. policy assumptions, zeroing in on the supposed danger and monolithic nature of communism, America's unilateral responsibility to contain it, and the nation's dependence upon military power to do so.[100] The team closed by reiterating the NCC's recommendation that the war be turned over to an international agency for mediation.

The report did not impress those who had expected it to cry out in a strong prophetic way against U.S. involvement in Vietnam. While its observations were sound, it forged little, if any, new ground. Some deemed it weaker than the NCC's June statement.[101] Dudley Ward thought it far too soft, for it raised concerns through questions rather than statements. He also wished it had "concluded with a prophetic challenge instead of a kind of theological assurance." From his perspective, "many readers of the report may feel that the time and cost [of the trip] were not justified."[102]

But the findings did help legitimate the NCC's position with firsthand observations by respected leaders. And Bilheimer admitted that, while the statement was "low key," he hoped it might influence Rusk.[103]

It didn't. Rusk greeted the report with vigorous disagreement.[104] Of course, the NCC's observations were nothing new to the State Department; they reflected the sentiments of many war critics that State had dismissed before. The fact that church leaders now leveled such criticisms did little to win them consideration. Thus, neither Bilheimer nor Rusk was able to persuade the other to adopt the presuppositions on which his own stance was based. Rusk knew the Council's Vietnam positions did not reflect those most popular in the pews, so he viewed the ecumenists as "generals without armies." He believed the NCC's positions reflected those of a coterie of elite liberal church bureaucrats, not millions of voting, churchgoing Americans.[105] This mattered. Clout with the Johnson administration correlated directly with ability to influence and represent voters.[106] When the NCC's influence with laity waned, its importance to government also declined; and Rusk had now failed to coax the Council back into useful partnership. As Rusk explained, had the NCC consulted with and gained its parishioners' blessings, "it would have made a difference in the impact and weight of their pronouncements in Washington."[107] Thus, as the Council tried to serve the denominations through prophetic leadership, it became isolated ideologically and strategically from its former sources of sociopolitical influence: the government and the pew. However, as Bilheimer stressed, the church was not a political organization or interest group. His primary purpose was not to play politics but, rather, to generate a true ecumenical witness to government and pew on Vietnam.

The summer months brought a crushing number of crises upon the Johnson administration. The Six Day War, tensions in Greece and Turkey over Cyprus, the USSR's Anti–Ballistic Missile activities, racial uprising in urban areas, and increasing antiwar protests all competed with Vietnam for the administration's attention. Using Henry Kissinger, then a State Department consultant, the White House made another effort to jump-start negotiations. But poor communication between the U.S. diplomatic corps and military leaders in Vietnam led to ill-timed bombing at delicate moments when restraint was vital. It seemed to the North Vietnamese that every time the United States sent a negotiator its way, it also bombed one of their cities. The mixed messages offended them.[108] By early autumn, the negotiation channel had closed.

Meanwhile, pressure from hawks rose within the U.S. government, supported by public polls that favored military escalation over withdrawal. McNamara saw this trend illustrated in the Senate's Armed Services Committee hearings at which he testified.[109] Increasing hard-line pressure from senators, the public, and the Joint Chiefs likewise hardened Johnson.

Robert Fangmeier (the Disciples of Christ chairman of SADIA) saw a conservative tide building in his home state. "Stimulated by the Vietnam War and by rising urban unrest," he wrote, "a spirit of 'mini-McCarthyism' seems to be rising in Indiana. So far it has apparently been responsible for the firing of a university and a high school teacher, for the request by an armed vigilante group for official recognition, and for an ominous revival of the Ku Klux Klan."[110] The public was turning toward strong-arm tactics at home and abroad to restore order.

Ecumenists grew discouraged. While Johnson planned to raise troop levels in Vietnam, the churches found rallying summer dissent difficult. As Schomer said to Bennett, "the President has shrewdly put forward his request in a season that is always hard for the mobilization of popular opposition, and this year finds the country irascible and frightened by reason of the riots."[111] Bilheimer wondered if the churches might have to exacerbate the strife by heightening their opposition to government policy. "The situation is indeed discouraging," he said. "When one thinks of the riots, the virtual defeat of the foreign aid bill, and the escalation in Vietnam, it becomes clear that we are in the middle of a profound crisis in the life of our people and nation. If it all keeps up in this way, I suspect that we shall need to precipitate a far-reaching church-state struggle."[112] So far, like good liberals, Bilheimer's staff had used polite persuasion and reason with the grass roots and the government. In late 1967, Bilheimer, as did others in the antiwar movement, seemed ready to ratchet up the intensity of the Council's witness.

The need to raise a loud, public, dove voice to counter that of the hawks had grown.[113] Negotiations Now! focused its summer efforts toward gathering at least one million signatures on its petition favoring negotiations by early autumn. Its coordinator told Schomer and Naylor that the "most important channel available to the campaign is the network of local congregations, . . . denominations and organizations whose leaders initiated this effort."[114] The Council and its members did what they could to publicize the petition. Negotiations Now! had also become successful in generating Catholic support.[115] Since Jewish interest had gravitated toward

Middle East issues, Catholic cooperation became especially important. So Elston urged the NCC to pursue Catholics too.

However, sitting on the guiding committee for Negotiations Now!, Elston noticed disturbing changes. He suspected its national leaders of crafting it into a political tool that attempted to use the churches for its own purposes. Elston warned SADIA's members that they should perhaps view Negotiations Now! as a helpful education medium at the local level but be wary of bonding with it at the national.[116] Fangmeier thought Elston was being overly critical. But Harry Applewhite (UCC) disclosed similar fears that Negotiations Now! had "betrayed our confidence" and suggested they leave the group.[117] As time passed, Elston wondered if its leadership might be tied with the CIA.[118] After all, earlier that year, the media had exposed widespread CIA infiltration into left-leaning groups, particularly student organizations.[119] Even the venerable peace activist Norman Thomas had been unwittingly manipulated by the CIA. Coming from Nazi Germany, Elston was sensitive to subversive government behavior.

Fear that government had co-opted church organizations compounded in August when the "politics of charity" issue arose again. The media revealed that Catholic Relief Services (CRS) was distributing food and clothing to South Vietnamese soldiers as part of their military salary.[120] General Westmoreland had requested this when South Vietnam's government failed to raise its soldiers' pay. To MacCracken's credit, he insisted that no Church World Service supplies be used to pay South Vietnamese troops.[121] The press excoriated CRS, and the scandal shamed the American Catholic community. Thomas Quigley, director of the United States Catholic Conference, said to Bilheimer that "we must voice the strongest oppositions" when relief gets tied in such ways with military programs. Quoting the *National Catholic Reporter*, Quigley continued, "CRS policy in Vietnam has been substantially determined by political and military considerations which have nothing to do with the great purposes for which the agency was founded."[122] Church entanglement (whether Catholic or Protestant) with the U.S. military overseas compromised the image and witness that churches sought to make. International affairs leaders knew that the church must serve humanity by advancing justice in the world; but this required that it never sell its soul, or rent its image, to any principality. The CRS scandal heightened internal pressure upon CWS to reduce its use of surplus government foodstuffs overseas and put more effort into generating supplies from church donations.[123]

South Vietnam's upcoming September elections rekindled some hope in church leaders. Truly democratic elections might bring to power a representative civilian government that could end its internal strife and perhaps launch negotiations with the North. But fair elections were already compromised by U.S. cooperation with the South's ruling generals. Schomer noted that Thieu and Ky received the added advantage of "tacit moral support" from the Johnson administration even though it claimed impartiality.[124] A skeptical Bilheimer asked Blake about sending a team of WCC representatives to serve as election observers.[125] If the Vatican could do likewise, observers might inspire more diligence from South Vietnamese officials.

On September 3, South Vietnam held elections for president, vice president, and senators. Johnson did appoint nine U.S. religious leaders to observe them.[126] The Methodist Peace Division, SANE's national committee, the FCNL, and the Unitarian-Universalist Association also sent their own pair of eyes in the form of David Wurfel. Professor Wurfel chaired the committee on Asian Studies at the University of Missouri and was well-suited for this role. He arrived in Vietnam three weeks beforehand in order to track the campaigns, gauge the level of political freedom allowed, and witness the balloting; he then stayed an additional week to study the results. Wurfel's report devastated those who had prayed for a clean election. While the U.S. government's Landsdale Commission declared it fair, Wurfel's account exposed crass corruption. His eight-page synopsis, as Herman Will summarized it, "criticized the exclusion of certain candidates, the closing of three newspapers, continuation of censorship, threatening of campaign workers, election day frauds involving 300,000 to 500,000 votes, rigging of the senate race, [and] the intervention of American officials in favor of government candidates." Thieu and Ky emerged as landslide victors. Those anticommunist ecumenists who pined for a truly democratic self-determining South Vietnam saw their dreams dashed. The Methodists circulated Wurfel's report to members of Congress and the media.[127]

Meanwhile, the intensification of military activity in recent months inspired the NCC to pass a stronger "Resolution on Vietnam." It argued that military escalation would "defeat our objectives" and any military victory would be meaningless apart from political solutions.[128] It also condemned America's attachment to "security and the status quo," because this position put the nation on the wrong side of world revolutions. Seeking security without building a bedrock of justice was like raising a house on sand instead of stone. Regarding military strategy, the resolution recommended that the United States resort to a defensive posture designed only to maintain areas already held by allied troops. While responsibility for the war and peacemaking fell to all sides, the statement urged the United States to do its part by terminating its northern bombing campaign and seeking negotiations. In concert with this, America should let South Vietnam forge its own peace with the Vietcong. And it still pressed Johnson to place the conflict before the UN General Assembly (which in two months heard over ninety speeches on Vietnam, even though the war was not officially on its agenda).[129] Copies went to all representatives and senators, Roman Catholic leaders, presidential candidates, the denominations, and local church councils.[130]

As students returned to campuses that autumn, antiwar activity surged across the nation, and public support for Johnson's war strategy dipped. On October 16, over one thousand draft-age men turned in or destroyed their draft cards while others stood in support. The popular Yale chaplain, William Sloane Coffin Jr., addressed over four thousand at a Boston interfaith rally where scores burned their cards in an altar candle's flame.[131] On October 21, about one hundred thousand demonstrators rallied at the Lincoln Memorial before fifty thousand people marched on the Pentagon in an attempt to shut it down. Elston said the Mobilization was "eager to draw people into a civil disobedience campaign."[132]

CALCAV complied. On October 25, it released a "Statement of Conscience and Conscription," which signaled its leaders' assent to civil disobedience on behalf of draft resisters. The statement directly related conscience-based civil disobedience with religious obedience.[133] Its most controversial section would soon get CALCAV leaders into legal trouble. It read, "We hereby publicly counsel all who in conscience cannot today serve in the armed forces to refuse such service by non-violent means. We pledge ourselves to aid and abet them in any way we can. This means that if they are now arrested for failing to comply with a law that violates their consciences we too must be arrested, for in the sight of that law we are now as guilty as they."[134] Gerhard Elston and David Hunter signed the document and presented it to the press, along with sixteen other high-profile religious leaders. Signing tied oneself to civil disobedience against the Selective Service Act. Within four months, over thirteen hundred clergy had inscribed their names.[135] Church leaders were slowly embracing this concept and the need for stronger action measures.

Clergy were also becoming more vocal. To recognize "World Order Sunday" on October 22, church executives asked pastors to preach on Vietnam—and across the nation they did so. Nearly everyone in the NCC climbed into a pulpit that Sunday.[136] In conjunction, church bodies world-wide continued to criticize U.S. Vietnam policy. As one example, the Fifth Assembly of the Conference of European Churches condemned a war they deemed defeatist for Americans, tragic for the Vietnamese, and a threat to world peace. Addressing the NCC, it wrote, "in spite of all your efforts, your convictions have not found any response as yet on the part of your government, but your brethren in the European churches most urgently recommend that you renew your endeavours."[137] While visiting San Francisco, the Archbishop of Canterbury also condemned the war.[138] In turn, the NCC asked the British Council of Churches to intensify pressure against its own government's support of U.S. policy.[139] From Canterbury Cathedral, the Anglican Bishop of Woolwich did just that, saying, "I still find it incredible that not one individual has resigned from the [British Labor] government on this issue."[140]

The draft hit home for Bilheimer when the army pursued his eldest son, Bobby. Fresh out of college, Bobby had traveled to East Kenya with the Presbyterian Church's Frontier Intern Program to work as a freelance journalist. There the army tracked him down, ordered him to fly to Italy at his own expense for the army physical, classified him 1-A (draftable), and soon commanded that he report for duty. When his alma mater Hamilton College offered him a teaching position, the army refused to defer him. "We were all hot in it," Bobby recalled, and "it was pretty clear to all of us [in the family] what my options were." Canada was a real possibility, for his father's colleagues knew how to get him there. Applying for CO status was another. Actually serving in the military was a consideration, too. Bobby visited with his father, Elston, and the others on the NCC's fifth floor to discuss his choices. "There were some pretty cool guys up there," he remembered. According to Bobby, no one pressured him in any particular direction, totally respecting this decision as his alone. "It was not like you gotta do this, or you gotta do that, or you're immoral if you do this or immoral if you do that. Nobody was on that page because everybody was getting drafted."[141]

Bobby hated the war, and the decision proved agonizing; but he decided to obey the draft and serve. He knew people who had gone to Canada and deemed that path problematic for both personal and professional reasons.

The CO option "had its own set of complications" for someone from a nonpacifist tradition. It finally came down to his belief that he should share the suffering and uncertainty of so many in his generation rather than take the privileged way out. As he said, "why should I, just because my dad had this job . . . take that out. . . . I wasn't prepared to just do that. I felt like this was a bitter pill that a lot of people were having to swallow . . . so I went." Bobby served two years in the army (1968–1969). It never deployed him to Vietnam, but he was prepared for that possibility. Rather, while stationed in the Panama Canal Zone and serving as a chaplain's assistant, he saw firsthand the psychological devastation of the war upon men moving in and out of Vietnam as well as upon those receiving jungle training. Bobby earned the Army Commendation Medal for excellence. "I served and I served well. . . . it was, to me, an expression of solidarity with other people who were being victimized by these [U.S. war] policies."[142]

As the Bilheimers faced the draft issue at home, the protesting spirit within the nation found its way into the NCC's Church and Society Conference in Detroit, October 22–26. The goal of the gathering was "to plan strategies which can help direct economic and social development for full opportunity in a technological age." Eight hundred delegates split into twenty-nine separate work groups focusing upon a wide range of issues. Comprised of people with diverse opinions and little common guidance, many groups seemed muddled. The spontaneous attempt of three hundred "left-leaning" attendees to revamp the conference's agenda to focus only upon Vietnam and the urban crisis enhanced the sense of parliamentary chaos. This "mini-revolt," combined with the fact that uninvited hippies were allowed to distribute fliers and summon attendees to a love feast, revealed the anti-establishment attitudes growing within certain church sectors that would burst forth again at the NCC's General Assembly in 1969. The conference's rebelliousness felt like an attack on the establishment. Even the NCC's staff evaluation admitted that the exclusivity of its organizational committees left many attendees feeling "manipulated" by a core of bureaucratic planners with agendas. Both *Christianity and Crisis* and the *Christian Century* gave the event poor reviews. However, many saw the Vietnam Working Group's report as a positive outcome.[143] Elston not only helped lead this group, he had also convinced the inspirational Vietnamese Buddhist monk and poet Thich Nhat Hanh to join it.[144]

While most in the working group were doves, they still represented a range of perspectives on dissent strategies. The main split separated those who advocated "coalition" strategies, which protested through established systems using lawful means, from those who felt the times called for "confrontation" tactics, including civil disobedience.[145] The final report, therefore, contained two sections. The first suggested moderate church activities, such as attempting to influence 1968 national party platforms on the war, providing pastoral care to men resisting military service, and creating "centers" geared toward enhancing dialogue between Protestants, Catholics, and Buddhists in Southeast Asia. The second included "proposals for those churches . . . that believe the present situation is so critical that the foregoing measures are inadequate." These more confrontational suggestions involved picketing or boycotting industries creating war materials, aiding and abetting draft dodgers, and even organizing a "general strike."[146]

Predictably, the last few suggestions made headlines, became attached to the NCC, and mired its name in deeper mud, especially to those already suspicious of it. Many news stories failed to mention that the strike was considered a last resort to be used only if nuclear bombs were dropped, North Vietnam was invaded by land, China was attacked, or North Vietnam's Red River dikes were bombed.[147] The strike would last for one day only and involve abandoning all business activities for massive prayer rallies and demonstrations. Media reports also often failed to clarify that the conference spoke for itself only (not the NCC), and that its attendees came as individuals, not representatives of their religious organizations. It was the same old media problem that skewed the Council's image further to the left than it actually was, thereby rousing the wrath of local Christians.[148]

Once again, scathing letters poured in from congregations, some of which urged denominations to withdraw their membership.[149] One minister, who supported ecumenism, pleaded for changes in the Council's relationship with the grass roots. The NCC's seeming disregard for lay opinions, combined with its publicized "way-out positions," were breeding resentment that he felt had reached a crisis point.[150] He suggested that, if the NCC wished to regain credibility, it encourage denominations to send more conservatives to the General Board. He also urged the Council to poll parishioners on issues prior to making public statements. While affirming the Council's forward-thinking nature, he warned its leaders against becoming so blindly prophetic that they ignored and alienated people in the pews.

The NCC could not interfere with denominational prerogatives in selecting board members. It also refused to base its interpretation of God's will on a popular poll. But it did recognize that it had a relational problem with laity and must improve communication with the public.[151]

Council staff tried to pinpoint the source of the problem. Burton Marvin, NCC Associate General Secretary for Communications, rooted it in public misperceptions about the NCC. The answer, therefore, lay in clarifications and corrections. For example, he wanted the Council to better explain what its official positions were and why. It also needed to reinforce that, while it was structurally representative of member denominations, it did not purport to speak for any Christian body other than itself. So, too, for conferences and their participants.

With respect to international affairs, Paul Dietterich (CCUN) traced the impasse to a lack of adequate education at the local level.[152] Parishioners based their foreign policy perceptions on presuppositions that ecumenists had largely abandoned. The solution, to Dietterich, called for church education programs designed to alter the popular ethnocentric, nationalistic worldview. Creating these programs, he knew, involved a catch-22; they would depend greatly upon the denominations, which ultimately could do only what their members would support. Such a foundation-shattering educational agenda for laity would take patience, time, and money, three things mainline churches saw shrinking in supply. Church bureaucrats had developed their faith foundations over decades and in intense ecumenical discussions of world crises; but church organizations had not "brought their people along" over the years, and this could not be rectified through some crash course.

Dean Kelley, the NCC's director for Religious and Civil Liberty, also pegged different worldviews as the problem. But rather than faulting a lack of international affairs teaching, he blamed church leaders for neglecting the spiritual and theological nurture of laity for twenty-odd years. He felt that most moderate-liberal Protestant denominations had failed to build an explicit faith connection between their members' spiritual lives and the broader world.[153] In *Why the Conservative Churches Are Growing*, Kelley attributed the decline of mainline religion in the late 1960s and early 1970s to this long-term pastoral inattention.[154] Ross Terrill, a Catholic who collaborated with the NCC on upcoming election activities, illustrated how this neglect now backfired on mainline leaders. "If the 20th century teaches us anything, it is perhaps that you cannot, from above, force political blueprints, ideal schemes, upon people who neither understand nor desire them. Political action can only evoke and cultivate what is already dormant in a people. Otherwise it becomes tyranny, with a small elite telling the people what they need, rather than shaping society according to what people say they want." He then warned that, "those who try, by politics, to bring down heaven upon earth manage, very often, only to raise hell."[155] Ironically, this approach also resembled that of the U.S. government in Vietnam.

The NCC's problems with parishioners resulted from all three dilemmas noted above. The NCC had not mastered the media or messaging. It had a very different worldview regarding foreign affairs than many laity; and the liberal churches had, for years, failed to tutor laity in new theologies as well as make them real and useful for people's navigation of daily life. Finally, the classic notion of representation, which involved trusting elites to know what was best for the masses, no longer received their assent. The mantra of the 1960s to "question authority"—which conservative evangelists had been urging Christians to chant against the elitist-seeming ecumenical movement for decades—permeated much of society, including churches. The NCC operated through a top-down structure at a time when bureaucratic establishments were under fire, mainline Protestant growth was flagging, and individualism was on the rise.

In the fall, Lyndon Johnson experienced his own public relations problems. Polls showed support for the war and his popularity sagging just as the air war intensified over North Vietnam. Internal dissention also plagued his administration.[156] By late 1967, McNamara had lost faith in the war policies he had helped design, signaling the end of his White House tenure. Within weeks his successor, Clark Clifford, would also harbor doubts, along with much of the nation. But as of November 1967, Clifford still expressed support.[157]

So too did a group of prestigious elder statesmen, dubbed the "wise men," whom Johnson summoned for advice that month. Its members had helped shape post–World War II foreign policy and were considered successful. Closing in on an important election year, and facing rising antiwar pressure, Johnson wanted their opinions. He failed to provide them a balanced slate of information on the war, however. They did not receive any written reports, nor did they hear from people with doubts about the policy. The wise men (except George Ball), therefore, advised Johnson to stay the course, wear down the enemy, and wait for its inevitable retreat. With regard to Johnson's public relations dilemma, they suggested that he shift the public focus from the negative to the positive, highlighting advances toward the goal rather than the war's hardships.[158] The wise men's confidence buoyed Johnson's. He quickly recalled General Westmoreland from the front and sent him on a nationwide speaking tour to boost the war's image. The general's overly optimistic reports set the stage for disillusionment after the New Year.

With Elston's help, the Methodists organized and funded a nationwide education tour of their own. Since spring, the Methodist Women's Division, World Division, and Social Concerns Board had sponsored a "Vietnam Education Project" (VEP), which, like the NCC's debate and action program, aimed to reach people with thought-provoking information about Vietnam. Among other activities, VEP had supported Negotiations Now! and sponsored Wurfel's investigation of South Vietnam's elections.[159] In September, a new education vehicle arose when four leaders of a relief agency in Vietnam, called International Voluntary Services (IVS), suddenly resigned. Its director, Don Luce, had lived in Vietnam since 1958 and understood its people as well as any American alive. When Luce, his assistant director Gene Stoltzfus, and two other staff members quit over America's Vietnam policy, they made national news.[160] These four had invested their lives with the Vietnamese and were not motivated by political agendas. Explaining, Stoltzfus said, "I'm a professional in community development. How can I develop community when it is US policy to destroy community?" Luce continued, saying, "For a long time I thought it was my job to build quietly, no matter what others did, so that at least some people would be building. But I was wrong. Now it is impossible to do anything—even what we do is being used to help justify what we can't approve."[161]

Luce and Stoltzfus not only spoke against the repercussions of U.S. Vietnam policy; they also exposed the awkward "politics of charity" situation over which many relief workers and religious agencies felt morally tested. Fifty IVS workers sent a statement to President Johnson describing their dilemma. The statement read in part:

> In the past IVS has made claims to political neutrality. Such claims are no longer tenable. We see ourselves being used in Vietnam and in the States to sell the validity of the US position in this country. . . . In the States public officials and the press . . . cite *our* work in Vietnam, as testimony to the essential benevolence of the American intervention.
>
> But this is not the testimony we want to make. . . . We're moved to set the

record straight and then to take what steps are necessary to get back where we started from, working with people because they're people, not because they're potential dissidents from American policy.[162]

The churches provided Luce with the means to share his story and correct that record.

Stoltzfus had informed Elston of the resignations before they occurred. Immediately recognizing their importance, Elston searched for ways to transform Luce and Stoltzfus into traveling speakers. They were not radicals and possessed rare firsthand information on the Vietnamese situation. Elston knew they made supremely reputable spokespeople to whom he thought the public would listen. To Elston's delight, the Women's Division of the Methodist Church agreed to bankroll the project.[163] With money in hand, VEP arranged speaking engagements for the former IVS leaders. Throughout the 1968 election year, they crisscrossed the country sharing their perceptions on over two hundred television and radio programs, with members of the press, at clubs, at universities, and of course, in churches. As Elston had predicted, the IVS speakers were hot items. When Luce appeared on a three-hour talk radio program, thousands called in with comments and questions.[164] Luce would also speak before the National Democratic Platform Committee that summer. And, along with Stoltzfus, he would provide contacts and information on Vietnam to the ecumenical community for the remainder of the war. Elston and CALCAV found them invaluable.

ELECTION YEAR PREPARATIONS

In mid-November, the denominations' international affairs secretaries began brainstorming election year activities for the churches. A SADIA subcommittee, led by Elston, drafted a strategy paper aimed at impacting the 1968 elections. It did so as part of a new Vietnam Action Committee (VAC), formed by SADIA and the Committee on Church Union (COCU) to make Vietnam a key election-year issue for candidates. It planned workshops in states with presidential primaries and candidates running for office. VAC also helped with the IVS tour, sought resources from the NCC's Peace Priority Program and denominations, and worked closely with CALCAV.[165] Elston served as the link between groups.

The election year fast became a major focus. While traveling through the United States, Elston casually inquired about support for the antiwar senator Eugene McCarthy should he enter the presidential race. After receiving many favorable reactions, Elston encouraged him to run. He sent him the NCC's most recent resolution on Vietnam, reminding him that, "Churches and other organizations would naturally bring to the attention of their membership any candidates' stands on issues that approximate those that they themselves have taken."[166] Political liberals were also pushing McCarthy to run.[167] Within days, he declared his candidacy.

As 1967 wound down, the NCC asked congregations to close their Christmas Eve services with candlelight prayers for peace in Vietnam. Elston hoped this would draw awareness to the issue in a nondivisive way as Christians contemplated the birth of the Prince of Peace.[168] Even conservative denominations could do this in good conscience. By year's end, the United States had reached a near peak of five hundred thousand combat troops in Vietnam.

CHAPTER EIGHT

Campaigns, Confrontations, and Civil Disobedience, 1968

POLITICS AND THEOLOGY

As the new year commenced, so did the NCC's election efforts. VAC's strategy paper, "Renewal Of American Dialogue: 1968" (known as ROAD '68), provided practical suggestions for how churches could influence the political process without crossing the delicate line separating church and state. Alan Geyer drafted it with Eugene McCarthy in mind, for the senator had inquired if the churches could promote his platform. Their institutional tax status prevented endorsements, and ecumenists were careful to protect the church's independent non-partisan identity. However, religious groups could encourage candidates to adopt positions favored by the ecumenical community and, if successful, publicize the correlation. By involving itself in the 1968 campaigns, VAC hoped to advance three goals: a political settlement ending the war, greater investment in urban poverty issues, and a reorientation of national political priorities.[1]

VAC wanted to sway candidates toward positions favorable to these goals as well as promote grassroots support of politicians who shared them.[2] It agreed with Negotiations Now! that a third-party antiwar presidential candidate could not win, so it focused on the two main parties.

VAC also steered clear of a "dump Johnson" strategy, which seemed too simplistic, negative, and personality-based.[3] In addition, it discouraged a single-issue platform on the war, preferring candidates who were strong on a range of issues. And it advised church people to nurture potential allies among both Democrats and Republicans. This agenda demonstrated VAC's loyalty to an ecumenical worldview rather than favoritism of any one political party, person, or pet wedge issue.

ROAD '68 urged widespread involvement in primary campaigns. Primaries allowed candidates to "test their strength," "generate momentum," craft their image, and build rapport with the public. This process provided a prime opportunity to influence candidates' platforms. Therefore the UCC, with SADIA's assistance, delivered a three-day training session in Washington, D.C., for religious persons interested in learning how to do so. VAC warned religious groups to keep the NCC's name out of the picture. To reduce any appearance of clerical domination, it also urged them to stimulate as much lay participation as possible.[4] And VAC counseled them to "strike a balance between radicalism and restraint, between prophecy and prudence" in their election activities.[5] At a time when extremism and fearmongering dominated public expressions, ecumenists preferred using judiciousness and reason to influence the public square.

On January 5, William Sloane Coffin Jr. gave a Protestant face to the stereotype of the radical antiwar cleric. Yale's chaplain was indicted for "conspiring to counsel young men to violate federal draft laws."[6] Back in October 1967 he had helped collect thousands of draft cards—for him, a faith-driven act of civil disobedience against an unjust war. He stood in good company. Baby doctor Benjamin Spock, Marcus Raskin, and two others were indicted as well. The ecumenical community rallied to his side. *Christianity and Crisis* published Coffin's justification.[7] Some, including Martin Luther King Jr., signed a "statement of complicity" with "the Boston Five" as they were called. In fact, all those who had signed CALCAV's October 1967 "Conscience and Conscription" (that is, the "aid and abet") statement could be considered complicitous. Elston, the first layperson to sign, heard that he might be arrested next.[8]

The NCC could help, Coffin said, by teaching how civil disobedience was a time-honored aspect of the Christian tradition.[9] So the NCC created the new Staff Advisory Committee on Selective Service and War Resistance (SACSSAWR) to discuss conscientious objection, civil disobedience, and the draft.[10] Elston and Dean Kelley served on SACSSAWR, as later would David Hunter, Burton Marvin, and Jim Hamilton of the NCC's Washington office. Lack of official policy meant the issue needed to pass through the General Board first.[11] This issue was touchy. As one committee member noticed, a selective CO policy would "require a reversal of [the NCC's] habitual 'liberal' stance" that frequently favored government intervention in the lives of individuals.[12]

Despite its policy gap on civil disobedience, the NCC possessed sufficient precedent to provide legal support to young men denied CO status. Along with the ACLU, the NCC sponsored legal suits by three clergy whose 4-D classification (deferment) was revoked and replaced with 1-A (draftable) after they turned in their draft cards to protest the war. One of the three, Henry Bucher, worked for the NCC. The court ruled in his favor and ordered the government to return his card and 4-D status. SAC-SSAWR also discussed the related issue of men who became conscientious objectors after military induction.[13] Several who were denied CO status consciously disobeyed military orders. Imprisonment and court-martials followed. An NCC delegation discussed this with General Lewis Hershey, director of the Selective Service, who viewed selective objectors as disingenuous opportunists. Kelley then probed the chief of chaplains about how chaplains dealt with conscience-convicted inductees. The chief's cool response showed little concern for providing compassionate counseling to such men. As a result of rising denominational appeals for draft-counseling workshops, the NCC created a series that churches could administer locally. Civil disobedience and meeting the pastoral needs of draft resisters, as well as AWOL soldiers, drew the NCC's attention throughout 1968.[14]

While others worked on political issues related to the war, Bilheimer returned to a topic that had bothered him since his first days on the job. The American ecumenical witness on Vietnam lacked an articulated theological rationale, and many coming from the civil rights movement seemed willing to slight this. The explicit reintegration of theology into the NCC's witness appeared critical to Bilheimer's mission; he saw it as the glue to bond the body of Christ at all church levels—and around the world.

American Christians had often disregarded the theological dimension of their convictions. Throughout the spiritual boom of the 1950s, a substantial proportion of laity (though not all) seemed content to rest their faith on comforting reassurances of heaven rather than on rigorous understandings of scripture. Laity who did engage theology tended to focus on topics related to the individual soul's condition rather than society's.[15] By the 1960s, many activist clergy had deemed theology largely irrelevant to those in need of social change. With few exceptions, Bilheimer mourned America's failure to nurture deep theological thinkers, and he did not want the theological aspect of the NCC's Vietnam efforts to go ignored. Neither did Elston, who felt the student Christian movement had stronger roots in a theology of justice than did the Council or denominations.[16] So did the Jewish community. As Bilheimer explained to theologian Colin Williams, "The present church struggle in the U.S. concerns justice. There is little really well worked out theological context for this struggle. . . . Probably most theological work is that done on the fly by people who are head over heels in the fight itself. Ecumenical work . . . is hindered by the lack of solid theological work on the subject."[17]

Therefore, Bilheimer collected a group of theologians in Chicago to explore justice issues raised by the war and to produce a substantial theological statement that would complement Bilheimer's own efforts on presuppositions. The proposed statement should help explain theologically *why* the ecumenical movement held its particular assumptions about world order, and *why* it was motivated by a different worldview than that which propelled America's foreign policy. Unfortunately, the theologians failed. The weakness of their initial statement did not justify the expenditure for a broader meeting. According to Elston, American theologians "were incapable of talking theology when talking about justice. . . . They were all geared to talking politics, sociology, history and theology in their own little field."[18]

J. Robert Nelson, chair of the NCC's Faith and Order Commission, was also frustrated by Americans' reluctance to integrate theology and action. He attributed this partially to habit, for the theologians in Faith and Order were used to working separately from and on different problems (such as doctrinal disparities between denominations) than the more activist leaders in the Council's Life and Mission division. However, since theological differences were becoming more prevalent within rather than between denominations (creating conservative/liberal splits within churches), and since these were growing more entwined with political issues, he urged theologians and activists to better integrate their work. This would require activists to put more emphasis upon theology, and theologians to "give priority . . . to the great controversies of the day."[19] For some reason, this stymied both. As historian Leonard Sweet explained, "Churches thus became little more than the sum and channel of human action. . . . A good church was not a believing church but a working church, . . . with lots of task forces."[20] Bilheimer feared this was becoming true, and he tried to circumvent it. Political action that did not germinate from a conscious, articulated understanding of the Christian faith was not a real ecumenical witness to Bilheimer. It made religious activism virtually indistinguishable from the secular variety, with little more to say than "stop the war."

This was not just a liberal oversight, however. Conservative Christians— who often used religious rhetoric to support U.S. efforts in Vietnam and saw the Cold War as a spiritual struggle between good and evil—rarely framed their arguments theologically either. Historian David Settje posits that this reflected their sense that their position was so obviously right, so commonsensical, that it needed no thorough theological justification.[21] Regardless of the reasons, American Christians on both sides of the Vietnam debate tended to neglect the theological angles of their arguments.

Bilheimer's frustration escalated with the war. The Johnson administration's inflexibility left little hope that liberals might convince it to shift assumptions and objectives.[22] Christian opinion also discouraged him. Nine Protestant magazines with 3.6 million total readers conducted an unscientific poll on the war.[23] Of 34,000 responses, 2,000 were from ministers. Results showed that, while 63 percent of the total criticized Johnson's war management, laypeople were far more hawkish than clergy about what should be done. For example, 60 percent of laity rejected a bombing halt, which 57 percent of clergy supported. Over half of those polled believed the United States should ensure victory using whatever military means were required, short of nuclear weapons—a position to which 66 percent of the clergy strongly objected. And 55 percent of all respondents opposed church advocacy of conscience-based protest, regardless of the repercussions. Scientific surveys confirmed this striking gap between clergy and laity over the war. Many laypeople stereotyped mainline clergy as dovish dissenters. They associated them generally with all antiwar protesters, a group type-cast as unpatriotic and immoral lawbreakers. At a consultation with Japan's National Christian Council, Bilheimer described the politically weak minority status of the peace movement, including the church component. "As concerns Vietnam my own feeling is that the protest movement is pretty well spent." Only a fraction of students, faculty, and church leadership comprised the "main sources of the protest." He continued, "The NCCCUSA has been more critical than any other institution in the U.S. . . . Right now I am not even certain about the National Leadership of our Churches. If I were to submit our September 1967 resolution on Vietnam to them now I would be afraid that the National Leadership would not approve it."[24] As Bilheimer addressed these delegates, a tidal shift was altering the very situation of which he spoke.

TET TURNS THE TIDE

In early February, a single wave of fighting called the Tet Offensive turned more public sentiment against the war than all previous antiwar efforts. It also soured Johnson's new defense secretary, Clark Clifford, to the president's war policy. Elston had learned of the Vietcong's planned attacks prior to their occurrence. His friend, Harry Haas, who lived in Vietnam, heard that a major offensive was planned for the cities and that he should flee Saigon before "all hell broke loose."[25] So he informed Elston. Shortly thereafter, on January 31, the Tet Offensive began. U.S. military intelligence failed, and combat troops were caught by surprise.[26] Americans watched it unfold on the evening news. Weeks earlier, General Westmoreland had boosted national confidence in a military victory, assuring the public that the Vietcong neared certain defeat. Now Americans saw the supposedly weak enemy invade major cities and assault the U.S. embassy. As Rusk described it, "When the networks broadcast footage of Vietcong sappers inside the walls of the American Embassy in Saigon, the inevitable impression was that the American effort in South Vietnam had simply gone to hell."[27]

Between late January and mid-April, a quick succession of events fueled widespread doubt about the war's prospects and Johnson's credibility. For example, Americans saw their military mired in a ghastly siege at Khe Sanh. Aired nightly on television, the battle exposed viewers to the stress and inhumanity of the war. When a South Vietnamese police chief, filmed live in the streets, suddenly executed a Vietcong suspect in civilian clothes with a gunshot to the head, Americans wondered whether democracy or a police state ruled the South. When a U.S. military officer explained the obliteration of an entire village by claiming he had "to destroy the town to save it," he illustrated for many Americans the unwinnable and morally ambiguous nature of this conflict.[28] As a result of the Tet Offensive and its repercussions, Vietnam Christian Service worked "around the clock" to meet the needs of some two hundred thousand new refugees in Saigon alone. Religious leaders voiced their concerns to Johnson.[29] Khe Sanh and Tet inspired misgivings within the United States about Johnson's military strategy. The enemy did not appear near defeat. The administration's credibility, already weakened by earlier publicized discrepancies, crumbled. According to Rusk, Tet "unleashed a tidal change in American opinion about the war."[30] Nationally trusted CBS news anchor Walter Cronkite embodied this shift when he confessed his own doubts about U.S. military policy on the air. After Tet, General Wheeler requested even more troops, and Clifford was summoned to reappraise the situation.[31]

Globally, people were reassessing the situation as well. Bilheimer liked an article in London's *Observer* that pinpointed America's unwinnable dilemma. "America is stuck with a war that is nonsense in military terms, counter-productive in diplomatic terms, dangerous in terms of its global implications and repugnant in moral terms. . . . the US has found that there is no effective democracy in Vietnam to defend and that it is the Communists who have most successfully identified themselves with Vietnamese nationalism." Bilheimer concurred with the conclusion: "In a real sense, the Americans are the prisoners of their own power and ideology."[32] These were the captives the ecumenical community sought to free. Recognizing Tet's impact on opinions globally, Elston began soliciting church positions on the war throughout the world, as well as interpreting the NCC's stance to European church leaders.[33]

Clifford noticed the pall that pervaded the White House and halls of Congress. "It is hard to imagine or re-create the atmosphere in Washington in the sixty days after Tet," he said. "The pressure grew so intense that at times I felt the government itself might come apart at its seams."[34] While Tet sapped spirits inside the beltway, it inspired national debate and inflated antiwar groups with hopes that negotiations might soon be sought.[35]

On February 5 and 6, 1968, CALCAV sponsored its second religious mobilization in Washington. Over two thousand participants visited congressional representatives, participated in workshops, and facilitated massive letter-writing to the administration. Martin Luther King Jr. added his voice at a special ceremony at Arlington National Cemetery. But government officials were largely unresponsive.[36] CALCAV used the mobilization to publicize the release of its book *In the Name of America*.[37] A team of Columbia University scholars and students led by Professor Seymour Melman had researched the conduct of U.S. troops in Vietnam. The resulting four-hundred-page book documented what the authors believed were violations of international laws of war. American lawmak-ers tended to dispute the implication of U.S. war crimes in Vietnam, but the book clearly illustrated a severe moral erosion in military behavior.[38] The My Lai massacre that occurred a month later (but which remained concealed until November 1969) helped confirm the charge of America's complicity in war crimes. Newspapers nationwide announced the book. CALCAV gave copies to senators in conjunction with their visits. While several NCC staff members participated in CALCAV's efforts, Espy care-fully distanced the NCC from CALCAV's stands, for Council members were still too divided on the issue to permit its support.[39]

The Council's relationship with CALCAV was also changing.[40] For the good of both organizations, CALCAV gradually became more indepen-dent of the NCC, and as it grew, the NCC began charging it for services. The NCC did, however, continue to process tax exempt donations on its behalf. Due to CALCAV's hefty debts and the expanding expense of its projects, its NCC credit line became a relational stress point between the two organizations, which approached finances very differently. The more cautious Council generally raised funds prior to spending them, whereas the action-based, independently run CALCAV charged expenses on faith, doing later what was necessary to raise funds for payment. CALCAV expected the NCC to cover its bills even when the Council's own budget remained tight.

While CALCAV, SADIA, Negotiations Now!, and other religious groups geared up for the coming elections, Bilheimer's hope that they might expedite peace faded. At the February convocation with Japanese Christian leaders, he raised doubts about McCarthy's lackluster one-issue campaign and Republican interest in altering the direction of U.S. Vietnam policy. He concluded that, "the American people will not have a choice on voting in relation to the Vietnam issue during the elections. I really don't think they care."[41] Geyer's prognosis was equally bleak. "It is a severe winter of discontent for the American political system. Seldom has an election year dawned with a more widespread sense of malaise and disillusionment in public attitudes toward the nation's politics." And even though the Council urged the international ecumenical community to press their home coun-tries to denounce U.S. Vietnam policy, Bilheimer knew that governments desiring U.S. cooperation generally remained mute.[42]

Bilheimer's pre-Tet pessimism had just cause. But Tet's repercussions changed the political landscape. Moderate antiwar positions gained more public legitimacy. Church statements on the war drew more attention from certain legislators who read several into the *Congressional Record*, including the NCC's.[43] The McCarthy campaign also surged to life with donations and volunteer support. Prior to the important New Hampshire primary, CALCAV distributed to voters' homes a fourteen-page brochure entitled, *Who's Right, Who's Wrong on Vietnam?* It did not endorse any candidate; rather, it included statements by prominent leaders from both parties that challenged the government's justifications for war, exposed its credibility gap, and praised antiwar activists as patriots. The pamphlet was later used in Wisconsin, Alaska, and Arkansas. In New Hampshire's primary on March 12, McCarthy came in a close second to the president, with 42.4 percent of the vote. Now the sitting president looked vulnerable.[44] This inspired Robert Kennedy to enter the race on March 16, providing doves with another antiwar choice. Kennedy's captivating style and competitive fire fueled people with energy. But the biggest political earthquake struck at the end of Johnson's televised address on March 31 when the incumbent unexpectedly withdrew from the race.

EXPANDING THE STRATEGY, CHALLENGING WORLDVIEWS

The NCC was also experiencing an equinox moment. Its February General Board meeting marked a turning point for its international affairs strategy. Bilheimer credited Ernest Gross with suggesting a broader strategic direction that would guide the Council during Nixon's reign.[45] This new approach moved the NCC beyond critiquing specific policies or facilitating debate and action on Vietnam toward framing that war explicitly within an outmoded worldview that needed revisioning. Doing so had always been central to Bilheimer's agenda. But it had not yet been woven overtly into the Council's methods or written statements on the war.

Ernest Gross was Bilheimer's mentor and counsel. Gross's extensive experience in government and understanding of Washington beltway politics proved invaluable to him. The two spent many afternoons strategizing over drinks at the exclusive Century Club where Gross was a member and establishment people hobnobbed together. Bilheimer distilled the choicest nuggets of their conversations into a paper designed to broaden the focus of the NCC's peace discussions. In fact, this paper was Bilheimer's answer to Rusk's earlier challenge that the Council conduct a new study on the components of a "just and durable peace." After months of review and revision, "Imperatives of Peace and Responsibilities of Power" became policy. The "Imperatives" statement sharpened significantly the articulated ecumenical worldview as it related to international affairs and provided a new basis for what the Council could do. While the statement's ideas were not new within ecumenical circles, their convergence into official NCC policy was momentous.

"Imperatives of Peace and Responsibilities of Power" asserted that justice must be the foundation for true national security and international peace in an increasingly interdependent world—not occupational military forces or bigger nuclear warheads. "We must strive for both order and justice," the statement clarified, "but in our world justice has a prior claim."[46] In conjunction, the statement challenged prevailing assumptions about U.S. power and its proper use by urging a redistribution through the enhancement of other nations' economic positions in the world. This concept of a justice-based peace required the United States to revamp almost totally its ways of perceiving security and conducting foreign policy. Such drastic change was not likely to appeal to those who wielded U.S. power, especially those who operated from a competitive and coercive view of national self-interest, rather than from one that saw America benefited by global justice. But Council leaders hoped that the vision and rationale underlying their statement would be compelling to a people at war with themselves and overseas.

Creating a just peace required three things, said the Council. The "use of military might" must be more constrained, for the military is limited in what it can and should be asked to do. While they can defend people from attack, guns cannot solve political problems or build justice. Yet the United States plunged its military into largely political situations, such as the Vietnam conflict, and asked soldiers to win local hearts and minds. This backfired. Additionally, in a world blossoming with nations newly freed from colonialism, the Council urged the United States to support the economic and cultural vitality of other peoples through the creation of indigenously chosen institutions rather than via puppets vulnerable to U.S. control. Finally, the United States must promote human rights as the bedrock for world order. Capitalism, communism, or even simple anticommunism, as ideologies, all neglected to make justice the top priority; therefore, when not grounded fully in human rights, they failed to secure peace.

U.S. policy often diverged from these three imperatives because it flowed from a different set of presuppositions that the NCC found faulty. These included U.S. adherence to a bipolar view of the world split into "communist" or "free," with Moscow stage-managing one side while the United States directed the other. This view saw Third World nations as mere pawns in a play, "hovering in a neutral vacuum" with little agency of their own. It also included the belief that America must police the world against communism, regardless of ability, real threat level, or global support. The United States then relied too much upon military power to maintain world order as if a military response was always the best defense of peace. The United States held too fiercely to the belief that it alone should decide how its power was deployed in the world. And it tended to favor the status quo regardless of whether that system was good for people. According to the NCC, order based upon privileged military, economic, or political might only bred resentment.

Therefore, the Council urged America to move in new directions. For example, it hoped the United States would use its strength "to increase trust among nations" rather than contain and isolate. As part of this, America should nurture "a new internationalism" that might help reconcile distrustful countries and should support a broader distribution of economic power while valuing distinct cultures, traditions, and histories. In the nuclear era, ecumenical leaders believed that humankind faced a dire choice: "find peace or perish." As the NCC's 1968 statement said, "Individual piety and morality are not enough. Choices for good and not evil, for life and not death, must be made in regard to matters that transcend the merely personal realms of life."

The NCC believed the church must help guide Americans toward this new way of seeing international affairs, which was merely an extension of loving one's neighbor as oneself. "Love," the statement explained, "enables men, confronted by enemies, to put themselves in the position of their enemies, understanding them as persons with different perspectives and legitimate needs and interests of their own." For example, Americans should not categorize the Vietcong as "'Cong' or 'communists' or 'guerrillas,' but [remember they are] individuals who, whatever their ideology or aspiration, react to life in their particular condition as human beings." This simple shift in perception was vital to increasing trust between peoples. The responsibilities of power, therefore, must also include acts that flow from this new view and aim to secure justice for everyone. Doing so was in every nation's self-interest, including America's.

During this time ecumenical circles were also buzzing about human rights struggles in South Africa. These further highlighted that America's policies often placed it on the wrong side of world revolutions and further illumined how justice, economic development, and racism intersected.[47] But "Imperatives of Peace and Responsibilities of Power" drew examples exclusively from the Vietnam War to illustrate its points, because Bilheimer viewed that conflict as a clear and direct repercussion of America's skewed presuppositions.[48] Stopping the war would *not* solve the deeper malady residing in the nation's justice-denying worldview. Therefore "Imperatives" called for church witness against the malady itself, as well as against its symptoms (the Vietnam War). This distinguished the NCC's approach from that of many antiwar groups for whom stopping the war was the ultimate goal. As Bilheimer explained, "We weren't just wild eyed activists; we weren't protesters only. We consciously tried to enter into the problem and see it . . . in light of the Christian faith."[49]

Bilheimer considered "Imperatives" the best statement produced on international affairs during his tenure at the Council. It contained analysis that mirrored and expanded Martin Luther King Jr.'s notion of "the beloved community" to a global scale. It did what Bilheimer thought churches should do: raise broad questions, a vision, and a frame of reference that prioritized humanity, justice, love, and peace—as he felt Jesus would—and then insert these into public debate. The statement also gave the Council its marching orders for even broader work on international affairs. The ideas within it still guide ecumenical approaches to global security.

The NCC circulated the "Imperatives" statement to government officials and churches, hoping that its analysis would inspire reflection and discussion. But, once again, the document was not crafted in a manner that enticed average parishioners to read it. As Elston said, the Council couldn't "sell it to the pews." Even some denominational leaders disliked it, because, according to Bilheimer, they thought "we were just being intellectual World Council of Churches types."[50] But Elston and Geyer helped generate more support and strategized ways of getting groups to discuss it.[51]

The Council implemented "Imperatives" by passing a related policy statement, "World Poverty and the Demands of Justice," as well as a new "Resolution on Vietnam." The first stressed the need for generous foreign aid, which, while plentiful after World War II, was greatly curtailed during the Cold War and manipulated for ideological purposes.[52] U.S. leaders channeled it too frequently to oppressive regimes. Since many Roman Catholic leaders shared the Council's interest in foreign aid and development, the NCC drafted a proposal for a Joint Protestant–Roman Catholic Action concerning International Aid, Trade and Development.[53] This provided a positive meeting ground for broader Christian cooperation.

The new Vietnam resolution expressed hope that negotiations were within reach and again urged all warring parties to pursue them. Holding peace talks up as the goal, it requested that the United States stop bombing, assure that nuclear weapons would not be used, and reaffirm its openness to inclusive talks with all parties. The resolution implored Hanoi to refrain from attacking Khe Sanh lest American attitudes be embittered further. It asked Hanoi to remain open to Johnson's recently softened negotiation position and "initiate in its own way the stabilization of the present confrontation in the South."[54] Then repeating the NCC's usual refrain, it urged churches to expand their debates and actions on the war. Christians especially should resist hardening their own hearts, for these could not foster reconciliation. Congressman George E. Brown Jr. read it all into the *Congressional Record.*[55]

In order to address the controversies over draft resistance and conscientious objection, the Council drew up a policy statement on "Religious Obedience and Civil Disobedience." CALCAV's Richard John Neuhaus captivated the General Board while making the case for it.[56] Nevertheless, the wary board referred it back to committee for further revision. Even though the civil disobedience statement had not come to a vote, the NCC continued planning a program to aid draft resisters. Subsequent events soon propelled both actions forward. Shortly after the board meeting, Bilheimer received a plea for help from an Episcopal priest in Canada who ministered to the needs of American refugees fleeing military service. Impressed by his work and his argument that American churches should help, Bilheimer asked Schomer to look into it.[57] NCC involvement in this ministry would blossom in late 1969. Meanwhile, Dean Kelley finally convinced the Department of Defense and the General Commission on Chaplains that chaplains should provide more sensitive and thorough assistance to young men who were filling out conscientious objector forms. The NCC even established a joint committee with the General Commission to develop counseling materials that the denominations could give to chaplains for use with conscience-torn servicemen.[58]

Meanwhile, White House attitudes had stiffened. U Thant told Schomer that Johnson seemed attentive to polls, which revealed that 41 percent of the public sought more hawkish tactics, 38 percent supported current policy, and only 21 percent favored either withdrawal or de-escalation.[59] At the administration's March briefing for nongovernmental organizations (attended by the NCC's Allan Parrent), Johnson made an unexpected appearance. Striding into the conference room, he delivered a fiery fifteen-minute impromptu speech exclaiming that the enemy aimed not only to conquer South Vietnam but also to win "the hearts and minds of the American people." He implied that the enemy was "seeking to achieve in DC what he could not achieve on the battlefield."[60] After imploring NGO leaders to rally Americans behind his "middle course" policy, Johnson closed with the cry, "We're number one and we're going to stay number one!"[61] Dean Rusk, Bill Bundy, Walt Rostow, and Averell Harriman spoke to participants as well. Parrent surmised that the administration was entrenching for a "hard-line campaign" that would continue painting dissenters as traitors.

Rocked by the Tet Offensive, Johnson brought the wise men back to Washington. Their latest advice reverberated the depth of Tet's impact. These elder statesmen who, months ago, had encouraged Johnson to stay the course now abandoned his failing policy. This time they had also received more balanced briefings. Like McNamara, most of them now recommended that the president exchange his military approach for a diplomatic one. The swing of Dean Acheson's opinion particularly affected Johnson, as did that of Cyrus Vance.[62] With few allies left, Johnson shifted stances. In his televised address on March 31, he curtailed the bombing of North Vietnam and expressed interest in beginning talks with its representatives. He closed with his stunning announcement that he would not seek or accept his party's nomination for another presidential term.

Ecumenical leaders were thrilled. The next day, Arthur Flemming wired Johnson an affirming message: "The National Council of Churches welcomes the initiatives for peace in Vietnam which you announced last night. We support you in them and in whatever additional consonant steps you may take in the interest of bringing hostilities to an end."[63] Bennett's article in *Christianity and Crisis* described the optimism that Johnson's announcement instilled. "His harshest critics could not avoid feeling with him in those last minutes of his broadcast. They . . . had to acknowledge that at this moment he had transcended himself. . . . One evening gave us more possibilities than we could have imagined in our most hopeful moments."[64]

The prospect of peace talks seemed closer than ever. Schomer, who maintained contact with Mai Van Bo, telegrammed Johnson to stress that a bombing halt over North Vietnam was an essential precursor to negotiations.[65] CALCAV called for a national fast that would extend from Good Friday through Easter. The fast's symbolic purpose was to cleanse America's spirit and signal a new beginning.[66] Anticipation now surrounded the upcoming elections, for, with popular support for the war eroding, many thought any presidential winner would have to end it. Therefore, some became dismissive or at least passive about the war, acting as if its demise was certain. Despite their optimism, liberal leaders also knew that, while Johnson was shifting tactics, he had not relinquished his ultimate objective: an independent anticommunist South Vietnam. Neither had Vice President Humphrey, who entered the presidential race carrying a similar message—that he would end the war, with honor.

Johnson selected Averell Harriman and Cyrus Vance to jump-start negotiations between warring parties. Despite Johnson's new push for talks (long advocated by the NCC), Bilheimer carefully protected the Council's autonomous confessing church posture with government. On April 15, Harriman met with five representatives of nongovernmental organizations, three of whom—Allan Parrent, Herman Will, and Dudley Ward—worked for or with the NCC. According to Parrent, Harriman and state department official Frank Sieverts probed for contacts the NGOs had made with the North Vietnamese and Vietcong that might prove fruitful in opening negotiations. Harriman also sought input, Parrent noted, on "how to allay . . . suspicions of U.S. policies and motives which exist in Vietnam. He hoped that maybe we, through some of our contacts, could help to do this."[67] Harriman admitted to them that "NLF representatives and North Vietnamese officials were much more frank and open with representatives of NGOs . . . [like theirs] than they were with U.S. officials" and Sieverts showed particular interest in accessing what the NLF was thinking through NGO contacts.[68] Harriman asked for the NGOs' help, short of "betray[ing] confidences" or "act[ing] as intelligence agents." Parrent described the request as emphatic and sincere. It seemed to attendees that the government was seeking the partnering help of NGOs, including the NCC, to provide it with information and connections that might benefit negotiations.

The three Council-affiliated representatives left the meeting feeling honored and eager to comply. In fact, they discussed sending a group of NGO leaders (which would include an NCC official) to meet with their NLF contacts and operate as an intermediary between warring parties.[69] They suggested meeting with Harriman again to identify questions that the government wanted pursued with the NLF. Throughout the interview, Harriman made clear to the church leaders that he shared McNamara's criticism of the bombing campaign, describing it as "senseless."[70] With administration officials clearly divided on policy, perhaps church leaders might help the dovish ones to prevail.[71]

The five NGO leaders did not question Harriman and Sievert's agenda. Nor did they express any wariness about church leaders working on behalf of government objectives. Was this not the sort of partnership that Council staff had once enjoyed, and that many secretly sought again, with government, but this time on behalf of a war-ending strategy they had long supported?

Bilheimer nixed this notion. Thinking that government had no shortage of contacts, he did not trust Harriman's motives and refused to let the NCC become a government lackey. Responding to Parrent, Bilheimer wrote, "In short, I suspect that we are being used in one way or another. It may well be that Harriman's office wants to use whatever contacts we or other people have, simply to see what they are likely to be up against before having to get themselves involved. . . . If that be true, I do not think it is a ploy to which we ought to be a part." He continued, "On the more objective level, it seems to me that errand-running of this sort is outside the role of the church, and certainly of a formally constituted agency of the churches like the NCC."[72] Bilheimer wanted to preserve the Council's independence, which mandated clear separation of church from state and a healthy suspicion of government. Further, he refused to risk compromising the NCC's relationships with overseas contacts by acting as a government informant. To Bilheimer, the Council's confessing church stance was critical to its Christian mission and its strength on controversial issues. Other church leaders prioritized differently, showing more willingness to do anything that might help stop the war, whether this meant collaboration with—or co-optation by—government in one instance and civil disobedience in another.

Harriman launched formal negotiations, in Paris, in May. Unfortunately, the talks began unproductively, with months of posturing and squabbles over issues such as table shapes. Meanwhile, the fighting in Vietnam intensified.

Events in spring 1968 signaled another violent year at home. On April 4, Martin Luther King Jr. was assassinated. This sparked waves of inner-city riots. Students, who had become more radicalized against the military-industrial complex, also began demonstrating in greater numbers on campuses. In late April, just blocks from NCC headquarters, Columbia University students occupied and trashed school buildings for several days. Ultimately the police ejected them. According to student activist and scholar Todd Gitlin, this uprising signaled the end of "deference and civility."[73] Angry students followed suit on campuses across the nation. John Bennett recognized that "moral revulsion" against U.S. Vietnam policy and the threat of being drafted had undermined student trust in authority and respect for the establishment.[74] The *Christian Century* sided with the establishment in Columbia University's case, albeit reluctantly. Calling it a "vexatious phenomenon," the *Century* said that "it seems to us better to limp along with the establishment than to follow the half-baked utopianism of the New Left. But it hurts us to say this. This week we make no claim to be prophets of the Lord."[75] In September, the NCC's General Board issued "A Letter to the Churches about the Crisis in Higher Educa- tion," asking churches to "listen to what young people are saying" about their frustrations with society even if in disagreement with their message or methods.[76] The NCC would live these words over the next year. Protest tactics were becoming more defiant and destructive. Even religious-based groups such as CALCAV were conducting more confrontational protests such as demonstrations against Dow Chemical, a maker of napalm, during its annual stockholders' meeting.

As radical protests escalated, Bilheimer again distinguished the NCC as a rational, respectable critic of the war. He highlighted the growing strength of its statements on Vietnam and described its consistent message as being unique among those of large national organizations. While recognizing the critiques of government policy "from academic circles, some members of Congress and some professional groups," he emphasized that the NCC "is the only major national institution to have developed and maintained a consistent policy of reasoned criticism of Government policy and of pressure for a negotiated peace."[77] Labor unions, the Catholic Church, and Jewish organizations had not done likewise, he noted. Unfortunately, the peace program's debate and action activities had drawn the NCC over budget by an estimated $103,000 throughout 1968 and would do so by even greater anticipated sums for 1969 and 1970. Therefore, the Council asked the denominations to increase their contributions and provide immediate assistance to cover the deficit.[78] After one and a half hours of what Tracey Jones described as "intense discussion," the Methodists agreed to grant the NCC $70,000 more for its 1968 budget because its peace work was critical.

The majority of this sum came from the Methodist Board of Missions. In turn, however, the Methodists flexed their muscles, airing grievances about the NCC's international affairs program that they wanted addressed. They sought a written promise that the NCC's three divisions (Christian Life and Mission, Christian Education, and Overseas Ministries) would devote seven total staff members to the Peace Priority Program rather than the current number of four.[79] They also demanded more consultation between Bilheimer and Methodist leaders such as Ward and Will, regarding program objectives, strategy, and staff selection. The Methodists were leveraging their size in order to shorten Bilheimer's leash and increase their voice in the Council's peace work. The NCC's increased budget requests of the denominations for international affairs drew their ire as well. From $93,863 donated in 1967, requests spiked originally to $227,000 for 1968; then they increased again to $340,000, which remained the figure for 1969.

According to the NCC's fund-raising tradition, it asked the Methodists and United Presbyterians to donate roughly one-third of this amount ($105,000 each), with the Disciples of Christ, United Church of Christ, Episcopal Church, Presbyterian Church U.S., and Reformed Church in America to contribute jointly an additional $105,000. Donations from the NCC's other communions often made up the difference. Speaking for the Methodists, Tracey Jones told Espy that they were "not prepared to consider an asking of more than approximately $75,000 for this budget." He reminded Espy that the Presbyterians and the other five main denominational contributors would have to agree to match that figure according to the traditional contribution ratio. Dale Fiers, of the Disciples of Christ, disliked the rising budget requests as well.[80] The funding problem festered over the next several years. As church budgets constricted, so did their ability to give to the NCC.

In June, the Council's General Board finally passed a policy statement on "Religious Obedience and Civil Disobedience."[81] It sanctioned civil disobedience when national laws conflicted with God's. However, the statement created certain guidelines for this sort of action and distinguished civil disobedience from the New Left's call for resistance and revolution.

Civil disobedience must remain nonviolent, and those violating the law should be willing to suffer the consequences. The church, which had always valued good order, must help determine when the government's laws undermined divine mandates. The policy affirmed civil disobedience as a legitimate Christian response to injustice. While law-breaking still bothered many Christians, most of the Council's denominations had official policies supporting it to some degree, which provided the NCC with sufficient precedent.[82]

Much of America's misguided foreign policy, certain ecumenists believed, was based upon outmoded assumptions about national and international security. Bilheimer's "Imperatives" paper had addressed this topic, but the NCC wanted to push the point further. Therefore, in September, the General Board passed the policy statement "Defense and Disarmament: New Requirements for Security," which analyzed negative repercussions of the bloated military-industrial complex. These included sapping resources from every sector of society and "influenc[ing] virtually all other national decisions." "Military necessity" often subordinated other important values in dehumanizing ways as military policies became "self-validating in actual practice." Additionally, the NCC attacked the dominance of ideological rationales to justify America's military approach to security. "An overly ideological approach to the world's ills," it asserted, "causes distorted interpretations of the facts to fit preconceived ideology."[83] Leaders who considered little else but ideology when assessing world problems often defaulted to using military means to solve them. Again, U.S. Vietnam policy offered the clearest example.

"Defense," the NCC warned, "should never become an end in itself." Thus, it called Christians to help "restore defense to its proper limits," so the civilian and political efforts that could foster genuine security might become preeminent. In accordance with this, the NCC pushed for nuclear arms control, reallocation of resources from defense to development, and empowering the UN to serve as originally intended, that is, "as a peace-keeping and peace-making" agency. Most important, this latest policy statement reiterated Bilheimer's call for a "re-vision" of the traditional American worldview, which still clung to preconceptions about itself and national security that threatened the well-being of both.[84]

This reexamination of America's use of power more sharply articulated why gun barrels could not provide the sort of international, multicultural, and justice-based security that ecumenists sought. America's militaristic approach to global crises stoked resentment throughout the developing world. Church leaders were receiving an earful about this within the international ecumenical community.[85]

CRIES FOR JUSTICE CHALLENGE CHURCH AND STATE

The NCC was set abuzz by the World Council's Fourth Assembly in Uppsala, Sweden, where the voices of marginalized people burst robustly onto center stage. They forced the white Euro-American power structure within the WCC to face its own elitism and Western-biased behaviors. Alan Geyer wrote, "At Uppsala there was a healthy outburst of political action on the part of the underrepresented: women, laymen, youth, black Americans, Third Worlders. It was only when such groups dared to organize, plan strategies and make concerted demands that the assembly became aware of the human issues at stake."[86] The trend had emerged two years earlier at the World Council's Conference on Church and Society. However, the continuing thrust from the margins drew attention to church responsibilities for advancing justice not only globally but also within church structures themselves.[87] Bennett described the WCC as being "shaken" by the pressure from "the neglected people," but, he added, the assembly had purposefully opened itself to face its complicity even though it steered clear of making a radical response.[88] Since renewal was central to the ecumenical mission, church structures must listen, reassess, repent, and adjust constantly, creating fuller unity, when the body of Christ called for it.

Uppsala foreshadowed the NCC's next General Assembly, when it would also be rocked by demonstrations from marginalized groups frustrated with the Protestant establishment. Underrepresented people were calling on the ecumenical councils to live more accountably by their own inclusive-sounding creeds. But as more church leaders adopted new breed approaches to issues, several ecumenists also felt that ecclesiastical bonds and the theological work of unity suffered. For example, Bilheimer said, after Uppsala the WCC became more captive to soapbox-issue pressures rather than being a leader among them.[89] Many who agreed blamed Eugene Carson Blake. Bilheimer and others felt that he privileged liberation action over nurturing the theological roots that held the ecumenical vision together.[90] Again, this was not a criticism of seeking justice for the oppressed but, rather, of using purely new breed approaches. These tended to prioritize one part of the ecumenical vision (that of service-oriented action) over another (that of theological clarity and a developed, articulated witness) when ecumenism required them to work in tandem. Yet, contrary to Bilheimer, many activists criticized the Councils for not being issue-oriented enough.

The Uppsala assembly focused on church responsibility for advancing global justice. It included a strong appeal for economic development and cooperation with the Roman Catholic Church. Debates raged over the Vietnam War as well. The assembly confronted the Vietnam conflict both within its conference halls and outside its doors. Inside, Robert McAfee Brown appealed for a united condemnation of U.S. policy.[91] Folksinger Pete Seeger, who performed there, pleaded for the same. Meanwhile, delegates affiliated with the NCC distributed its Vietnam statements to international church leaders. Elston drew parallels between the German church struggle against Hitler's regime and the American church struggle against the U.S. government over the Vietnam War. These swayed some German Lutheran delegates who had backed the U.S. war effort.[92] Elston felt that the NCC's statements carried weight with the WCC's seven hundred attendees and assisted passage of the assembly's own official condemnation of the war. The assembly endorsed selective conscientious objection as well.[93] Outside its halls, Swedish students had marched forty miles to protest the war there, while local supporters of the Vietcong's NLF solicited donations at the entrances.[94]

Anti-Western sentiments also spewed from the assembly's searing rebuke of the WCC's Commission of the Churches in International Affairs (CCIA), long headed by the American O. Frederick Nolde and the Briton Sir Kenneth Grubb. Many developing world and eastern European delegates, who resented that Americans and Britons had dominated most of the CCIA's leadership positions since its inception, charged it with functioning like "a NATO front." They condemned it for being overly friendly with the U.S. State Department and captive to the U.S. government's worldview. The retirements of both Nolde and Grubb helped quell discontent.[95] The NCC paid particular attention to these international opinions.

The summer of 1968 also opened NCC leaders' eyes to the growing ranks of American deserters overseas. Between sessions at Uppsala the NCC's executive director of the Department of Youth Ministries, John Wood, convinced about thirty American delegates to meet with four young men who had fled to Sweden as draft deserters or AWOL soldiers. Later, about fifty American delegates—including several NCC leaders—signed a statement expressing "general solidarity and concern for these men."[96] This action corresponded with the NCC's and CALCAV's interests in draft counseling and amnesty, drawing attention to the needs of deserter communities and their families.[97] Their work in these areas would expand greatly over the next several years.

On the home front, more violence punctuated the summer campaign season. In June an assassin killed Robert Kennedy the night he won the California primary. The antiwar candidate mostly likely to capture the presidency was dead. With Hubert Humphrey as the new Democratic front-runner, United Methodist leaders and antiwar groups including CALCAV begged the Democratic platform committee to include a peace plank. Methodists admitted later that peace plank supporters erred in assuming that delegates to the Democratic National Convention were accurately informed about the war.[98] The knowledge gap hampered their efforts, as did Humphrey's supporters, and the plank failed. While the leading candidates hoped to end the war, the Republican approach remained hawkish, and Humphrey still stood too closely by Johnson's policies. Negotiations seemed stalled. Frustrations erupted into a violent confrontation between demonstrators and the Chicago police outside of the Democratic National Convention. Television coverage of Humphrey's acceptance speech was interrupted by footage of police in riot gear gassing and beating protesters. The public divided disproportionately between persons horrified by police actions and an apparent silent majority who applauded their get-tough tactics.[99] Reports from church leaders coughing out gas-filled lungs inspired the NCC to pass a resolution on "Justice, Law, Order and Freedom." It addressed both insufficient police training for demonstrations and the police's abuse of authority against "lawful assembly and protest by citizens."[100]

Espy called the summer of 1968 "three months of trauma."[101] But he saw progress, too. The NCC's position on Vietnam had become more popularly accepted, yet he mourned how the war and unresolved racial issues were ripping America apart. He credited the NCC with making issues of power, order, and freedom more central in church discussions. And he told his colleagues that, while ideological and power differences fueled leftist street violence, their own ecumenical motivation to address controversial issues came instead from a Christian desire to enhance people's basic welfare.

While true, ideological and power differences were also tearing at the ecumenical fabric.

For those who ached for constructive change and dared to hope the 1968 elections might bring it, disillusionment became profound. The status quo seemed destined to continue regardless of which political party won the White House. Elston thought the public's popular understanding of the war, as well as its near total rejection of a possible U.S. defeat, blocked progress.[102] In Paris, negotiation teams remained stalemated in entrenched positions.

The New Left was divided, discredited, and growing more violent. Liberals were also divided, despondent, and somewhat directionless.[103] A few radical leaders such as Sid Lens and Dave Dellinger hoped to rejuvenate cooperative antiwar efforts and asked SADIA members for assistance.[104] Specifically, Lens suggested possible church involvement in the Mobe's upcoming "national day of mourning." Interested, ecumenical leaders also flirted with the thought of using Dellinger's influence to secure visas for a church-sponsored visit to North Vietnam.

As confrontation-style protests increased, Americans whom Nixon dubbed the "silent majority" expressed disgust at those labeled radical revolutionaries. Johnson implied that dissent was communist-inspired. Rusk claimed it encouraged enemies to continue fighting a war in which they were being militarily defeated. Nixon and his running mate, Spiro Agnew, called for a return to law and order, insinuating that protesters were subversives who deserved rough treatment. As the public tired of constant conflict and lost patience with activists, the law and order theme appealed to a cross-section of people seeking limits on systemic societal change and a reprieve from domestic chaos. In a paper for SADIA, Elston accurately predicted that post-election U.S. policy would reflect the growing strength of right-wing pressure groups and public conservatism.[105]

So, too, would strained relations between local laity and the NCC. To many Americans, the Council's antiwar statements identified it with the despised dissidents. Laity also resented the NCC's articulation of seemingly unrepresentative views and its perceived disregard for lay opinion.[106] As a result, in September, the Council launched a three-year project to listen to laity.[107] It scheduled a series of consultations around the nation at which churchgoers could express their views on a plethora of subjects. NCC and denominational representatives collected lay input at each one. A lay committee later compiled this data into recommendations for the churches.

Ineffective communication between church bureaucracies and layper-sons certainly contributed to the gap. Not only did the media frequently misrepresent NCC positions, but the Council's communication style was not nimbly adapted to different audiences. Thus, documents crafted for ecumenists' tastes often appeared stylistically dull, elitist, and outdated to others. Stanley Rowland, a communications consultant for the Pres-byterians, criticized the Protestant churches' overdependence upon dry documents to communicate its messages. He cited the NCC's debate and action multimedia packet as an example. In a time of "fluid, fast-changing sounds and images," he observed, "the N.C.C. produced a packet, destined for tens of thousands of churches, which contained printed material plus a record that used sound in the least effective way: printed material voiced on a recording."[108] Rowland wanted church organizations to employ more emotionally engaging media such as television, radio, films, and graphics along with marketing techniques such as catchy logos and tag lines. Con-servative religious bodies, motivated to proselytize, mastered such things far more effectively than liberal ones.[109]

The Council's intellectual policy statements did engage religious institu-tions themselves and held great meaning for church executives; they also provided foundations for action and made the Council's positions clear to government. But as educational and motivational tools for the grass roots, Rowland dubbed them a flop. Why the Council did not transform these into gripping forms for lay audiences is unclear. And, as stated earlier, the NCC relied completely upon the denominations to purchase, use, and interpret its materials to their membership. Its effectiveness, therefore, depended significantly upon the denominations with whom it worked.[110]

The NCC was still waging a public relations image battle against right-wing Christian groups that argued for a different church role in society and tried to discredit the National and World Councils. In the late fall, the conservative Clergymen's Committee on China spent ten thousand dollars to run a full-page ad in the *New York Times*. Boasting thousands of signatures, its central message attacked the foreign affairs stands of the two bodies. The statement, which began, "Millions of Americans are Distressed and Confused By [sic] the political and economic drift to the left by the National and World Councils of Churches," compared ecumenical policy to positions held by communists.[111] It charged the Councils with trying to weaken America's status in the world and undercut its fight against com-munist oppression. The ad then accused the NCC of hypocrisy in its struggle for justice because it paid too little attention to the persecuted within communist nations. "How can we help the poor and oppressed peoples who are the victims of Soviet imperialism, if we continue to dignify and bolster the cause of their oppressors?" it asked.[112] The statement urged the Councils to "return to their most important role as leaders in national and international evangelistic and missionary endeavors." It also encouraged them to steer youth away from "revolutionary activity" and toward respect for authority and country. The Clergymen's Committee felt peace could be more quickly achieved by saving souls and defending current national policy than by promoting protest against it. It was a nationalistic evangelical cry that held sway with people who were tired of strife and eager to return to conservative values and a familiar order. This long-running debate over the church's proper role and relationship with government was as divisive for Christians as were the social issues themselves. Ironically, about ten years later, conservative evangelicals would press themselves heavily into politics to roll back liberal influences on sociocultural affairs.

The gap between the NCC and parishioners was particularly grave in certain denominations. The largely southern Presbyterian Church U.S. seriously debated leaving the Council. Ed Grant, a member of its Inter-Church Relations Committee and a supporter of remaining with the NCC, nevertheless condemned Council leadership for drifting too far from popular sentiment. "As a layman with not too conservative views, I find it more and more difficult to be patient and sympathetic with the ultra-liberal group which now appears to be in control of the National Council of Churches and appears also to regard their function to be that of spokesmen for the liberal social-economic-political wing in the churches. In my judgment," he continued, "they have ceased to be representative of the main stream of our Churches and are risking their position of leadership to become 'Pioneers' in the new order. . . . Pioneers ordinarily work alone. Leaders, on the other hand, have people following them!"[113] Like Rusk, Grant concluded that NCC leaders operated as "generals without armies." Loss of grassroots support led to impotence with parishioners and government regardless of the rightness of Council positions. Then again, Old Testament prophets never took polls to determine God's will. Whether this impotence should matter in a true ecumenical witness or be a barometer of success caused some contention. So did what to do about it.

The Methodist Board of Missions was also dismayed by the Council, but for different reasons. It felt that the NCC should serve the denominations as their "agent." Yet it saw the Council acting more as an autonomous entity that created its own expensive long-term programs, then asked the denominations to fund and rubber-stamp them. Additionally, Methodist leaders resented that NCC staffers received a "much higher salary" than those in member churches. Since the Methodists supplied a substantial proportion of the Council's budget, its discontent carried clout. Lutheran, American Baptist, and Episcopal Churches shared these concerns.[114]

As noted earlier, relations between the NCC and government officials were also strained. The Council's antiwar stand had soured Johnson on the organization, so he refused to meet with its leaders about the war. While Rusk remained cordial with them, he had already dismissed them as lonely bureaucrats of little political use.

Hubert Humphrey who, when senator, enjoyed the enthusiastic support of ecumenists, now saw them disassociating just when he needed them. A few, such as John Bennett and Reinhold Niebuhr, considered presidential candidate Humphrey as the lesser of two evils and gave him their public endorsement. But many others refused to forgive Humphrey for being Johnson's apologist on Vietnam policy and quieted their campaign efforts.[115]

With the election pending, peace negotiators Averell Harriman and Cyrus Vance failed to secure an agreement with the South Vietnamese, who had heard that a Nixon victory might yield them a better deal. On November 5, Richard M. Nixon won the presidency in a tight vote. Recognizing that ecumenical organizations were politically insignificant to him and in apparent league with his enemies, his administration would treat them with icy contempt. Being shut out by the Executive Branch was unusual and puzzling for them. Nixon embraced the religious counsel of evangelist Billy Graham and others of his persuasion, who seemed more in touch with the masses and tacitly supportive of the president's policies. Frustrations caused by lack of White House access would force the Council to develop different strategies for speaking truth to power.

By the end of 1968, the Vietnam War had become unpopular, even though old worldviews remained fixed in the public mind, as did resentment against antiwar activism. The right wing still hoped to end the war through military and political victories. Few Americans were willing to accept defeat and withdraw; they desired the honorable end that Nixon pledged to pursue. Most also wanted U.S. casualties reduced and expected Nixon to seek a quick resolution to the conflict. Therefore, the ecumenical mood in November grew guardedly hopeful. The NCC's longtime appeal for negotiations and a bombing halt had finally become government policy. The Council had also fostered a denominational consensus largely critical of U.S. Vietnam policy. Since the war seemed near to a negotiated conclusion, NCC planning shifted further toward postwar concerns. Little did they know that Nixon would expand the war and commit U.S. troops to four more years of ground combat.

Harder times also lay ahead for the Council. In 1968 it hit its peak in terms of budget and staff size. The declining fortunes of its member churches, combined with dissatisfaction among white constituents, would soon erode its programs and influence. The difficulty of holding a moderate position amid criticism from both left and right, while dealing with an unresponsive Nixon White House, exasperated the Council and necessitated another strategic shift.

PART FOUR

REVOLUTION AND

REVELATION,

DECEMBER

1968-1969

CHAPTER NINE

Courting Nixon, December 1968–Fall 1969

GIVING NIXON THE BENEFIT OF THE DOUBT

Ecumenists approached the 1968 Christmas holiday with the desperate hope that, after a year of heightened violence and division, peace would return soon to Vietnam and America. Allan Parrent thought the war had become such a political albatross that Nixon would seek to end it.[1] John Bennett also rejoiced at what seemed to be clear signals of closure for that wrenching conflict. He wrote, "this new stage in the war and in the negotiations, this new hope that a peace of some kind may be significantly nearer, has been the best news that we have had in many months."[2] Even the antiwar movement quieted substantially. Certain Council leaders took satisfaction in the knowledge that, of the Council's seven points in its December 1965 statement against U.S. policy in Vietnam, the government had adopted four by 1968, and the other three were components of the current Paris peace talks.[3] Therefore, concern shifted toward the stalled talks themselves, the content of a future settlement, postwar healing, and America's postwar policy in Asia.[4]

Since Bilheimer had failed to secure visas to North Vietnam, he and Schomer pondered the possibility of meeting with the North Vietnamese in Paris. A consultation with them and perhaps the NLF might help fulfill the church's responsibility to listen to the "enemy." They were also anxious to discuss factors involved in a peace settlement, Vietnamese views of their country's future, and perhaps the church's role in postwar reconstruction.[5] They wanted new information to update their witness to government or, as Schomer said, "to speak fresh truth on Vietnam to new power, i.e., the Nixon administration."[6]

Schomer worked with Mai Van Bo to complete the arrangements. All four delegations (North Vietnamese, NLF, United States, and South Vietnamese) agreed to separate, parallel consultations with NCC leaders. Each banned the media but permitted the Council to forward meeting content to church leaders and the U.S. government. Bo advised Schomer that any questions regarding the political future of South Vietnam and the representation of "third force" groups (that is, nonaligned noncommunist southerners) should be raised with the NLF, not the North. Therefore, Schomer worked with NLF leaders Nguyen Thi Binh (Madame Binh) and Tran Van Tho to outline an agenda regarding South Vietnam's future.[7]

While making these arrangements, Schomer was stunned to learn of the North Vietnamese's bitter reaction to Johnson's 1965 Johns Hopkins speech that had delighted so many liberal Christians. The Vietnamese, it turned out, did not welcome big U.S. development programs of the sort that the NCC had encouraged Johnson to offer. As Schomer told Bilheimer: "You must hear from his own lips the ugly reception accorded Johnson's Johns Hopkins speech to grasp as I suddenly did on hearing him that all our 'good hearted' American Christian notions of post-war relief, reconstruction or even development schemes are simply not on wave-lengths that Vietnamese who are not on our USA payroll will even tune in on. I think it is very important that Tracey Jones especially hear him," he continued, "for the Methodists are as you know dreaming of many millions to be spent by Jim MacCracken and CWS in 'post war R & R in Vietnam.' I am afraid that our 1945 German (or even Czech and Polish) experience is so irrelevant to the eventual post-war situation in Vietnam that it could lead us into dangerous mistakes in our approaches even now." For Schomer, this wake-up call clearly illustrated that ecumenists, like most other Americans, tended to interpret situations and create solutions from a presumptive Western worldview that did not necessarily match Vietnamese wishes. Such information also reinforced the IAC's reservations about CWS's approach to service work in Vietnam.[8]

The NCC delegation that arrived in Paris on January 4 included Bilheimer, Elston, and Schomer, as well as four members of the NCC's constituency: Harold Berman (IAC member and Harvard Law professor), Rev. Edward Carothers (General Board member, United Methodist), Rev. Paul Empie (DOM member, Lutheran World Federation), and Richard Riseling (IAC member, American Baptist Convention). Over six days, they met for hours with leaders of the four Paris delegations, including Cyrus Vance and Philip Habib for the United States, and with former cabinet officials from the Ngo Dinh Diem, Bao Dai, Thieu/Ky, and Ho Chi Minh governments. They also talked with several Buddhist leaders, Vietnamese neutralists, and French experts.[9] The Vietnamese emphasized the overriding importance of nationalism, not communism, and their desire to be free from foreign interference.

Some within the NCC drew hope from the prospect that third force elements in South Vietnam might help bring peace. By "third force," they were referring to noncommunist nationalists who were not allied with Thieu's government. These included popular Buddhists and other religious and secular leaders such as students, labor organizers, and intellectuals who might help create a peaceful solution to the conflict. Some church officials believed that American and third force religious groups might cooperate toward this end. In fact, certain liberals had entertained this prospect back in 1965, but by mid-1967 many pacifists had abandoned the notion as unrealistic. Al Hassler and others in FOR still clung to it, however. Liberal antiwar anticommunists were especially drawn to this idea because it presented a truly Vietnamese solution without playing into communist hands.[10]

While the NCC did not officially endorse the third force option, Schomer favored it, as did Homer Jack (of the Unitarian Universalist Association and SANE), Barton Hunter (Disciples of Christ), and many within Negotiations Now! Elston and Bilheimer doubted the idea's practicality. Aware of the diversity among South Vietnam's Buddhists and other noncommunist religious groups, and knowing that these entities held more political and cultural significance than religious power, they questioned whether an interreligious third force coalition was possible or politically useful. Nevertheless, Bilheimer promised he would not automatically discount any idea about resolving the war.[11]

Some who traveled to Paris in early 1969 still saw possibilities for a third force role. The NCC report made clear that these particular ecumenical leaders favored preserving an independent South, provided that it was truly nationalist, representative, and free from foreign (especially Western) manipulation. As they affirmed in their confidential notes, "we believe that a new national government, formed as a result of the negotiations, would not result in a communist takeover, but would provide time . . . for peaceful competition between communist and non-communist elements." They added that, "The best wisdom of the knowledgeable Vietnamese people with whom we have talked is that there is still a chance for the war to be ended with relative political independence for South Vietnam, under a mixed socialist-capitalist economy and within the framework of a constitutional government. . . . [T]he power of southern regionalism would seem to be a strong factor in keeping any new national government independent of Hanoi and in providing a milieu in which a 'southern' political evolution might take place."[12] The Council's right-wing critics, who type-cast it as a naïve supporter of communist revolutions, were flat wrong. Unlike some antiwar activists, the NCC never glorified communism. But unlike many on the right, Council staff did not let their anticommunist preferences trump their dedication to self-determination and justice for people.

South Vietnam's success, they felt, depended upon the ability of third force elements to organize politically. But the Thieu/Ky regime prevented this through intimidation and imprisonment. And the hobbling of third force groups eliminated all competition for the NLF, which remained the only viable nationalist alternative to that perceived puppet government. Therefore, it seemed essential to expose and discredit the Thieu/Ky regime while encouraging the politically active nationalism of other South Vietnamese groups.[13] Nondelegation Vietnamese and French experts told Elston that NLF leaders were realists willing to share political power with third force nationalists. Paul Empie and Richard Riseling agreed that the NLF seemed more open to the notion of a "broadly based government in South Vietnam" than did the North Vietnamese.[14] Therefore, it puzzled church leaders that U.S. officials ignored or discounted these pockets of regional noncommunist nationalism in the South, as well as the inherent nationalism within the Vietcong, while pursuing American objectives through corrupt autocrats. The NCC team raised this matter with the State Department's William Bundy.[15] It also shared its findings at a confidential gathering of the Advisory Committee on Peace to which U Thant spoke. The General Board received the team's report during its January meeting, recognizing "that this is one of the most complex problems ever to have existed on this planet."[16]

While in Paris, the NCC delegation met Paul Tran, a former pupil of Schomer's, who had established Vietnamese contacts both in Paris and Vietnam, particularly with third force Buddhists.[17] Bilheimer hired Tran to serve as the NCC's informal confidential "agent," charged with keeping the Council appraised of changing dynamics within the peace talks and South Vietnam. Bilheimer told Tran he was interested in "any developments . . . which might have a bearing upon a peaceful and good solution to the conflict." Tran's detailed reports would help the NCC shape its positions on South Vietnam.[18] He also became a fruitful source of Vietnamese contacts for Elston.

To aid third force elements, the NCC supported Hoa Binh, a group that sought to expose the Thieu regime's undemocratic nature and stimulate American rejection of it. Back in late 1968, the NCC had helped create this independent ad hoc group in order to explore the viability of a third force option. "Hoa Binh" meant "Peace." Despite his skepticism, Elston joined, along with Rodney Shaw (Methodist), Robert Fangmeier (Disciples of Christ), Barton Hunter, Gene Stoltzfus, Homer Jack, Al Hassler, and Buddhist leader Tran Van Dinh. The group met monthly to explore what American and Vietnamese religious groups might do to advance negotiations and publicize the truth about Thieu's government.[19]

Many gifted third force leaders languished in jail as political prisoners. This situation was unlikely to change as long as the United States tacitly supported Thieu's police state tactics. And Nixon would have little motivation to challenge the regime if U.S. officials and voters remained silent, ignorant, or apathetic about Thieu's undemocratic practices. Throughout the first part of 1969, Hoa Binh brainstormed ways to raise public awareness and convince Nixon to retract support from Saigon's military regime. They knew it would be difficult but felt compelled to try.[20]

Hassler urged the ecumenical community to send a study team of influential religious and secular leaders to South Vietnam to investigate and expose its corrupt repressive nature. The group could also meet with third force leaders, assess their strength, and bring them more international attention. Elston and Schomer helped refine this idea and recruit financial sponsors. South Vietnam's human rights violations and the imprisonment of popular Buddhist leaders were drawing increased press coverage as well as the ire of antiwar activists.[21] Don Luce's shocking article entitled "Behind Vietnam's Prison Walls" did much to validate the need for investigation.[22] The piece described young people imprisoned for months for merely advocating peace, and it told of torturous interrogations and horrific prison conditions endured by the South's political dissidents. The fact that the world's premier democracy was defending such brutality seemed like a strong leverage point to woo the public. With peace activity and congressional interest in a post-election lull, Hoa Binh hoped these revelations might refuel the peace process. At the same time, they took care to ensure that their presentation of the third force option did not fuel anticommunist hysteria.[23] Plans for a late spring study team trip to South Vietnam gathered momentum.

CALCAV jumped on board as a sponsor. Concern for human rights, promoting political freedom, and exposing America's hypocritical support of dictators in Vietnam and Central America were key agenda items for CALCAV in 1969. Its interest in the rights of dissenters in Vietnam was mirrored by its efforts to expand their numbers in America.

During CALCAV's third religious mobilization in Washington, it created a ministry to U.S. draft deserters and AWOL soldiers in Sweden. On the steps of the Justice Department, several CALCAV leaders and Coretta Scott King laid hands upon the young Episcopal priest, Tom Hayes, to commission this work. Hayes spent the year helping deserters navigate the Swedish legal system, assimilate into its society, and meet basic needs. This outreach grew out of the earlier NCC-led visit to the deserter community during the World Council's Uppsala assembly. Throughout the year, Fernandez also investigated the situation of American deserters in Canada. By year-end, he and Elston would draw the NCC into a joint ministry with the Canadian Council of Churches.[24]

CALCAV leaders failed to meet with Nixon, but they secured an audience with Henry Kissinger, the president's National Security adviser, instead. Gerhard Elston, Richard Fernandez, William Sloane Coffin Jr., Richard John Neuhaus, Coretta Scott King, and Rabbi Abraham Heschel questioned Kissinger about Nixon's objectives in Paris and potential amnesty for resisters.[25] According to the *New York Times*, "it was the first such prearranged visit to the White House by militant spokesmen for any organization of vocal dissent—on either the peace or civil rights issues—in three years."[26] Elston credited Coretta Scott King's presence as the sole reason the meeting was granted. He relished watching Heschel, another German Jew, "wrestle for Kissinger's soul." Heschel confronted Kissinger with a subject that cut to the core of German Jewish history: the abuse of state power. Kissinger remained unmoved. He also defended the credibility of South Vietnam's constitution, which barred the political participation of communists. South Vietnamese officials used this to justify suppressing all dissent. Fresh from Paris, Elston replied that a third force peace government could probably be framed under that constitution. Kissinger feigned interest and asked Elston to call him later with input. When Elston tried, however, the new White House staff would not forward his call. This foreshadowed a pattern. In a follow-up letter, Elston enclosed the NCC's Paris report and mentioned that church leaders sometimes received information beyond that given to government officials. He closed with words designed to distinguish civic-minded, reasonable church leaders from antiwar revolutionaries. "In seeking to put our views before you, let me assure you that we are moved by slowly and painfully achieved insights and convictions and a deep concern for the United States integrity and security."[27]

In February 1969 Nixon and his administration remained unknown commodities. This is strange to say about a politician who had worked under the public's critical eye for decades. Since his inglorious defeat and ignoble press conference following the 1962 California governor's race, Nixon had resurrected and reshaped his image.[28] As Roger Shinn described in *Christianity and Crisis*, "This has been the mature Nixon, claiming the middle of the road as adroitly as Lyndon Johnson before him. . . . Curiously this veteran of two decades of public controversy enters the White House without disclosing his hand on the major issues he must face."[29] The cold warrior curtailed his combative comments enough to evoke a more stately, relaxed, likable air in the presidential campaign. Ecumenists waited for this statesmanlike Nixon to provide a peaceable direction on Vietnam. Johnson, who had been so accessible on civil rights, had denied NCC leaders audiences after they criticized his Vietnam policy. Would Nixon be more open to them? His administration's style also remained a mystery. Shinn said that William Rogers, who replaced Dean Rusk as secretary of state, possessed a reputation for "skill and integrity." The new defense secretary, Melvin Laird, had a hawkish past. But like Nixon, Laird had remained tactful and unprovocative enough to instill hope that recent events had made him wiser. In this "period of crossed fingers," Bennett indicated that peace advocates tentatively gave Nixon the benefit of the doubt.[30] The NCC hoped that Nixon might even turn his ear its way.

Council optimism about relations with Nixon blossomed because it assumed it had an inside contact within his administration, and personal connections usually meant a great deal in Washington. Arthur Flemming, NCC president, had served in Eisenhower's cabinet as secretary of health, education, and welfare along with Rogers while Nixon was vice president. These three Republicans had worked side by side and still addressed each other on a familiar basis. Council leaders presumed that Nixon and Rogers would respect Flemming's expertise and not dismiss him outright as an uninformed liberal churchperson. They hoped Flemming's credibility and connections with the president's administration might provide an entrée through which to impact the thinking of policy makers.

Nixon fostered the entertainment of that possibility. Shortly after the election, Flemming wrote Nixon to share the Council's Vietnam policy concerns. Nixon responded graciously and encouraged more detailed discussion. His new team was taking a fresh look, he said, and welcomed others' insights. Nixon also assured Flemming "that this will be an open Administration sensitive to a wide variety of efforts and ideas."[31] Promising that the Council's concerns would be given "careful consideration," Nixon suggested Flemming might pursue discussions with Bill Rogers. The invitation seemed genuine, and Nixon's open demeanor sincere. It thrilled Flemming and other Council staff, who began brainstorming about how to maximize this prized opportunity.

Bilheimer was eager to make the most of their White House witness. He saw the nation as suffering a severe identity crisis, compounded by shifting worldviews, and believed that the church must help "interpret the nation to itself." As he elaborated in the *Christian Century*, "the church's task is to hold before that nation in transition the highest source of identity and the best concepts of national interest."[32] But ecumenical leaders no longer held sway as in past years. Not wishing to appear again as isolated bureaucrats and still trusting that big names get heard, the Council assembled a "wise men's" meeting of its own. This included over thirty prestigious cultural leaders who gathered to discuss U.S. Vietnam policy and draft recommendations to Nixon for ending the war.[33] From mid-April through June, Schomer coordinated the details while Elston traveled to South Vietnam to collect updated information for this conference.

MALAISE DAYS—FINANCIAL DECLINE, STRUCTURAL CHALLENGE, AND ANGRY PARISHIONERS

As with the nation itself, identity concerns also rocked the NCC. While unhappy traditional churchgoers denounced the Council's inattention to their spiritual desires, left-leaning youth and minorities disliked the Council's devotion to the establishment. For example, to escape bureaucratic entanglements and compromises, the University Christian Movement voted itself into extinction. The UCM had operated as an independent part of the Council and was the progeny of the Student Christian Movement, a prolific seedbed for ecumenical leadership.[34] Its loss removed a vital training ground for young ecumenists. The left was attacking the "old white-male" establishment everywhere, and the NCC embodied it as well as any institution. To many on the left, the stodgy denominations and their church councils were betraying the cause of justice by adhering to their institutional, insular, old-boys-club methods instead of joining the activist revolution to restructure—or better yet, dismantle—the "establishment."[35] These realities converged at a time when the nation was torn by violent protests and bold demonstrations. Situated in upper Manhattan near Columbia University, Union Theological Seminary, Riverside Church, and Harlem, the NCC had a front row seat to many of them. By year-end, the Council itself would become a major stage.

Eugene Carson Blake advised America's ecumenical churches to focus more on joint action and less on institutional turf wars. Addressing the NCC's General Board in January, the WCC leader said, "If any of you here want the world or young people or poor people or the business community to take you seriously, break out of the denominational straightjacket that still is the most crippling factor in the church of Jesus Christ."[36] Weeks later, Methodist Dudley Ward complained of an "'institutional malaise' afflicting both the N.C.C. and some, if not all, denominations." He cited a spiritless "casual kind of resigned action" in the Council's administrative committee work that produced poor results. Ward knew this problem pervaded the mainline churches, but he still urged the NCC to reappraise its own "role, function and purpose" and attend to its "inner sickness." The denominations had a head start, he claimed, for "It is natural for us to take our responsibilities on our home base more seriously." He then challenged the NCC staff's effectiveness. "I can recall the time when the people who were serving the National Council, as representatives of their denominations, were really very, very serious and dedicated in the work they performed for the N.C.C. While our motivation may still be present, there is a deep seated resistance, reaction, and evidently less than serious attempts to deal with some of the crucial issues facing us in this arm of the ecumenical movement."[37]

While Espy agreed with Ward's identification of certain symptoms, he rejected Ward's diagnosis and defended the Council's dedication to quality. "To whatever extent motivation can be measured by input of time, energy and commitment," he rebutted, "I never have known a time in my fourteen years with the Council when the staff has shown a greater dedication. / This is not to say that there are not many frustrations. You are quite right in your basic thesis that there is a malaise both in the bureaucracy of the churches and those of the National Council."[38] Espy tied the trouble to both internal church dynamics and the "external forces of our time." Responsively, the NCC formed an internal "Reappraisal Committee" to explore the malady's origin as well as the funding shortfall that exacerbated it.

The committee's preliminary report noted sharp drops in funds for all Council programs, which reflected the denominations' growing financial difficulties. This shortage compounded an "already critical efficiency and productivity problem."[39] The report urged immediate "substantive and comprehensive budget cuts" as well as restructuring to slim down the NCC's unwieldy bureaucracy. This would require the reassessment of its functions and roles. It also recommended a reevaluation of current programs to see how well they met the needs of NCC "clients." Both of the two major Council-wide projects—the Peace Priority Program and the Crisis in the Nation Program, which dealt with poverty and race relations—were criticized for falling short of expectations. Some General Board members blamed a "crisis of confidence between denominational and N.C.C. personnel." Charles Spivey, director of Crisis in the Nation, pointed his finger back at denominational leaders, charging them with being too absorbed in "their own programs without any coordination" through the NCC. Bilheimer had leveled similar complaints. Conversely, Geyer blamed a systemic cause. "Whatever the personality factors involved," he said, "there appears to be a structural contradiction in such crash programs: it takes a mighty upsurge of moralistic bombast to turn the ecumenical establishment toward new priorities, but that very bombast raises hopes which cannot be realized within existing styles and structures."[40] With respect to Vietnam, denominational leaders' expectations of what the Council could accomplish regarding mass education and impact on government policy were probably unrealistic. Nevertheless, the Reappraisal Committee began investigating such matters. Its work would take several years, but its initial analysis foreshadowed sources of snowballing struggles.

The financial plight especially worried Bilheimer because he knew cuts might hit his department hardest. He told denomination heads that the Council could not depend upon laity to support the church's international affairs programs. "Peace and international affairs is not, in spite of much lip service to the contrary, a popular subject among the rank and file of the churches."[41] Money for that work, he believed, must be dedicated by a group of denominational executives personally committed to it. Bilheimer was being realistic. He felt the critical world situation made his department's work essential. In fact, he recommended increased funds, commitment, and staff. While the "rank and file" might not understand this, Bilheimer hoped that his enlightened brethren would see as he did and not balance their thinning budgets by slashing disbursements to his program. But this was wishful thinking. The Methodists were already asking Bilheimer to spend more conservatively and eliminate the expensive Advisory Committee on Peace, which Ward felt had outlived its usefulness.[42]

The ecumenical press was also pondering problems within organized Protestantism and, in early 1969, produced a stream of articles eager to analyze its maladies. A writer for the *Christian Century* created a causal list with which many observers (including Dean Kelley) agreed. These included a future-shock effect fed by information and action overload; "ecumenical doldrums" or a "ho-hum" attitude about the ecumenical movement after the natural demise of its newness; a reactionary fatigue by church people "tired of hearing how awful we are as a church"; and perhaps most important, a "devotional emptiness" that was reflected in a tepid, shriveled, unmotivated piety. The last could mean death to a religious community. As the writer aptly described, "We Protestants have invented many rationalized substitutes for devotional discipline: social activism, parish therapies, intellectual thirst, ecclesiastical 'Monopoly' games. . . . without devotional life they will pall and turn into parlor calisthenics rather than the acts of a redeeming community. / . . . In theology, [Jesus] has become a bloodless noun, bandied about more like a 'concept' than a person."[43]

To Kelley, the mainline denominations had not nurtured the spiritual connection between personal faith and social action that was apparent in the lives of ecumenists like Bilheimer and Elston. He felt that these denominations tried to browbeat (and sometimes guilt-trip) their parishioners into social action without having engendered a mutually enriching link between one's love for Jesus and working for justice, both domestically and in international affairs. Another writer for the *Century* illustrated the problem by saying that parishioners "are tired of hearing about the United Nations on Sunday instead of Jesus Christ." It was "a conflict in lay-clergy relations" that magnified the "widening chasm between the conservers and the renewers of American Protestantism."[44]

The Council itself was suspended over this chasm and being wrenched in two by forces tugging from both sides. Conservative Christians criticized the NCC for being too socially active, distant, unresponsive, elitist, and unrepresentative of most believers while liberal clergy rebuked it for being too invested in the status quo, bureaucratic structures, and an old boys' network that stymied necessary cultural changes. Then there were leaders such as Grover Hartmann of the Indiana Council of Churches, who encouraged the NCC to stay the middle course. Fearing it was more responsive to critics on the left and hence sliding in that direction, he implored the NCC to cling to its main constituency and financial source: those occupying the moderate, law-abiding middle ground.[45]

An ecumenical council with over thirty diverse communions had little choice but to strike a moderate pose. Yet surprisingly, its blend of relaying a prophetic message using establishment-based methods made it more adversaries than friends. Most Council leaders assumed that "speaking truth to power" required a reasoned nonpartisan stance if one wanted to be heard and heeded by government. With this in mind, in the spring of 1969, the Council helped orchestrate two major projects designed to challenge Nixon's thinking on Vietnam.

AMBITIOUS ATTEMPTS TO ATTRACT WHITE HOUSE ATTENTION

Sending the high-profile "Study Team on Religious and Political Freedom" to South Vietnam was not an NCC-sponsored project. However, certain NCC leaders such as Elston and Schomer—as well as denominational staff—were centrally involved.[46] Hoa Binh had originally proposed the idea of deploying a group of American civic leaders to investigate reports of religious and political oppression in South Vietnam. This study team aimed to execute that mission as well as interview Vietnamese religious leaders about the potential connection between "free religious expression . . . and the possibilities for a political solution that would bring peace."[47] The information gathered would then be shared with Nixon's administration and the media. As with the NCC's earlier Mission of Concern, study team members were chosen for their unique expertise, status, perspective, and respectability. They included John Pemberton (ACLU executive director), John Conyers (Michigan congressman), Rabbi Seymour Siegel (Jewish Theological Seminary professor), Robert Drinan

(Boston College Law School dean), Rear Admiral Arnold True (U.S. Navy, retired), Bishop James Armstrong (United Methodist Church), Anne Bennett (active layperson, wife of John Bennett), and Allan Brick (FOR associate secretary). It was a remarkable group, whose observations, organizers felt, should draw serious attention.

Prior to its departure on May 25, the team met with a Kissinger aide who insisted that Saigon was opening up to free expression and reducing its number of political prisoners. After a week's investigation, the team rejected this claim. It had interviewed President Thieu, Interior Minister Khiem, Ambassador Bunker, General Abrams, and several student, Buddhist, Catholic, university, and other cultural leaders, not to mention current and past prisoners. It had also toured prisons, including the infamous Con Son Island where political inmates languished. As a result, the team determined that South Vietnam's widespread repression was worsening. Meanwhile, the United States was funding a $1.3 million addition to the overcrowded Con Son Island, expanding its capacity to house more victims.[48]

Thieu defended his constitutional right to lock up anyone who advocated a coalition or peace government, because coalition-building implied cooperation with communists. Enforcing the constitution Thieu-style involved police state tactics and torture to ply confessions. The team concluded that his government survived on U.S. money and authority, not popular support, and did not represent the will of the people. Additionally, America's military interference was destroying the nation it claimed to save. Regarding the viability of third force groups, the team confirmed that, while unorganized, Buddhist leaders clearly sought reconciliation and peace, and they reflected sentiments shared by large segments of the population.[49] Its final analysis was clear. The United States was party to a travesty of flouted democratic values and human rights.

Team members spent days discussing, evaluating, and drafting their report. From Saigon, they telegrammed their conclusions to Nixon just before he departed for Midway Island to meet Thieu.[50] "There must be no illusion that this climate of political and religious suppression is compatible with either a representative or stable government," they stated pointedly. "We respectfully request that you consider this in weighing any commitments to the Thieu government." Nixon knew the public expected him to disengage U.S. troops from the war. At Midway, he declared the beginning of what Laird tagged the "Vietnamization" process.[51] This involved the slow withdrawal of some ground troops, to be replaced by South Vietnamese soldiers, combined with an escalation of U.S. air support. Twenty-five thousand Americans would come home in the first batch. Nixon added later that he would not "impose a purely military solution on the battlefield." To the delight of ecumenists, he also claimed that the United States would "accept any government in South Vietnam that results from the free choice of the South Vietnamese people themselves," including the possibility they might elect to reunify with the North.[52] But while seeking to reduce U.S. casualties through Vietnamization, Nixon concurrently tried to bomb the enemy into submission. Thieu reluctantly accepted Nixon's approach. According to information the NCC received from an anonymous Vietnamese third force scholar, "Thieu obtained no guarantee whatsoever for his government, and he had to face a series of demands from President Nixon tending to liberalize his regime."[53]

Days before the study team's departure, on May 22, Allan Parrent and four other church representatives met with Kissinger's primary staffer on Vietnam, Dean Moor, to share their impatience with the stagnant peace process. Moor stated flatly that the United States was committed to Theiu's government and would not push faster than it could tolerate. However, the United States was encouraging greater flexibility. Like Johnson, Moor said, Nixon used military might to maintain America's bargaining power. He insisted that this did not imply Nixon would escalate the war or seek a military victory. Moor admitted that the administration saw little potential in a third force option that seemed factious and weak, although the possibility of an "expanded GVN" (that is, Government of [South] Vietnam) remained. But the administration remained opposed to creation of a coalition government that included the NLF prior to Thieu-administered elections. Moor doubted as well that South Vietnam's political repression was as severe as peace groups claimed. This especially disturbed his visitors. So too did his adherence to Rusk-like presuppositions, including the domino theory and the necessity of projecting America's winning image globally to bolster world order and national security.[54]

The official report of the U.S. Study Team on Religious and Political Freedom failed to capture Nixon's attention. According to the *New York Times*, it "received a routine acknowledgment but no indication of any action" from the administration.[55] The group secured an audience with the undersecretary of state, Elliot Richardson. However, Representative Conyers described Richardson's reaction as "stiff, formal and unsympathetic." This lackluster response sorely disappointed the visitors. So did the paucity of media coverage. Determined to expose Saigon's repression to his colleagues, Conyers transcribed the team's report into the *Congressional Record* and rallied seven other legislators to promote the findings with statements.[56] But this was not the groundswell of interest planners had sought.

Meanwhile, the Council's IAC was following a similar strategy of gathering a competent, culturally elite group to study the Vietnam issue, reach consensus, and then present findings to Nixon that might affect his policies. In June, under Bilheimer's direction and Schomer's coordination, the Council hosted over thirty business, legal, educational, religious, civil rights, media, military, and government leaders at the prestigious Century Club to discuss America's Vietnam policy options.[57] Its official name was the NCC's Consultation on Vietnam Policy Options, but staff tagged it the "Wise Men's Conference" after those held by Johnson before and after the Tet Offensive.

Schomer spent months organizing it. As Bilheimer said, "Schomer had a real flair for dealing with the big boys, and he got them."[58] He even persuaded the notable Korean War commander, retired general Matthew Ridgway, to contribute a paper outlining his assessment of America's Vietnam options for group consideration.[59] While serving as army chief of staff, Ridgway had urged Eisenhower not to rescue the French at Dien Bien Phu in 1954, for he knew how precarious such a mission would be. His input to this consultation drew high respect. Meanwhile, Bilheimer sent Elston to assemble current information on both the peace process and the war for use as background materials.[60]

Paul Tran provided Elston with up-to-date information from Paris. Through secret advisers to the three Vietnamese delegations there, Tran learned that all parties expected Nixon to strive for an end to the war. U.S. negotiators wanted to resolve it by the midterm elections. So they pressed the South Vietnamese to clean up their government, contribute more strongly to their own war effort, and prepare for the postwar political participation of the NLF. This embittered Theiu's representatives. While Tran hoped for a settlement, he foresaw at least eighteen more months of difficult diplomacy ahead.[61]

Flying to Paris, Bilheimer talked with Mai Van Bo directly about negotiations, Nixon's approach, and the POW situation.[62] There he heard Bo call Nixon "perfidious," explaining that his talk of peace was betrayed by actions designed to preserve U.S. colonialism. Bo did not trust Nixon or believe that he wanted a quick end to the war. Nixon's meeting with Thieu at Midway fueled Bo's suspicions, for Thieu subsequently declared to the press that he would persecute supporters of a coalition or peace government. It did not appear, then, that Nixon had scolded Thieu about his oppressive policies. Regarding the peace process, Bo insisted upon U.S. withdrawal without preconditions, settlement negotiations based upon the NLF's ten-point program, and formation of an interim coalition government to administer free elections in the South. The notion of legitimate Thieu-administered elections struck him as ridiculous.

In early May, Elston had flown to South Vietnam to study the scene; it was his fourth trip to the war zone in two years. Based upon discussions with Vietnamese contacts in Saigon and surrounding provinces, Elston determined that GVN efforts to increase its control, operational efficiency, and political base were largely superficial.[63] The White House interpreted these too optimistically. What mattered most, he emphasized, were the deep feelings of the Vietnamese people, which American officials routinely dismissed. Elston thought the United States lacked competent interpreters and a realistic appraisal of the country's dynamics. It was overly dependent upon statistics and too ego-invested in South Vietnam's operational "success" to see objectively. Functioning as a police state, and dependent upon a foreign power, Thieu's regime lacked significant public support. In Vietnamese terms, it did not possess the "will of Heaven."[64] Without this, it engendered little respect or confidence that it would endure.

Meanwhile, the NLF was preparing to enter the political arena. With the onset of peace talks, Elston knew the NLF assumed that "the military phase of the war is over and that the political engagement is about to become decisive." Therefore it shifted some of its attention to infrastructural, political, cultural, and economic planning. (This may have led to recently touted "allied military progress" in some areas, Elston surmised.) The South Vietnamese government, however, had "nothing to match this." With regard to Vietnamese popular sentiment, Elston found anticommunist feelings among the educated ranks and in religious communities. But most people wanted the NLF involved in an open political process. Elston also discerned general apathy about the type of postwar government that might be formed. Peace was the dominant desire. Not surprisingly, citizens exhibited little faith in the electoral process, which, for South Vietnam, had long been corrupt. Few expressed admiration for the GVN's constitution, which many seemed eager to scrap. Gauging third force possibilities, Elston found masses of people ready to back a nationalist "popular movement," but leaders had not been able to organize. Buddhists were eager to try, provided they could do so without retribution.[65]

The NCC's wise men received Elston's report prior to the consultation of June 20–21. On June 30, the Council sent Nixon a formal letter summarizing their recommendations for settling the Vietnam conflict. It urged that Nixon seek to end the war justly rather than simply de-Americanize it.[66] To do so, consultation members suggested that he reduce the military aspect of the conflict rather than use it to increase U.S. bargaining power; additionally, Nixon should strive via the Paris talks to assemble a truly representative "interim body" empowered to create a viable permanent South Vietnamese government, order foreign forces to leave, and then decide South Vietnam's future relative to the North. The letter also asked Nixon to call Thieu's bluff by declaring that America would no longer assist a government that denied basic political freedoms, access, and involvement. Regarding Vietnamization, the wise men wanted Nixon to set a final troop withdrawal date. And they requested that the United States be generous with humanitarian relief and development aid for both South and North Vietnam after the war.

Flemming attached a cover note that explained how North Vietnam's hardening of positions since the consultation had mildly altered some participants' perspectives.[67] Congressmen Morse and McCloskey, specifically, recognized the increased difficulty of setting a withdrawal date as well as pursuing negotiations in the demilitarized manner suggested. But they held to their basic objectives. The Council's Executive Committee endorsed the wise men's letter as fitting with official NCC policy, and Bilheimer supported using it as the NCC's "platform."[68]

Careful to observe proper decorum, Flemming did not want the letter made public until Nixon had had time to read it, nor until the Council had secured an appointment with him or Rogers.[69] Therefore, the NCC delayed publication until July 3. The day before the July 4 holiday was an exceedingly poor release date, drawing negligible media attention. Schomer, who was in Chicago, found no mention of the letter in that city's four main papers. "Wise man" and former ambassador Edwin O. Reischauer echoed the same about Boston's papers. The *Washington Post*, *Wall Street Journal* and *Christian Science Monitor* ignored it as well. Schomer was apoplectic over this missed opportunity. Frustrations would rise further.

On July 11, Rogers met with Flemming, Schomer, Bilheimer, and three others for an hour to discuss the consultation's proposals. He had received a copy of the recommendations days before the meeting, but when they sat down to discuss it, Rogers obviously had not read it. This shocked them, for Rusk had always greeted NCC delegations with their statements in hand and red-marked full of comments. Since Flemming had served with Rogers in Eisenhower's cabinet, he assumed they could discuss policy respectfully with one another. But Rogers did not let Flemming, Bilheimer, or other church leaders talk, and he showed little interest in listening to their ideas. Rather, he lectured them about their patriotic duty as "potential public opinion makers" to support Nixon's initiatives while scolding them for not chastising Hanoi enough.[70] Clearly, Rogers cared little about the policy recommendations of the Council's delegation or the prestigious cultural leaders whom they represented. Rather, he tried to use the meeting "to enlist the churches" in the administration's agenda. At times, Rogers even vented his anger about William Fulbright's and George McGovern's supposed "collusion with the enemy." Schomer felt that Rogers's demeanor was "very defensive [and] reminiscent of the Rusk performance in his latter days of fatigue." All of Bilheimer's attempts to refocus Rogers upon Vietnam policy questions, Schomer said, were "brushed aside without any evidence of either interest [or] comprehension." Rogers was clearly annoyed by the NCC's refusal to be useful to the government. Flemming was personally offended by his discourtesy, and Bilheimer was livid. Adding insult to injury, as of July 14, Nixon had not yet acknowledged the wise men's letter. Afterward, Schomer insightfully surmised that Kissinger was really the person to pursue on Vietnam. He told Bilheimer, "Rogers and Lodge maintain[ed] the public show while Nixon and Kissinger direct[ed] the real action behind this facade."[71]

Desperate to garner some positive result from what seemed a fiasco, Schomer asked Bilheimer, "how can we possibly re-coup on the failure to accomplish what we set out to do in April with our intense Vietnam policy-changing drive? I do feel that our next steps had better be based on the awkward recognition that neither of our two objectives—'to prod Nixon toward indispensable changes of direction in his Vietnam policy' and 'to mobilize public support for these changes'—has been advanced in any significant way." Furious with Flemming for nixing the idea of a press conference after meeting Rogers, Schomer said, "it looks as if he closed out our last opportunity to make a direct impact on the public with the group statement."[72]

As with the 1967 Mission of Concern, the study team and wise men efforts both aimed to witness to and influence the Nixon administration by winning its respect. To do so, they all used high-ranking, moderate, knowledgeable elites from several fields of expertise to collect data and assemble recommendations undergirded by Christian concerns. The wise men's consultation especially exuded a nonpartisan spirit and bent over backward to show the president every courtesy. Nixon had signaled early to the NCC that he would welcome such advances. Yet this proved to be a ruse. While the study team received a little attention from Congress and the media, all told the Council failed to garner much public interest or even be heard by an administration that had deemed the Council politically useless. Indeed, as Nixon made his condescension clear, Bilheimer shifted strategies again. Respectful elite delegations armed with facts and polite discussions of presuppositional differences had failed to move either Johnson or Nixon. This freed the NCC to focus upon making a pure ecumenical witness—without having to genuflect as it tried to get presidential attention. Soon Bilheimer began to unite the churches in crafting a moral witness that was designed to challenge the president's own moral authority.

Planning sessions of the antiwar movement's "Fall Offensive" still bubbled with hope for making a positive national impact. Elston and Fernandez were already organizing for upcoming "New Mobe" and Moratorium events. The Council was also preparing for its next triennial General Assembly in December. However, James Forman's Black Manifesto and occupation of NCC offices complicated matters.[73]

THE BLACK MANIFESTO AND QUESTIONS OF JUSTICE

James Forman and the Black Manifesto became unavoidable preoccupations from May through December. This issue also illustrated the bind in which the Council found itself as a liberal, justice-minded bureaucracy dominated by white men faithfully invested in the establishment. The NCC strove to help end injustice; but Forman declared that the NCC and its white churches were part of the problem, and he demanded financial restitution. In May and June, Forman staged disruptive sit-ins not only in NCC offices but also at the headquarters of the United Presbyterian Church, the United Methodist Church, the United Church of Christ, and the Reformed Church in America.[74] In addition, he seized the pulpit during a Sunday service at

Riverside Church in order to publicize the manifesto. It demanded five hundred million dollars in reparations from white churches to the black community for their collaboration in repression. Several seminarians at Union, as well as persons involved in the religious organizations above, sympathized with Forman and the Black Economic Development Conference, which adopted him as leader.

Yet church leaders split over how to handle Forman and respond to the manifesto's demands. Forman and his sympathizers caused such disruption at the Interchurch Center that its trustees threatened Forman with a court injunction and refused to discuss issues until his entourage left the premises, which it did. The injunction idea was dropped, but the Interchurch Center did secure a temporary restraining order against Forman. This created terrible dissension among the staff. Espy helped facilitate an open meeting where workers assembled to discuss the affair. Forman showed up spontaneously with a coterie of media to make his case. Church leaders, in turn, explained why they had obtained the restraining order. Ultimately, the employees voted against using such tactics. As one NCC official explained, "the legal route was a dead end for institutions that believe in moral suasion."[75]

At one point, Forman's followers spread their sit-in to Bilheimer's office.[76] They accused him of "selling out" by focusing on Vietnam rather than on racism at home. Bilheimer found that accusation tough to handle. He took to heart their resentment that churches had budgeted hundreds of thousands of dollars to the Peace Priority Program but nowhere near that amount to black churches, economic conferences, and caucus programs administered by blacks. He understood their discontent. He also knew that white guilt was an effective button to push at the Council. Race was the hottest issue in the churches then—and people's attention shifted on a dime from Vietnam to race when triggered by events like this.

While Forman's abrasive style made most church leaders uncomfortable, many understood his argument and recognized some validity therein. But white laity roundly rejected the rude radical, his Marxist-like criticisms of America, and his reparation demands. They also fumed at the Council's willingness to entertain them. As historian James Findlay states, "Many of the communicants with the Council made it clear that if the churches endorsed Forman even partially, their response would be . . . to withdraw economic support and personal commitments from the National Council."[77] The NCC chose a middle ground solution that appeased its conscience but pleased neither parishioners nor Forman. It agreed to raise at least five hundred thousand dollars for urban programs administered by blacks. But it did not channel the money specifically to his group.[78] The NCC also promised to pay greater attention to institutionalized racism in America and the churches. But five hundred thousand dollars was nowhere near the five hundred million dollars in reparations he demanded, and Forman left dissatisfied. He would reappear at the NCC's General Assembly in December.

Bilheimer did not see domestic racism and Vietnam policy as entirely separate issues. Both were grounded in people's presuppositions about justice, power, security, and peace. Changing these would affect how they perceived both America's racial diversity and its foreign policy. In the *Christianity and Crisis* article "What Kind of People Are We?" Bilheimer explained the connections: "no verbal or policy commitment to justice and peace abroad different in substance from our solution of the race and poverty problem at home will be credible or effective. . . . The basic character that governs our use of power is the same." Bilheimer knew that together the Vietnam War and the civil rights movement put a mirror before the nation. He wanted Americans to consider what sort of image gazed back—and to question whether that reflection really embodied the kind of character they could embrace. Both issues called for national soul-searching. As he repeated, the church had a unique role here. "Perhaps the deepest ministry of the church to the nation today is to provide a sensitive, certainly non-judgmental, interpretation of the search for selfhood and identity which the nation is now undergoing."[79] The unfolding irony was that the NCC and its churches, as vested parts of American society, were undergoing their own self-examinations. The Black Manifesto helped fuel that process.

POSTWAR PLANNING AND THE FALL OFFENSIVE

In the fall of 1969 the Council's Vietnam efforts flowed in three main directions. The mission wing kept planning its postwar relief project called "Tomorrow's Vietnam," while the WCC launched a similar program. With Nixon's honeymoon over, peace groups were poised to participate in the largest antiwar protests to date. Elston, SADIA, and CALCAV turned their attention there. Meanwhile, the Council geared up for its grand triennial General Assembly, which would be unlike any in its history. The tensions of the times and issues on people's minds would not be tamed by the rules of parliamentary order into obeying any fixed agenda. The year 1969 promised a wild ride to the finish.

Church World Service had begun its proposal on the churches' postwar service role back in 1968 when the war's end seemed imminent. In mid-1969 revisions continued at a two-day NCC staff consultation of both the Division of Overseas Ministries and the IAC. Bilheimer's suggestions paralleled Elston's earlier ones. Tactfully, he conveyed that CWS's draft "seems to me to contain too many unexamined presuppositions about the needs in Vietnam; it seems to presuppose a time scheme and pace which many aspects of the situation call into question."[80] Bilheimer recommended that they build in more flexibility, given a host of potential outcomes, needs, restrictions, and opportunities. To resist imposing what the churches felt they knew how to do so well, he understood, required "authentic Christian humility."[81] David Stowe, the head of the DOM, somewhat surprisingly agreed and urged further research on the matter. CWS kept collecting input and shaping this postwar project throughout the year.

The World Council wanted to provide postwar assistance too. Bilheimer suggested that, since Protestants lacked an indigenous base in Vietnam as well as the trust of the people, it might begin by listening to Vietnamese opinions and keeping its blueprint loose. The WCC recognized that it could not consider postwar reconstruction plans apart from the peace process or the future of the entire region. Therefore, it decided to make its own pilgrimage to the Paris delegations while gathering input from Vietnamese in Vietnam. Schomer lent his services to arrange meetings between WCC leaders and the Paris delegations in October. The World Council also sent Don Luce and Nguyen Tang Canh to South Vietnam for three months in order to gather information and outline recommendations regarding postwar relief.[82]

Luce and Canh's findings basically echoed Elston's advice. They stressed that aid must be channeled through indigenous groups, particularly at the village level, with no strings or agenda attached.[83] Current relief supplies flooding into South Vietnam were largely co-opted by its government, trapped in its bureaucracy, and siphoned off by corruption. Therefore, the Vietnamese often identified Western aid and the voluntary agencies that distributed it with the Thieu government's war effort. They also viewed relief as a means by which Western governments encouraged dependence and tried to control the populace. Luce and Canh emphasized that Western agencies must give aid without conditions. They should not come into the country and set up the usual Western-dominated relief operation.

The results of the WCC's meetings in Paris made a big impression on both Councils' postwar planning efforts. Seven NCC representatives had attended, returning with pointed responses to their basic questions. The Vietnamese were less interested in ecumenical postwar relief than in what churches were doing to help end the war and secure Vietnamese independence from foreign interference. They never asked for aid and, when pressed about it, insisted that all development programs be administered by locals. "We must remake our own country," they insisted. And missionizing efforts were unwelcome. The history of Western, and now American, involvement in Vietnam had so scarred Vietnamese culture that further involvement, even on the humanitarian level, was suspect. As Schomer explained, "some Buddhists and some Catholics were particularly overwhelming in their anguished reports of what the massive American governmental presence, both military and civilian, had done to dislocate, erode and even destroy traditional personal and social morality among their people." Bilheimer knew that demonstrating real respect for Vietnamese nationalism would be vital to any successful humanitarian venture. This meant that America's churches might be barred from types of development work they liked to do.[84] Flexibility and humility must guide postwar preparations. The fact that ecumenical leaders struggled with this suggests a paternalism that many found difficult to shed.

While CWS pursued postwar plans, the IAC and its cohorts in SADIA, CALCAV, FOR, SANE, and Negotiations Now! readied themselves for the coming antiwar demonstrations called the Fall Offensive. The fractured antiwar movement, which had quieted in the wake of the Paris negotiations and Nixon's election, was rallying its disparate parts and demanding U.S. withdrawal. Even though Nixon's popularity was still high, his slow Vietnamization program, which included greater bombing, angered the left. So did his animosity toward antiwar activists. Shortly after his inauguration, Nixon aimed the IRS, FBI, and CIA at dissident groups in an effort to intimidate and weaken them.[85]

The IRS audited CALCAV and the Council, looking for evidence with which to challenge the NCC's tax exempt status.[86] Elston and CALCAV suspected their office phone lines were wiretapped. While calling home one day, Elston heard his previous day's conversation playing back to him. Since answering machines were not yet in use, this evidence seemed conclusive.[87] Nixon declared war on the antiwar movement as he escalated the one in Vietnam. So the movement prepared to release its floodgates on the White House.

The Fall Offensive comprised two complementary programs: the Moratorium and the New Mobilization. The same building housed both coordinating offices, just one floor apart. Both sought and received church group involvement.

The Moratorium was the pet project of Sam Brown and David Hawk, two student leaders from Eugene McCarthy's campaign.[88] Hawk, a Union Theological Seminary alumnus, had organized seminarians against the war. The Moratorium was based upon the idea of a short general strike; it asked people to pause during a workday, in effect placing a moratorium on "business as usual" in order to reflect upon the situation in Vietnam. It began October 15. If Nixon pursued military victory in Vietnam beyond that date, the Moratorium committee hoped people would observe it again each month, adding one more day to that of the previous month in escalating fashion until the administration sought peace. Like Vietnam Summer, these Moratorium days would include "teach-out" activities to educate people about the war and inspire mass expressions for peace. Elston encouraged SADIA to advocate it, for "If this is ever to get off the campuses, the denominations will have to provide platforms in the community! And there is that opportunity!"[89] The Moratorium promised to be the kind of well-organized, respectful, reflective demonstration that appealed to liberals and their spiritual communities. Thus, the NCC, CAL-CAV, SANE, FOR, the Central Conference of American Rabbis, Boston's Catholic bishop Richard Cardinal Cushing, and several denominational leaders got involved. It also received endorsements from John Kenneth Galbraith, Noam Chomsky, Hans Morgenthau, the New Republic, Americans for Democratic Action (ADA), the Republican Ripon Society, the UAW and the Teamsters, Averell Harriman, and twenty-four democratic senators. George McGovern and Al Lowenstein gave it nationwide publicity.[90]

On October 15, the Moratorium's varied and dignified observances mushroomed across the country. Several workplaces gave employees permission to take time off to join in. Others did so on their own initiative or organized special observances at their job sites. The NCC did both. Espy encouraged staff to take part, and the Interchurch Center assembled a Moratorium Ad Hoc Committee to arrange activities within the building. These included two showings of the documentary film Year of the Pig about the history of Vietnam's struggle, a talk by former IVS staff member John Sommer and co-author of *Vietnam: The Unheard Voices*, a vigil outside the building with the donning of black arm bands, the tolling of Riverside Church's large bell, and a worship service in the chapel.[91]

These Council activities were surrounded by a flurry of Moratorium events throughout New York City involving hundreds of thousands of people. CALCAV asked the religious community to visit hospitalized servicemen. New York's mayor attended fifteen different rallies and ordered the flag lowered to half-mast. After the midday performance of *Fiddler on the Roof*, its Broadway producer invited the audience to join its cast at a rally; many did. Woody Allen called off scheduled shows of *Play It Again, Sam*. Several Broadway actors led a candlelight march to Times Square, and St. Patrick's Cathedral overflowed with attendees for a night-time vigil who prayed for peace and sang "America the Beautiful" by candlelight. Up and down the Eastern Seaboard, through the Midwest and along the West Coast, Moratorium events peppered the country. Only the South lacked significant observance. Media spin of these events noted their patriotic "stillness" and shared sense of sad distress in the war's continuation.[92]

But advocates of Nixon's war policies countered with a showing of flags, which his administration encouraged. As part of this, some Moratorium participants were harassed; others lost their jobs. Disturbed by the Moratorium's widespread success and sense of deep feeling, Nixon sent Vice President Spiro Agnew on a campaign of verbal attacks to discredit those with antiwar sentiments. In a November 3 speech appealing to his silent majority, Nixon skillfully painted the protesters as objects of rebuke, diverting focus away from his own actions. He blamed them for the war's failures. And people who already held protesters in low esteem listened. Nixon convinced some recognizable Hollywood and business stars to take similar postures. Ronald Reagan, H. Ross Perot, Bob Hope, and Art Linkletter all allied behind Nixon's military efforts to prevent a communist takeover in South Vietnam.[93] Nixon stunned antiwar activists with his ability to turn the public mood so forcefully in his favor. But the second, and more radical, wave of antiwar activity had not yet broken upon Nixon's beach.

By 1969, the New Left was severely fractured. Nevertheless, the New Mobe drew radicals and liberals together for a major three-day November demonstration in the nation's capital and San Francisco. Their agenda drew support from Senators Charles Goodell, Frank Church, Mark Hatfield, George McGovern, Harold Hughes, and Thomas Eagleton who sponsored various resolutions and bills to disengage U.S. troops from Vietnam and American aid from the Thieu/Ky regime. The Mobe concurrently lost the backing of people suspicious of radicalism and fearful of violence. But it was committed to legal nonviolent demonstrations and used experts from the AFSC and FOR to train thousands of peace-keeping marshals.[94]

Stewart Meacham, of the AFSC and a cochair of the New Mobe, recruited Elston to the Mobe's steering committee. Its members were invited to "express their organizational viewpoint" in planning sessions, which appealed to Elston. He joined Richard Fernandez, Allan Brick (FOR), Jesse Jackson (Operation Breadbasket), Phil Berrigan (radical Catholic priest), Benjamin Spock, and intellectuals Howard Zinn and Noam Chomsky on the committee. Elston's involvement did not imply NCC sponsorship. The Council's constitution barred such a move without official vote and policy coverage. Nevertheless, CALCAV, SADIA, and several churches, led by their denominations' leaders, got involved in Mobe events.[95]

Some denominational leaders participated despite personal disagreements with the Mobe's agenda of immediate withdrawal. For example, Robert Moss, president of the United Church of Christ, invited other UCC executives to attend Mobe activities such as the Washington National Cathedral prayer service and the next day's rally, even though he—and probably they also—did not advocate immediate withdrawal. As he saw it, "participation . . . does not constitute endorsement of the New Mobilization or of any or all of the sponsoring groups. But religious groups concerned for peace will be joining other groups who also desire an end to our participation in Vietnam."[96] Ironically, Moss viewed Mobe participation as a means of showing support for Nixon's assumed peace interest. "The March on the 15th," he said, "could be a clear demonstration of support for the President as he works for peace just as the March on Washington in 1963 was a clear indication of support to the administration as it worked for passage of the Civil Rights Bill." Others in the Mobe used it to vent frustration at the president's lack of peace initiative. The Mobe united people with vastly different opinions about the war to urge a rapid end to the killing.

Mobe events began with the dramatic "March Against Death," a thirty-six-hour nonstop reminder of those who had died in the war. Originally Stewart Meacham's idea, the march was administered by Susan Miller (Episcopal Peace Fellowship) and drew many church-related groups to help coordinate it.[97] Over forty thousand people with candles in hand, led by Coretta Scott King, marched single file through the rain from Arlington National Cemetery to the White House. Each carried a placard with the name of a soldier who had been killed or a Vietnamese village that had been demolished. Seven drummers led the procession with a solemn funeral cadence. As each person passed the White House, they yelled out the name they carried, then continued to the Capitol, where they laid their signs in open coffins and extinguished their candles. The laden caskets were later carried to the rally. For many who participated or watched, the Death March was a potent spiritual experience. As it moved through Washington, Eugene Carson Blake and William Sloane Coffin Jr. helped lead a prayer service at Washington's National Cathedral. Blake delivered the main address. As Elston recalled, when Blake flashed the peace sign, it "brought the house down." Pete Seeger led the audience in a chorus of "We Shall Overcome." According to Coffin, "more than five thousand people stood motionless, their fingers raised in the V sign of the peace movement. The silence was awesome."[98] Carl McIntire and about a hundred counter protesters failed to disrupt the service.[99] It was preceded by a meal of rice and tea, the eight-dollar individual price of which went to the Committee of Responsibility to help bring Vietnamese youth seriously injured in the war to the United States for medical treatment.[100]

On November 15, over half a million people processed down Pennsylvania Avenue behind the caskets and assembled at the Washington Monument. It was one of the largest and most diverse demonstrations in the nation's history. Coffin, who co-chaired the rally with Spock, was disappointed by the quality of most of the speeches, to which few apparently listened anyway. Musical performances from the cast of Broadway's *Hair*, Pete Seeger, and Peter, Paul, and Mary were a hit, and culminated in the crowd's repetitive chanting of John Lennon's line "All we are saying / is give peace a chance." Swept up by the mood, Bilheimer found the demonstration "dominated by a spirit." The call to "give peace a chance," he felt, was "evidence of profound inner aspiration." He saw embodied in the Mobe's crowd the shift in worldview that he desired for the nation. "No longer sharing the perceptions of the international world which underlay the Cold War, no longer satisfied in conscience that war could be justified for the objectives announced in Vietnam," Bilheimer explained, "this vast throng asserted simply that they wished a different relationship to other peoples than that signified by the Vietnam War."[101] For him, it was a high moment.

A few fringe groups protested through confrontational or illegal means, but these did not distract much from the Mobe's main thrust. The most disheartening and destructive blows came from Nixon's cold shoulder and the sparse television coverage. Public opinion remained critical of both the war and its protesters, including the upstanding Moratorium and Mobe participants. When the president's poll numbers remained high, and pro-war demonstrators defended his policies, Nixon declared jubilantly, "We've got those liberal bastards on the run now, and we're going to keep them on the run."[102] The country wanted an end to U.S. casualties in Vietnam as well as the marching in America. But most citizens did not want to lose the war or abandon U.S. objectives. Neither did Nixon, who refused to let foreign policy be made in the streets and denigrated those who tried.

While assisting with CALCAV's Thanksgiving Fast, the Council geared up for its 1969 triennial General Assembly in Detroit, Michigan. Throughout the fall, the NCC kept taking heat from perturbed clergy, laity, and local churches for its Vietnam-related activities and proclamations. Its relationship with conservative parishioners was seriously strained. As the assembly neared, organizers sensed the Council would become a focal point of criticism from the left as well.

CHAPTER TEN

Ecumenical Erosion, Fall–December 1969

PUBLIC RELATIONS PROBLEMS RIGHT AND LEFT

Burton Marvin was desperate to improve public relations with local Christians. As communications director, he saw the flood of protest letters that inundated the NCC that fall. The bulk came from Presbyterians and Methodists at the congregational level.[1] These included clergy who felt the Council burdened rather than benefited local churches, and who resented having to explain Council actions to angry parishioners. Reacting to an NCC appeal for funds, Rev. Paul Woudenberg of First United Methodist Church in Santa Monica, California, vented his annoyance. His opinions typified those who penned critical letters.

> On balance, the National Council is a detriment to the local church, in my opinion. The distance of the Council from any real confrontation with "the people," and the sense of isolation of the Council from any possible influence in the grass roots, is profound. The democratic processes are simply not available to Christians who are concerned about the Council.
>
> Furthermore, the political utterances often have a sense of arrogance about them which is offensive to the local churchmen. It is all well and good to say that the General Board of Assembly speaks *to* the churches in the way of guidance. The local church wishes that it could speak from time to

time *to* the Board of Assembly in the way of guidance, for the pronouncements have a consistency to them which, in my judgment, represent but
political commentary. Without regard to specific conclusions, this is most
embarrassing to me, and necessitates much labor on my part to convince
my people that I am not associated with you.

You claim in Section 8 [of your brochure] that you are the main point
of contact in helping member denominations keep in touch with secular
organizations. My guess is that the precise opposite is true, and from where
I view the Council, you are working in spectacular isolation from the Christians you supposedly serve (who are, indeed, secular).

I frankly despair of ever hoping to believe that the Council could positively help the local church, and at the moment feel that my task would be
much easier if you would quietly disperse.[2]

Espy feared such sentiments had grown more common in the Council's
largest denomination. NCC staff member William Walzer heard similar
concerns from Methodist ministers in Ohio.[3] Local clergy attributed part
of the NCC's image problem to the media's over-reporting (sometimes
misreporting) of the Council's more controversial peace and justice activities, and its sparse coverage of the Council's popular missions work. This
perpetuated its image as a radical, politicized organization run amok.

In the South, skewed reporting contributed to the greatest perversion of
the Council's image for parishioners, many of whom viewed the organization as communist friendly. After returning home from a church conference in Virginia, Rev. Odell Brown of Chatham Heights United Methodist
Church penned a letter to the NCC expressing his district's disgust for it,
especially when asked to give money. "We are wholly opposed to the way
you have the budget so tied up that in order to support missions through
you we are forced to support all these perfectly diabolical communistic
ungodly stances of yours, as you have done over the years!"[4] This desire
of conservative churches to donate to CWS's work but not to that of the
Council's social justice and peace division continued through the 1990s,
fueling tensions between the Council's two wings that eventually resulted
in CWS's financial and operational divorce from the NCC in 2000.

Less constructively than Woudenberg, Brown railed against the Council for its lack of interest in lay opinion as well as its claims to speak "to the
churches" as Protestant America's voice. But it was the Council's socially
active liberalism that disturbed him most.

I am 100% sick and tired of the rotten Communistic Oriented national council of churches [*sic*], as are untold thousands of other church leaders over this land. You are a disgrace to us!

You use the gimmick of palming off your "radical" *soft on communism* policies by saying you are "SPEAKING TO THE CHURCHES"! This is worse than professional politicians do. At least they come back home and seek to get grass roots opinions on what their constituents want them to vote and propose in Washington! Why don't you send questionnaires to all local churches to ask how they feel about various issues and from this give out these facts, instead of *going to the press (first) with your notions* to the chagrin and embarrassment of all of us in the local church? The National Council of Churches is just a dirty word in this whole area! . . .

You are repeatedly making pronouncements that do not show expertise in the subjects. On Vietnam or the admission of Red China to the UN or other issues, it appears that all you read are time [*sic*] and Life Magazines.

You have consistently taken a liberal perspective on the problems of society and antoganized [*sic*] the more conservative elements of society. You have failed to become a place where both sides can talk with *RESPECT!* . . .

The Council, originally formed for people to talk across denominational lines, has laid that aspect aside and become social critics.

In short, I would be most happy to see you move your headquarters to moscow [*sic*] and operate from there, or if you prefer—Peking!

At least, then you would for once be honest![5]

While more extreme, Brown's concerns paralleled Woudenberg's. Biased incomplete news reporting did not discount the fact that the NCC usually advocated positions to the left of those held by most of its members' parishioners. Combined with its perceived disregard for lay opinion, this upset local churchgoers. As seen here, church people also often red-baited the Council instead of addressing its positions intellectually or theologically.

Espy admitted to Woudenberg that the Council struggled to communicate effectively with the grass roots, especially since it lacked a direct channel to them. "We are under a great handicap . . . as a national body whose contacts with local congregations necessarily are indirect—through the channels either of the denominations or the local councils of churches."[6]

But after chatting further with Methodist leaders, Espy concluded the problem was not the NCC's alone. Rather, the clergy-laity gap gaped widest within the denominations themselves and sprang from there. Specifically, he noted, "a more significant gap [exists] between the local pastor and his own national denominational leadership."[7] Robert Huston, one of those Methodist leaders, agreed. Writing to his colleagues he said, "Though the catalyst in these letters is the NCC, as Ed comments, the mood is part of a larger whole which includes us all."[8] Espy then explained to Wouden- berg that the board, which pastors often criticized, was comprised of delegates selected by the denominations in their own ways. Many chose to forgo direct local elections and, instead, used other procedures that they determined themselves. Therefore, while the NCC relied upon democratic "representative" methods, it had no authority to tell denominations whom to send to the General Board or Assembly, nor did it have any author- ity to "jump over" denominational leaders in order to deal directly with parishioners.[9]

Upon further examination, Woudenberg conceded Espy's point. "I am astonished at the high number of institutional bureaucrats on our repre- sentation. . . . [They] make up almost half of our delegation. I can hardly conceive of them representing, or even understanding, local church inter- ests. Therefore, I think the fault lies with the sort of persons that we send to the National Council, rather than something intrinsic in the Council itself. I hope you will forgive my overstatement here." As a result, Wouden- berg shifted blame for negative lay impressions of church authority to his denomination, pointing a finger at "bureaucratic directives [that] tend more toward the fatherly rather than brotherly spirit."[10]

When Woudenberg wrote Espy in 1969, he may have forgotten that he had discerned the denominational source of the clergy-laity problem himself back in 1966. He complained then that the Methodist Church's rules and structure left local congregations without direct representation to annual conferences. Woudenberg accused his denomination of taxation without representation; as a result, parishioners disregarded statements put forth by annual conferences.[11]

A conservative Methodist layperson, Michael Watson, reached the same conclusion: that the denominations bore great responsibility for the clergy-laity gap. Initially critical of the NCC and ready to scapegoat it, he agreed to study the organization on behalf of his like-minded brethren and eventually served a term on the General Board for an inside view. Like Woudenberg, Watson learned that the NCC depended upon the denominations to appoint balanced representatives to Council boards and then urge good attendance. This lay leader accused his denomination of letting the NCC down on both counts. Even though the Council asked the denominations to make laity 50 percent of their representatives, only nine of the Methodists' forty-four board members were not clerics. The proportion of laity to clergy mirrored what he saw at his church's annual conference. He noted as well that Methodist attendance at Council board meetings was poor, and he faulted his church for this laxity.[12] Both situations worsened the sense of lay disconnect from the NCC and their denominations. They also fed laity's growing frustration with institutional church statements and communication styles.

Several additional factors compounded the clergy-laity gap. As one Presbyterian pastor noted, this gap actually contained several subdivisions, such as a "seminary-parish gap" and a "hierarchy-working pastor gap."[13] For example, church leaders with seminary or executive jobs within denominations did not have congregations. Thus, their pay and job performance were not tied to pleasing those in the pews. This allowed them to risk stirring controversy with less direct penalty. Oftentimes, they received praise for their prophetic boldness. Many local pastors, however, felt trapped in a congregational lion's den, poised to be eaten alive if they riled their parishioners while their superiors sat safely in East Coast offices urging clergy to whip their congregants awake. This created considerable clerical stress. One minister admitted that pastors were the primary bottlenecks preventing "debate and action" materials from being utilized in local churches—for their job situations were not conducive to obedience here.[14] They might join groups such as CALCAV and protest as individuals, but they often censored themselves in the pulpit and balked at pushing the war issue into adult education classes.

Besides, laity often resented clergy who ignored their spiritual nurture in order to focus on saving the oppressed. Many saw social action projects as set in competition against their own needs or favored congregational programs when it came to resources and the pastor's time. Gallup polls in 1957 and 1968 questioning laity about whether they thought churches should speak out on sociopolitical issues showed a sharp drop in affirmative answers (from 47 to 40 percent between 1957 and 1968) and an increase among those declaring that churches should stay silent (from 44 to 53 percent).[15] This helps document the rise of a lay revolt against liberal church activism rather than any growing tolerance for church engagement in social justice activities. So too do the 1968 findings of sociologists Rodney Stark and Charles Glock, who confirmed that churches "seem to be held in captivity by a comfort-seeking laity" who wanted to be released from attention to peace and justice issues while in the pews.[16] To these laity, the church should be a bulwark against the changing secular world. This clashed with the official movement of most Catholic and mainline Protestant denominations in the 1960s to cease hiding behind stained-glass windows and join God's work in the streets.

Local clergy, whether personally leaning to the left or right on socio-political issues, felt caught in an uncomfortable untenable bind between their discordant hierarchy and congregation, a position that was precarious relationally to navigate and at times fraught with perceived dangers to one's career. Many clergy resented both laity and denominational leaders for this. To avoid sanction, conservative clergy frequently silenced themselves on controversial politics and theological interpretations in denominational meetings, while many liberal clergy did the same within their congregations. On top of this, tightening budgets meant low pay and shrinking advancement opportunities. In denominational clergy journals, they complained about burnout, declining morale, and thoughts of leaving the profession while they pleaded for more tolerance of diverse opinions and a better balance between spiritual nurture and activism in denominational emphases. On the latter point, few clergy knew how to weave these well. And even if their own personal feelings about the war and the church's role in social issues matched that of denominational leadership more so than laity, most still resented how the leadership failed to relate to local churches. All in all, clergy writings paint the Vietnam era as an agonizing time for local pastors. Their experiences help explain why the NCC's educational efforts on Vietnam floundered as well as how mainline churches struggled internally in the 1960s. It is also no wonder that the large clergy-laity gap within the denominations would become more pronounced for the National Council; it was further removed from local churches and, while answering to the denominations, also possessed a bureaucratic mind of its own. The Council clearly stood as the easiest target for those seeking to rage against the mainline Protestant machine.[17]

Despite Woudenberg's revised understanding of the NCC's role in the clergy-laity divide, Espy took the charge of arrogance seriously for it denoted a real NCC problem, and he promised to discuss it with the board.[18] This grassroots impression of the Council as elitist, disinterested, and overly "fatherly" in tone was a major liability during this period when rebellion against authority rippled through society. In "The Unresponsive Pew," published during the Woudenberg-Espy exchange, Jeanne Richie said that laity wanted more autonomy and empowerment within their churches. They resented prophetic tactics that clergy often used to stimulate congregational action on social issues. These inspired resistance, not cooperation. In her opinion, the "sociopolitical" or "economic" sermon also bored people. And guilt-tripping usually backfired.[19] Richie aimed her article at local clergy, not church institutions. Nevertheless, her critique of the prophetic strategy and her insights into lay desires shed light on the laity's waning affection for the NCC, not to mention their own denominational boards. Both were perceived as using the same pushy methods.

As Council leaders began to realize, more people, whether conservative or liberal, American or non-Western, wanted greater individual empowerment and less heavy-handed bureaucratic control. In the late 1960s and early 1970s, the Council was getting socked by all sides. Some church executives wearied of the attacks—especially those launched from within the liberal Protestant community itself. Lutheran executive Franklin Clark Fry was irritated by those who condemned the institutional church while also trying "to take the church into every social movement in the community."[20] Nevertheless, criticism continued to mount. In October and November 1969, as the Council readied itself for another General Assembly, its leaders learned that forces on the left were preparing to bring their grievances to the floor.

The radical renewalist Stephen Rose drew the most attention. A graduate of Union Theological Seminary, Rose was ordained in the United Presbyterian Church. He worked in an interracial ministry before founding *Renewal* magazine in 1962. A prolific author, he penned scores of articles and books and had even served as a staff writer for the WCC in 1966–1967.[21] Rose criticized church leadership for growing too far removed from laity, for conducting "social action" too bureaucratically in terms of statements, and for failing to work on the cutting edge of social justice movements. Council leaders knew that their organizational structure, methods, and mission needed retooling in light of changing times, slashed budgets, and conflicting expectations. But Rose advocated a grander overhaul that would alter the Council's character and function. He introduced his proposals to NCC executives in November, warning that he would direct an uninvited theatrical presentation of his vision at the assembly itself.

A week before the assembly, *Christianity and Crisis* provided Rose with a forum through which to present his ideas. In "The NCC: Phoenix on the Hudson?" he argued that the Council was dead and required rebirth. Specifically, it had emerged "still-born" in 1950 due to the denominations who denied it an autonomous mission; they kept it their servant by empowering it only to "conduct studies" and provide forums for ecumenical discussions. Rose complained that the NCC never received a constitutional mandate to run action programs nor did the denominations grant it the strong "maverick-like" executive leadership necessary to spearhead them. While Rose credited Espy with possessing a kind, socially liberal, justice-seeking heart, he also said that Espy retained "sympathy with the conservative older denominations' leaders who form the basic power bloc within NCC boards. His manner," Rose continued, "has been cautious, noiseless, befitting the highest official of a Council whose mandate must be eked from the denominational domains." By not granting the NCC the requisite independence and talent to lead, he contended, the communions had reduced it to a status similar to themselves, which forced it to compete with denominational programs for personnel and funds. Rose credited the NCC with performing well under these circumstances. "In the face of great odds—notably those posed by her constituency, which turns out to be herself wearing a different hat—she has done rather well, like the UN faced with the nations." Nevertheless, he felt changes in the relationships between Protestant bodies—and the role of the church in the world—necessitated a revolutionary overhaul for the Council too.[22]

Rose had little faith that the status-quo-bound church could be an effective transformative agent in a revolutionary world. Therefore, he proposed burying the "still-born" Council, then resurrecting it with a new life, structure, and mission that cut it free from the denominations. Sponsored by his Jonathan Edwards Tithing and Church Extension Society, Rose created a theatrical project called "Jonathan's Wake" to dramatize this at the assembly. The resurrected Council he envisioned would be essentially a secularized, diversely staffed, lay-focused, mission service center to organize action programs. To this end, he urged the NCC also to elect a black general secretary, fill its executive board with youth, and channel the majority of its funds "to the poor and oppressed" so they might self-administer programs relevant to their needs through the NCC. He hoped this would help fulfill the core of the Black Manifesto's demands. The denominations, he said, could focus on providing spiritual nourishment to parishioners, and the task of structural ecumenical unity could be assumed fully by another organization called the Consultation on Church Union (COCU).

While several of Rose's colleagues agreed generally with his diagnosis of the Council's problems, few officials concurred with his remedy.[23] In fact, most deemed it unwise, impractical, and destructive to the ecumenical vision. J. Edward Carothers, a Methodist member of the Council's Reappraisal Committee, claimed that "Steve Rose is one of the most naïve men we have running around right now" and called his proposals "immoral." Carothers criticized Rose's blind faith in the virtue of youth leadership. Youth had not proved to be superior leaders, he asserted, and "engaged in narcissistic behaviour." He also called Rose's suggestion of turning Council assets over to the poor and oppressed "the starkest folly one can imagine." "The needed task," he continued, "is infinitely more difficult than surrendering control over money and organization."[24] Carothers pleaded with Espy not to fall prey to the pressure tactics of Rose's renewalists. Bilheimer also worried about rising pressures upon Espy from the religious and secular left to reduce the Council to an action and service center, a thought that horrified him. It appeared to many that the Detroit General Assembly would trigger a battle over the identity, mission, and structure of the NCC.

The Council did make some prior concessions to its critics. Back in January, it had increased the number of youth at the assembly as well as on its nominating and credentials committees. It also encouraged denominations to appoint a significant number of lay delegates. Long before the event, staff discussed how they would handle probable disruptions from the floor, and they stressed flexibility and permissiveness in allowing people to be heard. The NCC committed also to "refrain from resorting to the police or the courts" in the face of protest. Council president Arthur Flemming, who would chair the assembly, appointed a liaison committee to advise and assist dissident groups seeking agenda time. The board's Executive Committee also invited Rose to its November meeting to share his proposals.[25] The Council even reserved time on the assembly's first day to hear people's presentations before working groups met. Flemming's posture of openness, respect, and flexibility from the chair served the NCC well. But its best-laid plans, which had included dedicated time to discuss its renewal and mission for the 1970s, were blown aside by a tempest of protesters and issues.

THE NCC'S TEMPESTUOUS 1969 DETROIT GENERAL ASSEMBLY

Ironically, Espy sprung the assembly's first surprise. In his opening address, he presented his own unsolicited, unreviewed suggestions for restructuring the NCC. He introduced these separately from, and in addition to, the Council's two formal committees on "Reappraisal" and "Mission in the 70s" that were commissioned to make recommendations. Perhaps Rose had affected him, for Espy proposed turning the NCC into what he called a "General Ecumenical Council," which would be a decentralized interchurch organization focused on collaborative issue-oriented actions.[26] Under Espy's plan, religious groups could choose which issues they wished to fund and engage in while ignoring the theological big picture.

Although some may have favored Espy's idea, most pilloried it. Alan Geyer saw in it "a contradiction between the claim of wholeness and the structure of fragmentation." Blacks, Geyer noted, tended to see it as "a dodge of the problems of power and priorities."[27] Bilheimer called it "disastrous" and was extremely disappointed by his old friend. He saw it as "an example of him buckling to those pressuring for an issue-oriented Council," which Bilheimer called interreligious but not ecumenical. In the former, Bilheimer explained, "you have everyone looking at the world through the lenses of their own issues, and not through the vision of all as members of the body of Christ. Everyone has a soapbox and all people can agree on is to let each person have their soapbox and write their own reports."[28] In other words, to Bilheimer, Espy proposed exchanging real ecumenism for a new breed model based upon self-interested cooperation and secular goals. The precious ecumenical grounding that Bilheimer fought to preserve, and which he thought Espy had hired him to maintain, would be lost.

Rose's group Jonathan's Wake peppered the next two days with performances and demands. It largely comprised white liberals and radicals (including the "Free Church of Berkeley" and some "Yippies") who supported the Black Manifesto and Rose's blueprint for the NCC. To dramatize

Rose's decree that a still-born Council required rebirth under new leadership, Jonathan's Wake disrupted the assembly with a Yippie-style theatrical funeral procession. About fifty demonstrators carried a coffin down the center aisle to the platform. Symbolizing the dead NCC, and draped with an American flag boasting peace symbols instead of stars, the casket sported a placard which read "In Memoriam NCC 1950–1969."[29] A lengthy liturgy followed, designed to decontaminate the place of demonic powers, such as "exploitation, suppression, and war."[30] Participants donned flowers, danced in the aisles, and sang hymns. Jonathan's Wake also held a mock draft lottery that summoned many delegates to fight in Vietnam, including the Episcopal Church's presiding bishop.[31] Later, during discussion of the Council's officer election procedures, Jonathan's Wake demanded that they be opened to alternative candidates and postponed for a few days, or it would declare the entire triennial meeting "undemocratic and invalid." It then threatened to "hold its own assembly for the remainder of the week at Central Methodist Church."[32]

The next day's events proved equally stunning. Bilheimer launched the morning session with a report on the peace program. Alan Geyer and Edwin O. Reischauer followed with presentations of a new proposed resolution on Vietnam and vivid descriptions of tragedies in Indochina. Geyer's powerful speech affirmed that the IAC was on the right track with a gutsy program and urged the denominations to dedicate more funds and personnel toward its success. However, a group of Yippies interrupted these presentations to read a statement by the "Youth of Amerika." Their demands included that the churches "give all church properties back to the Indians, . . . support the legalization of marijuana and other sacramental drugs, . . . help free all draft resisters, . . . support the Black Manifesto, . . . pay a minimum of $300 million to the youth of Amerika in reparation for the years of lies we've been forced to listen to, . . . no longer condemn any sexual activity as being immoral," and provide "free pay toilets."[33]

Continuing the interruption, Rev. Calvin Marshall, president of the National Black Economic Development Conference, called James Forman to the podium, where he again outlined his demands. Then, hijacking the chair from Flemming, Marshall called upon a Jonathan's Wake minister to present a resolution asking the NCC to pledge never to act against supporters of the Black Manifesto. Marshall tried to force a vote. But delegates refused to recognize takeover tactics that they deemed out of order. Rose suddenly ran through the assembly hall yelling, "Crucify me! Crucify me!"[34] Flemming patiently tolerated the outbursts until presentation of the Vietnam resolution could continue. The Youth Caucus then received time to read its prepared statement, which harshly condemned the war. It asked the NCC to support "demilitarization of the chaplaincy," "elimination of 4-D exemptions for seminarians and ministers," and a conscientious objector in their midst (James Rubins) by holding his draft card and providing counsel and legal aid.[35] Unlike the Yippies' demands, each of these represented serious issues with which the NCC was prepared to engage.

The afternoon session and next day's meetings turned attendees' focus to conscientious objectors. Discussions and votes revolved around two issues brought before the assembly: launching a new cooperative ministry by the National and Canadian Councils of Churches for draft resisters in Canada, and whether to hold Rubins's draft card in trust.

Just across the U.S. border in Windsor, Canada, CALCAV and NCC assembly representatives met with the Canadian Council to create a joint ministry to U.S. draft resisters. Delegates discussed how the Canadian Council might help meet resisters' needs while the NCC did the same for their relatives back home. Elston and Fernandez also arranged for about fourteen denominational leaders to talk with actual deserters in Canada.[36] The two considered this the most significant offshoot of the assembly.[37] It forced church bureaucrats to put a personal face on deserters, people frequently labeled cowards and traitors.

Herman Will met a young AWOL soldier whose parents worked in the defense industries. His blue-collar family was not well educated or deeply analytical about the nation's turmoil. The young man, a high school dropout, was not a polished speaker, nor was he a devout Christian or a social activist. When drafted for Vietnam, he went, fought, and was shot. The military shipped him back to the States for surgery and recuperation; once he had recovered, they planned to return him to the fighting. After witnessing the war firsthand, the young man saw no purpose in it. He did not wish to risk losing his life again for what seemed a senseless folly. So, while still being treated for his wounds, he snuck out of the hospital and made his way to Canada. Will did not think him a coward or a traitor but, rather, a responsible steward of the life God had given him, one who refused to waste it in a useless war.[38]

The assembly approved the consultation's plan for a joint Canadian-U.S. ministry project for war resisters. In February 1970, the General Board formalized this as the "Emergency Ministry Concerning U.S. Draft Age Emigrants in Canada," and Rich Killmer left CALCAV to direct it.[39] This NCC ministry to draft-age men grew, evolved, and changed names over the years, becoming a significant and long-lived program.

Meanwhile, many deemed the turmoil surrounding James Rubins's request to be the most spiritually gripping aspect of the assembly. The twenty-one-year-old Hope College student had been reared in the Reformed Church in America (RCA). Elston said that the cautious, conservative RCA came out slowly against the war; but when it did, it spoke from a strong biblical basis and had a real consensus of its parishioners. Rubins's faith, nurtured by his church, led him to take a conscientious objector's position on the war and a civil disobedience stance on the draft. Since his faith was the driving force behind his convictions, he asked the assembly to receive and hold his draft card in trust and to provide him with spiritual support, even legal counsel, if necessary. Rubins's request tested the assembly's willingness to act upon its stated policies on selective conscientious objection, civil disobedience, and the war. The NCC's attorney warned that the Council "would be subject to prosecution for violation of the Selective Service Act" if it accepted Rubins's card.[40]

Rubins's request was not an isolated incident. Back in June, five RCA members asked its General Synod to accept their draft cards in protest against the selective service system. Three of them had attended Hope College, the same school as Rubins, and all five had entered seminary. The seminarians explained to the synod that the body that molded their views, and to which they belonged, should share responsibility for the repercussions of its teachings. As they put it, "we have violated the law. We are willing to accept the consequences for our action. But we realize that our church who has been a great factor in our making this decision is partially responsible and obligated to accept us. To reject us would be to alienate us, to drive us from your community. . . . if you accept our cards, your action may possibly be interpreted as illegal. We ask you to take this risk."[41] While the synod declined their cards, it passed resolutions on selective civil disobedience and promised to provide "pastoral counsel . . . the love and nurture of the church; . . . ecclesiastical counsel in their stand and . . . voluntary legal aid on their behalf."[42]

This issue was fresh in RCA leader Marion deVelder's mind when he arrived at the General Assembly to be confronted by yet another RCA member seeking the church's intercession. Rev. Raymond Pontier, father of one of the earlier five, had presented a resolution calling the NCC to accept Rubins's card. A vigorous debate ensued over an individual's responsibilities to conscience and the law. In the midst of it, the usually reserved deVelder shouted that the body of Christ should stand with individuals of conscience and "stop being preoccupied with consequences."[43] The assembly then voted 228 for and 184 against, a clear majority supporting Rubins's resolution.[44]

Flemming quickly announced that it passed. But, just as supporters began to celebrate, others reminded the assembly that they needed a two-thirds majority to approve a resolution, and the "yeas" had fallen short. Someone moved that the motion to adopt the resolution be reconsidered for a later vote. After dinner, they amended and fiercely debated Rubins's resolution once more. On its second vote, the motion failed again. With frayed emotions, Rev. Jack York of Jonathan's Wake and the Free Church of Berkeley usurped the podium and shouted something to the effect that "This is despicable. The blood of the Vietnamese and Americans is dripping from the minutes [of this meeting] and from our hands. By God, wash off the blood of your brothers." Then he emptied a can of red paint over the speakers' table.[45] Papers were drenched, and Flemming's clothes were coated. By contrast, Rubins remained humble and composed. He simply told the audience, "I hold no grudge against people who did not stand with me. I believe in the church. I stand by the church. May God help us all."[46]

On the assembly's final day, well over one hundred people gathered around Rubins in support. These delegates signed an independent statement opposing the earlier vote and offering to hold his draft card as a group of individuals. They knew that doing so violated the law. Rubins, who then felt "too emotionally upset" to decide what to do, simply expressed gratitude for their offer.[47] There in protest, and ready to exploit any opportunity to discredit the NCC, Carl McIntire and his fundamentalist followers telegrammed U.S. Attorney General John Mitchell's office, urging "an immediate investigation of this criminal act which is a subversion of national security."[48] McIntire claimed that faithfulness to Christianity mandated such notification.

Faithfulness to Christian teachings was exactly the dilemma raised by Rubins's request. It tested the institutional church's willingness to risk its valued ties with the political establishment by standing instead with the lawbreaker who had acted upon the church's faith principles. While Rubins's resolution did not pass, the fact that a solid majority supported it does illustrate that the Council was reaching beyond the establishment's mainstream toward the margins where those who felt unrepresented stood. It remained the ever cautious, rational, respectable Council; but it was hearing the voices of those who felt repressed by hegemonic forces that the NCC had long embodied. By listening to people of color in the United States and in Asia, as well as its own conflicted youth, the Council kept reevaluating who its constituency included and how the ecumenical community could become more faithful to its beliefs.

The assembly also passed a powerful new "Resolution on Vietnam," which, for the first time, moved the Council toward advocating withdrawal. After complaining that America's reliance upon military solutions subverted the nation's chance to create a viable government in Vietnam, the resolution asked Nixon to call a cease-fire and withdraw U.S. troops by the end of 1970. Withdrawing risked less prestige than continuing the fight at this point. It also urged the White House to stop supporting the corrupt Thieu/Ky regime, and to end the war rather than simply replace American soldiers with Vietnamese. As one step, the resolution backed creation of "a comprehensive interim government in South Vietnam" and the eventual "formation of a new government broadly representative of all major elements in South Vietnam."[49] In addition to this resolution, the assembly passed another on chemical and biological weapons and a statement on civilian massacres in Vietnam. Shocking revelations of U.S. military massacres and cover-ups triggered the latter, drawing more attention in coming months.

The election of new officers and delegates at the assembly also created controversy. For the first time, the Council's proposed slate of officers included a female candidate for president. Dr. Cynthia Wedel had served previously as associate general secretary and, in 1968, had led several women's groups on an antiwar march in Washington, D.C.[50] A caucus of black churchmen who wanted the next president to be black challenged her nomination. This was the first time that any group had challenged an official slate of nominees. Rather than selecting a liberal black candidate such as Andrew Young, who might have had broad appeal and a real chance to beat Wedel, the caucus nominated the more radical Rev. Albert Cleage Jr., a black power advocate. He pastored a Detroit church called the Shrine of the Black Madonna and preached that Jesus was black. Cleage and the black caucus pressured Wedel to step aside, saying "the women's liberation movement must not stand in the way of the black liberation movement."[51] This exemplified the fractious nature of soapbox politics that often pitted one group's empowerment against another's. It also illustrated that blacks thought whites were using gender to block systemic change related to race. Wedel refused to withdraw and was elected, receiving 387 votes to Cleage's 93. The Council's first female president came to office at a time when several of its denominations, such as the Episcopal Church, did not yet ordain women. A number of blacks gained other important posts, including the NCC vice presidency, two program vice presidencies, and three vice presidencies at-large. The chair of the General Board's important nominating committee went to Theressa Hoover, a black woman. Nevertheless, upset by his defeat, Cleage proclaimed that "The N.C.C. is the Antichrist in this generation!" and "You better make the most of these establishment Negroes while you've got 'em."[52]

Recognizing the divisions within the Council, even among minority groups seeking to speak their truths to power, Wedel recommended creating permanent caucuses for them. Over the course of the assembly, the Council heard statements from several marginalized groups, including women, blacks, youth, Hispanics, Native Americans, and migrants. Each sought church support for their liberation agenda, illustrating that they valued church backing, recognition, and its remaining clout even while they attacked it as part of the establishment. Most challenged the NCC to become more inclusive of diversity, more reflective of society's pluralism within its structure, and more conscious of their perspectives and concerns. The NCC took these matters seriously. In order to ensure broader representation of its full constituency, it postponed the election of board leaders for a month so that Hoover's nominating committee could recruit more diverse candidates.[53] The Council also amended its procedures to expand the number of youth, women, and lay people involved in its leadership.

Thus, in this sense, assembly confrontations by disadvantaged groups did advance their objectives. In two other ways, however, they ultimately backfired. First, the Council's move toward the margins failed to persuade the young and victimized to stay in the churches and work for justice through them. Many activists left the churches, feeling they could accomplish more through secular organizations and arguments. Indeed, over time, the loss of young people contributed significantly to numerical drops in liberal church membership.[54] This decline of liberal activist Christianity, and rising debates over its meaning, created more cultural space for conservative evangelicals to define the faith according to their own theological and political interpretations as they sought greater leverage within the political establishment in the 1970s and 1980s. Second, to white conservative laity, it appeared as though the NCC was retreating further from "Main Street" Christian values. In actuality, the NCC was becoming *less* elitist—shifting from close identification with the establishment and top-down management styles toward a new recognition that it must listen to, see through the eyes of, and empower those on the margins. Nevertheless, as the Council awakened to such things and moved to the left on sociopolitical issues, much of the nation's white majority backlashed against the so-called rioters, bra burners, hippies, and draft dodgers, and liberal East Coast elites who coddled them.

While the discontent and challenges presented to the assembly surprised few NCC leaders, their convergence and force stunned all. The Council's planned agenda to discuss its "Mission in the 70s" was shoved aside by the continual series of unscheduled events. Some who witnessed this saw it as a healthful wake-up call. Others were disgusted by the Council's loss of control and viewed the chaotic assembly as its death knell. Summarizing its impact, one member wrote presciently, "we were pounded by wave after wave of a turbulent sea and as a result the NCCC will never be the same." It all signaled the rise of new voices and a rejection of automatic deferment to traditional authority. "We saw for the first time candidates from the floor against a slate; we were challenged to take a possibly illegal act; we heard that we were too sensitive to rules, too insensitive to human needs; we saw youth speaking up to elders, black, brown, and red to white, women to men. We were told the Council was preacher oriented rather than people oriented, that structures must serve functions, that we must utilize our great resources for justice." Interpreting the upheaval as a freshening, this member concluded: "All in all, it was the liveliest of all General Assemblies. Whether the tumult was that of birth pains or death for the Council remains to be seen, but it seemed to me we saw the stirring of new life."[55]

To traditional ecumenists, this was simply part of the ongoing molting process that was essential to ecumenism. The NCC was genuinely listening to groups that had previously received little attention; this required institutional and spiritual renewal as the church sought to become more internally true to itself, even as it witnessed to the broader nation. The structural nature and shape of this renewal became the most contentious, however. Fractious new breed models seemed to ecumenists to threaten the very core of the ecumenical vision.

Traditional ecumenists feared the new breed models reflected popular views that diversity, or pluralism, was best empowered through separatist causes and caucuses. Separatism arose as an understandable reaction to earlier national "consensus narratives" that whitewashed and masculinized U.S. history as well as to integrationist ideas of the 1940s, 1950s, and early 1960s that threatened to scatter or bury minority voices within a melting-pot model of unity. In practice, these often blended minorities in with a largely unchanged, white, middle-class male hegemony. Minorities risked becoming token faces within a status quo that still denied them opportunities to shape institutions unless they mimicked the white male power bloc. Therefore, they carved out autonomous areas in which to build their own influence. Separatist groups focused upon empowering themselves, both from within (that is, tackling internalized racism, sexism, classism, and homophobia) and as blocs within the larger society. Separate groups, movements, caucuses, and academic programs played essential roles in helping oppressed populations and transforming America's consciousness. But the fractious and sometimes competitive dynamic these often sustain—where groups focus on their own needs to the exclusion and sometimes at the expense of others—continues to concern some progressive activists.[56]

In the mid- to late twentieth century, many liberals mourned the loss of a "cultural center," or sense of community, even as they celebrated multiculturalism.[57] Therefore, progressives began connecting various empowerment movements to a broader human rights, environmental, and multi-issue paradigm that stressed their interdependence and fueled mutual support within a global family. The ecumenical vision holds this idea at its heart. In 1969, the NCC's structure, leadership, and even worldviews reflected much of the Western white male hegemony of the society around it, and these needed the same shake-up as U.S. society did in general on issues of age, race, class, gender, abilities, sexual orientation, and so forth. But traditional ecumenists such as Bilheimer also believed that the ecumenical vision gave it the conceptual and theological tools to bring fully empowered diversity into the body of Christ (renewing the church from within) without sacrificing its devotion to unity, the most central concept within ecumenism. The mere cooperation of separate caucuses working on singular disconnected issues was not unity to Bilheimer. Feeling interconnected as one diverse body that recognized everyone's interdependence and that worked on all justice issues as a part of a whole was essential to ecumenism. Of course, this was easier said than done. The voices of disgruntled white laity who felt ignored and disempowered, and who wanted preference over the needs of minorities, also challenged ecumenism. In addition, many disagreed with Bilheimer over whether the traditional ecumenical vision was still appropriate for changing times. Debates over how best to renew the church and NCC would fracture these communities further in coming years. These debates continue.

Another cloud hanging over the Council, dampening its future prospects, was its dramatically shrinking bank account. Its 1969 income fell about five hundred thousand dollars below the total in 1968. This forced the Council to slash budgets and programs midyear, lay off forty-two staffers, and brainstorm ways to cut additional positions for 1970. Several analysts blamed its financial predicament on its liberal activism, which many churchgoers found unacceptable. As one reporter claimed, "less money is coming to denominational headquarters and to the N.C.C., partly because of 'a backlash among conservative local congregations' against these bodies' liberal policies 'in such areas as race and opposition to the war in Vietnam.'" Bob Gildea saw the Council caught "in a squeeze play between militant liberals . . . and aggravated conservatives," both of whom had decided to give their money elsewhere: conservatives to more traditional evangelical endeavors and liberals to secular agencies that focused more forcefully on creating social change.[58] Some urged the Council to sidle either to the left or to the right in order to chase the cash.[59] However, NCC leaders cited other studies showing little correlation between Council stands and its financial woes; they stated that the NCC merely reflected the financial hardships of its denominations, which were experiencing membership fluctuations and thus altering their disbursements to the Council.

Amid its budget crisis, the NCC's 1968 and 1969 books were audited by the IRS; this continued into early 1972.[60] Fernandez believed the Council's funneling of CALCAV's donations had triggered suspicion in the IRS, which, under Nixon, used audits to intimidate tax exempt organizations that supported antiwar efforts. Smiling, Fernandez explained, "I was filtering money through [the NCC] for every demonstration you could think of."[61] Kelley questioned the legality of this practice, but Fernandez did not think such "conduits" were unlawful as long as the receiving organization used the money as publicly stated. CALCAV was also audited. IRS reports on both came up clean; but while the hassle and labor costs incurred levied their own penalty, neither organization felt intimidated.

The Democratic Party was also engulfed in an identity crisis. In 1968 Democrats had splintered over the war and presidential candidates. The failure of liberals to get an antiwar plank inserted into their party platform, combined with the police riot against protesters at the Democratic National Convention in Chicago, inspired many not to vote in that year's election.[62] Humphrey's close loss to Nixon left Democrats discouraged and in disarray. Since the party had also backed the Civil Rights and Voting Rights Acts, southern white Democrats began a mass defection; several voted independent while others swung Republican as the GOP embraced states' rights in its platform to lure Dixiecrats their way. The ascendancy of the Democratic Party and its liberal establishment, which had begun with Franklin Roosevelt in 1932, was over. Along with geographic white flight, many whites also withdrew their support from social programs such as welfare and affirmative action, and the taxes that fueled them. This is significant because liberal mainline Christianity and its ecumenical movement had risen in tandem with the political liberal establishment, often collaborating on social programs, while sometimes serving as its gadfly on international affairs. But in 1968 and 1969, the liberal establishment, as expressed both in religious and political forms, visibly fractured, appeared to lose constituents, and declined in influence. Meanwhile, political and religious conservatives grew in numbers and visibility. Later, these forces would cooperate to elect Ronald Reagan for president, as religious conservatives boldly engaged politics to help repair the moral damage they felt liberals had done to the nation. In this new conservative era, religious and political liberals, including the NCC, found themselves marginalized, demonized, and struggling. In the early 1970s, the Council tried to process and cope with its decline in cultural clout as internal fracturing escalated. It continued wrestling with how best to be the church on issues of war, peace, race, class, gender, and economics. And it launched a decades-long exploration of how conciliar ecumenism might need to transform itself for a new era.

A DISMAL END TO A DEPRESSING YEAR

The war remained ugly and persistent as 1969 drew to a close. Stories of GIs massacring Vietnamese civilians in My Lai village, and of the military's elaborate cover-up, broke just before Christmas. To many peace activists, this epitomized the corruption of the entire military-industrial complex. As the *Christian Century* stated, "Mylai was not a criminal incident in an otherwise 'just' war, it simply represents the ultimate logic of a criminal war."[63] Signs of sagging troop morale became public as well when GIs at Pleiku and Saigon demonstrated against the war during the holidays. Meanwhile, Nixon carried the government's alleged covertness to new heights. To the frustration of antiwar activists, though, he proved skillful at retaining public support. Nixon pacified his silent majority with the Vietnamization program, promises of continued troop withdrawals, and transformation of the draft into a lottery system. And he encouraged the displacement of public discontent onto antiwar protesters. Militarily, he grew more aggressive with North Vietnam, hoping it would see him as an anticommunist "madman" capable of unleashing massive destruction unless it surrendered.[64]

He also mocked the seriousness of the Paris peace talks and insulted its delegates by supporting Philip Habib to operate as "acting head" of the U.S. delegation. Although Habib knew Vietnamese history and spoke a bit of the language, his interpretation of the war's issues offended North Vietnamese and NLF representatives. Elston's Vietnamese contacts complained that Habib was the only one they could not talk to. "What motivates this bastard?" they asked him. Paul Tran concurred that Vietnamese delegates viewed Habib's appointment as a "maladresse without precedent," adding that Nixon's "downgrading" of the Paris talks seriously offended Asian dignity. Tran also felt Nixon's "Vietnamization" would result in the communization of South Vietnam, for he heard that communist opponents to the Thieu/Ky regime were preparing to strike militarily once the United States had withdrawn from the ground. Thieu sabotaged General Duong Van Minh's attempts to organize third force groups while Nixon turned a disinterested blind eye. To Tran, this mistake became a costly lost opportunity.[65] Nixon's upper hand with the public, his continuing aversion to action that might bring real peace, and the depletion of the antiwar movement's emotional and financial resources, left liberal church leaders frustrated and despairing as the decade ended.

Serving as apologist for Johnson's Vietnam policy, Vice President Hubert H. Humphrey addresses a public session of the NCC's General Assembly, 1966. (Fontainebleau Photography, Inc., Miami Beach, FL, NCC Records, Presbyterian Historical Society, Presbyterian Church (USA), Philadelphia, PA)

The NCC's multimedia packet for stimulating congregational engagement on the Vietnam War included a vinyl record album and copies of the "Appeal for Debate and Action" pamphlet, 1967. (copies in author's possession)

From left to right: Rev. Dr. William Sloane Coffin Jr., Gerhard Elston, Rev. Dr. John Bennett, Rev. Richard Fernandez, and Rev. Dr. Robert McAfee Brown attend an executive meeting of Clergy and Laymen Concerned About Vietnam (CALCAV), circa late 1960s. (CALC Records, Swarthmore College Peace Collection, Swarthmore, PA)

CALCAV participates in an anti–Vietnam War demonstration in Washington, D.C., circa late 1960s. From left to right: unknown, Richard Fernandez, Rabbi Abraham Heschel, and Robert McAfee Brown. (CALC Records, Swarthmore College Peace Collection, Swarthmore, PA)

Members of the NCC's "Peace Team" delegation to Paris in 1969, which met with nego-
tiating teams for North Vietnam, South Vietnam, the National Liberation Front, and the
United States, report back to the NCC's General Board. From left to right: Rev. Dr. Howard
Schomer, Rev. Dr. J. Edward Carothers (United Methodist Board of Missions), and Robert
S. Bilheimer. (Religious News Service Photo, NCC Records, Presbyterian Historical Soci-
ety, Presbyterian Church (USA), Philadelphia, PA)

Standing outside the Roman Catholic Archdiocese of New York, James Forman burns a court order temporarily preventing him from disturbing services at Riverside Church, 1969. Through his Black Manifesto, Forman was pushing for millions in reparations from white church organizations. (Religious News Service Photo, NCC Records, Presbyterian Historical Society, Presbyterian Church (USA), Philadelphia, PA)

Fundamentalist minister Rev. Dr. Carl McIntire (right) of the American Council of Christian Churches protests consideration of the Black Manifesto by the mainline churches on the steps of Riverside Church, New York City, 1969. He reads his own Christian Manifesto, which demanded three billion dollars in reparations from "modernist" churches. (Religious News Service Photo, NCC Records, Presbyterian Historical Society, Presbyterian Church (USA), Philadelphia, PA)

Jonathan's Wake protesters join in a procession of delegates to the NCC's General Assembly in Detroit, 1969. (John Fulton photographer, John Fulton Photo/Art, Indianapolis, IN. NCC Records, Presbyterian Historical Society, Presbyterian Church (USA), Philadelphia, PA)

Jonathan's Wake protesters led by Episcopal priest Malcolm Boyd (third from front, with flower in mouth) urge "new life" for the churches while theatrically declaring the NCC "dead" in its current form at the NCC's General Assembly, 1969, Detroit, MI. (John Fulton photographer, John Fulton Photo/Art, Indianapolis, IN. NCC Records, Presbyterian Historical Society, Presbyterian Church (USA), Philadelphia, PA)

Jonathan's Wake protesters hold a mock "draft lottery" of delegates during the NCC's General Assembly, 1969, Detroit, MI. (John Fulton photographer, John Fulton Photo/Art, Indianapolis, IN. NCC Records, Presbyterian Historical Society, Presbyterian Church (USA), Philadelphia, PA)

NCC President Arthur Flemming tries to maintain order from the moderator's table at the NCC's General Assembly, 1969, Detroit, MI. From left to right: NCC Vice President Rev. Dr. Edwin Tuller, Arthur Flemming, and General Secretary Dr, R. H. Edwin Espy. Jonathan's Wake protesters doused them with red paint to express their disappointment that the NCC had done too little to stop the war. (NCC Records, Presbyterian Historical Society, Presbyterian Church (USA), Philadelphia, PA)

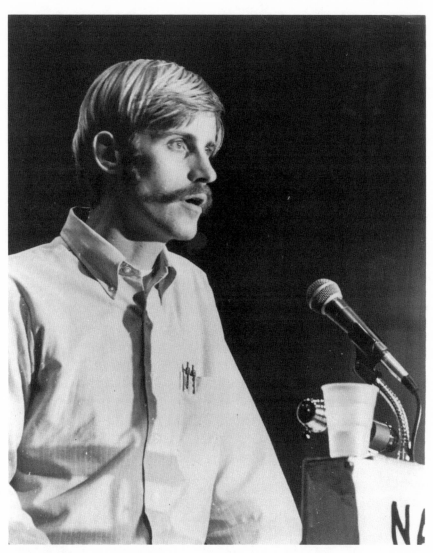

James D. Rubins asks delegates at the NCC's 1969 General Assembly to hold his draft card "in trust," Detroit, MI. (Religious News Service Photo, NCC Records, Presbyterian Historical Society, Presbyterian Church (USA), Philadelphia, PA)

Dennis Banks, a leader of the American Indian Movement, asks delegates at the NCC's 1969 General Assembly for $750 million to be used to aid American Indians. AIM was one of many activist groups either protesting or making requests of the NCC at this assembly. In the 1970s, the NCC helped mediate AIM's armed stand-off against the U.S. government at Wounded Knee and provided them with legal aid. (Religious News Service Photo, NCC Records, Presbyterian Historical Society, Presbyterian Church (USA), Philadelphia, PA)

Dr. Cynthia Wedel, Ed Espy, and Rev. Albert Cleage share a light moment before the balloting for NCC president at the General Assembly, 1969. (Religious News Service Photo, NCC Records, Presbyterian Historical Society, Presbyterian Church (USA), Philadelphia, PA)

(left) Religious leaders maintain a weeklong Easter vigil in front of the White House to protest the ongoing war in Vietnam, 1971, Washington, D.C. Methodist Board of Christian Social Concerns leader Rev. A. Dudley Ward reads from the Bible (center) while William P. Thompson, general secretary of the United Presbyterian Church, stands second from the left against the fence, in glasses and a tie. (United Methodist Church Archives, GCAH, Madison, NJ)

(below) Rev. John Adams, director of the Law, Justice, and Community Relations Department of the United Methodist Church, works through the auspices of the NCC to help negotiate a peaceful resolution to the Wounded Knee stand-off in 1973. (United Methodist Church Archives, GCAH, Madison, NJ)

NCC General Secretary Rev. Dr. Robert Edgar meets with Iraqi foreign minister and fellow Christian Tariq Aziz as part of an ecumenical coalition that sought to help avert the United States' preemptive war against Iraq, December 31, 2002. (NCC photo, National Council of Churches, New York, NY)

PART FIVE

VIETNAM AS A

MORAL ISSUE,

JANUARY 1970-

JANUARY 1973

Fighting Nixon and Seeking a New Strategy, January 1970–March 1971

BESIEGED

The Council stepped into the new decade punch-drunk from the frontal assaults it had absorbed at the recent General Assembly. Declining budgets hurt too. These forced it to explore questions about revamping itself and its relationships with various groups. Nevertheless, it retained enough forward momentum to continue attempts at transforming government policy as well as Americans' hearts and minds. In 1970 the Council grew more aware that its place within the establishment was shifting as Nixon treated it like others on his enemies list. His behavior toward the NCC and his actions related to the war baffled ecumenical leaders. Despite feeling more frustrated and ineffectual than ever before, the Council members kept trying to make a meaningful, public, ecumenical witness.

Still buffeted by the assembly's wake, in January, the General Board attended to lingering issues. First, it turned to the contentious job of restructuring the NCC. The board assembled a fifteen-member task force to evaluate the criticisms, suggestions, and long-range planning report "Mission in the 70s."[1] In mid-1970, the NCC weighed four different restructuring options proposed by this task force, which ranged from increasing centralization in the General Board to transforming the Council into a social justice coalition ministry. None was adopted. Restructural planning continued for three long years, culminating at the next triennial General Assembly in 1972.

The January board also expanded the number of youth, women, and ethnic and racial minorities in the NCC's legislative bodies. Theressa Hoover's nominating committee selected over five hundred people to serve potentially on the Council's program boards and committees, guided by the directive to "arrange a more equitable distribution of minority groups in decision-making positions of the Council."[2] The NCC's shrinking budget, which left several of its units in the red, forced the board to explore stricter financial controls as well.

Finally, the NCC had to cope with a new surge of criticism from those within the ecumenical movement who saw the recent assembly as symptomatic of the institution's maladies. Back in mid-1968, Alan Geyer had succeeded Kyle Haselden as editor of the *Christian Century*. He began using its opening editorial page as a vehicle through which to assess the Council and coax it toward certain reforms. Shortly after the assembly, Geyer summarized some widespread doubts about the NCC. For example, while he praised Espy's personal integrity, he described Espy's leadership as weak, passive, and unimaginative. He blasted the Council's inefficient bureaucracy, audacious array of programs, and wasteful spending. Like the Pentagon and other administrative bureaucracies that ballooned chaotically after World War II, the NCC needed streamlining, belt-tightening, and stronger centralized management. He questioned whether the Council's rapid additions of minorities to power positions were token gestures. But, of all its problems, Geyer most rebuked the Council's communication methods and style.[3] To him, communication ability could make or break the ecumenical movement. The NCC's overreliance on pronouncements, study papers, reports, and resolutions to share its work failed to connect with those in "the hinterland." It aimed its messages primarily at clergy and executives rather than laity. Its communication and programs were not well integrated with or inclusive of local church councils. All of this resulted in disconnections at various levels of the ecumenical community.[4] Geyer's editorials displeased Espy, and their relationship grew strained, but the *Century*'s new editor hoped to influence the Council's restructuring process in a positive manner.

Geyer did recognize that the NCC's troubles reflected those within its member denominations.[5] The United Presbyterian Church was a prime example. By 1967 panic had erupted over declining memberships and budgets, which the denomination attributed largely to lay protests against its social policies.[6] In 1970 it laid off 113 overseas staffers and an additional thirty within its home office, for its budget fell a million dollars short of the previous year. Church income had dropped 15 percent in three years, with inflation robbing an additional 18 percent of buying power. Things worsened the following year when its 1971 General Missions budget fell almost six million dollars from 1970; its other budgets took deep cuts as well. Presbyterian giving to the NCC dropped by two thousand dollars.[7] Interestingly, its 1971 General Assembly was much like the NCC's in 1969, complete with demonstrations by "Jesus Freaks," the United Presbyterian Liberation Front, the Submarine Church, blacks, Hispanics, and women. An attendee described it as "not just a polarized Assembly; . . . [but] an atomized Assembly."[8] Its decision to grant the controversial black communist and civil rights advocate Angela Davis ten thousand dollars for her legal defense fund sparked an uproar among angry white laity.[9]

Meanwhile, as mainline churches lost revenue and cut funds to the Council, the NCC was forced to slash staff and programs across units, including within the general secretary's office. By 1971 the NCC had trimmed elected staff from 181 to 120 and largely terminated its program at the Church Center for the United Nations. Several denominations did likewise.[10] And the NCC and its denominations were not the only ones in financial crisis. Between 1970 and 1974 so too was Union Theological Seminary, which parted with half its faculty, and *Christianity and Crisis*, which pondered folding.[11] Mainline Protestant institutions of all types were against the ropes. According to the *Century*, the NCC became a popular scapegoat at which to hurl frustrations, for it stood as "the most convenient symbol of the Protestant-Orthodox establishment in the U.S." Geyer surmised that church executives sometimes encouraged this in order to "deflect attention" from flaws within their own organizations. The former UCC official admitted that the denominations had also burdened the NCC at times with "excessive clearance and coordination" requirements, and by treating it like another denomination competing with them for resources. He described the NCC as "caught between the sterile ecclesiologies of managerial consultants and the unyielding sovereignties of denominational establishments." Geyer concluded, "Ultimately, the failures of the N.C.C. are the failures of its member communions to forge a common ecumenical thrust and to shape structures which will carry that thrust."[12] Lost confidence made it harder for the Council to recruit and retain people. In essence, the Council became trapped in a catch-22. While dependent upon the denominations' generosity for its viability, it was unable to inspire much from them while hamstrung by its negative image— an image that member churches sometimes did little to help rectify.

DISCORD AND DISSONANCE

The Council's problems with laity worsened as a conservative rejection of the social revolutions of the 1960s swept the country. People who packed the pews often identified with Nixon's silent majority, and he energized them both within and outside of religious confines. Disgruntled conservatives organized to counter the activism they felt had taken over their churches.[13] Angry Presbyterians created the Presbyterian Lay Committee to fight what they viewed as a socialist and secular drift. Within the Methodist Church, the like-minded "Good News" movement emerged. It even drafted a Methodists' bill of rights, which insisted that parishioners had the right to hear the traditional gospel preached from the pulpit, receive spiritual nurture for their individual souls, and not lose the bulk of their pastor's attention to "secular" social issues.[14] Smelling blood, the John Birch Society and other right-wing groups aggressively targeted mainline congregations. They used radio, print, film, and direct mail to attack the NCC and its communions in order to aggravate the local clergy-laity conflicts that already existed. The Birchers purposefully worked to foment divisions within congregations, creating crises in Methodist and Presbyterian churches, among others, that drew warnings from denominational officials.[15] Nixon played a contextual role in this. He inspired Vice President Agnew to spearhead the White House counterattack against dissident forces. In order to discredit them, Agnew launched a media blitz of invectives designed to crush the credibility of antiwar groups. This included the ecumenical churches.[16]

To satirize the ecumenical movement, Agnew exploited a common lay criticism: that it had sacrificed theology and nurturing individual faith to advance social change on the political front. Agnew also insinuated that liberal churches helped radicalize young people. He described modern youth as "children dropped off by their parents in Sunday school to hear the modern Gospel from a progressive preacher more interested in fighting pollution than fighting evil; you know, one of those pleasant clergymen who lifts his weekly sermons out of old newsletters from a National Council of Churches that has cast morality and theology aside as not relevant and set as its goal on earth the recognition of Red China and the preservation of the Florida alligators." George Cornell, the Associated Press religion editor, noticed Agnew's shrewd exploitation of a long-standing debate within Protestantism over the role of the church in society—specifically, "whether theology and morals involve only conditions of individuals, or also conditions in their societies."[17]

Bennett explained how this polarization fueled the churches' funding crisis. When parishioners felt their spiritual needs went unheeded, they hit church organizations in the pocketbook. Laity reduced donations to national agencies in favor of giving more to local, state, and regional bodies, and toward designated giving for particular pet programs. The Council's peace program suffered as a result. In 1970 it received $99,340 compared with $145,246 in 1969 and $172,034 in 1968.[18]

The new NCC president, Cynthia Wedel, ventured into this fray. Signaling that she heard laity's cries, she accepted blame for herself and her colleagues who admittedly ignored local views, leaving churchgoers behind in the quest for social justice. Wedel understood that sixties-era people no longer wanted to be told what to do or how to think, and that sparse two-way dialogue had become unacceptable. Therefore, she counseled that more receptivity to lay opinions would make churches' social action more effective. She also urged ecumenists to explain in plainer, more basic biblical terms *why* they felt led to seek particular goals and use certain methods to promote justice. Then she questioned their collective hypocrisy: "We know now that we have been unjust and unfeeling toward minorities, the poor, the young. But have we also been insensitive to the average man and woman in the pew? . . . Are we as leaders in the churches today arrogant and contemptuous of members of the Body of Christ who do not understand or agree with us?" As many local clergy and now Wedel suggested, perhaps church hierarchies had discounted and excluded parts of the body that did not pass a kind of social justice litmus test. Wedel knew this perception had crippled the church's clout with government. "When church leaders must give endless hours to explaining their actions and cutting their budgets," she explained, "the witness of the church is not helped.

When a statement by church leaders is criticized and rejected by millions of Christian voters, it has small effect on Congress or the President or the world outside."[19] Her solution, however, assumed that more upper-level tolerance and top-down education would solve the problem—not more lay-driven bottom-up shaping of positions—and this was not the remedy laity sought.

Besides, NCC and denominational leaders had tried and failed to educate successfully. As local pastors knew, laity often rejected information that did not fit their current religious or political frames of reference, and they resented paternalistic teaching efforts. In addition, conservative politicians such as Nixon nurtured the notion that the white working and middle classes were noble, self-made citizens (not beneficiaries complicit in a racist and sexist power system); they were a responsible "silent majority" that establishment liberals had shunted to the side while coddling lazy minorities seeking handouts, selfish feminists that abandoned their families, and insolent children courting media attention for their latest unlawful protest. Conservative strategists consciously crafted and pushed this frame and then exploited it politically; this was not something that merely bubbled up from the grass roots.[20]

Ecumenical leaders were uncertain how to adapt. Declining dollars tempted some to back away from the prophetic edge, to appease those who filled the offering plates. Others warned against this. With budgets gutted and criticism strong, the Council was forced to self-reflect.[21] Even the Division of Overseas Ministries was giving its relief methods a fresh look and detecting internal strains of imperialism that had long concerned Bilheimer and Elston. CWS was finally under its own microscope.[22]

MANEUVERING FOR THE UPPER HAND

In 1970 Nixon tried to neutralize the war as a midterm election issue. His obstinacy and ability to outmaneuver critics in the battle for public support fatigued peace movement leaders.[23] Nixon virtually declared war on the antiwar movement. As one White House staffer recalled, "You were either for us or against us, and if you were against us we were against you." William Sloane Coffin admitted, "I was tired of the whole affair . . . I was fed up with the war, already the longest in our history, and I was tired of fighting Nixon."[24]

Engendering further ecumenical dismay, Nixon began sponsoring Sunday morning worship services at the White House. Invitations were jealously sought, and Nixon used them to demarcate friend from foe as well as to woo political support. Preachers were chosen for their electoral, not spiritual, impact.[25] Given that the mainline Protestant leadership had largely distanced itself from his war policies, Nixon drew a different religious phalanx around him that would give his administration an aura of religious blessing. Although a tiny minority of evangelical leaders vocally opposed the war, many others such as Billy Graham complied (despite private qualms about Vietnam), commencing creation of a new conservative religious establishment that traded blessings with a political one, buoying the prestige of both. Most evangelicals took a nationalistic position on Vietnam—choosing to support elected authorities, stand behind America, and trust God rather than analyze the war.[26] Nixon aide Charles Colson was told to court and dazzle evangelicals at White House events, persons who might also fortify Nixon's electoral support in the white, NCC-hating, Bible-believing Sunbelt. This was part of Nixon's strategy to draw disaffected white Dixiecrats into the Republican tent. Colson said, "I found them [evangelicals] to be about the most pliable of any of the special interest groups that we worked with."[27]

Some Christians found the blend of "religion and private presidential politics . . . repugnant," said clergyman Michael Novak. He characterized Nixon's White House services as "not very American, not very Christian," and "not just worshipful in nature" for "they involve politics, prestige and an indication of intimacy with the people at the center of power." They peddled a "private, antiseptic, deodorized religion, full of illusions about God, country and the human heart." Reinhold Niebuhr derided them in a piece mockingly called "The King's Chapel and the King's Court." Nevertheless, the services were popular and became another deft means to surround Nixon with an aura of divine approval. They served to drain public power from the moral punch of his liberal Christian critics. A group of offended ministers and laity tried unsuccessfully to sue Nixon for what they called his unconstitutional blend of church and state.[28] Ironically, many years later, Colson tried to dissuade fellow evangelicals from succumbing to White House siren songs, saying that, "One of the reasons I have written books and given speeches warning Christian leaders not to be seduced by the wiles and the attractiveness of power in the White House, and to keep our distance and never mix the gospel with politics, is that I saw how well I exploited religious leaders when I was in that job. But that's what politicians do."[29]

Like his predecessor, Nixon ordered the IRS, FBI, and CIA to use investigations and even illegal surveillance to intimidate antiwar groups, including church organizations.[30] By late 1970 the FBI was dedicating 40 percent of its work to political investigations, and 95 percent of this focused on dissident groups. The CIA invested considerable resources in its similarly oriented "Operation Chaos." Surveillance was kept obvious in order to exacerbate the pressure felt by activist organizations.[31] This revealed Nixon's own paranoia about the power of his domestic "enemies" to undercut his policies and executive power. Elston was keenly aware of wire-tapped phones on his floor of the Interchurch Center. A friend swept for bugs and detected twenty-eight on the fifth floor, where the NCC had its IAC offices, and another on Elston's home phone. Elston also spotted government informants at planning meetings of antiwar groups.[32]

While formally cooperating with IRS auditors, the NCC and its legal counsel made it logistically difficult and physically uncomfortable for them to do their work. For example, they led IRS agents into a disorganized NCC warehouse with little guidance about how to find what they needed. The tiny cubby hole they were given in which to work exuded an atmosphere, Kelley joked, that was reminiscent of "early Attica prison." (Kelley suspected Strom Thurmond's hand behind the investigation.) The NCC passed its audit with flying colors. Only 8 percent of NCC activities were deemed "not exempt," which fell well below the allowable range of between 15 and 18 percent for organizations such as the Council.[33]

The audit was triggered in part by CALCAV's use of the NCC as a conduit for donations. A battle ensued between the two organizations when Daniel Bernstein, one of CALCAV's millionaire sponsors, died of leukemia, leaving roughly $1.8 million to the NCC with vague instructions that Fernandez "knew his wishes." This pitched the two financially starved organizations into a nasty squabble that once again drew IRS attention.[34] Fernandez was under the impression that using the NCC as a conduit for the bequest was legal, provided that CALCAV spent the money as declared. But the NCC was not convinced and grew more nervous about the tangled financial relationship between the Council and CALCAV. With respect to the bequest, Fernandez knew that Bernstein intended the full amount to go to CALCAV. However, Kelley and the Council's lawyers felt that, since Bernstein had given the money to the NCC and not CALCAV, he must have wanted it categorized as a charitable donation, protecting it from taxation. They also knew the bequest would become taxable if the entire sum went to CALCAV. Therefore, the General Board kept the money in the NCC's coffers and appointed a committee to decide how to apply it toward the peace purposes Bernstein favored.[35] Much of Bernstein's gift did, over time and in increments, go to CALCAV. But, because of the IRS investigation and other issues, Bernstein's money was not releasable to CALCAV for years. This hassle riled Fernandez, who had already spent much of the bequest on CALCAV projects prior to receiving any money. By the early 1970s, CALCAV faced a severe debt crisis. It owed over $150,000 to the NCC alone.[36] The fact that the Council was also strapped for funds strained the relationship even further; nevertheless, the two organizations kept cooperating on the war.

A dank mood began to infect Bilheimer and his staff, who doubted their ability to alter the Vietnam situation, at least until after the midterm elections. Even though antiwar groups planned activities for the week of April 15, which drew many ecumenical participants, Elston mourned how the loose Moratorium and Mobilization coalitions from last fall were crumbling.[37] Radical elements splintered, leaving the antiwar stage largely to liberals.[38] Nixon also maintained the upper hand in shaping public opinion. As Bilheimer remarked, "we could discover no indication that church people are continuing on the Vietnam issue. The total picture seems to indicate rather clearly that the Administration has defused the Vietnam peace movement, at least for the time being, pretty thoroughly." Republicans seemed headed toward midterm victories and Democrats appeared reluctant to question Vietnam policy, fearing such a strategy might backfire. Wall Street executives who favored disengagement also held their tongues. Bilheimer's team planned to do whatever it could to keep pressure on Congress for ending the war.[39]

Due to budget cuts, however, Bilheimer terminated the Council's relationship with its Paris informant, Paul Tran.[40] In his last note, Tran spoke pessimistically of the war's expansion and the hardening positions of each peace delegation.[41] Both the North Vietnamese and the United States sought outright military victory. U.S. invasions into Laos made explicit the widened regional context of the war. So too did the overthrow of Cambodia's neutralist leader Prince Norodom Sihanouk by Prime Minister Lon Nol who allied with the United States. The North Vietnamese accused the United States of instigating that coup (and Elston soon reached the same conclusion).[42] A negotiated peace still seemed distant. Nevertheless, CWS continued to plan church-assisted reconstruction in "Tomorrow's Vietnam," as did the World Council.[43] It was one way those bodies could express their desire to help end the suffering in a manner that was not yet fraught with a sense of futility.

As spring arrived, the popularity of Nixon's Vietnam policy waned. Polls revealed that only 38 percent of Americans supported his strategy (with 7 percent favoring escalation), down from about 70 percent the previous November. Conversely, about 46 percent now favored withdrawal, either immediate or gradual. Still, Nixon appeared to hold the initiative while antiwar movement activists fought internally and suffered from a poor public image. Whatever vitality remained now resided with moderate elements "whose goal," historian Charles DeBenedetti asserted, "was not revolution but reform, not to transform America in a revolt over Vietnam, but rather to save the society from the effects of further war."[44] Bilheimer's goals were broader. He wanted the war to trigger a national transformation in self-awareness and worldview. Shifting poll results revealed that a growing number of Americans desired a quick end to the conflict, albeit with as much "honor" as possible. About a week after the Mobe's spring events, Nixon appeased this public desire by announcing he would bring an additional 150,000 soldiers home from Vietnam.

AN EXPANDED WAR EMBOLDENS THE PEACE MOVEMENT

Most Americans seemed unaware that, in recent months, the war had spread to Cambodia. Following Sihanouk's overthrow and Nol's capture of the leadership, South Vietnamese troops, supported by U.S. forces, had entered Cambodia in order to eliminate communist staging and supply bases. Communist units counterattacked South Vietnam. Therefore, on April 30, Nixon publicly declared that U.S. troops would assist South Vietnam's massive offensive in Cambodia. Nixon presented the decision as a mandatory move to prevent the spread of communism, protect freedom and democracy, and preserve America's image.[45]

This time Nixon's rhetoric rang hollow. People focused instead on his executive decision to expand an unpopular war. Spontaneous bitter reactions rippled across the country and through the Capitol. Weary antiwar activists put aside their differences and found renewed energy for mass protest. On May 1, Cynthia Wedel and Ernest Gross went to the press to oppose America's role in the invasion, calling it "self-judging" and "self-defeating."[46] Bilheimer's team mobilized clergy for emergency congressional visits. They also generated a flurry of telegrams to denominations and local councils of churches encouraging people to speak out. As a result, a week later about seven hundred church people amassed in Washington. Kissinger said the size and nature of the demonstrations that week "shell-shocked" the White House.[47] A month of intense protest followed.

Campuses nationwide staged hasty demonstrations. Tensions ran high. On May 4, national guardsmen shot into a crowd of angry students at Kent State University, killing four and wounding nine. The fact that U.S. guardsmen turned weapons upon their own citizens moved many Americans to condemn their government for the first time. Students on campuses went ballistic with rage, and about 20 percent of the nation's colleges closed for varying periods as a result of uncontainable demonstrations.[48] A week and a half later, a similar incident at Jackson State University, which left two students dead at the hands of national guardsmen and state police, reinforced the growing sense that America's democracy was more threatened by its own government than by communists in Southeast Asia. Nixon had an enlivened peace movement on his hands, flush with new supporters. In addition, legislators began debating the constitutionality of Nixon's power to expand the conflict. Momentum grew in Congress for amendments to cut off war funding; some deemed this the only way to end it.[49]

On May 6, in an atmosphere of national chaos, protest, and campus revolt, leaders of the United Presbyterian Church, United Methodist Church, United Church of Christ, and the NCC released a press statement lambasting Nixon's contribution to a widened war, both at home and abroad. "Once again the U.S. has acted militarily in a situation which has increasingly revealed the futility of military measures," it said. "Once again the U.S. has by-passed constitutional procedures and ignored international agreements and institutions. In doing so it has acted contrary to its own declaration that it is seeking a de-escalation of the war and a political solution." The repetition of failed methods gave them little hope for a peaceful result.[50]

Throughout the month of May the Council and many of its denominations operated in a crisis-response mode, with a flurry of meetings to organize broad-based responses to the widening of a war that was supposed to be winding down.[51] Denominational and Council executives quickly drafted and released to the press a special "Message to the Churches" regarding Nixon's war policy and its ramifications. It discussed the crisis from moral, presuppositional, and practical perspectives and urged Christians to respond.

The message moved the dialogue with laity to new levels. First, it pushed the touchy point of repentance, asking Christians to see the current crisis as a call to national and personal contrition for perpetuating an unjust war. This would require courage to examine and alter basic assumptions, including those listed in the NCC's "Imperatives of Peace" statement. Second, it asserted Martin Luther King's and Reinhold Niebuhr's points that sociopolitical change needed creative conflict to move the status quo toward justice. Whereas most lay Christians still interpreted the command to be peacemakers as requiring them to quell discord, the message affirmed that, "True peace-making is not merely the stilling of conflict, but the achieving of right relations and . . . justice in social and political structures. . . . The times call for . . . new forms of constructive dissent, as well as new forms of social order."[52] It was a rather radical notion for the Protestant mainstream and still a tough sell in the pews. Twenty-five church leaders (theologians, communion heads, and Council executives) affixed their names to the message. As clergy without congregations, they enjoyed a unique shield from direct lay rebuke.

To put these beliefs into action the NCC, along with denominations and religious groups such as CALCAV, organized a large "Emergency Convocation on Southeast Asia" in Washington, D.C., on May 26 and 27. Over a thousand people arrived to press for legislation to cut off funds fueling the war. Afterward, the Council's IAC offered to help church agencies voice concerns via political channels.[53] The spread of U.S. troops into Cambodia followed by renewed public protests awakened more dovish sentiments in Congress, and peace activists took notice. Writing to a contact in Saigon, Elston described the changing political tides. "I have rarely seen such anger among Congressmen and Senators [toward U.S. policy]—even among those who are still supporting the President in public. Also, people on the Hill are shaken by the fact that neither the volume of visitation nor letters is letting up appreciably—they have never had such a sustained period of reaction to *anything* before!"[54]

The Senate approved the Church-Cooper amendment to halt funding for America's military foray into Cambodia by June 30, 1970. The House failed to follow suit, however. Congress did repeal the Tonkin Gulf Resolution, which had given Johnson authority to engage U.S. troops overseas indefinitely. Even though this did not significantly alter Nixon's course, people's hope for ending the war shifted toward the legislative branch. As Congress and the public grew more vocal, Nixon entrenched further into his hard-line policies and suspicions.[55]

Both the *Christian Century* and *Christianity and Crisis* celebrated the paradoxical adrenaline boost that Nixon's invasion gave a tired peace movement. The *Century* called it poetic justice. "With more than 400 campuses marked by student strikes, with Congress in an uproar, with the communications failures of a divided administration publicly exposed, and with church leaders more actively working for peace than they have been in many months. . . . What a turnabout it is," the *Century* observed, "for a regime in Washington which has been gloating over the weakening of the peace movement . . . to find itself suddenly facing the greatest crisis of confidence in national leadership in 40 years!"[56] *Christianity and Crisis* highlighted how Nixon's paranoid, self-absorbed personality twisted the meaning of this national response into a personal political attack. "It was an eerie indication of the isolated atmosphere that surrounds the White House to realize with a start that the President thinks that the great contest over the soul of America that is literally tearing this nation apart is somehow about him, Richard Nixon, and his political future."[57]

Nixon's intractability convinced antiwar groups, including the NCC, to increase their pressure upon Congress. For example, Bilheimer and Elston favored a petition drive by the National Coalition for a Responsible Congress, which asked legislators to condemn the war and force the president to end it.[58] An ecumenical convocation held later in Washington, D.C., which Elston helped plan, launched a campaign to "free political prisoners in South Vietnam" and pressure Congress to disengage American support from Thieu.[59]

The churches and the Council's Washington offices also worked the legislative angle through IMPACT, a self-described "interfaith legislative action network" that lobbied the legislature on a number of justice issues, including several related to the war. IMPACT monitored legislation that was of moral interest to the churches, helped prepare written materials summarizing legislative positions for constituents, and built local citizens' networks in key congressional districts that it could mobilize to action.[60] As influencing Congress gained importance and the NCC's funding dropped,

Bilheimer and Elston also channeled fewer departmental resources toward stimulating debate and action at grassroots levels. Besides, mobilizing local support had become CALCAV's forte.[61]

PUSHING PERCEIVED PRESSURE POINTS

The NCC kept pushing the issue of South Vietnam's repressive government before the public. At a June press conference, Council leaders condemned the perversion of American values reflected in U.S. support of Thieu and spotlighted mounting protests by students and monks. Don Luce wrote a graphic article detailing the torture of young dissidents.[62] A month later, Luce led two congressmen and congressional aide Thomas Harkin to see South Vietnam's prisons firsthand. Luce secured maps of the infamous Con Son Island prison from students who had been tortured there. When the team arrived, they spied a door that a guard warned was off-limits. One of them pushed it open anyway, and the group entered. The guard did not stop them. Inside the team discovered the infamous tiger cages that held political inmates. Harkin's photographs appeared in *Life* magazine and on television.[63] Here was proof that Thieu violated human rights to stifle political protest.

From June through year's end, the Council continued to publicize its positions, work toward a just peace, and engage international issues raised by the war.[64] Even though the NCC kept recommending use of the UN to facilitate peace and reconstruction in Vietnam, Bilheimer admitted to Schomer that he saw the Paris peace talks as the only real hope for ending the war in a just manner. He defended the Council's public advocacy of the UN, however, as a vehicle through which international opinion could speak on Vietnam. He wanted the global community to analyze U.S. actions in Indochina, and for Americans to hear its judgments.[65]

Through Schomer's services, the National and World Councils cooperated to collect fresh data from Paris on the status of the talks and postwar reconstruction possibilities. The NCC had lent Schomer to the WCC to coordinate its October 1969 meetings with the four delegations. After America extended its military involvement further into Indochina, the WCC requested Schomer full-time to coordinate all of its Vietnam-related efforts. This he did well into the following year.[66] From Paris, Schomer channeled his findings to the NCC, too, which helped replace Paul Tran's lost services.

In mid-1970, negotiations were deadlocked. When America invaded Cambodia, NLF and North Vietnamese representatives abandoned the peace table, threatening to stay away until America withdrew from that country.[67] Nixon, in turn, stonewalled the talks by delaying for eight months the appointment of a new lead negotiator to replace Ambassador Lodge who had departed in 1969.[68] NCC leaders worried that Nixon was losing interest in, if not purposefully sabotaging, negotiations. The United States removed its ground troops from Cambodia by June 30, and the talks eventually resumed, returning to their stalemated situation. Meanwhile, U.S. commitment to Nol's efforts against the North Vietnamese and Khmer Rouge grew.[69]

The Nixon administration's actions in Indochina disturbed and baffled ecumenists who remained frustrated by their lack of White House access. Schomer did all he could to probe for possible entrée into Nixon's thinking as well as for ways churches might help propel the peace process forward. For example, he met with General Matthew Ridgway, whose voice also went unheeded.[70] Ridgway told Schomer that if the White House refused to listen to sound advice, there was little one could do to penetrate its thinking. Schomer sought an appointment with Secretary of State Rogers but, instead, was "shunted to [William] Sullivan," a deputy assistant secretary for Far Eastern Affairs. Nixon had just selected David Bruce to head up the U.S. negotiating team, and Schomer hoped to glean insights into "the posture Washington would be taking" under Bruce's leadership.[71]

From Sullivan, Schomer learned that Nixon planned to continue the same hard line in Paris, which included fervent support of Thieu, no mention of a timetable for withdrawal, and the intention to push North Vietnam militarily toward compromise. North Vietnam, likewise, seemed prepared to hold on indefinitely until domestic strife within the United States weakened Nixon's stance.[72] Sullivan also dismissed the viability of an organized third force in the South that was capable of leading a peace cabinet or coalition government.[73]

The peace talks drew new attention in September when the Vietcong's Provisional Revolutionary Government's leader, Madame Binh, put forth an eight-point peace proposal offering a cease-fire and to negotiate the return of U.S. prisoners of war (POWs) in exchange for a set U.S. withdrawal date of June 30, 1971.[74] The PRG was also willing to accept a role in a future coalition government that might arrange general elections, as long as Thieu was deposed from power.[75]

Nixon did not respond directly to Binh's proposal, which insulted the PRG. Instead, on October 7, he took to the airwaves with a five-point proposition of his own. It aimed not only to steal the PRG's initiative but also to stifle the American peace movement and capture public support. It worked. Nixon offered a package that on the surface sounded reasonable and generous; but it was also diplomatically impracticable and further hardened the other side. For example, he proposed a mutual cease-fire and prisoner release that would require the enemy to lay down arms in most areas under its control. He called for an international conference on Vietnam, which Schomer knew that the North Vietnamese and PRG would reject as unfeasible, especially without the presence of China and the USSR. And he promised the United States would withdraw its troops from Vietnam, but only if the North and PRG accepted the current South Vietnamese government, allowed its people to create their own political solution via existing leaders and structures, and removed their (PRG and North Vietnamese) troops from South Vietnam, Cambodia, and Laos.[76] Posturing for the upcoming midterm elections, Nixon called for a show of support from his silent majority to "win a just peace in Vietnam," stave off military or political defeat, and isolate antiwar forces who wanted to "tear America down."[77] Although the war raged on, U.S. casualties were the lowest in years.

Several liberal politicians and periodicals praised Nixon's speech. But critics such as the *Century* called it "a major propaganda victory," not a substantive effort to promote negotiations.[78] Despite the recent exchange of proposals, Schomer noted that "nobody had come to Paris bearing gifts for anyone else," and "the adversaries were farther apart than at any time" since negotiations began.[79]

Schomer reached this conclusion after meeting with representatives from each of the Paris negotiating teams. He spent nearly two hours with Ambassador Habib, to get his interpretation of Nixon's proposal, and described the atmosphere as "prickly." Habib was visibly irritated by Schomer's queries and perturbed that the ecumenical movement had not thrown its moral weight behind Nixon's so-called peace efforts. Schomer also described the U.S. delegation as smug about the "broad domestic and . . . Western acclaim of the Nixon speech" and "outright ang[ry] with Madame Binh's acid rejection of the Nixon Five points." Habib viewed Nixon's proposal as generous and flexible. After all, Nixon introduced the possibility of total U.S. withdrawal and respect for an indigenous political settlement between Thieu and the PRG. But the United States adamantly refused to overthrow Thieu and the constituted republic of South Vietnam.

As Schomer departed, Habib threw a parting barb his way. Knowing that Schomer was scheduled to talk with the other side's delegations next, Habib said that, while Schomer "was better qualified to probe their thinking on the matter [peace proposals] than 99.5 percent of the people who would be calling on them, . . . they were certainly not going to negotiate with or through [Schomer], not esteeming [him] an 'interlocuteur valuable. They know, to put it baldly,' [Habib told Schomer] 'that your organization cannot deliver the goods.'"[80] So once again, a U.S. government official described the Council as impotent and useless, even while admitting that its staff member was clearly competent to explore the negotiations' complexities. Government officials did not generally dismiss the Council because they felt it lacked expertise or even sufficient realism on Vietnam. They dismissed it because it criticized U.S. policy and lacked enough public influence to be either useful or politically dangerous.

North Vietnamese negotiator Xuan Thuy explained his government's perspective to Schomer frankly. After reviewing how Nixon had rudely reciprocated their genuine and flexible negotiation efforts with a string of discourtesies, Thuy declared that Nixon's proposals still camouflaged America's intent to control Indochina's destiny through South Vietnamese puppet mercenaries. More surprisingly to Schomer, he stated bluntly that his people put little stake in the helpfulness of the American peace movement. They had witnessed how easily American liberals could be duped by their president's slick ways of cloaking imperialist intentions within altruistic-sounding speeches, such as Nixon's five points and Johnson's earlier appeal for the Tonkin Gulf Resolution. Binh's deputy also told Schomer that the PRG was ready to settle the war quickly, if the United States would meet two demands (which Nixon ignored): begin withdrawal of foreign troops with a deadline for total removal, and form a broad provisional coalition government in South Vietnam with the aim of organizing truly free democratic elections. Because Thieu and Ky were seen as impediments to free elections, the PRG insisted they be ousted and denied a place in that government. Many in the ecumenical community saw these stipulations as a reasonable basis for negotiation, for they were similar to peace ideas circulating within the churches.

Conversely, the South Vietnamese delegation told Schomer that the PRG and North Vietnamese sought Thieu and Ky's removal because the communists desired domination, which current leadership prevented; their talk about free elections was a ruse.[81] The South Vietnamese also reminded Schomer of Thieu's concessionary offer to share power with the PRG via a coalition government, suggesting that this illustrated their own will to negotiate peace.

Schomer described the peace talk atmosphere as bitter, polarized, and full of "propaganda feints."[82] Yet he also sensed that greater flexibility toward compromise might lie under the surface. His own anticommunist leanings may have colored his interpretation of the delegations' positions, for his notes reveal personal distrust of communist intentions and a partiality for the South Vietnamese–U.S. "willingness" to allow the communists an "opposition party" role in a noncommunist coalition government. And he retained his faith in the potential of third force assistance.[83]

Schomer still agonized over the NCC's fumbling of his orchestrated wise men's project as well. Therefore, he asked to try something similar at the World Council, using information he had gleaned from Paris.[84] Other than shaping their own positions, the churches had not been able to do much with it. Despite—or, perhaps, not fully recognizing—this, Eugene Carson Blake acted on Schomer's suggestion by inviting European leaders to the WCC to discuss what Europeans could offer toward a peaceful settlement.[85] While not expecting much from it, Bilheimer gave courtesy support.[86] His similarly skeptical counterpart at the WCC sensed these leaders were too tied to an imperialist mindset and preserving America's goodwill to speak truth to power.[87] Financial consultants recommended that this costly conference be deferred, however, which it was. As with the NCC, a budget crisis was subsuming the WCC. Program expansion, economic inflation, and reduced donations had plunged it into the red. This forced the WCC to retract and examine restructuring options "in light of its changing needs and resources."[88]

TIME AND SPACE

Bilheimer still hoped that the ecumenical movement could use the war to create a *kairos* moment and transform American worldviews. Part of this process involved stimulating international discussions about U.S.

foreign policy so as to build a prophetic global witness that might shake America free from its self-idolatry.

In December 1970, Bilheimer presented a paper at a Korean-American ecumenical consultation in Seoul.[89] He asked non-Western Christians to help push America beyond its exceptionalist sense of itself in relation to the world. Events that had rocked American society over the last five years had revealed "a fundamental confusion at the very base of foreign policy" where Americans previously had been self-assured, he said. This created a teachable moment. "Americans are not accustomed to being confused and uncertain of themselves in the world; they need discussion of the situation leading to acceptance of it and the emergence of new perceptions." Bilheimer wanted the nation to experience the same conversion that the NCC was undergoing, so he hoped the international community would tutor the United States here, perhaps serving as America's bridge toward a more compassionate, responsible, and mature understanding of itself.

This required lessons in cultural sensitivity and pluralism; for he explained that traditionally Americans had approached the world spatially in terms of conquering territory, expanding boundaries, tackling the environment, and exploiting continental resources. In essence, they experienced the setting of life as "space" where they could pursue their interests. However, others, like the Vietnamese, Bilheimer observed, were oriented not so much in "space" as in "time." Such cultures, he felt, had a stronger sense of history. Their place in and connections to history became the stage where life was lived. Americans were so spatially focused that they did not know how to honor this.

But catalytic events were forcing Americans to reexamine their basic assumptions. Bilheimer explained the collapse of America's Cold War consensus in light of transformations involving time and space. "The specific American perception of the free world environment, threatened by the communists, crumbled under the impact of modern events, just as peoples everywhere refused to be treated as an environment, asserting their own vitalities and aspirations, even in the face of overwhelming American wealth and power." Bilheimer recognized and celebrated the assertive agency of other peoples, seeing a divine purpose in it. "Fundamentally," he concluded, "the American mentality, even though buttressed by unique power, has been challenged to its depths by the vitality and intractability of peoples." It was time, therefore, for the global ecumenical community to help the United States find its way through this confusion and rebuild its premises upon a more humble, just, culturally respectful basis—one that Bilheimer also perceived as more Christian.

Youthful rebellion disturbed Bilheimer. (He and his youngest son argued vociferously over the boy's hair length.) However, he felt it functioned like a canary in a coal mine, signaling the country's cultural stress and confusion. As a result of the civil rights movement and the Vietnam War, he saw America's youth rebelling against their nation's actions and questioning certain traditional values, because these had failed to advance justice and freedom as promised. This revolt included resistance to organized Christianity, which had seemingly also failed to create a moral nation. Youth then pursued love and justice through alternative secular or spiritual avenues.[90] The church's troubles were part and parcel of the nation's. Thus, according to Bilheimer, they each needed the same awakening, the same repentance, and the same transformation. Both also needed the world's voices and God's presence to guide them forward.

Bilheimer wanted the churches to lead and learn at the same time. Yet he also doubted the ability of American Christians to do so. "[A]re they too much a part of the problem?" he wondered, sensing, to a large degree, that they were. To his dismay, American Christians tended to be as deeply tied to traditional, spatial, bipolar ways of thinking as were non-Christians—and perhaps even more so. Nevertheless, Bilheimer told his Korean audience that, "As Christians, we believe that power, whether political, economic, military or other forms, is not autonomous but subject to God. Therefore, those who lack power must demand justice and those who possess power bear a heavy responsibility to use power to create the relationships of justice, freedom and peace in which peoples find their true identity." The church had to do its part here, wherever it could and regardless of support from laity or governments.

Change felt stiflingly slow as 1970 ended. About 335,000 U.S. troops were still fighting in Vietnam. Although casualties had dropped following the withdrawal of some soldiers, the war had spread into Cambodia, and negotiations remained stuck and polarized. The peace movement was fragmented, exhausted, and limited in resources.[91] Liberal doves kept working through political channels, pressing Congress to end the war. Meanwhile, Nixon continued to disregard critics, rally support from his silent majority, and pursue a military answer in Vietnam.[92]

DIGGING IN AGAINST DEAFNESS AND DISINTEREST, 1971

Nixon launched the new year with contradictory actions on the war. While signing Congress's repeal of the Tonkin Gulf Resolution and assuring the public that he would continue to remove U.S. ground troops, he intensified the bombing over all war-torn areas.[93] A month into the year, South Vietnamese military units began amassing along the Laotian border, and American commanders agreed to support a planned invasion of Laos to attack North Vietnamese supply runners down the Ho Chi Minh Trail. No U.S. ground troops would be used. For the first time, the South Vietnamese military would fend for itself on the ground, albeit with devastating American air cover. The United States had been bombing Laotian targets secretly since at least 1965. But the public did not know this.[94] The potential invasion of yet another neutral country and further extension of the war outraged antiwar activists and ecumenists.

Frustrated by public apathy and Nixon's obstinacy, Howard Schomer, Robert Bilheimer, John Coventry Smith, and Eugene Carson Blake began planning Council responses. Schomer captured their mood in a letter to Blake. "I have just had direct word from the Hill that the top Senators are as much in the dark and as angrily frustrated as we are. . . . As the weary public ceases to react, Nixon will feel free to do almost anything he wishes on the battlefield."[95] Rising fears that China might enter the conflict if the war expanded further also gnawed at their nerves.

On February 8, the South Vietnamese invaded Laos with U.S. air support. But the North Vietnamese countered and drove their opponents into retreat. Vietnamization had apparently failed. Without U.S. ground forces, the South's army crumbled. As his poll ratings plummeted and fearing a public outcry, Nixon tried to put a positive spin on the battle.[96] Surprisingly, the invasion of Laos did not spark the kind of mass demonstrations that had followed the Cambodian controversy less than a year earlier. The lack of U.S. ground involvement seemed to have helped mute public protest. John Coventry Smith of the WCC said "the whole atmosphere on the television and in the newspapers is one of apathy and acceptance. There is deep-seated dismay but no particular expression of it because no one has any practical suggestion that he thinks has a chance of being approved."[97] On February 25, Wedel, Espy, Gross, and Bilheimer railed against the government's "lack of candor."[98] They argued that security concerns did not justify the secrecy of the recent invasion into a supposedly neutral nation. Nixon had cultivated his own credibility gap.

The McGovern-Hatfield amendment calling for a set date for troop withdrawal suddenly received a 73 percent public approval rating.[99] On February 24, representatives of twenty-four churches, synagogues, and religious agencies officially initiated their "Set the Date Now" campaign designed to garner widespread support for the amendment. Elston described Set the Date Now as a natural outgrowth of Negotiations Now!, which had become irrelevant once talks started. He, Schomer, David Hunter, Fernandez, and several denominational executives joined the steering committee.[100] They selected December 31, 1971, as the deadline for complete withdrawal. Democratic presidential candidate George McGovern and his running mate, Edmund Muskie, adopted this goal as well.[101] Hershal Halbert, international affairs director for the Episcopal Church and head of Set the Date Now, noted, "This is the first time that Catholics, Jews and Protestants have banded together in a program of education on the moral, spiritual, political and economic implication of U.S. involvement in South East Asia."[102] It was a program with a simple, popular goal.

Nixon countered by announcing further troop withdrawals and disparaging the dangerous inflexibility of a set withdrawal date. He warned that communists might inflict a bloodbath upon South Vietnam's people if Americans withdrew before its nationhood was secure. He also warned that a premature pullout might destroy America's chance to establish peace with honor, that is, a peace that won some key objectives. Anything less would be a defeat, and this should be unthinkable to patriots. Nixon also reasserted his right to bomb the North if it persisted in imprisoning U.S. servicemen. Like Johnson before him, Nixon rationalized his hawkish stance by citing the potentiality of right-wing attacks if he softened against the communists.[103] He hoped his rhetoric would make peace activists appear procommunist and weak on the POW issue. And yet, ironically (for those who knew Nixon's hawkish reputation), he also began warming relations with China.

During the winter of 1970–1971, antiwar groups collected once again to plan their spring protests. Collaboration was loose, as factions fought one another over ideology, tactics, and details. Nevertheless, they agreed to stage a series of events during April and May. Elston attended planning meetings and, along with Set the Date Now, found most promising the plans for a student-driven People's Peace Treaty and for large bicoastal peace marches in late April. Various religious groups were also preparing a series of Holy Week demonstrations.[104]

Another creative antiwar effort, "Unsell the War," had already launched its first ad. Some Yale students proposed this idea after watching a CBS television special called *The Selling of the Pentagon*, which unveiled military tactics to market the war. Over three hundred advertising professionals donated time, material, and creativity to a massive ad campaign to "unsell" the war. The ads promoted troop withdrawal by December 31, thereby supporting Set the Date Now. Hugh Heffner donated an entire page of *Playboy*'s March issue to an unsell ad that highlighted combat medals returned by GIs who had turned against the war. The ads were powerful, even chilling, in their ability to expose the war's hypocrisy and carnage. Radio, television stations, and magazines ran several free of charge. Organizers of Unsell the War needed a national organization with connections to help facilitate the project. They chose CALCAV.[105]

While Elston and Fernandez coordinated spring protest events, Schomer, Bilheimer, and colleagues at the WCC kept talking with White House officials and Paris peace delegates in an effort to break the deadlocked negotiations.[106] In mid-February, Defense Secretary Laird met with Schomer and Smith to discuss them. Schomer saw Laird as a confident, intelligent man who seemed dedicated to withdrawing U.S. troops but who displayed little understanding of races and cultures different from his own. He described Laird as "an old time American isolationist who has become an American imperialist."[107] Schomer and Smith emphasized their desire to see the war ended—not just to save American lives (through Vietnamization) but to save lives, period. They noticed that Laird immediately registered the point. Interestingly, a few days later, Nixon delivered a speech in which he echoed this sentiment.[108] At the end of the meeting, Laird had said he would welcome their suggestions for negotiations.[109] Given Nixon's and Rogers's previous uncongenial treatment of NCC executives, they gratefully jumped at the invitation and promised to offer some soon.

When approaching Laird a second time, ecumenical leaders wanted to do more than merely provide him with "refined rhetoric" to purify Nixon's image and appease consciences. Rather, the WCC's international affairs director, Leopoldo Niilus, urged the group to present practical "steps that could bring about new processes geared towards peace." Schomer agreed that, while churches should try to transform policy makers' worldviews, only practical, knowledge-based, actionable suggestions would appeal to Laird.[110]

Schomer considered Laird the strongest administration figure outside of the White House. Thus, like the NCC previously, the WCC now came bearing a careful, somewhat conservative, list of suggestions for Laird to help break the deadlock in Paris.[111] These proposals tried to thread a compromise between the various delegations' key demands that Schomer had heard expressed in late 1970. For example, to appease Thieu and the United States, they did not recommend that the United States remove Thieu and Ky, as demanded by the PRG and North Vietnam. However, to address the PRG's valid concerns about Thieu, they stressed that Thieu and Ky be stripped of all control over the upcoming elections in South Vietnam—suggesting it be given to an international supervisory body—and that campaign resources be regulated and equalized. The World Council also supported changes in the South's constitution to allow candidates representing the PRG and/or neutralist groups to run for and hold office. With regard to the peace talks, it suggested that an independent, well-respected person be appointed to revise procedures and perhaps assist with mediation. Although Schomer did not mention it to Laird, he also felt Nixon should appoint a whole new U.S. negotiation team. Schomer held little hope that a new message would be considered viable coming from "the same old faces." For their part, the WCC representatives felt as though they were already playing the role of "unofficial courier" between the four delegations, which allowed them to test ideas on those they visited.[112]

On March 17, Blake, Bilheimer, and Smith met for an hour with Laird, but they left uncertain about the degree to which he had heard, understood, or considered their message. Those in the WCC pursued follow-up discussions with Ambassador Bruce.[113] Bilheimer had grown quite skeptical of the Councils making any headway with the administration or in Paris.[114] Nevertheless, he thought it necessary that they push for total U.S. withdrawal, combined with a political settlement because, to him, Vietnamization was prolonging the war in favor of a military solution. He also felt the churches could do little to speed the release of prisoners. The administration promised to keep fighting forces in Vietnam as long as the North held U.S. prisoners, and the North refused to negotiate the release of prisoners until the United States committed to withdrawal. Responding to an inquiry about NCC efforts on behalf of POWs, Bilheimer said, "It has become clear to us that further work specifically on behalf of prisoners is largely futile, pending some political settlement of the war itself." After years of pushing for a negotiated settlement, Bilheimer had come to believe privately that U.S. military disengagement from Indochina was the most immediately realizable and necessary objective for the peace movement to push. If the warring parties could not reach an agreement soon it was time for America simply to get out.[115]

Despite inner doubts, ecumenical leaders continued publicly to endorse the goal of a negotiated political settlement to end the fighting. On March 20, about 170 Americans, including roughly 50 Protestant leaders from ecumenical denominations and agencies, spent a week exploring peace prospects with the four Paris negotiating teams. Elston helped lead the trip, while Allan Parrent and Jim Hamilton from the NCC's Washington office attended. They spoke with Vietnamese priests, monks, ex-government officials, French journalists, academics, and other knowledgeable people. Afterward, the fifty visiting church leaders issued a unanimous media statement about the need to take risks for peace. They supported a set timetable for U.S. military withdrawal from Indochina, for this might dislodge the blockage that was preventing productive negotiations. This particular position was already popular among antiwar liberals. These church leaders' verbal support simply gave it additional respectability. Several attendees carried the group's positions into congressional offices and urged local church members to do the same.[116] Elston was pleased that their statement received "a fair amount of response" both in the press and from members of Congress.[117] It was heartening that church actions could still make the news. Any press coverage at all—let alone good press—was a shrinking commodity for the NCC.

CHAPTER TWELVE

Waging a Moral Argument, March 1971–January 1973

STRATEGY SHIFT

By spring 1971, Bilheimer wanted to shift Council strategies again, and in a manner that would complement the work of congressional doves. Previous approaches had borne too little fruit, including the NCC's debate and action efforts as well as its attempts to transform the presuppositions undergirding U.S. foreign policy. While Bilheimer cared more about making the ecumenical witness than winning desired ends, pursuing the latter did matter, as long as those ends did not compromise the means.

One might assume that church leaders would have adopted a moral approach from the beginning. But they did not. Reinhold Niebuhr and other Christian realists had deemed moral arguments ineffectual in persuading institutions, which cared most about power and self-preservation. Therefore, ecumenists had opted instead to argue against the war on practical, political, and presuppositional terms, thinking this tactic would best capture the attention of government and affect policy. Realizing, however, that the Nixon administration had no interest in such dialogue, and no intention to listen to dissenters, ecumenists began moving back toward a moral argument. Since the government had always rested part of its justification for war on a moral framework of doing God's work to help free the vulnerable people of Southeast Asia from an atheistic tyrannical communist invasion, the churches felt sufficiently qualified to challenge this premise. Bilheimer suggested this strategy shift to Blake.

Bilheimer knew that congressional doves planned a major bipartisan spring thrust to halt appropriations for Vietnam. The most helpful thing churches could do, he told Blake, would be to surround this effort in a solid moral argument.[1] Drawing from "just war" theory long used by Christians, Bilheimer's premise argued essentially that America's military involvement in Vietnam was unjust because the United States lacked an achievable, defensible, beneficial objective and was using excessively destructive measures toward unreachable ends.[2] His ideas built upon earlier testimony that John Bennett, Catholic bishop John Dougherty, and Jewish professor Irving Greenberg had given to Senator Fulbright's Foreign Relations Committee about the war's impact on moral values.[3] Raising up a global ecumenical voice to condemn the immorality of U.S. policy became Bilheimer's next big project. This proved challenging, in part because the conservative counterargument, endorsed by the White House, was widely popular.

The relationship between racism and U.S. foreign policy also permeated morality discussions. In March, the Council's international affairs and social justice departments hosted a "Strategy Board" to explore this subject. Among other things, this group pointed out that nonwhite nations received much less foreign aid than those with white populations, and the aid came attached to strings designed to keep puppeteer-like power in U.S. hands. The board noticed as well that all State Department officials were white, and Nixon's speeches reflected the relative "unimportance of the non-white world." Global justice for nonwhites clearly seemed less urgent to Americans; for example, the U.S. government remained relatively silent on apartheid in South Africa and reluctant to pressure Britain there. Participants noted strong ties between America's economic interests and its political system, both of which were white-dominated and white-serving.[4] As Bilheimer considered the various moral aspects of U.S. Vietnam policy, race became central. It would receive greater attention in the Council's foreign policy discussions over the next eighteen months.

Members of CWS's Consultation on Christian Concerns in Tomorrow's Vietnam were beginning to see how racism and colonialism were embedded in long-practiced forms of overseas mission work. For example, Newt Thurber, who had recently held Westernized understandings of church mission, showed how much he had revised his opinions as a result of internal NCC discussions. "In tomorrow's Vietnam," he wrote, "the Christian churches will have to expiate grievous historical mistakes, disentangling themselves from a seriously compromising historical relationship. To many Vietnamese the Christian faith is something which goes with colonialism, imperialism and militarism." Thurber then recommended the "emergence of new forms of mission and relationships," which would abandon triumphalism, respect native religions, expose Christian values through service activities rather than proselytizing, take the shape of and be rooted in indigenous Vietnamese structures, and "be responsive to . . . Asian Christian leadership."[5] This internal renewal gave Bilheimer's staff something to celebrate.

As Bilheimer began preparing the Council for a strategy shift toward a moral argument, the NCC engaged in several spring antiwar events. Religious groups organized protests for Holy Week that included moral reflection and spiritual repentance related to the war. An interfaith vigil and fast in front of the White House by a small group of high-ranking religious officials drew the most attention. William P. Thompson was among them. The Presbyterian Stated Clerk, whom Bilheimer had found so valuable on the 1967 Mission of Concern trip because he could not be mistaken for a left-winger, was now standing outside of the Oval Office fasting for days in penitence. So too were the influential Methodist bishop James Armstrong, the Episcopal bishop Robert L. DeWitt, the president of the Washington Board of Rabbis, Eugene Lipman, and two college executives. The six released a statement that admitted complicity, expressed inner agony over useless destruction, called for repentance, and pleaded for new paths toward peace.[6] In the midst of despair, they prayed that America would find a "spirit generous enough to admit the wrong we have done to Asians, and large enough" to recommit to the unfinished business of addressing poverty, prejudice, and problems in the cities.

These six secured permission to stand before the White House. But near them a group of seminarians—without permission—chained themselves to the White House and Justice Department gates. After attempting to raise a charred crucifix on the executive lawn, eighty other religious leaders were removed and booked by police.[7] Partaking in this Holy Week fast left a deep impression upon Thompson. It propelled him concretely for the first time, via his conscience, to the front lines of the home-front battlefield. His memories remained vivid and impassioned decades later. Elston admitted he had always wanted CALCAV to do a huge exorcism around the White House with clergy in their religious garb sprinkling water and praying; to him, this event came the closest to realizing that vision.[8]

Pastors nationwide supplemented the Holy Week demonstrations with special sermons and local protests. In addition, the editors of *Christianity and Crisis*, the *Christian Century, Commonweal,* and the *National Catholic Reporter* released a joint interfaith appeal for penitence and action. Contrary to the judgment of conservative laity, these journals argued that Christians had been overly passive and easily appeased by the government; "we are convinced that the American church has been too patient—not too polemical—toward national leaders. We Christians have been too tolerant of American men of power, too forgetful of foreign victims of such power. Too often we have been manipulated into ineffectiveness by a sophisticated political machinery."[9] The editors joined the seminarians in their weeklong vigil before the Executive Mansion.[10] Ninety-two, including the editors, were arrested for blocking the sidewalk. While mild by New Left standards, this was a bold step for mainline Protestant leaders, especially given that most churchgoers still condemned civil disobedience as a tactic.

A variety of protests followed these Holy Week events. At one, veterans threw their combat medals onto the Capitol's steps. On April 24, massive demonstrations on both coasts drew huge crowds that rivaled the 1969 Mobilization. Those who endorsed the marches spanned the spectrum from Trotskyites to the ADA, CALCAV, SANE, the Teamsters, and twenty-six congressional representatives. Several groups, including CALCAV, FOR, and the American Friends Service Committee, spent several more days lobbying to set a withdrawal date while the People's Peace Treaty, which Elston supported, was presented as a House Resolution by four legislators. Liberals dominated these events and kept them nonviolent and respectable. As activities moved into May, however, radicals briefly reclaimed center stage. Thousands of young people, such as members of the May Day Committee, who had long supported the idea of a national strike to shut down the system, gathered in Washington with that intention.[11] They hoped to stop traffic and business operations, grab the attention of policy makers, and confront them with the option "End the war or face social chaos."[12] Elston had long advised his radical friends against a general strike, considering it ineffective. Once he realized they were committed to it, however, he urged them to plan it well and stop using the telephone, for they were telegraphing their tactics through bugged lines to the government.[13]

The Nixon administration was indeed aware of the radicals' intentions and was not about to let their plans succeed. On May 2, authorities descended upon a crowd of young people lingering after a rock concert and made massive arrests. Protesters used nearby churches and colleges to plan strike actions for May 3. But Nixon's deputy attorney general ordered the military and police to squelch any efforts to disrupt the nation's capital. Helicopters and marines toting loaded machine guns blanketed the city. Nixon intended it to be a "military attack" upon protesters, and to many it seemed as though the war had reached the nation's capital. Confused citizens and protesters alike skirted through streets dodging tear gas. Arrests were plentiful and arbitrary. Approximately seven thousand people were incarcerated in RFK Stadium and the Washington Coliseum. Scattered strike efforts continued through May 4 and 5, with arrests following each attempt. While some violence occurred on both sides, it was not prevalent. Nixon, who contemplated the idea of using "Teamster goons to beat up antiwar demonstrators" and verbalized vivid images of crushing such enemies with his heels, might have preferred more.[14] Elston avoided the May Day events. He saw the whole thing as a clash of misguided egos: those of radicals more interested in creating a confrontation than in planning an effective demonstration, and the ego of President Nixon who misunderstood people's agony over the war as being personal treason against his leadership.[15]

During the first half of 1971, public debates over several related issues fueled the formation of a morality-based antiwar argument for the ecumenical churches. First, the subject of U.S. war crimes in Vietnam had grown more prominent. The previous December, a citizens' commission that explored war crimes had sponsored a publicized hearing at which veterans told stories of atrocities committed under order.[16] The reports were so serious that the military then conducted formal hearings of its own. This coincided with the trial of Lieutenant Calley, the officer who had ordered the execution of several hundred unarmed My Lai villagers. The trial helped inspire Vietnam veterans against the war to conduct their own study into war crimes; several hundred veterans recounted incidents that verified the regularity and brutality of such acts in Vietnam, as well as military efforts to conceal them. CALCAV helped fund this project.

Calley was convicted in March and condemned to life in prison at hard labor. The ruling angered Americans across the country and political spectrum. Antiwar liberals felt that higher-ranking personnel who created the mentality and policies that Calley embodied were really to blame for the massacre. To them, Calley became the sacrificial lamb for a corrupt system seeking to hide its own culpability. Americans who backed U.S. Vietnam policy criticized the conviction of a soldier who thought he was "doing his duty." After all, body counts were the military's preferred sign of success; destroying the Vietcong's village support system was a military goal. This controversy highlighted further problems within the military, which included declining morale, increasing drug problems, rising desertion rates, and fragging incidents. The selective service system came under heightened attack, and Nixon planned to end the draft. No one, naval officer John Kerry told Congress, wanted to be the last person "to die for a mistake."[17]

Back in February, William P. Thompson had represented the NCC's General Board when testifying before the Senate Armed Services Committee on various ethical problems related to the draft. The Council had grown more aware of the draft's damaging effects through its Emergency Ministries program to resisters in Canada and Sweden.[18] Thompson asserted that the perversions of this war were exposed by the Calley-like actions of U.S. troops as well as by protesting young people whose lives were impacted by the draft.

Revelations of the military's attempts to cover up its own excesses magnified the credibility gap between citizens and their government. The extent to which Nixon was using the nation's intelligence agencies to harass and spy on dissenters came to light when stolen FBI files hit the press in March. In May, noted Catholic scholar Rosemary Ruether published the article, "Who'll Investigate the Investigators?" in which she railed against what she saw as the growing fascism within America's government and the narrowing of its citizens' minds. Much of this, Ruether said, "must be blamed on the Vietnamese war, to be sure. But," she continued, "public disgust over the war merely brought this corruption out in the open." Like Niebuhr, Ruether scrutinized Americans' sense of innocence, which undergirded blanket assumptions that Americans were somehow incapable of committing war crimes. "It does not take monsters to create national atrocities," she stressed, "but only ordinary people, pious and good in their private life, who are nevertheless willing to condone murder when confronted with 'foreign' matter which they cannot understand. The fascist goose-step is the product of fear of the unknown, deliberately cultivated through Manichaean interpretations of past political power and thwarted national pride. These elements are all abundantly present in the current American scene."[19]

Ruether called upon the NCC to investigate the full scope of America's Vietnam War–related actions and "distorted priorities."[20] She asked the greater church to create a public forum for discussion and assimilation of the findings. "I can see no other national institution of sufficient power, independence and concern for reconciliation capable of doing such a job, except that joint religious institution. . . . It may be heroic to imagine oneself a Bonhoeffer, underground and in prison as a resister of the Confessing Church. Far more important is for the churches to act now to prevent the necessity for such an underground church."[21] Like Elston, Ruether saw a church-state struggle emerging, similar to that in Nazi Germany, where the church must stand against the fascism of the state. Unbeknownst to her, Bilheimer was already planning an event to answer her request. In June, when the *New York Times* began publishing the Pentagon Papers, public faith in government plummeted lower, and Nixon resolved to plug all leaks of secret U.S. activities.[22]

The desire to dissect and publicize war's moral aspects was swelling among ecumenists. In a sermon Allan Parrent urged the church to "deal with it." Like Elston, Ruether, and Bilheimer, Parrent called upon the body of Christ to help the nation face the repercussions of its moral failures in Vietnam. "This is where the church has a role to play, if it has been able to withstand the constant temptation to be a captive of the culture or chaplain to the status quo. If it has retained its integrity and autonomy, it can then question basic assumptions, provide broader perspectives for a more adequate worldview, and raise the level of debate and understanding." He felt government officials often overlooked moral considerations because they dubbed such sensitivities incompatible with "hard-nosed realism." This led to tragedies such as that in Vietnam. But, in Niebuhrian fashion Parrent explained, "the problem today is that the national success story of American history has not prepared our nation to deal very well with tragedy, with irony, with frustration, with limitations. Just as the church ministers to individuals in time of personal tragedy or crisis, it must now minister to a nation facing fully for the first time that tragic element in history which its good fortune has until now allowed it to avoid."[23] Speaking before the Presbyterian General Assembly about America's moral crisis in Indochina, the renowned Buddhist monk and peace activist Thich Nhat Hanh agreed.[24] The chorus for such a strategy grew loud.

Reinhold Niebuhr died in June 1971. During World War II, Niebuhr had tried to move the church away from social action strategies reliant upon pure moralizing into the realm of realistic power politicking in the cause of justice. But his heirs at the NCC, who had spent years arguing the practical data points of Vietnam policy with unheeding officials, were ready to recover more of the church's traditional role as the moral gadfly of the nation.

BOB'S BABY—BACK TO BASICS

In 1966 Bilheimer had accepted Espy's offer to head the International Affairs Commission because he felt compelled by his faith to generate a true ecumenical witness against U.S. Vietnam policy. This had proved harder than anticipated. Even though most NCC denominations had passed statements of varying degrees against U.S. military involvement there, these tended to be weaker than the Council's and still suspect to parishioners.[25] Bilheimer remained frustrated by American Christians' lack of ecumenical perspective and theological understanding. Even many denominational leaders seemed so bound to cultural biases that they appeared partially blind to the experiences, visions, and needs of people in other nations. To Bilheimer, the American ecumenical "giants" of earlier years, such as Van Dusen and Cavert, had been succeeded by ecumenical "pygmies" more buffeted and confused by the times than able to spearhead a foresightful and theologically based witness amid them. When religious leaders tried to be prophetic, he said, they often forgot to be "churchmen," or rather, they did not know how to turn their vocation as churchmen into a prophetic witness on social issues. Instead, they simply took an issue, made political pronouncements, and called for action on it, thus becoming just "another activist screaming in the wind."[26] As a *Christian Century* article explained, this strictly activist approach to social issues threatened to turn Christianity into a culture-bound civic religion from the liberal side just as Billy Graham and Nixon had done from the conservative. It was "The Kingdom Reduced to 'Causes.'"[27]

Years of trying to stimulate an ecumenical witness against U.S. Vietnam policy had left Bilheimer weary. Public and media criticism attacked the liberal churches' style, structures, strategies, interpretations, and assumed roles. Funds dried up and pews became emptier. The Council and its denominations agonized over declining staffs and budgets as well as losing supporters from the government and grass roots. In desperation Bilheimer felt they often abandoned real ecumenical leadership to support a variety of "soapbox" stands in order to please the left while moderating other aspects to appease a public that was swinging politically and economically to the right. Disillusionment over the future of organized ecumenism weighed upon him. So few seemed aware of what the body of Christ, as "a people amidst peoples," really meant. Instead, organizations helped cloister Christians into narrow politicized groups, which encouraged them to see only their favored issue and listen only to others in their caucus. The National Council was falling prey to the same cultural forces that had fractured American society. Bilheimer had also lost confidence in Espy's leadership; the compassionate Espy had been so eager to please everyone that he had allowed the NCC to be swept up by divisive forces intent on splitting the Council in competing factions.[28]

In 1971 Bilheimer prepared to lead one last effort to generate an ecumenical witness against U.S. Vietnam policy. He urged the General Board to sponsor a huge conference focused on the moral issues involved. As a young man, Bilheimer had discovered his gift for organizing conferences, and his years at the World Council confirmed their value. They were a useful tool for orally based church people accustomed to listening and persuading. Ecumenical conferences had fostered cohesion, unity, and strength of witness. One centered on moral questions arising from the war might do so in America. Polls indicated that the public would be receptive to a moral approach. The board concurred that such an event might help reignite Vietnam as an election-year issue with tired voters.[29]

Therefore, the June General Board authorized holding "An Ecumenical Witness" conference.[30] This event would aim to use the church's authority to remove any appearance of moral blessing for U.S. Vietnam policy. As organizers explained, despite the NCC's and CALCAV's "actions, programs and pronouncements [these] have not yet succeeded in withdrawing the moral sanction from the war for the average churchgoer."[31] Perhaps the conference could inspire the nation to transform tragedy into wisdom and initiate the healing and reconciliation process. Organizers expected to invite between 600 and 850 delegates from around the world. Jewish and Roman Catholic leaders would also participate. Discussions would center on the human repercussions of the war, the role of racism in it, and the "consequent responsibilities of this country" both in Indochina and the

United States.[32] Additionally, conference designers envisioned the Ecumenical Witness as a springboard event for creating local cells of ongoing study groups to send continuing ripples of "debate and action" through grassroots communities.[33] Bilheimer hoped this consensus-building event would complement CALCAV's more localized efforts. Elston called the project "Bob's baby"; it would be his boss's climactic attempt to fulfill his calling at the NCC.

CHANGING TIMES AND SHIFTING SANDS

Times were changing, creating new challenges for groups still interested in rallying mass demonstrations for peace. As U.S. casualties declined and the public tired of protests, the Vietnam War shrank as a campaign issue. Nixon knew how to turn public opinion against antiwar activists, which he had done repeatedly over the last year. In mid-1971, Nixon captured even more of the foreign policy offensive when China extended him a sought-after invitation to visit. It seemed strange that the staunch cold warrior would seek reconciliation with the reds, but current tensions between China and the USSR made such diplomacy appealing—a move that the NCC had long recommended. Uncompromising anticommunism faded as Nixon legitimized a new détente relationship with those nations. His savvy step also mellowed the liberal criticism of his foreign policy. Prior to Nixon's Peking trip, Elston and about thirty church leaders met with Chinese officials in Ottawa, Canada. They expressed dismay that the Chinese would be so "soft" on Nixon and, in effect, play into his 1972 electioneering strategies. The Chinese resented this allegation but cordially interacted with members of what they called the "new church," which included blacks and women, so different from the old missionary "China hands" that the communists had once expelled from their country.[34]

Other changes affected the church's witness, too. In May, South Vietnam ousted Don Luce for unspecified reasons. He had lived there for thirteen years. With his removal the churches lost perhaps their most discerning and connected Vietnam observer. In September, South Vietnam also barred Luce's former organization, International Voluntary Services. Despite official denials Director Hugh Manke knew that IVS was ordered out "for political reasons and at the urging of the U.S. government." As Manke explained, IVS volunteers were in a "good position to spot irregularities in the [coming South Vietnamese] election," and many had become openly critical of Thieu's regime.[35]

In August 1971, CALCAV sponsored a weeklong conference in Ann Arbor, Michigan, to take stock of itself and shape a future direction that was appealing to both its local chapters and its national office. While CAL-CAV's membership contained mostly moderate liberals, it also included radicals who pushed the group further to the left than the NCC. In Ann Arbor, radical members carried a Vietcong flag in a conference peace parade and established communication links with Madame Binh and Xuan Thuy. What seemed to be CALCAV's growing advocacy of an "enemy" victory and blanket criticism of America as oppressor alienated two former supporters. (It also drew noticeable FBI surveillance.)[36] Peter Berger severed his membership; he was followed later by Richard John Neuhaus, once one of CALCAV's most outspoken long-time advocates. As the country moved in a more conservative direction, so did Neuhaus and Berger. Elston sensed that Neuhaus's move was motivated less by principle than by his opportunistic interest to stay in the religious limelight. Elston recalled Neuhaus confessing that those who wished to retain influence must be willing to follow the conservative trend. Elston resented Neuhaus's shift, and the two parted on sour terms after Ann Arbor. In subsequent decades, Neuhaus became one of the Council's most virulent and notable foes.[37]

While CALCAV lost some old supporters, including a few Jewish members, it gained new adherents, especially Roman Catholics. It hired two new national leaders, Trudi Young and Carl Rogers, to work with Fernandez and help revitalize the organization. The Ann Arbor conference and CALCAV's new leadership did succeed in forging stronger links between local chapters and the national office.[38] They also stimulated a flurry of creative social justice projects that both included and went beyond the war.

During 1971 and 1972, the Council was inundated with critical evaluations as both conservative laity and leftist groups levied complaints.[39] Analyzing the latter for the General Board, Dean Kelley pinpointed the Council's "New Deal" worldview as being an impediment in the 1970s. The NCC's top-down, government-trusting social justice model was falling out of step with the demands of those it aimed to champion. Radicals scrutinized assumptions from that bygone era, including the value of bureaucratization, the goal of cultural integration, and the paternalistic protection of vulnerable persons. Bottom-up, decentralized, self-empowerment approaches that valued a certain amount of cultural separatism were now popular. Perhaps the NCC should reevaluate its own assumptions about how best to foster justice, Kelley suggested. It was doing so somewhat on the international scene; domestically it had done less.[40]

In his report, Kelley tried to place the Council's problems into a broader historical context than others had done. The NCC and much of its executive staff were products of that earlier era, when the premises that shaped liberal thinking hit their creative apex and when conciliar ecumenism was waxing. Groups from both left and right were now questioning the goals and methods of Roosevelt-era liberals. Battles over Vietnam-related issues had also shaken some of the triumphalism out of the ecumenical movement, especially when it came to international affairs and mission work. These confrontations helped expose that the elitist attitudes inherent in America's globalistic policies were also present in the ecumenical movement's means of advocating and enacting its own social justice agenda. Some wondered whether the NCC was learning these lessons too late. Ironically, as the NCC and WCC struggled, several local councils of churches were thriving. William Cate, of the Church Council of Greater Seattle, called it the best of times for local interfaith dialogue and interchurch cooperation.[41]

Throughout the fall and winter Bilheimer's international affairs team prepared for the Ecumenical Witness conference that was slated for mid-January 1972.[42] The staff assembled national "inquiry groups" to hold follow-up hearings on issues emphasized by the conference, and it commissioned background papers to help launch discussions. The conference format would revolve around small working group discussions punctuated by multimedia presentations, distribution of resource material, and featured speakers.[43] As of December 30, the conference had 132 sponsors, making it a huge interfaith event. Elston said that he "originally thought it would be a much smaller thing, but it snowballed."[44] It was a mammoth undertaking, and Bilheimer's expectations ran high.

By year's end, the United States had 156,000 troops left in Vietnam. Its air war over Indochina still thundered in support of South Vietnam's efforts on the ground. But as U.S. troops slowly returned home, communist forces increased their attacks. In October, Thieu was returned to power for another four years in a corrupt election where he stood as the only candidate. The United States still refused to abandon him. Over the year Kissinger and Le Duc Tho had engaged in secret peace negotiations, but official talks remained stalled.[45] The war-weary public had shifted its attention to other things. Many religious groups, including the NCC, paid more attention to postwar concerns, like the needs of Vietnam veterans and amnesty for war resisters. But the Council also hoped a large moral outcry from America's religious communities would stimulate a ground-swelling plea for peace as the 1972 election year commenced.

AN ECUMENICAL WITNESS, 1972

On January 13, the Ecumenical Witness conference opened in Kansas City, Missouri, purposefully tucked away in America's heartland, far from the centers of eastern elitism. The event's official "Call" invited participants to assume a confessing church stance in addressing moral aspects of the Vietnam War. It challenged attendees to approach the subject more theo-logically—more biblically—than liberal clergy had done in recent years, and to transcend nationalism in doing so. In addition to "clarify[ing] the moral issues" involved, the conference also aimed to discern action steps for Christians regarding the war and its repercussions.[46]

Bilheimer designed the conference both to teach and to enact ecumen-ism. Its "Call" distinguished between "national religion" and a more tran-scendent loyalty to God that witnessed against the immoralities committed by earthly powers, including one's own country. He hoped the conference would clarify the difference for American Protestants—and stress how imperative it was for the church to be an international community rather than just a spiritual rubber stamp for American culture.

Speeches and papers designed to spark working group debates touched upon a number of subjects. Foremost among them was the human cost of war. William Sloane Coffin Jr. explained how the Vietnam conflict had slowly deadened Americans' sensitivity to others' suffering, thus dehu-manizing them. He urged the church to stress saving lives rather than sav-ing face, which he deemed no longer possible anyway.[47] Similarly, Arthur Walmsley, general secretary of the Massachusetts Council of Churches, wrote of the crisis of hope, the cloud of despair, and the numbed condition of people's hearts resulting from the war. "For an increasing number of Americans, the issue has . . . [triggered] a search for a deep truth about themselves as Americans, as human beings."[48] Herein, his analysis mir-rored Bilheimer's belief that the war could become a catalyst for repen-tance, growth, and renewal. Human rights activist Marion Wright Edelman pointed her finger at the attendees themselves. How could Christians, who were once appalled by the use of dogs and fire hoses against Birmingham's black children, passively accept the napalming of Vietnamese and the shootings at Kent State? She received a standing ovation when she said the war had "deadened our sense of moral outrage." In conjunction with a film on the destruction caused by the air war, Don Luce described how bombing villages inflicted profound spiritual pain upon Vietnamese, not just physical hardship.[49] Rich Killmer, who administered the NCC's Emergency Ministries program, reminded participants of the spiritual, psychological, and physical distress experienced by veterans and draft resisters who had different needs than men affected by earlier wars.[50] These presentations highlighted the multifaceted, multilevel damage done to a whole generation in Vietnam and the United States as a result of the war.

Other speakers, such as Eugene Carson Blake, focused on how the United States had forfeited leadership through its misuse of power and hypocritical betrayal of values. Blake said that America no longer stood for freedom, democracy, or justice but for an oppressive status quo, and he appealed to Christians to call the nation back to itself.[51] Sterling Cary, who would become the Council's next elected (and first African American) president, described America's globalistic policies as another form of racist imperialism that was not acceptable in an interdependent multicultural world. Cary reminded attendees that one's patriotism should be tied to the world community, no longer to a single nation.[52] The civil rights and ecumenical leader Andrew Young reiterated the connection between racism and militarism.[53] True security required peace based upon justice, not power. International delegates including André Dumas of France and Jurgen Hilke of Germany also challenged Americans to face their sinfulness, cultural weaknesses, excesses, and twisted values, just as European nations had been forced to do after regretted wars.[54] Altogether, the speakers articulated what religion scholar Robert Wuthnow called a second or alternative civil religion, which rejected American exceptionalism and religious nationalism in favor of membership within and responsibility toward the global community.

Conference participants also received shocking evidence of church complicity in the war from an extensive NCC-sponsored study on church investments in the military-industrial complex. Basically, the churches had garnered sizeable profits. The investments of major Protestant agencies in the nation's sixty main military contractors in 1970 totaled about $203 million and had earned the churches $6.2 million. The report concluded that, "These investments are big business for the churches representing an important if not the most important portion of their holdings." This damaging information had circulated through certain church leadership circles back in 1970 but was now reaching the public for the first time.[55] These facts hit the front page of the *New York Times* a week before the conference, causing quite a stir among congregations. First, the *Times* story opened with a line suggesting that the NCC "accused" ten of its members of hypocrisy related to the war.[56] That verb was incendiary and not reflective of the NCC's intended tone, for the document included the NCC's own complicity in investment choices. The Council had over $2.3 million invested in companies doing business for the Defense Department, which comprised 34 percent of its total stock value. Profits made from these stocks accounted for 41 percent of the Council's annual stock income.[57]

Second, the data itself was stunning, and the report received significant press coverage. The United Methodist Church, as the biggest mainline denomination with the largest investments, topped the list. Questions flooded Herman Will's office from laity and clergy demanding answers and help in dealing with the fallout.[58] Will explained that, although the Methodists invested only in companies that limited their military contracts to 10 percent or less, this still resulted in a large sum, and the church was now reconsidering its policy. He also admitted frankly that the churches had not thought deeply about how their investment choices should reflect their social positions. This marked a new step in their awareness.

As *Christianity and Crisis* noted, this sticky issue also touched back upon James Forman's accusations about where the churches got their money— that "they are businesses involved in business."[59] In May the NCC decided to sell 50 percent of these questionable holdings, informing companies' chairmen that the sale was a protest against their roles in the Vietnam War. The Council saw this as an important symbolic action. It justified holding onto the remaining 50 percent as leverage to work "for change from within the corporations who have contrary policy" to the NCC. It saw complete divestment as a measure of last resort. Other religious bodies, like the Brethren, divested from all of their military stock holdings.[60]

CALCAV's method of dealing with such investments reflected Fernandez's belief that institutional change required groups to wield power against power. Therefore, CALCAV boldly confronted corporations at stockholders meetings.[61] Earlier, at the Ecumenical Witness conference, Fernandez reiterated his emphatic belief that churches must stir creative conflict in the face of injustice, rather than appeasing it with passive statements and hand-wringing. As he often said, church people must "act their way into thinking" rather than "think their way into acting" if they wished to advance social change.[62] However, this notion ran somewhat counter to Bilheimer's, and Fernandez purposefully exposed this tension. He challenged conference participants to do more, study and pontificate less, and generate the kind of congregational conflict that engaged people's moral passions. He wanted them in touch with their hearts and humanity, not just with their intellects. He also encouraged them to develop empowering relationship-building communication with the grass roots in order to effect social change; church organizations were realizing the importance of this.

Fernandez felt that government officials would keep treating church leadership lightly as long as it failed to bring its own people along. He held up CALCAV as an example of what action-based creative conflict and strong grassroots relationships could do. Ecumenical Witness organizers hoped this conference would indeed spark a communication network of local-based cells that could increase political pressure for an end to America's role in the war. But Bilheimer also felt it critical that the church know its own mind *first*; the church must be unified regarding how its actions emerged from theologically grounded beliefs before it could make an effective witness. The difference between Fernandez and Bilheimer was perhaps as much about priority as strategy. Fernandez's primary aim was to create social change in the world. Bilheimer's was to build a strong ecumenical community that could distinguish itself as the church in its worldly witnesses. For Fernandez, the tediousness and insular nature of the conference discussion process removed the church from the front lines of social change, making it irrelevant to and even absent from the world. For Bilheimer, it was in those consensus-building discussions that the church found and rejuvenated itself, as an institution different from secular organizations, so that it could fulfill its theologically based justice-seeking mission in the world. In hindsight, both men were correct.

The Ecumenical Witness generated a public "Message" as well as a list of possible "Actions" that Christians might consider as part of their witness against the war. The message summarized conference themes. Recalling America's stated intentions, it also declared the war lost on numerous fronts. "We have not defeated communism in Indochina nor have we defended freedom. Imposing our will on distant lands and poor and non-white peoples, we have participated in their destruction while thwarting their self-determination. The guilt is not ours alone, but guilt is ours." In addition, it condemned how the nation had "squandered our wealth and misused our power" and neglected human need at home while sanctioning violence by example. "Our present national humiliation is the judgment of God upon us."[63]

Finally, the message outlined how and why the conference deemed America's role immoral. Retracing the war's history, it highlighted specific points where the United States demonstrated racism, disrespect for international agreements and law, unilateral abuse of power and weaponry, devaluation of the life and lands of non-Americans, support of dictatorial corruption to squelch the self-determinative freedom of people, and a hubristic useless pursuit of military victory rather than a negotiated settlement. For these "sins," the message called church communities to lead America toward a national act of repentance and restitution. Citing biblical precedent, it reminded people that "Prophets of old called their nations to repentance. So must we. They cleansed their temples. So must we. They identified with the sins of their people and pled for mercy. So must we. / But words . . . are not enough. All of these are nothing unless they issue forth deeds of peace."[64]

Therefore, six pages of action strategies followed. Since attendees could not reach consensus they included a smorgasbord of suggestions ranging from mild to radical. They clustered actions into specific categories, including ending America's role in the war, combating racism, channeling religious power into the political arena, using economic power in morally responsible ways, fostering repentance and reconciliation, and supporting basic freedoms.[65]

Most attendees spoke positively about the Ecumenical Witness in its immediate aftermath. The conference exceeded Elston's expectations, benefiting from "wonderful people," good materials, and decent press coverage.[66] Both he and Bilheimer felt it truly was an *ecumenical* meeting. The *New York Times* described it as "the most comprehensive religious gathering ever assembled in the United States over the peace issue, largely because of increased support among Catholics."[67] (About 200 of the conference's 650 delegates were Catholic, of which seven were bishops.) Allan Parrent and James Hamilton considered it one of the most significant NCC events during the entire Vietnam period.[68] The *Christian Century* hailed it for achieving "a degree of moral consensus beyond the expectations of many participants and observers."[69] The conference did assert the ecumenical community's authority on moral issues, not ceding this ground to those evangelicals whom Nixon courted as allies and moral counterweights.

While still in the afterglow, Bilheimer hailed the conference's rejection of America's "culture religion" in favor of the God of history's word on Vietnam.[70] In this he felt the Ecumenical Witness made a greater stride than its social gospel forebears toward breaking with the "accepted premises of U.S. society." He also thought it significant that the conference illuminated connections between domestic and foreign policy. Operating as "two sides of a coin," he wrote, "[t]he sickness of the one reveals the illness of the other."[71] Bilheimer had finally seen the flicker of his long-held desire for an ecumenical witness against the war become a flame.

But in later years, as Bilheimer recalled the conference and its months of stressful preparation, what stood prominently in his memory was the bitter, even exasperating, struggle to unite diverse groups in ecumenical consensus. While he admitted that "it was a pretty good show," which "got attention" and achieved its "basic purposes," he also described it as an administrative nightmare. By the early 1970s, the nation's anti-establishment mood had thoroughly penetrated religious circles. Bilheimer recalled that, after conference plans had been finalized in consultation with many different people who agreed to its final form, a group of participants revolted over its organization. To Bilheimer it felt like an "irrational anger at authority," which resulted in people not liking whatever others, who might have represented the establishment, had arranged. He noted that some attendees "were angry, very angry; at me but not just me. I stood for 'establishment,' and the conference was against all that." Bilheimer changed the conference proceedings "in about twenty minutes on the platform in a plenary session" to please the group. Recollecting, he said, "I can't remember how we reorganized the whole show. But it did come out very much like the original organization. Here was a crowd that had to tell the authorities to go to hell. They did. After they got it off their chests, we had a meeting. But I came back disillusioned, exhausted, and fed up." For church leaders who were used to wielding ecclesiastical power and who were raised to respect authority, the unceasing questioning of top-down leadership methods created considerable frustration.

In an interview decades later, Bilheimer's was still palpable. "I hoped [the Ecumenical Witness] would make an impact on church life and cause churches to think through and become part of the antiwar movement. I was naïve," he admitted. "I wanted the conference to be a real point where the churches exercised self criticism of themselves, their country, and its policies. I hoped they'd do that in such terms that people in churches and government would listen. It was predominantly a young conference. I had no idea of the depth of the spirit of revolt that was present," he realized. It was hard for this establishment leader bred in an earlier generation to fathom. "I came home saying I don't understand things anymore. People were just mad. Anything that was proposed was 'wrong.' None of us could figure out how to get people to work together. It was a sad, sad experience. . . . I came away feeling that what I was resenting was that they didn't like the schema that I had set up. But," he recalled, "the conference did some good things. . . . That was the last big thing I did [at the NCC]." Tired and burned out, "I left [the Council] not long after that," he said. "I felt that I had done what I could do on Vietnam . . . and I needed to get into a whole new ballgame." When Bilheimer returned from Kansas City, he told his wife, Dorothy, "we have to get out of here."[72] But it would be another year before he left the Council. In the meantime, he worked to maximize and focus the positive energy generated by the conference at national, regional, and local levels.

Liberal critics of the Ecumenical Witness complained of poor planning and communication, lack of local involvement, and the relative "lateness" of a moral message that said little new.[73] Conservatives attacked it for making extreme statements filled with preconceived biases and for letting radical hippie-types disrupt conference order.[74] Schomer and some of his colleagues in the Board for World Ministries also nitpicked, spreading the impression that it "did not achieve much." Bilheimer explained that Schomer's strong anticommunist "view of Vietnam is very different from that which the conference took."[75] But general feedback confirmed that the event helped reenergize and recommit battle-weary attendees to the urgent issues arising from the war, and to pursue peace and justice more broadly. As a result, they created several ongoing local and regional network groups across the country. Bilheimer nurtured communication between them, hoping they would hold mini ecumenical witness meetings of their own that spring to discuss conference themes and inquiry groups' findings. He set aside five thousand dollars as matching funds for such gatherings and urged local organizers to "call us collect if you need contacts, materials, or speakers." Several of these did take place in areas such as Seattle, Minnesota, Houston, Boston, and Richmond.[76] The communication links he developed proved useful in April when Nixon escalated the air war and church groups sought to renew pressure upon Congress.

PEACE WITH HONOR! APRIL 1972–JANUARY 1973

On April 7, Elston's "Indochina Update" reported the following: "Saddest development: U.S. unwilling to negotiate in Paris, except on basis of our own proposals, despite recent further concessions by Hanoi. . . . This leaves only military options to create conditions for a political settlement."[77] South Vietnam's government seemed more hated by and alienated from its people than ever. That spring, North Vietnam's General Giap launched several military offensives against the weakening South Vietnamese army. In order to prevent the South's collapse, Nixon ordered his commanders to "use whatever air you need to turn this thing around." This renewed the air war against North Vietnam, which Johnson had suspended in 1968, and expanded it across the South.[78] Fundamentalists like Carl McIntire and Billy Hargis were thrilled, believing that the only way America could lose this war was through a decided lack of will to win.[79] Even though extracted U.S. troops were not returned to battle, this signified further escalation. On the day of Nixon's order, Bilheimer shared a private, desperate thought: "the big offensive by Hanoi and the PRG is underway. It is terrible to have to hope that they will smash the Saigon army, but at this point, I see no other way except by destroying 'Vietnamization' that this war will really end."[80] Bilheimer did not glorify Hanoi or the Vietcong. His qualified reaction here was, for him, a painful choice of lesser evils in his desire to see the war ended.

On April 16, U.S. aircraft mistakenly bombed Soviet ships off North Vietnam's coast, killing several onboard. Church leaders watched Nixon's bold attacks with trepidation, fearing that such inevitable errors might provoke Russia and potentially China to engage troops. The international ecumenical community also grew anxious about Nixon's rumored intention to bomb the dikes along North Vietnam's Red River, one of the most extensive systems in the world, which would precipitate catastrophic flooding, death, and destruction.[81]

The next day Wedel and Espy released a statement protesting the irresponsibility and immorality of recent actions. "These latest developments indicate that the only thing that is winding down is United States ground troop participation," they stressed. "In the name of God the killing of Vietnamese by Americans must be stopped by any means except more killing. A peace or negotiations produced by automated mass bombing offends against humanity and cannot be just."[82] The *Christian Century* decried offensives mounted on both sides and mourned the futile military effort "to preserve the illusion of America's capability to control the destiny of Vietnam."[83] On April 20, twenty-two denominational executives echoed Wedel's and Espy's appeal and urged Christians to speak out.[84]

In response to Nixon's actions, Bilheimer coordinated a high-profile worship service at the stately National Cathedral called "An Ecumenical Witness of Prayer, Repentance and Commitment."[85] Representatives, senators, and other government officials received invitations, but the service was open to anyone in the Washington area. Many notables attended, including Kennedy's former attorney general, Nicholas Katzenbach, who brought his wife and children. The press covered it well. The powerful three-hour service made religious opposition to the war highly visible.[86] Local churches and synagogues around the country were asked to hold similar services between May 3 and 10, as well as keep their doors open between noon and 2:00 p.m. for persons interested in observing "a continuing vigil of prayer, repentance and commitment."[87] Contributions to aid victims of the bombing were collected at these sites. Set the Date Now called for "an Emergency Convocation to End the War" in Washington to lobby legislators to terminate war funding.[88] During this sensitized week of religious vigils, Nixon ordered the mining of Haiphong in North Vietnam, along with a naval blockade and continued air strikes. Honor mandated such moves, he said, and he appealed for the people's support.[89]

In reaction, the NCC formed an ad hoc staff task force from its key units. It used its various network channels to publicize participation in two major protest activities: CALCAV's congressional lobbying effort to terminate funding for the war, and the ecumenical Interdict Project in which churches closed down in an "ecclesiastical strike" to demonstrate "moral repudiation of the nation's policy in Vietnam."[90] The Interdict Project resurrected this practice from centuries ago when churches withheld sacraments from the people as "a sign of moral distress."

On May 11, religious leaders released another press statement condemning Nixon's expanded bombing campaign.[91] Blake, Bilheimer, Wedel, William Thompson, James Armstrong, Robert Moss (UCC president), and

John Hines (presiding bishop, Episcopal Church) all signed. They hoped the group's prestige would attract major press coverage. It did not. Dismayed, Bilheimer momentarily contemplated civil disobedience to grab media attention and sought Wedel's advice. "We cannot be heard inside the White House, and I think it is now clear that the President simply does not want to receive us. . . . To be virtually ignored [by the press] raises very real questions for us," he asserted. "Are we driven to the point that we must engage in some act, whether of civil disobedience or near civil disobedience, simply in order to be heard? And if we are driven to that, should we undertake it . . . ?"[92] It was a clear sign that the liberal Protestant establishment no longer commanded a dominant bully pulpit. Like the oppressed groups with which it chose to stand, the NCC felt more and more like an outsider looking in, banging on the door trying in vain to get attention.

Bilheimer knew the place of ecumenism in America had changed considerably since his heady days at the World Council. "'Who cares?' was the [new] attitude." William P. Thompson agreed. When asked who was listening to the NCC during the late 1960s, he replied, "I'm not sure anybody was." Bilheimer understood that, in the eyes of the people, the church had gone from being perceived as a central part of society to "part of the bureaucracy and on the margins."[93] Blake dispelled Bilheimer's notion that Protestant leaders take "to the streets to be heard," recommending that he stay focused on the constituencies. Bilheimer agreed.[94]

Even though religious leaders rebuked Nixon's escalation, his risky move paid dividends both militarily and politically. Haiphong's harbor contained ships from the USSR, but luckily the bombing did not provoke confrontation with that country or China.[95] Neither wished to upset the new détente they were establishing with the United States. Militarily, the bombing and blockade wounded the North and prevented the collapse of the South. Nixon also won in the polls. Americans still did not want to lose a war. Nixon's willingness to fight for peace "with honor" appealed to them. On top of this, the Democratic Party's presidential campaign, led by candidate George McGovern, was in trouble. A *Christian Century* article dubbed it "The Worthless Circus of '72."[96]

Positioned well, Nixon did not need the blessing of ecumenical leaders. Rather, he found it easy to shun them. Since his inauguration they had sought a presidential meeting about Vietnam, all to no avail. After the recent April escalation, Blake began a series of personal letters to Nixon appealing more strongly for a meeting between Nixon and ecumenical executives. In his first letter, Blake noted that Nixon willingly met with conservative evangelical leaders about Vietnam, but he had repeatedly dodged requests by ecumenists associated with the National and World Councils.[97] Blake received a response only after his office called to inquire about one.

The White House personnel assigned to answer Blake's letters explained that no meeting with Nixon was possible. Blake was furious. He retorted sharply, "Am I and my colleagues to understand from this that you have decided to ignore the major Protestant church leadership of the nation, even when they wish to discuss with you the important moral issues involved in your Indo-China foreign policy? / I could have understood a prompt reply suggesting another date. I could have understood the postponement of a tentative date due to the great pressures upon you. But I cannot understand or easily accept the obvious implications of this correspondence." He continued, "It is clear that you regularly discuss affairs, foreign and domestic, with leaders of the Roman Catholic Church and with anti-ecumenical Protestants. The fact that these ecumenical leaders have been refused appointments on several previous occasions was one of the reasons I was asked to write for this most recent appointment."[98] Blake's shock was clear. He saw himself and his colleagues as weighty individuals representing important constituencies that the president should heed. Nixon and his political base apparently disagreed.

Blake also wrote John McLaughlin, Nixon's deputy assistant for church affairs, inquiring about Nixon's cold shoulder. "We do not know whether this is a considered policy and whether it is a conscious attempt upon his and your part to neutralize the leadership of the main-line Protestant churches as against their own constituencies. It is hard to draw any other conclusion."[99] Blake knew this shunning was retaliation for their stance on Vietnam. But he also suspected Nixon was playing politics with religious communities, wooing some while dismissing others. As he explained to the *Christian Century*, "It is quite clear that President Nixon has religious advisers who have no respect for the mainline Protestant leadership. From the beginning, the actions of the Nixon White House have worked to downgrade the basic mainline Protestant leadership. And that is because this leadership was critical of the government's Vietnam policy—was critical before Nixon came in and still is. That is the issue. / I don't charge conspiracy," he continued, "but the Roman Catholic Church has been neutralized on Vietnam by the administration's support of its position on abortion and parochial schools."[100] McLaughlin told Blake that Nixon was very busy and that his request was "under 'active consideration.'" But after waiting for what Blake felt was an inordinate amount of time, he surmised that he was being given the administrative run-around. John Coventry Smith appealed to Laird for help in securing a presidential meeting. This also proved fruitless.[101] Bilheimer advised Blake to quit. The "White House letters are such as to make it degrading to pursue them in any substantial way."[102] The options were clear and sad—be co-opted for the president's purposes or be marginalized. Nixon was playing his political hand, and Bilheimer did not want the ecumenical church to bow, beg, or scurry after him.

But Blake could not let it go. This insult cut deep. It was incomprehensible to a person whose life, self-conception, and professional roles embodied the notion of a triumphal, hegemonic mainline church that could not be ignored. Nixon's shunning of the National and World Councils symbolized clearly the mainline Protestant establishment's loss of prestige and political clout. As a measure of last resort, Blake went to the press with copies of the letters. A few newspapers such as the *New York Post* carried stories about the "evasion."[103] Blake wrote Nixon a final letter, which he released simultaneously to the press, venting his frustration and how he felt pushed now to make their correspondence public. He also expressed the growing global concern over America's bombing near the North's Red River dikes.

Fearing that the United States intentionally might be trying to rupture the dikes and cause a "natural" disaster that could wipe out millions, Blake challenged the administration's explanation of the weakened dikes— which blamed Vietnamese "neglect"—as patently false. As a result, "The American protest that no intentional bombing has occurred and that only 'accidental' bombs have fallen on or near the dikes must also be untrue," he concluded.[104] Surprisingly, and to the Councils' delight, the *New York Times* reported Blake's comments. It took Blake's charges seriously and supported his appeal that Nixon ensure no dikes would be hit.[105] Bilheimer forwarded copies of Blake's last letter and the *Times* article to congressmen, senators, and Ecumenical Witness participants. Some congressmen commended Blake for increasing national awareness of this issue.[106] Others condemned him for "spreading this kind of lie and propaganda."[107] Bilheimer got Swedish film footage documenting the bombing and dike danger aired on NBC-TV's Chancellor news program.[108]

Along with pressing Congress to terminate war funding and the executive branch to stop bombing, the NCC joined other religious groups in filing an amicus curiae brief in a U.S. District Court case "challenging the legality of an undeclared war."[109] Questions centered around the fact that Congress had never officially declared war, as required by the Constitution. In June, the General Board passed a formal resolution requesting court investigations. It had also joined several denominations in a more forceful call for amnesty for war resisters.[110]

Meanwhile, the Council's Emergency Ministries program expanded in size and popularity. It was one of the first anywhere to attend to the unique needs of Vietnam veterans. Rich Killmer secured fifteen thousand dollars in grants from the National League of Cities and a variety of local churches nationwide to administer local-based Vietnam veterans' education, counseling, and work programs across the country. These successful efforts tapped local churches, veterans, and experts to aid former service personnel. Pastors found the program particularly helpful when desperate vets appeared on church doorsteps.[111]

Also the three national inquiry groups each researched an assigned topic arising from the Ecumenical Witness conference. Inquiry Group 1, on "U.S. Responsibility to the People of Indochina," followed Bilheimer's lead in analyzing the repercussions of questionable presuppositions. "We must examine what it is in the U.S. psyche that drives us into crusades, makes us seek 'victory' rather than solutions, and makes us so fearful of competing thoughts and systems. Within the religious community we must examine the idolatries, fears and ambiguities that have kept us from decisive action in the face of morally recognized imperatives." Its report then pointed out that Nixon's détente efforts with Red China neutralized anticommunist rhetoric used to justify the war, for such hyperbole had become "not only morally invalid but anachronistic in terms of public policy."[112] The group felt unable to deal with the question of responsibility toward the Indochinese until after the war ceased. So they deferred that topic.

Inquiry Group 2, on "American Racism Exported Abroad," described how America's ideas about its own superiority and manifest destiny cultivated a racist foreign policy. It also illustrated how racist attitudes—rooted deep in the American psyche and expressed domestically—fed directly into foreign affairs. "In international relations, the assumptions of white racial superiority translate into policies of cultural, military and economic dominance when confronted with people not of the white world."[113] The group's report exposed the specific relationship between imperialism and racism in U.S. Indochina policy and discussed how this exacerbated racial tensions among U.S. citizens.

Inquiry Group 3, on "War Crimes: U.S. Priorities and Military Force" and chaired by William P. Thompson, wrote the most detailed, impressive report of all. Nearly fifty pages in length, the NCC eventually published it in booklet form along with a study guide and film strip. Allan Parrent served as the group's secretary; he worked hard to finish the massive project before leaving the Council to assume a professorship at Virginia's Protestant Episcopal Theological Seminary. Bilheimer and Ernest Gross also served on this team. Using information already derived from trials, media reports, and other inquiries, they probed the causes of war crimes as well as links between such conduct and governmental policies in the post–World War II period.[114] Like the other two, this paper explored aspects of the American cultural mindset that facilitated the justification and cover-up of war crimes by U.S. troops.

Collectively, the three reports comprised an in-depth exploration into the psychological and sociological sides of America's worldview and how these may have contributed to the immoralities stemming from U.S. military involvement in Indochina. They analyzed how Americans who saw their nation as an altruistic and divinely led example for the world could commit inhumanities on a colossal scale. These were the types of analytical moral connections that Bilheimer sought from the church. The War Crimes Group hoped such studies might spark self-examination and inspire greater bonds with humanity. As stated in the concluding words of its study, "In the Judeo-Christian tradition fate does not control man. Though men often lose control to evil forces, God can deliver those who are willing to change. . . . In this there is hope."[115] This statement reflected many ecumenists' faith in H. Richard Niebuhr's vision of Christ as Transformer of Culture—the model that had so inspired Bilheimer in seminary.[116] It also embodied a basic Christian belief in redemption, reconciliation, and renewal for the repentant. These reports were distributed broadly for study and consideration.

At the June General Board meeting, Bilheimer acknowledged that Christian peace activism seemed more widespread and finally based upon something deeper than mere disagreement with aspects of U.S. policy. It was starting to reach a theological and moral level that "signifies a new dimension and direction of the witness of the church." Therefore, he urged Christians to go further and engage in rigorous theological efforts to transform national self-perceptions.

> The task is theological in the sense of discovering what kind of new beings we must be, what a Christian identity is in contemporary America. The task is to discover what it means in active obedience to examine, criticize and help formulate new assumptions for the society of which one is a part. The task is to discover in a new way what it means to be in but not of our society. If Christian efforts are aimed only at stopping the war, we may sink into apathy and we shall miss the main point. A nation's foreign policy is a projection of itself. A nation's foreign policy betrays or exemplifies the way in which it orders its own society. That is what "Vietnam" has done. The crucial question therefore is: upon what assumptions shall American society proceed? To speak, act and live from the Gospel to the assumptions and bases of American life, in scrutiny, criticism and reformulation, is the mandate which comes to us from the Indochina experience.... [T]hat is the task required of us by God.[117]

Bilheimer used the general word "Christians" without specifying a particular subset. Given the audience, it is likely he was talking to and about the liberal-leaning Christians who had answered the Councils' call to peacemaking on Vietnam. The ranks of this group were indeed growing. And the NCC's member denominations had become quite strong in their consensus opposition to U.S. policy. But "silent majority" Christians tended not to feel similarly. When Bilheimer's presentation unexpectedly hit the press, he received a startling number of angry letters claiming he did not speak for "them" nor for the "Christians" they knew. As one said, "Until Dr. Bilheimer's remarks made national headlines, most of us had never heard of him, and yet he purports to represent us all because we are 'Christians'!"[118] Bilheimer, who despaired at the paucity of media attention given to important ecumenical statements on the war, now suddenly received publicity for a presentation intended for the board only. Some newspaper articles also connected his statements to the board's recommendation that courts investigate the war's legality.[119] Grassroots fury punctuated the clergy-laity gap looming before the Council.

Several letter-writers stated that, while they sought a quick end to the war, they preferred Nixon's methods and goal of an honorable result.

Some condemned the NCC's attempt to "stab him [Nixon] in the back during an election year."[120] Most did not condemn the war for the reasons the ecumenical movement ultimately did and instead recoiled from the NCC's penitent message that America had sinned in Vietnam. Some spat criticism through insults as did this anonymous letter: "Why don't you Ministers tend to your own business and let the President tend to his. He is doing a fine job what with you Ministers, Democrats and Commies trying to take over. / You yap about the Church membership dropping off. Of course it is. We have lost all confidence and respect for such as you. / Are you a sob Sister, a Democrat, a Commie or just plain bored with the job you once thot [sic] you were called for?"[121] Conversely, evangelical churches that maintained an outward patriotic faith in presidential policies and America's mission (personal qualms notwithstanding) thrived.[122]

Even by 1972, John Bennett felt the atmosphere in most local churches still discouraged open discussion about Vietnam. "I am troubled by the enormous difficulty that individual congregations encounter when the issue of the war in Indochina is raised," he said. As individuals, ministers seemed aware of the immoralities of U.S. Vietnam policy. However, "when they try to bring their convictions on this subject to their congregations . . . they soon become frustrated. More often than not they and their churches have paid a high price in conflict and loss of support." He understood that divided congregations generally wished to err on the side of trusting the president. "What is troublesome," he clarified, "is the silence, the fear of controversy, that is often so paralyzing."[123] The frustrations of local clergy continued. While the war had been a catalyst for mainline religious organizations and leadership, inspiring self-reflection, the extent to which this occurred at the congregational level seemed slight, in their opinion.

In September, Bilheimer and Elston championed a touring education program called the Indochina Peace Campaign. Jane Fonda, Tom Hayden, and Daniel Berrigan launched it at Riverside Church. Bilheimer thought it might help motivate the inactive. He wrote, "despite the radical reputation of some participants, . . . Jane Fonda really communicates. The message is powerful, an unmistakable note of sincerity and commitment comes through. The program grabs middle America and the unconverted are moved." Since the churches' intellectual paperbound means of communication had not resonated, Bilheimer and Elston jumped at this colorful multimedia presentation. The program began just months after Fonda had traveled to Hanoi where reporters photographed her atop a North

Vietnamese anti-aircraft gun. This misjudgment (by her own admission) inspired hatred of her among some veterans that continues to this day.[124]

Also that fall, an NCC leader finally received a visa for North Vietnam. The Committee for Solidarity with the American People invited David Hunter to join Tom Hayden, professor Howard Zinn, Susan Miller, Fred Branfman (Project Air War), and two others on a fact-finding trip there. Hunter saw his role extending from the NCC's original Mission of Concern to Vietnam (1967), which aimed, he said, to "strengthen people-to-people relations between our country and a country with which we are at war." While there, the group spoke with eleven American POWs and brought home 150 of their letters. Hunter also explored the extent to which North Vietnam permitted free religious expression. He quipped that "religion is as free to practice its faith in the Democratic Republic of Vietnam as in the USA, with the limitation in both places that when it deviates from the policy of the government it meets opposition on the part of the state and pays a price, and this no more in the DRV than in the USA."[125] His jab here at Nixon's harassment of the NCC was unmistakable, except for those on the far right who cited his comment as an example of liberal naïveté about communism.

With official peace talks stalled in Paris, Kissinger negotiated secretly with Vietnamese representatives. On October 26, Kissinger announced to a war-weary public that "peace is at hand." Thieu would forestall this, however. A few weeks later, Nixon won a second term in a landslide victory. Several ecumenists shared Bennett's surprise at the public's noticeable lack of moral revulsion over Nixon's Vietnam policy. "It is clear," he wrote, "that the majority of voters have been convinced that President Nixon is ending the war and that they care very little about the destruction visited on the people, the culture and the land of Indochina since he took office. . . . Now the President is given the benefit of the doubt as he pursues 'peace with honor.'"[126]

Meanwhile, the Council focused on its December 1972 triennial General Assembly in Dallas, where the thinning organization revamped itself as requested by the previous one in 1969. The biggest structural change made by the 800-member assembly was to dissolve itself and the General Board in favor of a 347-member Governing Board, which would meet twice a year.[127] This would save scarce funds. The restructure also centralized more decision-making, budget, and administrative authority in this body rather than in the NCC's divisions and donor denominations. In addition, the assembly enacted a quota system for board delegates to ensure they would reflect the church's true diversity. Denominations had to send delegations comprised of at least one-quarter women, half laity, one-eighth persons under twenty-eight years old, and a percentage of minorities equaling that within their membership. The Council's divisions and commissions were also retooled. Alan Geyer, the gadfly who while editor of the *Christian Century* had criticized communication and structure issues, seemed pleased with the plan.[128]

But streamlining created casualties. The Council eliminated its controversial Division of Christian Life and Mission (DCLM), of which the IAC was a part. Much of its staff was laid off. Vestiges were merged into another division. Elston recalled that sometime in 1973 a few denominations withheld a large chunk of money previously budgeted to the Council, and this seemed to pound a final nail into the DCLM's coffin. According to Elston, Bilheimer received a verbal promise from Espy that, should the DCLM be gutted, the IAC would be taken under the general secretary's office. But this did not happen. Elston saw this as the last straw for Bilheimer, which drove him from the Council. Elston soon left as well. And Espy announced his retirement.[129] It was all part of a major transition for the Council, which would never again approach its 1960s peak of financial and personnel resources.

This was symptomatic of the cuts and restructurings that were rippling through panicked member denominations. For example, the United Presbyterian Church's 1972 restructuring included shrinking then burying its socially active Church and Society division within another office. The church claimed that the changes were motivated, in part, to demonstrate responsiveness to laity.[130] It was telling that the most prophetic wings of the churches were those often clipped.

The NCC's 1972 assembly received mixed reviews. Several participants praised its inclusiveness and effort to air minority issues.[131] But other church people, particularly at the grass roots, criticized it for going too far in this direction with one of its slated speakers.[132] The assembly allowed its black caucus to select its own spokesperson. The caucus chose the militant, anti-Semitic Imamu Amiri Baraka (alias LeRoi Jones) who, one observer described, "delivered a 90-minute, obviously ill-prepared, rambling hate-America-and-whitey war dance with the flatulence of a poison gas bag." When Baraka called for revolution and condemned capitalism, an Orthodox bishop predicted, "This is the end of the National Council of Churches."[133] Jewish groups protested the caucus's selection, but the assembly supported the black delegates' uncensored right to pick their own presenter.[134] Herb Philbrick, of the U.S. Press Association, described Jones as one of "the nation's filthiest of all the scum-level pornographic writers."[135] When news broke of Baraka's high speaking fee of fifteen hundred dollars while better prepared and more easily heard speakers received no compensation, rebukes hit the Council from several sides. The assembly's own press report put a positive spin on it, stating that "More openness and honesty was achieved by both black and white at the assembly than has been true in the past. Mr. Baraka said his piece and the delegates welcomed him and listened." It also argued that Baraka's critics were perhaps more turned off by his manner than by his words and concluded that, "in comparison with the appearance of black militant James Forman three years ago, the level of conflict between black and white had remarkably cooled down."[136]

Unlike in 1969, this assembly conducted its business with little disruption. It elected new leadership, including the mild-mannered Reverend Dr. W. Sterling Cary (a signer of the Black Manifesto) as the Council's first black president. It also passed several statements related to the war. These supported an array of actions such as amnesty for war resisters, religious donations to help fund the legal defense of eight vets charged with conspiracy to cause riots at the Republican Convention, church aid to North Vietnamese war wounded, and a CALCAV/FOR-sponsored Christmas program to aid bombing victims.[137]

Perhaps the most interesting review of the assembly came from Albert McClellan, the program planning secretary of the conservative and anti-ecumenical Southern Baptist Convention. The 1972 assembly was McClellan's fifth as an invited guest. He described for Espy the dramatic changes he had seen since the Council's 1960 assembly in San Francisco. "Gone are the religious processions with ecclesiastical garb and with them the long addresses and the interminable papers. / The old leaders are also gone and with them the messianic preoccupation with ecumenism as the sole answer to all church problems. The new order seems to be more democratic, more open, more understanding and more accepting, as well as less radical, less exclusive, less critical and less formal." He added, "I am not sure as a whole the new order is more articulate, but I am certain that it is more understanding of Christians outside ecumenical circles. I am also sure that its spirit is genuinely the spirit of Christ."[138] The Southern Baptist observer seemed pleased by what he saw as the Council's less pompous style and greater receptivity to evangelicals. This assessment is ironic given that laity often judged the Council to have become more radical and out of touch. It is also intriguing in light of the fact that ecumenists like Bilheimer mourned the early days, for they saw true ecumenism being lost in the NCC even as they celebrated its growing diversity.

In mid-December Kissinger's secret talks stalled. Hoping to pressure North Vietnam to accept Kissinger's settlement, and to reassure Thieu of U.S. support, Nixon blanketed the North with the severest bombing of the war. Hanoi and Haiphong were targeted. Civilian deaths skyrocketed. This purported "terror bombing" did not resonate well at home or abroad.[139] Members of Congress promised to return from Christmas break with a renewed thrust to cut off the war's funds. On December 21, Espy and William P. Thompson issued a joint statement condemning Nixon's holiday bombing spree. "We believe the new bombing of Vietnam to be immoral and evil beyond any options open to our nation and its leaders," they said. "We pray that the conflict between our loyalty to our Government and our faith in Christ may not deepen."[140] Thanks to the World Council, this statement circulated widely in Europe. Bilheimer noticed that European churches even "read it from their pulpits on Christmas."[141]

Nixon credited the Christmas bombing for bringing Hanoi back to the peace table in early January, although historians find this debatable. Regardless, within a week, Kissinger and Lu Duc Tho had reached a compromise agreement.[142] Its terms were nearly identical to those worked out the previous October, which Thieu had refused. The United States permitted North Vietnam to stay involved in South Vietnam militarily and politically. In other words, the White House no longer demanded that the communists leave the South. In turn, North Vietnam allowed Thieu's government to remain in power and to receive U.S. aid. But the U.S. military would disengage and leave the country. Nixon forced Thieu to accept this agreement by threatening to cut all American aid and to sign without him if need be. If he cooperated, Nixon promised Thieu continued supplies and U.S. attacks on the North if it defied the treaty. A cease-fire was announced January 21, the day after Nixon's second inauguration. The next day a broken-hearted Lyndon Johnson died of a massive heart attack at his Texas ranch.[143]

On January 27, 1973, all four parties met in Paris to sign the Peace Accords. The United States then began military disengagement. Within two months, the North released American POWs. The South Vietnamese government was supposed to restructure and include a council containing equal representation of the "GVN [Thieu's people], the PRG [Vietcong], and 'third force' elements." This council would then administer the political aspects of the treaty. One task would include holding an election for South Vietnam's future leadership. Signing parties also agreed that any future reunification of the two Vietnams would occur willingly, peaceably, and slowly. However, the treaty contained inherent problems, which all signing parties understood meant a return to military conflict after the Americans left. The political future of Vietnam's southern half was left unresolved, and the Vietnamese would eventually determine it themselves with guns. Yet Nixon claimed that he had brought America its "peace with honor in Vietnam."[144] Kissinger and Le Duc Tho received the Nobel Peace Prize for the settlement, which Kissinger accepted but Tho refused on the grounds that Vietnam was still not at peace.[145] A *New York Times* writer dubbed it "The Nobel War Prize."[146]

Ecumenical leaders agreed. They saw little honor or peacemaking in America's management of the war or negotiation process. A *Christian Century* editorial entitled "'Honorable' Peace: Final Self-Deception" captured their feelings of guilt, shame, failure, and shock, as well as their desire for America to heal its sin-sick soul. "There is no escape from the sickness of our national soul until we acknowledge that the sin was our own, and not that of some external evil or a misguided political leader. . . . [A]s the war ends, there is still an inability in the land to confront the absolute sin of self-deception that started, sustained and finally ended this war." That healing would require national reflection, assessment, repentance, and real renewal—something the churches should lead. But the editorial also asked antiwar Christians to self-reflect, noting where their activism became more political than faith-driven and where they became simply another activist "screaming in the wind."[147]

As Reinhold Niebuhr had pointed out years before, America needed to learn the same lesson European nations did after moral failures in war— that America had the capacity to commit corruptible, even genocidal, sins against humanity and the Earth; it was not pure, innocent, intrinsically superior or righteous; and God did not necessarily bless, favor, guide, or justify it more than any other nation. America's involvement in Vietnam illustrated this fact. As a result of the war, the country's mainline Protestant leadership had to face similar revelations about itself.

By January 1973, as the Paris Peace Accords were signed, the Council was spinning in a downward cycle. Staff members were stunned, sad, tired, frustrated, and bickering. For the next three decades, the NCC continued to struggle amid shrinking resources, to self-evaluate and restructure, to fend off conservative attacks, and to try to shape a prophetic ecumenical witness on social justice and peace issues.

So, what had the National Council of Churches accomplished with respect to its extensive, devoted, and costly effort to make a witness against the Vietnam War? It united many mainline Protestant denominations behind the antiwar position and even in moral condemnation of the war. It provided vital support to other antiwar church groups and programs, most notably CALCAV. It helped spearhead well-researched probing critiques, not only of the war but of the nature of U.S. security, militarism, racism, and power, while putting these in the context of Christian values. Church leaders created an ecumenical international witness rooted in these ideas. Similar to the ways in which clergy had participated in the civil rights movement in far greater percentages (and supported more systemic changes) than laity, religious leaders were also more willing than their own parishioners to criticize the war. To many, the Council did act courageously as a confessing church—witnessing its positions to government, the courts, and the people in a non-partisan fashion—when it was costly and unpopular to do so. The NCC had also pioneered programs to help both war resisters and Vietnam veterans when few programs existed to meet their unique needs. Finally, the ecumenical movement was an active and legitimizing part of the overall antiwar movement, and whatever credit this larger force receives for advancing peace should be shared with its religious participants.

Forty Years in the Wilderness

Embattled Ecumenism, Vietnam's Legacy, and

Hard Times for the NCC

DENOUEMENTS AND TRANSITIONS

In early 1973, American combat troops came home from Vietnam. However, the United States kept funding Thieu's government and an air war over Cambodia. In an article titled "The Depth of Militarism," Bilheimer once again attacked his country's dependence on military means for creating "security." For years ecumenists had insisted that genuine security depended upon peace with justice, not brinkmanship or arms superiority. Bilheimer was no pacifist. Rather, he wanted more emphasis placed on international relationship-building than on arms posturing. To him, this was biblical and realistically smart. "When a people believes its security to be provided by military force, it denies that security is to be found in relations with others."[1]

Bilheimer's warning was timely. So too was his prescription, for despite the NCC's failure to communicate this message persuasively regarding Vietnam, it soon tasted success when it helped avert massive bloodshed during a domestic crisis. On February 27, 1973, about two hundred Indians from the

Oglala Nation and the American Indian Movement (AIM) began a seventy-one-day armed occupation of the historic Wounded Knee battle site in South Dakota. The occupiers hoped to draw attention to Indians' economic plights, the repercussions of broken treaties, and political oppression from the Bureau of Indian Affairs (BIA) and its complicitous friends in the Oglala Tribal Council.[2] Indian veterans from Vietnam used their skills to establish a defensible perimeter. The U.S. government responded with an unprecedented display of martial might. Whereas the Indians were armed largely with rifles, shotguns, revolvers, and little ammunition, the government's daunting array included army units from the Eighty-Second Airborne, two F4 Phantom jets, several National Guard helicopters, seventeen armored personnel carriers, machine guns, flares, about 150 FBI agents, over 200 U.S. marshals, at least 100 BIA police, several Justice Department officials, CIA investigators, and Secret Service agents.[3] To many, this assemblage looked as if the Vietnam War had come home.

The NCC's Governing Board took quick action. Working through a small leadership team comprised largely of Methodists, the Council served an intermediary role in the crisis. It helped broker cease-fires, facilitate dialogues, and convince both parties that negotiations could best secure mutually desired ends. It also ensured that the occupiers' basic needs for food, blankets, and medical supplies were met for as long as its representatives were allowed on the scene. This involved perilous acts of shuttle diplomacy amid gunfire, deft negotiation, long hours, and a willingness to take risks at a time when the NCC and the United Methodist Church were themselves experiencing institutional hardships.[4]

Even though the Nixon administration had dismissed ecumenists as impotent foes on Vietnam and AIM's leaders had condemned the churches' complicity in past government land grabs and attempts to eradicate their culture, both deemed the NCC useful to mediate this particular situation. Many hardliners within Nixon's administration preferred to subdue protesters using strong-arm, militaristic, "law-and-order" tactics. Nevertheless, the negative fallout from doing so earlier at Kent State and Attica prison, not to mention American failures in Vietnam, inspired others in the administration to seek alternatives at Wounded Knee. So too did polls, which suggested that a government assault would be unpopular, even though white ranchers, the tribal council, and certain military personnel appeared eager for one.[5] In this instance, therefore, ecumenical leaders' relationship-building methods seemed valuable. AIM, meanwhile, recognized that mainline Protestants were gaining a new understanding of Indian issues and their own participation in past wrongs. From a practical perspective, AIM also sought a prominent institutional ally with money and moral clout in its fight against the government, and despite the NCC's present difficulties, it still fit that bill.[6]

To ecumenists, they were able to do at Wounded Knee what they had failed to accomplish in eight years of thwarted efforts on Vietnam. They demonstrated the church's relevance as an institution engaged in society for peace with justice, and positive results finally validated their methods and motivations. Given the swirl of declining budgets, staff, and member-ships that mainline churches faced, their accomplishment at Wounded Knee was immensely meaningful to them. Laity seemed largely supportive of their efforts here, too. But the victory was brief and overshadowed by the Watergate scandal breaking in the news.

Over the next two years, the Council pursued its reconciliation goals for Vietnam. For example, it sought an end to America's financial support of corrupt anticommunist regimes in Indochina, complete amnesty for U.S. draft and war resisters, relief for Indochinese war victims, and aid for Vietnam veterans reintegrating into American society.[7] Congress finally passed legislation limiting funds for South Vietnam's military efforts and the air war over Cambodia. Nixon, who swore he would find loopholes in the restrictions, became too mired in Watergate to give circumvention much attention. As U.S. support declined, Theiu's military and government crumbled under North Vietnamese offensives. After Nixon resigned in April 1974, President Gerald Ford could not persuade legislators to grant funds that might prevent South Vietnam's collapse. The North Vietnamese and Vietcong took control of the South in spring 1975 and reunified their country. The communist Khmer Rouge also wrested control from Lon Nol's government in Cambodia. A decade of U.S. military efforts to shape the po-litical fate of Indochina had failed. Therefore, Kissinger morphed them into an economic assault as the U.S. imposed punitive sanctions upon Vietnam, blocked relief aid from entering, and denied it UN recognition. This fueled widespread famine. The NCC urged an end to economic warfare, hoping instead for U.S. recognition of and reconciliation with that country.[8]

Meanwhile, the Council watched as scandal destroyed Nixon's presi-dency and the remnants of trust Americans placed in their government. Some declared it poetic justice that Nixon's combative paranoia, which drove his war policies in Indochina and against his critics at home, also led to his Watergate downfall. At the time, religion scholar Martin Marty suggested (perhaps wishfully) that Watergate had unraveled the patriotic cloak of morality woven by the union of Nixon and Graham and donned by "mildright politicians."[9]

But the union of conservative religion and politics did not slide into moral discredit along with Nixon. Instead, evangelicals sponsored a huge outreach campaign called "Key '73." It united 140 denominations in a huge national effort to refocus religious attention back upon the individual soul rather than society.[10] This was evidence of an ongoing revival that soon (and ironically, given the aims of Key '73) moved evangelicals more dominantly into public square activism. In 1979, evangelicals engaged politics with organizational force behind Ronald Reagan's presidential bid. This all foreshadowed the fact that evangelicals would soon become a critical voter base within the Republican Party and major players within the sociopolitical establishment.[11]

At the same time, the Council and its mainline members recognized that revitalizing lay support would require overt attention to people's spiritual hunger, while connecting this more effectively to their justice work. By 1974, in order to make the NCC more palatable to the grass roots, its new Division of Church and Society (DCS) reemphasized evangelism and launched a listening ministry to laity.[12] A conflict-weary and no longer silent block of Americans, who felt ignored by church bureaucrats, wanted their own needs made central again. This was part and parcel of the silent majority's broader resentment of elite, liberal, northeastern bureaucracies that apparently heeded the screaming radicals rather than them.[13] The NCC had, in some sense, sacrificed positive relations with its own parishioners and government to nurture bonds with people in the global ecumenical community and with marginalized groups in the United States. It is important to remember that the NCC perceived being prophetic on justice issues as its mandate and duty; this derived from the expectations of denominational leaders affiliated with the NCC—those who financed its programs and helped set its policy. However, by 1974, the Council clearly stood on the opposite side of the nation's conservative political ascendency, even as it attempted to stand on the right side of social justice movements. The growth of conservatives' power over the next three decades would have a huge impact on the NCC.

After undergoing years of attack from left and right and suffering severe budget cuts, the Council continued to downsize. When the DCLM was eliminated and blended into the DCS, core people on Bilheimer's team either quit or were laid off, including Bilheimer himself.[14] In the new division, only one staffer was allotted for international affairs, down from five. When asked about his departure, Bilheimer said, "That period was so distasteful that I can hardly remember it." He could not recall if Espy fired him or if he quit in anticipation. He did remember that "The demise of the NCC in the eyes of the people was tremendous," and that the Council was on "a real downward spiral when I left." To Bilheimer, the Council's ecumenical spirit and leadership quality had weakened. Its theologians lacked sufficient ecumenical experience and prophetic drive while its activists failed to grasp that their activism should emerge from their theological grounding as Christians. "My mood was utter despair of anything significant happening in the NCC." It had become "nothing more than a playground of second-rate people politicking with each other to get some kind of resolution passed," when its loss of stature had made its resolutions largely impotent. Bilheimer's own faith in the power of well-reasoned statements by the church's best and brightest had been decimated. He said, "we were all operating on the assumption that if the General Board came to a conclusion on a matter, it would make a difference in the churches, and it took years of turmoil to see that that was not true." Bilheimer concluded pessimistically, "The churches did their own thing on matters and the General Board didn't make any difference; it had no impact."[15]

Bilheimer described it as one of the most dismal periods of his life. The job market also proved difficult, as he found himself overqualified for many positions while simultaneously being associated with a declining and, to some, outmoded trend in church leadership.[16] Nevertheless, Bilheimer kept hoping that America's sense of guilt or failure arising from the war might become a source of redemption. Only such a tragedy, he thought, could infuse people with humility and a desire to self-reflect. In 1977 he wrote optimistically, "I believe that we are just now entering a new stage in which Christians in America have the historical possibility of rising above the dynamics of our society and culture. We have always had the theological possibility of doing so, but our history has been against us. Now our history [the Vietnam failure] pushes us in that direction. I believe that the Church in the United States is for the first time entering a truly ecumenical era."[17] His hopefulness was probably buoyed by President Jimmy Carter's address months earlier that criticized militarism and called Vietnam "the best example of its [America's] intellectual and moral poverty." As Carter bluntly explained, "The Vietnamese war produced a profound moral crisis, sapping worldwide faith in our own policy and our own system of life." Carter then asserted that a new world, which had repudiated colonialism, "calls for a new American foreign policy—a policy based upon constant decency in its values."[18] Recognition from a sitting president seemed significant. However, by the 1980s Bilheimer realized that this hopeful sign had proven illusory.

In 1974 the Institute for Ecumenical and Cultural Research in College-ville, Minnesota, hired Bilheimer as its executive director—a position he found richly satisfying and from which he retired ten years later.[19] During that time he published *A Spirituality for the Long Haul: Biblical Risk and Moral Stand* and later *Breakthrough: The Emergence of the Ecumenical Tradition*. Both were ecumenical treatises that perpetuated his vision. The first explained the ecumenical worldview and process that he feared was being forgotten, including how ecumenism wedded theology and action. *Breakthrough* celebrated the development of international ecumenism during its pre-1960s heyday; it was a work of love that took him back to his cherished Geneva years at the World Council. For his accomplishments, Bilheimer received three honorary doctorates and St. John's University's prestigious Pax Christi Award.[20]

Gerhard Elston also mourned changes he saw overtaking the Council. He admitted that it had probably overextended itself when tackling issues too divisive for the denominations. But the NCC's mission was precisely to "stick its neck out" on controversial subjects, he insisted. When money became scarce, Elston feared the Council was abandoning this mission in favor of a more conciliatory one with parishioners. He was disappointed that Claire Randall, who succeeded Espy as general secretary in 1974, tried to lead the NCC in a less public-offending direction.[21] This mirrored the denominations, many of which retrenched and eliminated activists from key positions. But to Elston, this threatened to render the NCC insignifi-cant. He also traced this trend back to Espy who tried to please too many people when controversy thickened.[22]

While Elston shared Bilheimer's disappointment with the Council's direction, he credited it with more success in the antiwar movement. To him, ecumenical antiwar efforts had helped educate the public on Viet-nam. When the peace accord was signed, Elston remarked that a "critical mass" of church people were solidly against the war. He wanted the NCC to receive some credit for this and noted that this long-growing Christian critical mass comprised a significant part of the population that had even-tually forced Nixon's hand.[23] Also, unlike Bilheimer, Elston viewed his years with the NCC as the most dynamic and meaningful of his life. His role had suited him, as had the times. When the Council dissolved the DCLM into the DCS, Elston continued to work within it for a brief time before becoming director of the Center for Ethics and Society at the Lutheran Church in America.[24] Then, in 1978, he assumed the reins of Amnesty International USA, which had received the Nobel Peace Prize the previous year. After retirement, he worked in Philadelphia as a translator, taught German, and spoke at various colleges, universities, and religious meetings. He remained an effervescent champion of social justice and peace.[25]

Even though the NCC reached out to laity in the early 1970s, it also continued its internal renewal by incorporating what it had learned from listening to people of color globally. For example, it integrated its understanding of injustice (as systemic problems requiring true empowerment of the marginalized) into its programs, staff hires, and restructuring. This affected Church World Service most dramatically.

CWS and the Council's social justice wing were often at odds. CWS's ties to government funds and efforts in Vietnam compromised the NCC's credibility when it stood against the war. Conversely, the social justice wing's controversial positions and alienation of laity threatened CWS's image and fund-raising ability by association. The two also clashed over postwar planning for relief efforts in Vietnam.[26] Bilheimer and Elston pressed service leaders to change their presuppositions and methods in dealing with Vietnam, and they experienced slow measured success. By the early 1970s, CWS showed a concerted decline in its use of surplus government foodstuffs overseas and an increased effort to source more supplies from church donations, even though these were less plentiful and more costly.[27]

Several other factors within the NCC, VNCS, and the nation at large may have influenced these developments. In 1965, CWS became a department within the NCC's Division of Overseas Ministries. According to former CWS associate director Robert Stenning, the DOM itself was split. Some favored a missions focus that included an immediate emphasis on "development" (that is, analyzing the root causes of problems, making systemic changes, and doing political advocacy). Others favored a "relief" approach that fed people first, no questions asked, and let development efforts emerge slowly only after the crises of need had subsided.[28] As a result of the civil rights movement and the Vietnam War, the NCC's sense of religious mission became more oriented toward social action. This inspired DOM leaders to move in that direction also by the early 1970s. So too did the rising number of DOM staffers who entered the NCC with Latin American missions experience, as liberation theology took hold. The growing resentment of VNCS fieldworkers toward the U.S. government's co-optive use of voluntary relief agencies to further its military objectives contributed as well.[29]

As social justice issues increasingly drove the NCC's agenda, Mac-Cracken budged under pressure but not by conviction. He maintained that CWS should stick to its relief role and not sabotage its effectiveness by becoming overtly political in ways that bit the hands that fed it.[30] Supporters argued articulately that there was no other way to distribute life-saving relief effectively in such a politically polarized world.[31]

Nevertheless, by the time the United States began its military withdrawal from Vietnam, the NCC had embraced a direction for itself that mandated protest of governmental policies that violated people's human rights. In 1973, even CWS approved a Council document making "matters of 'justice and liberation'" a consideration when providing relief.[32] With regard to Asia, the social justice and missions wings agreed, "There is a need for sensitive, generous and respectful American response to the efforts of the East Asian peoples to secure liberation in the determination of their own life-style and justice in their economic and social development. This human need," they confirmed, "overarches all others."[33]

These statements articulated the united objective of the Council's departments henceforth, even though the strategies of CWS remained fiercely debated.[34] While the 1973 document was drafted under Mac-Cracken's leadership, it was not applied with his blessing. In fact, amid great controversy in 1974, MacCracken was forced to resign for not implementing that strategy in the manner desired by his superiors.[35]

His dismissal sparked anger within certain CWS circles and became a proof point for conservatives who claimed that the Council had been overtaken by Marxist-loving revolutionaries. The controversy worsened when, shortly thereafter, the *Christian Century* published the slanted but thought-provoking article "The Politics of Charity," which detailed how cooperative ties between CWS and the government did bind that church agency to the government's questionable policies in Vietnam and elsewhere.[36] Pressures to make an ecumenical witness on the Vietnam War and the Council's new focus on heeding the voices of the oppressed, even over the preferences of its government and parishioners, had compelled the Council to face its own credibility gap between its words and deeds. It also set the entire Council on a human rights course that emphasized systemic economic and political empowerment for the poor and marginalized.

Paul McCleary replaced MacCracken. A Methodist with Latin American missions experience, he quickly enforced the blending of justice advocacy with relief aid. CWS even opened an Office on Development Policy in Washington to educate government officials about hunger issues.[37] Development and global education became part of CWS's mandate. Therefore, by 1974, the NCC's social action wing had established hegemony in terms of integrating a justice focus into the entire Council. Also, by the war's end, both the Council's social justice and missions wings were listening to "third world" voices in ways they hadn't before, recognizing people's aspirations for themselves as preeminent over what the United States or churches might prescribe. The NCC hoped this new sensitivity would build the Council's credibility with nonwhite peoples as well as fulfill its prophetic directive to advance peace with justice.

As Edward Fiske of the *New York Times* noted, Council "leaders who once spent much of their time worrying about the loss of financial support from conservatives on the right are now more worried about losing touch with minorities on the left."[38] In truth, they agonized over both; however, the Council did not want to retreat too far from the prophetic edge while attempting to restore better relations with laity. Budget cuts, more than a lack of willingness, stifled its peace and justice programs. By 1975, and largely as a result of its work on the Vietnam War, the NCC no longer considered itself a central part of the establishment. Its self-identity had shifted toward finding unity with those on the margins as the nation swung politically to the right. The Council's declining clout, resources, and influence with respect to the establishment reaffirmed this; it was no longer the government insider of bygone years. By virtue of who and what institutions made up the Council, it would always have a foot planted within establishment circles. But the location of that foot slid toward the left edge as it stood closer to those who felt excluded.

A BELEAGUERED INSTITUTION SEARCHES FOR IDENTITY AND RELEVANCE, 1975-2000

The impact of the Vietnam War, and the tumultuous era that encompassed it, has continued to resonate within the NCC's life and work, just as it has within the nation itself. Three manifestations are worth noting as the NCC's story moves toward the twenty-first century.[39] First, the war exposed and exacerbated fissures within the ecumenical community that ruptured in subsequent years. The most significant was that between CWS and the rest of the NCC. Their problems were enmeshed in the clergy-laity gap. The substory of CWS's eventual separation and divorce from the NCC illustrates the limitations that constituencies, sociopolitical contexts, and institutional structures place upon ecumenical achievement of transcendence and unity. The difficulty (if not impossibility) of escaping these limitations contributed to a major reconfiguration of institutionalized ecumenism, which in turn has continued to irritate the debate over ecumenism between new breeders and traditional ecumenists.

Second, while the war fueled soul-searching transformations within the ecumenical community, Bilheimer's hope that it would do so nationally faded in the 1980s. The country largely recoiled from messages that challenged its exceptionalist self-narrative. This dovetailed with the rise of the far religious right within the establishment as well as destructive attacks on the NCC, while the White House's political use of religion proliferated.

Finally, the war influenced NCC policies and actions in future decades, most notably regarding Central America and the Middle East. Memories of Vietnam affected the perceptions and decisions of twenty-first-century NCC leaders when President George W. Bush launched a preemptive war against Iraq in 2003. These Vietnam-related influences will be highlighted as we follow the NCC forward.

One might assume that CWS's forced assimilation into the Council's more liberation-focused culture solved the NCC's problems with CWS and healed the breach between them. It did not, for the shifting political climate imperiled the NCC in ways that worsened its financial, image-based, and constituency tensions with CWS. MacCracken, and CWS's denominational board of overseers, had wanted to save CWS from the DCLM's fate by retaining its more nonconfrontational ways.[40] Nevertheless, its new leadership took risks. For example, in the late 1970s, CWS defied the U.S. government in order to feed those starving in the reunified communist Vietnam. Despite restrictive U.S. sanctions that perpetuated famine there, CWS sent a huge shipment of wheat to Ho Chi Minh City's (formerly Saigon's) hospitals and orphanages. Midwestern farmers in eight states donated the wheat, and CWS raised two million dollars to ship it.[41] Conservatives insinuated later that this illustrated support for the brutal regime ruling Vietnam, even though CWS gave the wheat directly to starving refugees and despite that regime. Primarily because CWS had the unique ability to raise its own funds locally and because its reputation as a relief agency played well in the pews, it survived the budget cuts of the 1970s in relatively good shape. Because of this it also remained tied and sensitive to laity in ways that other NCC departments did not (and, in many instances, were not structured to) do.

Nevertheless, the Council's radical image threatened its financial health during the Reagan years, and this hurt CWS as well. The NCC had an adversarial relationship with the Reagan White House, particularly on foreign policy. Tension points included Reagan's reluctance to sanction South Africa for apartheid, his nuclear arms buildup, and especially his support of despotic anticommunist leaders in Nicaragua and El Salvador while denying asylum to refugees fleeing their death squads.[42] Despite sharp cuts in funds for social justice and peace projects, the Council created a global Human Rights Office in 1977, from which it coordinated attention-grabbing efforts to address abuses worldwide. This included supporting the Sanctuary Movement, which hid Central American war refugees within church buildings; protesting U.S. backing of oppressive regimes; spearheading church efforts against South Africa's apartheid while mobilizing pressure on companies doing business there; urging self-determination for Palestinians; and assisting negotiations that settled Guatemala's civil war in the 1990s. Many of the churches' human rights and peace advocates of this era emerged from the anti–Vietnam War movement.[43] Similarly, NCC opposition to U.S. buttressing of anticommunist police states and imperialist involvement in Central America built directly upon policies it had forged on Vietnam.

Deriving lessons from the Vietnam War was just as divisive for Americans as the war itself. Complicating this process was the fact that most did not understand the history or causes of the war (the mass media rarely explained these), many people avoided the hard questions during the conflict, and once the tragedy ended, the nation seemed eager to forget it. When soldiers returned home, silence became the unwritten rule. No questions; no discussion.[44] These knowledge vacuums, combined with Americans' longing to feel good about their country again, made people ripe for Reagan's revisionist narrative. Additionally, the Vietnam War did not destroy American power or its way of life, as World War II had done to European countries. Therefore, Americans could continue business as usual while ignoring deep questions and self-examination.

Reagan's favored narrative of the conflict, spun originally by conservatives and bitter military brass such as Westmoreland, holds considerable popular resonance today even though most professional historians debunk it.[45] Reagan did an important, overdue thing: he thanked, praised, and welcomed home the Vietnam veterans. But his war narrative overlooked U.S. errors in mission, motives, and military methods. Calling the war a noble and just cause, he and his coterie blamed its "loss" (a word he also contested) upon liberal spoilers: peaceniks, the media, and weak-kneed politicians. He implied they had undercut popular support through biased reporting, gutted America's morale while upholding the enemy's, and forced the military to fight with one hand tied behind its back. In other words, the United States would have won if proper resolve, military might, and political non-interference had been employed. This narrative, dubbed the "stab-in-the-back" thesis, echoed that of Christian fundamentalists such as Carl McIntire and Billy Hargis; it also preserved America's nationalistic, exceptionalist identity.[46] And it served to batter antiwar democrats who, while largely correct about Vietnam, were painted as lacking patriotism and requisite martial backbone. This sort of spin did not challenge Americans to alter their self-understanding but, rather, invited them to reshape the facts to fit personal presuppositions. In 1970, Richard John Neuhaus astutely predicted that religious nationalists might triumph in the war of public opinion; for, if America lost Vietnam and popular sentiment still denigrated peaceniks, churches that appeared patriotic and retained public approval would "be in a position to congratulate themselves on their foresight." Those who opposed the war and critiqued its systemic causes, however, would be rejected by a citizenry desperate to retain its national myths.[47]

This all signaled a cultural retreat from Bilheimer's desire that the war serve as a catalyst for self-reflection, humility, and wisdom. The Reagan-era Vietnam narrative remained popular when George W. Bush ordered a pre-emptive U.S. attack on Iraq in 2003 and rallied citizens, the press, and even Democratic legislators to his side. As presumed weapons of mass destruction went unfound and as military conditions turned sour after the initial invasion, Bush urged "staying the course," alluding to a lesson drawn from the Reagan-era Vietnam narrative which asserted that loss resulted from flagging willpower. As seen in Iraq, American hubris, militarism, disregard for world opinion, and globalistic desires had changed little since those elements contributed to U.S. engagement in Vietnam. As illustrated in the Abu Ghraib prison scandal (2004), when U.S. military guards humiliated and tortured Iraqi prisoners, the government sought to blame a few bad apples (similar to targeting Calley for My Lai) while the nation resisted admitting that it had erred, in a systemic national sense, in Iraq.

Additionally, the antiwar movement of the 1960s remained tainted as wrong and unpatriotic, so much so that, in 2004, when decorated Vietnam War veteran John Kerry ran for president, he downplayed his leadership of Vietnam Veterans Against the War while his opponent's advocates used this to tarnish his image. Kerry emphasized his military service in a misguided war rather than his efforts to end it, for this played better in Peoria. Finally, and more explicitly than Nixon, Reagan wooed leaders of the New Christian Right while snubbing those of the liberal mainline and helped build a powerful coalition of religious and political conservatives in the Republican Party, which became the new establishment. Many moderate mainline Protestant voters liked Reagan, too, especially early on in his administration.[48]

In the 1980s, just as in previous decades, right-wing groups attacked the NCC in ways they hoped might sink it, and such groups felt energized by the rising fortunes of conservative organizations. Foreshadowing what was to come, in August 1982 the conservative periodical *Reader's Digest* published a biting attack on the World Council of Churches that claimed to expose its Marxist tilt.[49] Then, in January 1983, the National Council received a double-barreled attack from *Reader's Digest* (circulation 17.9 million) and CBS's hit television show *60 Minutes* (22.9 million households).[50] An article titled "Do You Know Where Your Church Offerings Go?" and a TV spot called "The Gospel According to Whom?" accused the NCC of funneling church offering plate donations to Marxist causes.[51] These attacks included criticism of CWS's postwar efforts to feed starving orphans in Vietnam, arguing that such action benefited or legitimated communist rulers there. In truth, CWS took care to ensure the wheat went directly into refugee bellies, not into government hands; a CWS team had accompanied the grain from dock to destination. The news pieces also painted the NCC as antagonistic toward capitalism and biased in its selective condemnation of human rights violations.[52] *Reader's Digest* mourned that MacCracken, who "refused to re-orient the agency [CWS] from its traditional mission of helping the poor and hungry . . . was summarily fired" and that "now CWS also engages in political advocacy, contributing churchgoer funds to programs designed to further strategic goals of governments with which CWS leaders sympathize." The story said that "money from hunger appeals . . . is funding political activists." Quoting an informant, *Reader's Digest* wrote,

"People just can't believe that their church, the church they've loved all their lives, can be financing all these Marxist-Leninist projects." Another informant accused the NCC of having "substituted revolution for religion." These stories sparked a flurry of conservative lay anger that a CWS official called "deafening."[53]

They also captured national attention. *Time, Newsweek, U.S. News and World Report,* and the nation's major newspapers carried articles on them and the NCC's rebuttal. Several investigative journalists noticed that *Reader's Digest* and *60 Minutes* based their charges on information gathered largely from one small neoconservative group bent on vilifying the NCC: the Institute on Religion and Democracy (IRD).[54] This organization succeeded Carl McIntire's ACCC as the lead pit bull—hungry to badger, bite, and incapacitate the NCC and its ecumenical movement, which it has done at nearly every opportunity since its creation. Founded in 1981 by Richard John Neuhaus, the IRD forged strong connections with the secular neoconservative American Enterprise Institute and has received major funding from right-wing organizations including the Bradley, Olin, Scaife, and Smith-Richardson Foundations. Morley Safer of *60 Minutes* interviewed Neuhaus, who accused the Council of doing "evil" things and being procommunist; but Safer failed to invite NCC spokespeople to address Neuhaus's charges.[55]

The journalists who investigated the *Reader's Digest* and *60 Minutes* stories also clarified that the NCC's monetary investment in political causes was small, as mandated by its 501c3 non-profit tax status, and that the 70 percent of the NCC budget earmarked for CWS was indeed spent on service work.[56] But they recognized how the Council's liberal image created disfavor with many local Christians, which hence threatened the organization's financial health.[57] *Newsweek* wrote, "in its effort to be a voice for the voiceless, the NCC failed to listen to the complaints of its own white, middle-class supporters. . . . concerns to which conservative Christians so effectively speak." It also described the NCC as "less a tyrant than an ecclesiastical Gulliver, a lumbering target for any Lilliputian group that dares to challenge its liberal political bent." Several articles faulted the NCC for its "romantic naïveté in relating to revolutions in developing countries" and of perhaps reacting to exposed injustices by swinging too far, too blindly, in the appease-all-activists direction.[58]

The NCC, as well as supporters at the *Christian Century,* rebutted the charges made by *Reader's Digest* and *60 Minutes* and rebuked their reporting as poorly researched and slanted.[59] In 2002 the retiring producer of *60 Minutes*, Don Hewitt, confessed that he regretted the flawed story.[60] While the attacks provided the Council with a public opportunity to address its image problems, they hit the financially weak Council at a vulnerable time, thus injuring it further.[61] The ramifications of these two articles aggravated stress points between CWS and the NCC, as CWS saw its ties with the Council create a credibility gap with its constituents.

In the late 1970s and early 1980s, a group upset by the NCC's weakened ecumenical state aimed to transform it into the center of a more organic, unified, ecumenical community. Led by longtime ecumenist and Governing Board member Paul Crow, these leaders tried to address the Council's lack of internal cohesion, its treatment as a mere agency of the denominations, its thin theological understandings of its work, and the turf-driven protectionism of denominations and program units. The idea was to move the Council from being a coordinator of interdenominational cooperation to being the catalyst for a real "community of communions," something Bilheimer had desired. By 1984 the board had adopted a restructuring plan to do so.

Also in 1984, the NCC hired a new general secretary, Arie Brouwer, who came from the World Council's social justice wing. That year CWS named a new executive director as well, J. Richard Butler, who had risen through CWS ranks.[62] Brouwer inherited the board's restructuring directive, which included integrating CWS and other departments—in identity and finances—more tightly under centralized NCC management.[63] One repercussion of integration involved charging offices a "common services assessment" to help finance shared NCC services that benefited each department. Because CWS now brought in and spent between 70 and 80 percent of the NCC's total budget, CWS complained that it was charged an excessive fee—one that subsidized other NCC programs for "common services" that CWS could perform for itself.[64] Exacerbating the problem, CWS had finally hit its own financial crisis. Contributions had remained flat for several years while expenses and salaries climbed.[65]

In 1987, Brouwer threatened to fire Butler for dragging his feet in completing the integration process.[66] Brouwer attributed CWS's reluctance to its unwillingness to share its bounty and be a team player. He was especially angry that CWS avoided using the NCC label in its fund-raising television ads when CWS's popular service image could be of help to the Council. Of course, CWS sought to distance itself and fought further integration in order to preserve that popularity. CWS feared that loyal contributors would refuse to give if they thought their money might flow into one of the NCC's supposedly radical programs. Thus, further blending of the NCC and CWS might scare off CWS's conservative patrons. It worried also that levying large common assessment fees on CWS was being dishonest to donors who had given funds for relief only.[67] In this politically polarized era dominated by conservative sentiments and shrinking mainline finances, the NCC's and CWS's different constituencies, structures, and foci created contradictory needs. Whereas the NCC needed CWS's popular image and resources, CWS wanted to evade the NCC's adversarial liberal image and monetary demands.

A long-simmering power struggle surfaced and exploded. With a budget and staff that dwarfed the combined rest of the Council, many in CWS resented being controlled and, to them, financially used by a now-desperate shrinking Council. The NCC was the parent body; yet, because of the size difference, one writer likened the situation to the tail (NCC) wagging the dog (CWS).[68] So, when Brouwer asked Butler to resign, Butler refused and received the "unanimous endorsement of the CWS Unit Committee," a group of denominational executives whose communions funded and shaped CWS policy.[69] The NCC created a committee to adjudicate the Brouwer-Butler dispute. Nevertheless, in June 1988, Butler suddenly quit, charging Brouwer with demeaning CWS in written communications and warning that his integration plan placed too much power in "too few hands."[70] Feeling that Butler had been driven out, an angry CWS committee asked to have Brouwer's leadership assessed, which drew Brouwer's vitriol.[71] Finally, in December, CWS requested a divorce from the NCC.[72] To appease CWS, which was the only department big enough to block Council directives, another NCC committee recommended that the Council delay further integration plans.[73] After a contentious board meeting at which Brouwer failed to receive a vote of confidence, Brouwer resigned (1989) bringing the personnel aspect of the crisis to a close. With Brouwer out and integration plans halted, CWS continued with the Council. However, points of conflict between CWS and the NCC remained unresolved and their futures troubled.[74]

To traditional ecumenists such as Crow, the NCC had lost an opportunity to move from being merely interdenominational to ecumenical; it let slip a chance to shift from its action-agency mentality left over from the 1960s into a truly prophetic one also grounded in theology. Crow blamed

Brouwer and felt the NCC abandoned its ecumenical moorings after that. An internal debate over the nature of "real ecumenism" waged vociferously not only within the NCC but also throughout the World Council. Traditional ecumenists, who favored integrating theological discussions with action and who longed for an organic unity of Christians operating as a "people amidst peoples" rather than separate interest groups, feared that the NCC and WCC were veering away permanently from the original vision.[75]

Between 1975 and 1987, the NCC's budget dropped in value by 53 percent. Its staff size was also decimated; in 1968 it boasted 187 elected staff members and by 1989 only 61.[76] Therefore, in 1990, the NCC restructured again. In a move that noted the popularity and fund-raising power of CWS relative to other departments, the NCC melded vestiges of its bygone International Affairs Commission (including its valuable "area desks" that staffed people with political expertise in various regions of the world) and DOM into CWS, creating a new NCC unit called "Church World Service and Witness."[77] But the new name became contentious, because "witness" connoted politicized advocacy work that CWS did not want prominently attached to it. So CWS chose to call itself "CWS/CROP" in correspondence with supporters while the NCC used "Church World Service and Witness" in its mailings.[78] The restructuring put CWS in the new unit's driver's seat and recognized that CWS—while charged with social justice goals—had strength because its mission was clear, and its service work resonated well with the public. The rest of the Council was still trying, as historian William McKinney wrote, "to ask what God is calling post-establishment churches to be about in a culture that no longer takes us as seriously as we take ourselves."[79] One former Council staffer turned critic blamed the NCC's troubles on "people with suicidal tendencies on the inside," explaining that "the triumph of their slogans is much more important to them than the survival of the organization they serve."[80]

In the 1990s, relations between CWS and the NCC finally strained to the breaking point. Four situations converged to compel CWS again to seek divorce. The first, and most publicized, was the NCC's massive budget deficit, which climbed to nearly ten million dollars and was, in part, the result of poor fiscal management.[81] CWS, which brought in the vast majority of NCC funds, resented that the NCC controlled them all. Its grassroots and denominational supporters had grown more distrustful of how church hierarchies managed donations, and amid reports of financial crisis at the NCC, these backers demanded separation.[82] The NCC, in its defense, contended that the head of CWS signed off on all expenditures in the 1990s, and that CWS's common services assessment merely reflected its fair share of NCC overhead costs.[83]

Second, General Secretary Joan Brown Campbell's personal friendship with President Bill Clinton and First Lady Hillary—combined with the NCC's liberal political stands—gave the appearance that the Council had now become a partisan supporter of the Democratic Party. (Never mind that Donald Argue, president of the National Association of Evangelicals, also befriended the Clintons, who courted a wide Christian gamut.)[84] After twelve years of being shut out by Republican administrations, the NCC took advantage of renewed White House access under Clinton. However, public assumptions of Council partisanship threatened CWS's ability to work constructively with future Republican administrations. Indeed, the NCC's subsequent criticism of George W. Bush's policies and Bush's refusal to meet with Council leaders put CWS in a tough position. Compounding this, the government's value as a CWS benefactor had grown again. Government support comprised about 25 percent of CWS's budget in 1999 and 28 percent in 2002.[85] CWS had to be able to work with every presidential administration, whether Democrat or Republican, and the NCC's love-hate rapports with presidents were not conducive to CWS's need for outward political neutrality.[86]

Third, in the late 1990s, after the CWS directorship had become a revolving door of short-term tenures, new director Rodney Page told denomination heads that the situation with the NCC had become unworkable. His candor caught people's attention. Leaders of denominational mission programs helped convince others that separation was necessary.[87]

Finally, in 2000, when Page retired, CWS was experiencing a resurgence of financial health.[88] It was supplying and utilizing 85 percent of the NCC's approximately seventy-seven million dollar budget. Instead of making this increased funding vulnerable to what appeared to be a sinking, mismanaged NCC, CWS demanded separation in order to protect both its funding and the organization itself.

In 2000, the NCC granted CWS's wish by freeing it financially from the Council at large. This stopped the NCC from laying common services charges on CWS without mutual agreement. CWS hoped separation would translate into greater "trust and transparency" with donors who wanted their money spent entirely on relief projects.[89]

Rev. John McCullough, who became CWS's executive director in 2000, spearheaded the establishment of its distinct identity. According to McCullough, CWS's name recognition and identity had slipped in the 1990s and was subsumed by the NCC's. He aimed to recover it by creating a unique logo and website for CWS.[90] Both were designed to position CWS as an organization in its own right and to exude an image that reflected its supporters' priorities. The website's intentional near absence of references to the NCC was striking. Sections titled "About CWS" and "History" contained no mention of its fifty-year tenure within the Council. In contrast, the NCC still promoted CWS activities and news prominently.[91] Its website and newsletter *Eculink* gave few clues that CWS was no longer part of the NCC. The Council's general secretary, Robert Edgar, dedicated an entire section of *Eculink* (with a circulation of eighty thousand) to the work of CWS. This positive publicity was paid for entirely by the NCC, which still benefited from connection with the CWS image. According to Edgar, however, CWS refused to add *Eculink* to its own mailing list, for overt ties with the NCC made it too difficult to raise funds.[92]

Edgar was also disappointed that, in a 1999 reorganization occurring just prior to his hire, CWS eliminated their area desks of political experts on various regions of the world, because they deemed them too political in appearance. Those desks had given the general secretary access to expertise and valued relationships with other nations' councils of churches. With those gone, the NCC's international staff network constricted further, hindering its ability to respond to global issues. As a result, much of the NCC's international work fell to him, his administrative assistant, and "one other staff person who handles the world."[93]

Disgruntled laity have tended to view CWS and the NCC in the simplistic polarized terms of "good guy" and "bad guy." Unbeknownst to parishioners, however, is the fact that several of the NCC's official statements on more recent political issues originated within the governance ranks of CWS. These include resolutions on Israel and Palestine, September 11th, Afghanistan, and the war in Iraq.[94] While the NCC often tried to leverage CWS's image to boost its own, CWS in turn used the NCC as a conduit through which to make political statements without grassroots knowledge. Indeed, Executive Director McCullough admitted that CWS leadership often had little disagreement with the NCC on its political stands.

The conflict derived, rather, from the NCC's hierarchical process and relational style, which was not conducive to CWS's grassroots-based structure. CWS saw the NCC as overly aggressive in its quick prophetic replies to controversial issues; it disliked that top NCC staff often generated these with little involvement invited of others. It also dreaded the NCC's appearance of partisanship in its attacks on Republican policies. This all threatened to hurt CWS's working relationship with its grassroots and governmental constituencies. If CWS is ever going to join the NCC visibly in confronting hot politicized issues, Reverend McCullough predicted the Council must become more consultative with and reflective of the various layers within the body of Christ; its statements must also be crafted in ways that will not invite charges of partisanship. McCullough admitted that CWS is a heavy grassroots organization that cannot afford to jump far ahead of its constituencies nor alienate the White House; because of these structural and financial links, Edgar called CWS "genetically nice." Conversely, under Edgar, the NCC still saw jumping ahead of laity and alienating the White House as sometimes part of its prophetic mission.

From Edgar's perspective, the NCC's identity, strengths, and function-ality came from its ability to react quickly and prophetically to political crises, and then to rally church support behind Council positions. Since the 1960s, several within the NCC have perceived this as one of its great-est and most underappreciated gifts to the ecumenical community.[95] Its hierarchical structure that links its funding and survival to denomina-tional bureaucracies rather than to parishioners provides it this freedom. Becoming more reflective of laity as well as neutral with government might muffle what the NCC perceives as its prophetic voice. It might also remove from the mainline denominations the service of this on-call snowplow organization that can spearhead responses to controversial issues—one that can counter those mobilized quickly on the Christian right. Conversely, others within NCC circles have renewed Bilheimer's old plea to infuse theology and a sharper focus on spiritual Christian unity more centrally into the backbone of its public social witness.[96] Still others contend that, if the NCC continues to project its own voice over that of parishioners, it cannot and should not survive.

ECUMENISM IN TRANSITION, 2000–2010

The Council's survival was indeed raised with a question mark during CWS's departure in 2000. At that time, the NCC saw its annual budget dwindle to seven million dollars, and its professional staff cut to forty-seven. Some feared it might fold. Yet, the NCC experienced a resurrection. Under the leadership of General Secretary Robert Edgar, the NCC balanced its budget. In 2002, armed with a generous grant from the Lilly Endowment for new program development, monetary assistance from the Methodist and Presbyterian Churches, and tighter internal oversight, the NCC turned an important financial corner.[97]

In April 2000, Edgar also called a meeting with NCC board members to help the Council rethink its future. With the aid of a consultant, who noted that the NCC lacked clarity about its mission, attendees experienced an epiphany. As Edgar described it, "Bruce Robins of the Methodist Church said something that was very profound.... [T]he vocational mission of all of us around this table is not to fix what's wrong with the National Council of Churches.... [It] is to restart the ecumenical movement with the same energy that our founding fathers and mothers had." By day's end they had crafted a multi-pronged strategy.[98] First, create a "larger table" of sorts at which the entire spectrum of Christian churches would feel welcome and willing to talk together. Second, make addressing poverty—and its correlating issues such as public education, health care, housing, children, and the capitalist economic model—a long-term focus of the ecumenical movement. Third, elevate environmental stewardship to a priority. And, fourth, retain an institutional arm that could tackle controversial peace and justice issues in a quick prophetic way. This approach reflected 1960s era new breed priorities. It downplayed and separated theological discussions of Christian unity from what these leaders highlighted as the NCC's main work: social justice action.

The first step led to the creation of a new ecumenical organization called Christian Churches Together in the USA (CCT). Since conservative churches have been disinclined to join anything connected to the NCC, the Council assumed an anonymous background role while helping its member denominations birth it. CCT aimed to bring together not only the NCC's members but also Catholics, Pentecostals, and other conservative Christians for discussion and perhaps cooperation on a few issues of mutual concern.[99] This larger "but thinner" table, as Edgar described it, has included voices from a broad spectrum of theological beliefs, and because CCT requires consensus for action, many expected it to be more a dialoguing and relationship-building vehicle than a driver of action programs. (Edgar described its mission as helping Christians "learn how to play in the sandbox together.") The new organization also operates as a medium for theological discussions between Christian groups, for some primarily seek that. Orthodox churches, for example, which have frequently opposed the NCC's liberalism, nevertheless retained membership because it united them in valued Christian dialogue with others. CCT has sought to do this on a broader scale.[100]

While some speculated initially that CCT might replace the NCC (as happened to councils in Great Britain and Australia that developed CCT organizations), this appeared unlikely to others who saw an ongoing need for NCC advocacy on peace and justice issues. Specifically, it can act quickly on hot-button issues like the Iraq War that CCT and CWS might not wish to touch. The NCC can also push further and deeper, in its traditional snowplow way, on issues such as poverty and the environment. Herein the NCC fills a niche much desired by its more socially active communions such as the UCC, Methodists, and Quakers.[101] Since the NCC's job, viewed through this lens, is a prophetic and catalytic one, and since its direct constituents remain the denominations, Edgar did not feel it vital that the NCC reflect the perspectives of laity. He noted that, "none of the prophets, none of the disciples ever had a majority; none of them ever took a vote to figure out what God's will is." It did not surprise him, either, "that there would be a disconnect between prophetic lay and clergy leadership and the general population."[102]

Reminiscent of Bilheimer's goal at the Ecumenical Witness conference, Edgar wanted churches to reclaim the moral high ground from George W. Bush's administration and the far Christian right, which he felt had willingly been co-opted by the GOP. He urged churches to take the moral lead by focusing upon three life-and-death justice issues: peace, poverty, and planet Earth. Edgar believed churches also needed to have their own foreign policy that reflected a worldview grounded in Christian values. They should transcend and question the actions and presuppositions of power groups such as governments. Edgar specifically wanted the NCC to function as a "chaplain of world opinion" as well as a visible counterforce to the religious right's dominance within America's political culture.[103] Although Edgar had made his political career in the Democratic Party before joining the NCC, he reached out to moderate Christians of both parties on issues of concern. Like Bilheimer, he hoped that moderates in the churches would be touched by human connections within the global community, inspiring them to put compassion and empathy before nationalism and religious self-interest. In the political climate of President George W. Bush's first term, when Democratic leaders often stifled their criticisms, Edgar hoped that churches, led by the NCC, could be a voice that still challenged worldviews and presuppositions. Therefore, under his leadership, the NCC did not change its process of political action from the prophetic to the consultative-reflective mode that CWS requested. In fact, for Edgar, the Iraq War illustrated why the NCC's prophetic role was so vital.

VIETNAM'S INFLUENCE: THE IRAQ WAR AND RELIGIOUS ACTIVISM

In late summer 2002, President George W. Bush grew impatient with UN inspectors for not finding the weapons of mass destruction that he felt sure lay in Saddam Hussein's possession, and he began hinting at America's right to initiate preemptive war. Many religious leaders spoke out against such potential action, including Edgar and the NCC.

Edgar wanted religious leaders to move quickly against Bush's impending attack, in part because he felt churches had been too slow to condemn the Vietnam War. Back in February 1968, as a twenty-five-year-old seminarian at Drew Theological School (Methodist), Edgar had participated in his first major antiwar event, one organized by CALCAV and William Sloane Coffin. He crossed an angry picket line of war supporters led by Carl McIntire who held signs reading "Kill a Commie for Christ's Sake." Martin Luther King gave the keynote address.[104]

The experience shaped Edgar's life. Like many seminarians in the 1960s, he was convinced that churches needed to make themselves relevant to people through "action-sermons," that is, by working for peace and justice through practical measures that made a difference in people's lives and embodied God's love for humanity. The new breed style and agenda captured him. As a young pastor in urban Philadelphia, he saw violence erupt over civil rights, economic justice issues, and U.S. Vietnam policies. Then, in April 1975 as a newly elected congressman from Pennsylvania, Edgar helped advance the effort in Congress to end America's remaining involvement in the war. He grasped, then, that the churches had been too cautious on Vietnam. "I realized how long it took . . . and how many body bags you needed to get organized religion to be concerned about the war."[105] This amplified his urgency to mobilize churches in 2002, on moral and "just war" grounds, to reject preemptive war with Iraq when it seemed clear that Bush was inching the United States toward it.

Edgar is proud of the fact that, in 2002 and 2003, a broad coalition of religious leaders and groups spoke out strongly against Bush's war plans, seven months before the U.S. attack on Baghdad. The churches condemned war as a solution, urged peaceful means of resolution, and tried to make the faces and voices of Iraqi civilians known to the American people. Specifically, on September 12, 2002, one year and a day after the 9/11 terrorist attacks on New York's Twin Towers and the Pentagon, nearly fifty religious leaders representing a plethora of organizations sent a joint letter to President Bush and British prime minister Tony Blair opposing a possible preemptive attack on Iraq. The signers included NCC staffers, leaders of various Catholic orders, evangelicals, black Baptists, CWS, Unitarians, leaders of the Syrian Orthodox Church, Quakers, Moravians, Brethren, and executives within several Protestant mainline churches such as the Methodists, Disciples of Christ, United Church of Christ, Baptists, Evangelical Lutherans (ECLA), Reformed Church in America, and the Presbyterian Church (PCUSA). The letter deemed it immoral, unjust, and a bad precedent to use a preemptive strike to topple a regime. It urged continued UN inspections, diplomatic efforts, and international sanctions to deal with Iraq. It suggested that an attack on Iraq might divert efforts against terrorism and in Afghanistan, while risking the destruction of untold numbers of civilian lives. And, if Bush truly sought peace, stability, and justice in the Middle East, the letter urged advancing an Israeli-Palestinian agreement instead.[106]

A day later, the U.S. Conference of Catholic Bishops also judged Bush's possible preemptive strike against Iraq morally illegitimate. It noted the lack of evidence connecting Iraq to 9/11. Presciently, it also raised the specter of negative consequences from an attack toppling Saddam Hussein, including civil unrest, a rise in terrorism, destabilization of the nation and region, and loss of resources for the Afghanistan mission.[107] The Vatican itself communicated gentle but suggestive opinions in the press during October 2002, urging diplomacy and international efforts, a focus on relevant justice issues, and a rejection of armed intervention in Iraq.[108] Also in October, over two hundred clergy from the Protestant, Catholic, and Jewish traditions conducted an antiwar protest in clerical dress on San Francisco's Golden Gate Bridge. Seminary presidents of the nine schools in the Graduate Theological Union even penned a joint letter confirming that Christian just war criteria were missing from Bush's plans.[109] And in conjunction with others, the NCC helped organize large prayer vigils, took delegations to Iraq, sent groups around the world in peace-seeking efforts, drafted joint letters and statements to heads of state, and spoke frequently in the news media.[110]

Edgar appeared on several television programs, including *Fox News* and *Hardball*, often counterpoised against an evangelical supporter of the war such as Jerry Falwell. Given the dominance of conservative Christian voices in the public square, Edgar hoped to make a different religious witness known on the war, as well as to help provide credibility to the antiwar movement, which, as in the 1960s, was stereotyped as traitorous, radical, and kooky. Similar also to the Vietnam War was the global outcry condemning U.S. policy, particularly by the citizens of other nations who took part in massive antiwar demonstrations. Like his predecessors, Edgar wanted the church's witness to reflect a global consciousness rather than merely a national sensibility on the war.

Interviewed in 2003, he connected his response on Iraq directly to his Vietnam era experiences. "I think perhaps the disciples of the sixties, people like me who were vaccinated by the courage of a Dr. King and the articulation of a William Sloane Coffin, were better prepared during this incursion to stand up and speak out earlier." To him, the prophetic voice of the ecumenical churches was more necessary than ever. "I think Jerry Falwell, Franklin Graham, Pat Robertson, Jesse Helms, and Newt Gingrich moved the Republican Party and the religious community to the right. Mainline religious leaders," Edgar noted, also "stepped to the right. . . . Having said that," he concluded, "it may be that the voice of those clergy and lay people who are stepping out and are courageous may be more important today than it was in the 1960s, because in the sixties you had both the religious and the political prophets. In the decade we live in now, the voices of the political prophets are really very thin."[111]

Mirroring Nixon's and Reagan's rejection of NCC leaders as personas non grata, Bush refused all NCC requests to discuss the impending war. He clung instead to statements like that of Southern Baptist leader Richard Land, who justified preemptive war against Saddam Hussein, saying it stood "well within the time-honored criteria of just war theory as developed by Christian theologians."[112] On the other hand, Bush's ally Prime Minister Blair met with an NCC delegation about Iraq in February 2003.[113]

With hindsight, several prominent news journalists and politicians have admitted that the media and leaders within both political parties failed to ask tough critical questions before the war.[114] And many of them later saw the war as misguided and mistake-ridden. As some church leaders warned in 2002, unforeseen repercussions such as civil conflict and regional instability burgeoned beyond the U.S. military's control, civilian casualties skyrocketed after Bush prematurely declared "Mission Accomplished" in May 2003, and U.S. military resources became stretched so thin that some questioned whether those for Afghanistan were compromised. On the Iraq War, perhaps even more so than on Vietnam, certain churches played an important, if unpopular, gadfly role as one of the few voices on the establishment's margins willing to raise tough questions about America's war policy. Their stated motives stemmed from a moral humanitarian base of religious traditions and beliefs rather than from political interests or economic power. Their suggestions stressed diplomatic solutions that might also generate greater justice, trust, and communication between nations. As Bilheimer observed, when men like Kissinger shaped policy, politicians often disregarded humanitarian, religious, and moral consider-ations during war. NCC leaders from both the Vietnam and Iraq War eras have argued definitively that when conformist political pressures silence popular criticism, the voices of religious gadflies become especially critical to include in the public square.

What qualifies as a "prophetic voice" or a prophetic message is debated within the broader Christian community, and determinations still often, though not exclusively, divide along liberal and conservative lines. How-ever, the appropriateness of clergy making specific political statements, doing activist work, and claiming to represent Christian values seems less controversial today than in the 1960s. Even though some clergy still avoid politics as secular, corrupting, and distracting from preaching the gospel, many conservative churches and their pastors have embraced political activism. In fact, studies show that evangelicals today are even more supportive of religious leaders engaging political issues than are mainline Protestants.[115] Research has also exposed what historian Darren Dochuk calls "the myth of the spiritual church," as it spotlights discrepan-cies between conservative pulpit condemnations of religious social activ-ism and considerable conservative Christian politicking throughout the twentieth century.[116]

Jerry Falwell, who denounced the activism and prophetic claims of Prot-estant liberals in the 1960s, later defended such actions when employed by clergy like himself in the service of conservative Christian political positions. Contrasting himself with the more moderate Billy Graham, who retreated from political pronouncements and partisanship with age, Falwell told Graham, "You are an evangelist; I am a pastor. I have prophetic responsibilities that you do not have." Falwell then described his political tasks to a *Newsweek* reporter: "I have spent the last 30 years forming the religious right," he noted. "I write a letter every week and send a newspaper every month to 200,000 pastors who are broadly called evangelicals, bringing them up to date on what is happening in Washington, in the state capitals, in the culture, and what we need to do about it."[117] Randall Terry, the founder of the anti-abortion group Operation Rescue, also admitted he deliberately incorporated the nonviolent civil disobedience tactics used so effectively by civil rights activists decades earlier for his own protests against abortion providers. Like new breeders of the 1960s, he preferred deeds to words.[118] Ironically, in more recent decades, secular liberal activists have often been first to tell religious ones that they should depart from pronouncing in the public square and remain sequestered within private spiritual settings.

Whereas conservative religious groups now boldly engage sociopolitical issues and claim to possess the secular expertise and theological justifications to do so (aspects they questioned of liberal religious activists in the 1960s), ecumenical communities are paying more attention to making explicit the connections between their issue-related stances, theological understandings, and spiritual values. Laity have also made clear that, while they favor inserting church positions on issues into the public square, they overwhelmingly want to reserve Sunday morning services for spiritual messages.[119] Many mainline clergy have heard and responded. Since the 1960s, these local clergy have also shifted their own political focus more to the local level and away from national politics, leaving the latter to denominational offices and the NCC.[120] Laity have approved. This has lightened some of the pinch that clergy felt over politics during the Vietnam War between their denominational headquarters and their congregations. Mainline churches are also working to improve communication with the public as well as their ability to mobilize their members, although they face an uphill climb in both areas.

Significantly, some progressive religious leaders have reached out to progressive political activists seeking inclusion again at their table, just as many Democratic politicians have realized, astutely, that they have hurt their party's connection with the public by explicitly excising spiritual images, language, and motives from their messages since the 1960s.[121] This had opened Democrats to charges of "Godlessness" while granting the Republican Party sole claim as public preserver of Christian morals.[122] In 2006, a few Democrats including then senator Barak Obama

(Illinois) began collaborating with religious leaders to better incorporate faith-sensitive language, priorities, worldviews, and strategies within the Democratic Party.[123] The re-creation of a strong "spiritual left" to contest the now formidable religious far right in the public square, and in supportive cooperation with political progressives, appears underway.[124] The challenge remains for the Christian left to create what religious studies scholar Mark Silk calls "a ground game," that is, the ability to mobilize the laity, which the Christian right possesses. Currently, as in the Vietnam era, it seems limited to an "air game" controlled by religious leaders who merely articulate positions and seek media forums.[125] The efforts exerted here from denominational and NCC Washington offices are hampered by having too few staff and minuscule funding.

Although mainline Protestant laity have been shifting slowly from the ranks of moderate Republicans to the Democratic Party over the last few decades, generating a ground game might prove difficult for several reasons. First, a clergy-laity gap still exists on sociopolitical issues, with the leadership generally leaning further left than its more moderate laity.[126] Organized conservative groups operating within the mainline Protestant community, which stand to the theological and political right of many laity, continue purposefully to fuel that divide with significant help from the IRD.[127] Second, mainline laity tend to prefer doing quiet, local, civic service behind the scenes (of which they do more than any other religious group) rather than public political advocacy. Third, because of their often comfortable place within the system, they tend to feel less desirous of change than evangelicals who still perceive themselves as marginalized from mainstream culture.[128] Finally, mainline Protestants fell as a percentage of the voting electorate from 46 percent in 1960 to 28 percent in 1996. Religious scholars explain that this was due more to demographic factors such as lower birth rates than to defections from mainline churches.[129] Nevertheless, this decline denotes a drop in electoral power, which is what most grabs the attention of Washington politicians. But renewed energy, leadership, optimism, and a broadened religious coalition that includes progressive evangelicals gives organizers of a new religious "left" some hope. So, too, does the rising discontent of political and religious moderates who have grown more alienated from the policies and practices of the Republican Party.[130]

The debate still rages over whether practical cooperation focused primarily around activist issues is really true ecumenism at work. Traditional ecumenists including Robert Bilheimer and Paul Crow argued the negative.

In fact, Crow criticized the NCC's new breed approach to building Christian unity around issues first, such as environmentalism, rather than starting with theological dialogue and church transformation. He denounced Edgar's direction as accelerating the Council's death as a real ecumenical organization. Other more friendly critics clarified that Edgar's main sin was one of omission rather than commission.[131] They applauded his fiscal management and energetic social witness. Nevertheless, seeing him as a new breeder shaped by the 1960s, they claimed that Edgar failed to integrate theological discussion and sufficient spiritual energy centrally into the NCC's justice work. Some even saw him as the last gasp of the Council's swing in the new breed direction.

A NEW FRACTURED ECUMENICAL MODEL

When the NCC was created in 1950 by merging the Federal Council with CWS and several other independent Christian agencies, it attempted as the World Council did to unite "Faith and Order," "Life and Works," and all of the other Christian agency programs under one organizational ecumenical roof. The idea behind this was that real ecumenism requires these things to be bound together and organically melded into one witness. For good or ill, this grand organizational experiment faltered, largely due to divisive factors that proved impossible to transcend during and after the Vietnam era.

Organized American mainline ecumenism has moved from the single conciliar "umbrella" model popularized after World War II into a series of smaller, overlapping, satellite organizations, each with its own specialty. CCT was designed primarily to facilitate dialogue and serve as the broadest reflection of American Christianity. It also aimed to embody the spirit of the "Faith and Order" branch of ecumenism, which emphasized theology.[132] CWS remains the churches' "apolitical" service and relief agency. The NCC has specialized in being the religious gadfly on the political scene, as well as the organizer of ecumenical action on political crises too controversial for the other two. In this, it has embodied the spirit of the "Life and Works" branch of ecumenism, which traditionally emphasized social justice. A fourth organization called Churches Uniting in Christ (CUIC) has aimed to enhance interdenominational relationships by bringing communions together in mutual recognition of one another's sacraments and clergy—as well as cooperation in common mission. Therefore, the ecumenical movement has splintered back into separate interest-group type organizations that overlap and cooperate, but which also allow those within them to ignore and dissociate from the others if they wish.[133]

Whether this multi-centered satellite model of mainline ecumenism will survive and thrive is speculative. John McCullough deemed it necessary in the short run; however, he also predicted that the satellites will need to move more closely together in the future. Even though the whole notion of bureaucratic national ecumenism has lost its sex appeal since the 1960s, it may be more necessary than ever. With mainline congregations aging, the need increases for churches to pool resources to accomplish shared goals. At the same time, however, shrinking denominational budgets have forced both the NCC and CWS to seek out new paying partners. These new partners, or constituent-benefactors, will bring their own binding expectations to the table.[134]

So, too, has the NCC's newest general secretary. When Edgar left that role in late 2007, the Council unanimously selected Rev. Dr. Michael Kinnamon, a longtime professor of theology and ecumenical studies, to replace him. Kinnamon, a theologian with experience in the WCC's Faith and Order Commission as well as in running CUIC, seems committed to weaving theological dialogue and prophetic action back together again at the NCC. In a keynote address in April 2008, Kinnamon asserted, "As long as I am General Secretary, Faith and Order will never be marginalized in the work of the National Council of Churches. . . . But as long as I am General Secretary, I will insist that racism, sexism, poverty, and violence are church-dividing issues that belong on the agenda of Faith and Order— and that our unity as Christians, though an end in itself, is also part and parcel of our witness to God's work of liberation and reconciliation in the world."[135] Kinnamon clearly seeks to make the NCC a "community of communions" rather than just an action agency of the denominations, something Bilheimer and Crow would applaud. What this will mean both structurally and relationally remains to be seen.[136]

As the NCC and CWS's rocky marriage revealed, ecumenical organizations became trapped within the political culture wars of the last forty years by the priorities and beliefs of their constituent-benefactors who provided them their funds, credibility, and mandates. In order to function effectively and preserve an established organizational identity, the "right arm" (CWS) and "left arm" (NCC) of American mainline ecumenism (as

Edgar called them) still cannot easily rise above this reality to act in ways that might offend their patrons. Their structures also serve to dictate what they can do as well as how they are perceived. Some might see the original ecumenical vision being compromised in the current satellite model. Nevertheless, from a purely practical organizational perspective, ecumenical cooperation between distinct religious organizations able to maintain their own unique identities, finances, and constituencies ultimately may prove more viable and sustainable for all. This structural model may also provide the flexibility to allow religious organizations to ride through America's polarizing political periods with less stress upon their relationships and institutional health.

The NCC is now struggling to reconfigure itself in an atmosphere where, since the 1960s, institutionalized ecumenism has become a lower priority. Two seemingly contradictory forces appear at work here. First, Alan Geyer argued that local churches have to some extent "retribalized," by which he meant efforts "to recover what is distinctive to their own denominational heritage."[137] This cultural phenomenon extends beyond the churches. Since the 1960s, the World War II generation's glorification of American unity gave way to celebrations of different cultural identities, including white Americans seeking to reclaim lost ethnic roots. The growth of ethnic parades and festivals in local communities illustrates this.[138] Geyer also attributed declining interest in ecumenism to the rapid growth of conservative churches, which have not generally supported the ecumenical vision. America's globalistic attitude toward other nations and cultures, as repopularized by Bush-era neoconservatives, did not help either. On the flip side, others call organized ecumenism a victim of its own success. For, along with some retribalization, Protestants also more readily recognize those in other denominations as equal members of the body of Christ; thus denominational lines have lost significance to laity. This reflects the broader culture's growing embrace of pluralism in many forms, yet this embrace still tends to flow along conservative and liberal fault lines. As ecumenists well know, pluralism is hard work. For when ecumenism has sought to unite different parts of Christianity, imbedded intra-Christian gripes, turf issues, expectations, and sociopolitical preferences have come with them. One can conclude that the NCC's troubles since the Vietnam era were not simply repercussions of internal maladies or missteps. Though ecumenism has sought to transcend cultural biases and self-serving loyalties, the American people have rarely been so inclined. Thus the political and historical climates in which the NCC operated have affected its work more profoundly than ecumenists might wish to admit.

Indeed, when CWS split from the NCC, and both CCT and CUIC were created to conduct theological and unity functions that the NCC could not, while the NCC provided the prophetic punch the others were missing—this all served as an admission of ecumenism's vulnerability to culture. To function in a post-Protestant, polarized, politically conservative America, the ecumenical body was cut up and then re-intersected in an almost Picasso-like form. Perhaps this is a fitting symbol of how wars blow bodies apart, whether they be physical, spiritual, or organizational ones—bodies that, if they survive, can learn to contribute in new ways while perhaps growing wiser and stronger from their scars.

The Ecumenical Way—A Reflective Review

In a world of revolution, rapid change, and sharp conflict of ideologies,
Christians have an opportunity and duty to be a reconciling and healing force
between nations and peoples and races where possible.
—"Policy Statement on Viet-Nam," NCC General Board, December 3, 1965

In 1950 the newborn NCC inherited an ecumenical vision forged amid
class strife, depression, and two world wars; it was fashioned during an era
when progressivism and New Deal–type approaches to problems shaped
establishment assumptions and bureaucratic structures. The ecumenical worldview of unity, transcendence, global compassion, cooperation,
peace, human rights, and renewal embodied the dreams of those who
wanted the church to serve as a catalyst for a new, better way of being
in relationship with others while becoming more truly a body of Christ
within itself. Despite early Cold War challenges and unrelenting attacks by
the religious far right, the NCC grew as the ecumenical idea drew sizeable
support. Government leaders paid it the attentive respect that was due to
an influential organization.

By its own account the NCC reached its peak of power, influence, and
sense of importance in 1965 when the U.S. "Americanized" the Vietnam
War. Ten years later, when Saigon fell, the United States had lost its first
war and a rapidly shrinking NCC was trying to pull out of a tailspin. The

impact of the war and the era that encompassed it has rippled through the NCC's history ever since, and continues to transform it. In a sense, battling the Vietnam War while dealing with the convention-breaking era itself served as the NCC's biggest trial by fire. Its mostly deeply held principle of unity was sorely tested during the century's most divisive years. Its ability to transcend culture was tested amid immense cultural upheaval and activist pressure, much of which rocked the NCC and compelled it to change. Its sense of its own ability as an establishment insider to move government, and as a religious authority to mobilize parishioners with a word from above, was tested at a time when people's trust of authorities collapsed in reaction to lies, violence, and scandals. Its self-confidence as a persuasive change agent was tested also when charged to help stop one of the most lengthy, obtuse, and morally ambiguous wars in U.S. history. Its conviction that the church must speak truth to power and maintain its independence was tested as government sought either to use or impair the NCC's influence with respect to the war, while the NCC's relief wing clung to the government's coattails. Its belief that it is part of a worldwide body of Christ was tested during a time when Christian nationalism and American exceptionalism spiked amid a unilateral hot war that the government saw as embedded in a global Cold War against atheistic communists. Thus, the period between 1965 and 1975 was perhaps the most trying and revealing period one could find for the NCC, particularly because the organization felt strong when the Vietnam era began. It provides a fascinating window through which to watch and assess the Council's work and ideas—and by extension, those of the ecumenical churches. If trial by fire is of any use, it can help expose core strengths and weaknesses while often significantly scarring and transforming that which survives the flames.

When evaluating the NCC through its Vietnam work, one must keep in mind the self-identity, vision, roles, and goals it embraced. The NCC often tried to address every problem through a program or task force, attempting to do and be all things to all people. Expectations often outran reality. This was clearly the case in 1965. Older leaders remembered the Federal Council's success in shaping ideas about a "just and durable peace," which helped birth the United Nations and later its Universal Declaration of Human Rights; they also recalled its effective mobilization of parishioners around those things. Younger new breeders believed the NCC had been a significant pioneering leader in the civil rights struggles since 1963. And ecumenists like Bilheimer—who saw the ecumenical movement as a second reformation with a global responsibility to be the prophetic voice and helpful hands for bringing peace, justice, and reconciliation to the planet—felt a powerful calling in their work; they sensed that miraculous strides had been made amid *kairos* moments. Each of these groups transferred high expectations and a triumphal spirit to the Council's efforts on Vietnam. At that time, a sense of mainline Protestant hegemony still reigned. Signs of erosion had long been apparent, but the mountaintop upon which the mainline churches stood was not yet crumbling.

In an attempt to examine the NCC and glean insights from its triumphs and tribulations as it tackled the Vietnam War, we'll use its own goals and roles as our focus. For the sake of organization, we can group them into six main categories: (1) learning and witnessing, which sought to develop positions and speak truth to power; (2) educating, mobilizing, and providing resources to others; (3) collaborating with and supporting other antiwar groups; (4) addressing the war's repercussions through service and advocacy; (5) ecumenizing, through listening and building consensus within the body of Christ; and (6) renewing the church and transforming worldviews. These categories dovetail well with key concepts underlying the historical ecumenical vision that include unity, witness, transcendence, renewal, justice, and service. The NCC's Vietnam agenda hewed closely to these traditional purposes of the ecumenical movement. The Council responded to the war as part of a diverse ensemble of antiwar groups: it tried to contribute in ways that drew upon its particular strengths and abilities while honoring its identity as a manifestation of the body of Christ. Let us now explore the NCC's goals, activities, and accomplishments within each of these categories.

LEARNING AND WITNESSING (SPEAKING TRUTH TO POWER)

One of the Council's primary goals involved witnessing to government with the hope of influencing U.S. Vietnam policy. Doing so was an expected delineated activity for an ecumenical body that represented over thirty denominations with a collective membership of more than forty million parishioners. The organization's status provided the necessary clout to secure audiences with top government officials. Its worldwide connections and resources gave it access to firsthand information on the war from a vast array of sources. Many other groups in the antiwar movement lacked these advantages.

Traditional ecumenists felt it essential that the church always be a "confessing church," one that asserted its independent voice before the nation's power brokers and brought its perspective as powerfully as possible into the debate.[1] To fulfill its prophetic responsibility, Bilheimer stressed, the church must make a tenacious, responsible witness to those in power. Whether the government listened was a matter of its own free will. Whether and how God used that witness was a matter of divine choice.

Most new breeders and secular activists had a different view. They emphasized the achievement of practical results and amassing pressure upon the government to force its hand. They deemed the witness a failure if it did not produce the desired outcome. Sociopolitical aims largely dictated the strategies they preferred. In fact, they were willing to use tactics that, to traditional ecumenists, threatened to dilute the power of the confessing church in order to win. For ecumenists such as Bilheimer the goal of being an independent confessing church through witness strongly influenced which methods they chose to employ.

The International Affairs Commission did craft, update, and press an ecumenical church witness upon government doggedly for nearly ten years. Even though it saw the government slowly adopting some of its (and others') recommendations, the NCC clearly did not have much effect upon U.S. foreign policy or those who made it. Then again, no particular peace group did. Pharaoh's heart remained hard and bent upon military victory—despite plague after plague, and whether that pharaoh be Johnson or Nixon. Scholars disagree as to whether the peace movement as a whole put limits on presidents and expedited an end to the war, whether it simply caused extra internal chaos, or whether it prolonged the war by buoying the enemy.[2]

Those who measure success from the activist new breed perspective would probably judge the NCC's efforts a failure. Secular historians who also use practical results as yardsticks for sound action might judge them naïve. Was it not ridiculous and prideful for church leaders already slipping in power to think they could move the White House? To Bilheimer, however, the church's greatest failure would have been to shirk its ecumenical duty by not speaking out—as continuously and intelligently as possible and regardless of the consequences or what one might deem possible. In God, were not all things possible? Bilheimer wanted desperately to see real success. He wanted to help move government officials to change both Vietnam policy and their more general presuppositions about world security.

He shifted message and approach whenever he thought this might better open the ears and eyes of those in power. But he wanted to ensure, in doing so, that the church preserved as much transcendence from government and cultural forces as possible. Its ability to be "the church" rather than a cultural or political pawn, he felt, depended upon this. Therefore, how one evaluates this aspect of the NCC's work depends upon one's biases in priorities and definitions of success.

The NCC blended the expectations and tactics of new breeders and traditional ecumenists when making its appeals to government, and it targeted all three branches. Bilheimer put considerable personal energy into White House appeals. His efforts included decorous polite visits with cabinet—officials that involved discussions of practical peace options, assumptions underlying ideas about security, and religious beliefs about concepts like "the enemy." The NCC also lobbied Congress with CALCAV, organized election-based efforts to affect candidate positions on peace, negotiated about CO counseling with the Selective Service, supported petition drives, opposed suppression of civil liberties or dissent, testified before Congress, and filed amicus curiae briefs for court cases on a range of war-related topics. Throughout, Bilheimer tapped church leaders who represented the diversity within ecumenical circles, including social gospel activists, neo-orthodox realists, anticommunists, anti-imperialists, those from just war churches, and pacifists.

When Bilheimer left the NCC, he was frustrated by its limited success with government, and he knew the Council's power had slipped. He also felt a personal sense of failure. But if one uses the measure of being a confessing church set upon speaking its truth to power, he and his staff warrant recognition. Like a bulldog, they never let go of the government's ankle. And they resisted government efforts to put a leash on the Council and command it to heel. Church World Service was the exception, yet NCC staffers deserve credit for persuading CWS to change its relationship with government over time. We've also seen several examples of Bilheimer's defensive protection of the church's independence from government. For instance, he demanded that the State Department respect the Council's freedom when conducting its Mission of Concern and got it. He also pulled Allan Parrent and Herman Will away from Averell Harriman when he suspected Harriman wanted to use the churches as lackeys. When Secretary of State Rogers scolded the NCC for its paucity of government loyalty, Bilheimer's team did not tuck tail and become obedient. When Vice President Agnew included the Council in his public barrages of insults, when the IRS targeted and harassed it, and when Council offices were wiretapped, the NCC remained undaunted and unintimidated. Bilheimer knew the Council was losing its prized influence and political access. The loss pained a staff used to both. But the NCC did not sell out for a box seat at Nixon's White House worship services or to regain some of the privileges that pleasing presidents can bring. When Eugene Carson Blake pursued Nixon via letters, demanding recognition and an answer, Bilheimer advised against it, judging it demeaning for the church at that point. For Bilheimer, church power and identity rested in its independence, prophetic truthfulness, theological awareness, and willingness to walk its talk.

Bilheimer's methods of witnessing to the White House raise questions, however. Clearly, he believed in the value of reasoned discussion, good data, real listening, and the power of persuasion to change hearts and minds, for he repeatedly employed these approaches. They had worked within the ecumenical community to create denominational consensus and renewal around controversial subjects, so he assumed they could succeed with government officials. Secular liberals had long favored such tactics, too.[3] However, in the 1950s and 1960s, civil rights and other activist groups quoted Reinhold Niebuhr, who said that only pressure, not persuasion, would move power-based institutions such as government. But until Nixon virtually slammed the door in the face of the ecumenical community, Bilheimer kept bringing positions, data, arguments, and elite-generated ideas to the executive branch. All his life he loved to debate, to press people to think rigorously. His son noted that he had a gift for being able "to challenge you to think more, better, harder."[4] Yet, with government, these efforts failed. And he may have waited too long to switch over to a moral argument, which seemed prime ground for the churches. Relying upon moral arguments was an old social gospel tactic and one that Niebuhr deemed useless upon institutions. Perhaps this affected Bilheimer, for he was more a product of Christian realism and neo-orthodoxy than the social gospel. Nevertheless, when Nixon shut the NCC out and tried to buoy his moral standing through conservative religious support, Bilheimer responded with a biting, massive, moral Ecumenical Witness against the war. Despite institutional struggles, Bilheimer drew the global ecumenical community together and pitched its voice into the burgeoning culture war over morality.

The NCC is often viewed as a liberal institution. Yet Bilheimer's efforts to speak truth to power were nonpartisan affairs. The Council criticized both Democratic and Republican officials who supported the war. The delegations Bilheimer assembled were also nonpartisan, containing a mix of Democrats and Republicans. This is often difficult for churches caught in America's culture wars to do. And delegations reflected the range of views within the NCC, from those of anticommunists such as Schomer, Geyer, and Kenneth Thompson to those favoring anti-imperialism over anticommunism, including Elston and Bilheimer himself. They included activist social gospel Methodists like Tracey Jones, lawyerly Presbyterians like William Phelps Thompson, and establishmentarians like the Episcopal bishop George Barrett. Bilheimer also hoped a diverse slate of church leaders would help dismantle simplistic stereotypes of who antiwar activists were and what they looked like. Since the media overemphasized antiwar radicalism, Bilheimer's strategy of using Council delegations to display the movement's establishment-respecting church side was not unwise when trying to sway government leaders and traditional white parishioners. After all, people more often listen to those who look and talk like themselves than to those who can be easily viewed as "other" and dismissed. But Johnson and Nixon were not inclined to listen to any contrary voices that they didn't need to heed for political reasons.

Finally, since the Council believed in the persuasive power of good data and demonstrated expertise, it did its homework when preparing public positions and presentations. It gathered records from the U.S. government, including those received directly from cabinet officials, ambassadors, and congresspersons. It paid close attention to the popular media. It also went beyond studying easily obtained information and conducted extensive independent efforts to collect data from primary sources. These efforts included sending staffers regularly to South Vietnam in order to amass onsite information from both supporters and opponents of U.S. policy. The Council even tried to go to North Vietnam though was denied access. When not in Asia, the NCC sent representatives to Paris to gather reactions and updates from all four peace delegations. To this, it added insights gleaned from ecumenical communities across the globe. It then brought this information back to its churches for use in formulating policy positions, which were later shared with government.

Laity commonly urged church leaders to stay quiet on Vietnam, accusing them of lacking sufficient knowledge. Leave policy to the experts, they argued, for they supposedly knew best and had the facts. But this charge is specious. The NCC went to greater lengths to be judicious and diligent in data collection than most other groups of private citizens. In the eyes of many within ecumenical circles, the Council was so concerned about being responsible that it often erred toward caution when crafting its positions on the war. Whereas government officials such as Dean Rusk and Philip Habib disagreed with its conclusions and recommendations, they never charged its leaders with being out of their league. They were far more upset by the NCC's lack of pliable usefulness and blind loyalty to the government. In fact, on the issue of expertise, it is an interesting exercise to compare Defense Secretary McNamara's list of eleven government mistakes on Vietnam from his book *In Retrospect* with the NCC's positions. Of the ten possible errors that could apply equally to civilian groups as to government, the NCC was far more correct on each issue than was the White House.[5]

The denominations expected their Council to take responsible and well-informed stands on controversial issues, and then speak these to power. It clearly did so.

EDUCATING, MOBILIZING, AND PROVIDING RESOURCES TO OTHERS

The NCC succeeded in providing an array of resources to its denominations, but it failed to educate and mobilize laity as hoped. Providing aid and information to its institutional members was part of its established role—and well within its ability. Educating and mobilizing laity, however, was more pragmatically the responsibility of the denominations. At best the NCC could inspire, support, and help coordinate efforts, but the denominations had to implement them, for the Council lacked direct access to the grass roots. It was designed, rather, to serve the denominations, to interact with their selected representatives and staff, and to interface on their behalf with other councils, religious organizations, and government officials. To reach parishioners, the NCC had to rely upon denominational channels or local councils of churches. Because the NCC felt as though it had succeeded in rallying them through these channels to support the UN's creation and civil rights legislation, church leaders encouraged the Council to repeat this on Vietnam. But that issue proved too complex and divisive for quick mobilization, and changing cultural attitudes toward authority hampered results.

The Council's educational "debate and action" program was a corollary to its efforts with government. Generating public support for negotiations, it thought, could provide cover for the doves in government to work toward a negotiated resolution to the conflict. Conversely, as Rusk and the Nixon administration made clear, if the NCC could not win over and marshal its people (that is, the voters), then the government could ignore it with no loss of political capital. In other words, the NCC's access to governmental power rested upon its clout with parishioners. Actual insider influence then hinged upon being willing to be useful to policy makers.

Therefore, the Council launched an ambitious debate and action effort and urged its denominations to run with that ball. It prepped affordable materials for their use. It created a forum whereby denominations could coordinate programs with one another. The NCC also took an education program on the road to several cities, working with local councils to deliver it. The organization helped source and support traveling speakers, as with the IVS tour and, later, Jane Fonda's program. And it urged continually—in statements, articles, and telegrams—that church people speak out on the war.

This debate and action program yielded weak results for several reasons. First, denominational efforts varied widely; some denominations tried to run with the ball, others walked with it, and a few barely touched it. Those who scurried, such as the Methodists, smacked hard into the wall separating clergy and laity; and by using top-down, bureaucratic, sometimes pushy methods Methodist leaders merely reinforced that wall. The clergy-laity problem was rooted within the denominations and was exacerbated by changing cultural times. Addressing it would have had to start there.

But the Council's narrowly pitched communication methods contributed to the crisis. The NCC failed to translate its thoughtful positions on the war into a language and medium that would catch and hold the laity's attention or appeal to multiple audiences. Rather, it used the same academic paperbound products and style with laity as it did with fellow church leaders. To laity the Council came off as preachy, authoritarian, elitist, and dull. Its 1967 multimedia album packet on Vietnam is a prime example. And, while the NCC sometimes made use of television and radio, it never mastered or utilized these media, including direct mail, as adeptly as Christian conservatives.[6]

The NCC also intensified the clergy-laity gap through the distant bureaucratic style that laity perceived from the "God Box," not to mention the contempt they felt emanating from there. Bilheimer's team and the staff with whom it worked was a highly passionate, warm, generous, sacrificial, hardworking, and devout group of people. But many of them, such as Bilheimer and Dudley Ward, were also elitists of a sort. Bilheimer certainly believed that most laity possessed a rudimentary faith that needed an ecumenical awakening of consciousness, and Ward showed no desire to slow down his hard-driving antiwar machine for laity who couldn't keep up. Stopping the war was his first priority. Neither thought ecumenical leaders had much to learn from laity. Besides, they felt sure they already knew what laity thought (decades of negative letters kept them informed) and how laity needed to change. Sensing all this, local Christians accused denominational executives of creating a new, intolerant, "pietistic" litmus test based upon social stands for determining true Christianity. Moderate conservatives resented this most because they felt as if denominational leaders lumped them unjustly with the far right if they expressed any discomfort with liberal religious programs. The NCC's staff did not seem directly culpable here; it had to hold together a Christian coalition ranging from moderate conservatives to left-leaning liberals, so it showed tolerance for a range of opinion even while advocating particular viewpoints. But, by virtue of its positions, it was perceived so. As Council staffers well knew (but perhaps most laity did not), the denominations paid the NCC to serve as their snowplow on stormy issues, absorbing the iciest resistance and helping clear a path through which the denominations could follow.

Dean Kelley, Alan Geyer, certain communications staff, and later Cynthia Wedel understood that NCC relations with laity had devolved to a tenuous state. But they also knew the problem ran through the entire mainline Protestant community. In fact, secular liberals suffered from the same problem. They—as well as conservative corporate elites—were cultural products of a modernist era that built bureaucracies, trusted authority, employed top-down management methods, and admired an educated professional style. This allowed conservatives such as Nixon, and later Reagan and George W. Bush (each of whom had no problem pandering to corporate elites), to paint themselves as populists by capitalizing on Nixon's savvy characterization of liberals as snooty, effete, wine-and-cheese intellectuals who romanticized the communists, feared a good fight, and gave the hard-earned tax dollars of patriotic Americans to lazy minorities who served as the liberals' latest bleeding-heart cause.

Related also to the problem of perceived contempt and bureaucratic distance was the lack of emotional and spiritual energy that laity felt coming from mainline churches. Again, the NCC was part and parcel of this problem. Scholars repeatedly describe the Vietnam War era as a time when people hungered for personal, emotional, mystical, and spiritual experiences. And this hunger drove both conservative laity, who were drawn in greater numbers to more expressive Christian modes such as Pentecostalism, and radical youth, who sought ecstasy and intimacy in a variety of religious and countercultural forms. But the NCC, like many denominational headquarters, was filled with leaders shaped by neo-orthodoxy. This emphasized the intellect over the emotions and the transcendence of God over personal desires to experience the divine in an immanent or self-indulgent way. The neo-orthodox were reacting in opposition to popular evangelicalism, which they felt often erred too far in the simplistic, anti-intellectual, self-absorbed direction where faith became a matter of warm fuzzy feelings. But a cold impersonal religion will attract and hold few. The NCC's failure to address this effectively was a major mistake. Granted, the Council and its churches were caught floundering within a complex cultural shift from a modern to a postmodern world they did not yet fully understand. The cultural rebellion against authority and the establishment also complicated their situation. Nevertheless, this remained a missed opportunity. Bilheimer felt deep passion for the ecumenical vision, which is richly warm and spiritually meaningful in its concepts of unity, interdependence, justice, communal self-reflection, and peace. However, the NCC through its stilted forms failed to communicate the spiritual vitality of this vision, and as Bilheimer feared, the ecumenical vision was really not being taught to the grass roots at all. Nor did he know how to reach American citizens effectively with it.

Clergy stood on the cusp between church bureaucrats and the average working people who occupied the pews. Few pastors found it possible or comfortable to bridge the gap. Communication styles and image issues were problems. So were the huge variations in education, theological orientation, and worldview—differences that proved too complex for many clergy to navigate. As a result, pastors on both sides of the liberal-conservative divide chose instead to go silent. Sociologist Robert Wuthnow has emphasized that the higher education gulf between conservative laity and liberal church people determined more strongly than any other factor which side of the gap one favored.[7] Higher education often correlated with theological openness. Add on top of this obstacle for clergy an obtuse and morally confusing war about which presidents secretly lied—a war that many citizens were told was not only traitorous but dangerous to the troops to oppose. Local pastors felt pressure rather than compassion from their denominational executives as they struggled daily with these divisions and found the remote, denomination-serving NCC of little help to them in this dilemma.[8]

Cognitive scientist and best-selling author George Lakoff has pinpointed liberals' overriding communication problem as one not just of language and style but also of "framing." His book, *Don't Think of an Elephant* (2004), has become a guide for many progressive politicians. One recurring liberal error, says Lakoff, is assuming that solid facts and good ideas are effective in educating and mobilizing followers. If this is indeed true, then the NCC certainly stumbled here. Lakoff argues that people bounce incoming data off the conceptual frames that are already fixed in their brains. If the data refutes the frame, people usually dismiss the data and keep the frame. If the data reinforces the frame, then it is accepted and assimilated as "true." Lakoff asserts that liberals must work to reshape people's frames through the language, stories, and arguments that they relate. When Bilheimer began to angle his arguments toward addressing the presuppositions underlying U.S. policy, he was starting to address those frames. But Bilheimer targeted his effort at government officials. His argument in the "Imperatives of Peace" document was never translated into a form useful for lay audiences. This policy statement suffered from the same style problems as other NCC treatises.

The Council's mass communications methods fell short. This being said, however, I cannot confidently assert that the NCC would have been significantly more successful in mobilizing laity around its ecumenical analysis of the war if it had been more dexterous and creative. For xample, conservative laity displayed a measure of disingenuousness in their rising criticism of clerical political activism. Laity became more opposed (not less) to church activism from the 1950s to the 1960s when the public spotlight focused on liberal churches' social issues. Yet, when conservative churches moved center stage in the late 1970s, they eagerly engaged national politics on matters they championed; and today, evangelicals are more supportive of church political action than mainline Christians. Is this simply a sign of changed minds? Or does it reveal that religious justifications follow ideology? In other words, did conservative laity oppose church activism in the 1960s because they rejected the positions and worldview of the liberal churches? Later, when conservative churches took political positions of which they approved, then did activism suddenly seem acceptable? It is hard to miss the fact that Protestant white laity comprised a sizable portion of the silent majority that backlashed against liberal politics in the late 1960s. Yes, they eventually became critical of the war along with the rest of the public but not for the reasons the NCC advocated. Therefore, would laity have stayed as close-minded toward the NCC regardless of its communication strategies? One can wonder.

From a purely logistical perspective, the ecumenical churches were also trying to activate churchgoers on Vietnam within a shorter and more nationally polarized time frame than when doing so on civil rights. By 1963, when the NCC sprung into action on civil rights, black churches had already provided years of educational groundwork. Therefore, it was easier for the NCC to mobilize white non-southern mainliners fairly quickly on civil rights in 1964 and 1965. Conversely, in 1965, antiwar activists were starting virtually from scratch in terms of educating Americans about the Vietnam conflict. In the second half of the 1960s, white Americans were also more divided and bending hard toward conservative policies. And unlike on civil rights, activists encountered a potent moral counterargument that defended the war and encouraged unquestioning support for one's country. Therefore, expectations that the NCC could mobilize laity quickly around an ecumenical analysis of the war—people who tended already to be more conservative than average nonchurchgoing Americans—likely exceeded the realm of possibility.

Perhaps the most productive thing the NCC did to help rally church people was through its support of Clergy and Laymen Concerned About Vietnam. Activating local clergy and laity was CALCAV's forte, and it had a freedom in this regard that the NCC lacked. The Council always remained CALCAV's reliable older sibling. Without the NCC's financial and administrative support, one wonders whether CALCAV would have been born or remained viable as an organization. Many scholars of the antiwar movement mention and praise the charismatic CALCAV, but few credit the Council that often kept it afloat.

Similarly, and by structural design, the NCC could potentially reach laity by working well with its denominational members. Yet the bureaucratic design, administrative linkages, and funding relationships that connected the denominations with the NCC formed part of their collective tensions in the 1960s. The contested definition of ecumenism played a role, too. Was the Council merely a servant of the denominations—a snowplow, a useful lightning rod on controversial issues, and a vehicle for church collaboration on projects that were more easily shared? Or was the Council the engine that transformed the denominations into an ecumenical communion—an organization that made ecumenism manifest by fusing denominational contributions into an organic new ecumenical endeavor? In this latter sense, then, were the denominations to be the servants of ecumenical efforts driven by the NCC? Many denomination heads assumed the first (that is, the NCC should facilitate their agendas) and did not want the Council competing with or stripping their church programs for resources. Bilheimer and other Council staff assumed (or wanted) the ecumenical mission to be preeminent and were distressed by the sense that denomination heads favored denominational power over producing real ecumenism. Tensions over turf and resources flared, as between SADIA and Bilheimer, and this dynamic was not unique. The same strains arose between NCC staff and denominational secretaries on the NCC's "Crisis in the Nation" program. Denominational leaders also expressed frequent displeasure at what their money bought them in NCC programming, while denominational restraints often frustrated the NCC. Overblown expectations certainly aggravated both responses. What people understood ecumenism to be (was it interdenominationalism or something more?) and how they thought it should function institutionally, financially, and administratively were ambiguous within ecumenical circles in the 1960s. This confusion complicated NCC work on Vietnam. It also exposed the messiness of translating the ecumenical vision into institutional bureaucratic forms. These never seemed to run smoothly or to anyone's satisfaction in the Vietnam era and after. Hassles, headaches, and morale problems became endemic.

The NCC provided resources to many organizations and groups while failing to educate and mobilize laity in a massive way. This was due in large part to problems within the denominations themselves. Nevertheless, the NCC's maladies contributed to them.

COLLABORATING WITH AND SUPPORTING OTHER ANTIWAR GROUPS

To the extent that he could, Bilheimer fiercely guarded the NCC's independent identity as the church, with respect to both government and secular groups. As he stated time and again, he did not want the church to become controlled by cultural pressures. Rather, he wanted it to stand as a catalytic leader and prophetic beacon amid those pressures. And they were immense in the 1960s, chaotic and large enough to swamp many boats seeking to sail through them.

The ecumenical movement was about unity, bridge-building, listening, and renewal. It also asserted the church's responsibility to engage societal issues. Therefore, the NCC collaborated with (or at minimum, supported) many groups, both religious-based and secular, whose antiwar projects seemed consonant with official Council positions. The largest among them included CALCAV, FOR, FCNL, Negotiations Now!, Set the Date Now, Vietnam Summer, the Moratorium, and the Mobe. The energetic Elston served as the Council's connection to these other groups, so he joined as many steering committees as possible, while keeping up with others via mailing lists, meetings, and networking.

The critical thing here is that this kept an ecumenical voice at the tables of many different groups—from Cold War establishment types to the radical left. It ensured that religious liberals and the secular left had to talk with and recognize each other as they discussed issues; traditional ecumenists and new breeders had to do the same within CALCAV. This active debate made them aware of each other's views, perspectives, and concerns, and it challenged them to find ways to include each other, which they did. Not that they didn't squabble. Rather, they frequently learned about and worked with each other through arguments.

Despite sharing mutual peace and justice goals, however, many young religious and secular activists found the churches too stodgy, bureaucratic, and slow for their tastes. They distrusted the establishment and the older white men who administered it, including the NCC. Besides, the mainline churches often provided insufficient space for youth to express themselves in the creative ways they desired. Activist left-leaning youth comprised the greatest post-1965 exodus out of mainline churches. When youth put to death the University Christian Movement, and with it the long legacy of the Student Christian Movement, they declared their impatient disillusionment with religious bureaucracies. This act also removed a crucial ecumenical training ground for new leadership and a once vital vehicle for creativity, direction, and energy within the movement. Youth who left mainline religion often experimented with other spiritual forms or embraced secular advocacy as more satisfying from a social change perspective. Decades later, some became part of the secular left wing that urged religion to sequester itself in the private sphere. So, too, did many young people who grew up in and later rejected conservative religion.

Nevertheless, during the Vietnam era we saw young activists working with the NCC on antiwar events. And at the Council's wild 1969 General Assembly in Detroit, groups of largely young activists came not only to protest but to ask for the Council's help. Young people who a year earlier had given up all hope that they could make a difference through the Democratic Party still came to make their voices heard at the NCC's General Assembly. Unlike the Democratic Party, the NCC listened and responded in ways that illustrated genuine openness and consideration. It did not dismiss the youth, showing instead both tolerance and respect in the face of disruptive rudeness. Conversely, it did not automatically acquiesce and strike a prostrate pose before every radical demand either. Stephen Rose's renewal ideas were given several platforms and seriously considered before being rejected. James Rubins lost his appeal for the NCC to hold his draft card in two separate close votes, illustrating that the NCC had wrestled with and agonized over the decision. The Council took seriously the Black Manifesto's often perceptive critique of white churches, and it gave a generous monetary sum—considering slashed budgets—to a group for black inner city projects along the lines that James Forman desired, albeit not to Forman's group specifically. The American Indians' confrontational appeal for help at this assembly resulted in a long-term productive collaboration between the NCC and various Native American groups working to restore Indian lands and serve their justice needs. This prepared the NCC to provide ready assistance later during the 1973 Wounded Knee standoff. Finally, the NCC responded swiftly and significantly to the cries for greater inclusion of youth, minorities, and women in the Council's governing ranks.

Radicals dismissed these responses as too weak. But anything short of full immediate compliance with their demands would have seemed so to them, and they often mixed sound ideas with crazy requests. Radicals failed to value where and how the NCC was changing. The Council was on the same journey as the rest of the nation, wrestling with racial, gender, class, and generational diversity as well as newly apparent problems inherent in modern corporate bureaucracies and top-down leadership styles. And on these issues it was more genuinely responsive, thoughtful, and open to learning and growing responsibly—moving toward true, not token, renewal—than much of America. Its ecumenical vision mandated this.

The NCC showed consistently during the Vietnam era that it wanted to maintain constructive dialogues between religious leaders and marginalized dissenters. The Council was shifting left, consciously and thoughtfully. As a sign of its own intentional renewal, it also sought to be a better ally for the oppressed and to embrace diversity amid unity. While the radical left rejected these important beginnings as meaningless, showing little grace, conservatives accused the NCC of sacrificing transcendent churchliness to become a groupie of secular revolutionaries. Both were wrong. Given its constituency, the NCC tried to traverse a difficult path at a time when it was nearly impossible for such liberals to please anyone.

Bilheimer felt the NCC lost the trail, not when it moved left positionally but when it failed to integrate sufficient theological and ecumenical consciousness into the process. New breed activism that favored action over ground-laying theological discussion appeared to overwhelm the Council, especially after 1968. And this new breed style came into the NCC largely from white civil rights activists. To Bilheimer, this type of activism reduced ecumenism to mere interdenominational cooperation, allowed works to trump spiritual understanding, and turned the church into a political action group, thereby sacrificing some of its power, meaning, and identity. New breeders thought that old-line ecumenists such as Bilheimer favored too much talk when God's work required people willing to walk. Many of them argued that action was more spiritually transformative than discussion. But Bilheimer didn't see much conscious, spiritual, theological processing happening, even upon completing actions. Impassioned debates in 1969 and subsequent years over the NCC's restructuring brought this internal debate into the open. The outcome reveals that the new breed approach gained a measure of hegemony within the Council, although the debate between new breed and traditional ecumenists still continues.

ADDRESSING THE WAR'S REPERCUSSIONS THROUGH SERVICE AND ADVOCACY

The NCC's consciousness of the war's repercussions grew with the war itself, and as the record shows, its responsiveness steadily expanded along with its awareness of needs. Protestants had few relief networks or personnel in Vietnam prior to the war, so delivering aid to Vietnamese war victims was challenging. The strings the U.S. government attached to humanitarian relief complicated matters further. The State Department and Pentagon successfully co-opted religious charities to do the government's "hearts and minds" work in South Vietnam, while largely restricting their ability to aid victims in areas under communist leadership. The NCC collaborated with Mennonite and Lutheran partners to create Vietnam Christian Service. CWS managed the NCC's contribution to it. Despite the fact that CWS was complicit in some of that governmental co-optation, the NCC also knew that it must help Vietnamese refugees and this presented the best way available. Therefore, the NCC supported VNCS's efforts while Bilheimer and Elston worked internally to awaken CWS to the compromising ecumenical costs of government entanglement with PL 480 commodities and restrictions. It was a tough catch-22. Helping refugees often meant turning a blind eye to the government's use of the church's good deeds for its own political ends. This proved morally and practically sticky when the church disagreed with the government's goals and when their relationship compromised ecumenical credibility with colonized peoples of color. On the other hand, refusing to work with the government often meant that churches could not get aid in at all. Then people starved while church and state bickered over politics. So, again, the NCC walked a difficult fence that did not fully please everyone, but it managed to get assistance in while trying to wean CWS from government dependency and assumptions.

The NCC also sought to aid Vietnamese peace activists, including Buddhist monks who might potentially generate a "third force" negotiated solution to the war. This notion particularly attracted U.S. anticommunists who did not want South Vietnam to fall under North Vietnamese control, but who knew that America's military solution was imperialistic and ntenable, and that an indigenous political solution must be found. Bilheimer and Elston supported programmatically those within NCC circles who wanted to pursue this possibility even though both of them doubted the practical viability of the third force as an organized power bloc. Regardless of staff differences over the third force idea, the NCC was united in its concern that Vietnamese peace activists were being routinely imprisoned, tortured, and killed by Thieu's government, with U.S. support, simply to stifle dissent. Therefore, the NCC vigorously supported ecumenical efforts to unmask the real police-state dictatorship behind the democratic veneer of the Thieu/Ky regime. The Council wanted the White House to withdraw support or require real reform, so that native Vietnamese peace activists—many of whom were spiritual leaders themselves—could help find solutions to their country's complex conflict.

Conservatives criticized the NCC for being more concerned about Vietnamese prisoners of war being tortured in South Vietnam's tiger cages than with captured U.S. servicemen languishing in North Vietnam's horrific "Hanoi Hilton."[9] The NCC did pay more attention to and articulate more overt criticism of the former because it felt it could make a real difference doing so. But it never negated the horror of the latter. The NCC felt it had far more leverage with the U.S. government and media to change policies at home than it did with the North Vietnamese. Had Bilheimer been permitted to enter North Vietnam in 1967, he would have requested to visit U.S. POWs to inspect their situation and, at minimum, be a conduit for letters to and from families back home. Barring this, Bilheimer said that the most effective thing the NCC could do to help stop the suffering of U.S. POWs in North Vietnam was to end the war so they could come home. Pushing the United States to terminate blanket support of the Thieu/Ky regime and to free Vietnamese peace activists might help speed an indigenous and negotiated end to a stalemated war.

The NCC tried to address American victims of the war through other means. Unlike some antiwar activists who demeaned Vietnam veterans, the NCC reached out compassionately with assistance. For these returning U.S. soldiers, it created one of the first aid programs in the nation, and one that received consistently high marks from those who witnessed it. The Council recognized in the early 1970s that Vietnam veterans experienced unique difficulties transitioning back into society that were not being addressed by current programs. Clergy witnessed these problems as veterans appeared in their pews or knocked on church doors seeking help. The Emergency Ministries program headed by Rich Killmer was probably the most successful NCC Vietnam-related program that worked with local communities.

The Council also recognized that an unfair conscription system and restrictive conscientious objection laws put young men of draftable age into a moral and legal bind. For those who disagreed with the war, responding dutifully to the nation's draft to kill Vietnamese compromised their consciences and humanity, as well as risked their psychological and physical health. Following one's conscience, particularly if one were not a member of a pacifist church, often forced one to become a criminal or to abandon family and nation to become a permanent refugee elsewhere. Draft-age men made it clear that their churches were complicit in this dilemma, for churches had often played a role in shaping their consciences with religious teachings. The NCC agreed. Therefore, it fought to change laws that limited a person's ability to find options consonant with their consciences. Because classist and racist draft laws put the poor and minorities into this bind far more often than white people of means, the Council argued against this moral unfairness, too. It appealed for changes in draft and CO laws while creating programs to help young men find what they needed, whether that be draft counseling or help transitioning to life in Sweden or Canada. In this work, the NCC collaborated with international ecumenical partners. It also championed people's right to dissent against draft laws, eventually supporting civil disobedience, which was a difficult concept for many church leaders who deeply respected the rule of law. After the war, it urged amnesty for all.

Young antiwar activists were often accused of self-interest in opposing the war, as if saving their own hides was their primary motivation. As evidence, critics point out that antiwar activity did quiet somewhat after Nixon instituted the lottery system and phased in Vietnamization. However, seminarians and clergy received draft exemptions, most NCC leaders were far past draft age, and they had the resources to save their own sons from the war if they so chose. The NCC also excoriated Vietnamization as a strategy to avoid ending the war, and for implying that Vietnamese lives were more expendable than those of Americans. As Elston explained, the ecumenical vision reminded people to see a Vietnamese child as equivalent to "my baby." Thus, NCC leaders labored against unfair draft and CO laws because they saw them as wrong and felt they had a responsibility here; self-protection was a non-issue.

CWS also planned to address the war's repercussions by aiding Vietnam's postwar reconstruction. This went nowhere, however, because the U.S. government banned such aid after communist reunification in 1975. But Bilheimer's team had helped convince CWS by that point that potential aid should honor the self-determining rights and indigenous leadership of the Vietnamese people enough to let them administer any rebuilding efforts. Colonialism in Western religious development work must end, it believed, along with U.S. imperialism in general. The Council's primary aims became reconciliation and showing overdue respect for Vietnamese independence. Vietnam's continuing tragedy after 1975 was compounded by more regional war, a hardened, brutal government, and harsh punitive U.S. sanctions that were designed to isolate and starve the nation. These made CWS's aims nearly impossible to accomplish until the mid-1990s when the U.S. government, under President Bill Clinton's leadership, began restoring relations with Vietnam.

The NCC threw a wide net in its attempt to address the war's effects, both in Vietnam and the United States. It focused where it felt it might be able to make a difference: on the repercussions of its own government's actions, without negating the horrors caused by those fighting the United States. It argued as well that the best way to end the war's suffering was to stop the war—a war that seemed to be creating more hardship than its supporters promised it could ease.

ECUMENIZING THROUGH LISTENING AND BUILDING CONSENSUS WITHIN THE BODY OF CHRIST

Bilheimer was an ecumenist, first and foremost. The ecumenical vision, undergirded by history and theology, motivated (he would say, mandated) his response to the war and all of the interconnected issues that violated ecumenical Christian premises. He took the NCC job directing its Peace Priority Program because he felt the Vietnam War created a teach-able *kairos* moment. If World War II could bolster Christian unity and transform European views about nationalism and exceptionalism while helping expose the injustices of imperialism, perhaps Vietnam could do so for America's churches and people. The earlier lesson had not stuck in America, and McCarthyism in many ways drove it backward. Bilheimer thought Vietnam provided a new moment of reckoning.

Bilheimer believed the NCC hired him to do what his predecessor Ken Maxwell apparently could not. This entailed uniting the denominations in transformative consensus-building dialogue about the war, bolstering similar international ecumenical dialogues for mutual learning and witness, and then speaking their churchly truths to power. He largely accomplished these goals.

The information the NCC gathered, the conferences and meetings it held, and the official statements it drafted on Vietnam, all served to stimulate discussion among denominational leaders. The NCC was uniquely suited for this work. As historian Mitchell Hall observed, on Vietnam the NCC's own statements "set the tone" for the denominations. Council pronouncements also gave the denominations cover to begin discussing a controversial topic that felt like a minefield to many Christian leaders. Data and debate among denominational representatives at NCC meetings trickled down to denominational settings and helped stimulate conversations there about the war, even if some communions were slow to take official stands.

By the end of 1967, most NCC member denominations were talking about the war, and a fair number had produced critical or questioning statements about it.[10] By 1971 even some of the NCC's most conservative members had moved from postures generally supportive of U.S. policy to criticism of the Vietnam War, and particularly of its morality. Two prime illustrations of this are the Reformed Church in America and the southern-based Presbyterian Church in the U.S. Each moved slowly and with considerable internal debate against the war.[11] Ed Espy noticed that denominational leaders were often far more open about Vietnam with one another in NCC settings, saying riskier things than they would dare utter within intradenominational meetings. Therefore, the NCC provided an important educational venue for candid discussion, denominational cross-pollination, and enhanced learning; this helped transform church leadership's understanding of the war as well as related issues such as globalism, security, the role of race and economics in war, militarism, and conscientious objection. Bilheimer was particularly pleased that most denominational executives eventually recognized that the United States had engaged in an unjust act of imperialism in Vietnam; the concept was difficult to convey at first, he said, because many simply assumed America was not that kind of nation.[12]

Bilheimer aided this learning process by accelerating the NCC's efforts to listen to people from other nations, particularly Asians. The Council had recognized its need for Asian help in comprehending the Vietnam conflict prior to Bilheimer's arrival, but he made such listening routine. He insisted that listening was vital to increasing understanding within and renewing the body of Christ. Respecting Asians as teachers and guides was a fruitful new experience. When American church leaders realized they needed Asians to help them grasp the nuances of a war that baffled them, and when they began to see U.S. actions through a different prism of experience, it reinforced how various parts of the Christian body required the wisdom, truths, insights, and skills of others to complete themselves. Church leaders began to experience this awakening. But it did not significantly trickle down to the pews or into the nation's political consciousness with respect to global human interdependence. Bilheimer had certainly hoped that it would.

Bilheimer networked regularly with church councils in other nations, not only to glean their insights but also to persuade them to pressure their governments into criticizing U.S. foreign policy. The British, Japanese, and South Korean church councils usually told Bilheimer regretfully that they were powerless to sway their national officials. They knew political expediency required their governments to support U.S. policy in public. But within the World Council, the international ecumenical outcry against the war and American imperialism was deafening by 1968.

Conservative critics have argued that the NCC bent its listening ear in a biased direction, seeking out voices from the left but not those from the right. Then they level the charge of hypocrisy, saying that ecumenism was not fully inclusive.[13] To some degree this is true. But when they try to imply that the ecumenical movement was consciously "pro-communist" and "anti-American," they go too far and reveal their own ideological prejudices. The initial charges also need more contextual background for full understanding.

First, by the 1960s, the progeny of early modernists and fundamentalists knew each other's religious arguments well. They had been debating one another for over half a century on religious, political, and social issues. The Federal and National Councils sat constantly in the crosshairs of conservative Christians eager to destroy an ecumenical movement that they demonized. Therefore, there is some credence to the sense that NCC leaders already knew the right's positions and how and why they disagreed with them. Need they talk more?

Second, for those who might argue "yes," it is important to understand that ecumenical leaders reached a friendly hand to those on the right far more frequently than vice versa. NCC leaders viewed their conservative brethren as misguided but, still, as Christians. They always invited evangelicals from outside their membership to attend their General Assemblies as observers. In 1966, they even hosted Billy Graham as a speaker. Behind the scenes, the NCC worked to expand its membership to include Pentecostals and evangelicals.[14] After all, the Council prized the fact that its numbers included conservative Orthodox churches and often treated them with kid gloves in order to keep them. (The Greek Orthodox Church strongly supported the U.S. government in Vietnam, and Archbishop

Iakovos's voice was heard loudly within NCC debates over the war.)[15] Conversely many conservatives denied that the NCC was truly Christian and therefore viewed dialogue with the Council as useless and corrupting. Some of Graham's fellow evangelicals vilified him for consorting with the NCC in 1966. A few fundamentalists such as Carl McIntire and Billy Hargis devoted their lives to attacking the NCC. Richard Neuhaus and the IRD have continued this tradition. They also encourage mainline conservative Christians to pursue "ecumenical unity" only with those who agree with them theologically; liberal Christians remain categorized as heretics.[16] By contrast, the NCC has never dedicated time or money specifically to harm a conservative religious group. It defends itself when it must, but it has not worked to annihilate another religious organization.

Third, the NCC leaned its ear leftward because its leaders and churches had largely been Cold War anticommunists in the 1950s, albeit not rigidly so; and it was from society's leftward margins that they heard God's challenge in the 1960s. The direction from which they felt church renewal must come beckoned from there. I will discuss this later.

Bilheimer not only nurtured interdenominational and ecumenical relationships; he also fostered interfaith dialogue and cooperation against the war. Reformed Jewish organizations came out officially against U.S. Vietnam policy about the same time as the NCC. With a plethora of Jewish organizations located in New York City, collaboration among Jewish and NCC leaders proved convenient. Jewish voices and activity against the war quieted, however, as the Six Day War refocused Jewish concerns inward and made protesting the president practically unwise. While the pope spoke in coded fashion against the Vietnam conflict early on, and while several notable priests and nuns took to the streets to protest it, organized Catholic opposition to the war and collaboration with the NCC emerged slowly and steadily. Such collaboration became fruitful just as Jews dimmed their involvement. I have skirted delving deeply into these interfaith relationships, for they invite research projects of their own.

Ecumenism also required that Christians pay attention to the interdependent relationships between justice and peace issues. Ecumenists had done this since the movement's early years. For Bilheimer, this meant the body of Christ must resist the temptation to put issues onto separate, competitive soapboxes—a temptation to which many activists succumbed in the fractured environment of the late 1960s and early 1970s. Instead, he stressed that the church must speak to both the shared underlying problems and the negated spiritual values that fueled the related issues manifested in U.S. Vietnam policy—such as imperialism, racism, classism, militarism, environmental destruction, war crimes, and the demonization of dissent. As the war progressed, the NCC became more proficient at connecting these issues in official statements. Bilheimer wove them together most skillfully at the Ecumenical Witness conference in 1972.

However, he felt the NCC failed to root its stances about the interconnectedness of issues sufficiently in theology. Doing so would have helped strengthen its arguments, its identity as a manifestation of the church, and the laity's understanding of Council positions. In 1968 Bilheimer tried and failed to get theologians and activists to produce a quality theological statement about justice and peace. Conservatives who condemned the NCC's failure here also largely neglected to put their own positions on the war, and critiques of the NCC, into theological terms. (Anticommunism is not a theology; it is an ideology.) Nevertheless, as Bilheimer noted, a new breed emphasis upon action over discussion, the isolation of activists and theologians from one another in the Council's work environment, and the rising popularity of a more "secular theology" that relied upon sociological and economic analysis to inform church positions on social issues, all helped make traditional theological analysis of them almost passé during the Vietnam era. Generating theological explanations that informed and anchored the work being done would have strengthened the NCC's overall ecumenical effort. Whether it would have helped win the hearts and minds of laity is unknown; so too is whether the NCC would have been able to communicate its theological grounding effectively if it had indeed been fully developed. Regardless, the fact that progressive Christian leaders today are more carefully citing scripture to support their positions on the Iraq War, poverty, global warming, and so forth is testimony to a lesson being learned.[17] There are signs within the NCC's mainline denominations that the pendulum may be swinging away from the new breed style and back toward Bilheimer's, perhaps pulling the current NCC with it.[18]

RENEWING THE CHURCH AND TRANSFORMING WORLDVIEWS

Renewing the church was—and still is—fundamental to the ecumenical process. Renewal happened as the body of Christ found and listened to its diverse members, discussed prayerfully the meaning of what was learned through such exchanges, repented for falling short of God's designs, then transformed in ways that lived its new understanding and reflected its broadened self. Renewal was the process by which the body of Christ more fully recognized and became unified as a Christian community of diverse churches, cultures, histories, and doctrines. It was a constant succession of conversations and conversions about who God is and what the church is meant to be. Realization always fell short of envisioned ideals. But renewal was seen as a continual journey toward real community and discovering the fullest face of God within it.[19] The civil rights movement, the anticolonial efforts of peoples overseas, and the Vietnam War were all important catalysts in the NCC's and WCC's own journeys of renewal—catalysts that Bilheimer hoped would stir transformation in the churches as a whole. Bilheimer wanted this renewal process to extend into the very fabric of American society as well, helping to broaden worldviews and self-understanding. The NCC and its denominations made some specific—albeit imperfect—steps toward renewal as a result of the Vietnam War. Its spiritual "worldview" renewal was more fruitful than its structural attempts, which have remained difficult, contentious, and uncertain since the war ended. Evaluating the ecumenical movement's new interrelated satellite model, as described in the epilogue, must await the test of time.

Now let us continue the discussion concerning the NCC's spiritual renewal of consciousness. Conservatives have criticized the NCC for losing its supposed transcendence when it favored and focused upon voices coming from its left; but the NCC's leaders heard God beckoning them to take the next renewing step by attending to those voices. They listened with curious, open, and often humble ears. At the same time, Bilheimer and others tried to remain self-critical and resist blindly jumping onto bandwagons. They were diligent collectors and processors of data. They conferenced things to death. They moved intentionally in the direction they chose because their religious teachings stressed that Jesus stood with the poor and oppressed, eschewed violence, questioned the authorities of his day, broke unjust laws, and advocated peace. Both the civil rights movement and the Vietnam War showed church leaders their own shortcomings in fulfilling Jesus' commandments. These events revealed how they had been seeing through a glass darkly. From the left they found insights that they felt helped pull clouds from their eyes. But for doing so, charges of communism resurfaced. As Archbishop Dom Helder Camara once said, "When I feed the poor they call me a saint. When I ask why the poor have no food, they call me a communist."[20]

The NCC emphasized a left-leaning critical perspective more than a centrist and establishment-based one because this reflected its own historical self-correction process. To ecumenical leaders, their new awakenings made them better Christians and more fully a part of the body of Christ. The NCC's perspective denoted the direction in learning that ecumenists desired for America's churches as a whole, which they felt suffered from biases similar to those they were trying to shed. The fact that nationalistic imperialist biases resurfaced and crescendoed among America's religious and political communities in the 1980s, and again during George W. Bush's administration, proved to the NCC that America had not learned from Vietnam. American religious and political views remained dangerously skewed to the right and still rooted in an exceptionalist—even warlike— civil religion. Therefore, they felt self-correction required loud prophetic voices summoning people to sidle further "left" in order to recover a lost aspect of divine truth.

This is the current message of Rabbi Michael Lerner. This progressive religious leader asserts that Americans need to be reminded of the "Left Hand of God," which embodies the nurturing, loving, compassionate, communal desires of the Divine. The "Right Hand of God," favored by the religious far right, exalts a warlike, authoritarian, free-market, individualistic deity. Lerner is not alone. Former NCC General Secretary Robert Edgar and progressive evangelical Jim Wallis (founder of Sojourners) have also been calling on Americans to rescue their faiths from what they deem perversions of the far right. They assert they are not trying to mimic the right's error by pulling religion totally into a political "left" or pairing it with any particular political party or partisan agenda. Rather, they are attempting to center it back within Judeo-Christian scripture, the "left hand" truths of which are being ignored. Similarly, during the Vietnam War, if the NCC did not criticize communist governments as frequently as it did the U.S. government, this was because the Council was trying to help America remove the log from its own eye first. Sadly, Bush's preemptive war in Iraq and early domestic support for it denoted a familiar blindness that the NCC was unable to heal.

This brings us back to Bilheimer's hope of using the Vietnam War as a catalyst to transform American worldviews. Bilheimer approached this task by challenging government leaders to question their presuppositions about the war and, from there, to explore the integral cause-and-effect relationships between justice (whether economic, social, or political), peace, and real national security in the world. To him, the Vietnam War emerged from a skewed racist, militaristic worldview, historical misconceptions, and a jingoistic form of Christianity that blessed uncritically an imperialist foreign policy. If the presuppositions underlying U.S. policy in Vietnam went unaddressed, Bilheimer felt sure that America would create another Vietnam-like conflict in the future. He certainly understood the urgency felt by antiwar activists who sought simply to stop the war, and he saw efforts toward that end as justified. But he wanted most of all for the body of Christ, and the nation at large, to process the war, learn, and mature from it—to see and relate to others in a more just and Godly way. What did America's words and behavior with respect to Vietnam say about Americans as a people? What did the churches' rhetoric and actions here reveal about them?

As a result of Vietnam, the NCC and denominations at executive levels transformed their understandings about U.S. foreign policy significantly.[21] This shift in thinking trickled down in different measures to local clergy. Robert Edgar's urgency to move preemptively against G. W. Bush's attack on Iraq and the early mobilization of church leaders in this case testifies to lessons learned from Vietnam. But the American people largely rejected deep introspection; many jumped quickly toward an explanation of the Vietnam War that preserved America's exceptionalist worldview in foreign policy and nationalistic civil religion, then transferred this thinking later to the war in Iraq. As Arthur Schlesinger Jr. noted in 2005, 9/11 may have "revived the myth of our national innocence," a concept against which Reinhold Niebuhr and the NCC had long inveighed. Conservative religious leaders helped wrap the Iraq War in Christian justifications much as they had done the one in Vietnam. As a result, Robert Edgar, Jim Wallis, and Michael Lerner, former anti–Vietnam War activists all, each published books condemning the popular use of Christianity once again to justify "Pax Americana" and a theology of empire.[22] They blamed President Bush, and the far right Christian leaders who counseled him, for re-popularizing this "bad theology" to serve destructive ends. Echoing Bilheimer from forty years earlier, Wallis wrote, "God on our side [thinking]—leads inevitably to triumphalism, self-righteousness, bad theology, and, often, dangerous foreign policy."[23]

The lessons that Bush drew from Vietnam for Iraq were practical ones about how to fight a war and "stay the course." They had little to do with self-understanding or identity. When conservatives spoke about shaking "the Vietnam syndrome" (that is, a fear of future military quagmires), they urged America to get back in the military saddle and win wars with massive shows of force. And so Bilheimer was right. The unexplored, unlearned lessons of Vietnam contributed to another specious quagmire in Iraq, another government credibility gap, and an American image that sank globally to one of its lowest points ever.

LESSONS, OBSERVATIONS, AND PROMOTING THE "ECUMENICAL WAY"

At the moment of this writing (2011), as in the Vietnam era, Americans live in a highly polarized time politically. The country is caught in questionable nation-building experiments and military mssions in the Middle East, and a crisis of global insecurity dominates our awareness. Amid all this, faith communities continue to engage these issues, and the topic of church-state relations remains as controversial as it was forty years ago. Those who wield influence within the establishment have changed, and this has affected how various groups feel about the proper relationship between faith and politics. Yet many of the questions, pitfalls, concerns, and arguments from forty years ago remain hotly contested and relevant.

The National Council of Churches today carries "virtually no political weight in conservative circles and just a little bit more than that in liberal circles," said the evangelical David Kuo, former official in President G. W. Bush's Office of Faith Based and Community Initiatives. It can't "flex any political muscle," he continued, noting that Christian conservatives on the rise in politics looked back at the NCC "with pity." Whereas Jesus commanded Christians to be "salt" and "light" to the world, it "was obvious to us," he concluded, "that [the NCC and its denominations] had lost their flavor."[24] What can today's political and faith activists learn from the story of that marginalized and transformed Christian organization? What truths or valuable insights did its own trial by fire during the Vietnam era expose that might be worthy of our heeding? Readers may draw a variety of conclusions from this complex story; let me highlight a few that I find particularly relevant.

What can we learn from the so-called decline of the National Council of Churches? This question inspires its own obvious corollary: in what manner and why did it "decline"? The NCC has shrunk in budget, staff, percentage of national population, and sociopolitical influence since the 1960s. But its coalition is still huge. As of 2010, it had thirty-six denominational members comprising over forty-five million parishioners. (This actually exceeded the raw numbers from the 1960s.) By contrast, the National Association of Evangelicals had forty denominational members comprising about thirty million parishioners.[25] Conservative critics often argue that the NCC slipped because it moved too far to the left—religiously toward "secularism" and politically toward "socialism." They argue that both God and people of faith punished the NCC and its churches by abandoning them, causing a loss of power and influence. To regain these, both religiously and politically, America's ecumenical community must turn and follow the conservative example. The lesson in the NCC's "decline," then, is a vindication of conservatives' own theology and political agenda.[26]

This is no surprise. Conservatives have stereotyped the NCC as being a left-wing secular political organization—Christian in name only—that served as the "lap dog" of the Democratic Party and blindly glorified and abetted communist revolution.[27] Its ecumenical agenda was perceived as seeking both world government and a world church that boiled Christianity down to its lowest common denominator and acquiesced to a host of cultural sins under the banner of tolerance.[28] Its elitist-seeming intellectualism combined with an assumed liberal gullibility became proof aplenty that it had little of value to say about practical real-life problems, including war, peace, racism, poverty, and the environment. Such distorted typecasting has endeavored to prevent the NCC and its ecumenical vision from being considered a viable alternative to the conservative, nationalistic, individualistic Christianity long questioned by the Council. It has aimed to convince people to reject the NCC as un-Christian and un-American and, therefore, to dismiss its queries, insights, and experiences as being unworthy of consideration. The Christian right's superior mass media talent, rich funding, and political prominence over the last three decades, combined with the ecumenical community's more limited communication capacity and fluctuating influence, have given conservatives considerable power in shaping public impressions of the NCC. The right has had little incentive to be fair in this. And secular liberals' own distaste for religion in the public square has left the NCC with few political allies. One clear fact emerges: religious divisions are rife with ideology. None is truly transcendent or free from cultural biases, agendas, and constraints, not the NCC or its conservative critics.[29] Conscious efforts to transcend ego, to be honest about biases, and to self-reflect critically are vitally important. When it comes to transcendent thinking, churches must remain aware of their own limitations and the constraints that political cultures, their constituencies, and their own administrative structures place upon them. The same is true of scholars; therefore, I do not claim objective purity either. I am but one historian with a set of data, analyses, and conclusions to share.

So, why did the NCC "decline" during the Vietnam era, and what insights can be gleaned from this? We often assume that a loss of money or power denotes failure. The conservative argument above implies that decline denotes error, and even sin. It is a social Darwinist assertion. It is also a theory of free market capitalism that inferior products or companies give way to superior ones—and religion in America operates in a voluntary market-type setting. This belief corresponds with the democratic idea that what is most popular deserves to win. Yet might does not always make right, bigger is not always better, and popular majority favorites may simply reflect that which blesses the majority's self-interests rather than the common or spiritual good. The recent boom of prosperity theology within wildly successful mega churches—which preach a materialistic gospel many liberal and conservative Christians agree is heretical—certainly illustrates this.[30] Had the NCC and its denominations wanted, above all else, to remain politically influential from the late 1960s through the 1980s, they might have done the following: made themselves useful to presidents in power, mirrored the conservative white laity's silent-majority sentiments, gotten political only on strategically useful wedge issues, helped preserve America's exceptionalist civil religion, and encouraged exclusivism among its members to generate a sense of extra-specialness among congregants. But this would not have been prophetic in a manner true to their understanding of scripture, ecumenism, or God's will.

Again, the NCC's "decline" does not necessarily mean it was wrong either religiously or politically. Even the NAE has struggled in the last decade, in part because of the plethora of competing evangelical organizations now in existence.[31] And the slimming of the NCC's bureaucracy through forced budget and staff cuts may prove positive if it offers the formerly bloated organization an opportunity to reshape itself into a more sustainable, focused, and effective institution. What its struggles do denote is a loss of some public and political appeal, which resulted from a variety of causes. The NCC saw itself called to a prophetic role in the 1960s, and prophets are rarely popular. Had the NCC shifted to the right and followed the crowd, it might have remained a central part of the establishment (albeit risking further loss of its youth).[32] Because of its ecumenical beliefs and the political positions that arose from them, the NCC made a conscious decision not to do this. To ecumenical leaders, the neoconservative bent of American politics and the far religious right's uncritical blessing of free market corporate capitalism and assertive U.S. military power were contrary to scripture and Christian values.

I do not count the NCC's prophetic stance or positions among its mistakes. In fact, the religious right would have done well to emulate the NCC's modeling of confessing church behavior with respect to the government on Vietnam. Nixon's administration looked for conservative Christian leaders to pimp for votes, and those eager for political power complied. In recent years, a few influential evangelicals have risked warning their fellows about the dangerous fusion between the religious and political right. In his book *Tempting Faith*, David Kuo related how Bush's administration used religious conservatives excited about his faith-based initiative to help him win evangelical votes and then failed to deliver on its promises. When Kuo entered the halls of power, he admitted his complicity. "I wasn't just a Christian trying to serve God in politics. Now I was a Christian in politics looking for ways to recruit other Christians into politics so that we would have their votes."[33] He likened the aura of political power to the corrupting ring in Tolkien's *Lord of the Rings*. "Today, there is no doubt that many Christians have been seduced. . . . Patriotism—a good thing—has become part of our religion. So has partisanship. We have been quietly and gradually nursed to the point where our faith and God himself are merely part of a political cause. Invoking God's name is just a rhetorical device. / That's bad news."[34] When Kuo broke his silence, the Bush White House threatened conservative Christian media sources with the loss of presidential access if they gave him publicity.[35]

Kuo is not the only evangelical who has learned recently the religious price of political power and the political price of speaking prophetically. In 2006, Rev. Joel Hunter was selected to lead the conservative Christian Coalition founded by Pat Robertson. When he announced his desire to shift the coalition's agenda away from a purely partisan (Republican) one toward a stance that also addressed poverty and environmental issues, internal resistance forced him to withdraw from that slated role. Fellow evangelical leaders considered his proposed agenda too liberal-sounding and therefore offensive to their base. A top executive in the NAE, Richard Cizik, received heat for similar reasons, inspiring an essay published on the IRD's website to ask, "Is it possible that the [NAE] has come to resemble its old nemesis, the National Council of Churches?"[36] Around this same time (2006), the famed evangelical pastor Rick Warren was excoriated by fellow evangelicals for inviting the Democratic senator and liberal Christian Barack Obama to his mega church in order to speak on behalf of AIDS work, something Warren also championed. Apparently it was politically blasphemous to have an avowed Democrat in the church. Many evangelicals have become so attached to the Republican Party, and the exchange of worldly influence that flows between them, that evangelicals have sacrificed their prophetic edge in order to reap partisan favors. Bilheimer would probably say they have traded away true churchly power, rooted in an independent moral witness, for the tempting temporal variety that politicians and popularity bestow. According to the ecumenical vision, this is a cardinal sin. But ecumenists can well understand the addictive forces within that temptation.

The NCC was once a powerful insider within the liberal establishment. Yet it was willing to condemn that establishment's foreign policy and risk the consequences when it felt its friends in the White House were violating Christian, moral, humanitarian, and democratic principles. As the NCC's story reveals, this was agonizing for its leaders. They did it imperfectly and haltingly. But they did it. And even though it offended their base, they still did it. When the Council had a leader (Ken Maxwell) who seemed too wedded to the State Department to be prophetic, they let him go and hired Bilheimer. He and Elston reminded colleagues continuously about the critical importance of keeping the church separate from the state. For the church must make its witness. It must speak its truth to power, insert its voice into public debate, and try to influence policies and political thinking. But it must also jealously guard its independence. Bilheimer was downright hawkish about ensuring that the NCC not get used politically by either the left or the right. As James Madison predicted when he urged separation between church and state, and as the ecumenical movement learned through its experiences, political organizations woo religious alliances for political ends. Religious groups all too often become seduced by the siren song of political power. It is a lesson the religious right needs to learn now, which signers of a recent "Evangelical Manifesto" recognize.[37] And it is one the ecumenical movement should be keen to remember.[38] Historically, this lesson has been easily forgotten, so bears constant repeating.

I do not see the NCC's prophetic stances as a problem. Nor do I fault its general positions on the war. If the reigning historical consensus on Vietnam is to be trusted, the NCC was largely correct in its criticisms of U.S. policy. History may prove it prescient again on the Iraq War. The NCC's denominations did see membership declines in the 1960s. But religious historians and sociologists have also been quick to point out that the mainline churches' greatest numerical defections came from youth fleeing toward the secular left and not into the bosom of the religious right. Demographic factors also played a major role. And rising religious pluralism meant that the old establishment churches comprising the NCC naturally lost some hegemony. The fact that these denominations tend to eschew a flashy entertainment-type worship style has also affected their numbers as Americans have grown more attracted to glitz and techno-logical stimulation. Finally, the fact that the Southern Baptist Convention (which has become more conservative in the last two decades) is also struggling to stem membership losses illustrates that conservatism and growth are not necessarily synonymous.[39] So where did the NCC stumble?

First, the NCC suffered from problems that permeated much of American society and the so-called establishment—issues that the 1960s-era rebellions attacked head-on. These included dismissive top-down leadership styles, bloated organizational structures and too much faith in bureaucratization as a solution to problems, racism, classism, sexism, age-ism, questionable financial investment practices, dependence upon an old boys' network as a means of sharing and exercising influence, ignorance of other cultures, and trust that data and reason alone could change policies, hearts, and minds. The Council was also complicit in several problems that permeated the mainline religious community. Its outmoded and narrowly pitched communication style must top the list, for this exacerbated every other malady. Triumphalism and naïveté fueled overly high expectations of what the formerly hegemonic churches could accomplish. But embed-ded in these shortcomings was an ambitious, tenacious, and generous courage that wrestled with principalities, powers, and policies and is hard not to admire. Insufficient emphasis upon the spiritual beliefs (including theology) and spiritual essence (the felt spiritual meaning) undergirding the Council's work proved to be a deficiency. To those outside of church hierarchies, the discourse often sounded as if liberal religion had become subservient to political ends, even if this was not necessarily the case. By its nature, politics is often spiritually dry; purely intellectualized theology can be, too. Most critically, then, the NCC and its churches failed to meet people's spiritual hunger for meaning and religious expression during the convulsive chaotic 1960s. What they tried to do on this front did not translate; it did not communicate.

Today, progressive Christian leaders are more careful to fuse scripture and religious values into messages that address sociopolitical issues. But I see continuing today a missed opportunity that slipped out of the NCC's grasp in the 1960s. The Council's rich ecumenical vision was never articulated or taught successfully to a broad base of people during the Vietnam era. Bilheimer certainly tried. Indeed it was his life's mission. But his top-down efforts didn't get past the upper echelon, where he met resistance over how to define and implement ecumenism. Internal debates of this sort exposed confusion among church leaders about the essential nature of ecumenism and their inability to talk about it fluently with colleagues—let alone with laity.

Most Americans from left to right did not know what ecumenism meant in the 1960s. For those who had some familiarity with the word, it usually connoted cooperation between people of different denominations or faiths. This very basic sense of ecumenism grew popular in the 1960s and remains so. But it misses the meat of the ecumenical vision; it purées it down to a preschool pablum of playing nicely in the sandbox. For others, the touted bureaucratic mergers of churches in the 1950s and 1960s, and indeed the conciliar structure of the NCC itself, served as the face of ecumenism. Thus, people saw ecumenism as an institutional thing. But when the NCC's bureaucratic structure proved problematic and when the denominational merger movement lost some public buy-in during the late 1960s, many took this to mean that ecumenism's vision had run its course. Lost again in all of this was the vitalizing essence of the ecumenical vision as it applied to people, policies, and the world beyond the churches. Finally, for many left-leaning political activists in the Vietnam period, ecumenism's emphasis upon unity and togetherness seemed too akin to tokenist integration schemes that diluted diversity within a preserved status quo power structure. To them diversity was real, unity was fake, so ecumenism was suspect. But again, this denotes a misunderstanding of the ecumenical vision; what it reveals is an accurate reaction to a largely white male church hierarchy.

After the Vietnam era, the national ecumenical vision as once carried by the NCC lost its popular steam. With no associated student movement, there was no farm-team training ground for new leaders. Except in its most basic sandbox form, ecumenism has fallen out of vogue. And the NCC and its denominations have done little in the last decade to resurrect or teach it at the grassroots level. The most shocking illustration of this can be seen in Robert Edgar's book *Middle Church*, which is his appeal for people of faith to rally around what are essentially ecumenical values and political goals in order to recover Christianity from the far right. Surprisingly, however, the word "ecumenism" is missing from the main body of the book (and index). It appears only in the acknowledgments. There is no effort in Edgar's discussion of scripture, values, and Christian works to connect those things explicitly to the broader historical vision called ecumenism. There is no attempt to rescue or revitalize the term itself through a clear discussion of what it has meant and continues to mean as a timeless *spiritual* vision and process.

The NCC and its member denominations should do so for two important reasons. First, groups of far right conservative Christians within the mainline churches (who call themselves "orthodox" or "classic" Christians and emphasize "right doctrine") have begun adopting the words "ecumenical" and "confessing church" to describe their own movements. They are actively reframing understandings of ecumenical history for their own purposes while undermining and disparaging the ecumenical vision as carried forth by people such as Bilheimer. These groups, many born out of the 1960s lay revolt, do this with the IRD's considerable help and set themselves up in virulent opposition to the Federal, National, and World Councils' ecumenical work.[40] As Lakoff asserts, the battle over language is critical in the struggle to educate and influence. If IRD conservatives seek to usurp the very meaning of ecumenism, the NCC should avoid getting caught asleep here.

Second, the ecumenical vision may serve as a potential bridge between various progressive religious communities, people who have fled to the secular left, and evangelicals who are growing frustrated by the far right's divisive partisan use of the gospel message. For, with factionalism rising both within and between political parties, sparked by political scandals, Wall Street fraud, recessions, and ill-begotten wars in the Middle East, some people speculate that the nation has entered another watershed moment. It could be a time of shifting political fortunes, hegemonies, and coalitions—a time when ears may hear different voices. If this be true, the ecumenical vision might rise again as a potent uniter of people who are tired of war and polarization, who put spiritual principles and connections before partisan ties, who recognize the global interconnections between people and issues, who feel called to work in compassionate ministries for peace, justice, and a sustainable environment, and who long for foreign policies that don't outright court Armageddon.

Bilheimer's eldest son, Bobby, sees signs of this within Rick Warren's ministry, which eschews rigid dogmatism and partisanship in favor of uniting Christians in the healing work of addressing poverty, AIDS, and environmental degradation. Bobby worked with the Warrens to educate Christians about the international AIDS crisis. He knows his father would have viewed Warren's theology as simplistic, even "fundamentalist," yet he is also certain his father would have found Warren's genuine emphasis upon Christian humility, bold action in the face of human suffering, and open-armed inclusive Christian unity in that service "enormously attractive." Bobby has less confidence in the NCC's ability to lead here, which he sees hampered by "bullshit and bureaucracy."[41] Like many of his generation, he has lost faith in institutional answers. Communication, bureaucratic processes, and lay relations still challenge the NCC, as does the task of remaking itself in a changing world. The Council is continually seeking and experimenting; General Secretary Michael Kinnamon seems eager to heal the breaches between the Faith and Order and Life and Works streams within ecumenism. And in October 2010, progressive youth reconstituted the long-dead Student Christian Movement in America.[42] But the best path into a revitalized future remains obscure.

Ecumenism has roots in a complex theology that, in its currently published forms, is obtuse for many of us who lack theological training. I suspect professional ecumenists have winced a time or two at my handling of the topic. Nevertheless, I argue that theologians have often put concepts such as ecumenism perilously beyond the grasp of laity, reserving rich discussions about it for themselves. Through this research, however, it has become clear to me that ecumenism is about more than merging denominations, or creating conciliar institutions, or bringing various types of Christians together for "tea parties," as Visser 't Hooft once quipped. The ecumenical vision, as espoused by those who created and sustained the Federal, World, and National Councils, is a particular *way* of being Christian. That manner of Christianity is often quite different from how Christians on the far right have expressed their faith. The "ecumenical way," as I'll call it, is compelling and quite ancient. It is not simply an invention of twentieth-century modernism as some critics charge. Nor is it a naïve or passé fad.[43]

The ecumenical vision taps into a deep, timeless spiritual wisdom and persistent longing for peaceful connections within the human family. Consider the collective wisdom of the spiritual sages who lived during the Axial Age, from 900 to 200 BCE. Religion scholar Karen Armstrong describes this era as "a time of spiritual genius."[44] It produced the Buddha, Socrates, Confucius, Jeremiah, Ezekiel, Euripides, and various notable mystics. If one stretches forward to approximately 650 CE, one sees that Rabbi Hillel (founder of Rabbinic Judaism), Jesus, and Muhammad each reasserted the basic spiritual precepts of their Axial predecessors. Together they expressed a spiritual ethic that is remarkably similar to the ecumenical worldview of the twentieth century.

As Armstrong summarizes it, the Axial sages stressed universal reverence and concern for everyone; compassion amid suffering, rather than vengeance; rejection of violence, hatred, greed, and egotism; self-criticism and transcendence of ego; practical acts of benevolence, rather than beliefs in particular doctrines, as a means of spiritual growth; uniting people through love into a common purpose and community; the idea that "all is one"; the need to question fundamental assumptions and reeducate the self; seeing things from other people's points of view; a belief that no one has the last word on truth; honoring the stranger; turning tragedy into a catalyst for good; loving and finding common ground with one's "enemy"; a willingness to be prophetic and "puncture the national ego"; and most universally a belief in the Golden Rule. The commonalties that the ecumenical vision shares with the Axial sages, Hillel, Jesus, and Muhammad, are striking. The ecumenical vision, which stems from the divine unity of the diverse body of Christ, also affirms the sacred unity of the human race. Accordingly, social issues are all interconnected; there is one human community. Listening to one another and working toward a more justice-based world together will complete and enrich us all. Relationships, compassion, and justice are the keys to peace. Through this work, we discover the full face of God. Transcending one's biases, culture, and nationalism along with undertaking continual self-criticism are key ecumenical principles. Constant spiritual renewal stems from these practices.

Coincidentally as well, each of the Axial sages arose during a convulsive time of violence and war within their respective cultures, and they spoke prophetically with intention to reject the values, lifestyles, and beliefs that perpetuated that violence. So, too, the current ecumenical movement emerged from fatigue with religious divisions, hatred, and violence; its vision flowered amid two world wars. No wonder Bilheimer saw the Vietnam War as a possible catalyst for transforming dangerous worldviews. The ecumenists sought to apply their faith to practical problems in the society at large. Many of them had careers that bridged politics and religion. This, too, reflects the Axial pattern. As Armstrong describes it, "The sages were not utopian dreamers but practical men; many were preoccupied with politics and government. They were convinced that empathy did not just sound edifying, but actually worked. Compassion and concern for everybody was the best policy." Bilheimer's "Imperatives of Peace" document asserted the same. Conservatives often paint the NCC as a modernist secularized offshoot of "true Christianity" that is destined to wither away. However, against the historical backdrop of the Axial sages and those who carried forward their spiritual vision, the ecumenical movement as embodied by the NCC appears to be a recent manifestation of an ancient, undying, global, spiritual movement that is wholly Christian—but not only. While the NCC has waned institutionally, this larger movement may be starting to wax anew. Both secular and religious voices are calling for it.

As violence again threatens the possibility of world peace, Armstrong urges those in the twenty-first century to remember the applicable spiritual genius of the Axial Age. "Today extremists have distorted the Axial traditions by accentuating the belligerent elements that have evolved over the centuries at the expense of those that speak of compassion and respect for the sacred rights of others . . . we should all strive to recover the compassionate vision and find a way of expressing it in an innovative, inspiring way—just as the Axial sages did. / This need not be a purely intellectual campaign; it should also be a spiritual process." During the Vietnam era, ecumenists sometimes forgot to accentuate that this work is indeed a spiritual process, not just one that inspires intellectual, bureaucratic, and structural transformations. But seeing ecumenism primarily as a bureaucratic manifestation of unity, containing primarily structural or institutional challenges, *was* one of the cultural manifestations of the modernist age in which ecumenism emerged. Today ecumenists are focusing more on creating a "community of communions," rather than bureaucratic forms of unity. Meanwhile, the spiritual principles, power, and potential within the ecumenical vision remain as timeless and potent as they did during the Axial Age.

Those who lead the NCC and mainline denominations should consider teaching the full ecumenical worldview proficiently, at a mass level, and by emphasizing the term itself. For the name gives the concept an important and necessary handle. Besides, the term's root meaning of "the whole inhabited Earth" is spiritually significant. The vision is still able to capture people passionately and revitalize their faiths, as it did Bilheimer's back at Yale. Today's ecumenical leaders should also consider not only anchoring discussion of the ecumenical way in Judeo-Christian scriptures but also showing how it reflects spiritual ideas that extend beyond Christianity. This characteristic may help create spiritual and historical bridges that might connect Christians to those of other faiths and traditions. It may restore spiritual relationships with activists who fled organized religion years ago. Evangelicals can find much common ground in these spiritual principles, too—if they can hold them in creative tension with their faith's assertion of specialness and doctrinal correctness.

Religious progressives tend to believe that divine truth exists in many different religious forms. Sociologists of religion have argued that such universalism fails to produce growing vibrant religious traditions. Rather, many assert that religious groups that maintain their distinctiveness and sense of specialness tend to grow most vibrantly. Scholars point to the rapid expansion of conservative churches that maintain exclusivity as convincing proof.[45] But there appear to be two enduring and sometimes dichotomous urges within human beings: to be unique or more "chosen" than others; and to rebel against the boxes and barriers that separate one from another. The American tradition itself embodies both. Individualism and competition are powerful American characteristics. But the nation's first motto, "E pluribus Unum" (Out of the many, one), expresses the desire to create a single unified people from one of the most diverse collections on the planet. It is much like the ecumenical image of the diverse yet interconnected Christian body. Consider also humanity's response to the first full photographs of Earth taken from space (1969, 1972), which impressed powerfully upon people how all of life shares a beautiful blue home. These are among the most published photographs in history, but they are not popular simply because they are pretty. Rather, the photographs capture the interdependent shared unity of life, and people often have a spiritual reaction to them.

Unity is a powerful, ancient, and enduring spiritual longing. Many secular human rights and environmental activists now are reaching out to collaborate rather than compete with each other in order to accomplish their sociopolitical goals, for as Bilheimer argued, shared values underlie much of what they seek, and success in one area can help all. In fact, within the American progressive community, as well as around the world, there is a mounting movement to shift, as David Korten says, "from Empire to Earth community" in terms of worldviews, presuppositions, and global actions. Doing so in this century may be essential, many assert, if humankind is to thrive.[46] Over sixty years ago, ecumenists who urged creation of the UN and its "Universal Declaration of Human Rights" understood their actions in those very terms, and as a spiritual imperative during a time of crisis.

Korten, a former USAID adviser and faculty member of Harvard's Graduate School of Business, is one of America's foremost progressive activists working toward a peaceful, just, sustainable world. To a group of religious leaders in Seattle after the 2004 presidential election, Korten connected that work to Christian history. "The historic Jesus stood against Empire and called on his followers to live into being a world of peace and justice. . . . However the religious movement Jesus founded was soon co-opted to the service of Empire during the rule of Emperor Constantine. / The struggle between the imperial and the egalitarian Christian traditions continues to this day."[47] Korten does not claim any specific religious affiliation. Nevertheless, he stressed that, "Virtually every progressive leader I know is working from a deeply spiritual place, but we rarely speak openly in our environmental, peace, and justice work of values or the sacred." As a result, he says that, "The time has come for the nation's mainstream churches to come out of the closet and speak publicly of the values and the spiritual foundations of the progressive agenda and to articulate spiritually grounded stories of human possibility and the world that the living Jesus called us to create." Korten seems not to realize that ecumenists have been doing so for much of the last century. Their ineffective communication style and limited media exposure have hampered their achieving a place in historical memory. Currently, the only spiritual voices of faith that Korten's community tends to hear are from the far religious right in support of a theology of empire. This repulses them. And this reminds us that, even though religious exclusivity and providentialism remain popular in the United States, these traits, when made militant, also repel people. They offend the enduring human impulse that longs for connection to others, that finds God reflected in the full diversity of creation, and that seeks peace through plowshares rather than swords.

As conservative Christians look through their interpretations of the Bible toward the future, many on the far right see an impending and inevitable bloody Armageddon. They gird their loins behind political forces bent on being and battling empires. Peace is not possible when war is foreordained. They invest their hope in Heaven, not on saving Earth.

As progressive Christians look through their interpretations of the Bible toward the future, many see Jesus' living example calling them to help turn humankind's community behavior toward operating from a different paradigm before it is too late. And to them, it isn't. Signs of both crisis and hope for creation abound globally. They invest their hope in the spiritual power of love, compassion, justice, and community that comes from the Divine and is modeled by everyday people working in concert with the Creator. With global warming, nuclear threats, state-supported genocides, and war in the Middle East, like many of their secular-spiritual counterparts, they feel a *kairos* moment of decision pressing upon the world's citizens in the dawn of the twenty-first century. The time may be ripe to question old assumptions and learn to live differently with one another, or risk human destruction of this shared Earthly home. From the Axial sages to the ecumenists, people of faith have felt called to be in the lead in such moments. After forty years in a wilderness dominated by political conservatives and entangled in their own internal strife, ecumenists and organizations such as the NCC may still have an important, critical, and influential role to play in what is not only a political, economic, and cultural transformation but also—and perhaps at the core—a spiritual one.

NOTES

INTRODUCTION—ECUMENISM AND THE VIETNAM WAR

1. Holy Bible, New Revised Standard Version (New York: Oxford University Press, 1989).

2. "NCC" and "National Council of Churches" are the original acronym and shortened name of the organization used during the Vietnam War. More recently, the Council has sometimes used "NCCC" for "National Council of the Churches of Christ."

3. James F. Findlay Jr., *Church People in the Struggle: The National Council of Churches and the Black Freedom Movement, 1950-1970* (New York: Oxford University Press, 1993), 48-75. Herman Will, Methodist leader, called the ecumenical churches' work on civil rights legislation their "high water mark not reached before or since." Herman Will Jr., "How Churches Influence National Policy," *Christian Advocate*, 24 December 1970, 9-10. Many saw religious mobilization for ratification of the UN charter similarly.

4. According to Jeff Manza and Clem Brooks, in 1960 mainline Protestants comprised 46 percent of the American electorate. By 1996, they made up less than 28 percent. "The Changing Political Fortunes of Mainline Protestants," in Robert Wuthnow and John H. Evans, eds., *The Quiet Hand of God: Faith-Based Activism and the Public Role of Mainline Protestantism* (Berkeley and Los Angeles: University of California, 2002), 160.

5. See Mark Hulsether, *Building a Protestant Left: Christianity and Crisis Magazine, 1941-1993* (Knoxville: University of Tennessee Press, 1999). In the 1960s the magazine's offices moved from Union into space a block or two away.

6. In terms of members, mainline Protestant churches had been losing religious market share slowly for decades, but their fortunes and sense of public political clout remained strong until the mid-1960s.

7. I draw parallels between the ecumenical vision and the Axial sages in the conclusion. For more, see Karen Armstrong, *The Great Transformation: The Beginning of Our Religious Traditions* (New York: Alfred A. Knopf, 2006); also Michael Kinnamon, *The Vision of the Ecumenical Movement and How It Has Been Impoverished by Its Friends* (St. Louis: Chalice Press, 2003).

8. Kinnamon in *Vision* confirms this.

9. For a few classic works on transformations in mainline Protestantism, see Robert Wuthnow, *The Restructuring of American Religion: Society and Faith since World War Two* (Princeton, NJ: Princeton University Press, 1988); Wade Clark Roof and William McKinney, *American Mainline Religion: Its Changing Shape and Future* (New Brunswick, NJ: Rutgers University Press, 1987); Robert S. Ellwood, *The 60s Spiritual Awakening: American Religion Moving from Modern to Postmodern* (New Brunswick, NJ: Rutgers University Press, 1994); David W. Lotz, ed., *Altered Landscapes: Christianity in America, 1935-1985* (Grand Rapids, MI: William B. Eerdmans, 1989); Amanda Porterfield, *The Transformation of American Religion: The Story of a Late-Twentieth-Century Awakening* (New York: Oxford University Press, 2001); Roger Finke and Rodney Stark, *The Churching of America, 1776-1990: Winners and Losers in Our Religious Economy* (New Brunswick, NJ: Rutgers University Press, 1992). Jeffrey K. Hadden, *The Gathering Storm in the Churches* (Garden City, NY: Doubleday, 1969) discusses the clergy-laity gap and the civil rights movement in detail. Wuthnow and Evans, in *Quiet Hand of God*, examine the public actions and status of mainline Protestantism from 1970 to about 2000. Most books on the antiwar movement barely

mention religious organizations. For one exception, see Charles DeBenedetti, *An American Ordeal: The Antiwar Movement of the Vietnam Era* (Syracuse, NY: Syracuse University Press, 1990); but it does not talk much about the churches themselves. Two books that focus on the antiwar activism of individual clergy and clergy groups are Michael Friedland, *Lift Up Your Voice Like a Trumpet: White Clergy and the Civil Rights and Antiwar Movement, 1954–1973* (Chapel Hill: North Carolina University Press, 1998), and Mitchell Hall, *Because of Their Faith: CALCAV and Religious Opposition to the Vietnam War* (New York: Columbia University Press, 1990). Among the first books to deal with church denominations and the Vietnam War are David Settje's *Lutherans and the Longest War: Adrift on a Sea of Doubt about the Cold and Vietnam Wars, 1964–1975* (Lexington, KY: Lexington Books, 2007) and *Faith and War: How Christians Debated the Cold and Vietnam Wars* (New York: New York University Press, 2011). A few studies have been conducted on church responses to the broader topic of national security and the Cold War. See, for example, Rick Nutt, *Toward Peacemaking: Presbyterians in the South and National Security, 1945–1983* (Tuscaloosa: University of Alabama Press, 1994); Randall Dean Austin, "Caution Christian Soldiers: The Mainline Protestant Churches and the Cold War" (Ph.D. dissertation, University of Arkansas, 1997). Studies have begun on churches and overseas relief work in Vietnam during the war. See Scott Flipse, "Bearing the Cross of Vietnam: Humanitarianism, Religion, and the American Commitment to South Vietnam, 1952–1975" (Ph.D. dissertation, University of Notre Dame, 2003); Scott Flipse, "The Latest Casualty of War: Catholic Relief Services, Humanitarianism, and the War in Vietnam, 1967–1968," *Peace and Change: A Journal of Peace Research* 27.2 (April 2002): 245–70; Perry Bush, "The Political Education of Vietnam Christian Service, 1954–1975," *Peace and Change: A Journal of Peace Research* 27.2 (April 2002): 198–224; David E. Leaman, "Politicized Service and Teamwork Tensions: Mennonite Central Committee in Vietnam, 1966–1969," *Mennonite Quarterly Review* 71 (1997): 544–70. For a study on evangelical churches and the Vietnam War, see Andrew LeRoy Pratt, "Religious Faith and Civil Religion: Evangelical Responses to the Vietnam War, 1964–1973" (Ph.D. dissertation, Southern Baptist Theological Seminary, 1988).

10. Insider accounts include Samuel McCrea Cavert, *The American Churches in the Ecumenical Movement, 1900–1968* (New York: Association Press, 1968); Paul Crow, "[Ecumenism in] North America," in *A History of the Ecumenical Movement*, vol. 3, *1968–2000*, ed. John Briggs, Mercy Oduyoye, and Georges Tsetsis (Geneva: WCC, 2004), 609–41; Kinnamon, *Vision*. For a survey of the broader movement, see Thomas E. Fitzgerald, *The Ecumenical Movement: An Introductory History* (Westport, CT: Praeger, 2004). Conservative writers with a clear bias against the NCC and ecumenical movement include Ernest Lefever, K. L. Billingsley, and most recently, Thomas C. Oden. Billingsley's *From Mainline to Sideline: The Social Witness of the National Council of Churches* (Washington: Ethics and Public Policy Center, 1990) describes the NCC's growing liberalization through a critical conservative bias. Oden's book, *Turning Around the Mainline: How Renewal Movements Are Changing the Church* (Grand Rapids, MI: Baker Books, 2006), is also strongly biased against the NCC and its ecumenical movement. Several organizations have made attacking the NCC and ecumenism a central part of their mission. These include American Council of Christian Churches, the John Birch Society, and more recently the Institute on Religion and Democracy (IRD). (Oden works in conjunction with the IRD.) Few balanced scholarly books have been written on the NCC. One of the earliest is Henry

J. Pratt, *The Liberalization of American Protestantism: A Case Study in Complex Organizations* (Detroit: Wayne State University Press, 1972). The NCC's civil rights work has received the most scholarly attention. Two excellent books are James Findlay's *Church People* and Mark Newman, *Divine Agitators: The Delta Ministry and Civil Rights in Mississippi* (Athens: University of Georgia, 2004). Neither of these explores the subject of ecumenism in great detail. There are a few important works that contain detailed discussion about the NCC's predecessor organization, the Federal Council of Churches. These include Gerald Sittser, *A Cautious Patriotism: The American Churches and the Second World War* (Chapel Hill: University of North Carolina, 1997), and John S. Nurser, *For All Peoples and All Nations: The Ecumenical Church and Human Rights* (Washington, D.C.: Georgetown University Press, 2005). These two, in addition to William Inboden's *Religion and American Foreign Policy, 1945–1960* (New York: Cambridge University Press, 2008), are among the few that include some in-depth treatment of the FCC's and NCC's responses to foreign policy issues.

11. Both Findlay, in *Church People*, and David Chappell, in *A Stone of Hope: Prophetic Religion and the Death of Jim Crow* (Chapel Hill: University of North Carolina Press, 2004), discuss the clear, singular moral argument that existed for those advocating civil rights. Settje summarizes the competing Christian moral arguments on the Vietnam War both in *Faith and War* and in *Lutherans and the Longest War*.

12. "Just war" criteria evolved over centuries and blended a combination of religious, philosophical, military, and political ideas into roughly seven principles. These usually include (1) having a just cause; (2) having a legitimate authority to wage the war; (3) obtaining an official declaration of war; (4) possessing a proper or "right" intention that seeks just, peaceful ends, rather than power and prizes; (5) using only the amount of force needed to achieve those ends, that is, avoiding excessive force; (6) employing war as a last resort, and only after all other means of conflict resolution are exhausted; and (7) having a reasonable probability of success. See Michael Walzer, *Just and Unjust Wars: A Moral Argument with Historical Illustrations* (New York: Basic Books, 1977).

13. Liberal and conservative religious ideas have roots going back much further. I am referring here to that which split Protestants into the general categories of "liberal" and "conservative" that engaged in the culture wars of the twentieth century.

14. These included the inerrancy of the Bible, the virgin birth of Jesus, and the literal second coming of Christ.

15. This is not to say that conservative Christians ceased talking about or being interested in politics. Rather, many conservative churches, as religious bodies, urged a focus upon spiritual issues rather than lobbying for specific political issues or measures. Yet, the historical record exposes some discrepancy between such positions and the considerable political involvement of many conservative Christian leaders and organizations. See Allan J. Lichtman, *White Protestant Nation: The Rise of the American Conservative Movement* (New York: Grove Press, 2008), 346.

16. Evangelicals also criticized the "universalism" of ecumenists who saw aspects of divine truth not only in every Christian group but also often in other cultures and religions. See the "history" section of the National Association of Evangelicals website, www.nae.net (accessed December 2006). The NAE would not allow dual membership in its organization and in the Federal or National Councils of Churches. Its criticism of the NCC grew especially harsh in the 1950s, when the NAE was quite nationalistic.

17. Wuthnow, *Restructuring*, ch. 10.

18. Both Alan Geyer and Reverend Dr. Robert Edgar expressed this sentiment in interviews. Alan Geyer, interview by author, 13 June 2003, in Washington, D.C. (hereafter Geyer interview); Reverend Dr. Robert Edgar, interview by author, 22 May 2003, in Boise, Idaho (hereafter Edgar interview). Manza and Brooks argue that conservative Christians have gained more leverage within the Republican Party in recent decades, largely because more moderate mainline Protestants have been moving from the ranks of moderate-conservatives (where they traditionally voted Republican) toward the political center; increasingly they are joining the Democratic Party. The defection of mainline Protestants from the GOP means Republican politicians no longer need to cater to as many moderate voices. Prominent liberal-leaning evangelicals include Jimmy Carter, Tony Campolo, Jim Wallis, and leaders within Sojourners.

19. A third branch was the international missionary movement. It does not figure much into this particular study.

20. See the NAE's website at www.nae.net (December 2006).

21. Since the mid-1990s, several conservative groups within the mainline churches (they call themselves "orthodox" or "classic" Christians) have begun trying to redefine and claim the words "ecumenical" and "confessing church" for themselves and their own movement. I'll discuss this briefly later, for this branched out of lay discontent that arose in the 1960s. For more see Oden, *Turning Around the Mainline*.

1—THE ROOTS OF ECUMANIA

1. Robert S. Bilheimer (hereafter RSB), *Breakthrough: The Emergence of the Ecumenical Tradition* (Grand Rapids, MI: William Eerdmans; Geneva: WCC Publications, 1989), 11–12. The epigraph is from Holy Bible, New Revised Standard Version (New York: Oxford University Press, 1989).

2. RSB, "Let American Ecumenism Be Ecumenical," *Worship* 51 (1977): 407–19; RSB, telephone interview by author, 14 December 1991, and personal interviews by author, St. Cloud, Minnesota, 5–9 August 1993. See also RSB, *A Spirituality for the Long Haul: Biblical Risk and Moral Stand* (Philadelphia: Fortress Press, 1984).

3. Kinnamon, *Vision*.

4. According to Paul Crow, "ecumaniac" was used in pejorative ways in the 1960s. Others attached the label to themselves with playful pride.

5. Kinnamon, *Vision*, 2–3. RSB said being "converted to Christ never meant anything to me, but being a member of the Body of Christ—that meant something to me." RSB interview, 5 August 1993.

6. RSB, *Breakthrough*, 15.

7. Pratt, *Liberalization*, 109–21.

8. "Key to my whole attempt . . . in the ecumenical enterprise," RSB remarked, "is in H. R. Niebuhr's chapter on church as transformer of culture." RSB interview, 9 August 1993. See H. Richard Niebuhr, *Christ and Culture* (New York: Harper and Row, 1951). This book was published after RSB finished seminary; however, H. R. Niebuhr was teaching these concepts prior to publishing them. RSB, *Breakthrough*, 18n3, 26.

9. RSB, *Breakthrough*, 27.

10. His future boss, R. H. Edwin Espy (hereafter EE), head of the SCM for the YMCA and a fellow Yale alumnus, recommended RSB for the Interseminary job.

11. RSB, *Breakthrough*, 28–29, 65.

12. RSB interview, 6 August 1993.

13. RSB biographical file, Presbyterian Historical Society, Philadelphia, PA.

14. The New Deal helped establish a pattern of leadership from above when tackling social issues. See Dean Kelley, *Social Justice*, report, Department of Social Justice, 10 September 1971, 13, Record Group (hereafter RG) 3, box 4, folder 14, NCC Records, Presbyterian Historical Society, Philadelphia, PA (hereafter NCC). Gerhard Elston attributed RSB's fondness for top-down conciliar methods to "the academic and Presbyterian in him." Elston, telephone interview by author, 11 December 1991, and personal interviews by author, Philadelphia, 13–22 October 1992.

15. RSB's program director job in New York City was to help educate American Protestant leaders about and involve them in the international ecumenical movement. Everyone in the WCC, he said, wanted to "get to the Americans." He became well acquainted with FCC and NCC leaders. There he witnessed the impact of the Cold War and McCarthyism upon U.S. churches. His son Bobby recalled his father's pastorate of Westminster Presbyterian Church in Jamaica, NY, saying "he was one of the very first . . . white pastors of an all black congregation in that part of the world." He added, "He was a real wonderful pastor to those people, preaching wonderful sermons, and they just adored him." Robert E. Bilheimer (hereafter REB), telephone interview by author, 9 March 2007; RSB interview, 5 August 1993.

16. See Mark Toulouse, *The Transformation of John Foster Dulles: From Prophet of Realism to Priest of Nationalism* (Macon, GA: Mercer University Press, 1985), 89–112.

17. RSB, "Let American Ecumenism."

18. RSB interviews, August 1993. See also Edward LeRoy Long Jr., "Christian Ethics as Responses to Social Conditions," in Lotz, *Altered Landscapes*, 296–98; Wuthnow, *Restructuring*, 138–43.

19. REB interview.

20. Elston interview, 22 October 1992.

21. RSB, *Breakthrough*, 35–39; Elston interview, 22 October 1992.

22. W. A. Visser 't Hooft, *The Wretchedness and Greatness of the Church* (London: SCM Press, 1944), 64.

23. RSB interview, 6 August 1993.

24. That was the crux of the Confessing Church's significance for American ecumenists who idealized it as a model. However, in recent years, historians have uncovered a more complicated and compromised history of the Confessing Church in Germany. They have argued that its main goal was to protect its own ecclesiastical authority and autonomy and that its own anti-Semitism led it to remain silent on Nazi policy relative to the Jews. Historians have argued, therefore, that church independence, not social justice, drove the Confessing Church's interest. After the war, German church leaders tried to hide their complicity on the Jewish question. This is discussed convincingly in Robert P. Ericksen and Susannah Heschel, eds., *Betrayal: German Churches and the Holocaust* (Minneapolis: Augsburg Fortress Publishers, 1999). Thus, the Confessing Church's own complicit anti-Semitism went unnoticed and uncriticized by Americans who, in the 1960s, combined a fight for church independence with a prophetic duty to seek social justice. How people remember, spin, and then use history is fascinating in this case, too; both the traditional ecumenists described here and recent (1990s) groups of mainline conservative opponents (who call themselves "classic" or "orthodox" Christians) have adopted the "confessing church" model for themselves. Conservatives are using it to justify purging denominations of liberal "heresies," seeing the Confessing Church primarily as a defender of pure

church doctrine. Many of these same conservatives supported neoconservative political policies and issues in President George W. Bush's administration, so were complicit in making the church a vocal defender of that administration's politics.

25. Information and quotes in this and the next seven paragraphs are from Elston interviews.

26. See also Gerhard Albert Elston biographical file, Swarthmore College Peace Collection, Swarthmore College, Swarthmore, Pennsylvania (hereafter SCPC).

27. The FCC's number of denominational members varied over its history from twenty-nine to thirty-three. The term "mainline" refers to Protestant denominations that were the most common and "mainstream" in America's early history. They became part of what was called the "Protestant establishment." These included Presbyterian, Methodist, Episcopalian, Congregational, Disciples of Christ, Reformed, United Lutheran, and American Baptist. Sydney Ahlstrom, *A Religious History of the American People* (New Haven: Yale University Press, 1972), 802–3. See also Pratt, *Liberalization*, 15–48.

28. "Plan of Federation," quoted in Cavert, *American Churches*, 48–49.

29. George Anderson, "Ecumenical Movements," in Lotz, *Altered Landscapes*, 94–95. The FCC became a champion of labor and, due to needs emerging from World War I, grew its services and bureaucratic structure enormously. See Ahlstrom, *Religious History*, 803–4.

30. Pratt, *Liberalization*, 15–48.

31. Ahlstrom, *Religious History*, 804. Not all ecumenists or FCC members were social gospelers. While this was strong among Methodists and to a lesser extent Presbyterians, it was fairly weak among Lutherans and Baptists. See Donald Meyer, *The Protestant Search for Political Realism, 1919–1941*, 2nd ed. (Middletown: Wesleyan University Press, 1988), 175.

32. Pratt, *Liberalization*, 27. In October 1932, Franklin Roosevelt proclaimed proudly that he was "as radical as the Federal Council." Ibid.

33. Meyer, *Protestant Search*, 314–16. Many Protestants were critical of the New Deal's "socialism" as well as FDR's ending of prohibition.

34. *The Church and the World* (1926), edited by Francis Miller, advocated a departure from culture-accommodating modernism.

35. Heather Warren, "The Theological Discussion Group and Its Impact on American and Ecumenical Theology, 1920–1945," *Church History* 62 (1993): 528–43.

36. Ibid.; RSB interviews.

37. Warren, "Theological Discussion Group." At the time, Cavert was the FCC's general secretary and would play a leadership role in founding the World Council.

38. Gabriel Fackre, "Theology: Ephemeral, Conjunctural and Perennial," in Lotz, *Altered Landscapes*, 246–67, discusses the distinctions between these.

39. Meyer, *Protestant Search*; H. Richard Niebuhr, *The Social Sources of Denominationalism* (1929; New York: World Publishing, 1971); H. Richard Niebuhr, Francis Miller, and Wilhelm Pauck, *The Church Against the World* (Chicago: Willett, Clark, 1935); H. Richard Niebuhr, *The Kingdom of God in America* (New York: Harper and Row, 1937); Paul Tillich, *The Religious Situation* (New York: Henry Holt, 1932); Paul Tillich, *Interpretation of History* (New York: Charles Scribner's Sons, 1936).

40. RSB interview, 9 August 1993; Reinhold Niebuhr, *Moral Man and Immoral Society* (1932; New York: Charles Scribner's Sons, 1960). See also Fackre, "Theology," 250.

41. Michael O. Emerson and J. Russell Hawkins, "Viewed in Black and White: Conservative Protestantism, Racial Issues, and Oppositional Politics," in Mark A. Noll and Luke E. Harlow, eds., *Religion and American Politics from the Colonial Period to the Present* (1990; New York: Oxford University Press, 2007), 297–325.

42. Meyer, *Protestant Search*, 360; see also Hulsether, *Building*. Van Dusen and Francis Miller were on the original editorial board, and Reinhold Niebuhr was editor; sponsors included John Bennett and Henry Sloane Coffin. Reinhold Niebuhr, "A Christian Journal Confronts Mankind's Continuing Crisis," *Christianity and Crisis* (hereafter *C&C*), 21 February 1966, 13–14.

43. Ahlstrom, *Religious History*, 937.

44. "A Message from the Oxford Conference to the Christian Churches," Oxford Report, 45–52, quoted in RSB, *Breakthrough*, 24. Meyer described this gathering as "the first of the great world conferences in which [modernist] liberalism stood on the defensive." Meyer, *Protestant Search*, 273.

45. Paul Gordon Lauren, *The Evolution of International Human Rights* (Philadelphia: University of Pennsylvania Press, 2003), 166–264.

46. Just war theory articulated clear parameters for wars to be deemed "just." The criteria evolved over centuries and blended a combination of religious and philosophical ideas, ancient laws, political theories, and military practices into roughly seven principles. These are listed in the notes to the Introduction.

47. Warren, "Theological Discussion Group"; Nurser, *For All Peoples*, 81–92. Theological Discussion Group members participated.

48. Guiding Principles from Bromley Oxnam, "Christian Responsibility on a Changing Planet," Fifth World Order Study Conference, Cleveland, 18 November 1958, RG 6, box 27, folder 24, NCC; John Foster Dulles to the commission membership, 12 March 1943, Dulles Papers, box 22, quoted in Toulouse, *Dulles*, 67.

49. Bennett cited in Toulouse, *Dulles*, 83.

50. Warren, "Theological Discussion Group," 540–42.

51. See Nurser, *For All Peoples*; Wuthnow, *Restructuring*, 49–50.

52. His FCC colleague Roswell Barnes noted that, at the UN's founding conference, Dulles "talked persuasively about human rights, economic justice, and the social and political advancement of subject peoples." Roswell P. Barnes, "John Foster Dulles," draft for *British Weekly*, 25 November 1952, RG 6, box 19, folder 16, NCC.

53. Nolde served as the CCIA's director until 1969 and helped shape the WCC's stands on the Vietnam War. Betty Thompson, "Tribute to a Diplomat," *Christian Century* (hereafter *CC*), 28 May 1969, 736; "Protestant Spokesman Nolde Dead at 72," *CC*, 19 July 1972, 771; RSB, *Breakthrough*, 150–51; Nurser, *For All Peoples*.

54. Oxnam, "Christian Responsibility."

55. President Truman to John Foster Dulles, 6 November 1945, from Toulouse, *Dulles*, 83f.

56. It stands in sharp contrast to many conservative Christians' current suspicions of the UN as a symbol of secular humanism and a dangerous attempt at creating world government. In fact, the best-selling apocalyptic writer Tim LaHaye predicts the anti-Christ will emerge from the United Nations. See LaHaye's *Left Behind* series.

57. Long, "Christian Ethics," 298.

58. Darren Dochuk, "Evangelicalism Becomes Southern, Politics Becomes Evangelical: From FDR to Ronald Reagan," in Noll and Harlow, *Religion and American Politics*, 297–325. Inboden, in *Religion*, discusses the interplay of religion with anticommunist beliefs and policies.

59. Amsterdam Report, 77–78, from RSB, *Breakthrough*, 167–69.

60. Amsterdam Report, 78–80, in ibid., 168–70. See Inboden, *Religion*, for a more critical view of WCC positions.

61. Ibid., 168.

62. Toulouse, *Dulles*, 197–201.

63. Wuthnow, *Restructuring*, 41.

64. John Bennett, editorial, *C&C*, 1 May 1972, 106–7; Ronald Stone, "An Interview with Reinhold Niebuhr," *C&C*, 17 March 1969, 48–52.

65. Richard Wightman Fox, *Reinhold Niebuhr: A Biography* (1985; Ithaca: Cornell University Press, 1996), 228–38, 252–56; Phillip Lloyd Hacker, *The Suicide of an Elite: American Internationalists and Vietnam* (Stanford: Stanford University Press, 1990), 26–28.

66. Elston interview, 15 October 1992.

67. Contributing editor, "China's Restoration of Religion: Intimations of a Christian Traveler," *CC*, 10 October 1973, 1007.

68. Elston interview, 15 October 1992.

69. Robert McNamara linked this loss to the subsequent short-sightedness of U.S. Vietnam policy. See Robert S. McNamara, *In Retrospect: The Tragedy and Lessons of Vietnam* (New York: Random House, 1995), 32–33.

70. Stephen Whitfield, *The Culture of the Cold War* (Baltimore: Johns Hopkins University Press, 1991), 86–87; Andrew Finstuen, *Original Sin and Everyday Protestants: The Theology of Reinhold Niebuhr, Billy Graham, and Paul Tillich in an Age of Anxiety* (Chapel Hill: University of North Carolina Press, 2009); Inboden, *Religion*. See Darren Dochuk, *From Bible Belt to Sun Belt: Plain-Folk Religion, Grassroots Politics, and the Rise of Evangelical Conservatism* (New York: W.W. Norton, 2011), for a discussion on the relationship between anticommunism, "the new gospel of wealth," battles against liberal Christians, and racial justice in the 1940s–1960s. On the myth of national innocence, see Reinhold Niebuhr, *The Irony of American History* (New York: Charles Scribner's Sons, 1952).

71. In 1957 Graham said, "My own theory about Communism is that it is master-minded by Satan. . . . I think there is no other explanation for the tremendous gains of Communism in which they seem to outwit us at every turn, unless they have supernatural power and wisdom and intelligence given to them." Whitfield, *Culture of the Cold War*, 81. See also William Martin, *A Prophet with Honor: The Billy Graham Story* (New York: William Morrow, 1991), 123–54.

72. Whitfield, *Culture of the Cold War*, 85. "G-man" stood for government man, also known as an FBI agent.

73. So did George Kennan. See Inboden, *Religion*, 1–25, chs. 3 and 7.

74. Ibid., 20; Roof and McKinney, *Mainline Religion*, 27, 83.

75. Reinhold Niebuhr is a prime example. See Fox, *Niebuhr*, 252–56. The NCC also tried repeatedly to prove its anticommunism in the early 1950s. See Settje, *Lutherans*, ch. 1.

76. It is interesting that "liberal" and "conservative" Christians each accused the other of being culture-driven Christians. Conservatives criticized ecumenists for engaging too much in the dirty issues of the world while neglecting spiritual duties. Ecumenists criticized conservatives for tying their faith too tightly to the nation's civil religion and way of life.

2—THE NCC AND THE AMERICAN WAY OF LIFE

1. For a list of the NCC's original members, see Nathan VanderWerf, *The Times Were Very Full: A Perspective on the First Twenty-Five Years of the National Council of the Churches of Christ in the United States of America, 1950–1975* (New York: NCC, 1975). Other agencies like Church World Service and the Protestant Radio Commission joined shortly following the NCC's formation.

2. Wuthnow, *Restructuring*, 81–82.

3. Communists were called "reds." "Pink" refers to someone seen as inclining in that direction.

4. "To the People of the Nation," *Christian Faith in Action: Commemorative Volume* . . . (New York: NCC, 1951), 150–53, in Edwin S. Gaustad, ed., *A Documentary History of Religion in America, since 1965* (Grand Rapids, MI: William Eerdmans, 1983), 456–59.

5. Wuthnow, *Restructuring*, 82.

6. Pratt, *Liberalization*.

7. McIntire was one of the most well-known separatist fundamentalists in the twentieth century. A former student of J. Gresham Machen at Princeton and Westminster seminaries, he became more extreme than his mentor. He created not only the American Council of Christian Churches (ACCC) in 1941 but also the International Council of Christian Churches in 1947 in response to the impending birth of the World Council. He founded several schools (many of which went defunct) and conducted a regular radio broadcast from 1955 into the 1970s. He also mentored prominent leaders of the religious right such as Billy Hargis and Francis Schaeffer. And he organized many prowar demonstrations for the Vietnam War. Historian Allan Lichtman lists him among the far right's major leaders. Lichtman, *White Protestant Nation*, 453 (on the ACCC, 123). Since McIntire often appeared at NCC conferences, regular delegates greeted him familiarly. According to Richard Fernandez, McIntire had an uncanny memory; he knew all of the NCC leaders by name, face, denomination, and role. Richard Fernandez, interviews by author, 31 October, 12 December 1991, in Philadelphia, Pennsylvania.

8. *How Red Is the Federal/National Council of Churches?* (New York: American Council of Christian Churches). I estimate the publication year to be 1951.

9. *Plain Facts about the National Council of Churches of Christ in the U.S.A.* (New York: NCC). I estimate the publication year to be 1953. In the October 1952 issue of *The Pastor*, Ralph Roy published an article, "A Ministry of Schism," discrediting Carl McIntire, the ACCC, and its accusations against the NCC.

10. The NCC and the NAE wrestled over the meaning and use of the words "evangelical" and "ecumenical." See Cavert, *American Churches*, 262; also Ahlstrom, *Religious History*, 958.

11. Lichtman, *White Protestant Nation*, 123–25. Lichtman cites the NAE as opposing "national health insurance, civil rights laws, and federal aid to education" (124). Graham said "Personal salvation must come before social reformation" (ibid., 215); yet he also courted Howard Pew's money, understanding that Pew had a political and economic agenda that he wanted advocated. Conservative evangelicals and fundamentalists appear inconsistent when criticizing liberal churches for engaging in worldly social activism while doing the same on their own issues. See also the history section of the NAE website; Dochuk, "Evangelicalism Becomes Southern" and *From Bible Belt*, 118–19, 161–62, 248; Settje, *Faith*.

12. Meyer, *Protestant Search*, 404–5. Pew headed up a laymen's committee within the NCC designed to keep a conservative check on the Council. When Pew failed to win veto power over the Council's policy-crafting process, he helped found *Christianity Today* in 1957, which was often critical of the Council. See Pratt, *Liberalization*, 86–104; E. V. Toy Jr., "The National Lay Committee and the National Council of Churches: A Case Study of Protestants in Conflict," *American Quarterly* 21.2 (Summer 1969): 190–209. Inboden, *Religion*, 55, 99.

13. Lichtman, *White Protestant Nation*, 194. Pew gave money to conservative religious groups that pushed his political and economic agenda, especially the evangelical journal *Christianity Today*. Ibid., 215–17.

14. Ken Maxwell, "The Philosophy and Objectives of Non-Governmental Organizations in Their Foreign Affairs Concerns," Conference on Foreign Affairs, Department of State, 26 May 1959, RG 6, box 25, folder 1.

15. Findlay, *Church People*, 11–12.

16. Roy Ross at the NCC General Assembly in St. Louis, 1954, in VanderWerf, *Times Were Very Full*, 36–37.

17. Bishop Oxnam served as president of the Federal Council (1944–1946), president of the World Council (1947–1953), and vice president of the National Council's social justice–minded Division of Life and Work (1957–1960). Ibid., 114.

18. J. B. Matthews, in Edwin Gaustad, *A Religious History of America* (1966; New York: Harper and Row, 1990), 295. Much in this paragraph and the next has been drawn from ibid., 294–96. See also Fox, *Niebuhr*, 253–54.

19. Hargis later ran into Oxnam at the WCC where, according to Hargis, Oxnam said to him, "I have completely forgiven you for what you did to me. I don't hold it against you." Hargis later wondered if he had done the right thing but finally concluded in the affirmative. "Evangelist Hargis 'Ghosted Attack on Oxnam,'" *Christian Advocate*, 6 April 1967: 23.

20. Gaustad, *Religious History*, 295.

21. Ibid., 296.

22. Ibid., 294–96. In the 1950s the NCC generally relied upon pronouncements and education programs rather than direct action to address social issues. In 1956 the NCC had a personnel policy that aimed to ascertain if employees had connections to communist groups; they tried to balance protecting individual rights with protecting the NCC's integrity. "Policy Regarding Communism," draft, 7 November 1956, RG 4, box 14, folder 25, NCC.

23. Pratt, *Liberalization*, 18–19, 37–44, 86–104, 108–21. Billingsley discusses, from a conservative, critical perspective, the Council's "lurch to the left" after its first decade. See Billingsley, *From Mainline to Sideline*.

24. Findlay, *Church People*, 14.

25. John Bennett, editorial response, *C&C*, 1 May 1972, 106–7.

26. Stone, "An Interview."

27. Bennett, editorial response. Fifty years later, the neoconservatives within President George W. Bush's administration revived many of Acheson's and Dulles's ideas about the benefits of U.S. power and globalism and applied them to Middle East policy.

28. As one example of a Council leader's balanced anticommunism, see Ernest Gross, "Illusions of our Asian Policy," address, 10th American Assembly, 17 November 1956, RG 6, box 14, folder 21, NCC.

29. The Eisenhower administration articulated this "domino theory." It believed if one nation was allowed to turn communist in a particular region, its conversion would likely precipitate the fall of its neighbors, like a row of dominoes.

30. Toulouse, *Dulles*, 252–53. Toulouse credits John Smylie's article "National Ethos and the Church," in *Theology Today* (October 1963), for the terminology and interpretation in this sentence. For a broader discussion of religious Cold War thinking within foreign policy circles, including Dulles, see Inboden, *Religion*.

31. John Foster Dulles to Walter Van Kirk, 20 November 1952, RG 6, box 19, folder 16, NCC.

32. Elston interview, 15 October 1992; Barnes, "John Foster Dulles," 2; John Foster Dulles, address to the NCC General Board, December 1952, in Willard Uphaus to "Friend," 19 February 1953, RG 6, box 19, folder 16, NCC. Dulles's address was also printed in the 24 December 1952 issue of the *Christian Century*.

33. Elston interview, 15 October 1992.

34. Dulles to Van Kirk, 6 March 1953, RG 6, box 19, folder 16, NCC.

35. Message from the Fourth World Order Study Conference, National Council of Churches, Cleveland, 27–30 October 1953, in Oxnam, "Christian Responsibility," 3.

36. Fourth World Order Study Conference, National Council of Churches, Cleveland, 27–30 October 1953, in Robert F. Smylie, "The China Issue: A Review of the Position of the National Council of Churches," *CC*, 10 October 1973, 1004.

37. Statement, General Board, 14 November 1954, RG 6, box 13, folder 19, NCC; Walter W. Van Kirk, "Report of Executive Director," Division of Christian Life and Work (DCLW), 21 April 1955, RG 6, box 14, folder 21, NCC.

38. Report, Department of International Affairs, 27 April 1955; Kenneth Maxwell, "What the Churches Are Doing in International Affairs in the Current Crisis," Report to the General Board, 4 December 1956; Report, "Re: Conference with President Eisenhower and Secretary of State Dulles by NCC Officers, April 3 1957, on Christian Concerns for Foreign Aid Programs and Other Developments to Date"; all in RG 6, box 14, folder 21, NCC. See also *Newsweek*, 18 March 1957. See Inboden, *Religion*, for a more critical perspective.

39. State Department policy statement, August 1958, in Smylie, "The China Issue," 1004. Smylie's article provides information summarized in this paragraph.

40. Specifically, he laid out the world situation using a strict bipolar model and reasserted America's duty to help noncommunist nations remain "free" at all cost. Contending that communists encouraged nationalist movements in developing countries as a step toward overtaking them later, he implied that America must therefore work to preserve people's freedom by ensuring that nationalist movements stay stalwartly anticommunist. Warning that the UN was virtually paralyzed by Soviet vetoes, he affirmed that the United States must use its power as a protective "shield" for peoples against communist aggression. He painted America as a good Christian nation motivated by democratic values to exercise its power altruistically on behalf of the world's best interests. John Foster Dulles, Fifth World Order Study Conference, 18 November 1958, RG 6, box 27, folder 24, NCC.

41. Oxnam, "Christian Responsibility."

42. Ibid.

43. Wallace C. Merwin, "Resume of Approaches to the Chinese Church," Report to the Annual Meeting of the China Committee, Division of Foreign Missions, 5 March 1958, RG 4, box 21, folder 15, NCC. See Inboden, *Religion*, for more on Christian divisions regarding U.S. China policy.

44. Oxnam, "Christian Responsibility."

45. "It [isolation] helps to preserve a false image of the United States and of other nations in the minds of the Chinese people. It keeps our people in ignorance of what is taking place in China. It hampers negotiations for disarmament. It limits the functioning of international organizations. We have a strong hope that the resumption of relationships between the peoples of China and of the United States may make possible also a restoration of relationships between their churches and ours." Message to the Churches, Fifth World Order Study Conference, in Smylie, "The China Issue," 1004.

46. Smylie, "The China Issue." See also Inboden, *Religion*.

47. Inboden also fails to make these distinctions clear.

48. The Hartford Appeal, policy statement, NCC General Board, 25 February 1959, National Council of Churches Communication and Research Department Office Files, New York, New York (hereafter NCCNYO).

49. Smylie, "The China Issue," 1005, taken from Eleanor Lansing Dulles, *John Foster Dulles: The Last Year* (New York: Harcourt, Brace and World, 1963); Ken Maxwell, "The Philosophy and Objectives of Nongovernmental Organizations in Their Foreign Affairs Concerns," Conference on Foreign Affairs, Department of State, 26 May 1959, RG 6, box 25, folder 1, NCC. For more on tensions between Dulles and ecumenists, see Inboden, *Religion*.

50. *Air Reserve Center Training Manual*, student text, NR 45-0050, Incr. V., vol. 7, reserve noncommissioned officer course, U.S. Air Force, New York, 4 January 1960, section 15, page 14.

51. The Revised Standard Version of the Bible, which the NCC produced in 1952, was controversial to a public used to the King James Version and suspicious of the liberal Council. Evangelicals largely refused to use it, creating their own New International Version thereafter.

52. *Air Reserve Center Training Manual*, 20.

53. The Councils opposed universal military training. The NCC opposed the arms race and America's policy dependence upon the military. Pratt notes that the Federal Council's peace program for disarmament after World War I alienated the military, which in turn charged the Council with communist collaboration. See Pratt, *Liberalization*, 25–33.

54. Elston interview, 15 October 1992.

55. James Wine to Honorable Thomas S. Gates Jr., 11 February 1960, RG 17, box 6, folder 1, NCC.

56. James Wine, "Report on Air Force Manual Issue, General Board, Oklahoma City," 24 February 1960, RG 17, box 6, folder 1, NCC.

57. "Issues Presented by Air Reserve Center Training Manual," Hearing before the Committee on Un-American Activities, House of Representatives, 86th Cong., 2nd sess., 2 February 1960, 1288, 1294–313, RG 17, box 6, folder 23, NCC.

58. Statement to Congressmen for the National Council of Churches, 23 March 1960, RG 17, box 6, folder 19, NCC.

59. "Issues Presented by Air Reserve Center Training Manual," Hearing before the Committee on Un-American Activities, House of Representatives, 86th Cong., 2nd sess., 2 February 1960, 1288, 1294–1313, RG 17, box 6, folder 23, NCC.

60. John Wicklein, "Extremists Try to Curb Clergy," *New York Times*, 28 March 1960, 1.

61. John F. Kennedy, from *Washington Post*, 19 April 1960, in "Interpretation Manual," Office of Information, 25 April 1961, RG 4, box 36, folder 30, NCC.

62. Finstuen says both, in *Original Sin*, and presents evidence of laity engaging theologically and positively with challenging sermons on original sin from Reinhold Niebuhr, Billy Graham, and Paul Tillich. But Finstuen's analysis revolves solely around discussions of original sin (1945–1965), a traditional, familiar, personalized, and accepted Christian topic. Finstuen does not deal directly with systemic institutionalized sin.

63. See Rodney Stark and Charles Y. Glock, *American Piety: The Nature of Religious Commitment* (Berkeley and Los Angeles: University of California Press, 1968); Hadden, *Gathering Storm*. The clergy-laity gap has been a widely discussed topic since.

64. Allan Parrent, personal interview together with James Hamilton and author (hereafter Hamilton/Parrent interview), 21 November 1991, Methodist Building, Washington, D.C.

65. E. Raymond Wilson, "Are We Serious about Social Action?" *CC*, 10 February 1965, 169–71.

66. VanderWerf, *Times Were Very Full*, 64; Ken Maxwell, CCIA Annual Report, May 1961–May 1962, RG 6, box 27, folder 10, NCC.

67. "Toward a Family of Nations Under God: Agenda of Action for Peace," pronouncement, General Board, 2 June 1960, RG 6, box 30, folder 1, NCC.

68. "Interpretation Manual," Office of Information, 25 April 1961, RG 4, box 36, folder 30, NCC.

69. "Toward a Family of Nations. To the Commission of the Churches on International Affairs," Annual Report, Department of International Affairs, May 1961, RG 6, box 27, folder 10, NCC.

70. Excerpt from the "Recording of the Proceedings of the Meeting of the General Committee of the Department of International Affairs, October 7, 1960, Containing Introduction of and Remarks by Harry W. Seamans, Officer in Charge," Organization Liaison Division, Office of Public Services, U.S. Department of State, RG 6, box 25, folder 1, NCC.

71. The one-year program was known as the "Nationwide Program of Education and Action for Peace." "Toward a Family of Nations. To the Commission of the Churches on International Affairs," Annual Report, Department of International Affairs, May 1961, RG 6, box 27, folder 10, NCC. The five-year "Program of Education and Action in Christian Responsibility for World Survival and Peace" emerged as a result of lay interest and financing.

72. They assured the Kennedy administration that the NCC was rallying support among its constituencies as well as stimulating communication with legislators. Maxwell to Rusk, 2 August 1963, RG 6, box 25, folder 1, NCC.

73. See Findlay, *Church People*; Newman, *Divine Agitators*.

74. Findlay, *Church People*, 37, 61, 62.

75. Ibid., 48, 50, 169–70. Kennedy, Rusk, and Harriman also met with a group of National and World Council leaders to discuss the nuclear test ban treaty—another area of cooperation. See Maxwell to Rusk, 2 August 1963, RG 6, box 25, folder 1, NCC.

76. The previous generation of Federal Council staff had also gathered non-American perspectives, but most had been sought from Europe. "Third World" voices, as they were called, remained muted within the WCC until the 1960s. Listening intently to Asian voices was new for many ecumenists in the 1960s.

77. DeBenedetti, *American Ordeal*, 158. DeBenedetti drew this from the *National Guardian*, 22 April 1967, 2.

78. EE letter to Lyndon Johnson (hereafter LBJ), 22 November 1965, RG 4, box 33, folder 14, NCC.

79. The Message to the Churches, Sixth General Assembly, Philadelphia, 1–7 December 1963, reprinted in *CC*, 1 January 1964, 12–14.

80. Ibid.

81. One deemed the war "just" because the United States was defending freedom against invading atheistic communist aggressors. The alternative position, eventually supported by most ecumenists, argued that the war was unjust, immoral, and impractical. With respect to civil rights, even segregation-supporting Christians could not find a clear defense of segregation in the Bible. For more, see Chappell's *A Stone of Hope*.

3—A BRIEF INTERLUDE ON VIETNAM, TO 1963

1. There are several excellent survey-type books on the Vietnam War. My favorites include George C. Herring, *America's Longest War: The United States and Vietnam, 1950–1975* (1979; New York: Alfred A. Knopf, 1986); Marilyn B. Young, *The Vietnam Wars, 1945–1990* (New York: Harper Perennial, 1991); and George Donelson Moss, *Vietnam: An American Ordeal* (Englewood Cliffs: Prentice Hall, 1990). I have used all of these in assembling this interlude. For an excellent concise treatment, see Mitchell Hall, *The Vietnam War* (Essex, England: Pearson Education, 2000). For more of a Vietnamese and cultural perspective, see Frances Fitzgerald's classic *Fire in the Lake* (New York: Vintage Books, 1972); and Li Ly Hayslip, *When Heaven and Earth Changed Places* (1989; New York: Penguin Books, 1990). For a look inside U.S. government circles as the war began, see David Halberstam, *The Best and the Brightest* (1969; New York: Random House, 1972); McNamara, *In Retrospect*; Fredrik Logevall, *Choosing War: The Lost Chance for Peace and the Escalation of War in Vietnam* (Berkeley and Los Angeles: University of California Press, 1999).

2. Officially, at first the Japanese allowed the French to continue administering Vietnam (and absorbing the costs of this), while the Japanese acquired control of the nation's resources, trade, and strategic areas. The area was, for all intents and purposes, now in Japan's grips. Then, in March 1945, the Japanese removed the French completely.

3. Young, *Vietnam Wars*, 10.

4. Vietnamese Declaration of Independence, 2 September 1945.

5. Young, *Vietnam Wars*, 15–21.

4—AWAKENING A LOYAL OPPOSITION, 1964–JULY 1965

1. "Johnson Addresses the World," editorial, *CC*, 1 January 1964, 3.

2. Reinhold Niebuhr, "President Johnson's Foreign Policy," *C&C*, 16 March 1964, 31–32.

3. Logevall, *Choosing War*, 375–414.

4. "Rift Deepens Between Peking and Moscow," *CC*, 19 February 1964, 230; O. Frederick Nolde, "A New Look at International Affairs," annual meeting of U.S. Conference for the World Council of Churches, Buck Hill Falls, 4 April 1964, RG 6, box 18, folder 6, NCC.

5. John Bennett, "Senator Fulbright Speaks Out," *C&C*, 13 April 1964, 57–58.

6. "Program of Education and Action for Peace 1964," NCC press release 57DLW, 26 May 1964, E. Raymond Wilson Papers (hereafter ERWP), CDG-A, box 3, SCPC.

7. LBJ letter, 14 May 1965, in *Nationwide Program of Education and Action for Peace* (New York: NCC, 1964), RG 6, box 30, folder 2, NCC.

8. Waldo Beach, "The Servant Church in the Revolution," *C&C*, 11 May 1964, 81.

9. Ryozo Hara letter to "Friend," 4 June 1964, RG 6, box 27, folder 1, NCC.

10. John S. Rounds confidential memo to Colin Bell et al., regional peace education secretaries, 25 June 1964, RG 6, box 27, folder 1, NCC. Chakravarty also briefed the executive and legislative branches of the government. Additionally, John Bennett wrote a perceptive article for *Christianity and Crisis* called "Questions about Vietnam," 20 July 1964, 141–42.

11. Stephen E. Ambrose, *Rise to Globalism: American Foreign Policy since 1938* (1971; New York: Penguin Books, 1993), 199.

12. Logevall, *Choosing War*, 375–414. Logevall argues that LBJ intentionally drove U.S. policy toward escalation in Vietnam.

13. Ambrose, *Rise to Globalism*, 199.

14. "Goldwater? No!" editorial, *CC*, 1 July 1964, 851.

15. "Antidote to Extremism," editorial, *CC*, 29 July 1964, 955–56.

16. Ibid., 956 (the others are "racism, rabid nationalism and resentment at controls on business"). See also "Churchmen Hold a Peace Conference," editorial, *CC*, 29 July 1964, 957.

17. John Bennett, "The Goldwater Nomination," *C&C*, 3 August 1964, 157–58. Bennett's ecumenical résumé and foreign affairs experience were extensive. He was secretary of the section on "Church and Economic Order" at the Oxford Conference in 1937, and of the section on the "Church and the Disorder of Society" at the Amsterdam Assembly in 1948. He was vice chair of a section on "Responsible Society" at the WCC's Evanston Assembly in 1954. He served on an FCC commission to study the moral implications of using mass destructive weapons during wartime in 1950, and as a member of both the NCC's Council on Foreign Relations and IAC. In 1962 Union Theological Seminary made him president (he was in his sixties) after years of service as its Reinhold Niebuhr Professor of Social Ethics. In 1965 he helped found Clergy and Laymen Concerned About Vietnam (CALCAV) and served on its national executive committee. A book on foreign policy from a Christian perspective followed in 1966. His wife, Anne Bennett, was a fervent antiwar activist, and often further to the left than he was on the war. See John Bennett's biographical file, compiled by the publicity office of Union Theological Seminary (hereafter UTS); John Bennett Papers, Burke Library, UTS.

18. McNamara, *In Retrospect*, 150–51; Dean Rusk, *As I Saw It* (New York: Penguin Books, 1990), 444–45.

19. LBJ address, American Bar Association, 12 August 1964, in McNamara, *In Retrospect*, 146.

20. Moss, *Vietnam*, 168–69. The domino theory asserts that, once communism gets rooted in a particular geographic region, it will try to infect its neighbors. Without some outside force "containing" it, communism is therefore likely to spread, toppling a region of nations like a row of dominoes.

21. McNamara, *In Retrospect*, 147–51. See also Logevall, *Choosing War*, which focuses entirely on the administration's decision-making process in what the author calls the "Long 1964."

22. "Is President Swayed by Talk of War?" *CC*, 12 August 1964, 1006; "An Echo, Not a Choice," *CC*, 19 August 1964, 1028–29; "Johnson? Yes!" editorial, *CC*, 9 September 1964, 1099–101.

23. "Johnson? Yes!" 1099–100. For more on Goldwater's ability to rally conservative Christians passionately behind his candidacy, see Dochuk, *From Bible Belt*, 226–30, 245–53, 271.

24. "Of Betrayal and Loyalty," *CC*, 30 June 1971, 792–93.

25. "On Presenting Both Sides," *CC*, 23 September 1964, 1163–64.

26. Editorial Board, "We Oppose Senator Goldwater," *C&C*, 5 October 1964, 181–83.

27. Editorial Board, "The Johnson-Humphrey Team," *C&C*, 19 October 1964, 193–94.

28. "A Time for Cool Heads and Steady Hands," *CC*, 28 October 1964, 1323–24.

29. "What Now?" *CC*, 11 November 1964, 1387; John Bennett, "Rejection and Election," *C&C*, 16 November 1964, 221.

30. James Sellers, "Our Reluctant Laity and the Seminaries," *CC*, 29 April 1964, 551–52.

31. "The Churches' Mandate," *CC*, 18 November 1964, 1419–20.

32. Leroy Davis, "The Clergy-Laity Schism," *CC*, 25 November 1964, 1455–56.

33. Dean Kelley used this phrase in his personal interview with author, 28 October 1991, in New York (hereafter Kelley interview). Apparently it was used often during the 1960s to describe the clergy-laity gap.

34. Reinhold Niebuhr, "Protestant Individualism and the Goldwater Movement," *C&C*, 14 December 1964, 248–49. See also Settje, *Lutherans*, ch. 3.

35. McNamara, *In Retrospect*, 161–63, 169.

36. DeBenedetti, *American Ordeal*, 101–7.

37. Editors, "About This Issue," *C&C*, 2 November 1964, 209.

38. Wayne Morse, "The US Must Withdraw," *C&C*, 2 November 1964, 209–13.

39. Frank N. Trager, "To Guarantee the Independence of Vietnam," *C&C*, 2 November 1964, 213–15.

40. Born in 1918, Kenneth L. Maxwell was an American Baptist who worked in the NCC's Department of Racial and Cultural Relations before becoming director of its International Affairs Commission. He served for over a decade before RSB assumed the position. Maxwell had also worked as a pastor. A longtime UN supporter, he helped found the United Nations Association of the USA. In his later years, he taught political science and international relations in Arizona. Maxwell died in August 1998. See *American Baptist News* for 4 September 1998 at http://www.wfn.org/1998/09/msg00000.html (20 October 2006).

41. Prior to working for the United Church of Christ (UCC), Geyer was employed by the Presbyterians, but he was a Methodist and the son of a Methodist minister. Geyer earned both a seminary degree and a doctorate in political science and ethics. Geyer began creating a Peace Priority Program for the UCC. Geyer interview.

42. Alan Geyer, "Vietnam's Greatest Need: Political Aid," *C&C*, 2 November 1964, 216–19. Geyer wrote an address in October 1967, which made similar points: that the United States had overly militarized what were essentially political struggles

in Vietnam, and that it didn't recognize differences within communism. He remained critical of communists and their brutality and hoped that a noncommunist government might prevail in South Vietnam. See Alan Geyer, "Vietnam: A Case Study in Ambiguity," 21 October 1967, delivered at Wisconsin State University, Oshkosh, given to author by Alan Geyer.

43. Kenneth Maxwell, "Why Are Christians Working for Peace?" *Peace . . . ? Man and Nations in a Changing Community* (New York: NCC Department of International Affairs, 1964), ERWP, CDG-A, box 1, SCPC.

44. U Kyaw Than, "The Crucified in Vietnam" (confidential notes on the EACC and Vietnam), 6 January 1965, RG 6, box 21, folder 1, NCC. All quotes in this and the next two paragraphs are from these notes.

45. Elston interview, 16 October 1992.

46. "Urge Cease-Fire in South Vietnam," *CC*, 13 January 1965, 37.

47. Wilson, "Are We Serious About Social Action?"

48. John Bennett, "Beyond Frozen Positions in the Cold War," *C&C*, 11 January 1965, 269–70; "Chinese Checkers," *CC*, 13 January 1965, 35–36; Betty Pilkington, "Chinese Puzzle in the UN," *CC*, 13 January 1965, 50–51.

49. Reinhold Niebuhr, "Vietnam: An Insoluble Problem," *C&C*, 8 February 1965, 1–2.

50. As one example, see John Bennett, "The United States and China," *C&C*, 19 April 1965.

51. Leonard Kramer to Reverend Ralph Galt, 2 November 1964, RG 6, box 27, folder 1, NCC; David Stowe, "What About Mainland China?" *CC*, 13 January 1965, 44–46. Stowe was executive secretary of the NCC's Division of Overseas Ministries.

52. Gross, address, Division of Christian Life and Mission Program board meeting, New York, 10 February 1965, press release 17DCLM.

53. Michael Maclear, *The Ten Thousand Day War: Vietnam, 1945–1975* (New York: Avon Books, 1981), 123–24.

54. Bishop A. Raymond Grant et al., telegram to LBJ, 8 February 1965, RG 6, box 30, folder 34, NCC.

55. U Thant, "Statement by the Secretary-General on the Situation in Viet-Nam," press release SG/SM/251, Office of Public Information, UN, New York, 12 February 1965, RG 5, box 17, folder 41, NCC.

56. Reuben Mueller to LBJ, 15 February 1965, RG 4, box 33, folder 5, NCC.

57. McNamara, *In Retrospect*, 174.

58. Harold Fey, "Is the UN Dying?" *CC*, 3 March 1965, 263–64.

59. Rusk, *As I Saw It*, 462–63; "Press Conference by the Secretary-General at U.N. Headquarters," note no. 3075, 24 February 1965, RG 5, box 17, folder 41, NCC.

60. "Resolution on Vietnam," General Board, 25 February 1965, RG 4, box 33, folder 14, NCC.

61. John Bennett, "Where Are We Headed in Vietnam?" *C&C*, 8 March 1965, 29–30.

62. "Alternatives in Vietnam," *CC*, 10 March 1965, 291–92; Sir Kenneth Grubb and O. Frederick Nolde, "South Vietnam: A Statement on Certain Lines of Action by the Chairman and Director of the Commission of the Churches on International Affairs," 10 March 1965, RG 5, box 21, folder 17, NCC; E. Raymond Wilson to Vice President Hubert Humphrey, 19 March 1965, RG 4, box 33, folder 14, NCC; "Bad News from Vietnam," *CC*, 7 April 1965, 419–20.

63. "Resolution on Vietnam Crisis," General Brotherhood Board, Church of the

Brethren, 19 March 1965, RG 6, box 30, folder 32, NCC. "The Epistle of the [225?]th Annual Session of Philadelphia Yearly Meeting of the Religious Society of Friends," 25–31 March 1965; and David G. Paul, clerk, Philadelphia Yearly Meeting of the Religious Society of Friends to President Johnson, 31 March 1965; both in RG 5, box 17, folder 40, NCC.

64. Mueller to Mr. Leon Shapiro, 1 April 1965, RG 6, box 27, folder 1, NCC.

65. McNamara, *In Retrospect*, 181.

66. LBJ, "Pattern for Peace in Southeast Asia," Johns Hopkins University, Baltimore, 7 April 1965, RG 5, box 17, folder 40, NCC.

67. Minutes of the Special Advisory Committee on Viet-Nam of the National Council of Churches (hereafter SACVN), 16 November 1965, NCC Washington Office Files (hereafter NCCWOF). Maxwell claimed the NCC was the first major organization to push the White House to offer development aid and that NCC efforts contributed to its inclusion in the speech. The Tennessee Valley Authority was a government-funded New Deal project that brought cheap electricity to rural areas in America.

68. Hubert Humphrey to E. Raymond Wilson of the FCNL, RG 4, box 33, folder 15, NCC.

69. Logevall, *Choosing War*, 375–414, esp. 393–94.

70. Maxwell memo to Members of the General Committee, IAC and Executives in Christian Social Education and Action, 5 May 1965, RG 4, box 33, folder 14, NCC. See also SACVN minutes, 16 November 1965, NCCWOF.

71. The *Christian Century* responded to the speech with cautious optimism, hearing in it an assurance that LBJ would not allow a local war to turn into "a more generalized war with catastrophic consequences." "The Doves' Chance in Vietnam," *CC*, 21 April 1965, 484–85. See also Roger Shinn, "Negotiation Without Capitulation," *C&C*, 3 May 1965, 89–90.

72. Maxwell to Members of General Committee, 5 May 1965, RG 4, box 33, folder 14, NCC.

73. RSB interviews; Gross to Rusk, February 9, 1966, Soc. 12-1 U.S., RG 59, box 3249, National Archives II, College Park, MD (hereafter NAII). A State Department staff member wrote Rusk, commenting, "Those of us in the Department who have worked closely with Ken Maxwell know how reasonable and how effective he has been in every matter involving U.S. foreign policy. His fine intelligence and education, and his gracious cooperation, made him one of our most valuable contacts. He initiated and carried out one of the largest and most thorough programs in foreign policy education in the last decade." See James L. Greenfield, memo to the Secretary (Dean Rusk), 1 March 1966, Soc. 12-1 U.S., RG 59, box 3249, NAII.

74. McNamara, *In Retrospect*, 181.

75. DeBenedetti, *American Ordeal*, 110–13.

76. Ibid., 112–13; McNamara, *In Retrospect*, 141–42.

77. Elston interview, 20 October 1992.

78. Gross to LBJ, 11 May 1965, RG 6, box 28, folder 18, NCC.

79. DeBenedetti, *American Ordeal*, 112–13.

80. "Washington Visitation by Religious Representatives on Vietnam," 4–6 May 1965, RG 4, box 33, folder 14, NCC. This lists the fourteen cooperating religious organizations and the names of individual participants (including NCC staffers and NCC-involved denominational leaders), as well as the names of White House and State Department officials, senators, and representatives with whom they met.

81. See "Call to Vigil on Vietnam," *CC*, 12 May 1965, 605, for the names of the committee members.

82. Mueller to U.S. Mitchell, 24 May 1965, RG 4, box 33, folder 5, NCC.

83. "Nothing Personal, Mr. President," *CC*, 26 May 1965, 667–68.

84. McNamara, *In Retrospect*, 188–89.

85. Editorial Board, "U.S. Policy in Vietnam: A Statement," *C&C*, 14 June 1965, 125–26.

86. Kyle Haselden, *CC*, 16 June 1965, 766–67.

87. Arthur J. Moore, "The Question of Credibility," *C&C*, 28 June 1965, 133–34.

88. Editors of the *Christian Century* and *Christianity and Crisis*, "On Foreign Policy: A Joint Appeal to the National Council of Churches," *CC*, 7 July 1965, 863. Mitchell Hall describes the two journals' circulation impact as follows: "*Christian Century* with 40,000 subscribers was probably the best-known and most widely quoted journal of the Protestant press. *Christianity and Crisis* with only one-fourth the circulation had an impact well beyond its numbers by influencing opinion makers and reaching a larger public through its citations in the secular press." Hall, *Because of Their Faith*, 7. See also Hulsether, *Building*, xi–xx. Portions of the text here appeared first in Jill K. Gill, "The Political Price of Prophetic Leadership: The National Council of Churches and the Vietnam War," *Peace and Change* 27.2 (April 2002): 271–300, © 2002 Peace History Society and Consortium on Peace Research, Education, and Development.

89. Geyer interview; Elston interview.

90. "Churches Speaking Out On Foreign Policy," *Time*, 30 July 1965, 53.

91. Clifford Earle to Kramer, 26 July 1965, RG 6, box 30, folder 34, NCC.

92. EACC Officers, "To the National Council of Churches and the British Council of Churches," circular, 21 June 1965, RG 6, box 27, folder 1, NCC.

93. "Japanese Peace Mission Ends American Tour," press release, August 1965; and Isamu Omura et al., statement, Japanese Christian Peace Mission to the U.S., 15 August 1965; both in RG 6, box 27, folder 1, NCC.

94. Vernon Ferwerda (NCC Washington office) said the Japanese viewed Ho Chi Minh "as the George Washington of Vietnam," emphasizing his nationalism over his communism; this stunned many Americans and impeded "any meeting of minds." Ferwerda helped arrange for the Japanese team to visit key State and Defense Department personnel, hoping to dispel the team's perception of Pentagon leaders as inhumane. American church leaders also tried to explain to the Japanese that America was not primarily imperialist but rather anti-aggression, and that most church people supported the government's basic policy to use force against imposed communist takeovers. Ferwerda memo to EE, August 9, 1965, RG 6, box 27, folder 1, NCC. Harold Fey, "Japanese Peace Mission," *CC*, 11 August 1965, 982–83. Interestingly, after spending two months in Asia in 1956, Roy G. Ross of the NCC had written an article explaining his astonishment that Asians were largely indifferent to communism; self-determination was their larger concern. He discovered as well how suspicious Asians were of imperialism within Western missionary activity. Roy G. Ross, "The Christian Mission in Asia," drafted September 1956 for publication in *CC*, October 1956, RG 4, box 14, folder 20, NCC.

95. Norman Baugher to EE, 26 July 1965, RG 4, box 33, folder 14, NCC.

96. Herman Will, memo to Dudley Ward, 26 July 1965, RG 4, box 33, folder 14, NCC.

97. Robert Spike, memo to EE, 26 July 1965, RG 4, box 33, folder 14, NCC.

98. McNamara, *In Retrospect*, 189–206. Lichtman argues that LBJ hoped to force

a diplomatic solution by showing the VC and the NVA that they could not win; *White Protestant Nation*, 271.

5—TAKING A STAND, JULY–DECEMBER 1965

1. "Meeting on Vietnam," 27 July 1965, RG 4, box 33, folder 14, NCC.

2. An article published in the *Christian Century* in 1974 claimed that the U.S. government and churches had long cooperated to advance one another's interests around the globe and dubbed this selective dissemination of relief efforts to bolster American interests "The Politics of Charity." Doug Hostetter and Michael McIntyre, "The Politics of Charity," *CC*, 18 September 1974, 845–50.

3. Ronald Stenning, *Church World Service: Fifty Years of Help and Hope* (New York: Friendship Press, 1996), 15–16.

4. James MacCracken, memo on CWS and Church-State Relationship, 11 April 1967, RG 8, box 96, folder CWS: Church and State, 1967, NCC. For another example of CWS's favorable disposition toward cooperating with government AID programs in Vietnam, see Hugh Farley to Hubert H. Humphrey, 8 November 1965, and attached report, RG 5, box 17, folder 41, NCC. See discussion of this report in Hostetter and McIntyre, "Politics of Charity"; Robert Sullivan, "The Politics of Altruism: The American Church-State Conflict in the Food-for-Peace Program," *Journal of Church and State* 11 (Winter 1969): 47–61; Robert Sullivan, "The Politics of Altruism: An Introduction to the Food for Peace Partnership between the United States Government and Voluntary Relief Agencies," *Western Political Quarterly* 23 (1970): 762–68; David S. Sorenson, "Food for Peace—Or Defense and Profit? The Role of P.L. 480, 1963–1973," *Social Science Quarterly* 60 (June 1979): 62–71.

5. Baugher to EE, 26 July 1965, RG 4, box 33, folder 14, NCC.

6. This was according to Dr. Harold Row, SACVN, taped presentation, 29 September 1965, RG 6, box 27, folder 4, NCC.

7. The NCC's Washington office representative warned leaders not to "let the left wing manipulate us," and to choose allies with caution. Another attendee warned of the same regarding the right. A third clarified that the church must act as an independent moral force that values justice and the quality of human life. A fourth said, yes, speak morally, but "be careful about criticism of the government." "Meeting on Vietnam," 27 July 1965, RG 4, box 33, folder 14, NCC. See also Logevall, *Choosing War*, 375–414.

8. Charles Tait, "Whatever Happened to the State Department?" *The Nation*, 13 September 1965, 137–41. This article, found in the NCC's Vietnam files, describes how the State Department had been taken over by a militaristic mentality on foreign policy after World War II.

9. From the outset, Methodist leaders were among the most activist-minded of the nonpacifist denominations in advocating an NCC witness against U.S. Vietnam policy. Elston described Ward wanting to "sound the trumpet" on Vietnam, but he had difficulty getting others to go along and was frustrated by the NCC's bureaucratic process. Elston interview, 20 October 1992. Bishop John Wesley Lord suggested to Espy that the NCC provide the kind of bold moral leadership on Vietnam that it did on civil rights. Lord to EE, 28 July 1965, RG 4, box 33, folder 14, NCC. See also Will memo to Ward, 26 July 1965, Church and Society Records (hereafter CS), box 33, 1444-2-1:08, General Commission on Archives and History,

United Methodist Church, Madison, New Jersey (hereafter GCAH).

10. EE to Mueller, 29 July 1965, RG 4, box 33, folder 14, NCC. As of 16 August 1965, panel members included (as listed) Arthur Flemming, Norman Baugher, John Bennett, Mrs. Fred Buschmeyer, Harold Bosley, Edwin Dahlberg, Dale Fiers, Ernest Gross, Ben Mohr Herbster, John E. Hines, J. Irwin Miller, John Coventry Smith, Mrs. Emlen Stokes, and Prince Taylor. Greek Orthodox Archbishop Iakovos, who opposed the NCC's "criticism" of the American government and religious political action, joined shortly thereafter. Consultants included Robert Bulkley, Harold Fey, Tracey Jones, Elmira Kendricks, O. Frederick Nolde, Eugene Smith, and Dudley Ward. For titles and affiliations, see NCC press release 92GA, 16 August 1965, RG 4, box 33, folder 14, NCC.

11. "Background Paper for the President's Special Panel on Vietnam," 5 August 1965, RG 4, box 33, folder 14, NCC.

12. Maxwell to Iakovos, 23 August 1965, RG 4, box 33, folder 14, NCC.

13. Mueller to EE, 20 August 1965, RG 4, box 33, folder 5, NCC.

14. SACVN meeting notes, 5 August 1965, RG 4, box 33, folder 14, NCC; Maxwell to Rusk, 23 August 1965, RG 6, box 27, folder 4, NCC.

15. SACVN minutes, 29 September 1965, RG 4, box 33, folder 14, NCC.

16. "Notes on Meeting of August 20, 1965 of NCC Staff Members Concerned with Viet-Nam," RG 4, box 33, folder 14., NCC.

17. "Christian Consensus on Vietnam," *CC*, 8 September 1965, 1083–84.

18. SACVN minutes, 29 September 1965, RG 4, box 33, folder 14, NCC; John Coventry Smith to Rev. Colin Williams, 9 September 1965, RG 6, box 27, folder 4, NCC.

19. "Vietnam—A Report by W. Harold Row," September 1965, RG 4, box 33, folder 14, NCC (a summary of this report is in SACVN minutes, 29 September 1965).

20. Ibid.

21. On 6 October 1965, the Division of Overseas Missions also announced expansion of a Mennonite service program in Vietnam, which would be cosponsored by the NCC's CWS and called Vietnam Christian Service (VNCS). Frank Hutchison to David Stowe, 14 October 1965, RG 4, box 33, folder 14, NCC.

22. Senator William Fulbright published *The Arrogance of Power* the following year.

23. DeBenedetti, *American Ordeal*, 124–32.

24. Logevall includes Hans Morgenthau, Walter Lippman, Mike Mansfield, Frank Church, William Fulbright, and several prominent newspapers in this group.

25. DeBenedetti, *American Ordeal*, 124–32.

26. The liberal ecumenical community was dividing between ecumenists and new breed activists, and between the social justice and service/relief wings of the NCC.

27. William Sloane Coffin Jr. to EE, 7 October 1965; and "Americans for Reappraisal of Far Eastern Policy Statement of Purpose," October 1965; both in RG 5, box 21, folder 17, NCC.

28. A. J. Muste to Bennett, 15 October 1965, DG 50, box 52, Muste Papers, reel 89.31, SCPC.

29. Gibson Winter, "A Theology of Demonstration," *CC*, 13 October 1965, 1249–52.

30. Elston interview, 22 October 1992.

31. The NSCF was a federation of SCM groups.

32. Leonard Clough, "The National Student Christian Federation: A Bridge between Independent Organizations and a Unified Movement," *Journal of Ecumenical Studies* 32.3 (Summer 1995), 331; Elston interview, 13 October 1992.

33. Elston interview, 13 October 1992; Sixth World Order Study Conference, survey results, RG 6, box 28, folder 19, NCC.

34. Kyle Haselden, editorial, "Red China at St. Louis," *CC*, 3 November 1965, 1343–44.

35. I could not find a copy of Kenneth Thompson's background paper, but other articles he authored echoed a strong traditional anticommunist perspective. Hulsether also describes Thompson as a "hawk" in 1966, and one increasingly "out of step" with his colleagues both at the Council and on the *Christianity and Crisis* editorial board. See Hulsether, *Building*, 126–27.

36. Sixth World Order Study Conference, survey results, RG 6, box 28, folder 19, NCC.

37. The Methodist Church sent a large delegation of 124 persons. Since its bishops and general board selected the vast majority of those sent, and since the bishops, especially, tended to be critical of U.S. Vietnam policy, their delegation was likely strongly bent toward action against the war. See Will memo to Ward, 1965, CS, box 32, 1442-2-3:31, GCAH.

38. Sixth World Order Study Conference, survey results, RG 6, box 28, folder 19, NCC. Also Haselden, "Red China at St. Louis," and Final Recommendations, Sixth World Order Study Conference, section 3, 23 October 1965, RG 4, box 33, folder 17, NCC.

39. Final Report, Sixth World Order Study Conference, section 2, 23 October 1965, RG 4, box 33, folder 17, NCC.

40. Meeting of the General Committee International Affairs Commission, minutes, NCC, 29 October 1965, ERWP, CDG-A, box 3, SCPC.

41. Elston interview, 13 October 1992.

42. E. Raymond Wilson to Maxwell and Kramer, 15 November 1965, RG 6, box 28, folder 19, NCC. Wilson said that "The Vietnam statement was achieved by cutting two corners sharply. One was any serious judgment of the war. The second was any adequate recognition of the great difficulty of settlement and reconstruction." He was disappointed that the conference was "short on humility" and on advice to the churches to advance peace.

43. Howard Schomer, "Genesis and Validity of This Mission, NCC Advisory Committee on Peace," 14 January 1969, RG 6, box 26, folder 11, NCC.

44. Final Recommendations, Sixth World Order Study Conference, section 3, 23 October 1965, RG 4, box 33, folder 17, NCC.

45. Elston interviews.

46. MacLear, *Ten Thousand Day War*, 143.

47. This process is outlined in the General Committee's meeting notes. Minutes of the Meeting of the General Committee, International Affairs Commission, NCC, 30 October 1965, ERWP, CDG-A, box 3, SCPC. It is also outlined in "Chronology Re NCC Activities Related to Viet-Nam," anonymous handwritten notes, SACVN, 1 December 1965, RG 6, box 27, folder 4, NCC.

48. MacCracken was later cited as perpetuating the "politics of charity" problem, contributing to his resignation in 1974. Hostetter and McIntyre, "Politics of Charity," 845–50; also James Wall, "Strategy Conflict at Church World Service," editorial, *CC*, 17 July 1974, 715–16.

49. MacCracken, "CWS and Church-State Relationship," 11 April 1967, RG 8, box 96, folder CWS: Church and State, 1967, NCC. *The National Council of Churches in Christ in the USA: What It Is and What It Does* (New York: NCC, 1965), RG4, box 36, folder 30, NCC. The percentage of the NCC budget generated and used by CWS would grow. See, for example, Rev. R. Odell Brown to EE et al., 6 October 1969, RG 4, box 36, folder 13, NCC.

50. John W. Abbott, "CWS's Mandate: A Look at the Other Side," *CC*, 4 September 1974, 823–24; "The National Council of Churches Under New Management," *Christianity Today*, 26 July 1974, 37.

51. David Hunter, telephone interview, 16 October 1992 (hereafter Hunter interview).

52. MacCracken, "CWS and Church-State Relationship," 11 April 1967, RG 8, box 96, folder CWS: Church and State, 1967, NCC. For another example of CWS's willingness to cooperate with government AID programs in Vietnam, see Farley to Humphrey, 8 November 1965, and its attached report. MacCracken to Howard Kresge, 17 August 1971, RG 8, box 98, folder: AID, NCC. For statistics of relief given, see Stenning, *Church World Service.*

53. See Abbott, "CWS's Mandate," 823–24.

54. See Hostetter and McIntyre, "Politics of Charity"; also Stenning, *Church World Service*, 32.

55. Farley to Humphrey, 8 November 1965, also Farley to Chester Cooper, 16 September 1965, RG 5, box 17, folder 40, NCC.

56. As an example, a 1970 USAID report said: "Starting in 1965, as the U.S. participation in the war effort in Viet Nam piled up momentum, there was U.S. mission acceptance of the premise that Title II food [PL 480] was one of the resources to be used in the massive U.S. support of South Vietnam's counterinsurgency and pacification effort." Berger airgram to USAID office, Department of State, 21 April 1971, AID-US 7-2 Viet S, RG 59, box 587, folder 1/1/70, NAII. An article in *EACC News* stated that "the situation is such that any operation involving the import and transport of supplies and personnel needs the active support and cooperation of the USAID authorities. These facts, together with the near impossibility of working in VC controlled territory, means that any such work of relief in South Vietnam can be interpreted as support of and identification with the war effort." "Saigon Reports over 100,000 New Refugees," *EACC News*, 15 February 1968, in RG 6, box 30, folder 30, NCC.

57. Hostetter and McIntyre, "Politics of Charity."

58. *The National Council . . . What It Is*. See also Pratt, *Liberalization*, 256–57.

59. As an early sign of this split, Frank Hutchison of the DOM visited South Vietnam and returned with a critical report of government activities there. Rev. Frank L. Hutchison to Marcy and Anne, 14 November 1965, RG 6, box 27, folder 1, NCC.

60. The Bangkok consultation actually lasted until 4 December 1965.

61. SACVN minutes, 16 November 1965, NCCWOF.

62. The seven were Norman J. Baugher, Edna Sinclair, Robert W. Mance, Edwin Tuller, David Hunter, David Stowe, and Leonard Kramer. O. Frederick Nolde served as consultant to the NCC and the EACC. William Bradley also served as a consultant. For affiliations and titles, see "Report on Visit of NCC Delegation to Southeast Asia," 17 December 1965, RG 4, box 32, folder 29, NCC (hereafter "Report on NCC Visit").

63. Ibid. Even though one member was female, the NCC delegation's report

spoke only in terms of churchmen and brothers, something typical of the era. In attendee lists, women were generally listed as "Mrs." followed by their husband's full name. The EACC delegation members were Rev. S. Marantika, Rev. H. L. Perkins, U Thaung Tin, Mr. T. B. Simatupang, Mr. Koson Srisang, the Rev. Alan A. Brash, Dr. S. Nababan, and U Kyaw Than. See ibid. for affiliations and titles.

64. Logevall qualifies this by saying that, of this group, only the Australians were unreservedly supportive of U.S. policy in Vietnam. *Choosing War*, 375–414.

65. "Report on NCC Visit."

66. For more on the "Will of Heaven," see the first chapter of Fitzgerald, *Fire in the Lake*.

67. "Report on NCC Visit."

68. Edna Sinclair, personal journal, RG 5, box 17, folder 39, NCC.

69. "Report on NCC Visit."

70. Smith from Norman Baugher, "Report on Vietnam to Executive Committee," General Board, 21 February 1966, RG 4, box 33, folder 26, NCC.

71. David Hunter to Paul Longacre, 21 December 1965, RG 5, box 17, folder 39, NCC; Hunter interview.

72. Kay Longcope, "NCC's General Board Urges Priority for Peacemaking," *Presbyterian Life*, 1 January 1966, 33.

73. "Policy Statement on Viet-Nam," General Board, 3 December 1965, RG 4, box 36, folder 15, NCC. A policy statement comes only from an NCC governing body, that is, the General Board or General Assembly. It is described as "a declaration of conviction or a statement of policy or position, formally approved, for one or more of the following purposes: (a) for guidance of the Council in its program operations; (b) for consideration of the member churches; (c) for the purpose of influencing public opinion." Policy statements must "be concise, concerned with items of major importance, and an expression of substantial preponderance of General Assembly or General Board opinion that the view expressed is a required part of the Council's witness to Jesus Christ." NCC policy statements are nearly always preceded by similar policies established within some of its member denominations. They require a two-thirds majority vote and voting delegates must have at least four weeks to consider the text prior to voting. Resolutions, on the other hand, can be adopted by a Council unit, as well as by the General Board or Assembly. Their purpose is "to provide implementation of previously approved policy or to recommend implementation by constituent members of the Council or its units." Resolutions are "'action' statement[s] rather than a statement of conviction." Resolutions do not have to follow the stricter presentation rules applying to policy statements. For more, see "The Nature of Council Statements" in "Interpretation Manual," Office of Information, 25 April 1961, RG 4, folder 36, box 30, NCC. 74. The day after the policy statement passed, McGeorge Bundy wrote a memo to President Johnson assessing the pros and cons of a bombing pause over North Vietnam. The NCC's recent statement supported a pause, so Bundy wrote, "we have the pronouncement of the National Council of Churches, but it is far from clear that they really represent their congregations." See "Memorandum from the President's Special Assistant for National Security Affairs [McGeorge Bundy] to President Johnson," 4 December 1965, in *Foreign Relations of the United States, 1964–1968*, vol. 3, *Vietnam, June–December 1965*, Department of State Publications 10289, ed. Glenn La Fantasie (Washington, D.C.: U.S. Government Printing Office, 1996), 600.

75. John E. Marvin, "The National Council Statement," *Michigan Christian Advocate*, 16 December 1965, 5, RG 4, box 33, folder 14, NCC.

76. "A Message to the Churches on Viet-Nam," General Board, 3 December 1965, RG 4, box 36, folder 15, NCC.

77. EE memo to Members of the NCC Delegation to Bangkok, 17 December 1965, RG 5, box 17, folder 39, NCC. By February 1966, the NCC had distributed ten thousand copies of the "Statement and Message" to denominations, councils of churches, and related groups. Over a hundred thousand copies had been distributed to a wider variety of groups. For this and other IAC actions between December and February 8, 1966, see "Aspects of International Affairs Commission Activities on the Viet-Nam Question," 8 February 1966, RG 6, box 26, folder 16, NCC.

78. The editors, [Policy Statement and Message] *C&C*, 27 December 1965, 282.

79. Harold Davis to David Hunter, 22 December 1965, RG 5, box 15, folder 33, NCC.

80. See Chappell, in *A Stone of Hope*, who argues that since churches had a hard time finding a convincing biblical argument in favor of segregation, segregationists urged churches simply to see the issue as political and not as church business.

81. See also the Vestry of Christ Episcopal Church in Bluefield, West Virginia, letter to the Executive Council of the Protestant Episcopal Church, 10 January 1966, protesting its membership in the NCC, RG 5, box 15, folder 34, NCC.

82. Rev. Francis W. Hayes Jr., address, St. John's Church, Hampton, Virginia, 10 January 1966, RG 5, box 15, folder 34, NCC.

83. "Statement by the Union of American Hebrew Congregations," November 1965, *Concern*, 1–15 January 1966, 3, RG 6, box 27, folder 1, NCC; "Policy Statement on Vietnam, Synagogue Council of America," January 1966, RG 6, box 30, folder 33, NCC.

84. "Excerpts from the Ecumenical Council's Constitution on 'The Church in the Modern World,'" *Concern*, 1–15 January 1966, 4–5, RG 6, box 27, folder 1, NCC.

85. "Pope Paul VI before the United Nations General Assembly," October 4, 1965, *Concern*, 1–15 January 1966, 5–6, RG 6, box 27, folder 1, NCC.

86. The American Catholic Church, with its many immigrant members, feared appearing unpatriotic on Vietnam. Being tied to Rome, it did not have the same freedom to speak independently as American Protestant bodies. Complicating matters, too, was the fact that many of the South Vietnamese who supported U.S. military involvement there were Catholic. Despite these issues, which tended to mute Catholic criticism of the war, there were many Catholic individuals who joined antiwar efforts and participated in civil disobedience according to their consciences regardless of the official position of the Catholic Church.

87. "War Hurting Conscience of American Public," Moscow Domestic Service in Russian 2030 GMT, 7 December 1965, USSR International Affairs, RG 4, box 33, folder 14, NCC.

88. "Open Letter to the NCC—From the Japanese Christian Council," *CC*, 6 April 1966, 430. See also "Open Letter to NCCC," April 1966, RG 4, box 33, folder 24, NCC.

89. While I did not uncover the full story behind his resignation, interviewees offered insights. Elston tied it to the rising call for a different approach to international affairs than Maxwell's, which gained voice at the sixth conference. RSB hypothesized that Maxwell did not seem ready or able to draw the denominations into ecumenical dialogue on Vietnam. Geyer recalled that Maxwell had had a "broad, inclusive agenda

on international affairs" that involved projects on a wide range of foreign policy issues. When people pushed for greater focus on the war, Maxwell resisted, fearing that his other projects might be subsumed. Geyer saw Maxwell as simply "protecting something that he created." Geyer also saw Maxwell as a victim of the increasingly shrill, harsh rhetoric within the antiwar movement. Geyer interview.

90. Kramer left around 15 July 1966, and Ferwerda departed the Washington office around 1 October 1966. See David Hunter, memo to EE, 19 May 1966, RG 5, box 16, folder 12, NCC; Jim Hamilton to Harriet Spangler, 14 November 1966, RG 4, box 33, folder 34, NCC.

6—BUILDING AN ECUMENICAL PEACE WITNESS, 1966

1. McNamara, *In Retrospect*, 226–230. See also Rusk, *As I Saw It*, 464.

2. Mueller telegram to LBJ, 30 December 1965, RG 4, box 33, folder 15, NCC.

3. Hulsether, *Building*, 130.

4. Elston interview, 11 December 1991; Fernandez interview, 31 October 1991; Hall, *Because of Their Faith*, 15–23.

5. Founders included John Bennett, William Sloane Coffin, Richard John Neuhaus, David Hunter, Martin Luther King Jr., Reinhold Niebuhr, Philip Berrigan, Kyle Haselden, Wayne Cowan, Eugene Carson Blake, Harold Row, and Abraham Heschel. Hall, *Because of Their Faith*, 15–17. William Sloane Coffin, draft letter to fellow clergy, 17 January 1966; press release, CCAV, 18 January 1966; both in RG 5, box 13, folder 31, NCC.

6. "Clergy Concerned About Vietnam," *CC*, 26 January 1966, 99–100.

7. David Hunter, memo to EE, 28 January 1966, RG 4, box 33, folder 26, NCC.

8. H. Leroy Brininger, memo to S. Feke and H. Newton Hudson, 19 January 1966, RG 4, box 34, folder 8, NCC. In May 1967 the financial and staff relationship between the NCC and CALCAV changed to some degree. See David Hunter, memo to The Executive Committee, CALCAV, 29 May 1967, RG 4, box 34, folder 8, NCC.

9. Flemming et al., night letter to Rusk, 24 January 1966, RG 5, box 21, folder 16, NCC. See also David Hunter's handwritten notes, 21 January 1966, RG 6, box 25, folder 1, NCC.

10. *Washington Post*, 31 January 1966, cited in McNamara, *In Retrospect*, 229.

11. "Renewed Bombing Paralyzes Security Council," *CC*, 16 February 1966, 196.

12. NCC Program Cabinet minutes, 19 January 1966, RG 4, box 33, folder 29, NCC; David Hunter, memo to Coates et al., 18 January 1966, RG 6, box 26, folder 16, NCC; SACVN Minutes, 8 February, 1966, RG 6, box 27, folder 3, NCC; "IV. Background Material," 21 February 1966, RG 4, box 33, folder 26, NCC.

13. Smith to Rusk, 24 January 1966, RG 6, box 26, folder 16, NCC; Hunter memo to SACVN, 11 February 1966, RG 4, box 33, folder 26, NCC.

14. J. Irwin Miller, in "Background Paper for General Board, IV," in "IV. Background Material," 21 February 1966, RG 4, box 33, folder 26, NCC.

15. Ibid.

16. Priority Program for Peace ("Peace Priority Program"), General Board, 24 February 1966, 3 March 1966, RG 4, box 35, folder 27, NCC.

17. General Board minutes, 22–25 February 1966, RG 3, box 4, folder 4, NCC. Regarding budget, see also Advisory Committee on Peace minutes, 28 March 1966; and Contributions from Member Denominations, Schedule D, Priority Program on

Peace and Church Center at United Nations, 18 May 1966; both in RG 4, box 33, folder 26, NCC. Unsigned letter to Lydia Stokes, 11 April 1967; Donald Landwer memo to EE, 20 September 1967; and EE letter to Mrs. S. Emlen Stokes, 21 September 1967; all in RG 4, box 34, folder 6, NCC.

18. General Board minutes, 22–25 February 1966, page 5, RG 3, box 4, folder 4, NCC.

19. Ibid, 2.

20. The proposal was drafted quickly, by a Committee of Seven, to meet the General Board deadline. As a result, members of the NCC "constituency were not adequately involved in that necessarily hasty process." Colin Williams to Jon Regier, 25 March 1966, RG 6, box 27, folder 3, NCC.

21. Priority Program for Peace, General Board, 24 February 1966, 3 March 1966, RG 4, box 35, folder 27, NCC.

22. For the Advisory Committee on Peace membership list (and their affiliations), see Priority Program for Peace Progress Report, as of June 1966, RG 4, box 33, folder 26, NCC.

23. "Rights and Responsibilities of Debate, Diversity and Dissent," policy statement, General Board, NCC, 22 February 1966, NCCNYO.

24. Smylie, "The China Issue."

25. The February General Board passed a resolution on Vietnam that reaffirmed its December policy statement while emphasizing aspects that came to seem more significant as the war evolved. The statement stressed the difficulty of being loyal to both God and nation. "Resolution on Viet-Nam," NCC General Board, 24 February 1966, NCCNYO.

26. Report to [*sic*] the executive director to General Board, Commission on Religion and Race, 22–25 February 1966, RG 4, box 33, folder 31, NCC.

27. Niebuhr, "Christian Journal," 11–13; John Bennett, "From Supporter of War in 1941 to Critic in 1966," *C&C*, 21 February 1966, 13–14.

28. Judy Austin, informal discussions with author, April–May 2007, Boise, Idaho. Austin sat at the Bennetts' table.

29. "Humphrey's Dilemma," *CC*, 16 March 1966, 325–26.

30. REB, telephone interview with author, 9 March 2007. (Bobby is RSB's eldest son.)

31. Eugene Carson Blake, "The Church in the Next Decade," *C&C*, 21 February 1966, 15–18.

32. Everett H. Jones to David Hunter, 28 February 1966, RG 5, box 15, folder 34, NCC.

33. EE to W. A. Visser 't Hooft, 14 March 1966, RG 4, box 33, folder 34, NCC.

34. REB interview.

35. Ibid. RSB did this while working for the WCC in New York.

36. RSB interview, 5 August 1993.

37. RSB interviews.

38. Ibid. See also RSB, *Spirituality*, 48–127.

39. RSB, "Transition in the American Identity," *CC*, 1 January 1969, 11–14; RSB, "Christian Opposition to the Indochina War," General Board, 10 June 1972, RG 6, box 26, folder 1, NCC; RSB, "What Kind of People Are We?" *C&C*, 23 June 1969, 176–78; RSB, "Let American Ecumenism"; RSB, *Spirituality*.

40. Minutes, Social Education and Action Section, DCLM, NCC Washington

Office, September 5–6, 1968, CS, box 7, 1439-3-1:36, GCAH. Scholars like Ngo Vinh Long and H. Bruce Franklin have illustrated in their research that the United States did indeed entertain imperialistic commercial designs for Southeast Asia.

41. RSB interviews.

42. Ibid.; RSB, "Sunday Morning Sermon," 24 April 1966, RG 4, box 33, folder 19, NCC.

43. REB interview. He described his father as a wonderful pastor and preacher but also as a "complete fish out of water" at the Rochester church. His father needed to get back into the ecumenical action.

44. RSB interview, 6 August 1993.

45. As examples, see the Denominational Staff Council memo to the Advisory Committee on Peace, 21 April 1966, RG 6, box 27, folder 3, NCC; Herman Will to David Hunter, 13 May 1996, RG 5, box 21, folder 16, NCC.

46. RSB to Colin Williams, 30 October, 17 November 1967, both in RG 6, box 27, folder 6, NCC; Leonard Sweet, "The Modernization of Protestant Religion in America," in Lotz, *Altered Landscapes*, 25–33; Elston interviews. See also Gordon L. Anderson, "The Evolution of the Concept of Peace in the Work of the National Council of Churches," *Journal of Ecumenical Studies* 21 (Fall 1984): 730–54.

47. RSB interviews; REB interview.

48. "Warns Against Danger of 'Empty' Ecumenicity," *Christian Advocate*, 1 July 1965, 23.

49. Elston interviews.

50. Priority Program for Peace progress report, June 1966, RG 4, box 33, folder 26, NCC. Whereas new breed clergy tended to define "A good church not [as] a believing church but [as] a working church" (Sweet, "Modernization of Protestant Religion," 33), RSB knew it must be both. See RSB, *Spirituality*, 62–63. So did Dieter Hessel of the United Presbyterian Church's Office of Church and Society. Hessel's book, *Reconciliation and Conflict: Church Controversy over Social Involvement* (Philadelphia: Westminster Press, 1969), reflects similar perspectives. Some liberal church executives did emphasize theological understanding.

51. RSB interviews; RSB, "Sunday Morning Sermon," 24 April 1966, RG 4, box 33, folder 19, NCC; RSB, *Spirituality*, 129–39, 149–52. Michael Corbett and Julia Mitchell Corbett, in *Politics and Religion in the United States* (New York: Garland Publishing, 1999), 347, 356–57, distinguish between the "witnessing" and "winning" models of religious lobbying. RSB embodies the witnessing model.

52. RSB to Kurtis Naylor, 8 September 1966, RG 5, box 16, folder 12, NCC.

53. RSB interviews, 6, 9 August 1993.

54. Will memo to Ward, 26 July 1965, CS, box 33, 1444-2-1:08, GCAH; Kenneth G. Neigh, "Don't Tear down the Wall," *Monday Morning*, November 1966 (special issue): 4–15.

55. The Church of the Brethren's Resolutions on the Vietnam War and China, 25 March 1966, RG 6, box 30, folder 32, NCC; Settje, *Faith and War.*

56. Geyer interview. For example, Methodist Herman Will argued adamantly with his boss Dudley Ward against cutting his budget in order to transfer funds into the NCC's Peace Priority Program. Ward forced his hand, replying, "If the Division of Peace is to maintain initiative in peace work ecumenically, it will need to be related directly and with cash to the National Council's Program." Will memo to Ward, and Ward's memo back, both 17 May 1966, in CS, box 33, 1444-2-1:43, GCAH.

57. Geyer interview. Geyer also noted that, in general, most denominational international affairs secretaries got along well, enjoying the camaraderie. He mentioned that RSB had been kind and generous to him personally, saying, "I owed him a great deal." Paul Crow, a longtime friend of RSB, connected RSB's difficulties with denominational staff to his ecumenical identity. Paul Crow, conversations with author at American Society of Church History Conference, Louisville, KY, 8–10 May 2003.

58. RSB interviews.

59. Carl G. Karsh, "National Council Mirrors Shifting Church Patterns," *Presbyterian Life*, 15 January 1967, 31.

60. See their exchange of memos cited above, 17 May 1966, in CS, box 33, 1444-2-1:43, GCAH.

61. On cognate funding, see James Findlay, "Glimpses of Recent History: The National Council of Churches, 1974–2004," *Journal of Presbyterian History* 84.2 (2006): 152–69.

62. Herman Will, *A Will for Peace* (Washington, D.C.: General Board of Church and Society of the United Methodist Church, 1984), 125.

63. "Wednesdays in Washington," *CC*, 27 April 1966, 518.

64. A Call to Commitment through the Peace Priority Program (New York: United Church of Christ, 15 March 1966).

65. Timothy Light, memo to CCAV Steering Committee, 8 April 1966, RG 5, box 13, folder 31, NCC.

66. Fernandez had protested against nuclear testing in 1957. A graduate of Andover Newton Seminary, he was chaplain at the University of Pennsylvania when CALCAV hired him. Fernandez interviews. "People for Peace: Vietnam Summer Co-Directors," *Vietnam Summer News*, 23 June 1967, 2, in CS, box 23, 1331-7-3:24, "Vietnam Summer," GCAH; Elston interview, 20 October 1992.

67. Both Will and Fernandez called RSB "cautious."

68. Jill K. Gill, "The Politics of Ecumenical Disunity: The Troubled Marriage of Church World Service and the National Council of Churches," *Religion and American Culture* 14.2 (Summer 2004): 175–212; Kinnamon, *Vision*.

69. "WCC Central Committee Speaks Out on Vietnam," *CC*, 2 March 1966.

70. "A Statement on Vietnam," National Inter-Religious Conference on Peace, Washington, D.C., 17 March 1966, RG 6, box 26, folder 16, NCC; Archbishop Iakovos of the Greek Orthodox Church (NCC member) and John Wesley Lord, both active in the NCC, co-chaired this.

71. RSB interview, 6 August 1993.

72. Naylor's specialty and responsibilities were largely with the Middle East and Europe departments. David Stowe, memo to Jon Regier, 3 June 1966, RG 5, box 16, folder 12, NCC; RSB to Paul Anderson, 31 August 1966, RG 6, box 15, folder 25, NCC.

73. Elston interview, 15 October 1992.

74. Elston interview, 11 December 1991. RSB interviews. Naylor memo to RSB, 23 November 1966, RG 6, box 15, folder 25, NCC; Elston appears clean cut in some pictures and bearded in others during his tenure at the NCC.

75. Elston interview, 22 October 1992.

76. RSB interview, 6 August 1993; Hamilton/Parrent interview. Parrent worked with the new head of the NCC Washington office, Jim Hamilton, who took over 1 October 1966 after Ferwerda departed. Jim Hamilton to Harriet Spangler, 14 November 1966, RG 4, box 33, folder 34, NCC.

77. Findlay observed that this team strongly resembled Robert Spike's team in the Commission on Religion and Race, hypothesizing that the CORR may have served as a model.

78. Editorial Board, "We Protest the National Policy in Vietnam," *C&C*, 7 March 1966, 33–34. Butterfield in ibid.

79. "Churches Default COs," *CC*, 30 March 1966, 389.

80. Advisory Committee on Peace minutes, 20 May 1966, RG 6, box 27, folder 3, NCC.

81. Local councils of churches were also a source, but they lacked the influence and access of the denominations; they were also often short-staffed. Generally, they played a minor role assisting with NCC programs on Vietnam.

82. Mueller to Denomination Heads, 22 June 1966, RG 4, box 33, folder 24, NCC.

83. John Coventry Smith thought that most denominations did not do as Mueller encouraged. See Smith to Members of the Division of World Mission and Evangelism Executive Committee, 11 July 1966, RG 6, box 26, folder 16, NCC. Supporting his observation, see Advisory Committee on Peace minutes, 24 August 1966, RG 6, box 27, folder 3, NCC.

84. The Lutheran Church in America's statement on Vietnam in June 1966 did not go as far as the NCC's. See "Memorial #26—Statement on Vietnam, Minnesota Synod, Lutheran Church in America," 28 June 1966, RG 6, box 26, folder 16; Franklin Clark Fry, memo to RSB, 5 July 1966, RG 6, box 30, folder 33, NCC.

85. Franklin Clark Fry to Mueller, 5 July 1966, RG 6, box 26, folder 16, NCC. According to David Settje, the Lutheran Church in America shied away from making church policy statements on the war, fearing division of its membership.

86. Lee Moorehead to Herman Will, 22 January 1965, CS, box 32, 1443-2-3:62, GCAH. For United Methodist periodicals, see *Concern Magazine*, the *Christian Advocate*, and *Together Magazine*; for the Presbyterians, see *Presbyterian Life* and *Monday Morning*. For specific evidence from 1965 and 1966, see the 1 October 1965 issue of *Concern Magazine* for several articles on the war; Edward B. Fiske, "We Must Question the Escalation Mindset," *Presbyterian Life*, 15 February 1966, 30, 32–33; also letter, 3 December 1965, from F. Paige Carlin, managing editor of the *Christian Advocate* and *Together Magazine*, with regard to the huge number of angry laity responding to Herman Will's article on Vietnam in CS, box 33, 1444-2-1:37, GCAH. See sample letters from the following laypersons expressing disgust at both the Methodists' and NCC's published statements on the war: Bertram E. Oughton to Ward, 28 December 1966; Erva Davis to Ward, 29 December 1966; R. L. Irmes to Ward, 31 December 1966; all in CS, box 33, 1479-1-1:48, GCAH.

87. DeBenedetti, *American Ordeal*, 154–58.

88. Greek Orthodox statement, in Smith to Members of the Division of World Mission and Evangelism Executive Committee, 11 July 1966, RG 6, box 26, folder 16, NCC. See also "Greek Orthodox Congress Backs United States Viet Nam Policy," press release, Greek Orthodox Archdiocese of North and South America, 1 July 1966, NCC.

89. Naylor to RSB, 15 July 1966, RG 6, box 26, folder 16, NCC.

90. RSB to Naylor, 20 July 1966, RG 6, box 26, folder 16, NCC.

91. Advisory Committee on Peace minutes, 24 August 1966, RG 6, box 27, folder 3, NCC.

92. Elston interview, 20 October 1992.

93. Geyer interview.

94. Advisory Committee on Peace minutes, 24 August 1966, RG 6, box 27, folder 3, NCC.

95. "World Council: Radical New Voice," *Time,* 5 August 1966, 69. Some scholars have claimed the Russian Orthodox Church served as a conduit for KGB infiltration of the WCC; they have also claimed that the Russians urged the WCC to focus more on human rights violations within colonialism than the oppressive nature of communist governments. See *The Churches, South Africa, and the Political Context,* ed. Gerhard Besier (London: Duncker and Humblot, 1999). The Russian Orthodox Church was also a member of the NCC, but I found no evidence that anything of this nature occurred within the NCC. The Russian Orthodox Church was largely a nonplayer within the NCC on Vietnam.

96. "World Council: Radical New Voice," *Time,* 5 August 1966, 69; Wayne Cowan, "Church and Society at Geneva," *C&C,* 19 September 1966, 201–3. See also Robert D. Bulkley, "Comments on World Conference on Church and Society," *Monday Morning,* 12 September 1966, 2, 7–10.

97. Logevall, *Choosing War,* says that, privately, Britain opposed U.S. policy in Vietnam.

98. Rt. Rev. Dr. Kenneth Sansbury to EE, 16 September 1966, RG 6, box 26, folder 15, NCC; Discussion on RSB's Paper, 14 September 1966, RG 6, box 18, folder 1, NCC; Rev. Paul Oestreicher, Vietnam, Consultation of British, U.S. and Canadian International Affairs Departments, 14–16 September 1966, RG 6, box 26, folder 15, NCC.

99. Final Itinerary for RSB, Sarah Marguk Travel Service, New York, 19 September 1966, RG 6, box 16, folder 16, NCC.

100. Tapes of RSB's Asian Trip, September–October 1966, RG 6, box 16, folder 16, NCC.

101. RSB to Naylor, 10 October 1966, RG 6, box 16, folder 16, NCC; RSB interview, 6 August 1966.

102. Elston interview, 20 October 1967.

103. H. Burgelin to the chairman, Commission on International Affairs, 13 February 1967, RG 6, box 26, folder 14, NCC.

104. CCIA Central Committee statement of February 1966, in O. Frederick Nolde to RSB, 2 March 1967, RG 6, box 26, folder 14, NCC.

105. Herman Will told me that the Methodist Church had the solid support of its people when it criticized America's Vietnam policy. I did not get this sense from the records I perused.

106. Alan Geyer, "Viet-Nam and the American Churches," Consultation of British, U.S. and Canadian International Affairs Departments, 14–16 September 1966, RG 4, box 33, folder 26, NCC.

107. Ibid. Other church leaders, such as John Bennett, did not think the divisions were that severe within progressive church circles and thought Geyer may be reflecting too much upon divisions within his own agency. John Bennett, On Vietnam, Consultation of British, U.S. and Canadian International Affairs Departments, 14–16 September 1966, RG 4, box 33, folder 26, NCC.

108. RSB felt Americans were overly inclined to tell people what to do and think, thus the importance of consultations, listening ministries, and conferences. RSB, "Christian Witness in International Affairs," General Assembly, December 1966, RG 2, box 4, folder 12, NCC.

109. David Hunter, memo to EE, 31 October 1966; EE memo to RSB, 31 October 1966; Jon Regier, memo to RSB, 1 November 1966; all in RG 6, box 18, folder 1, NCC.

110. They also wanted to mobilize congressional districts, with the hope that moving Congress might erode the president's ability to wage war. Shaw noted that protests didn't seem to affect members of Congress, but constituent pressure did. See Rodney Shaw to Fernandez, August 26, 1966, CS, box 34, 1444-2-2:11, GCAH.

111. Robert Fangmeier to RSB, 11 October 1966, RG 6, box 18, folder 1, NCC.

112. Oren Baker to EE, 4 October 1966, RG 6, box 26, folder 15, NCC.

113. Naylor to Baker, 27 October 1966, ibid.

114. Robert Bulkley to Ward, 2 September 1966, ibid.

115. Kramer once explained to a concerned pastor the NCC's motivations when it produced controversial statements on Vietnam. "We are not trying to make up anybody's mind for them, but we are interested in having people use their minds. We are not trying to have people agree with us but we are trying to have people focus on the questions." Kramer to Rev. Howard H. Groover, 14 July 1966, RG 6, box 26, folder 16, NCC.

116. Will interview, 3 December 1995.

117. For more details, see Naylor memo to David Hunter, 28 September 1966, NCC. See also David Hunter to Fernandez, 26 September 1966, RG 5, box 13, folder 31, NCC; Fernandez to constituency, October 1966, CALC Records, box 2, series 2, SCPC.

118. De Benedetti, *American Ordeal*, 156; Robert Greenblatt to "friend," November 1966, RG 6, box 26, folder 15, NCC.

119. "Reading Election Tea Leaves," *CC*, 23 November 1966, 1431.

120. Fernandez to denominational leaders and peace groups, 29 November 1966, RG 5, box 13, folder 31, NCC; "Vietnam: Challenge to Conscience," FCNL minutes, 23 November 1966, RG 6, box 26, folder 15, NCC.

121. RSB, "Christian Witness in International Affairs," General Assembly, December 1966, RG 2, box 4, folder 12, NCC.

122. Ibid.

123. Ibid.; General Assembly minutes, 8 December 1966, RG 2, box 4, folder 12, NCC.

124. Will, *A Will for Peace*, 129–30. See also NCC, General Assembly, *An Appeal to the Churches Concerning Vietnam* (New York: Council Press, NCC, 9 December 1966).

125. Kyle Haselden, "NCC Holding Operation," *CC*, 21 December 1966, 1562–64. See "Danger on the Home Front," *CC*, 25 January 1967, 99–100; also Harold Bosley "letter to the editor" [Haselden], 3 January 1967, RG 6, box 26, folder 14, NCC. Bosley described the assembly's reaction to Graham as coming "close to being a complete betrayal of the National Council's avowed concern to formulate an intelligent approach to the problems being put to faith by an increasingly critical world." Inviting Graham was controversial, but the move appealed to laity who felt that mainline leaders judged Graham too harshly. Graham received considerable flack from his own evangelical constituency for attending the "modernist" NCC's assembly. And EE fended off criticism from mainline Protestants for inviting Graham. The two shared their amusement over this with one another. See Graham to EE, 4 January 1967, RG 4, box 33, folder 41, NCC; EE to Graham, 9 January 1967, RG 4, box 33, folder 41, NCC; also Vice President Hubert Humphrey

in Press Conference, press release GA C-25, 8 December 1966, RG 2, box 4, folder 16, NCC. Graham's willingness to attend illustrated his own personal collegiality toward his more liberal brethren. Interacting with recognized mainline Protestant leaders also helped lend evangelicals sought-after cultural respectability. George Marsden, *Religion and American Culture* (1990; Orlando: Harcourt, 2001), 226–27.

126. Bennett to Haselden, 22 December 1966, RG 6, box 26, folder 14, NCC.

127. RSB to Dr. David L. Stitt, 4 January 1967, RG 6, box 26, folder 14, NCC; *An Appeal to the Churches Concerning Vietnam,* New York: Council Press, 9 December 1966, 10. RSB did not like Haselden's article on the assembly.

128. "The NCC Elite: A Breakdown of Beliefs," *Christianity Today,* 21 July 1967, 46–47; "A Study Report on the Miami Assembly," NCC, 6 May 1967, RG 2, box 4, folder 15, NCC.

129. Topics of Major Concern to the General Public Writing to the National Council's Department of Information, January–December 1966, RG 3, box 4, NCC.

130. EE to the Honorable Burke Marshall, 5 December 1966; EE to the Honorable Robert McNamara, 9 December 1966; both in RG 4, box 33, folder 32, NCC.

131. General Assembly minutes, 2–3 December 1966, RG 3, box 4, folder 4, NCC; "Students Merge Religious Groups," *New York Times,* 11 September 1966, RG 5, box 15, folder 60, NCC. The UCM general secretary, Leonard Clough, said in this article, "Students aren't attracted to a denominational organization anymore. . . . But they are interested in social action, in international affairs and other issues, and we are interested in making the resources of the churches available to them." For more on the history of the broad and multifaceted Student Christian Movement, including the UCM, see an entire special issue of the *Journal of Ecumenical Studies* 32.3 (Summer 1995) devoted to this topic. On the UCM in particular, see especially articles by Leonard Clough, 319–34, and Paul E. Schrading, 340–52.

132. See Sara M. Evans, ed., *Journeys that Opened Up the World: Women, Student Christian Movements, and Social Justice, 1955–1975* (New Brunswick, NJ: Rutgers University Press, 2003), 129–38. For more on the UCM's vision and purposes, see "An Open Letter from the Central Committee of the NSCF," 30 April 1966; and "Official Revised Version as Voted by Central Committee 4/29/66 Articles of Operations of the University Christian Movement in the USA"; both in Elston files, box 35, SCPC. Students were rebelling against existing church structures in a variety of ways. As examples, see "New Structures and Guidelines for Mission," *Presbyterian Life,* 15 June 1967, 30; "A Mood of Questing," *Christian Advocate,* 14 January 1965, 2.

133. When Arthur Flemming was elected NCC president, the professor of political science was also serving as president of the University of Oregon. He was a Methodist layperson long involved in FCC and NCC leadership. His government experience included serving as secretary of health, education and welfare in Eisenhower's cabinet (1958–1961) and as director of the Office of Defense Mobilization (1953–1957), in which he also operated as a member of the National Security Council. He served as a member of Eisenhower's Advisory Committee on Government Organization (1953–1961) and as a member of the International Civil Service Advisory Board (1950–1964). During World War II, he was for three years a member of the War Manpower Commission and worked as chair of the Labor-Management Manpower Policy Committee. One Cleveland newspaper editor stated that "Arthur Flemming . . . practically carried on his shoulders the whole personnel problem of the American government at war. . . . Few men outside the armed forces made so great a

contribution to the prosecution of the war. No college president in the United States knows as much about the practical working of the government." Since 1961, Flemming had also served as a member of the National Advisory Committee of the Peace Corps. He was a member of the U.S. Civil Service Commission (1939–1948) and chair of the advisory committee on personnel management of the Atomic Energy Commission (1943–1953). He also served as a member of the first and second Hoover commissions on organization of the executive branch of the government. All the above is from NCC press releases GA C-7, GA C-10, RG 2, box 4, folder 16, NCC.

134. Arthur Goldberg, in EE telegram to Church Officials throughout the USA, 27 December 1966, RG 6, box 26, folder 15, NCC.

135. Flemming and EE, telegram to LBJ, 20 December 1966, RG 6, box 26, folder 15, NCC.

136. "Activities on 20 December 1966 and Following Concerning Vietnam," 22 December 1966; and RSB to approximately 590 heads of councils of churches with volunteer staffs, 27 December 1966; both in RG 6, box 26, folder 15, NCC.

137. For examples of earlier appeals, see Lee Edwin Walker (United Presbyterian) to EE, 5 January 1967; Robert Bulkley, telegram to Judicatory Executives and Christian Education Field Directors, United Presbyterian Church, 27 December 1966; Herman Will (Methodist), Methodist Action on Vietnam Appeal of the National Council of Churches, 6 January 1967; Roy Short to Flemming, 28 December 1966; Fangmeier (Disciples of Christ) to EE, 30 December 1966; all in RG 6, box 30, folder 19, NCC. For more summaries of denominational responses to the NCC telegrams as well as to the appeal for debate and action, see Ad Hoc Meeting on Vietnam Action, Notes in Lieu of Minutes, 7 January 1967, RG 6, box 26, folder 14, NCC.

138. Will, *A Will for Peace*, 128–29. See also RSB, "Record of Activities of 31 December 1966 Concerning Vietnam," 5 January 1967, RG 6, box 26, folder 15, NCC.

139. Geyer interview. Will, *A Will for Peace*, 130–31. See Rusk's account in *As I Saw It*; and Herring, *Longest War*, 166–68.

7—SPARKING DEBATE AND ACTION, 1967

1. "Reporting the Ad Hoc Meeting on Vietnam Action, Notes in Lieu of Minutes," 7 January 1967, RG 6, box 26, folder 14, NCC. Appendix A lists those who attended; Appendix D describes "Strategy Suggestions for Action on Vietnam"; Appendix E is a telegram sent January 9 to LBJ signed by sixty-six meeting attendees expressing strong support for Goldberg's and U Thant's peace initiatives. See also RSB, letter to "The approximately 200 people the telegrams went to," 22 December 1966, RG 6, box 26, folder 15, NCC.

2. Harold Row to Naylor, 10 January 1967; "Reporting the Ad Hoc Meeting on Vietnam Action, Notes in Lieu of Minutes," 7 January 1967; both in RG 6, box 26, folder 14, NCC.

3. *A Multi-Media Album to Encourage Debate and Action on Vietnam* (New York: Council Press, NCC, 1967); "Now Available: A Multi-Media Album to Help in Discussing the National Council of Churches 'Appeal for Debate and Action' on Vietnam," February 1967, RG 6, box 26, folder 14, NCC; Elston memo to MacCracken, 10 April 1967, RG 6, box 26, folder 13, NCC; Elston memo to Participants in Ad Hoc Meeting on Vietnam, etc., 12 May 1967, RG 6, box 30, folder 23; David Hunter, memo to Elston, 15 May 1967, RG 6, box 26, folder 13, NCC.

4. Elston interviews. Elston made these changes before he officially joined the IAC on 1 January 1967.

5. Ibid.

6. Elston to Deborah Brewster, 17 January 1967, RG 6, box 30, folder 13, NCC.

7. Kurtis Naylor, Staff Council—International Affairs, 13 January 1967; for a list of members, see "Staff Council (SADIA) Members as of 20 January 1967"; both in RG 6, box 15, folder 3, NCC.

8. "Summary Notes of a Strategy Meeting Held in the Interchurch Center," 6 January 1967, RG 6, box 26, folder 19, NCC. See also Elston to Rabbi Henry Siegman, 26 January 1967, RG 6, box 30, folder 33, NCC.

9. "Notes for Further Discussion which Arise from an Interview with the Secretary of State by Ernest A. Gross, Kenneth W. Thompson, and Robert S. Bilheimer," 9 January 1967, RG 6, box 25, folder 1, NCC. See also Margaret Bender, memo to Bishop Lloyd Wicke, 8 May 1967, CS, box 23, 1441-7-3:19, GCAH.

10. "Notes for Further Discussion," 9 January 1967, RG 6, box 25, folder 1, NCC. Harry Seamans, the NGO's contact person in the State Department, admitted to Naylor that, after the meeting, Rusk felt uneasy about how open he had been with the church leaders, as if he might have breached some line of security. See Naylor memo to RSB, 11 January 1967, RG 6, box 25, folder 1, NCC.

11. Referring to the lack of common presuppositions, Regier wrote RSB saying, "The frightening aspect of this gap is that there is also an enormous gap even between the World Council of Churches and National Council of Churches and the parallels of poverty and discrimination in the USA and the peoples of so many of the emerging nations. Is there any wonder that the gap compounded makes a mockery out of a war on poverty and the war in Vietnam?" See Regier, confidential memo to RSB, 27 January 1967, RG 6, box 25, folder 1, NCC.

12. "Notes for Further Discussion," 9 January 1967; see also Ernest Gross to RSB, 23 January 1967; both in RG 6, box 25, folder 1, NCC.

13. RSB, "Christian Witness in International Affairs," General Assembly, December 1966, RG 2, box 4, folder 12, NCC. RSB, "Achievements and Hopes of the Peace Priority Program: A Progress Report from the Director of International Affairs," General Board, 20–24 February 1967, RG 4, box 33, folder 44, NCC. Dieter Hessel, a Presbyterian church executive, also emphasized the need to explore presuppositions. See Dieter Hessel, "Probing Vietnam Policy," *Monday Morning*, 27 February 1967, 3–6; also RSB, "Vietnam: The Fundamental Issue," 7–10, in the same issue.

14. "Conscientious Objection to Military Service," policy statement, General Board, 23 February 1967, NCCNYO.

15. For more information, see Hall, *Because of Their Faith*, 44–45; DeBenedetti, *American Ordeal*, 181–85; Elston to Philip Farnham, 8 May 1967, RG 6, box 26, folder 13, NCC.

16. For example, see Barton Hunter, memo to Dale Fiers, 17 March 1967, RG 6, box 26, folder 13, NCC; Fiers to EE, 24 March 1967, RG 4, box 34, folder 8, NCC; Grover Hartmann to RSB, 12 April 1967, RG 6, box 26, folder 13, NCC.

17. See the Negotiations Now! flier dated 28 March 1967, listing the names of the guiding committee members, which included Bennett, Elston, Heschel, Row, Will, and several others. RG 6, box 26, folder 13, NCC. See also "Negotiations Now! Claims Broad Backing for Moderate Appeal," *Vietnam Summer News*, 25 August 1967, 12, CS, box 23, 1441-7-3:24, GCAH. Planning for a grand Spring Mobilization was in full

swing. See RSB to top twenty-five church leaders, 21 March 1967, RG 6, box 26, folder 14, NCC.

18. Three divisions within the national church (the Women's Division, World Division, and Peace and World Order Division) collaborated toward this end with considerable energy. Several local councils of churches also were responsive to circulating the NCC's materials.

19. A "district" is a local judicatory area comprised of staff members who oversee a collection of Methodist congregations within a local area. Several districts make up a single regional annual conference.

20. See Will memo to Ward, 27 March 1967, CS, box 33, 1444-2-1:43, GCAH. "Two Boards Launch Viet Nam Emphasis," *Christian Advocate*, 13 July 1967, 21. Vietnam Emphasis materials, February 1967; "Memorandum on Proposed Joint Action Program on Vietnam," 6 March 1967; Rodney Shaw, Carl Soule, and Herman Will to Conference Chairmen, 5 May 1967; and Margaret Bender to Will, 29 June 1967; all in CS, box 23, 1441-7-3:21, GCAH.

21. Hall summarizes several denominational positions from spring 1967 in *Because of Their Faith*, 46–47.

22. See minutes in RG 6, box 15, folder 3, NCC; Elston to Stewart Meacham, 21 March 1967, RG 6, box 26, folder 14, NCC; Naylor to Rev. George Wilson, 6 April 1967, RG 6, box 26, folder 13, NCC. See also a listing of NCC interactions with local and regional church councils on Vietnam from December 1966 through June 1968 on two separate lists in RG 6, box 27, folders 5 and 6, NCC. For a list of nine Vietnam meetings sponsored by church councils with the help of the NCC, see Correspondence with Councils of Churches, RG 6, box 27, folder 5, NCC.

23. Elston, "Debate and Action on Vietnam: The Situation in the Churches," Appendix 2, 13 February 1967, RG 6, box 26, folder 14, NCC. Biheimer failed to get church leaders in Missouri to arrange a Vietnam discussion meeting. "The basic reason is that they do not feel they could get a large meeting together because of a basic lack of concern in the churches about Vietnam, or else because there are not sufficient people who disagree with the government. It is, I believe, a pretty serious and deepgoing situation." RSB to Fangmeier, 8 March 1967, RG 6, box 15, folder 3, NCC.

24. Elston interview, 20 October 1992; Elston memo to Naylor, 11 April 1967, RG 6, box 26, folder 13, NCC.

25. See also Hessel, *Reconciliation*, 8–9.

26. Wuthnow and Evans stress this point, in *Quiet Hand of God*.

27. Alfred Hero, "Christian Churches and World Affairs, United Presbyterian Consultation," 7–8 March 1967, RG 6, box 22, folder 17, NCC.

28. Ed Grant to EE, 8 March 1967, RG 4, box 35, folder 15, NCC. See also Marshall C. Dendy to EE, 4 March 1967, RG 4, box 34, folder 4, NCC.

29. EE to Grant, 22 March 1967, RG 4, box 35, folder 15, NCC. Also R. H. Edwin Espy, interview by author, 26 August 1991, in Doylestown, Pennsylvania. A biographical document given to the author by EE, titled "R. H. Edwin Espy World Ecumenist Led the National Council," says, "[I]n the public mind the civil rights movement, the recognition of the People's Republic of China, student uprisings, anti-Vietnam war demonstrations and other controversial issues which were more visible tended to distort the perception of the Council among much of the churches' membership. Yet the national leadership of the member churches were firm in their support of the Council and of course controlled its policies."

30. This consultation was part of a new one-year United Presbyterian Church program called the Institute on the Church and International Responsibility (ICIR), which would complement the NCC's Peace Priority Program. See its description attached to the March consultation's meeting notes: "Peace Seeking through Voluntary Organizations: What and How Can the Church Contribute?" Consultation, Office of Social Education and Evangelism, United Presbyterian Church, USA, 7–8 March 1967, pt. 2, 14, RG 6, box 22, folder 17, NCC.

31. Those who emphasize "winning" want to affect policy first and foremost, and they are willing to strike compromises in order to eek out partial piecemeal wins. Those who emphasize "witnessing" focus on speaking their undiluted truth to power and holding their prophetic vision before the public. Corbett and Corbett, *Politics and Religion*, 347, 356–57.

32. "Peace Seeking through Voluntary Organizations," RG 6, box 22, folder 17, NCC.

33. Will, "How Churches Influence National Policy," 9–10; Editors, "Mandate for Involvement," *Christian Advocate*, 11 January 1968: 2; Hessel, "Probing Vietnam Policy."

34. George W. Bush used the phrase "staying the course" during the Iraq War; for him, the U.S. government's failure to do so in Vietnam was one of its greatest mistakes.

35. Will, "How Churches Influence National Policy"; Hessel, "Probing Vietnam Policy."

36. Will, "How Churches Influence National Policy."

37. Dean Rusk telephone interview with author, 15 January 1992 (hereafter Rusk interview).

38. Rusk to RSB, 27 February 1967, RG 6, box 25, folder 1, NCC.

39. RSB to Flemming, Gross, Thompson, 21 March 1967, RG 6, box 26, folder 14, NCC.

40. Fernandez interview, 31 October 1991; Andrew Young, "Andrew Young," *C&C*, 3 May 1971, 80–81; RSB, interviews; Hall, *Because of Their Faith*, 41–45; DeBenedetti, *American Ordeal*, 172–74.

41. Prior to the Riverside Church speech, on 25 March, King spoke against the war at the Chicago Coliseum, but his speech at the Riverside Church made the largest impact and drew much attention.

42. Fernandez interviews.

43. Hall, *Because of Their Faith*, 42. Fernandez said that he penned that famous phrase "the greatest purveyor of violence in the world today." Fernandez interviews.

44. Ibid., 43–44.

45. DeBenedetti, *American Ordeal*, 173–76.

46. This description is summarized from Hall, *Because of Their Faith*, 45, and DeBenedetti, *American Ordeal*, 182–88. See also Elston memo to Henry Bucher, 20 April 1967, RG 6, box 30, folder 44, NCC. Robert J. Nelson, "Vietnam Summer," *CC*, 24 May 1967, 678–79.

47. Elston to Rev. Richard Mumma, 24 April 1967; Elston memo to Rich Killmer, 20 April 1967; both in RG 6, box 30, folder 44, NCC. See also Elston to Gar Alperovitz, 24 April 1967, RG 6, box 30, folder 4, NCC; Elston memo to SADIA, Department of International Affairs, Councils of Churches, 4 May 1967, RG 6, box 26, folder 13, NCC.

48. "Fernandez Attacks Clergy Silence," *Vietnam Summer News*, 23 June 1967, 2, CS, box 23, 1441-7-3:24, GCAH.

49. Elston interviews. See Robert Pickus to RSB, 22 April 1967, RG 6, box 26, folder 13, NCC.

50. Hall, *Because of Their Faith*, 45–46; DeBenedetti, *American Ordeal*, 182–88.

51. MacCracken memo to RSB, 13 December 1966, RG 5, box 21, folder 17, NCC.

52. David Stowe, memo to RSB et al., 7 April 1967, RG 6, box 26, folder 13, NCC.

53. RSB memo to EE and Tracey K. Jones Jr., 22 March 1967, RG 4, box 33, folder 44, NCC.

54. Will interview, 8 December 1996.

55. Schomer memo to EE, 3 May 1967, RG 6, box 26, folder 13, NCC.

56. Elston interview, 11 December 1991. RSB said Schomer was brilliant, but also difficult to work with. RSB interview, 6 August 1993. Fernandez noted his strong anticommunism. Fernandez interview, 31 October 1991.

57. As an exception, Elston noted that David Stowe, the head of DOM, was "with us," but that MacCracken, however, was perhaps most protective of and tied to relationships with the government.

58. Tracey Jones, memo to David Stowe, 28 April 1967, RG 6, box 26, folder 13, NCC.

59. Frank Hutchison, memo to Mr. John Mullen, 9 February 1967, RG 6, box 26, folder 14, NCC. This perspective also is evident at the denominational level among relief staff. See "Plan for Post-War Vietnam, Churchman Urges," *Presbyterian Life*, 1 January 1968, 24.

60. "Saigon Reports over 100,000 Refugees," *EACC News*, 15 February 1968, RG 6, box 30, folder 30, NCC.

61. Elston memo to Naylor and RSB, 5 April 1967, RG 6, box 26, folder 13, NCC. RSB memo to MacCracken, 21 October 1969; and Schomer memo to MacCracken, 22 October 1969; both in RG 6, box 26, folder 9, NCC.

62. RSB interviews. MacCracken, like RSB a member of the United Presbyterian Church, first came onto the CWS staff as director of its immigration services in 1959.

63. See "A Report to the Consultation on Christian Concerns in Tomorrow's Vietnam," 9 January 1970, RG 6, box 26, folder 8, NCC; Newt Thurber, "Mission in Vietnam—A Report to the Consultation on Christian Concerns in Tomorrow's Vietnam," 5 March 1971, RG 6, box 26, folder 7, NCC. In *Church World Service*, Stenning stresses that CWS always had a policy that emphasized self-help and indigenous control of relief programs once indigenous groups were ready to take over. But the records indicate that only time and debate took the CWS's Commission on Tomorrow's Vietnam in that direction.

64. Clark Clifford, *Counsel to the President: A Memoir* (New York: Anchor Books, 1991), 447.

65. McNamara, *In Retrospect*, 234.

66. "United Presbyterian General Assembly," *CC*, 14 June 1967, 788–90. See also "A Declaration of Conscience," 179th General Assembly, United Presbyterian Church, RG 4, box 34, folder 7, NCC.

67. David Hunter to members of General Secretariat, 15 June 1967, RG 6, box 26, folder 13, NCC.

68. Resolution on Vietnam, NCC General Board, 2 June 1967, NCCNYO.

69. Resolution on Counseling Men Eligible for Military Service, General Board, 2 June 1967. See also General Board minutes, June 1967, RG 3, box 4, folder 6, NCC.

70. RSB, "Objectives and Responsibilities in USA Foreign Policy: A Christian Critique," draft, June 1967, RG 6, box 27, folder 2, NCC.

71. As one example, see Flemming telegram to LBJ, 6 June 1967, RG 4, box 33, folder 40, NCC.

72. Naylor memo to Bruce Hanson, 16 January 1969, RG 4, box 35, folder 18, NCC.

73. Bishop George Barrett, journal, June–July 1967, RG 6, box 16, folder 15, NCC.

74. Elston interviews. RSB interviews. Elston and RSB both recalled the details in this section in the same way. RSB, "Confidential Report on Interview with [Rusk]," 4 March 1967; and RSB, notes [from Rusk meeting], 4 April 1967; both in RG 6, box 16, folder 15, NCC.

75. RSB interview, 14 December 1991.

76. Geyer mentioned that Christian relief workers in Vietnam were helping to develop a "theology of the enemy" at this time. It involved the idea that Christian service should not be politically conditioned for those whom the government labels "allies" and "enemies."

77. "Niemoeller Reports on Vietnam," *CC*, 15 February 1967, 215–16.

78. See the State Department documents discussing the NCC's request for State Department assistance in visiting South and North Vietnam in 1967. Barbara Watson of the State Department's Bureau of Security and Consular Affairs recommended to Rusk that he authorize the NCC's request for the reasons summarized here. Rusk initialed approval of the passport request (dated 22 May 1967). See Watson, memo to The Secretary [Dean Rusk], Department of State, 18 May 1967, on the subject of "Validation of Passports for Travel to North Viet-Nam by Study Group from the National Council of Churches," located in Pol. U.S. 27 Viet S, RG 59, box 2784, NAII.

79. Itinerary, 1 August 1967; and Sarah Marquis Travel Service, Itinerary for RSB, 7 June 1967; both in RG 6, box 16, folder 15, NCC.

80. Elston interview, 20 October 1992.

81. RSB interviews; RSB to Blake, 7 June 1967, RG 6, box 16, folder 15, NCC; Elston interviews; RSB to Andre Philip, 14 July 1967, RG 6, box 26, folder 13, NCC. William P. Thompson followed Blake into the State Clerk position in 1965. A devoted ecumenist, Thompson helped create the World Alliance of Reformed Churches in 1970. After the Vietnam War, Thompson served a term as NCC president (1975–1978) and then played a critical role in uniting the northern and southern branches of the Presbyterian Church in 1983. See "William P. Thompson, Presbyterian and ecumenical leader, dies at 87," 27 April 2006, ncccusa.org/news/06051billthompson.html (1 September 2006).

82. RSB to Blake, 7 June 1967, RG 6, box 16, folder 15, NCC; Elston interview, 20 October 1992.

83. Elston interview, 20 October 1992.

84. Barrett journal, 7 June 1967, RG 6, box 16, folder 15, NCC.

85. RSB memo to Naylor, 8 June 1967; EE memo to Naylor, 12 June 1967; both in RG 6, box 16, folder 15, NCC.

86. Naylor memo to RSB, 23 May 1967, RG 6, box 16, folder 15, NCC.

87. Barrett journal, 7, 28 June 1967, RG 6, box 16, folder 15, NCC.

88. See RSB's handwritten appointment schedule, June 1967, RG6, box 16, folder 15, NCC.

89. Russell Johnson to Prince Sihanouk, 6 June 1967, RG 6, box 16, folder 15, NCC. See Thompson's and Barrett's trip notes.

90. William P. Thompson, "Notes on Trip to South East Asia," 15 June–5 July 1967, RG 6, box 16, folder 15, NCC.

91. Barrett journal, 27 June 1967, ibid.

92. Leaman, "Politicized Service."

93. Barrett journal, 29 June, and epilogue, 20 July 1967, RG 6, box 16, folder 15, NCC.

94. I found no evidence to confirm or deny this theory.

95. Mai Van Bo told Schomer (via Paul Tran) that denial of the visas was due to "slow communications." See Schomer memo to RSB, 25 September 1967, RG 6, box 26, folder 13, NCC. RSB made another unsuccessful attempt at visas after release of the NCC's September Resolution on Vietnam. RSB, memo to Flemming, 29 September 1967, RG 6, box 26, folder 13, NCC.

96. RSB interview, 5 August 1993.

97. Barrett journal, 3 July 1967, RG 6, box 16, folder 15, NCC.

98. RSB to William P. Thompson, 28 July 1967, RG 6, box 16, folder 15, NCC.

99. Barrett journal, epilogue, 25 July 1967, ibid.

100. "NCC Delegation to South East Asia Report," 5 July 1967, RG 6, box 26, folder 13, NCC; "NCC Delegation Returns from Vietnam," International Issues, Department of International Affairs, NCC, 21 July 1967, RG 4, box 33, folder 44, NCC. A copy of the report is also in the State Department files, soc 12-1, RG 59, box 3110, NAII.

101. Paul Leatherman, director of Vietnam Christian Service, was also disappointed by the statement. See Paul Leatherman to RSB, 26 July 1967, RG 6, box 16, folder 15, NCC.

102. Ward to RSB, 14 July 1967, RG 6, box 16, folder 15, NCC.

103. RSB to Andre Philip, 14 July 1967, RG 6, box 26, folder 13, NCC.

104. Barrett journal, epilogue, 20 July 1967, RG 6, box 16, folder 15, NCC.

105. Rusk interview.

106. See also Rhodri Jeffreys-Jones, *Peace Now: American Society and the Ending of the Vietnam War* (New Haven: Yale University Press, 1999).

107. Rusk interview.

108. See McNamara, *In Retrospect*, 273–303.

109. Ibid., 284–95.

110. Robert Fangmeier, "Shades of the '50s Haunt the Hoosiers," *CC*, 23 August 1967, 1074.

111. Schomer to Bennett, 10 August 1967, CALC Records, Bennett letters, box 1, series 2, SCPC.

112. RSB to Richard Wood, 30 August 1967, RG 6, box 26, folder 13, NCC.

113. While the war was unpopular, more people favored ending it through escalation rather than through diplomatic means. Roger Shinn, "Whom the Gods Would Destroy . . . ," *C&C*, 18 September 1967, 197–98.

114. Mary Temple to Naylor and Schomer, 26 June 1967, RG 6, box 26, folder 13, NCC. Vietnam Summer volunteers took the petition with them door to door, but

they disliked its rejection of direct action. "Negotiations Now! Claims Broad Backing for Moderate Appeal," *Vietnam Summer News*, 25 August 1967, 12, CS, box 23, 1441-7-3:24, GCAH.

115. Elston memo to RSB, 28 July 1967, RG 6, box 26, folder 13, NCC.

116. Elston memo to SADIA, 21 September 1967, RG 6, box 15, folder 3, NCC. See also Elston to Fangmeier, 3 October 1967, RG 6, box 30, folder 13, NCC.

117. Fangmeier to Elston, 25 September 1967, RG 6, box 30, folder 13, NCC; Harry C. Applewhite to Elston, 6 November 1968, RG 6, box 30, folder 8, NCC.

118. Elston interview, 20 October 1992.

119. Stories broke widely in the press and periodicals. For two examples, see Reinhold Niebuhr, "Politics, Patriotism and Integrity," *C&C*, 20 March 1967, 45–46; Leon Howell, "Growing Up in America," *C&C*, 20 March 1967, 49–52. The NCC learned that three foundations allegedly linked with the CIA had provided some financial assistance to three NCC-related programs. General Board minutes, 21–24 February 1967, RG 3, box 4, folder 6, NCC.

120. Thomas Quigley to RSB, 1 September 1967, RG 6, box 30, folder 32, NCC. See also "Chauvinistic Catholic Charity," *Commonweal*, 10 November 1967, 159–60; Flipse, "Latest Casualty."

121. Ronald Stenning, telephone interview by author, 1 February 1998 (hereafter Stenning interview).

122. Quigley to RSB, 1 September 1967, RG 6, box 30, folder 32, NCC.

123. David Stowe, summary of church-state discussion in NCC, presented to DOM Program Board, 3 March 1967, RG 8, box 96, folder: CWS: Church and State, 1967, NCC; Thomas J. Liggett to MacCracken, 16 February 1972, RG 8, box 98, folder: Denominations, NCC. See MacCracken, "CWS and Church-State Relationship," 11 April 1967, RG 8, box 96, folder CWS: Church and State, 1967, NCC. In the 1950s and early 1960s, CWS projects might receive two-thirds of their funding and supplies from government. Stenning says that, by 1974, CWS had cut PL 480 commodities to 15 percent of its budget, and by 1975 to 10 percent. Stenning, *Church World Service*, 25, 65.

124. Schomer memo to RSB, 13 July 1967, RG 6, box 26, folder 13, NCC.

125. RSB to Rev. Ralph E. Smeltzer, 20 July 1967; and RSB to Blake, 12 July 1967; both in RG 6, box 26, folder 13, NCC.

126. Will, *A Will for Peace*, 134–38. I also discussed the 1967 elections with Will in person. Elston to Staff Associates, 29 August 1967, RG 6, box 15, folder 3, NCC.

127. Will, *A Will for Peace*, 136–37. See also David Wurfel, "Dr. David Wurfel Reports on Vietnam," *United Methodist*, 21 September 1967, RG 6, box 30, folder 34, NCC.

128. Resolution on Vietnam, General Board, 15 September 1967, RG 4, box 36, folder 15, NCC.

129. "Viet-Nam in the General Debate of the 22nd UN General Assembly," International Affairs Reports from Quaker Workers, American Friends Service Committee, November 1967, RG 6, box 30, folder 5, NCC.

130. Elston memo to RSB, 18 September 1967, RG 6, box 30, folder 24, NCC.

131. DeBenedetti, *American Ordeal*, 194–95.

132. Elston to Mr. Peter Standish, 21 September 1967, RG 6, box 30, folder 44, NCC.

133. Hall, *Because of Their Faith*, 55–58. A few months earlier CALCAV had published a book titled *Vietnam: Crisis of Conscience*.

134. "Conscience and Conscription, CALCAV," released 25 October 1967, RG 5, box 17, folder 5, NCC.

135. Hall, *Because of Their Faith*, 57.

136. Elston interview, 20 October 1992.

137. Glen Williams to NCC, 17 November 1967, RG 4, box 34, folder 8, NCC.

138. "Anglican Condemns British Support of U.S. Policy in Vietnam War," Religious News Service (foreign service), NCC, Allan Parrent Personal Papers, private collection (hereafter APP).

139. RSB to Paul Oestreicher, 5 October 1967, RG 6, box 30, folder 35, NCC.

140. "Anglican Condemns British Support of U.S. Policy," APP.

141. REB interview.

142. Ibid.

143. "Summary Staff Evaluation of the Detroit Conference on Church and Society," RG 4, box 33, folder 38, NCC; Franklin Sherman, "Church and Society at Detroit," *C&C*, 27 November 1967, 275–78; Kyle Haselden, "Sense and Psychedelics," *CC*, 15 November 1967, 1452–54. Thanks to Chip Berlet, a participant, for sharing his memories and his file on the event.

144. Elston interview, 20 October 1992.

145. Haselden, "Sense and Psychedelics." Haselden says this kind of division plagued many civil rights and peace groups of the time. See "A SANE Warning," *CC*, 8 November 1967, 1419–21.

146. Sherman, "Church and Society at Detroit."

147. Wales Smith to EE, 27 October 1967, RG 4, box 34, folder 6, NCC.

148. Haselden, "Sense and Psychedelics." The various independent reports from the Detroit conference were merely forwarded to the NCC for consideration by its upcoming February General Board.

149. For examples, see Gilbert Hopkins to NCC, 28 November 1967, RG 5, box 15, folder 34, NCC; Wales Smith to EE, 27 October 1967, RG 4, box 34, folder 6, NCC; Marshall C. Dendy to EE, 3 November 1967, RG 4, box 34, folder 4, NCC; see also the Session of Philadelphia Presbyterian Church to Our Representatives on the Board of the National Council, December 1967, RG 4, box 35, folder 30, NCC.

150. Wales Smith to Burton Marvin, 13 November 1967, RG 4, box 34, folder 6, NCC.

151. "Progress Report on the Relationship between the NCCCUSA and Roman Catholicism," agenda item 4, General Board, 1–2 June 1967, RG 3, box 4, folder 6. Marvin to Wales E. Smith, 9 November 1967; Marvin memo to EE, 15 November 1967; Marvin to Smith, 15 November 1967; all in RG 4, box 34, folder 6, NCC.

152. Paul Dietterich, *Some Dimensions of International Affairs Education*, Monographs in International Affairs Education (New York: Department of International Affairs, NCC, December 1967).

153. Kelley interview.

154. Dean M. Kelley, *Why the Conservative Churches Are Growing*, 3rd ed. (1972; Macon: Mercer University Press, 1986). Evangelicals were outpacing ecumenical churches by formulating new methods of outreach, growth, and authority. These included entrepreneurial innovation and an embrace of technology that would produce what some called the "electric church." Adding entertainment value and modern cultural elements worked. See for example Dochuk, *From Bible Belt*, 341–42.

155. Ross Terrill, Turku '68 speech, RG 6, box 30, folder 38, NCC.

156. McNamara, *In Retrospect*, 307–9.

157. Clifford, *Counsel*, 455–57, 465.

158. McNamara, *In Retrospect*, 306–9; Moss, *Vietnam*, 232; Herring, *Longest War*, 184.

159. Will, *A Will for Peace*, 134–46.

160. Michael Novak, "Latest Casualty in Vietnam: Voluntary Agencies," *C&C*, 30 October 1967, 250–52. One of their first television appearances was on *Face the Nation*. For more on IVS in general, see Paul A. Rodell, "International Voluntary Services in Vietnam: War and the Birth of Activism, 1958–1967," *Peace and Change: A Journal of Peace Research* 27.2 (April 2002): 225–44.

161. Stoltzfus and Luce quoted in Novak, "Latest Casualty in Vietnam."

162. Ibid.

163. Elston memo to SADIA and Councils of Churches, 2 October 1967, RG 6, box 30, folder 15, NCC; Elston memo to RSB, 4 March 1968, RG 6, box 30, folder 37, NCC; Vietnam Education Project, April 1968, RG 6, box 30, folder 34, NCC; Elston interview, 11 December 1991.

164. Will, *A Will for Peace*, 141–46.

165. Richard Riseling, SADIA minutes, 19 November 1967, RG 6, box 15, folder 3, NCC; Ray Gibbons, memo to COCU Executive Directors, 20 November 1967, RG 6, box 30, folder 22, NCC. See also a VAC memo, 12 December 1967, RG 6, box 15, folder 3, NCC. VAC quickly became a subcommittee of SADIA. SADIA minutes, 12 December 1967, RG 6, box 15, folder 3, NCC. Vietnam Education Project, Methodist Church, April 1968, RG 6, box 30, folder 34, NCC. Additionally, EE, Gross, RSB, Naylor, and Ward decided that the NCC should present its Vietnam resolution before government officials, including the White House. Flemming to David Cassat, 20 November 1967, RG 6, box 30, folder 25; Ward to Flemming, 29 November 1967, RG 4, box 34, folder 8; Advisory Committee on Peace minutes, 4 December 1967, RG 6, box 27, folder 2; all in NCC.

166. Elston to Eugene McCarthy, 27 November 1967, RG 6, box 30, folder 17, NCC. See also Elston interview, 20 October 1992.

167. Hall, *Because of Their Faith*, 70.

168. Elston memo to RSB and David Hunter, 22 November 1967, RG 6, box 27, folder 5, NCC. See also RSB and John Ketcham to Colleagues, 5 December 1967, RG 6, box 15, folder 3, NCC.

8—CAMPAIGNS, CONFRONTATIONS, AND CIVIL DISOBEDIENCE, 1968

1. Alan Geyer, ROAD/68, 30 November 1967, RG 6, box 30, folder 22, NCC; Geyer interview.

2. Geyer, ROAD/68, 30 November 1967, RG 6, box 30, folder 22, NCC.

3. Al Lowenstein's Americans for Democratic Action pursued this tactic.

4. SADIA minutes, 12 January 1968, RG 6, box 15, folder 3, NCC.

5. Geyer, ROAD/68, 30 November 1967, RG 6, box 30, folder 22, NCC.

6. DeBenedetti, *American Ordeal*, 208–9.

7. William Sloane Coffin, "Civil Disobedience, the Draft, and the War," *C&C*, 5 February 1968, 8–11.

8. Elston interview, 20 October 1992.

9. "Rough Draft for Theological Statement," 31 January 1968, RG 6, box 27, folder 6, NCC.

10. SACSSAWR minutes, 22 January 1968, RG 5, box 17, folder 5, NCC.

11. Kelley, draft letter to Coffin, 22 January 1968; Flemming and EE to Coffin, 27 March 1968; both in RG 5, box 17, folder 5, NCC.

12. SACSSAWR minutes, 22 January 1968, ibid.

13. Ibid.; "Churchmen Challenge Hershey Draft Ruling," *Presbyterian Life,* 1 January 1968, 24–25. Henry Bucher had worked with the UCM coordinating field staff.

14. Also in January, RSB began nurturing cooperation between American Roman Catholic leadership and the NCC on foreign affairs. See steering committee notes of the Working Group of Bishops' Committee for Ecumenical and Inter-Religious Affairs and the NCC, 8 January 1968; also notes for 9 April, 27 May 1968; all in RG 4, box 35, folder 9, NCC.

15. In *Original Sin,* Finstuen does not refute the notion that a majority of Americans bypassed theological questions; rather, he highlights a substantial lay revival during this period (1945–1965) that did engage in theological questions focused primarily on the doctrine of original sin, a very traditional and personal Christian topic. His research does not show laity engaged in theological explorations related to systemic or institutionalized sin, or questions of social justice.

16. Elston interview, 15 October 1992. UCM students had a "Theological Reflections Committee" and did seem to take theological discussion seriously, although they wished to see such work taking place more in the midst of social justice work than sequestered away from those front lines. For more on theological discussions within the UCM, see Clough, "The National Student Christian Federation," 330–31, 334. Paul E. Schrading confirms that both theology and activist politics were important to students in the UCM; Paul E. Schrading, "The University Christian Movement: A Personal Remembrance," *Journal of Ecumenical Studies* 32.3 (Summer 1995), 345, 347. Schrading cites a UCM document that read in part, "UCM's theology emerges from anthropological, sociological and historical assumptions. We do not see God apart from the world. We know [God] as the actualizer of all human possibilities who is involved with [human beings] in time and in the world. . . . We know [God's] will as we are engaged in [human] liberation."

17. RSB to Colin Williams, 30 October; also 17 November 1967; both in RG 6, box 27, folder 6, NCC. Hessel agreed; see *Reconciliation.*

18. Elston interviews.

19. "Activists and Theologians Should Work Together, NCC Told," *Presbyterian Life,* 1 July 1968, 30.

20. Sweet, "Modernization of Protestant Religion," 33.

21. Settje, *Lutherans,* chs. 3, 4, 5, 7. In *Faith and War,* Settje discusses the roots of conservatives' convictions about the war and communism. He highlights, in particular, how communist persecution of evangelicals' missionaries fueled their furor.

22. RSB to Paul Oestreicher, 16 January 1968, RG 6, box 30, folder 24, NCC.

23. Hall, *Because of Their Faith,* 65–67.

24. RSB, in Program for NCCCUSA-NCCJ[apan] Consultation on "Peace in Vietnam," 9–10 February 1968, RG 6, box 30, folder 37, NCC.

25. Elston interview, 22 October 1992.

26. Clifford, *Counsel,* 468–69.

27. Rusk, *As I Saw It,* 477.

28. DeBenedetti, *American Ordeal,* 210.

29. Letter written to Johnson from "fellow Americans," dated 20 February 1968, in RG 4, box 35, folder 1, NCC; also MacCracken's report in General Board minutes, 20–22 February 1968, RG 3, box 4, folder 7, NCC.

30. Rusk, *As I Saw It*, 475; Rusk interview.

31. DeBenedetti, *American Ordeal*, 210; Clifford, *Counsel*, 481.

32. "What the *Observer* Thinks: The American Tragedy," *London Observer*, 4 February 1968, RG 6, box 30, folder 13, NCC.

33. Elston memo to John Wood, 24 January 1968, RG 4, box 36, folder 15, NCC. Elston memo to RSB, 21 March 1968; Elston to Prof. Helmuth Gollwitzer, 20 March 1968; both in RG 6, box 30, folder 37, NCC.

34. Clifford, *Counsel*, 476.

35. See DeBenedetti, *American Ordeal*, 211.

36. Ibid., 60–65; William MacKaye, "Clergy in the Capitol," *C&C*, 3 March 1968, 36–37.

37. Working Group of the Bishops' Committee for Ecumenical and Inter-Religious Affairs and the NCC, Steering Committee notes, 7 February 1968, RG 4, box 35, folder 9, NCC.

38. CALCAV, *In the Name of America* (New York: CALCAV, 1968); Hall, *Because of Their Faith*, 61–62.

39. EE to David Kidwell, 8 February 1968; also Kidwell to EE, 5 February 1968; both in RG 4, box 36, folder 15, NCC. See also EE memo to David Hunter, 22 November 1967, RG 4, box 34, folder 8, NCC.

40. DCLM Executive Committee minutes, 3 January 1968, E. Raymond Wilson Papers, CDG-A, box 1, SCPC. David Hunter, memo to Jon Regier, 29 November 1967; William Carhart to Rev. Paul Slinghoff, 22 November 1967; both in RG 5, box 13, folder 32, NCC. EE memo to David Hunter, 22 November 1967, RG 4, box 34, folder 8, NCC.

41. RSB, in Program for NCCCUSA-NCCJ[apan] Consultation, RG 6, box 30, folder 37, NCC.

42. Alan Geyer, "The Politics of Discontent in 1968," *C&C*, 19 February 1968, 18–22.

43. Hon. Lester L. Wolff, House of Representatives, in *Congressional Record*, 20 February 1968, E991, APP; the Honorable George Brown Jr., House of Representatives, in *Congressional Record*, 26 February 1968, E1151–52.

44. Hall, *Because of Their Faith*, 71; Elston interview, 20 October 1992; Reinhold Niebuhr, "A Time for Reassessment," *C&C*, 1 April 1968, 55–56.

45. RSB interviews.

46. "Imperatives of Peace and Responsibilities of Power," policy statement, NCC General Board, 21 February 1968, NCCNYO. Quotations in this and the next four paragraphs are from this document.

47. "A Position Paper Concerning Southern Africa," Department of International Affairs, NCC, March 1968, NCC.

48. The February General Board also passed a new "Resolution on Vietnam," with specific recommendations to which the "Imperatives" document directed readers' attention.

49. RSB interview, 6 August 1993.

50. Elston interview, 20 October 1968; RSB interview, 9 August 1993.

51. "Outline of a Proposed Three-Year International Affairs Program of

Encounter, Study and Education in USA/Asia Relations," RG 6, box 30, folder 21, NCC.

52. "World Poverty and the Demands of Justice," policy statement, NCC General Board, 22 February 1968, RSB files.

53. Joint Protestant–Roman Catholic Action Concerning International Aid, Trade and Development, March 1968, RG 4, box 35, folder 27, NCC. See the later draft proposal for a joint NCC-Catholic five-year program, "Church Action for World Development," 7 October 1968, RG 6, box 36, folder 21, NCC.

54. "Resolution on Vietnam," NCC General Board, 22 February 1968, NCC-NYO. Johnson's new "San Antonio" formula retreated from his previous insistence upon a mutual de-escalation. For the first time, Johnson suggested that he would be open to including the Vietcong politically in South Vietnam.

55. Hon. George E. Brown Jr., House of Representatives, *Congressional Record*, 28 February 1968, E1297.

56. Richard John Neuhaus, "Obedience and the Political Order," 22 February 1968, RG 5, box 17, folder 5, NCC.

57. RSB memo to Schomer, 13 March 1968, RG 6, box 30, folder 42, NCC.

58. Kelley memo to EE, 19 March 1968, RG 4, box 34, folder 28, NCC.

59. Schomer, "Notes on Conversation with U Thant, UN Secretary-General," 6 March 1968, RG 6, box 26, folder 12, NCC.

60. Parrent memo to RSB, 26 March 1968, RG 6, box 25, folder 1, NCC.

61. Ibid.; LBJ quoted in Hamilton/Parrent interview.

62. Rusk, *As I Saw It*, 480; Clifford, *Counsel*, 507, 511–14.

63. Flemming, telegram to LBJ, 1 April 1968, RG 4, box 36, folder 17, NCC; RSB, memo to Advisory Council on Peace and denomination heads, 2 April 1968, RG 4, box 35, folder 27, NCC. Frederick Nolde sent communication to Mai Van Bo. See Blake to RSB, 5 April 1968, RG 6, box 30, folder 28, NCC.

64. John Bennett, "The President's Surprise," *C&C*, 15 April 1968, 70–71.

65. Schomer telegram to LBJ, 3 April 1968; Schomer telegram to William Bundy, 3 April 1968; Schomer to Ambassador at Large Averell Harriman, 4 April 1968; all in RG 4, box 36, folder 17, NCC.

66. "A Call for a National Fast," April 8–10, CALCAV, RG 4, box 36, folder 15, NCC.

67. Parrent memos to RSB, 15 April 1968, RG 6, box 30, folder 10, NCC. These are subtitled "Discussion with Ambassador Harriman on Vietnam Negotiations" and "Follow Up to the Harriman Conversation." A National Student Association leader and Sanford Gottlieb of SANE were the other two attending.

68. Ibid. Participant David Hartsough's set of notes recorded that Harriman criticized LBJ's bombing. Harriman also apparently said that LBJ was cautious about the idea of a coalition government in South Vietnam because, as Harriman described it, "the U.S.'s fingers were burned in Laos." David Hartsough, "Discussion with Governor Harriman," 5 April 1968, CS, box 22, 1441-7-2:33, GCAH.

69. Parrent memo to RSB, 15 April 1968, RG 6, box 30, folder 10, NCC; Hartsough, "Discussion with Governor Harriman," 5 April 1968, CS, box 22, 1441-7-2:33, GCAH. Will contacted a member of the Vatican's staff for tips regarding possible NLF contacts for the churches should they seek to play an intermediary role. See Will to Monsignor Joseph Gremilion, Vatican, 16 April 1968, CS, box 23, 1441-7-3:21, GCAH.

70. Hartsough, "Discussion with Governor Harriman," 5 April 1968, CS, box 22, 1441-7-2:33, GCAH.

71. A later meeting between Methodist leaders and Assistant Secretary of State William Bundy confirmed these divisions. "Conversation with William Bundy," handwritten confidential notes by Rodney Shaw and Sanford Gottlieb, 8 August 1968, CS, box 23, 1441-7-3:23, GCAH. Bundy told them that the administration was divided between hardliners, who wanted a Korea solution for Vietnam, and those who would accept a Vietnamese solution, with Bundy favoring the latter. With respect to the NLF, Bundy disclosed, "We now reject formal dealings with the NLF. There is public hardness in Saigon, but private realism." Bundy also made it clear that he saw and favored ways in which communists could be incorporated legally into South Vietnamese society.

72. RSB memo to Parrent, 17 April 1968, RG6, box 30, folder 10, NCC.

73. Todd Gitlin, *The Sixties: Years of Hope, Days of Rage* (New York: Bantam Books, 1987), 306–9.

74. John Bennett, "The Columbia Revolution: II," *C&C*, 24 June 1968, 38.

75. "Insurrection in the Groves of Academe," *CC*, 8 May 1968, 607–8.

76. "A Letter to the Churches about the Crisis in Higher Education," General Board, 12 September 1968, RG 3, box 4, folder 8, NCC.

77. RSB, "International Affairs and Peace Priority Program: Accomplishments June 1966–April 1968," 1 May 1968, RG 4, box 35, folder 27, NCC.

78. "Denominational Support Received in 1967 for Total International Affairs Program," 6 May 1968; and EE to Denominational Participants in May 6 meeting, 14 May 1968; both in RG 4, box 35, folder 27, NCC.

79. This number failed to count Dietterich at the CCUN.

80. Dale Fiers to EE, 17 May 1968, RG 4, box 35, folder 17, NCC.

81. The statement was over six months in the making; CALCAV's controversial "aid and abet" declaration and Coffin's subsequent support of draft evaders had helped inspire it. RSB memo to Kelley and Elston, 31 October 1967, RG 6, box 30, folder 42, NCC.

82. "Religious Obedience and Civil Disobedience," policy statement, General Board, 7 June 1968, NCCNYO; "Denominational Policies Relative to Civil Disobedience," 7 June 1968; both in RG 5, box 17, folder 5, NCC.

83. "Defense and Disarmament: New Requirements for Security," policy statement, General Board, 12 September 1968, NCCNYO.

84. Ibid.

85. They were also becoming aware of this resentment in the mission fields. See Jose Bonino, "Missionary Planning and National Integrity," *C&C*, 24 June 1968, 140–43.

86. Alan Geyer, "Toward Justice and Peace in International Affairs," *CC*, 21 August 1968, 1049–53. Geyer mentioned that this assembly was difficult for several reasons. Martin Luther King Jr. was scheduled to speak at it but had been assassinated. The United States was on the defensive due to the war. Russia's increased pressure on Czechoslovakia since the "Prague spring" resistance movement there was also a hot topic. Geyer interview. See also Frank Heinze, "Toward a Moral World Community," *Monday Morning*, 9 September 1968, 11–12.

87. Robert McAfee Brown, "The Lessons of the Assembly," *C&C*, 16 September 1968, 205–7.

88. John Bennett, "An Immense Event," *C&C*, 16 September 1968, 207–8. See also Arthur J. Moore, "Uppsala, 1968: Was It Transitional Enough?" *C&C*, 16 September 1968, 203–5, where he says that, like the NCC, the WCC did not wish to alienate its Orthodox members.

89. RSB interview, 6 August 1993. See Kinnamon, *Vision*, for a similar perspective.

90. For example, see Kinnamon, *Vision*, 112–18.

91. Brown was a leading member of CALCAV, a strong supporter of its "aid and abet" statement, and a key force behind the United Presbyterian's Declaration of Conscience. Alan Geyer, "Old and New at Uppsala," *CC*, 21 August 1968, 1031–36.

92. Elston interviews.

93. Robert McAfee Brown, "The WCC and Selective Objection," *C&C*, 16 September 1968, 195–96.

94. Geyer, "Toward Justice."

95. Ibid. For a description of the changes in CCIA structure in 1969, see CCIA 1969, RG 6, box 27, folder 9, NCC. A South American lawyer, Leopoldo Juan Niilus, succeeded Nolde as director. Nolde had played a critical role in the passage of the Universal Declaration of Human Rights back in 1948; he also largely drafted its article protecting religious liberty. For more information, see Nurser, *For All Peoples*.

96. John Wood, memo to Kelley, 14 August 1968, RG 5, box 17, folder 5, NCC.

97. Regarding deserter communities in Canada, see RSB memo to Schomer, 13 March 1968; RSB to Dr. Samuel McCrea Cavert, 9 September 1968; both in RG 6, box 30, folder 42, NCC. Regarding the manual on the draft from the Department of Youth Ministries, see Henry Bullock to EE, 24 July 1968, RG 4, box 36, folder 13, NCC. Regarding efforts to repeal the draft, see SADIA minutes, 18 June 1968, RG 6, box 15, folder 3, NCC. Regarding amnesty, see Kelley memo to RSB, 23 September 1968; RSB memo to Kelley, 24 September 1968; both in RG 6, box 30, folder 42, NCC. For CALCAV's interaction with the deserter community in Sweden at Uppsala, see Hall, *Because of Their Faith*, 81.

98. Will, *A Will for Peace*, 143; Hall, *Because of Their Faith*, 72–73; Stuart Marshall Bloch, "Report from Democratic National Convention," 5 September 1968, CS, box 22, 1441-7-2:17, GCAH. The Methodists had also appealed before the Republican platform committee.

99. DeBenedetti, *American Ordeal*, 223–31.

100. General Board minutes, 12–13 September 1968, RG 3, box 4, folder 7, NCC. The board also resolved that the NCC would not schedule meetings in any city before investigating the "policies and practices of the local police." Executive Committee minutes, 21 January 1969, RG 3, box 4, folder 12, NCC.

101. Report of the General Secretary to the General Board, 12 September 1968, RG 3, box 4, folder 8, NCC.

102. Elston, "Vietnam Action: Prepared for SADIA," 16 September 1968, RG 6, box 15, folder 3, NCC.

103. DeBenedetti, *American Ordeal*, 229–37.

104. Elston memo to RSB, 26 September 1968, RG 6, box 30, folder 15, NCC.

105. Elston, "Vietnam Action II," 21 October 1968, RG 6, box 15, folder 3, NCC.

106. John Swomley, "Who Speaks for the Church?" *CC*, 6 March 1968, 291–93. In the spring of 1968, lay anger had reignited with the belated release of the Detroit Church and Society Conference report. Elston to Maynard Moore, 17 May 1968, RG 6, box 30, folder 13, NCC.

107. J. Allan Ranck, "General Secretary's Report to the General Board," part 2, 12 September 1968, RG 3, box 4, folder 8, NCC. Burton Marvin, "A Statement on the Task of the Office of Communication," 31 March 1968, RG 5, box 34, folder 32, NCC.

108. Stanley Rowland, "Crisis in Church Communication," *CC*, 2 October 1968, 1240–43.

109. See, for example, Sara Diamond, *Roads to Dominion: Right-Wing Movements and Political Power in the United States* (New York: Guilford Press, 1995), 162.

110. Many NCC leaders felt that their debate and action program did raise people's consciousness about the war. RSB memo to Parrent, 17 June 1968, RG 6, box 30, folder 16, NCC.

111. See "Dissent Yes–Smear No!" *Tempo*, 1 January 1969, 12.

112. Clergymen's Committee on China, "Millions of Americans Are Distressed and Confused," *New York Times*, 18 November 1968, C12.

113. Edward Grant, "Report to Inter-Church Relations Committee, Presbyterian Church, U.S.," 1 October 1968, NCC.

114. See untitled, undated document on the Methodist Board of Missions' concerns about the NCC, discussing a meeting held on 19 September 1968; also Tracey K. Jones Jr., memo to the Cabinet, 23 October 1968; both in RG 4, box 36, folder 13, NCC. For an interesting opinion on denominational motivations for this criticism, see "Secretariat for Relationships with Christian Councils: Report 53 A, The NCCCUSA," January 1969, RG 4, box 36, folder 20, NCC.

115. "Tiamat and Marduk: Babylon Politics in 1968," *CC*, 30 October 1968, 1359–60; Jim Hamilton and Allan Parrent, Hamilton/Parrent interview.

9—COURTING NIXON, DECEMBER 1968–FALL 1969

1. Allan Parrent, "International Affairs in the Nixon Administration," *C&C*, 20 January 1969, 342. Arthur J. Moore, "Back to the Status Quo?" *C&C*, 25 November 1968, 277–78.

2. John Bennett, "The End of the Bombing," *C&C*, 25 November 1968, 278–79. Roger Shinn, "After Viet Nam, What Next?" *C&C*, 9 December 1968, 293–94.

3. Leon Howell, "The Pause that Refreshes?" *C&C*, 3 February 1969, 14. Schomer to Arthur Schlesinger Jr., 27 January 1969; Schomer, "Genesis and Validity of This Mission, NCC Advisory Committee on Peace," 14 January 1969; both in RG 6, box 26, folder 11, NCC.

4. Elston to Rev. Harry Haas, 17 December 1968, RG 6, box 30, folder 11, NCC.

5. RSB memo to Schomer, 20 November 1968; RSB memo to Dr. William P. Thompson, 25 November 1968; both in RG 6, box 26, folder 12, NCC.

6. Schomer memo to RSB, 18 November 1968, ibid.

7. Xuan Oahn to Schomer, 9 November 1968, RG 6, box 30, folder 40, NCC. Schomer to RSB, 2 December 1968; RSB to William Bundy, 26 December 1968; also RSB memo to Berman et al., 26 December 1968; all in RG 6, box 26, folder 12, NCC.

8. Schomer to RSB, 5 December 1968, RG 6, box 26, folder 12, NCC. Schomer got this information from trusted French contact Charles Fourniau. Elston to Barton Hunter, 11 December 1968, RG 6, box 30, folder 5, NCC.

9. "Comments Following the Visit of a National Council of Churches Delegation to Paris, confidential," 10 January 1969, RG 6, box 26, folder 11, NCC.

10. Al Hassler and Gerhard Elston, memo on the "Third Solution to the Viet-

namese War," Hoa Binh Ad Hoc Committee (hereafter Hoa Binh) minutes, 3 March 1969, RG 6, box 30, folder 5, NCC; DeBenedetti, *American Ordeal*, 117, 189–90, 242, 353, 378; Hoa Binh minutes, 11 October 1968, RG 6, box 30, folder 5, NCC.

11. Elston interview, 20 October 1992. See also Elston memo to Barton Hunter, 13 January 1969, RG 6, box 30, folder 5, NCC; Elston memo to Members of Special Delegation, 14 January 1969, RG 6, box 26, folder 11, NCC; RSB interview, 6 August 1993.

12. "Comments Following the Visit . . . to Paris, confidential," 10 January 1969, RG 6, box 26, folder 11, NCC. See also "Report of the Delegation to Meet in Paris with Persons and Groups Concerned with the Current Conflict in Vietnam," 17 January 1969, RG 3, box 4, folder 11, NCC.

13. "Report of the Delegation to Meet in Paris with Persons and Groups Concerned with the Current Conflict in Vietnam," 17 January 1969, RG 3, box 4, folder 11, NCC. Schomer memo to RSB, 10 January 1969; RSB memo to Schomer, 10 January 1969; both in RG 6, box 26, folder 11, NCC. Elston's notes on "Report on Vietnam Negotiations," International Relations Committee, Council for Christian Social Action, United Church of Christ, 21 January 1969, RG 6, box 30, folder 40, NCC.

14. Elston memo to Members of Special Delegation, 14 January 1969; Paul Empie, memo to RSB, 14 January 1969; both in RG 6, box 26, folder 11, NCC. Richard Riseling, "Having Met with the Enemy," *Mission* (March 1969): 22.

15. Schomer memo to RSB, 10 January 1969; RSB memo to Schomer, 10 January 1969, both in RG 6, box 26, folder 11, NCC. RSB memo to Flemming, Gross, Jones, et al., 13 January 1969, RG 6, box 30, folder 40, NCC; also RSB, "Points Arising from Paris Meetings to Be Communicated to the State Department," 10 January 1969, RG 6, box 26, folder 11, NCC.

16. "Report of the Delegation to Meet in Paris," 17 January 1969, RG 3, box 4, folder 11, NCC.

17. Elston interviews. Elston said that Tran had great contacts through Duong Van Minh, who was involved in the coup against Diem in 1963 and appeared as a political rival to Thieu and Ky in the late 1960s.

18. RSB to Tran, 17 January 1969; Tran to RSB, 12 February 1969; both in RG 6, box 26, folder 11, NCC.

19. Hoa Binh minutes, 11 October 1968, RG 6, box 30, folder 5, NCC.

20. Hoa Binh minutes, 6 January, 12 February, 3, 22 March 1969, all in ibid. See also Al Hassler and Gerhard Elston, "Memorandum on the 'Third Solution' to the Vietnamese War," 3 March 1969, ibid.

21. Hoa Binh minutes, 6 January, 12 February, 3, 22 March 1969, all in RG 6, box 30, folder 5, NCC; Will, *A Will for Peace*, 146.

22. Don Luce, "Behind Vietnam's Prison Walls," *CC*, 19 February 1969, 261–64. Hoa Binh also circulated thousands of copies of "America's Political Prisoners in South Vietnam," a "white paper" drafted by FOR on the repression fostered by the Thieu regime. See Barton Hunter, memo to Elston, 6 March 1969, RG 6, box 30, folder 5, NCC.

23. Hoa Binh minutes, 22 March 1969, ibid.

24. Hall, *Because of Their Faith*, 79–89.

25. Ibid., 80.

26. Ben Franklin, "Opponents of Vietnam War Meet with Kissinger," *New York Times*, 6 February 1969, RG 6, box 30, folder 12, NCC.

27. Elston interviews; Elston to Henry Kissinger, 17 February 1969, RG 6, box 30, folder 69, NCC.

28. Michael B. Friedland, "New, Newer, Newest: The Transformation of Richard Nixon in the Popular Media, 1962–1968," *Viet Nam Generation* 7.1–2 (Winter 1996).

29. Roger Shinn, "The New Administration Moves In," *C&C*, 20 January 1969, 337.

30. John Bennett, "The Period of Crossed Fingers," *C&C*, 3 March 1969, 33–34.

31. Richard Nixon to Flemming, 22 February 1969, RG 4, box 35, folder 12, NCC.

32. RSB, "Transition in the American Identity," *CC*, 1 January 1969, 11–14.

33. "Memo of Understanding: Special Vietnam Program, April 16–June 1, 1969," 21 April 1969, RG 6, box 26, folder 11, NCC.

34. For more, see Paul Schrading, form letter to friends, March 1969; Nell Sale, "Speech Delivered to Advisory Council," March 1969; both in RG 4, box 36, folder 11, NCC. See Executive Committee minutes, 24 March 1969, RG 3, box 4, folder 12, NCC, for the UCM's reasons for disbanding, which included "the general atmosphere of mistrust of the bureaucracy, mistrust of national structures."

35. "Some Reflections and Recommendations from the International Caucus on the UCM Paper on Ideology, General Committee Meeting, 27 February–1 March, 1969," RG 4, box 36, folder 11, NCC.

36. Eugene Carson Blake, in "NCC in Memphis," *CC*, 12 February 1969, 204.

37. Ward to William Thompson, 13 February 1969, RG 4, box 36, folder 13, NCC.

38. EE to Ward, 18 February 1969, RG 4, box 36, folder 13, NCC.

39. "A Preliminary Report Outline Describing Major Work Directions of the Committee on Reappraisal of Role and Function of the NCC," Executive Committee, 19 April 1969, RG 3, box 4, folder 12, NCC.

40. Alan Geyer, "May Day in Manhattan," *CC*, 14 May 1969, 671–72. Charles Spivey is quoted in the same.

41. RSB, "The Peace Priority Program, 1966–1969," draft, 17 April 1969, RG 4, box 35, folder 27, NCC.

42. Ward to Tracey K. Jones Jr. and RSB, 14 January 1969, RG 6, box 27, folder 2, NCC.

43. Walter Wagoner, "Thoughts for Protestants to Be Static By," *CC*, 19 February 1969, 249–51.

44. "The Misplaced Ministry of the Laity," *CC*, 19 February 1969, 243.

45. Grover Hartmann, "Statement on Policy of National Council of Churches," 25 March 1969, RG 4, box 35, folder 31, NCC.

46. Initial funding came from FOR, CALCAV, the Disciples of Christ, the Episcopal Church, and the Church of the Brethren. Barton Hunter, memo to RSB, 22 May 1969, RG 6, box 26, folder 11, NCC. Methodists did not contribute funds because they were "in the red" financially; however, they donated staff and coordinated press contacts. Gene Stoltzfus to Barton Hunter and Allan Brick, 11 May 1969, CS, box 47, 1444-4-3:08, GCAH.

47. Statement by Barton Hunter, press release, U.S. Study Team on Religious and Political Freedom in Vietnam, 25 May 1969, RG 6, box 26, folder 11, NCC.

48. Anne Bennett, "A Visit to Viet Nam," *C&C*, 7 July 1969: 187–88. See also her files in the Burke Library Archives, series 9 Faculty, subseries H, box 3, folder Anne

Bennett's trip to Vietnam, Union Theological Seminary (hereafter UTS). See also Hall, *Because of Their Faith*, 88–89.

49. Will, *A Will for Peace*, 146–48. "Findings of Trip to Vietnam, U.S. Study Team, 25 May–10 June 1969," RG 6, box 30, folder 6, NCC.

50. Rep. John Conyers on behalf of the U.S. Study Team, telegram to President Nixon, 5 June 1969, RG 6, box 30, folder 6, NCC.

51. Stanley Karnow, *Vietnam: A History* (New York: Viking Press, 1983), 594–96.

52. "Model for Eventual Letter, Public or Private, to President Richard Nixon," 21 June 1969, RG 4, box 36, folder 15, NCC.

53. "The Perspective of a Vietnamese Scholar on the Current Diplomatic and Political Evolution," 12 June 1969, RG 4, box 36, folder 15, NCC.

54. Ibid.

55. Cleve Mathews, "Support of Thieu by Nixon Underscored," *New York Times*, 18 July 1969, RG 6, box 30, folder 6, NCC.

56. James Armstrong and John Conyers, "Vietnam: Sojourn and Sequel," *CC*, 15 October 1969, 1307–9; "Spotlight on Vietnam," editorial, *Nation*, 7 July 1969, RG 6, box 30, folder 6, NCC. The Methodists were overseeing press contacts. Will, *A Will for Peace*, 146–48. For a detailed description in the mainstream media of the team's findings, see Tom Foley, "Torture on Cong Son," *New York Daily World*, 3 July 1969, clipping in the Burke Library Archives, series 9 Faculty, subseries H, box 3, UTS.

57. See "Consultation on Vietnam Policy Options, 20–21 June 1969," RG 6, box 26, folder 10, NCC, for a list of scheduled attendees and their organizational affiliations. Attendees included Representatives John Anderson, John Conyers Jr., Paul Findley, Paul McCloskey Jr., Jeffrey Cohelan, and Bradford Morse; Senators Jacob Javits and Joseph Tydings; along with Ernest Gross, Cyrus Vance, Coretta Scott King, Harrison Salisbury, Edwin O. Reischauer, Hans Morgenthau, several university professors, John Sommer, and several NCC and denominational leaders.

58. RSB interview, 6 August 1993.

59. Matthew Ridgway, "Vietnam Options," 20 June 1969, RG 6, box 26, folder 10, NCC.

60. Elston to Tran, 27 February 1969, RG 6, box 30, folder 12, NCC.

61. Tran to Schomer, 18 April 1969, RG 6, box 26, folder 11, NCC.

62. "Summary of Interview, Ambassador Mai Van Bo and Robert S. Bilheimer," 13 June 1969, RG 6, box 26, folder 10, NCC.

63. Elston, "Observations of a National Council of Churches Staff Member in South Vietnam in May 1969," RG 4, box 36, folder 15, NCC.

64. See Frances Fitzgerald, *Fire*, for more.

65. Elston, "Observations of a National Council of Churches Staff Member in South Vietnam in May 1969," RG 4, box 36, folder 15, NCC.

66. Schomer to Members of the Vietnam Policy Consultation, 13 June 1969, RG 4, box 36, folder 15, NCC; Flemming et al. to Nixon, 30 June 1969, RG 3, box 4, folder 12, NCC.

67. Flemming et al. to Nixon, 30 June 1969, RG 3, box 4, folder 12, NCC.

68. Elston to Rev. R. N. Usher-Wilson, 25 July 1969, RG 6, box 30, folder 12, NCC; RSB memo to Flemming, 24 June 1969, RG 6, box 26, folder 10, NCC.

69. Schomer to RSB, 14 July 1969, RG 6, box 26, folder 10, NCC.

70. Ibid.; Elston interview, 15 October 1992. Rogers specifically accused the NCC of not condemning Hanoi's secrecy regarding American POWs. But Rogers was

mistaken. RSB had met with Mai Van Bo on June 13 to appeal for the release of POW names, as well as permission for a general "Christian delegation" visit. The Council had also raised the POW issue with Bo in January. Summary of interview, Ambassador Mai Van Bo and RSB, 13 June 1969, RG 6, box 26, folder 10, NCC.

71. Elston interview, 15 October 1992; Schomer to RSB, 14 July 1969, RG 6, box 26, folder 10, NCC.

72. Schomer to RSB, 14 July 1969, RG 6, box 26, folder 10, NCC.

73. Findlay, *Church People*, 199–225; General Board minutes, 1–2 May 1969, RG 3, box 4, folder 9, NCC.

74. Findlay, *Church People*, 199–225.

75. Ibid., 205.

76. RSB interview, 6 August 1993.

77. Findlay, *Church People*, 207.

78. "Response of the General Board of the National Council of Churches to the Black Manifesto," General Board, 11 September 1969, RG 3, box 4, folder 9, NCC.

79. RSB, "What Kind of People Are We?" *C&C*, 23 June 1969, 176–78.

80. MacCracken memo to EE, 21 May 1969, RG 4, box 36, folder 15, NCC; RSB memo to MacCracken, 16 May 1969, RG 6, box 26, folder 11, NCC.

81. Consultation on Christian Concerns in Tomorrow's Vietnam minutes, 27 May 1969, RG 4, box 36, folder 15, NCC.

82. RSB to Blake and John Coventry Smith, 22 May 1969, RG 6, box 26, folder 11, NCC; Schomer to Ambassador Cyrus Vance, 19 September 1969, RG 6, box 26, folder 9, NCC; Don Luce and Nguyen Canh, "An Approach to Post-War Service Priorities in South Vietnam," WCC, fall 1969, RG 6, box 30, folder 28, NCC.

83. Luce and Canh, "Approach to Post-War Service Priorities in South Vietnam." Canh's middle name appears as both Tang and Lang

84. Schomer, "Draft Statement Requested for GS Report to Phoenix General Board," 20 August 1970, RG 6, box 26, folder 8, NCC; Schomer memo to MacCracken, 22 October 1969, and RSB memo to MacCracken, 21 October 1969, RG 6, box 26, folder 9, NCC.

85. "The Ides of October," *CC*, 29 October 1969, 1369; DeBenedetti, *American Ordeal*, 246–47.

86. Hall, *Because of Their Faith*, 92.

87. Elston interviews; a friend of Elston's later swept for bugs and confirmed their existence.

88. DeBenedetti, *American Ordeal*, 248–50.

89. Elston memo to SADIA, 28 June 1969, RG 6, box 26, folder 10, NCC.

90. DeBenedetti, *American Ordeal*, 249–50.

91. Ibid., 255. David Hunter and Charles Lutz for the Ad Hoc Joint Agency Moratorium Committee, memo to Personnel of Participating Agencies, 15 October 1969, RG 4, box 36, folder 15, NCC.

92. DeBenedetti, *American Ordeal*, 255–57; Robert McAfee Brown, Father Theodore Hesburgh, and Rabbi Maurice Eisendrath, "Call to Clergy to Visit the Vietnam Wounded," 1 October 1969, RG 4, box 36, folder 15, NCC.

93. DeBenedetti, *American Ordeal*, 257–59.

94. Ibid., 253–61.

95. Stewart Meacham to Elston, 6 September 1969; New Mobilization Committee to End the War in Vietnam steering committee minutes, 30–31 July 1969; Elston

to Meacham, 20 September 1969; all in RG 6, box 30, folder 7, NCC. Richard Riseling, memo to SADIA members, 24 October 1969, RG 6, box 15, folder 2, NCC.

96. Robert Moss to Conference Executives of United Church of Christ, 28 October 1969, RG 6, box 30, folder 35, NCC.

97. DeBenedetti, *American Ordeal*, 261–62; Elston memo to Communication System, 15 November 1969, RG 6, box 30, folder 15, NCC.

98. Blueprint for the Churches, CALCAV, fall 1969, RG 6, box 15, folder 2, NCC; DeBenedetti, *American Ordeal*, 261–62; Elston interview, 20 October 1992; Hall, *Because of Their Faith*, 95 (Coffin).

99. Pratt, "Religious Faith," 224–55.

100. Fernandez to RSB, 31 October 1969, RG 6, box 30, folder 44, NCC.

101. RSB, "The Changing Domestic Base of U.S. Foreign Policy," for presentation at the "Consultation on Korean-American Relations: Dilemmas and Opportunities in the Future of Northeast Asia, Seoul, Korea, 2–5 December 1970," RSB's Personal Papers, private collection (hereafter RSBP). See also Hall, *Because of Their Faith*, 92–93; DeBenedetti, *American Ordeal*, 262–63.

102. DeBenedetti, *American Ordeal*, 263–65. Herring, *America's Longest War*, 230 (Nixon).

10—ECUMENICAL EROSION, FALL-DECEMBER 1969

1. Program Cabinet minutes, 5 September 1969, RG 4, box 36, folder 1, NCC.

2. Paul Woudenberg to EE, 10 October 1969, RG 4, box 36, folder 13, NCC.

3. William Walzer, memo to Fletcher Coates, 14 October 1969, RG 4, box 36, folder 13, NCC.

4. R. Odell Brown to EE, Flemming, et al., 6 October 1969, RG 4, box 36, folder 13, NCC.

5. Ibid.

6. EE to Woudenberg, 15 October 1969, RG 4, box 36, folder 13, NCC.

7. EE to Robert Huston, Tracey Jones, and Ward, 30 October 1969, ibid.

8. Huston to Jones, EE, and Ward, 10 November 1969, ibid.

9. EE to Woudenberg, 15 October 1969, ibid.

10. Woudenberg to EE, 20 October 1969, ibid.

11. Reverend Paul R. Woudenberg, "Lay Members Don't Represent Local Churches," *Christian Advocate*, 19 May 1966, 14.

12. Michael C. Watson, "A Layman and the National Council of Churches," *Christian Advocate*, 28 December 1967, 11–12.

13. Alex Orr, "The Clergy-Laity Gap," *Monday Morning*, 10 February 1969, 8–9.

14. Alex Orr, "Why Are Ministers Bottlenecks?" *Monday Morning*, 15 January 1968, 6–7.

15. "New Gallup Poll: 53% Say Church Should Not Become Involved in Social or Political Issues: Sharp Change from the Minority Opinion of 44% in 1957 Survey," *Presbyterian Layman* (May 1968): 1.

16. "Wide Bias Found in 'Church Members,'" *Presbyterian Life*, 1 May 1968, 28.

17. For more, see Jill K. Gill, "Caught in the Middle: Navigating the Clergy-Laity Gap during the Vietnam War," *Journal of Presbyterian History*, forthcoming. Parts of this section come from this article.

18. EE to Woudenberg, 15 October 1969, RG 4, box 36, folder 13, NCC.

19. Jeanne Richie, "The Unresponsive Pew," *CC*, 8 October 1969, 1278–81.

20. "Lutheran Fry: Moratorium on Criticism," *Christian Advocate*, 2 November 1967, 23.

21. Biographical information on Rose is drawn from "An Announcement," *CC*, 9 June 1971, 513.

22. Stephen Rose, "The NCC: Phoenix on the Hudson?" *C&C*, 24 November 1969, 295–301.

23. A. Dale Fiers to EE, 25 November 1969, RG 4, box 35, folder 17, NCC; David Colwell, "New Leadership Needed," *C&C*, 24 November 1969, 302–3.

24. J. Edward Carothers to EE, 24 November 1969, RG 4, box 36, folder 13, NCC.

25. General Board minutes, 21–24 January 1969, RG 3, box 4, folder 9; James Stoner to J. A. Ranck, W. Parry, EE, 21 August 1969, RG 2, box 4, folder 17; "Preparation for Unscheduled Events at the General Assembly," 20 November 1969, RG 2, box 5, folder 3; Executive Committee minutes, 28 November 1969, RG 3, box 4, folder 11; all NCC.

26. Edwin Espy, "Christian Obedience and the NCC," General Secretary's Address, General Assembly, 30 November 1969, RG 2, box 5, folder 1, NCC.

27. Alan Geyer, "Joy Box with No Joy: The NCC at Detroit," *CC*, 17 December 1969, 1601–5.

28. RSB interview, 6 August 1993.

29. Report from Association of Council Secretaries, General Assembly, Detroit, 30 November–4 December 1969, RG 2, box 5, folder 14, NCC; General Assembly minutes, 2nd Plenary Session, 1 December 1969, Detroit, 30 November–4 December 1969, RG 2, box 4, folder 18, NCC.

30. "Top Church Post Urged for Negro," *New York Times*, 2 December 1969, RG 4, box 35, folder 13, NCC; Free Church of Berkeley, "Part II: The Exorcism, Jonathan's Wake," General Assembly, 30 November–4 December 1969, RG 2, box 5, folder 3, NCC.

31. Edward Fiske, "Church Council's Parley: Several Steps Further to the Left," *New York Times*, 8 December 1969, RG 4, box 35, folder 13, NCC.

32. General Assembly, 30 November–4 December 1969, RG 2, box 5, folder 3, NCC.

33. General Assembly minutes, Seventh Plenary Session, 3 December 1969, Detroit, 30 November–4 December 1969, RG 2, box 4, folder 18, NCC; Youth of Amerika, YIPPIE! General Assembly, Detroit, 30 November–4 December, RG 2, box 5, folder 3, NCC.

34. General Assembly minutes, Seventh Plenary Session, RG 2, box 4, folder 18, NCC; Geyer, "Joy Box."

35. Youth Caucus Statement, General Assembly, Detroit, 30 November–4 December 1969, RG 2, box 5, folder 3, NCC.

36. Hall, *Because of Their Faith*, 84–85; Elston interview, 15 October 1992; Elston memo to RSB, 13 November 1969, RG 6, box 30, folder 12, NCC. See also Donald W. Maxwell, "Religion and Politics at the Border: Canadian Church Support for American Vietnam War Resisters," *Journal of Church and State* 48.4 (2006): 807–29. "Proposed Joint CCC-NCC Consultation on 'Pastoral Service with U.S. Draft-Age Emigrants in Canada' for presentation to the Executive Committee," 28 November 1969, RG 2, box 5, folder 1, NCC; "At a Glance," NCC press release GA-26, RG 2, box 5, folder 4, NCC;

"Canadian Council of Churches / National Council of Churches Joint Consultation on Pastoral Service with U.S. Draft-Age Emigrants in Canada," December 1969, RG 6, box 15, folder 2, NCC.

37. Elston interview, 15 October 1969.

38. Will interview, 17 March 1996.

39. Hall, *Because of Their Faith*, 84–85.

40. Elston interview, 13 October 1992; General Assembly minutes, Eighth Plenary Business Session, 3 December 1969, Detroit, RG 2, box 4, folder 18, NCC.

41. Glenn Pontier, "Statement by Students, General Synod, Reformed Church in America," June 1969, RG 5, box 17, folder 5, NCC.

42. Glenn Pontier to Dr. Marion deVelder, 1 December 1969, RG 5, box 17, folder 5, NCC.

43. Marion deVelder, in Fiske, "Church Council's Parley."

44. Geyer, "Joy Box"; General Assembly minutes, Eighth and Ninth Plenary Business Sessions, 3 December 1969, Detroit, RG 2, box 4, folder 18, NCC.

45. Geyer, "Joy Box"; Nancy Manser, "NCC Elects First Woman President," *Detroit News*, 5 December 1969, RG 4, box 35, folder 13, NCC. Geyer and Manser quote York slightly differently. I have used Manser's version of the quotation in the text. Geyer quotes York as saying, "The blood of the Vietnamese is upon you!" I do not know which is correct.

46. Geyer, "Joy Box."

47. General Assembly minutes, Ninth Plenary Business Session, 3 December 1969, Detroit, RG 2, box 4, folder 18, NCC; Geyer, "Joy Box."

48. ACCC telegram to John Mitchell, in Geyer, "Joy Box."

49. Proposed Resolution on Vietnam, 3 December 1969, General Assembly, RG 3, box 4, folder 10, NCC. General Assembly minutes, Twelfth Plenary Business Session, 4 December 1969, RG 2, box 4, folder 18, NCC.

50. "Church Council Victor: Mrs. Cynthia Clark Wedel," *New York Times*, 5 December 1969, RG 4, box 35, folder 13, NCC.

51. Geyer, "Joy Box." See also Fiske, "Church Council's Parley."

52. Cleage in Geyer, "Joy Box."

53. Associate Council of Secretaries, General Assembly, Detroit, 30 November–4 December 1969, RG 2, box 5, folder 14, NCC.

54. Several sources document this. For one, see Hulsether, *Building*, 145–46. Meanwhile evangelical groups had, since the 1950s, been actively courting conservative youth, and rather successfully. See Diamond, *Roads to Dominion*, 164; William Martin, *With God on Our Side: The Rise of the Religious Right in America* (New York: Broadway Books, 1996).

55. Grover Hartmann, Review of the 8th General Assembly of the NCCCUSA, General Assembly, Detroit, 30 November–4 December 1969, RG 4, box 35, folder 1, NCC. Everyone I interviewed credited Flemming for his deft handling of the chaos. Geyer said, "He handled it with as much skill and grace as anybody could do."

56. For an interesting related discussion, see the introduction to Hulsether, *Building*.

57. Arthur Schlesinger, *The Disuniting of America: Reflections on a Multicultural Society* (New York: W. W. Norton, 1992). RSB's interviews stressed that the ecumenical movement had lost its sense of being "a people amidst peoples"; he saw the loss of connectedness manifested nationwide.

58. Roy Branson, "Time to Meet the Evangelicals?" *CC*, 24 December 1969, 1640–43. Branson cites several studies to support his thesis. Bob Gildea, untitled and undated article, RG 4, box 35, folder 1, NCC.

59. For reflections on this type of no-win situation for liberals, see Mark Hulsether, *Religion, Culture and Politics in the Twentieth-Century United States* (New York: Columbia University Press, 2007), 159.

60. Kelley interview. Documents in Kelley's files substantiate this.

61. Fernandez interview, 31 October 1991.

62. This included some new breed clergy. Alternatively, liberal ecumenists affiliated with the NCC tended to support voting, even during this discouraging time. See Hulsether, *Building*, 156.

63. "Carnage and Incarnation," *CC*, 24 December 1969, 1633.

64. DeBenedetti, *American Ordeal*, 252–68.

65. "Tran, Notes 11, 12, and 13, summarized," 26 November 1969, RG 6, box 26, folder 9 NCC; Elston interview, 15 October 1992.

11—FIGHTING NIXON AND SEEKING A NEW STRATEGY, JANUARY 1970–MARCH 1971

1. "Round-up Report," press release, General Board, 23 January 1970, RG 3, box 4, folder 13, NCC.

2. "Options for Conciliarism," *CC*, 17 June 1970, 747.

3. Geyer wrote most of the uncredited "Stance" pieces in the *Christian Century* from mid-1968, when he became editor, to 1972 when he departed. Geyer interview.

4. See also "Ecumenism as Communication," *CC*, 13 November 1969, 1441; "Who's Listening to Lay People?" *CC*, 11 August 1971, 943; Geyer, "May Day in Manhattan," *CC*, 14 May 1969, 1071–72; "More Power to the NCC!" *CC*, 10 February 1971, 179; "Misplaced Ministry of the Laity."

5. "Suffering Ecumenical Cats," *CC*, 11 February 1970, 163.

6. "Fifty Million Fund Triumphs; General Mission Giving Puzzles," *Presbyterian Life*, 15 June 1967, 32–34, and "Regarding Vietnam: A Declaration of Conscience," *Presbyterian Life*, 15 June 1967, 24–25. The articles note a sharp decline in giving since 1961, and a loss of ten thousand members in five years. Some studies have contested the assertion that most laity opposed church participation in social action and that church stands on issues led to significant decline in memberships and funding. See Hadden, *Gathering Storm*; "Why Church?" *CC*, 12 January 1972, 27. However, laity often argued that these things put them off, and many church leaders believed them.

7. "'71 COEMAR Budget Cut Three Quarters of a Million," *Presbyterian Life*, 15 December 1970, 46. See United Presbyterian Church in the United States of America, General Assembly minutes, Part I, Journal, for 1969 (909–11) and 1970 (834–35), Presbyterian Historical Society (hereafter PHS).

8. Articles in *Monday Morning* dated 1 July 1971, quote in "Despair and Hope," 4, "Vietnam Statement Causes Anguish," 14–17, "Among Young Christians: Not One Style But Many," 26.

9. "Reaction Following the 183rd General Assembly," *Monday Morning*, 15 July 1971, 16–19.

10. James L. Stoner, memo to denominational approvals executives, 16 Novem-

ber 1970, Elston Papers, box 36, SCPC; Alan Geyer, "NCC on the Boardwalk," *CC*, 30 June 1971, 791–92; Paul Dietterich, "Phased Withdrawal," *CC*, 10 November 1971, 1326–27; "The UN's Disastrous Situation," *CC*, 24 November 1971, 1373.

11. Hulsether, *Building*, 242–43, 255.

12. "Ecumenism as Communication," 1441; "More Power to the NCC!"; "Suffering Ecumenical Cats."

13. Aubrey Haines, "Polarization within the Churches," *CC*, 2 September 1970, 1039–41.

14. "A Call to Presbyterian Laymen," *Presbyterian Life*, 1 December 1965, 18–19; "Portland Presbyterians Register an Objection to the Vietnam Declaration," *Presbyterian Layman* (March 1968): 3; Haines, "Polarization within the Churches." Both the Presbyterian Lay Committee and the Good News Methodists continue today as leaders of a conservative movement within mainline Protestantism to turn those denominations back toward what they call "orthodox" or "classic" doctrines, beliefs, and practices. See Oden, *Turning Around the Mainline*; Robert Tapp, "On the Rise of Demotheology," *CC*, 3 February 1971, 153–55. Harold Bosley noted correctly that "The churches' concern for social issues is alienating many of the older generation of churchmen without winning the support of an appreciable number of those— younger and older alike—who, while deeply concerned about social issues, refuse to get involved in the churches." Harold Bosley, "The Quiet Storm in the Churches," *CC*, 2 December 1970, 1449–52; see also Robert E. Van Dusen to Dr. Frank W. Gunn, 3 December 1970, RG 6, box 30, folder 33, NCC.

15. Articles in *Monday Morning*, "Far Right Attacks the Church," and John Coventry Smith, "It Still Happens," both dated 20 April 1970, 26; Reverend Richard Ittner, "Moving Forward in the Age of Malaise," 1 January 1973, 3–4.

16. George Cornell, from AP news features, *Religion in the News*, 17 June 1970, RG 6, box 30, folder 16, NCC.

17. Ibid. (Agnew). Some called this a polarization between "pietist" and "pragmatist" schools of Christian thought. George Docherty, "The Gospel of the Dynamic Middle," *CC*, 15 July 1970, 863.

18. John Bennett, "The Great Controversy in the Churches," *CC*, 27 May 1970, 659–63; also Bosley, "Quiet Storm in the Churches"; "Data for Possible Inclusion in the Report of the GAFC to the General Board in Washington, D.C.," June 19–20 1970, Denominational Support Committee, 18 June 1970, RG 3, box 4, folder 14, NCC.

19. Cynthia Wedel, "The Church and Social Action," *CC*, 21 August 1970, 959–62.

20. For one discussion of this, see Hulsether, *Building*, 149–52; also David Farber, "The Silent Majority and Talk About Revolution," in *The Sixties: From Memory to History*, ed. David Farber (Chapel Hill: University of North Carolina Press, 1994); George Lakoff, *Don't Think of an Elephant: Know Your Values and Frame the Debate* (White River Junction, VT: Chelsea Green, 2004); Diamond, *Roads to Dominion*, 115–17, 127–28; Mary C. Brennan, *Turning Right in the Sixties: The Conservative Capture of the GOP* (Chapel Hill: University of North Carolina Press, 1995).

21. Meanwhile, the IAC organized convocations and workshops to help Christian education specialists create lay international affairs curriculum. For more, see "Current Program of the National Council of Churches in International Affairs and Peace, Department of International Affairs," 8 June 1970, NCCWOF; also "Consultation on New Perspectives on National Security: The Educational

Task," CCUN, 24 August 1970, RG 6, box 15, folder 1, NCC; Elston memo to Boyd Lowry and Ed Luidens, 25 November 1970, RG 6, box 30, folder 15, NCC.

22. "Consultation on Christian Concerns in Tomorrow's Vietnam" minutes, DOM, 14 October 1970, RG 6, box 26, folder 8, NCC.

23. DeBenedetti, *American Ordeal*, 292–95; Moss, *Vietnam*, 322–24. See also Schomer's advance text of "Is the Vietnam War Really Ending?" for *Tempo*, 1 December 1970, given to RSB, 19 November 1970, RG 6, box 26, folder 8, NCC.

24. Coffin in DeBenedetti, *American Ordeal*, 289, 294.

25. Charles Colson, *God and Government: An Insider's View on the Boundaries between Faith and Politics* (Grand Rapids, MI: Zondervan, 2007), 348. For more on Nixon's partisan wooing of evangelicals, especially across the southern Sunbelt, see Dochuk, *From Bible Belt*, 332-37.

26. Martin writes, "none ever made such a conscious, calculating use of religion as a political instrument as did Richard Nixon," in *God on Our Side*, 97; see 97–99 for his description of these White House services and Nixon's political use of them. Although Graham harbored private concerns about the war that grew with time, he remained publicly supportive of Nixon's policies, as did most evangelicals. Fundamentalists such as Carl McIntire went further, actively promoting the war as God's battle with Satanic forces. They were more than religious nationalists; they were crusaders. For more on such distinctions, see Jill K. Gill, "Religious Communities and the Vietnam War," in Mitchell Hall, ed., *Vietnam War Era: People and Perspectives* (Santa Barbara, CA: ABC-CLIO, 2009), 97–116.

27. Colson, in Martin, *God on Our Side*, 99; Colson, *God and Government*, 345–55. See also Dochuk, "Evangelicalism Becomes Southern." Although Nixon had his eyes on the suburban Sunbelt, he also pursued disaffected Democrats nationally.

28. Michael Novak, "White House Religion: A Tricky Business," *CC*, 23 September 1970, 1112. Novak identified as a liberal then. Elston interviews; Reinhold Niebuhr, "The King's Chapel and the King's Court," *C&C*, 4 August 1969, 211–12. Hulsether comes to a similar conclusion, *Building*, 147–48.

29. Colson, in Martin, *God on Our Side*, 99; Colson, *God and Government*, 345–55.

30. Moss, *Vietnam*, 231, 322.

31. DeBenedetti, *American Ordeal*, 287–88.

32. Elston interviews.

33. Kelley interview.

34. Fernandez interview, 31 October 1991. The figure quoted is from Fernandez's memory. Hall, *Because of Their Faith*, 104, describes the bequest amount as equaling one-eighth of Bernstein's estate. Kelley interview. See part of a quotation from the will in "Acceptance and Management of a Legacy," Office of Administration, 25 February 1971, RG 5, box 13, folder 32, NCC.

35. Kelley interview; Fernandez interview, 31 October 1991.

36. Hall, *Because of Their Faith*, 104–6.

37. RSB to Bishop James Armstrong, 17 February 1970, RG 6, box 26, folder 8, NCC; also DeBenedetti, *American Ordeal*, 269–71. Elston memo to Church and Synagogue–Related "Moratorium" Types, 24 February 1970; Elston to Phillips, 14 March 1970; Rev. John Boyles to Elston, 20 March 1970; all in RG 6, box 30, folder 7, NCC.

38. DeBenedetti, *American Ordeal*, 270–73.

39. RSB to Armstrong, 17 February 1970, RG 6, box 26, folder 8, NCC; IMPACT

Quarterly Narrative Report, 1 January–31 March 1970, RG 5, box 21, folder 19, NCC.

40. RSB to Tran, 31 March 1970, RG 6, box 26, folder 8, NCC.

41. "Highlights of Tran Note no. 14," 19 March 1970, RG 6, box 26, folder 8, NCC.

42. Elston to William C. Gausmann, 8 June 1970, RG 6, box 30, folder 17, NCC.

43. N. Canh, "Coordinating Conference for Reconstruction in Vietnam, Confidential, World Council of Churches," March 1970; "Vietnam Consultation Minutes, Consultation on Christian Concerns in Tomorrow's Vietnam," 9 January 1970; both in RG 6, box 26, folder 8, NCC.

44. For more on Vietnamization, see Moss, *Vietnam*, 305–18; DeBenedetti, *American Ordeal*, 271–72.

45. DeBenedetti, *American Ordeal*, 277–80.

46. Cynthia Wedel and Ernest Gross, press release statement, 1 May 1970; also "Recommended Program of Action Concerning Cambodia and Vietnam, Report to General Board," 20 June 1970; both in RG 3, box 4, folder 14, NCC.

47. "Cambodian Crisis Congressional Visits Briefing, Washington, D.C.," 5 May 1970, RG 6, box 30, folder 15, NCC; "A Brief Report of Activities Regarding Cambodia and Vietnam," 14 May 1970, RG 6, box 26, folder 8, NCC; "Current Program of the National Council of Churches, Department of International Affairs," 8 June 1970, NCCWOF; Kissinger, in Hall, *Because of Their Faith*, 100.

48. DeBenedetti, *American Ordeal*, 280.

49. "Act Now Against Expanded War in Cambodia and Vietnam," FCNL, 4 May 1970, RG 6, box 30, folder 33, NCC.

50. Dr. William P. Thompson et al., "Press Statement on Cambodia and Southeast Asia," 6 May 1970, RG 6, box 26, folder 8, NCC.

51. EE memo to All NCC Staff, 11 May 1970; David Hunter, memo to RSB, 13 May 1970; both in ibid.

52. "A Message to the Churches," 20 May 1970, ibid.

53. "A Brief Report of Activities regarding Cambodia and Vietnam. A Call to an Emergency Religious Convocation on the War in South East Asia," 26 May 1970, NCCWOF; Hall, *Because of Their Faith*, 100–101; "Current Program of the National Council of Churches, Department of International Affairs," 8 June 1970, NCCWOF; "Recommended Program of Action Concerning Cambodia and Vietnam, Report for Presentation to the General Board," 20 June 1970, RG 3, box 4, folder 14, NCC.

54. Elston to William C. Gausmann, 8 June 1970, RG 6, box 30, folder 17, NCC.

55. Moss, *Vietnam*, 320–21; DeBenedetti, *American Ordeal*, 285–88, 322.

56. "Costly Blessings at Kent State?" *CC*, 20 May 1970, 620–21.

57. "On the Brink," *C&C*, 25 May 1970, 105.

58. Elston memo to SADIA, 17 September 1970, RG 6, box 30, folder 15, NCC.

59. Allan Brick et al. to RSB, 12 November 1970, RG 6, box 26, folder 8, NCC.

60. D. Ackerman to SEAS, SADIA, and selected Councils of churches, 2 October 1970, RG 6, box 15, folder 1, NCC. Frederick Routh, "An Evaluative Report on Impact," 1 September 1970; "Sources for Impact Materials 5/27/68–9/1/70"; both in RG 5, box 21, folder 19, NCC. For a listing of IMPACT's interdenominational funding sources, see "IMPACT Budget Quarterly 7/1–9/30/70," RG 5, box 21, folder 19, NCC. For more on the Washington Interreligious Staff Council (WISC) with which IMPACT was connected, see Edward Snyder, "The Churches' Role in Washington," *CC*, 20 January 1971, 69–70; RSB to Armstrong, 17 February 1970; "IMPACT Quarterly Narrative

Report, 1 January–31 March 1970," RG 5, box 21, folder 19, NCC.

61. Elston funneled his updated Vietnam information into CALCAV's new weekly newspaper, *American Report*. Elston to Vo-Dinh, 25 September 1970, RG 6, box 30, folder 17, NCC.

62. "Statement for June 10 Press Conference," 10 June 1970, RG 6, box 30, folder 5, NCC; Don Luce, "Torture in Saigon," 18 May 1970, RG 6, box 30, folder 23, NCC.

63. The story about discovering the tiger cages comes from Will interview, 8 December 1995. See also Will, *A Will for Peace*, 153. "The Tiger Cages of Con Son," *Life*, 17 July 1970, 24–29. The congressmen were William Anderson of Tennessee and Augustus Hawkins of California.

64. See "Resolution on Cambodia-Vietnam Situation, General Board," 21 June 1970, NCCNYO.

65. RSB memo to Schomer, 3 August 1970, RG 6, box 26, folder 8, NCC.

66. Schomer, "Draft Statement Request for GS Report to Phoenix General Board," 10 August 1970; Niilus memo to Blake, 25 August 1970; both in RG 6, box 26, folder 8, NCC.

67. Moss, *Vietnam*, 320–25. See also Schomer, "Is the Vietnam War Really Ending?" *Tempo*, 19 November 1970, RG 6, box 26, folder 8, NCC.

68. Schomer memo to Niilus, 17 October 1970, RG 6, box 26, folder 8, NCC.

69. Moss, *Vietnam*, 320–25.

70. Melvin Laird also ignored Ridgway. Schomer memo to RSB; Niilus, "Private Conversation with General Matthew B. Ridgway," 11 June 1970; both in RG 6, box 26, folder 8, NCC.

71. Schomer memo to Blake, 29 July 1970, RG 6, box 26, folder 8, NCC. Sullivan had been ambassador to Laos while the CIA was running its covert military operation there prior to the South Vietnamese and American offensive in 1971. See Schomer memo to Blake, 15 March 1971, RG 6, box 26, folder 7, NCC.

72. Schomer to Ambassador Habib, 20 August 1970, RG 6, box 26, folder 8, NCC.

73. Schomer to Blake, 29 July 1970, ibid.

74. DeBenedetti, *American Ordeal*, 292–93.

75. Schomer, "Is the Vietnam War Really Ending?" The PRG was created by the NLF in 1969.

76. Ibid.

77. Nixon in DeBenedetti, *American Ordeal*, 292–93.

78. Ibid.; "A Way Out?" *CC*, 21 October 1970, 1244.

79. Schomer, "Is the Vietnam War Really Ending?"; Herring, *Longest War*, 238–40.

80. Schomer to Niilus, 17 October 1970, RG 6, box 26, folder 8, NCC.

81. Ibid.

82. Schomer to Dahlen, 26 October 1970, RG 6, box 26, folder 8, NCC.

83. Schomer to Niilus, 17 October 1970, and Schomer to Dahlen, 26 October 1970, ibid.

84. Blake, draft letter, 2 November 1970, and Schomer to Niilus, 3 December 1970, ibid.

85. Blake, draft letter, 2 November 1970, and Schomer to Dahlen, 26 October 1970, ibid.

86. Schomer to Blake, 5 February 1971, RG 6, box 26, folder 7, NCC.

87. Niilus memo (draft) to Blake, Schomer, N. Canh, and D. Epps, 2 March

1971; also Dwain Epps, memo, 3 March 1971; all in ibid.

88. Trevor Beeson, "Hard Times for the WCC," *CC*, 26 August 1970, 1008.

89. RSB, "The Changing Domestic Base of U.S. Foreign Policy," Korea-American Consultation, Seoul, Korea, 2–5 December 1970, NCC, RSBP. Unless otherwise noted, all RSB quotations in this and the next four paragraphs are from this paper.

90. Hessel, *Reconciliation*, 18.

91. David Hunter to Rev. Hugh C. White, 12 March 1971, RG 6, box 26, folder 7, NCC.

92. More precisely, Nixon was pursuing military leverage to create at least a temporarily self-defensible state in the South so the United States could declare victory and disengage with honor.

93. DeBenedetti, *American Ordeal*, 298–300.

94. Moss, *Vietnam*, 324–28.

95. Schomer to Blake, 5 February 1971, RG 6, box 26, folder 7, NCC.

96. DeBenedetti, *American Ordeal*, 298–300; Moss, *Vietnam*, 324–28.

97. John Coventry Smith to Blake, 18 February 1971, RG 6, box 26, folder 7, NCC.

98. RSB, EE, Gross, Wedel, "Statement on the Indochina War," 25 February 1971; RSB to Dr. Harold Bosley, 3 March 1971; both in RG 6, box 26, folder 7, NCC.

99. DeBenedetti, *American Ordeal*, 298–99.

100. "New Interreligious Coalition Launches Campaign to Stop the War," press release, 26 February 1971, NCCWOF. See also Hall, *Because of Their Faith*, 112–14. Elston interview, 15 October 1992. "Steering Committee for Interfaith Campaign to Set the Date," December 1970; Allan Brick, memo to invitees, 18 December 1970; both in RG 6, box 26, folder 8, NCC.

101. DeBenedetti, *American Ordeal*, 301. For information on the role of church leaders (including from the NCC and CALCAV) in McGovern's campaign, see Mark A. Lempke, "A Caucus of Prophets: George McGovern's 1972 Campaign and the Crucible of Protestant Politics" (Ph.D. dissertation, University at Buffalo, 2011).

102. "New Interreligious Coalition," press release, 26 February 1971, NCCWOF.

103. DeBenedetti, *American Ordeal*, 298–99.

104. Ibid., 299–307; Elston memo to RSB, 18 January 1971, RG 6, box 26, folder 7, NCC.

105. Hall, *Because of Their Faith*, 127–28; "Medals for Peace—Help Unsell the War," *Playboy* (March 1971), RG 5, box 13, folder 31, NCC.

106. Smith to Laird, 17 February 1971, RG 6, box 26, folder 7, NCC.

107. Schomer, in Niilus memo (draft) to Blake, Schomer, N. Canh, and Epps, 2 March 1971, RG 6, box 26, folder 7, NCC.

108. The phrase about saving not just American lives but human lives comes from ibid.

109. Smith to Laird, 17 February 1971, RG 6, box 26, folder 7, NCC.

110. Niilus to Blake et al., 2 March 1971; Schomer memo to Niilus, "Assignments Recorded in Minutes of Staff Meeting of 12–13 February 1971," 3 March 1971; both in RG 6, box 26, folder 7, NCC.

111. Niilus, Canh, Schomer, Epps memo to Blake, 5 March 1971, ibid.; "Memorandum for Secretary Laird," 17 March 1971, ibid. (although this memo lists no author, it is from the World Council's CCIA).

112. Schomer memo to Blake, 15 March 1971, RG 6, box 26, folder 7, NCC.

113. RSB to Niilus, 23 April 1971; Epps to RSB, 29 April 1971; both in ibid.

114. RSB to Niilus, 24 March 1971, ibid.

115. RSB to Mr. A. M. Hart, 16 March 1971, ibid.

116. DeBenedetti, *American Ordeal*, 303. Hall, *Because of Their Faith*, 110. Consultation Participants, "Paris Consultation on Vietnam," March 1971; "A Message from the Protestant Church Leaders Consultation on Vietnam in Paris March 20–27, 1971," 26 March 1971; both in RG 6, box 26, folder 7, NCC. See also "Churchmen Meet Paris Peacemakers," *Presbyterian Life*, 15 April 1971, 8–9, 27–29. When the travelers visited congressional offices, they also echoed the WCC's recommendations that negotiation procedures be revamped to allow for a more casual, honest, and fluid exchange of ideas. For Elston's thoughts about changes in negotiation procedures, see Elston to N. Tang Canh, 8 April 1971, RG 6, box 30, folder 14, NCC.

117. Elston to Niilus, 2 April 1971, RG 6, box 30, folder 28, NCC.

12—WAGING A MORAL ARGUMENT, MARCH 1971–JANUARY 1973

1. RSB to Blake, 8 April 1971, RG 6, box 26, folder 7, NCC.

2. RSB, draft, 7 April 1971, and RSB to Blake, 8 April 1971, ibid.

3. "Moral and Military Aspects of the War in Southeast Asia," U.S. Senate, Committee on Foreign Relations, Washington, D.C., 7 May 1970, APP.

4. "Strategy Board on Race as a Factor in U.S. Foreign Policy," Department of International Affairs and Department of Social Justice, NCC, 19–20 March 1971, RG 6, box 26, folder 4, NCC.

5. Newt Thurber, "Mission in Vietnam: A Report to the Consultation on Christian Concerns in Tomorrow's Vietnam, Exhibit A," 5 March 1971, RG 6, box 26, folder 7, NCC.

6. "Text of a Statement Issued by Participants in the Interfaith Vigil and Fast before the White House, Washington, D.C. during Holy Week 1971 (April 4–9)," press release, 4 April 1971, RG 6, box 26, folder 7, NCC.

7. William P. Thompson, personal interview with author, 3 September 1991, Princeton, New Jersey (hereafter Thompson interview); DeBenedetti, *American Ordeal*, 303.

8. Thompson interview; Elston interview, 20 October 1992.

9. Editors, "A Call to Penitence and Action," *C&C*, 19 April 1971, 66–68.

10. Robert Harsh, "Holy Week in Jail," *C&C*, 17 May 1971, 99.

11. DeBenedetti, *American Ordeal*, 303–7 for this and previous paragraph.

12. Quoted in ibid., 305.

13. Elston interview, 20 October 1992.

14. DeBenedetti, *American Ordeal*, 303–6.

15. Elston interview, 20 October 1992.

16. DeBenedetti, *American Ordeal*, 307–8.

17. Kerry, in ibid. Fragging refers to the intentional murder of one U.S. soldier (generally an officer) at the hand of another during battle.

18. William P. Thompson, "Testimony on Selective Service to the Senate Armed Services Committee," 8 February 1971, NCCWOF; "A Report on the Swedish Ecumenical Council Conference on U.S. Draft Age Immigrants in Sweden," 24 May 1971, RG 3, box 4, folder 16, NCC; "The U.S. Churches and the War in Vietnam, Swedish Ecumenical Council, Stockholm, Sweden," 23 May 1971, RG 6, box 26, folder 7, NCC.

19. DeBenedetti, *American Ordeal*, 307; Rosemary Ruether, "Who'll Investigate the Investigators?" *Worldview* (May 1971): 9–11, copy also in NCC files.

20. See also Arthur Walmsley to RSB, 16 June 1971, RG 6, box 26, folder 2, NCC. Walmsley was the general secretary of the Massachusetts Council of Churches.

21. Ruether, "Who'll Investigate?" 11.

22. See "Of Betrayal and Loyalty."

23. Allen Parrent, "The Vietnam War as a Moral Issue," sermon, Alexandria, Virginia, 2 May 1971, APP.

24. "The Moral Crisis of the United States in Indochina," *Presbyterian Life*, 1 July 1971, 14–17.

25. Press release C-5, General Board, 12 June 1971, RG 3, box 4, folder 16, NCC; RSB to Mrs. Constance Henry, 29 August 1971, RG 6, box 26, folder 7, NCC.

26. RSB interview, 6 August 1993.

27. James Hitchcock, "Religion and American Culture—The Next Phase," *CC*, 20 September 1972, 915–22.

28. RSB and Elston were both dismayed by Espy's seemingly lost ecumenical priorities and weak leadership during times that they felt required clarity and strength of vision. RSB and Elston interviews.

29. "Concerning the Proposed Meetings on the Vietnam War," General Board, 11–12 June 1971, RG 6, box 26, folder 7, NCC; General Board minutes, 11–12 June 1971, RG 3, box 4, folder 16, NCC.

30. General Board minutes, 4 June 1971, RG 3, box 4, folder 16, NCC; "Action by the General Board for a Conference on Vietnam," 12 June 1971, RG 6, box 26, folder 7, NCC. See also Geyer, "NCC on the Boardwalk."

31. "Concerning the Proposed Meetings," 11–12 June 1971, RG 6, box 26, folder 7, NCC.

32. "Action by the General Board for a Conference on Vietnam," 12 June 1971, ibid.

33. "Concerning the Proposed Meetings," 11–12 June 1971, ibid.

34. Elston interview, 20 October 1992.

35. "Let Politics Live in Vietnam," *CC*, 9 June 1971, 511.

36. My description of this conference comes from Hall, *Because of Their Faith*, 116–25. Regarding plans for this conference, see Naylor memo to RSB, 26 May 1971, RG 6, box 26, folder 7, NCC. For more on FBI surveillance of CALCAV, see http://www.fbi.gov/.

37. As an example of his changing opinions, see Richard John Neuhaus, "The Loneliness of the Long-Distance Radical," *CC*, 26 April 1972, 477–81. Elston interview, 20 October 1971. Along with Michael Novak and Peter Berger, Neuhaus became a strong conservative in the 1970s and helped found the neoconservative Institute on Religion and Democracy (IRD) in 1981, which has become one of the NCC's main adversaries since that time.

38. Hall, *Because of Their Faith*, 116–25.

39. The gap between NCC leadership and parishioners remained the top concern. See Dean Kelley, "The Un-Service Station," *CC*, 30 June 1971, 799–801; John Crossley, "Second Chance for the Neo-Orthodox," *CC*, 8 September 1971, 1048–51. See also Joseph C. Hough Jr., "The Church Alive and Changing," *CC*, 5 January 1972, 8–12. In November, the NCC received its commissioned report about "Today's Church," which pinpointed discrepancies of viewpoints between clergy and laity. "Clergy and Laity Speak Out on Today's Church," *Tempo* 1.9 (December 1971), RG 6,

box 26, folder 6, NCC.

40. Dean Kelley, "Social Outlook," report, General Board, 10 September 1971, RG 3, box 4, folder 16, NCC.

41. William Cate, "Ecumenism on Main Street, USA," *CC*, 17 November 1971, 1339–40. Interfaith and interdenominational activities did not denote full ecumenism, however, according to RSB's definition. Many locals assumed they did.

42. Efforts in other related areas continued, too, such as the Emergency Ministries program for draft-age persons, particularly in the United States, Canada, and Sweden. This program was redesigned (and renamed Emergency Ministries Concerning the War) to include the needs of Vietnam veterans. See "Emergency Ministries Concerning the War," *Department of Higher Education News Notes* 17.6 (November–December 1971); "The Emergency Ministries concerning the War, for Presentation to NCC Executive Committee," 16 December 1971. NCC staff also took supportive roles in CALCAV's fall actions such as the Daily Death Toll in November and began to champion amnesty.

43. For more on national inquiry group preparations, see documents in the NCC dated 1 November 1971 in RG 6, box 26, folder 4. For more on RSB's goals for the conference, see RSB, memo to the Planning Committee for "An Ecumenical Witness" on the Indochina War, 6 December 1971, RG 6, box 26, folder 5, NCC; RSB memo to Blake, 5 August 1971, RG 6, box 26, folder 7, NCC; Press release from An Ecumenical Witness, 30 December 1971, RG 6, box 26, folder 6, NCC.

44. Elston interview, 20 October 1992.

45. Moss, *Vietnam*, 327–30.

46. "A Call to an Ecumenical Witness, Kansas City," NCC, 13–16 January 1972, RG 6, box 26, folder 2, NCC.

47. William Sloane Coffin, "Wanted in 1972: The Truth," January 1972, APP. I could not determine in which journal this appeared. For a shortened version, see "Truth and the War," RG 6, box 26, folder 6, NCC.

48. Rev. Arthur E. Walmsley, "The Search for Moral Competence," January 1972, ibid.

49. Edelman and Luce in a press release from the Ecumenical Witness, Kansas City, 14 January 1972, ibid.

50. Rich Killmer, "An Action Paper for the Church on Vietnam Era Veterans and War Resisters Abroad," Ecumenical Witness, 13 January 1972, ibid.

51. Blake, address, Ecumenical Witness, Kansas City, 15 January 1972, RSBP.

52. Sterling Cary, "Why I Am Against the War in Vietnam," Ecumenical Witness, January 1972, RG 6, box 26, folder 6, NCC.

53. Press release C-6, Ecumenical Witness, Kansas City, 13 January 1972, ibid.

54. André Dumas, "Whether These Were Sins, Not Simply Mistakes," Ecumenical Witness, Kansas City, 16 January 1972, RG 6, box 26, folder 3, NCC. Jurgen Hilke, address, Ecumenical Witness, Kansas City, 16 January 1971, RG 6, box 26, folder 2, NCC.

55. "Church Investments, Technological Warfare and the Military-Industrial Complex," Ecumenical Witness, January 1972, RG 6, box 26, folder 6, NCC; Elston to Cornell West, 5 October 1970, RG 6, box 30, folder 12, NCC; Stephen Rose, "The Coming Confrontation of the Church's War Investments," *CC*, 14 October 1970, 1209–11.

56. Douglas Robinson, "Churches Profit off War," *New York Times*, 5 January

1972; "Church Agency Raps Arms Investments," *Modesto Bee* (AP story), 5 January 1972; both in CS, box 41, 1444-3-3:21, GCAH. See also "Church and Armament Profits," *Christian Advocate*, 1 January 1972.

57. Investment Portfolio Account BX505 F4, 31 March 1972, RG 6, box 26, folder 1, NCC.

58. Winslow to Will, 11 January 1972; Mr. and Mrs. Ted Gribas to Will, 9 March 1972; Rev. William Harvey to Board of Christian Social Concerns, 8 February 1972; Will to Mrs. Ben Phillips, 24 October 1972; all in CS, box 41, 1444-3-3:21, GCAH.

59. James McGraw, "Prophecy, Research and the CIC," *C&C*, 7 February 1972, 14–19.

60. Action Statement, 19 May 1972, RG 6, box 26, folder 1, NCC; "For the 'Clearest Possible Witness,'" *CC*, 26 April 1972, 471.

61. Campaign Honeywell Workshop at St. Stephen and the Incarnation Church, 8–9 September 1972, CS, box 41, 1444-3-3:21, GCAH.

62. Richard Fernandez, "An Experiment in Creative Conflict," Ecumenical Witness, January 1972, RG 6, box 26, folder 6, NCC.

63. Message, Ecumenical Witness, Kansas City, 16 January 1972, ibid.

64. Ibid.

65. Action Strategies, An Ecumenical Witness, Kansas City, 13–16 January 1972, RG 6, box 26, folder 6, NCC.

66. Elston interviews.

67. Edward Fiske, "Religious Assembly Terms Vietnam Policy Immoral," *New York Times*, 17 January 1972, APP.

68. Hamilton/Parrent interview.

69. "Ecumenical Witness: Withdraw Now!" *CC*, 26 January 1972, 81–82.

70. RSB, "No Violin, But Not Yet a Trumpet," January 1972, RG 6, box 26, folder 6, NCC.

71. RSB to Bishop A. James Armstrong, 20 January 1972, RG 6, box 26, folder 2, NCC.

72. RSB interview, 6 August 1993. Dorothy verified RSB's misery during this period.

73. Poikail George, Ecumenical Witness in Kansas City, January 13–16, 1972, RG 6, box 26, folder 2, NCC; Stephen Brown to Bishop James Armstrong, 22 January 1972, RG 6, box 26, folder 4, NCC.

74. Eugene Pulliam, "Social Action and the Pulpit," *Arizona Republic*, 30 January 1972, RG 6, box 26, folder 2, NCC; Lester Kinsolving, "Disruptions," newspaper article (newspaper unknown), 5 February 1972, RG 6, box 26, folder 6, NCC.

75. RSB to Mrs. Renuka M. Somasekhar, 6 April 1972, RG 6, box 26, folder 2, NCC.

76. Ecumenical Witness Planning Committee minutes, 7 February, 6 March 1972, RG 6, box 26, folder 5, NCC. Also Anima Bose to RSB, 24 February 1972; Naylor to John Loney, 25 February 1972; Sara Ashley to RSB, 23 March 1972; RSB memo to Participants in the Ecumenical Witness Conference at Kansas City, 13 April 1972; and Ecumenical Witness Update, 8 June 1972; all in RG 6, box 26, folder 2, NCC. Report on Kansas City Follow-up, Appendix 1, Planning Committee, 6 March 1972, RG 6, box 26, folder 5, NCC.

77. Elston memo to Southeast Asia Working Group, 7 April 1972, RG 6, box 26, folder 1, NCC.

78. Moss, *Vietnam*, 332–36 (Nixon, 334).

79. Pratt, "Religious Faith."

80. RSB to Mrs. Renuka M. Somasekhar, 6 April 1972, RG 6, box 26, folder 2, NCC.

81. Blake to the President, 17 July 1972, RG 6, box 26, folder 1, NCC. Yves Lacoste, "American Aviation Can Cause Flooding in the North without Directly Hitting the Dikes," *LeMonde*, 7 June 1972, RG 6, box 26, folder 2, NCC. Niilus memo to N. Canh and Epps, 10 July 1972; Epps memo to Blake, 13 July 1972; both in RG 6, box 26, folder 1, NCC.

82. Cynthia Clark Wedel and EE, statement, 17 April 1972; Blake to EE, 17 April 1972; both in RG 6, box 26, folder 1, NCC.

83. "This Old and New War," *CC*, 19 April 1972, 439.

84. Untitled, signed statement, 20 April 1972, RG 6, box 26, folder 1, NCC.

85. "So Long as the U.S. Participates in the Indochina War," 21 April 1972, RG 6, box 26, folder 1, NCC.

86. Elston interview, 15 October 1992.

87. "So Long as the U.S. Participates," RG 6, box 26, folder 1, NCC. For an agenda of one of these local observances, see the Church Council of Greater Seattle board of directors, 9 May 1972, RG 6, box 26, folder 2, NCC.

88. "Emergency Convocation to End the War," 10–11 May 1972, RG 6, box 26, folder 1, NCC.

89. Moss, *Vietnam*, 335–36; "Back to the Brink?" *CC*, 24 May 1972, 58. Nixon also softened his settlement terms.

90. David Hunter, memo to Agencies in the Interchurch Center and Other Networks, 11 May 1972; RSB memo to Ecumenical Witness participants, 17 May 1972; RSB to "Network" Friends, 19 May 1972; all in RG 6, box 26, folder 1, NCC. RSB to "Network" Friends, 22 May 1972, RG 6, box 26, folder 2, NCC. Defense Secretary Laird said that, if Congress cut off funding, he would bypass its legislation under the authority of an old Civil War law called the Deficiency Operations Act. Natalie Gawdiak, memo to RSB, 8 June 1972, RG 6, box 26, folder 1, NCC.

91. Statement by Church Leaders, St. John's Church, Washington, D.C., 11 May 1972, RG 6, box 26, folder 1, NCC.

92. RSB to Cynthia Wedel, 15 May 1972, RG 6, box 26, folder 1, NCC.

93. Thompson interview; RSB interviews.

94. Blake to RSB, 19 May 1972; RSB to Blake, 31 May 1972; both in RG 6, box 26, folder 1, NCC.

95. Moss, *Vietnam*, 335–36.

96. "The Worthless Circus of '72," *CC*, 22 March 1972, 327.

97. Stephen Rose, "Eugene Carson Blake: A Welcome-Home Interview," *CC*, 18 October 1972, 1036–39; Blake to Nixon, 26 April 1972, RG 6, box 26, folder 1, NCC.

98. Blake to the President, 16 May 1972, RG 6, box 26, folder 1, NCC.

99. Blake to Dr. John McLaughlin, 6 June 1972, ibid.

100. Rose, "Eugene Carson Blake."

101. Smith to Laird, 27 April 1972, RG 6, box 26, folder 1, NCC.

102. RSB to Blake, 13 July 1972, ibid.

103. James A. Wechsler, "A Studied Evasion," *New York Post*, 25 July 1972, ibid. Apparently the *Washington Post* carried a story about Nixon's refusal to meet with ecumenical leaders back in May. See Carroll Shaw to Nixon, 30 May 1972, ibid.

104. Blake to the President, 17 July 1972, ibid.

105. "Bombing the Dikes," *New York Times*, 22 July 1972, ibid.

106. Frank Denholm to RSB, 28 July 1972, ibid.

107. William L. Springer to RSB, 26 July 1972, ibid.

108. RSB to Blake, 24 July 1972, ibid.

109. "Proposal for Brief Amicus Curiae," May 1972, ibid. See also VanderWerf, *Times Were Very Full*, 109–11.

110. "Resolution on Illegality of Vietnam War," NCC General Board, 10 June 1972, NCCNYO; "Statement to Accompany the Document, Proposed Policy Statement on Amnesty," NCC General Board, Spring 1972, RG 3, box 4, folder 17, NCC.

111. Press release 62DCE, Department of Information, 4 October 1972, NCCWOF; "Grant from the National League of Cities/U.S. Conference of Mayors to the Emergency Ministries Concerning the War of the National Council of Churches," report, spring or fall 1972, RG 6, box 26, folder 1, NCC. For description of the contract, see Bob Hill, memo to John Gunther, 22 August 1972, RG 5, box 15, folder 59, NCC; "Suggested Program for the Emergency Ministries Concerning the War, January 1–June 30, 1972," General Board, 11–15 February 1972, RG 6, box 26, folder 1, NCC; Richard Kilmer, "No Victory Parades," *Event Magazine* (April 1972), in CS, box 42, 1443-4-1:02, GCAH. The Methodists used the NCC's program. See Will, letter to Rev. Jonathan Gosser, 21 January 1972, CS, box 41, 1444-3-3:21, GCAH. The United Presbyterian Church created its own program for veterans in March 1972. See *Monday Morning*, 7 February 1972, 42.

112. "Draft Statement by National Inquiry Group 1," 14 March 1972, RG 6, box 26, folder 3, NCC.

113. "The Indochina War: American Racism Exported Abroad," 6 June 1972, RG 6, box 26, folder 4, NCC.

114. William P. Thompson (chair, National Inquiry Group), *War Crimes: U.S. Priorities and Military Force* (New York: National Council of Churches, 1972), RG 2, box 5, folder 25, NCC; Charles McCollough, *Study Guide for War Crimes, U.S. Priorities and Military Force* (New York: Friendship Press, 1972), RG 6, box 27, folder 5, NCC.

115. Thompson, *War Crimes*.

116. H. Richard Niebuhr, *Christ and Culture*.

117. RSB, "Christian Opposition to the Indochina War," General Board, 10 June 1972, RG 6, box 26, folder 1, NCC. Ironically, the conservative-moving Richard John Neuhaus asked the same thing of the churches in Neuhaus, "The War, the Churches, and Civil Religion," *Annals of the American Academy of Political and Social Science* 387 (January 1970): 128–40.

118. Victor Rockhill to RSB, 4 August 1972, RG 6, box 26, folder 1, NCC.

119. RSB to Victor Rockhill, 18 August 1972; also RSB to Roy Kale, 28 June 1972; both in ibid.

120. Roy Kale to RSB, 12 June 1972, ibid. For other examples, see Burke Baker to RSB and Ken Neigh, 12 June 1972; Frank Maher to RSB, 14 June 1972; both in ibid.

121. Anonymous letter to NCC leaders, 12 June 1972, ibid.

122. Pratt, "Religious Faith"; Settje, *Faith and War*, ch. 4.

123. John Bennett, "The War and the Local Church," *C&C*, 2 October 1972, 215–16.

124. RSB to "Participants in Ecumenical Witness in: California, Illinois, Michi-

gan, New Jersey, New York, Ohio, Pennsylvania, and Peace Action Network in above States," 15 September 1972, RG 6, box 26, folder 2, NCC. Nothing in the records indicated whether this affected the program's reception.

125. Tracy Early, "Dr. Hunter Reports on Week's Visit to North Vietnam," *Religious News Service*, 16 November 1972.

126. John C. Bennett, "Election Reflections," *C&C*, 27 November 1972, 257–58.

127. "New Council Structure," *CC*, 20 December 1972, 1288–89; "New Structure," press release GA-21, General Assembly, 6 December 1972, RG 2, box 5, folder 35, NCC; James Wall, "The Quota: A Necessary Aberration," *CC*, 20 December 1972, 1287; Betty Thompson, "No Signs of Death for NCC," *CC*, 20 December 1972, 1287–88.

128. "NCC Upbeat in New Orleans," *CC*, 22 September 1971, 1100–101.

129. On the DCLM situation, see Elston interviews; also "Proposed Administrative Organization of the National Council of the Churches of Christ in the United States of America," Organization and Management, November 1972, RG 2, box 5, folder 25, NCC. With respect to Espy's retirement, he had worked for the NCC in various capacities since 1955. Although some criticized his leadership during the Council's most volatile years, all spoke of him with great personal affection, especially for his dedication to his work, his commitment to social justice and reconciliation, and his big-hearted kindness toward others. After he retired, he focused upon fostering interreligious cooperation and served in leadership roles within the American Baptist Convention; "R. H. Edwin Espy, World Ecumenist Led National Council" given to author by EE.

130. Articles in *Monday Morning*, "Toward Strengthening Mission," 12 February 1973, 9–10; J. Harold Thomson, "It Ain't What It Used to Be," 17 April 1972, 12; Caroll Jenkins, "Much to Do about Life in the Future," 17 April 1972, 13; see also the 15 January 1973 issue for more.

131. "Summary of Concerns, Issues and Strategies which Resulted from the General Assembly, NCCCUSA in Dallas, TX," draft, 12 January 1973, RG 2, box 5, folder 33, NCC.

132. As one example, see Alwen Neuharth to David Hunter, 23 December 1972, RG 2, box 5, folder 33, NCC.

133. Lester Kinsolving, "Can Council of Churches Survive?" *Rapid City Journal*, 24 December 1972, RG 2, box 5, folder 33, NCC.

134. "New Structure," press release GA-21, General Assembly, 6 December 1972, RG 2, box 5, folder 35, NCC.

135. See several collected articles in RG 2, box 5, folder 33, NCC. One is by Herb Philbrick of the U.S. Press Association and was printed in a Florida newspaper.

136. General Assembly, press release or follow-up report, December 1972, RG 2, box 5, folder 33, NCC.

137. "Resolution on Racial Tensions and Violence in the Armed Forces" and "Policy Statement on the Indochina War: Healing the Divisions of the Nation," both General Board, 2 December 1972, NCCNYO; "Resolution on Vietnam Veterans Against the War: Conspiracy Indictments" and "Resolution on Military Force and Foreign Policy," both General Assembly, 6 December 1972, NCCNYO; "Resolution on Medical Aid to Indochina," and "Resolution on Peace in Indochina," both General Assembly, NCC, 7 December 1972, NCCNYO. "Resolution on Call to a Religious Convocation in Washington, D.C.," General Assembly, 7 December 1972, RG 2, box 5, folder 6, NCC. "Resolution of Action on the Christmas Campaign 'For the Victims'

of the Vietnam War," General Assembly, NCC, 7 December 1972, in VanderWerf, *The Times Were Very Full*, 107.

138. Albert McClellan, letter to EE, 22 December 1972, RG 2, box 5, folder 33, NCC.

139. Moss, *Vietnam*, 337–44.

140. "Statement by Dr. Thompson and Dr. Espy," 21 December 1972, RG 6, box 27, folder 5, NCC.

141. RSB memo to EE and David Hunter, 5 January 1973, RG 5, box 16, folder 4, NCC.

142. Moss, *Vietnam*, 339–42.

143. Doris Kearns, *Lyndon Johnson and the American Dream* (New York: Signet, 1976), 382.

144. Moss, *Vietnam*, 339–42.

145. Maclear, *Ten Thousand Day War*, 310.

146. Moss, *Vietnam*, 344.

147. "'Honorable' Peace: Final Self-Deception," *CC*, 7 February 1973, 139.

EPILOGUE—FORTY YEARS IN THE WILDERNESS

1. RSB, "The Depth of Militarism," *CC*, 28 February 1973, 259–62. The Council's new Governing Board agreed and encouraged Americans to aid war victims in Indochina in a relationship-building effort. The WCC established the Fund for Reconstruction and Reconciliation in Indochina, and the NCC's Governing Board urged its members to give. Half of the board members selected to administer the fund were Indochinese persons, and the board was committed to letting the Indochinese determine the use of collected donations. "Resolution on Indochina," Governing Board, NCC, 1 March 1973, NCCNYC.

2. "Pastoral Letter from Bishop Armstrong to Be Read in All United Methodist Churches in the Dakota Area Sunday, March 18, 1973," CS, 1479-2-3:21, GCAH; Leonard Crow Dog and Richard Erdoes, *Crow Dog: Four Generations of Sioux Medicine Men* (New York: HarperCollins, 1995), 185–243; Paul Chaat Smith and Robert Allen Warrior, *Like a Hurricane: The Indian Movement from Alcatraz to Wounded Knee* (New York: New Press, 1996), 194–279.

3. "American Indian Movement, Box 147, Rapid City, South Dakota," CS 1445-3-3:13, GCAH; Smith and Warrior, *Like a Hurricane*, 196, 211–13; Crow Dog and Erdoes, *Crow Dog*, 192; Rolland Dewing, *Wounded Knee II* (Freeman, SD: Pine Hill Press, 1995), 56, 92.

4. Parts of this section appeared first in Jill K. Gill, "Preventing a Second Massacre at Wounded Knee, 1973," *Methodist History* 43.1 (October 2004): 45–56. After the conflict, the NCC provided legal aid for Indians who were prosecuted.

5. John P. Adams to Rev. Mr. Ray Woodruff, June 7, 1973, CS, 1445-3-1:26, GCAH; "Crisis Facilitator Sums Up Wounded Knee," *Christian Advocate*, 5 July 1973, 19, CS, 1445-3-2:40, GCAH; Smith and Warrior, *Like a Hurricane*, 200–214, 230, 254–55; John Kifner, "U.S. Removes Roadblocks in Wounded Knee Vicinity," *New York Times*, 11 March 1973, CS, 1485-4-1:14, GCAH; Rolland Dewing, *Wounded Knee II* (Freeman, SD: Pine Hill Press, 1995), 60–61. In September 1971, inmates at Attica prison took hostages and began to protest poor conditions and treatment at the facility. After a period of negotiations, state troopers stormed the building. Ten hostages and

twenty-nine inmates were killed by the police with roughly another eighty wounded. Later, the inmates won a class action lawsuit against the state of New York. This made many question the efficacy of heavy-handed, violent, "law and order" tactics of the type that Nixon had championed.

6. Dennis Banks, "Consciousness Raising," *Engage/Social Action* 3 (January 1975): 37–39, CS, 1445-3-3:13, GCAH.

7. "Resolution on Ending Further Involvement in Indochina War," Governing Board, 27 February 1974, NCCNYO. Thompson, Cary, Moore, Lord, and Gumbleton, telegram to Nixon, 13 December 1973; Sterling Cary, memo to religious community, 18 January 1974; both in RG 5, box 15, folder 59, NCC. Amnesty and Discharge Legislation, Special Ministries, 11 February 1974, NCCWOF; Press release 22 DEM, NCC Department of Information, 14 March 1973, RG 5, box 15, folder 59, NCC; Rich Killmer [and others], "Doing Theology through Special Ministries," 1975, NCCWOF.

8. "Resolution on Vietnam," Governing Board, 10 October 1976, NCCNYO.

9. Martin Marty, "Watergate Year as Watershed Year," *CC*, 26 December 1973, 1272–74.

10. Donald Bloesch, "Key 73: Pathway to Renewal?" *CC*, 3 January 1973, 9–11. See also Cornish Rogers, "NCC Tests New Structures," *CC*, 14 March 1973, 307–8; Marty, "Watergate Year."

11. Lyman Kellstedt, John Green, Corwin Smidt, James Guth, "Faith Transformed: Religion and American Politics from FDR to George W. Bush," in Noll and Harlow, *Religion and American Politics*, 269–96; Lichtman, *White Protestant Nation*, 341–49.

12. VanderWerf, *Times Were Very Full*, 93–97; "NCC Unit to 'Listen,'" *CC*, 27 March 1974, 334–35. The NCC had launched a "Listening-to-lay people project" in 1968; the findings were distributed in 1971. See "Who's Listening to Lay People?" *CC*, 11 August 1971, 943. In 1972, the NCC completed a "North American Interchurch Study," which surveyed lay and clergy attitudes about church. See "Why Church?" *CC*, 12 January 1972, 27.

13. James Wall, "The Unread World of an NCC Meeting," *CC*, 19 March 1975, 275–76. Parts of the epilogue appeared first in Jill K. Gill, "The Politics of Ecumenical Disunity: The Troubled Marriage of Church World Service and the National Council of Churches," *Religion and American Culture* 14.2 (Summer 2004): 175–212.

14. RSB left sometime in 1973. His son Bobby said the NCC shut down RSB's entire IAC operation under funding pressure. The NCC's racial justice staff also took a hit, as did those in many of its member denominations. See Bradford Verter, "Furthering the Freedom Struggle: Racial Justice Activism in the Mainline Churches since the Civil Rights Era," in Wuthnow and Evans, *Quiet Hand of God*, 181–212; Findlay, *Church People*, 213.

15. RSB interview, 6 August 1993.

16. According to his son Bobby, he applied for several pastorates during this time and at one point was seriously considered for a top administration job at Princeton Theological Seminary.

17. RSB, "Let American Ecumenism," *Worship*, September 1977, 407–19 (417).

18. President Jimmy Carter's address at Notre Dame University, 22 May 1977, from Robert J. McMahon, ed., *Major Problems in the History of the Vietnam War* (Lexington: D.C. Heath, 1990), 600–601.

19. William P. Thompson said that he recommended RSB for the role. Thomp-

son interview. Bobby Bilheimer called the institute an "ecumenical think tank," noting that the job was perfect for his father. REB interview.

20. RSB passed away December 2006 from Alzheimer's at the age of eighty-nine. See Patrick Henry's obituary of RSB, http://www.yale.edu/divinity/notes/061220/bilheimer.shtml (11 January 2007).

21. Randall, a layperson herself, felt a strong need to connect better with laity.

22. Elston interviews.

23. Elston interview, 20 October 1992.

24. There is record of him in this role, June 1975; see Gerhard Elston collection, DG 165, SCPC.

25. A week after my last extensive interview with him in October 1992, Elston died of a massive heart attack in New York City. He was sixty-eight years old.

26. Hunter interview. David Hunter described the large rift between the "social service" and "social action" people as being partly rooted in budgetary competition. Both groups saw their own financial needs as paramount, and as Hunter said, they couldn't get excited about the other's ministry.

27. David Stowe, "Summary of Church-State Discussion in NCC," presented to DOM Program Board, 3 March 1967; also MacCracken, "CWS and Church-State Relations;" both in RG 8, box 96, folder CWS: Church & State, 1967, NCC. Thomas J. Liggett to MacCracken, 16 February 1972; and MacCracken to Liggett, 24 February 1972; both in RG 8, box 98, folder: Denominations, NCC. In the late 1950s and early 1960s, CWS projects might receive two-thirds of their funding and supplies from government sources, but Stenning says that by 1974 CWS had cut its use of PL 480 commodities to 15 percent of its budget and to 10 percent by 1975. See *Church World Service*, 25, 65. In 1989 Linda-Marie Delloff listed government aid at 9 percent of the CWS budget. Linda-Marie Delloff, "The NCC in a New Time (II)," *C&C*, 9 January 1989, 466–72. CWS still accepts government help for specific relief projects. In *Church World Service*, Stenning emphasizes that CWS always had a policy stressing self-help and indigenous control of relief programs once indigenous groups were ready to take over. But the records indicate that it was both time and debate that took the CWS's Commission on Tomorrow's Vietnam in that direction.

28. Stenning interview; Stenning, *Church World Service*, 23–105. Staff members in the NCC's International Affairs Commission recalled that "old China hands" within the DOM tended to side with CWS, while other DOM executives understood the IAC's "confessing church" suspicion of government entanglements.

29. Leaman, "Politicized Service." Even though VNCS leaders quelled the upstarts and smoothed relations with government, the issue grew more divisive as the war continued to sour. Events that fueled general suspicion of government operations may have also contributed to CWS's decision to reduce government aid. These included the credibility gap revealed by the Tet offensive, media exposure of corruption within the South Vietnamese government, and the uncovering of secret CIA funding for certain student and religious organizations in the United States.

30. For MacCracken's biting response to the VNCS personnel director who was beginning to criticize the war and advocate more political involvement for VNCS, see Leaman, "Politicized Service," 563. MacCracken to Howard Kresge, 17 August 1971, RG 8, box 98, folder: A.I.D., NCC. For statistics on numbers served and food distributed over its history, see Stenning, *Church World Service*.

31. See Abbott, "CWS's Mandate," 823–24.

32. See Stenning, *Church World Service*, 63–64; CWS Consultation, Stony Point, New York, 20–21 June 1973.

33. *The United States and East Asia: A Christian Context for the Development of New Relationships Among Peoples*, Program Boards of Division of Christian Life and Mission and Division of Overseas Ministries, NCC, December 1971, RSBP.

34. Peter Kihss, "Church World Service Repudiates Promotion of Revolutionary Change," *New York Times*, 16 July 1974, 71.1. See also Abbott, "CWS's Mandate"; "Is Relief Enough?" *Time*, 21 October 1974, 97–98.

35. James Wall, "Strategy Conflict at Church World Service," *CC*, 17 July 1974. Specifically, Eugene Stockwell—recently appointed head of the DOM, and a Methodist with a missions background in Latin America—pressed for MacCracken's departure, with the support of NCC executives.

36. Hostetter and McIntyre, "Politics of Charity." Interestingly, Hostetter (Mennonite) had worked for VNCS in Vietnam from 1966 to 1969. For more on Hostetter's work with VNCS, see Leaman, "Politicized Service."

37. This was done in conjunction with Lutheran World Relief, which paid 40 percent of the cost; CWS paid 60 percent. See Stenning, *Church World Service*, 64–87.

38. Fiske wrote this after the NCC's 1969 General Assembly; see Fiske, "Church Council's Parley."

39. As of 2010, the NCC's archival records after 1973 were not yet publicly available to scholars. Therefore, I have pieced together the relevant continuing threads of the Council's more recent history using other sources.

40. CWS was overruled by its superiors in the DOM. See also Kihss, "Church World Service"; Abbott, "CWS's Mandate"; "Is Relief Enough?"

41. Stenning, *Church World Service*, 79–84. CWS also assisted Vietnamese refugees who were seeking to emigrate in order to reunite with family. It provided relief in Cambodia (Kampuchea) after Pol Pot's regime fell, and this with U.S. permission. (The U.S. government allowed only relief aid, no development assistance.)

42. See Lester Kurtz and Kelly Goran Fulton, "Love Your Enemies? Protestants and United States Foreign Policy," in Wuthnow and Evans, *Quiet Hand of God*, 364–80. Reagan refused to meet with NCC leaders to discuss Central America policies.

43. Kurtz and Fulton, "Love Your Enemies?"

44. RSB's son Bobby said that Vietnam-era vets were treated just like Vietnam War vets. When he returned from the army, no one asked him questions or wanted to talk about it. Once he was out of the military, people expected him to move on with his life and showed little interest in hearing about his experiences. "This included members of my own family," he clarified, "including my father. And it was very deep and very pervasive." REB interview.

45. For three examples, see Herring's, Moss's, and Marilyn Young's histories of the war. For some discussion of various lessons and narratives, see Herring, *Longest War*, 272–81; Thomas G. Patterson, "Vietnam and Central America," in McMahon, *Major Problems*, 621–34. Nixon largely agreed with Reagan's spin. See Richard Nixon, "No More Vietnams," in McMahon, *Major Problems*, 601–3. Robert McNamara's lessons refute Reagan's and Westmoreland's; see the last chapter of *In Retrospect*. For one historian's analysis of the revisionist process, see H. Bruce Franklin, *Vietnam and Other American Fantasies* (Amherst: University of Massachusetts Press, 2000). See especially Mitchell Hall's marvelous short historiographical discussion of Vietnam

War narratives in *The Vietnam War*, 83–87.

46. Pratt, "Religious Faith," 275–350. See also Hargis's book *Our Vietnam Defeat! What Happened: A Study in International Defeat, Shabby Betrayal, Shameful Retreat* (Neosho, MO: Operation God and Country; Tulsa, OK: Christian Crusade, 1975). Hall discusses the "stab-in-the-back" thesis in *The Vietnam War*, 84–85.

47. Richard John Neuhaus, "War, Churches, and Civil Religion," *Annals of the American Academy of Political and Social Science* 387 (January 1970): 128–40. Parts of this section were published earlier in Gill, "Religious Communities and the Vietnam War."

48. Geyer interview. See Manza and Brooks, "Changing Political Fortunes," 159–78. Even though the essay's argument asserts the gradual growing liberalism of mainline voters from the 1960s to the 1990s, its voting charts reveal a mainline dip toward conservative ideas in 1980 when Reagan was elected. Lichtman, *White Protestant Nation*, 341–78. Dochuk traces Reagan's wooing of evangelicals back to his days as governor of California; Reagan's relationship with and mobilization of evangelicals politically was stronger than Nixon's. See Dochuk, *From Bible Belt*, 263, 269–74, 295–306, 357–61, ch. 13, 405–6.

49. Joseph A. Harriss, "Karl Marx or Jesus Christ?" *Reader's Digest* (August 1982): 130–34; Kinnamon, *Vision*, 1–4.

50. Richard N. Ostling, "Warring over Where Donations Go," *Time*, 28 March 1983, 58–59.

51. Rael Jean Isaac, "Do You Know Where Your Church Offerings Go?" *Reader's Digest* (January 1983): 120–25; Robert McAfee Brown, "The Gospel According to Morley Safer," *CC*, 2 March 1983, 183–86; "'60 Minutes' Preview," *CC*, 9 March 1983, 209–10; James M. Wall, "A Religious Mandate to Be Involved," *CC*, 9 March 1983, 203; Isaac C. Rottenberg, "Why Did the NCC Get Such Bad Press?" *Christianity Today*, 20 May 1983, 25–26.

52. For example, they said it denounced United States–supported dictatorial regimes in Latin America but muted its criticism of communist governments such as those in Cuba, Vietnam, China, and the Soviet Union. When the NCC sent food into communist Vietnam to feed starving refugees, they accused it of helping Vietnam's communist government, arguing that its repressive regime benefited as well. For more on CWS's wheat shipment to Vietnam, see Stenning, *Church World Service*, 79–81.

53. Stenning, *Church World Service*, 98.

54. Marjorie Hyer, "Interfaith Conference Spurs Debate on Religious Liberty," *Los Angeles Times*, 27 April 1985, 5.

55. Alan Geyer, *Ideology in America: Challenges to Faith* (Louisville: Westminster John Knox Press, 1997), 69–82. Geyer details the IRD's long history of attacks on mainline Protestant churches and ecumenical organizations, especially the NCC. He also notes that the IRD helped create several conservative organizations within mainline Protestant communions—such as Presbyterians for Democracy and Religious Freedom; United Methodist Action for Faith, Freedom, and Family; and Episcopal Action for Faith, Freedom, and Family—and that these are based in and run from the IRD headquarters in Washington, D.C. See also Oden, *Turning Around the Mainline*, especially page 74. See also Bob Edgar, *Middle Church: Reclaiming the Moral Values of the Faithful Majority from the Religious Right* (New York: Simon and Schuster, 2006), 23–24. Edgar says that the IRD was created specifically to attack the NCC.

56. Hyer, "Interfaith Conference"; Kenneth L. Woodward with David Gates,

"Ideology Under the Alms," *Newsweek*, 7 February 1983, 61–62.

57. See also Rottenberg, "Bad Press."

58. Woodward with Gates, "Ideology"; Wall, "Religious Mandate."

59. See Brown, "Gospel According to Morley Safer"; "'60 Minutes' Preview"; Wall, "Religious Mandate."

60. "Death of Former NCC General Secretary Claire Randall Invokes Memories of a Gracious and Decisive Leader," NCC News Service, 12 September 2007, http://www.ncccusa.org/news/070912clairerandall.html (3 June 2008).

61. Delloff, "NCC in a New Time."

62. Stenning, *Church World Service*, 99; James Wall, "'Integration' Sparks NCC Showdown," *CC*, 4 November 1987, 955–56.

63. In the early 1970s, Brouwer led one of the task forces charged with proposing a restructuring plan for the NCC after its 1969 General Assembly. Ironically, most of the options that his group pushed would have decentralized the NCC into something like the General Ecumenical Council that EE had suggested at the 1969 assembly. Yet when Brouwer's group proposed these, EE and W. Sterling Cary argued against them, charging they would diffuse and fracture the ecumenical mission and vision. See "More Power to the NCC!" *CC*, 10 February 1971, 179; "CWS Chief Endorsed," *CC*, 28 October 1987, 936–37. The expressed goals were to create a more unified ecumenical organization, reduce the "turf-driven culture" of the NCC, and keep closer tabs on programs and budgets. See Jean Caffey Lyles, "The National Council of Churches: Is There Life After 50?" *CC*, 10 November 1999, 1086–93; Arie Brouwer, "The Real Crises at the NCC," *CC*, 27 June–4 July 1990, 641–45.

64. Wall, "Integration"; Brouwer, "The Real Crises"; Wesley Granberg-Michaelson, "Time for New Wineskins?" *CC*, 10 November 1999, 1076–77; Lyles, "National Council of Churches."

65. Delloff, "NCC in a New Time." This article also puts some of the blame upon poor financial management and planning.

66. "CWS Chief Endorsed."

67. Brouwer, "The Real Crises"; Wall, "Integration"; Delloff, "NCC in a New Time"; Jean Caffey Lyles, "NCC Officials Put Dispute on Hold," *CC*, 18 November 1987, 1021–22; Stenning, *Church World Service*, 114–15.

68. Lyles, "National Council of Churches"; Brouwer, "The Real Crises"; William Lawson and Roger Schrock, "Interpreting the Crisis at the NCC," *CC*, 27 June–4 July 1990, 637–38.

69. "CWS Chief Endorsed."

70. "Butler Resigns from CWS," *CC*, 8–15 June 1988, 567 (quote); "Figure in the National Council of Churches' Power Struggle Quits," *Los Angeles Times*, 28 May 1988, 6.

71. Gustav Spohn, "NCC Leader Stuns Board," *Christianity Today*, 16 June 1989, 52. For Brouwer's perspective, see Brouwer, "The Real Crises."

72. Spohn, "NCC Leader," 52; Brouwer, "The Real Crises"; "CWS Seeks Independence," *CC*, 21–28 December 1988, 1176. CWS had considered independence at other times in the past.

73. Delloff, "NCC in a New Time"; Brouwer, "The Real Crises."

74. Granberg-Michaelson, "Time for New Wineskins?"; "Embattled Head of National Council of Churches Quits," *Los Angeles Times*, 1 July 1989, 7; "Council of Churches' Head to Resign Today," *Washington Post*, 27 June 1989, A6; David Kling-

hoffer, "National Council of Churches Eschews Reform," *Wall Street Journal*, 15 May 1989, 1; "Split Vote over Leadership Reflects National Council of Churches' Rift," *Los Angeles Times*, 20 May 1989, 6. For more, see Findlay, "Recent History."

75. Paul Crow, email to author, 19 May 2003. For more on this general debate, see Kinnamon, *Vision*.

76. Delloff, "NCC in a New Time"; "Split Vote."

77. Stenning, *Church World Service*, 116–17. Sarah Vilankulu differs slightly in her recollections of this, emphasizing that Church World Service and Witness was a blend of CWS and the DOM. She clarifies that the DCLM became the DCS, which later became the "Prophetic Justice Unit" and, later, the "National Ministries Unit." When CWS split from the NCC in 2000, the remaining NCC was, in effect, the National Ministries Unit, so the unit disbanded. At the time of my conversation with Vilankulu, she noted that the NCC was then restructuring into five commissions: Faith and Order, Interfaith Relations, Communications, Education and Leadership Ministries, and Justice and Advocacy (which took over former DCS functions). Sarah Vilankulu, conversation with author, 17 June 2003 (hereafter Vilankulu conversation).

78. John H. Adams, "NCC Wants to Divert Hunger Funds to Reduce Budget Shortfall," *The Layman Online*, 18 November 1999, www.layman.org (30 January 2003); Vilankulu conversation. Vilankulu served in the Communications Department for both organizations. Another reason perhaps to use "CWS/CROP" was that "CROP" had good name recognition among laity. CROP was originally an acronym for "Christian Rural Overseas Program." The acronym is no longer pertinent to the program (so is no longer treated as an acronym), yet CWS retained the name CROP due to its historical roots and popularity.

79. William McKinney, "The NCC in a New Time (I)," *C&C*, 9 January 1989, 465–66. Some questioned whether this expression of Christianity had ever been popular beyond the bureaucratic ranks and seminaries of the mainline denominations. See Kenneth S. Kantzer, "Liberalism's Rise and Fall," *Christianity Today*, 18 February 1983, 10–11.

80. Rottenberg, "Bad Press."

81. The deficit figure comes from Rev. Dr. Paul Crow Jr., who served on the NCC's Governing Board for about thirty years. Edgar interview. See also Peter J. Pizor to GAC Executive Committee [Presbyterian Church USA], 14 February 2000, www.pforum.org/wupdates/gac2000/pizor.htm (30 January 2003).

82. John McCullough, personal interview with author, 27 July 2003, New York, NY (hereafter McCullough interview).

83. The first point is from Edgar interview; the second point is in Clifton Kirkpatrick to the Presbyterian Church (USA), 19 November 1999, www.pcusa.org/oga/sclerk/nccletter.htm (30 January 2003).

84. See NAE website, history section.

85. CWS budget information is posted on its website at www.churchworldservice.org.

86. McCullough interview. See also Diane L. Knippers and Joan Brown Campbell, "Have American Churches Politicized Their Religious Mission?" *Insight on the News*, 12 February 1996, 26–28.

87. McCullough interview.

88. "Rev. Dr. Rodney Page Retires from CWS Director Post," NCC News Service, 31 May 2000, www.ncccusa.org/news/00archives.html (30 January 2003). Page had expanded CWS's annual income from forty-two to sixty-two million dollars, in four

years, by increasing government funds, foundation gifts, and grassroots donations.

89. Jean Caffey Lyles, "Dollars and Signs," *CC*, 7–14 June 2000, 638–39; "$500,000 Lilly Endowment Development Grant Caps National Council of Churches' Financial Turnaround," NCC News Service, 1 August 2002, at www.ncccusa.org/news/02archives.html (30 January 2003); Lyles, "National Council of Churches."

90. "Church World Service Launches New Identity," NCC News Service, 29 November 2001, at www.ncccusa.org/news/01archives.html (30 January 2003). McCullough interview.

91. See the CWS website at www.churchworldservice.org/ and the NCC website at www.ncccusa.org/ (30 January 2003).

92. Edgar interview. As of 2003, the NCC and CWS still held joint General Assemblies.

93. Ibid.

94. McCullough interview; Vilankulu conversation.

95. Sarah Vilankulu said the NCC is at its best when serving as a quick-response task force on crisis issues; this is when the churches most need and seek cooperation with the NCC. Vilankulu conversation.

96. Barbara Brown Zikmund, conversation with author, 13 April 2007, Salt Lake City, Utah (hereafter Zikmund conversation). At the time of the conversation, she was a member of the NCC's executive committee.

97. As president of the Claremont School of Theology, Edgar helped restore that institution financially. The NCC hired him, in part, to do the same. "$500,000 Lilly Endowment Grant"; Edgar interview; "National Council of Churches," Presbyterian Church (USA), 2001, www.pforum.org/ga213/primer/issues/ncc.htm (30 January 2003).

98. Edgar interview.

99. Ibid. Poverty and the environment have been identified as the two most popular social issues for Americans. See Robert Wuthnow, "Beyond Quiet Influence? Possibilities for the Protestant Mainline," in Wuthnow and Evans, *Quiet Hand of God*, 381–403. For more on CCT, see "Plans for 'Christian Churches Together in the USA' Move from Vision toward Reality," 29 January 2003, www.ncccusa.org/about/cctusa.html (1 September 2006). An idea similar to CCT was floated in 1971 among NCC staff and even proposed by a special NCC committee. See "National Council May Be Widened," *Monday Morning*, 15 February 1971, 4. Although CCT has drawn Roman Catholic, evangelical, and Pentecostal involvement, conservative churches remained suspicious because of its perceived connection to the NCC. John Dart, "New Funds Boost NCC," *CC*, 14 August 2002, 12–13.

100. Edgar interview. See CCT website at www.christianchurchestogether.org.

101. Both Edgar and Vilankulu confirmed the sensed need for continuation of the NCC's special advocacy role. Edgar interview; Vilankulu conversation.

102. Edgar interview.

103. Edgar made numerous television appearances, going toe-to-toe in interviews with Jerry Falwell and other leaders of conservative Christian organizations such as the Christian Coalition and the IRD.

104. Edgar interview; see also Edgar, *Middle Church*, preface and page 11.

105. Edgar interview. He was a six-term member of the U.S. House of Representatives, serving from 1974 to 1987, where he was the first Democrat in over a century from Pennsylvania's largely Republican Seventh District. See also Edgar, *Middle Church*, 82–84.

106. Later, more leaders signed it. Letter from U.S. Church Leaders to George W. Bush, 12 September 2002, at www.ncccusa.org/news/02news83.html (1 September 2006). This letter was preceded on 29 August 2002 by one from thirty-eight church leaders from the United States, Britain, and Canada, who drafted it while attending a meeting at the WCC. In this letter, they noted that the "United Nations Charter does not permit states to engage in pre-emptive war." See "Leaders from American, Canadian, British Churches Appeal to U.S. Government: 'Stop the Rush to War,'" 29 August 2002, at www.ncccusa.org/news/02news82.html (1 September 2006). Edgar, *Middle Church*, 65–75.

107. Bishop Wilton D. Gregory to President George W. Bush, "Letter to President Bush on Iraq," 13 September 2002, at www.ncccusa.org/iraq/iraqlinks.html (November 2002).

108. John L. Allen Jr., "Vatican Will Not Support American War on Iraq," *National Catholic Reporter*, 20 September 2002.

109. Don Lattin, "Clerics Question Whether Pre-Emptive Iraq Strike Would Be 'Just War,'" *San Francisco Chronicle*, 15 October 2003, A-16.

110. For more on the NCC's humanitarian mission to Iraq from 29 December 2001 to 3 January 2002, which took thirteen religious leaders to Iraq, see "NCC-Led Religious Leaders Mission to Iraq Concludes," 3 January 2002, at www.ncccusa.org/news/02news104.html (1 September 2006). Edgar also discusses the mission in *Middle Church*, 65–75. Additionally, the NCC organized a religious delegation to visit five capitals in Europe (including Paris, London, Berlin, Rome) on a peace-seeking mission; see "NCC Delegation to Paris Surprises Many with Opposition to War," 12 February 2003, at www.ncccusa.org/news/03news10.html (1 September 2006).

111. Edgar interview.

112. Lichtman, *White Protestant Nation*, 442. Richard Land, et al., to President George W. Bush, 3 October 2002, http://erlc.com/article/the-so-called-land-letter/.

113. Edgar interview. The request for a meeting came from forty-six religious leaders who were unhappy about Bush's stance on Iraq. See one letter by a member of Bush's staff declining Edgar's request for a meeting, Bradley A. Blakeman to Dr. Edgar, 5 March 2006, at www.ncccusa.org/news/03news4.html (1 September 2006). On the meeting with Blair, see "U.S. Church Leaders Meet Blair in Third of Five NCC-Led Peace Delegations," 18 February 2003, at www.ncccusa.org/news/03news14.html (1 September 2006). Jim Wallis includes a useful description of the meeting in *God's Politics: Why the Right Gets It Wrong and the Left Doesn't Get It* (New York: HarperCollins, 2005), 133–36.

114. Peter Jennings and John Kerry were two who did.

115. Wuthnow, "Beyond Quiet Influence?" 395.

116. Dochuk, "Evangelicalism Becomes Southern," 303; Lichtman, *White Protestant Nation*, 346; Hulsether, *Religion*, 182–83.

117. Jon Meacham, "Pilgrim's Progress," *Newsweek*, 14 August 2006, 37–43.

118. Martin, *God on Our Side*, 299–328.

119. In all, 76 percent of Americans do not want religious leaders expressing political views from the pulpit, but they support airing those views in other forums. Wuthnow, "Beyond Quiet Influence?"

120. Laura Olson, "Mainline Protestant Washington Office and the Political Lives of Clergy," ibid., 54–79.

121. On Democrats' seeking to change the party's anti-religious reputation, see "Moral Values: God Is a Liberal," in James Carville and Paul Begala, *Take It Back: Our*

Party, Our Country, Our Future (New York: Simon and Schuster, 2006), ch. 2.

122. For example, see Ann Coulter, *Godless: The Church of Liberalism* (New York: Crown Forum, 2006).

123. See, for example, the Conference on Spiritual Activism in May 2006 cosponsored by organizations such as Tikkun, All Souls Church in Washington, D.C., Pacific School of Religion, Buddhist Peace Fellowship, New Dimensions, the Board of Church and Society of the United Methodist Church, The Shalom Center, Christian Alliance for Progress, Progressive Muslim Union, CrossWalk America, Human Rights Campaign, Pax Christi, Share International Magazine, and a group the NCC helped found, FaithfulAmerica.org.

124. For example, the NCC was involved with "Ecumenical Advocacy Days," which drew together over nine hundred Christian activists to talk about strategies on issues of concern, as well as to visit members of Congress about domestic and foreign policy. See "Ecumenical Advocacy Days: Church leaders seek solidarity as they tackle the tough issues facing the nation," 8 March 2006, at www.ncccusa.org/news/06030 9ecumenicaladvocacydays.html (1 September 2006). For another example, see the Network of Spiritual Progressives (NSP) nurtured by Tikkun and other groups. See www.Tikkun.org.

125. "Religion Taking a Left Turn?" *CBS News*, 10 July 2006, at www.ncccusa. org/news/newshome.html (1 September 2006).

126. Olson, "Mainline Protestant Washington Offices," 54–79.

127. See Oden, *Turning Around the Mainline*. Oden even provides tips on how "orthodox" Christians within the mainline churches can attempt to take control of mainline church property.

128. Manza and Brooks, "Changing Political Fortunes," 159–80; Wuthnow, "Beyond Quiet Influence?" 381–404; Nancy Ammerman, "Connecting Mainline Protestant Churches with Public Life," in Wuthnow and Evans, *Quiet Hand of God*, 129–58.

129. In addition to bearing fewer children, which Hulsether says explains about 80 percent of the difference between liberal and conservative growth rates, mainline Protestants tend to marry later than evangelicals and to wait longer before having kids. They also tend to be older than evangelicals, often past child-bearing years. Hulsether, *Religion*, 158; Manza and Brooks, "Changing Political Fortunes"; Peter Thuesen, "The Logic of Mainline Churchliness," in Wuthnow and Evans, *Quiet Hand of God*, 27–53. Mainline conservatives, eager to disparage liberal leaders within their ranks, continue to push the idea that mainline decline is due to defections to the right. See Oden, *Turning Around the Mainline*, and the IRD website.

130. Manza and Brooks, "Changing Political Fortunes." For information on evangelicals' moving away from GOP politics and toward issues such as poverty, see, for example, Holly Lebowitz Rossi, "Poverty Is Rick Warren's Passionate New Purpose," Religion News Service, 12 June 2005, at http://pewforum.org/news/display. php?NewsID=4938 (2 March 2007). During the 2006 midterm elections, Democrats drew some evangelical former Bush supporters their way as part of a public outcry against the war. Democrats won back both congressional houses. A minority of evangelicals opposed the war from the beginning. In 2008 Democrats increased their margin further and won the White House with Barak Obama reaching out to people of faith (including evangelicals) and Republican moderates.

131. Crow conversations; Zikmund conversation.

132. CCT drew participation from some Pentecostal denominations, such as the Church of God in Christ. However, some became angry and alienated because of what they perceived as pushiness and impatience from the leadership, which drove the group forward on certain measures without allowing sufficient dialogue, processing, and input from members new to these kinds of ecumenical forums. Other smaller churches have found it difficult to be members of both CCT and the NCC, for they lack sufficient resources. In such instances, their loyalty has tended to flow toward their traditional affiliation with the NCC. Zikmund conversation.

133. See the CUIC website at www.eden.edu/cuic/cuic.htm. Edgar interview. It is important to note that the NCC still contains within it a powerful Faith and Order Commission, which often demonstrates a mind of its own but which some have charged was marginalized within the NCC under Edgar. And CCT's official plan includes hope that it might generate cooperative action on social justice issues. But Edgar felt CCT would largely specialize in "dialogue" while the NCC would specialize in "action." Throughout the NCC's history, a handful of people have worked, often unsuccessfully, to integrate theology and action more organically in accord with the original ecumenical vision. For a 2006 effort, see "Celebrating 50 Years of Faith and Order," 6 January 2006, www.ncccusa.org/news/060106faocelebration.html (1 September 2006). Nevertheless, some worried in 2007 that the Faith and Order Commission had developed an arrogant and independent attitude that complicated efforts to heal the internally fractured NCC. Zikmund conversation.

134. Edgar and McCullough interviews. The NCC also receives invaluable income from sales of the NRSV Bible, of which it holds the copyright. Zikmund conversation.

135. Michael Kinnamon, "Pray Without Ceasing," address, National Workshop on Christian Unity, 15 April 2008, www.ncccusa.org/MK.keynote.nwcu.html (3 June 2008). For biographical information on Kinnamon, see www.ncccusa.org/news/BIOmkinnamon.htm. As of 2008, the NCC had thirty-five Protestant, Orthodox, and Anglican denominational members, containing about 45 million total parishioners.

136. Conservative "orthodox" Christian groups within mainline churches have launched what they call an ecumenical effort of their own—to unite those who adhere to their recognized "classic" Christian doctrines while excluding as heretics those Christians who do not. See Oden, *Turning Around the Mainline*.

137. Geyer interview. Nancy Ammerman and others have also argued that religious institutions often find strength and lay support by maintaining their distinct identities.

138. James S. Olson, Equality Deferred: Race, Ethnicity, and Immigration in America since 1945 (Belmont, CA: Wadsworth Thompson, 2003), 128–38.

APPENDIX: THE ECUMENICAL WAY

1. Some "orthodox" mainline conservatives interpret and apply the "Confessing Church" story in a different way from most ecumenists who have affiliated with the NCC. Those associated with the IRD argue that the Confessing Church of Germany focused on ensuring that doctrinal truth was preserved in the face of secularization in Germany. As a result, IRD-related groups use the Confessing Church as a model and term for their own movement, which seeks to purge the mainline denominations of "liberalism." Ecumenists associated with the National and World Councils, however, have generally seen the Confessing Church as a shining example of the church holding

its ground in the face of a struggle with the state for control of the church. They see it as a model for how to remain both prophetic and separate from state control and a nationalistic culture. See Oden, *Turning Around the Mainline*, and the IRD website.

2. Adam Garfinkle, *Telltale Hearts: The Origins and Impact of the Vietnam Anti-war Movement* (New York: St. Martin's Press, 1995); Melvin Small, *Johnson, Nixon, and the Doves* (New Brunswick, NJ: Rutgers University Press, 1988).

3. Chappell, *A Stone of Hope*.

4. REB interview.

5. See McNamara, *In Retrospect*, 321–23. McNamara lists eleven total mistakes. The ten government mistakes I refer to are (1) misjudging NVA and VC aims, and exaggerating their threat to the U.S.; (2) imposing American views upon the Vietnamese, rather than understanding Vietnamese worldviews and desires; (3) underestimating the role of nationalism and anti-imperialist sentiments while overemphasizing the role and threat of communism; (4) misjudging the Vietnamese because of a lack of cultural expertise in the U.S. government; (5) misjudging what the military could actually accomplish; (6) not engaging the nation in a frank debate about the war; (7) [not applicable to the NCC]; (8) committing hubris by trying to remake another nation in one's own image; (9) supporting a unilateral war and dismissing international opinion; (10) underestimating the war's complexity while overestimating our ability to control events; and (11) failing to self-reflect and self-analyze within the government.

6. Since Christian conservatives proselytized heavily while mainline ecumenical Christians did less so, this may have played a role in more strongly motivating conservatives to master and invest in popular media. The fact also that the Federal and National Councils received free radio and television time combined with frequent easily obtained coverage in major newspapers in the 1940s and 1950s, unlike conservatives, may have made them less inclined to study how to win attention through engaging various audiences.

7. Wuthnow, *Restructuring*, ch. 7.

8. See Jill Gill, "Caught in the Middle: Navigating the Clergy-Laity Gap during the Vietnam War," *Journal of Presbyterian History*, forthcoming.

9. K. L. Billingsley, "A Vietnam Memorial: The National Council of Churches in Indochina," *This World* 23 (Fall 1988): 25–39. The "Hanoi Hilton" was a North Vietnamese prison.

10. These included the Methodists, the United Church of Christ, the American Baptists, the United Presbyterians, The Disciples of Christ, the Society of Friends (Quakers), the Church of the Brethren, the Evangelical United Brethren, the Lutheran Church in America, the Mennonites, and the Episcopalians. See "Churches' Statements on Vietnam—in hand Sept. 1, 1967," RG 6, box 30, folder 25, NCC; Hall, *Because of Their Faith*, 46–47.

11. See Rick Nutt's discussion in *Toward Peacemaking*, 69–92, 111–24; Elston interviews.

12. RSB interviews.

13. See Billingsley, *From Mainline to Sideline*, and "A Vietnam Memorial."

14. Some black Pentecostal groups became angered and alienated within CCT by what they viewed as an overly pushy and impatient leadership; this put their continuing involvement in jeopardy. Zikmund conversation.

15. Iakovos was even a member of SACVN. The Orthodox knew the value of their membership to the NCC, and they leveraged their power occasionally on par-

ticular issues. The most notable example occurred in the late 1980s and the 1990s when the Orthodox threatened to leave the NCC if it accepted a gay denomination into its membership. The NCC agreed not to act upon the denomination's application in order to keep the Orthodox within the Council.

16. See Oden, *Turning Around the Mainline*.

17. Edgar's and Wallis's recent books contain scriptural references and biblical arguments when discussing the Iraq War and social issues. However, Edgar's sidesteps references to ecumenism (which I will discuss later).

18. Zikmund conversation.

19. Conservative or "orthodox" mainline Christians active within what they are calling their own "confessing movement" oppose this definition of renewal. Rather, they seek to "renew" the church by grounding it back in conservative or "orthodox" doctrines. They reject renewal that includes theological perspectives other than their own. See Oden, *Turning Around the Mainline*.

20. Dom Helder Camara was the Roman Catholic archbishop of Recif, Brazil, and a pioneer of liberation theology in Latin America. He contributed to RSB's Ecumenical Witness in 1972.

21. Rick Nutt, for example, explains how the Vietnam War helped transform the leadership's view of U.S. foreign policy in the Presbyterian Church U.S. See *Toward Peacemaking*, 69–124.

22. Arthur Schlesinger Jr., "Forgetting Reinhold Niebuhr," *New York Times*, 18 September 2005; Edgar, *Middle Church*, 63–100; Wallis, *God's Politics*, esp. 108–71; Michael Lerner, *The Left Hand of God: Taking Back Our Country from the Religious Right* (New York: HarperCollins, 2006), 112–13. On Bush's exceptionalist, Pax Americana views, see Lichtman, *White Protestant Nation*, 439–43.

23. Wallis, *God's Politics*, xviii.

24. David Kuo, *Tempting Faith: An Inside Story of Political Seduction* (New York: Free Press, 2006), 38.

25. These figures were taken from the NCC's and the NAE's respective websites in 2010. Oden estimates the conservative "orthodox Christian" base within mainline churches to be one million active participants, with several more million "sympathizers." *Turning Around the Mainline*, 74. He cites no sources and is probably generous in his estimate. Even given his figures of one to "several" million, and subtracting them from the NCC's member base number of around 45 million, what one might call the "centrist moderate to liberal" Christian population is still massive. In *Religion*, Hulsether argues that people have often exaggerated the degree of decline experienced by mainline churches.

26. I have heard this argument articulated to me time and again by evangelical and fundamentalist Christians, including those in scholarly circles. Oden makes the same argument in *Turning Around the Mainline*. However, he fails to provide evidence to support his assertions, treating them as if they are obvious. His book also contains few endnotes of a scholarly nature.

27. Kuo says that he and his colleagues described it as such, back (I believe) in the 1990s. On the issue of communist revolution, see Billingsley's writings. For another example from the 1960s that is very typical of right-wing attacks, see David Emerson Gumaer, "Apostasy: The National Council of Churches," *Studies in Reformed Theology* 9.1 (1998); this piece was reprinted from the late 1960s, www.reformed-theology.org/html/issue07/apostasy.htm (September 15, 2006).

28. As one example, see a website that is highly critical of ecumenism. Jeremiah Project, "Modern Ecumenical Movement," at http://www.jeremiahproject.com/prophecy/ecumen01.html (13 December 2006).

29. Oden claims that his mainline movement of "orthodox Christians" is focused on scriptural truth and authority, not partisan politics. However, his book contains several statements that frame certain political positions as the truly Christian ones; and the IRD, on whose board Oden serves, is and has always been both political and partisan. Its funding sources alone reveal its allegiances (see epilogue). So, too, does its website.

30. This comes from Anderson Cooper's television program "What Is a Christian?" which aired on CNN in December 2006. Both progressive evangelical Jim Wallis and Southern Baptist Richard Land agreed that prosperity theology is contrary to their understandings of scripture. The largest church in the United States, Lake Wood Ministries in Houston, preaches prosperity theology. Joel Osteen, its minister, was called "America's top TV preacher." See http://transcripts.cnn.com/TRANSCRIPTS/0612/14/acd.02.html (30 December 2006).

31. See history section of NAE website.

32. Hulsether argues that, if liberal churches move right, they risk alienating their youth further. *Religion*, 159.

33. Kuo, *Tempting Faith*, 168. See also Lichtman on the partisanship and economic interests of the new religious right.

34. Kuo, *Tempting Faith*, 250, 264.

35. Ibid., 255.

36. Alan Wisdom, "Uncertain Future: The National Association of Evangelicals after Ted Haggard," *Ecumenical News*, IRD, 18 March 2007, www.ird-renew.org/site/apps/nl/content2.asp?c=fvKVLfMVIsG&b=470197&ct=3640743 (19 March 2007).

37. Evangelical Manifesto Steering Committee, "An Evangelical Manifesto: A Declaration of Evangelical Identity and Public Commitment," Washington, D.C., 7 May 2008. This manifesto declares, "Called by Jesus to be 'in' the world but 'not of' the world, we are fully engaged in public affairs, but never completely equated with any party, partisan ideology, economic system, class, tribe, or national identity." It was signed by over eighty scholars and theologians who were concerned about evangelical identity and behavior. See also Lichtman, *White Protestant Nation*, 455–56.

38. Some within ecumenical circles think, at times, that Edgar crossed that line into partisanship. Zikmund conversation.

39. Jacqueline L. Salmon, "Southern Baptists Struggle to Maintain Flock," *Washington Post*, 8 June 2008, A02; Brigid Schulte, "Shrinking Flock Examines Its Identity," *Washington Post*, 8 June 2008, C01.

40. Oden is an engineer of this effort. He is closely tied to the IRD, having served as its board chair. His book is full of invective against liberal Christians and groups affiliated with the NCC. His vision of ecumenism is designed to unite only those who agree with "orthodox" Christians' doctrinal interpretations and application of scripture. Other Christians, in his words, are "heretical." While urging conservatives to stay within mainline churches, he also urges liberal Christians to leave them if they are not willing to convert to "orthodox" doctrinal beliefs, for he wants the orthodox to take control of mainline institutional properties, resources, and endowments. He even provides strategies for how the orthodox can file suits for that property.

41. REB interview. Bobby produced a documentary in 2003 called *A Closer Walk* about the international AIDS crisis. He and the Warrens collaborated to get the film into churches.

42. The new SCM of the USA will join the ecumenical World Student Christian Federation. See http://sites.google.com/site/scmusanow/ (3 May 2010).

43. Oden characterizes the Councils' ecumenism as a now dying product of "modernism." Warren Vinz is one scholar who argues that religious ideas about unity in America in the mid-twentieth century were products of an atypical time in American history. See his rich discussion in *Pulpit Politics: Faces of American Protestant Nationalism in the Twentieth Century* (Albany: State University of New York, 1997).

44. Armstrong, *Great Transformation*, 397. Quotations and information in this and the next three paragraphs are from ibid., 390–99.

45. Finke and Stark, *Churching of America*.

46. See David C. Korten, "The Great Turning: From Empire to Earth Community," *Yes! A Journal of Positive Futures* 38 (Summer 2006): 12–21; David C. Korten, *The Great Turning: From Empire to Earth Community* (San Francisco: Berrett-Koehler, 2006).

47. David Korten, presentation, "Imperial Politics, Christianity and the True Jesus: Reflections on the 2004 Election," November 2004, www.davidkorten.org/Talks/talks_imperialpolitics.htm (25 January 2007).

SELECTED BIBLIOGRAPHY

INTERVIEWS BY AUTHOR

Austin, Judy. Informal conversations and email exchanges, April–May 2007, Boise, Idaho.

Bilheimer, Robert E. (REB). Telephone interview, 9 March 2007.

Bilheimer, Robert S. (RSB). Telephone interview, 14 December 1991. Interviews, 5–9 August 1993, Collegeville, Minnesota.

Cate, William. Informal conversation, 1997, Seattle, Washington.

Crow, Paul. Conversations, 8–10 May 2003, Louisville, Kentucky. Discussions by email, 14, 19 May 2003.

Edgar, Rev. Dr. Robert. Interview, 22 May 2003, Boise, Idaho.

Elston, Gerhard. Interviews, 11 December 1991, 13–22 October 1992, Philadelphia, Pennsylvania.

Espy, R. H. Edwin. Interview, 26 August 1991, Doylestown, Pennsylvania.

Fernandez, Richard. Interviews, 31 October, 12 December 1991, Philadelphia, Pennsylvania.

Geyer, Alan. Interview, 13 June 2003, Washington, D.C.

Hamilton, James. Interview (with Allan Parrent), 21 November 1991, Washington, D.C.

Hunter, David. Telephone interview, 16 October 1992.

Kelley, Dean. Interview, 28 October 1991, New York, New York.

McCullough, John. Interview, 27 July 2003, New York, New York.

Parrent, Allan. Interview (with James Hamilton), 21 November 1991, Washington, D.C.

Rusk, Dean. Telephone interview, 15 January 1992.

Stenning, Ronald. Telephone interview, 1 February 1998.

Thompson, William P. Interview, 3 September 1991, Princeton, New Jersey.

Vilankulu, Sarah. Informal conversations, 1991–2003, New York, New York.

Will, Herman. Interviews, 3 December 1995, 17 March 1996, Seattle, Washington. Telephone interview, 8 December 1995.

Zikmund, Barbara Brown. Informal conversation, 13 April 2007, Salt Lake City, Utah.

PRIVATE PAPERS

Bilheimer, Robert S.
Elston, Gerhard
Kelley, Dean
Parrent, Allan

MANUSCRIPT SOURCES

American Friends Service Committee Records. Philadelphia, Pennsylvania.

Anne and John Bennett Papers. Burke Library, Union Theological Seminary, New York.

Clergy and Laity Concerned Records (CALC). Swarthmore College Peace Collection, Swarthmore, Pennsylvania.

Department of State, U.S. Government. National Archives II, College Park, Maryland.

General Commission of Archives and History, United Methodist Church. Special Collections and Archives, Madison, New Jersey.

Gerhard Elston Papers. Swarthmore College Peace Collection, Swarthmore, Pennsylvania.

A. J. Muste Papers. Swarthmore College Peace Collection, Swarthmore, Pennsylvania.

National Council of Churches Communications Department and Research Department Files. National Council of Churches, New York.

National Council of Churches Records. Presbyterian Historical Society, Philadelphia, Pennsylvania.

National Council of Churches Washington Office Files. National Council of Churches, Washington, D.C.

Presbyterian Historical Society, Presbyterian Church (USA) National Archives. Philadelphia, Pennsylvania.

Student Protest Papers. Burke Library, Union Theological Seminary, New York.

E. Raymond Wilson Papers. Swarthmore College Peace Collection, Swarthmore, Pennsylvania.

PUBLISHED CHURCH RECORDS

Journal of the Last Session of the General Conference of the Evangelical United Brethren Church, Last Session of the General Conference of the Methodist Church, and the General Conference of the United Methodist Church. Vols. 1 and 2. Dallas, Texas, 21 April–4 May 1968.

Journal of the 1972 General Conference of the United Methodist Church. Vols. 1 and 2. Atlanta, Georgia, 16–28 April, 1972.

Minutes of the General Assembly of the United Presbyterian Church in the United States of America. Part 1, *Journal.* One Hundred and Seventy-eighth General Assembly, Boston, Massachusetts, 18–25 May, 1966; One Hundred and Seventy-ninth General Assembly, Portland, Oregon, 18–24 May, 1967; One Hundred and Eightieth General Assembly, Minneapolis, Minnesota, 16–22 May, 1968; One Hundred and Eighty-first General Assembly, San Antonio, Texas, 14–21 May, 1969; One Hundred and Eighty-second General Assembly, Chicago, Illinois, 20–27 May, 1970; One Hundred and Eighty-third General Assembly, Rochester, New York, 17–26 May, 1971.

SELECTED PERIODICALS AND NEWSPAPERS

Christian Advocate (Methodist/United Methodist)
Christian Century (Independent Mainline Protestant)
Christianity and Crisis (Independent Mainline Protestant)

Christianity Today (Independent Evangelical Protestant)
Congressional Record (U.S. Government)
Los Angeles Times
Monday Morning (United Presbyterian Church)
Newsweek
New York Times
The Presbyterian Layman (Presbyterian Lay Committee)
Presbyterian Life (United Presbyterian Church)
Time

SELECTED WORKS

Abbott, John W. "CWS's Mandate: A Look at the Other Side." *Christian Century*, 4 September 1974, 823–24.

Abrams, Elliott, ed. *The Influence of Faith: Religious Groups and U.S. Foreign Policy.* Lanham, MD: Rowman and Littlefield, 2001.

Ahlstrom, Sydney. *A Religious History of the American People.* New Haven: Yale University Press, 1972.

Aiello, Thomas. "Constructing 'Godless Communism': Religion, Politics, and Popular Culture, 1954–1960. *Americana* 4.1 (Spring 2005). At http://www.american-popularculture.com/journal/articles/spring_2005/aiello.htm (1 May 2010).

Air Reserve Center Training Manual. Student Text, NR 45-0050, Incr. V., vol. 7. Reserve Non-Commissioned Officer Course. U.S. Air Force. New York, 4 January 1960, section 15, page 14.

Alpert, Rebecca, ed. *Voices of the Religious Left.* Philadelphia: Temple University Press, 2004.

Ambrose, Stephen E. *Eisenhower: Soldier and President.* New York: Touchstone, 1990.

———. *Rise to Globalism: American Foreign Policy since 1938.* 1971. New York: Penguin Books, 1993.

Ammerman, Nancy. *Pillars of Faith: American Congregations and Their Partners.* Berkeley and Los Angeles: University of California Press, 2005.

Anderson, Gordon L. "The Evolution of the Concept of Peace in the Work of the National Council of Churches." *Journal of Ecumenical Studies* 21 (Fall 1984): 730–54.

Anderson, Lois J. "R. H. Edwin Espy: An Ecumenical Layman with a Calling." *American Baptist Quarterly* 16.4 (December 1997): 399–412.

Andrew, John A., III. *The Other Side of the Sixties: Young Americans for Freedom and the Rise of Conservative Politics.* New Brunswick, NJ: Rutgers University Press, 1997.

Armstrong, Karen. *The Great Transformation: The Beginning of Our Religious Traditions.* New York: Alfred A. Knopf, 2006.

Atkinson, Rick. *The Long Gray Line: From West Point to Vietnam and After—The Turbulent Odyssey of the Class of 1966.* New York: Pocket Star Books, 1989.

Banks, Dennis. "Consciousness Raising." *Engage/Social Action* 3 (January 1975): 37–39.

Bennett, John. Editorial response. *Christianity and Crisis*, 1 May 1972, 106–7.

Bentley, Eric, ed. *Thirty Years of Treason: Excerpts from Hearings before the House Committee on Un-American Activities, 1938–1968.* New York: Viking Press, 1971.

Berg, Thomas C. "Proclaiming Together? Convergence and Divergence in Mainline and Evangelical Evangelism, 1945–1967." *Religion and American Culture* 5.1 (Winter 1995): 49–76.

Berkowitz, Edward D. *Something Happened: A Political and Cultural Overview of the Seventies.* New York: Columbia University Press, 2006.

Berman, Larry. *Lyndon Johnson's War.* New York: W. W. Norton, 1989.

Bernstein, Carl, and Bob Woodward. *All the President's Men.* New York: Warner Books, 1975.

Beschloss, Michael. *Reaching for Glory: The Johnson White House Tapes, 1964–1965.* New York: Simon and Schuster, 2002.

———. *Taking Charge: The Johnson White House Tapes, 1963–1964.* New York: Simon and Schuster, 1998.

Bilheimer, Robert Sperry. *Breakthrough: The Emergence of the Ecumenical Tradition.* Grand Rapids, MI: William B. Eerdmans; Geneva: WCC, 1989.

———. "The Changing Domestic Base of U.S. Foreign Policy." Paper for presentation at the "Consultation on Korean-American Relations: Dilemmas and Opportunities in the Future of Northeast Asia." Seoul, Korea, 2–5 December 1970. Bilheimer's Personal Papers.

———. "The Depth of Militarism." *Christian Century,* 28 February 1973, 259–62.

———. "Let American Ecumenism Be Ecumenical." *Worship* 51 (September 1977): 407–19.

———. *A Spirituality for the Long Haul: Biblical Risk and Moral Stand.* Philadelphia: Fortress Press, 1984.

———. "Transition in the American Identity." *Christian Century,* 1 January 1969, 11–14.

———. "What Kind of People Are We?" *Christianity and Crisis,* 23 June 1969, 176–78.

Billingsley, K. L. *From Mainline to Sideline: The Social Witness of the National Council of Churches.* Washington, D.C.: Ethics and Public Policy Center, 1990.

———. "A Vietnam Memorial: The National Council of Churches in Indochina." *This World* 23 (Fall 1988): 25–39.

Black, Conrad. *Richard Nixon: A Life in Full.* New York: Public Affairs, 2007.

Blake, Eugene Carson. "In His Own Words." *Journal of Presbyterian History* 76.4 (November 1998): 260–84.

Blum, John Morton. *Years of Discord: American Politics and Society, 1961–1974.* New York: W. W. Norton, 1991.

Bonhoeffer, Dietrich. *Letters and Papers from Prison.* 1953. New York: Macmillan, 1979.

Bosley, Harold. "The Quiet Storm in the Churches." *Christian Century,* 2 December 1970, 1449–52.

Boyer, Paul. *By the Bomb's Early Light: American Thought and Culture at the Dawn of the Atomic Age.* Chapel Hill: University of North Carolina Press, 1985.

Brennan, Mary C. *Turning Right in the Sixties: The Conservative Capture of the GOP.* Chapel Hill: University of North Carolina Press, 1995.

Briggs, John, Mercy Oduyoye, and Georges Tsetsis, eds. *A History of the Ecumenical Movement.* Vol. 3, *1968–2000.* Geneva: WCC, 2004.

Brouwer, Arie. "The Real Crises at the NCC." *Christian Century,* 27 June–4 July 1990, 641–45.

Brown, Robert McAfee. "The Gospel according to Morley Safer." *Christian Century,* 2 March 1983, 183–86.

Brown, Robert McAfee, Abraham Heschel, and Michael Novak. *Vietnam: Crisis of Conscience*. New York: Association Press, 1967.

Bush, Perry. "The Political Education of Vietnam Christian Service, 1954–1975." *Peace and Change: A Journal of Peace Research* 47.2 (April 2002): 198–224.

Buzzanco, Robert. *Masters of War: Military Dissent and Politics in the Vietnam Era*. Cambridge: Cambridge University Press, 1996.

Capizzi, Joseph E. "Selective Conscientious Objection in the United States." *Journal of Church and State* 38.2 (Spring 1996): 339–63.

Carter, Dan T. *From George Wallace to Newt Gingrich: Race in the Conservative Counter Revolution, 1963–1994*. Baton Rouge: Louisiana State University Press, 1996.

Carter, Jimmy. *Our Endangered Values: America's Moral Crisis*. New York: Simon and Schuster, 2005.

Carville, James, and Paul Begala. *Take It Back: Our Party, Our Country, Our Future*. New York: Simon and Schuster, 2006.

Cavert, Samuel McCrea. *The American Churches in the Ecumenical Movement, 1900–1968*. New York: Association Press, 1968.

Chadwick, Owen. *The Christian Church in the Cold War*. New York: Penguin Books, 1992.

Chappell, David. *A Stone of Hope: Prophetic Religion and the Death of Jim Crow*. Chapel Hill: University of North Carolina Press, 2004.

"Chauvinistic Catholic Charity." *Commonweal*, 10 November 1967, 159–60.

Clergy and Laymen Concerned About Vietnam. *In the Name of America*. New York: CALCAV, 1968.

Clifford, Clark. *Counsel to the President: A Memoir*. New York: Anchor Books, 1991.

Clough, Leonard. "The National Student Christian Federation: A Bridge Between Independent Organizations and a Unified Movement." *Journal of Ecumenical Studies* 32.3 (Summer 1995): 319–35.

Coffin, William Sloane. *Credo*. Louisville, KY: Westminster John Knox Press, 2004.

Colson, Charles. *God and Government: An Insider's View on the Boundaries between Faith and Politics*. Grand Rapids, MI: Zondervan, 2007.

Corbett, Michael, and Julia Mitchell Corbett. *Politics and Religion in the United States*. New York: Garland Publishing, 1999.

Cox, Harvey. "The 'New Breed' in American Churches: Sources of Social Activism in American Religion." *Daedalus* (Winter 1967).

———. *The Secular City*. 1965. New York: MacMillan, 1966.

Crow Dog, Leonard, and Richard Erdoes. *Crow Dog: Four Generations of Sioux Medicine Men*. New York: HarperCollins, 1995.

Cummings, D. Duane. *Dale Fiers: Twentieth Century Disciple*. Fort Worth: Texas Christian University Press, 2003.

"CWS Chief Endorsed." *Christian Century*, 28 October 1987, 936–37.

Dallek, Robert. *Flawed Giant: Lyndon Johnson and His Times, 1961–1973*. New York: Oxford University Press, 1999.

———. *Lyndon B. Johnson: Portrait of a President*. New York: Oxford University Press, 2005.

———. *Nixon and Kissinger: Partners in Power*. New York: Harper Perennial, 2007.

Danielson, Leilah. "'It Is a Day of Judgment': The Peacemakers, Religion, and Radicalism in Cold War America." *Religion and American Culture* 18.2 (Summer 2008): 215–48.

Dayton, Donald W. "The Ecumenical Significance of Oberlin." *Journal of Ecumenical Studies* 42.4 (Fall 2007): 511–26.

DeBenedetti, Charles. *An American Ordeal: The Antiwar Movement of the Vietnam Era.* Syracuse: Syracuse University Press, 1990.

Delloff, Linda-Marie. "The NCC in a New Time (II)." *Christianity and Crisis,* 9 January 1989, 466–72.

De Santa Ana, Julio. *Religions Today: Their Challenge to the Ecumenical Movement.* Geneva: WCC, 2006.

Dewing, Rolland. *Wounded Knee II.* Freeman, South Dakota: Pine Hill Press, 1995.

Diamond, Sara. *Roads to Dominion: Right-Wing Movements and Political Power in the United States.* New York: Guilford Press, 1995.

Di Leo, David. *George Ball: Vietnam and the Rethinking of Containment.* Chapel Hill: University of North Carolina Press, 1991.

Dionne, E. J., Jr. *Souled Out: Reclaiming Faith and Politics after the Religious Right.* Princeton, NJ: Princeton University Press, 2008.

Dochuk, Darren. "Evangelicalism Becomes Southern, Politics Becomes Evangelical: From FDR to Ronald Reagan." In *Religion and American Politics,* ed. Noll and Harlow, 297–325.

———. *From Bible Belt to Sun Belt: Plain-Folk Religion, Grassroots Politics, and the Rise of Evangelical Conservatism.* New York: W.W. Norton, 2011.

Duiker, William J. *Sacred War: Nationalism and Revolution in a Divided Vietnam.* New York: McGraw-Hill, 1995.

"Ecumenism as Communication." *Christian Century,* 13 November 1969, 1441.

Edgar, Bob. *Middle Church: Reclaiming the Moral Values of the Faithful Majority from the Religious Right.* New York: Simon and Schuster, 2006.

Ellwood, Robert S. *The 60s Spiritual Awakening: American Religion Moving from Modern to Postmodern.* New Brunswick, NJ: Rutgers University Press, 1994.

"Embattled Head of the National Council of Churches Quits." *Los Angeles Times,* 1 July 1989, 7.

Emerson, Gloria. *Winners and Losers: Battles, Retreats, Gains, Losses, and Ruins from the Vietnam War.* 1976. New York: W. W. Norton, 1992.

Ericksen, Robert P., and Susannah Heschel, eds. *Betrayal: German Churches and the Holocaust.* Minneapolis: Augsburg Fortress Publishers, 1999.

Evans, Sara M., ed. *Journeys that Opened Up the World: Women, Student Christian Movements, and Social Justice, 1955–1975.* New Brunswick, NJ: Rutgers University Press, 2003.

Fackre, Gabriel. *Believing, Caring, and Doing in the United Church of Christ: An Interpretation.* Cleveland: United Church Press, 2005.

———. "Theology: Ephemeral, Conjunctural and Perennial." In Lotz, *Altered Landscapes,* 246–67.

Farber, David. "The Silent Majority and Talk about Revolution." In *The Sixties: From Memory to History,* ed. David Farber. Chapel Hill: University of North Carolina Press, 1994.

Farber, David, and Jeff Roche, eds. *The Conservative Sixties.* New York: Peter Lang, 2003.

Feldman, Noah. *Divided by God: America's Church-State Problem—and What We Should Do about It.* New York: Farrar, Straus and Giroux, 2005.

Fey, Harold E., ed. *A History of the Ecumenical Movement.* Vol. 2, *1948–1968.* Geneva: WCC, 2009.

"Figure in the National Council of Churches' Power Struggle Quits." *Los Angeles Times*, 28 May 1988, 6.

Findlay, James. *Church People in the Struggle: The National Council of Churches and the Black Freedom Movement, 1950-1970*. New York: Oxford University Press, 1993.

———. "Glimpses of Recent History: The National Council of Churches, 1974-2004." *Journal of Presbyterian History* 84.2 (2006): 152-69.

Finke, Roger, and Rodney Stark. *The Churching of America, 1776-1990: Winners and Losers in Our Religious Economy*. New Brunswick, NJ: Rutgers University Press, 1992.

Finstuen, Andrew. *Original Sin and Everyday Protestants: The Theology of Reinhold Niebuhr, Billy Graham, and Paul Tillich in an Age of Anxiety*. Chapel Hill: University of North Carolina Press, 2009.

Fiske, Edward. "Church Council's Parley: Several Steps Further to the Left." *New York Times*, 8 December 1969.

———. "Religious Assembly Terms Vietnam Policy Immoral." *New York Times*, 17 January 1972.

Fitzgerald, Frances. *Fire in the Lake*. New York: Vintage Books, 1972.

Fitzgerald, Thomas E. *The Ecumenical Movement: An Introductory History*. Westport, CT: Praeger, 2004.

"$500,000 Lilly Endowment Development Grant Caps National Council of Churches' Financial Turnaround." NCC News Service, 1 August 2002, at www.ncccusa. org/news/02archives.html (30 January 2003).

Flipse, Scott. "Bearing the Cross of Vietnam: Humanitarianism, Religion, and the American Commitment to South Vietnam, 1952-1975." Ph.D. dissertation, University of Notre Dame, 2003.

———. "The Latest Casualty of War: Catholic Relief Services, Humanitarianism, and the War in Vietnam, 1967-1968." *Peace and Change: A Journal of Peace Research* 27.2 (April 2002): 245-70.

Fox, Richard Wightman. *Reinhold Niebuhr: A Biography*. 1985. Ithaca: Cornell University Press, 1996.

Frank, Thomas. *What's the Matter with Kansas? How Conservatives Won the Heart of America*. New York: Metropolitan, 2004.

Franklin, Ben. "Opponents of Vietnam War Meet with Kissinger." *New York Times*, 6 February 1969.

Franklin, H. Bruce. *Vietnam and Other American Fantasies*. Amherst: University of Massachusetts Press, 2000.

Friedland, Michael. *Lift Up Your Voice Like a Trumpet: White Clergy and the Civil Rights and Antiwar Movements, 1954-1973*. Chapel Hill: University of North Carolina Press, 1998.

———. "New, Newer, Newest: The Transformation of Richard Nixon in the Popular Media, 1962-1968." *Viet Nam Generation* 7.1-2 (Winter 1996).

Fry, Joseph A. *Debating Vietnam: Fulbright, Stennis, and Their Senate Hearings*. Lanham, MD: Rowman and Littlefield, 2006.

Fulbright, Senator William. "The War and Its Effects—I." *Congressional Record*. Senate, 8 December 1967, S18178-81.

———. "The War and Its Effects—II." *Congressional Record*. Senate, 13 December 1967, S18485-88.

Garfinkle, Adam. *Telltale Hearts: The Origins and Impact of the Vietnam Antiwar Movement*. New York: St. Martin's Press, 1995.

Gaustad, Edwin S. *A Religious History of America*. 1966. New York: Harper and Row, 1990.

———, ed. *A Documentary History of Religion in America, since 1965*. Grand Rapids, MI: William B. Eerdmans, 1983.

Gettleman, Marvin E., Jane Franklin, Marilyn B. Young, and H. Bruce Franklin, eds. *Vietnam and America: The Most Comprehensive Documented History of the Vietnam War*. 2nd ed. New York: Grove Press, 1995.

Geyer, Alan. *Ideology in America: Challenges to Faith*. Louisville, KY: Westminster John Knox Press, 1997.

———. "Joy Box with No Joy: The NCC at Detroit." *Christian Century*, 17 December 1969, 1601–5.

———. "May Day in Manhattan." *Christian Century*, 14 May 1969, 671–72.

———. "NCC on the Boardwalk." *Christian Century*, 30 June 1971, 791–92.

———. *Piety and Politics: American Protestantism in the World Arena*. Richmond, VA: John Knox Press, 1963.

———. "Toward Justice and Peace in International Affairs." *Christian Century*, 21 August 1968, 1049–53.

Gibbons, William Conrad. *The U.S. Government and the Vietnam War: Executive and Legislative Roles and Relationships, Part III: January–July 1965*. Princeton, NJ: Princeton University Press, 1989.

Gill, Jill K. "Caught in the Middle: Navigating the Clergy-Laity Gap during the Vietnam War." *Journal of Presbyterian History*, forthcoming.

———. "The Decline of Real Ecumenism." *Journal of Presbyterian History* 81.4 (Winter 2003): 242–63.

———. "Peace Is Not the Absence of War but the Presence of Justice: The National Council of Churches' Reaction and Response to the Vietnam War, 1965–1972." Ph.D. dissertation, University of Pennsylvania, 1996.

———. "The Political Price of Prophetic Leadership: The National Council of Churches and the Vietnam War." *Peace and Change: A Journal of Peace Research* 27.2 (April 2002): 271–300.

———. "The Politics of Ecumenical Disunity: The Troubled Marriage of Church World Service and the National Council of Churches." *Religion and American Culture* 14.2 (Summer 2004): 175–212.

———. "Preventing a Second Massacre at Wounded Knee: 1973, United Methodists Mediate for Peace." *Methodist History* 43.1 (October 2004): 45–56.

———. "Religious Communities and the Vietnam War." In *Vietnam War Era: People and Perspectives*, ed. Mitchell Hall, 97–116. Santa Barbara, CA: ABC-CLIO, 2009.

Gitlin, Todd. *The Sixties: Years of Hope, Days of Rage*. New York: Bantam Books, 1987.

Granberg-Michaelson, Wesley. "Time for New Wineskins?" *Christian Century*, 10 November 1999, 1076–77.

Gutterman, David S. *Prophetic Politics: Christian Social Movements and American Democracy*. Ithaca, NY: Cornell University Press, 2005.

Hadden, Jeffrey K. *The Gathering Storm in the Churches*. Garden City, NY: Doubleday, 1969.

Haines, Aubrey. "Polarization within the Churches." *Christian Century*, 2 September 1970, 1039–41.

Halberstam, David. *The Best and the Brightest.* 1969. New York: Random House, 1972.
————. *The Fifties.* New York: Fawcett Columbine, 1993.
Hall, Mitchell K. *Because of Their Faith: CALCAV and Religious Opposition to the Vietnam War.* New York: Columbia University Press, 1990.
————. "A Time for War: The Church of God's Response to Vietnam." *Indiana Magazine of History* 79.4 (December 1983): 285–304.
————. *The Vietnam War.* Essex, England: Pearson Education, 2000; revised 2nd ed., New York: Longman, 2008.
————, ed. *Vietnam War Era: People and Perspectives.* Santa Barbara, CA: ABC-CLIO, 2009.
Hall, Simon. *Peace and Freedom: The Civil Rights and Antiwar Movements in the 1960s.* Philadelphia: University of Pennsylvania Press, 2005.
Hamilton, Michael P., ed. *The Vietnam War: Christian Perspectives.* Grand Rapids, MI: William B. Eerdmans, 1968.
Haselden, Kyle. Editorial. "Red China at St. Louis." *Christian Century,* 3 November 1965.
————. "Sense and Psychedelics." *Christian Century,* 15 November 1967, 1452–54.
Hatcher, Patrick Lloyd. *The Suicide of an Elite: American Internationalists and Vietnam.* Stanford: Stanford University Press, 1990.
Hein, David. "The Episcopal Church and the Ecumenical Movement, 1937–1997: Presbyterians, Lutherans, and the Future." *Anglican and Episcopal History* 66.1 (March 1997): 4–29.
Herring, George C. *America's Longest War: The United States and Vietnam, 1950–1975.* 2nd ed. New York: Alfred A. Knopf, 1986.
Hess, Gary R. "The Unending Debate: Historians and the Vietnam War." In *America in the World: The Historiography of American Foreign Relations since 1941,* ed. Michael J. Hogan, 358–94. Cambridge: Cambridge University Press, 1995.
Hessel, Dieter. "Probing Vietnam Policy." *Monday Morning,* 27 February 1967, 3–6.
————. *Reconciliation and Conflict: Church Controversy over Social Involvement.* Philadelphia: Westminster Press, 1969.
Holy Bible. New Revised Standard Version. New York: Oxford University Press, 1989.
Hope, Samuel R. "Vietnam Christian Service." *Journal of Presbyterian History* 47 (June 1969): 103–23.
Horsfield, Peter G. "And Now a Word from Our Sponsor: Religious Programs on American Television." *Revue Française d'Etudes Américaines* 6.12 (October 1981): 259–74.
Hostetter, Doug, and Michael McIntyre. "The Politics of Charity." *Christian Century,* 18 September 1974, 845–50.
Hubert, Porter W. "Ecumenical Concerns among American Baptists." *Journal of Ecumenical Studies* 17.2 (Winter 1980): 21–37.
Hulsether, Mark. *Building a Protestant Left: Christianity and Crisis Magazine, 1941–1993.* Knoxville: University of Tennessee Press, 1999.
————. *Religion, Culture and Politics in the Twentieth-Century United States.* New York: Columbia University Press, 2007.
Hyer, Marjorie. "Interfaith Conference Spurs Debate on Religious Liberty." *Los Angeles Times,* 27 April 1985, 5.
Igleheart, Glenn A. "Ecumenical Concerns among Southern Baptists." *Journal of Ecumenical Studies* 17.2 (Winter 1980): 49–61.

Inboden, William. *Religion and American Foreign Policy, 1945–1960: The Soul of Containment.* New York: Cambridge University Press, 2008.

Isaacson, Walter. *Kissinger: A Biography.* New York: Simon and Schuster, 1992.

Isaacson, Walter, and Evan Thomas. *The Wise Men: Six Friends and the World They Made.* New York: Touchstone Books, 1988.

"Is Relief Enough?" *Time,* 21 October 1974, 97–98.

Issac, Jael Jean. "Do You Know Where Your Church Offerings Go?" *Reader's Digest* (January 1983): 120–25.

Jackson, Miles W. "Churchmen Help Gain Impasse at Wounded Knee." *Christian Advocate,* 15 March 1973, 24.

Jeffreys-Jones, Rhodri. *Peace Now: American Society and the Ending of the Vietnam War.* New Haven: Yale University Press, 1999.

Jespersen, T. Christopher. "Analogies at War: Vietnam, the Bush Administration's War in Iraq, and the Search for a Usable Past." *Pacific Historical Review* 74.3 (August 2005): 411–26.

"Johnson? Yes!" Editorial. *Christian Century,* 9 September 1964: 1099–101.

Kahin, George McT. *Intervention: How America Became Involved in Vietnam.* Garden City, NY: Anchor Books, 1987.

Karnow, Stanley. *Vietnam: A History.* New York: Viking Press, 1983.

Katznelson, Ira. *When Affirmative Action Was White: An Untold History of Racial Inequality in Twentieth-Century America.* New York: Norton, 2005.

Kearns, Doris. *Lyndon Johnson and the American Dream.* New York: Signet, 1976.

Kelley, Dean M. *Why the Conservative Churches Are Growing.* 1972. 3rd ed., Macon: Mercer University Press, 1986.

Kihss, Peter. "Church World Service Repudiates Promotion of Revolutionary Change." *New York Times,* 16 July 1974, 71.

Kimball, Jeffrey. *The Vietnam War Files: Uncovering the Secret History of Nixon-Era Strategy.* Lawrence: University Press of Kansas, 2004.

Kinnamon, Michael. *The Vision of the Ecumenical Movement and How It Has Been Impoverished by Its Friends.* St. Louis: Chalice Press, 2003.

Kinsolving, Lester. "Can Council of Churches Survive?" *Rapid City Journal,* 24 December 1972.

Klatch, Rebecca. *A Generation Divided: The New Left, the New Right and the 1960s.* Berkeley and Los Angeles: University of California Press, 1999.

Klinghoffer, David. "National Council of Churches Eschews Reform." *Wall Street Journal,* 15 May 1989, 1.

Knippers, Diane L., and Joan Brown Campbell. "Have American Churches Politicized Their Religious Mission?" *Insight on the News,* 12 February 1996, 26–28.

Korten, David C. "The Great Turning: From Empire to Earth Community." *Yes! A Journal of Positive Futures* 38 (Summer 2006): 12–21.

———. *The Great Turning: From Empire to Earth Community.* San Francisco: Berrett-Koehler Publishers, 2006.

Kosek, Joseph Kip. *Acts of Conscience: Christian Nonviolence and Modern American Democracy.* New York: Columbia University Press, 2009.

Kruse, Kevin M. *White Flight: Atlanta and the Making of Modern Conservatism.* Princeton, NJ: Princeton University Press, 2005.

Kuo, David. *Tempting Faith: An Inside Story of Political Seduction.* New York: Free Press, 2006.

Kurtz, Lester, and Kelly Goran Fulton. "Love Your Enemies? Protestants and United States Foreign Policy." In Wuthnow and Evans, *Quiet Hand of God*, 364–80.

Lakoff, George. *Don't Think of an Elephant: Know Your Values and Frame the Debate*. White River Junction, VT: Chelsea Green, 2004.

Landers, James. *The Weekly War: Newsmagazines and Vietnam*. Columbia: University of Missouri Press, 2004.

Lauren, Paul Gordon. *The Evolution of International Human Rights*. Philadelphia: University of Pennsylvania Press, 2003.

Leaman, David E. "Politicized Service and Teamwork Tensions: Mennonite Central Committee in Vietnam, 1966–1969." *Mennonite Quarterly Review* 71 (1977): 544–70.

Lempke, Mark A. "A Caucus of Prophets: George McGovern's 1972 Campaign and the Crucible of Protestant Politics." Ph.D. dissertation, University of Buffalo, 2011.

Lerner, Michael. *The Left Hand of God: Taking Back Our Country from the Religious Right*. New York: HarperCollins, 2006.

Lewy, Guenter. "The Moral Crisis of American Pacifism." *This World: A Journal of Religion and Public Life* 20 (1987): 3–25.

Lichtman, Allan J. *White Protestant Nation: The Rise of the American Conservative Movement*. New York: Grove Press, 2008.

Lieberman, Robbie. *The Strangest Dream: Communism, Anticommunism, and the U.S. Peace Movement, 1945–1963*. Syracuse: Syracuse University Press, 2000.

Lienesch, Michael. *Redeeming America: Piety and Politics in the New Christian Right*. Chapel Hill: University of North Carolina Press, 1993.

Logevall, Fredrik. *Choosing War: The Lost Chance for Peace and the Escalation of War in Vietnam*. Berkeley and Los Angeles: University of California Press, 1999.

Logevall, Fredrik, and Andrew Preston, eds. *Nixon in the World: American Foreign Relations, 1969–1977*. New York: Oxford University Press, 2008.

Long, Edward Leroy, Jr. "Christian Ethics as Responses to Social Conditions." In Lotz, *Altered Landscapes*, 296–98.

Lotz, David W., ed. *Altered Landscapes: Christianity in America, 1935–1985*. Grand Rapids, MI: William B. Eerdmans, 1989.

Lukas, J. Anthony. *Nightmare: The Underside of the Nixon Years*. 1976. New York: Penguin, 1988.

Lyles, Jean Caffey. "The National Council of Churches: Is There Life after 50?" *Christian Century*, 20 November 1999, 1086–93.

MacLear, Michael. *The Ten Thousand Day War: Vietnam, 1945–1975*. New York: Avon, 1981.

Manser, Nancy. "NCC Elects First Woman President." *Detroit News*, 5 December 1969.

Manza, Jeff, and Clem Brooks. "The Changing Political Fortunes of Mainline Protestants." In Wuthnow and Evans, *Quiet Hand of God*, 159–80.

Marsden, George M. *Religion and American Culture*. 1990. Orlando: Harcourt, 2001.

Martin, William. *A Prophet with Honor: The Billy Graham Story*. New York: William Morrow, 1991.

———. *With God on Our Side: The Rise of the Religious Right in America*. New York: Broadway Books, 1996.

Marty, Martin E. *Pilgrims in Their Own Land: 500 Years of Religion in America*. New York: Penguin Books, 1984.

———. "Watergate Year as Watershed Year." *Christian Century*, 26 December 1973, 1272–74.

Mathews, Cleve. "Support of Thieu by Nixon Underscored." *New York Times*, 18 July 1969.

Matusow, Allen J. *The Unraveling of America: A History of Liberalism in the 1960s.* New York: Harper and Row, 1984.

Maxwell, Donald W. "Religion and Politics at the Border: Canadian Church Support for American Vietnam War Resisters." *Journal of Church and State* 48.4 (2006): 807–29.

McGirr, Lisa. *Suburban Warriors: The Origins of the New American Right.* Princeton, NJ: Princeton University Press, 2001.

McGlothlen, Ronald. *Controlling the Waves: Dean Acheson and U.S. Foreign Policy in Asia.* New York: W. W. Norton, 1993.

McKinney, William, ed. *The Responsibility People.* Grand Rapids, MI: William B. Eerdmans, 1994.

McLeod, Hugh. *The Religious Crisis of the 1960s.* New York: Oxford University Press, 2007.

McMahon, Robert J., ed. *Major Problems in the History of the Vietnam War.* Lexington: D. C. Heath, 1990.

McNamara, Robert S. *In Retrospect: The Tragedy and Lessons of Vietnam.* New York: Random House, 1995.

McQuaid, Kim. *The Anxious Years: America in the Vietnam–Watergate Era.* New York: Basic Books, 1989.

Meyer, Donald. *The Protestant Search for Political Realism, 1919–1941.* 2nd ed. Middletown, CT: Wesleyan University Press, 1988.

"The Misplaced Ministry of the Laity." *Christian Century*, 19 February 1969, 243.

Moon, Penelope Adams. "'Peace on Earth—Peace in Vietnam': The Catholic Peace Fellowship and Antiwar Witness, 1964–1976." *Journal of Social History* 36.4 (Summer 2003): 1033–58.

Moore, Lt. Gen. Harold G. (Ret.), and Joseph L. Galloway. *We Were Soldiers Once . . . And Young: Ia Drang—The Battle that Changed the War in Vietnam.* 1992. New York: Harper Perennial, 1993.

"More Power to the NCC!" *Christian Century*, 10 February 1971, 179.

Morrison, Joan, and Robert K. Morrison. *From Camelot to Kent State.* New York: Times Books, 1987.

Moss, George Donelson. *Vietnam: An American Ordeal.* Englewood Cliffs, NJ: Prentice Hall, 1990.

Muller-Fahrenholtz, Geiko. *America's Battle for God: A European Christian Looks at Civil Religion.* Grand Rapids, MI: William B. Eerdmans, 2007.

Muravchik, Joshua. "The National Council of Churches and the USSR." *This World* 9 (1984): 30–53.

Murray, Peter C. *Methodists and the Crucible of Race, 1930–1975.* Columbia: University of Missouri Press, 2004.

National Council of Churches. "Separation and Interaction of Church and State." *A Journal of Church and State* 6.2 (1964): 147–53.

"The National Council of Churches under New Management." *Christianity Today*, 26 July 1974, 37.

"The NCC Elite: A Breakdown of Beliefs." *Christianity Today*, 21 July 1967, 46–47.

Neuhaus, Richard John. "The War, the Churches, and Civil Religion." *Annals of the American Academy of Political and Social Science* 387 (January 1970): 128–40.

Neuhaus, Richard John, and Michael Cromartie, eds. *Piety and Politics: Evangelicals and Fundamentalists Confront the World.* Washington, D.C.: Ethics and Public Policy Center, 1987.

Newman, Mark. *Divine Agitators: The Delta Ministry and Civil Rights in Mississippi.* Athens: University of Georgia, 2004.

Niebuhr, Gustav. "Church Council Meets amid Financial Crisis." *New York Times,* 13 November 1999, A13.

——. "Council of Churches Proposes Meeting with Christian Groups." *New York Times,* 23 October 2000, A14.

Niebuhr, H. Richard. *Christ and Culture.* New York: Harper and Row, 1951.

——. *The Kingdom of God in America.* New York: Harper and Row, 1937.

——. *The Social Sources of Denominationalism.* 1929. New York: World Publishing, 1971.

Niebuhr, H. Richard, Francis Miller, and Wilhelm Pauck. *The Church Against the World.* Chicago: Willet, Clark, 1935.

Niebuhr, Reinhold. "A Christian Journal Confronts Mankind's Continuing Crisis." *Christianity and Crisis,* 21 February 1966, 11–14.

——. *The Irony of American History.* New York: Charles Scribner's Sons, 1952.

——. "The King's Chapel and the King's Court." *Christianity and Crisis,* 4 August 1969, 211–12.

——. *Moral Man and Immoral Society.* 1932. New York: Charles Scribner's Sons, 1960.

——. "Politics, Patriotism and Integrity." *Christianity and Crisis,* 20 March 1967, 45–46.

——. "President Johnson's Foreign Policy." *Christianity and Crisis,* 16 March 1964, 31–32.

——. "Protestant Individualism and the Goldwater Movement." *Christianity and Crisis,* 14 December 1964, 248–49.

——. "A Time for Reassessment." *Christianity and Crisis,* 1 April 1968, 55–56.

——. "Vietnam: An Insoluble Problem." *Christianity and Crisis,* 8 February 1965, 1–2.

Noll, Mark A., and Luke E. Harlow, eds. *Religion and American Politics from the Colonial Period to the Present.* 1990. New York: Oxford University Press, 2007.

Novak, Michael. *A Theology for Radical Politics.* New York: Herder and Herder, 1969.

Nurser, John S. *For All Peoples and All Nations: The Ecumenical Church and Human Rights.* Washington, D.C.: Georgetown University Press, 2005.

Nutt, Rick. "For Truth and Liberty: Presbyterians and McCarthyism." *Journal of Presbyterian History* (Spring 2000): 51–66.

——. *Toward Peacemaking: Presbyterians in the South and National Security, 1945–1983.* Tuscaloosa: University of Alabama Press, 1994.

Oates, Stephen B. *Let the Trumpet Sound: The Life of Martin Luther King, Jr.* New York: Mentor Books, 1982.

Oden, Thomas C. *Turning Around the Mainline: How Renewal Movements Are Changing the Church.* Grand Rapids, MI: Baker Books, 2006.

"Of Betrayal and Loyalty." *Christian Century,* 30 June 1971, 792–93.

Oppenheimer, Mark. *Knocking on Heaven's Door: American Religion in the Age of the Counterculture.* New Haven: Yale University Press, 2003.

Orr, Alex. "The Clergy-Laity Gap." *Monday Morning,* 10 February 1969, 8–9.

———. "Why Are Ministers Bottlenecks?" *Monday Morning*, 15 January 1968, 6–7.

Orwin, Clifford. "The Unraveling of Christianity in America." *Public Interest* 155 (Spring 2004): 20–36.

Ostling, Richard N. "Warring over Where Donations Go." *Time*, 28 March 1983, 58–59.

Oxnam, Bromley. "Christian Responsibility on a Changing Planet." Fifth World Order Study Conference, Cleveland, 18 November 1958. RG 6, box 27, folder 24, NCC.

Pells, Richard H. *The Liberal Mind in a Conservative Age: American Intellectuals in the 1940s and 1950s*. New York: Harper and Row, 1985.

Perlstein, Rick. *Nixonland: The Rise of a President and the Fracturing of America*. New York: Scribner, 2008.

Piper, John F., Jr. "The Formation of the Social Policy of the Federal Council of Churches." *Journal of Church and State* 11.1 (1969): 63–82.

Porterfield, Amanda. *The Transformation of American Religion: A Story of a Late-Twentieth-Century Awakening*. New York: Oxford University Press, 2001.

Prados, John. *Vietnam: The History of an Unwinnable War, 1945–1975*. Lawrence: University Press of Kansas, 2009.

Pratt, Andrew LeRoy. "Religious Faith and Civil Religion: Evangelical Responses to the Vietnam War, 1964–1973." Ph.D. dissertation, Southern Baptist Theological Seminary, 1988.

Pratt, Henry J. "The Growth of Political Activism in the National Council of Churches." *Review of Politics* 34.3 (July 1972): 323–41.

———. *The Liberalization of American Protestantism: A Case Study in Complex Organizations*. Detroit: Wayne State University Press, 1972.

———. "Organizational Stress and Adaptation to Changing Political Status." *American Behavioral Scientist* 17.6 (July/August 1974): 865–84.

Quigley, Thomas E., ed. *American Catholics and Vietnam*. Grand Rapids, MI: William B. Eerdmans, 1968.

Raskin, Marcus G., and Bernard B. Fall, eds. *The Viet-Nam Reader: Articles and Documents on American Foreign Policy and the Viet-Nam Crisis*. New York: Vintage Books, 1965.

Riseling, Richard. "Having Met with the Enemy." *Mission* (March 1969): 22.

Rodell, Paul A. "International Voluntary Services in Vietnam: War and the Birth of Activism, 1958–1967." *Peace and Change: A Journal of Peace Research* 27.2 (April 2002): 225–44.

Roof, Wade, and William McKinney. *American Mainline Religion: Its Changing Shape and Future*. New Brunswick, NJ: Rutgers University Press, 1987.

Rose, Stephen. "Eugene Carson Blake: A Welcome-Home Interview." *Christian Century*, 18 October 1972, 1036–39.

Rottenberg, Isaac C. "Why Did the NCC Get Such Bad Press?" *Christianity Today*, 20 May 1983, 25–26.

Rotter, Andrew J. "Christians, Muslims, and Hindus: Religion and U.S.–South Asian Relations, 1947–1954." *Diplomatic History* 24 (Fall 2000): 593–640. With commentary by Robert Dean, Robert Buzzanco, and Patricia R. Hill.

Rowe, John Carlos, and Rick Berg, eds. *The Vietnam War and American Culture*. New York: Columbia University Press, 1991.

Roy, Ralph. "A Ministry of Schism." *The Pastor*, October 1952.

Ruether, Rosemary. "Who'll Investigate the Investigators?" *Worldview* (May 1971): 9–11.

Rusch, William G. *Ecumenical Reception: Its Challenge and Opportunity.* New York: William B. Eerdmans, 2007.

Rusk, Dean. *As I Saw It.* New York: Penguin Books, 1990.

Schmitz, David F. *Thank God They're on Our Side: The United States and Right-Wing Dictatorships, 1921–1965.* Chapel Hill: University of North Carolina Press, 1999.

——. *The United States and Right-Wing Dictatorships, 1965–1989.* Cambridge: Cambridge University Press, 2006.

Schneider, Robert A. "The Federal Council of Churches and American Presbyterians, 1900–1950." *Journal of Presbyterian History* 84.2 (1997): 103–22.

Schrading, Paul E. "The University Christian Movement: A Personal Remembrance." *Journal of Ecumenical Studies* 32.3 (Summer 1995): 340–52.

Schulman, Bruce J., and Julian E. Zelizer, eds. *Rightward Bound: Making America Conservative in the 1970s.* Cambridge: Harvard University Press, 2008.

Schultze, Quentin J. *Christianity and the Mass Media in America: Toward a Democratic Accommodation.* East Lansing: Michigan State University Press, 2003.

"Separation and Interaction of Church and State." *Journal of Church and State* 6.2 (Spring 1964): 147–53.

Settje, David. *Faith and War: How Christians Debated the Cold and Vietnam Wars.* New York: New York University Press, 2011.

——. *Lutherans and the Longest War: Adrift on a Sea of Doubt about the Cold and Vietnam Wars, 1964–1975.* Lexington, KY: Lexington Books, 2007.

Sheehan, Neil, and the *New York Times* Staff. *The Pentagon Papers.* 1971. New York: Bantam Books, 1971.

Sheerin, John B. "Who Speaks for the Church on Vietnam?" *Catholic World* 204.1220 (November 1966): 72–76.

Sherman, Franklin. "Church and Society at Detroit." *Christianity and Crisis,* 27 November 1967, 275–78.

Sincere, Richard E., Jr. "The Politics of Sentiment: U.S. Churches Approach Investment in South Africa." *South Africa International* 114.3 (1984): 453–66.

Sittser, Gerald. *A Cautious Patriotism: The American Churches and the Second World War.* Chapel Hill: University of North Carolina Press, 1997.

——. "Expanding Democracy on the Home Front: Religion in World War II." Unpublished paper.

——. "The Great Debate." Unpublished paper.

"'60 Minutes' Preview." *Christian Century,* 9 March 1983, 209–10.

Small, Melvin. *Antiwarriors: The Vietnam War and the Battle for America's Hearts and Minds.* Lanham, MD: Scholarly Resources, 2003.

——. *Johnson, Nixon, and the Doves.* New Brunswick, NJ: Rutgers University Press, 1988.

Smith, Paul Chaat, and Robert Allen Warrior. *Like a Hurricane: The Indian Movement from Alcatraz to Wounded Knee.* New York: New Press, 1996.

Smylie, James H. "American Religious Bodies, Just War, and Vietnam." *Journal of Church and State* 11 (Autumn 1969): 383–408. Reprinted in *American Presbyterians* 73.3 (Fall 1995): 187–202.

Smylie, Robert. "The China Issue: A Review of the Position of the National Council of Churches." *Christian Century,* 10 October 1973, 1003–7.

Sorenson, David S. "Food for Peace—Or Defense and Profit? The Role of P.L. 480, 1963–73." *Social Science Quarterly* 60 (June 1979): 62–71.

"Split Vote over Leadership Reflects National Council of Churches' Rift." *Los Angeles Times*, 20 May 1989, 6.

Spohn, Gustav. "NCC Leader Stuns Board." *Christianity Today*, 16 June 1989, 52.

"Spotlight on Vietnam." Editorial. *The Nation*, 7 July 1969.

Stammer, Larry B. "Church Councils Seek to Speak with One Voice." *Los Angeles Times*, 5 September 2000, A1.

Staub, Michael E., ed. *The Jewish 1960s: An American Sourcebook*. Waltham, MA: Brandeis University Press, 2004.

Stenning, Ronald. *Church World Service: Fifty Years of Help and Hope*. New York: Friendship Press, 1996.

Stone, Robert. "An Interview with Reinhold Niebuhr." *Christianity and Crisis*, 17 March 1969, 48–52.

Stormer, John A. *None Dare Call It Treason*. New York: Buccaneer Books, 1964.

"Suffering Ecumenical Cats." *Christian Century*, 11 February 1970, 163.

Sugrue, Thomas J. *Sweet Land of Liberty: The Forgotten Struggle for Civil Rights in the North*. New York: Random House, 2008.

Sullivan, Robert. "The Politics of Altruism: An Introduction to the Food for Peace Partnership between the United States Government and Voluntary Relief Agencies." *Western Political Quarterly* 23 (1970): 762–68.

———. "The Politics of Altruism: The American Church-State Conflict in the Food-for-Peace Program." *Journal of Church and State* 11 (Winter 1969): 47–61.

Summers, Anthony. *The Arrogance of Power: The Secret World of Richard Nixon*. New York: Penguin Books, 2000.

Sweet, Leonard. "The Modernization of Protestant Religion in America. In *Altered Landscapes*, ed. Lotz, 25–33.

Tait, Charles. "Whatever Happened to the State Department?" *The Nation*, 13 September 1965, 137–41.

Taylor, Kay. "Bishop Discusses Role: NCC at Wounded Knee." *Rapid City Journal*, 4 April 1973, CS, 1485-4-1:17, GCAH.

Tillich, Paul. *Interpretation of History*. New York: Charles Scribner's Sons, 1936.

———. *The Religious Situation*. New York: Henry Holt, 1932.

Timberg, Robert. *The Nightingale's Song*. New York: Touchstone, 1995.

Tollefson, James W. *The Strength Not to Fight: Conscientious Objectors of the Vietnam War in Their Own Words*. Washington, D.C.: Brassey's, 2000.

"Top Church Post Urged for Negro." *New York Times*, 2 December 1969.

Toulouse, Mark G. *The Transformation of John Foster Dulles: From Prophet of Realism to Priest of Nationalism*. Macon, GA: Mercer University Press, 1985.

Toy, E.V., Jr. "The National Lay Committee and the National Council of Churches: A Case Study of Protestants in Conflict." *American Quarterly* 21.2 (June 1969): 190–209.

U.S. Senate. *Report on the U.S. Senate Hearings: The Truth about Vietnam*. San Diego: Greenleaf Classics, 1966.

Van DeMark, Brian. *Into the Quagmire: Lyndon Johnson and the Escalation of the Vietnam War*. New York: Oxford University Press, 1995.

VanderWerf, Nathan. *The Times Were Very Full: A Perspective on the First Twenty-Five Years of the National Council of the Churches of Christ in the United States of America, 1950–1975*. New York: NCC, 1975.

Vinz, Warren. *Pulpit Politics: Faces of American Protestant Nationalism in the Twentieth Century*. Albany: State University of New York, 1997.

Wall, James. "'Integration' Sparks NCC Showdown." *Christian Century*, 4 November 1987, 955–56.

———. "The Quota: A Necessary Aberration." *Christian Century*, 20 December 1972, 1287.

———. "A Religious Mandate to Be Involved." *Christian Century*, 9 March 1983, 203.

———. "Strategy Conflict at Church World Service." Editorial, *Christian Century*, 17 July 1974, 715–16.

Wallis, Jim. *God's Politics: Why the Right Gets It Wrong and the Left Doesn't Get It.* New York: HarperCollins, 2005.

Walzer, Michael. *Just and Unjust Wars: A Moral Argument with Historical Illustrations.* New York: Basic Books, 1977.

Ward, Hiley H. "Broad New Church Council Urged at U.S. Meeting Here." *Detroit Free Press*, 1 December 1969, A:1, 6.

Warner, R. Stephen. *New Wine in Old Wineskins: Evangelicals and Liberals in a Small Town Church.* Berkeley and Los Angeles: University of California Press, 1988.

Warren, Heather. "The Theological Discussion Group and Its Impact on American and Ecumenical Theology, 1920–1945." *Church History* 62 (1993): 528–43.

Watson, Michael C. "A Layman and the National Council of Churches." *Christian Advocate*, 28 December 1967, 11–12.

Wechsler, James A. "A Studied Evasion." *New York Post*, 25 July 1972.

Weigel, George. *The Final Revolution: The Resistance Church and the Collapse of Communism.* New York: Oxford University Press, 1992

Wells, Ronald A. *The Wars of America: Christian Views.* Macon, GA: Mercer University Press, 1991.

Whitfield, Stephen. *The Culture of the Cold War.* Baltimore: Johns Hopkins University Press, 1991.

Wicker, Tom. *JFK and LBJ: The Influence of Personality upon Politics.* 1968. Chicago: Ivan R. Dee, 1991.

Wicklein, John. "Extremists Try to Curb Clergy." *New York Times*, 28 March 1960, 1.

Will, Herman. "How Churches Influence National Policy." *Christian Advocate*, 24 December 1970, 9–10.

———. *A Will for Peace.* Washington, D.C.: General Board of Church and Society of the United Methodist Church, 1984.

Willbanks, James H. *Abandoning Vietnam: How America Left and South Vietnam Lost Its War.* Lawrence: University Press of Kansas, 2004.

Wills, Garry. *Nixon Agonistes: The Crisis of the Self-Made Man.* 1969. New York: Mentor Books, 1979.

Wilson, E. Raymond. "Are We Serious about Social Action?" *Christian Century*, 10 February 1965, 169–71.

Wittner, Lawrence S. "Peace Movements and Foreign Policy: The Challenge to Diplomatic Historians." *Diplomatic History* 11 (Fall 1987): 355–70.

Wogaman, J. Philip. *Christian Perspectives on Politics.* 1988. Louisville, KY: Westminster John Knox Press, 2000.

Wood, James R. "Unanticipated Consequences of Organizational Coalitions: Ecumenical Cooperation and Civil Rights Policy." *Social Forces* 50.4 (May 1972): 512–21.

Woodger, Mary Jane. "Commentary on the Leadership of the Church of Jesus Christ of Latter-Day Saints during the Vietnam War." *Journal of American and Contemporary Cultures* 23.1 (Spring 2000): 53–61.

Woods, Jeff. *Black Struggle Red Scare: Segregation and Anti-Communism in the South, 1948–1968.* Baton Rouge: Louisiana State University, 2004.

Woodward, Kenneth L., with David Gates. "Ideology under the Alms." *Newsweek,* 7 February 1983, 61–62.

"World Council: Radical New Voice." *Time,* 5 August 1966, 69.

Woudenberg, Paul R. "Lay Members Don't Represent Local Churches." *Christian Advocate,* 19 May 1966, 14.

Wuthnow, Robert. "Beyond Quiet Influence? Possibilities for the Protestant Mainline." In Wuthnow and Evans, *Quiet Hand of God,* 381–403.

———. *The Restructuring of American Religion: Society and Faith since World War Two.* Princeton, NJ: Princeton University Press, 1988.

Wuthnow, Robert, and John H. Evans, eds. *The Quiet Hand of God: Faith-Based Activism and the Public Role of Mainline Protestantism.* Berkeley and Los Angeles: University of California, 2002.

Young, Marilyn B. *The Vietnam Wars, 1945–1990.* New York: Harper Perennial, 1991.

INDEX

Abu Ghraib, 367–68
Acheson, Dean, 46, 53, 212
Advisory Committee on Peace, 141, 152, 163, 232, 239
Afghanistan, 374, 379, 381
African Americans, 17, 272, 335. *See also* Black Manifesto; civil rights movement; Forman, James; racism
Agnew, Spiro, 221, 253, 300–301, 394
Air Force Reserve Center Training Manual, 59–61
American Baptist Convention, 224, 231, 379
American Civil Liberties Union (ACLU), 152, 201, 240
American Council of Christian Churches (ACCC), 18, 47–48, 369. *See also* McIntire, Carl
American Friends Service Committee (AFSC), 149, 254, 325
American Indians, American Indian Movement (AIM), 272, 290, 293, 356–58, 404
American way of life, 42, 49, 53. *See also* nationalism, Christian
Americans for Democratic Action, 252, 325
amnesty, 220, 234, 334, 346, 352, 358, 408
Anglicans, 185, 191
anticommunism: of conservative Protestants, 40–41, 44; early impact on ecumenism, 37, 40–52; of ecumenists, general, 41, 45, 115, 169; influence on views of Vietnam War, 71–73, 90, 103, 114, 120–21, 346; of NCC, 46–47, 53, 100, 115, 118, 156–57, 178, 184, 231–33, 395, 412, 441n22. *See also* McCarthyism
anti-Iraq War movement, 380, 416; and respectability of religious groups, 380
anti-Vietnam War movement, 186, 205–6, 249, 251; beginnings, and Johnson administration, 89–90, 99–100; criticism of, 112–13, 203, 212, 221, 224, 253, 256, 306, 367–68, 380; divisions within, 89–91, 112–13, 139, 221, 253, 278, 305–6, 318, 403; ecumenical approach to, 140, 147, 210, 355; government

harassment of, 221, 251, 253, 303–5, 326–27; and prowar protestors, 253, 255; religious involvement in, general, 100, 112, 140, 150, 167, 203–04, 215, 234, 254, 305–9, 324–25, 401; and respectability of religious groups, 113, 125, 138, 176, 183, 321, 325, 355, 395; and veterans, 325–27. *See also* draft; Mobilization (Mobe); Moratorium; protests spring of 1971
Appeal to the Churches Concerning Vietnam (NCC's), 161–62, 165–66
Archbishop of Canterbury, 191
Argue, Donald, 373
Armstrong, James, 241, 324, 342
Asians. *See* East Asia Christian Conference; NCC: listening to Asians
audits. *See* Internal Revenue Service
Axial Age, sages: and ecumenical way, 5, 426–27, 430

Baraka, Imamu Amiri (LeRoi Jones), 351–52
Barmen Declaration, 29
Barrett, George, 168, 183, 185
Baugher, Norman, 104, 107
Bennett, Anne, 143, 241
Bennett, John, 35, 38, 112–13, 280, 446n17; on campaign of 1964, 83; on communism, Cold War, 42, 52–53; on General Assembly 1966, 161–62; on Humphrey's candidacy, 224; on mobilizing laity, 349–50; on morality of the war, 323, 350; pushing NCC on Vietnam, 80, 95–96; and Riverside Church antiwar speech, 176; on U.S. Vietnam policy, 142
Berger, Peter, 332
Bernstein, Daniel, 304–5
Berrigan, Daniel, 349
Berrigan, Philip, 254
Bilheimer, Robert E. (Bobby), 191–92, 409, 412–13, 425
Bilheimer, Robert S., 341–43; on addressing injustices, 146, 275, 412–13; on anti-

401–2; resources for international affairs, 93, 108–9. *See also* clergy-laity gap; Bilheimer, Robert S.; *denominations by name*; Staff Associates for Departments of International Affairs

deserters. *See* resisters, draft and war

DeVelder, Marion, 270

Diem, Ngo Dinh. *See* Ngo Dinh Diem

Dietterich, Paul, 151, 194

Disciples of Christ, 158, 216, 231, 233, 379

dissent: NCC's defense of, 54, 56, 58, 60, 116, 141, 308, 393, 408

Division of Christian Life and Mission (DCLM, NCC's), 63, 202; elimination of, 351, 359, 362

Division of Christian Life and Work (DCLW, NCC's), 55, 63

Division of Church and Society (DCS, NCC's), 351, 359, 362

Division of Overseas Ministries (DOM, NCC's), 107, 111, 117, 119, 177, 362–64, 372. *See also* Church World Service

Dominican Republic, 99

draft, conscription: civil disobedience and, 190, 200–201, 211, 268–69, 408; and Congressional hearings on, 168; and lottery system, 277, 327; and NCC, 180, 190, 200–201, 211, 288, 327, 407–8; protests of, 112, 190, 288. *See also* civil disobedience; conscientious objection; resisters

Dulles, John Foster, 50, 129, 181; and anti-communism, 41; critiqued by ecumenists, 52–59, 156; and Fifth World Order Study Conference, 55, 422n40; influence of, 167; and a "Just and Durable Peace," 38; and United Nations, 38–40

Dumas, Andre, 335

East Asia Christian Conference (EACC): Bangkok meeting of 1965, 109, 119–22; influence on NCC, 91–93, 103–4; influence on WCC, 156

economics: conservative Protestant views of, 33, 47–49; ecumenical views of, 17, 323, 338, 376. *See also* capitalism; labor

Eculink, 374

ecumania, ecumaniac, 25, 435n4

ecumenical way: author's reflections on, 425–30

Ecumenical Witness conference: build-up to, 323, 328–30, 333; evaluations of, 338–40; and investment profits from

war, 335–36; local network and inquiry groups, 333, 340, 346–47; message and actions, 337–38; new breed versus traditional ecumenism, 336–37; preparation and purpose of, 333–34, 377, 394, 413; speeches and topics, 334–37

ecumenism: on communism, 80; and communication methods, 26, 298; conferences, role of, 26, 36–37, 330, 410; conservatives' use of term, 412, 424; decline of interest in, 386, 398–99; decline of real ecumenism, 6, 146, 218–19, 266, 274, 329–30, 353, 360, 370–72, 384–85, 405, 422–23; definition of, 5–6, 147, 149–50, 384, 401–2; divisions between traditionalists and new breeders, general, 146, 149–50, 218–19, 274–75, 329–30, 337, 354–55, 365, 370–72, 403; divisions between traditionalists and new breeders in NCC, 149, 360, 385, 392–93, 405; divisions within, general, 7, 28, 274, 364–65, 424; Faith and Order, Life and Work movements, 18, 24, 37–38, 360, 384–85, 425; history of, 18–19, 24–25, 32–37; image problem in Asia, 92–93, 107, 111; and imperialism (*see* imperialism); institutional and structural issues, 298–300, 384–87, 401–2, 423, 427; listening to non-western perspectives, 81, 410; malaise in, 237–39; misunderstanding of, 5–6, 147, 423, 425; renewal and unity, processes of, 6, 160–61, 218, 249, 274–75, 334, 354, 413–14, 426, 513n19; teaching of, 399–400, 423–25, 428; on theology (*see* theology); triumphalism of, 29, 37, 47, 333, 345, 391; vision, goals and manifestations of, 5–6, 8–9, 23–28, 33, 35–37, 44, 210, 236, 274–75, 314, 316, 384, 389–91, 423–26, 428. *See also* Bilheimer, Robert S.; clergy-laity gap; Confessing Church; NCC; prophetic voice; "peace with justice," Student Christian Movement

Edelman, Marion Wright, 334–35

Edgar, Robert: and CWS, 374–75; critiqued, 384; departed NCC, 385; and the Iraq War, 294, 378–81, 415–16; and the media, 380; and *Middle Church*, 424; new breed style of, 377–80, 384; on prophetic role, 377–78; vision for NCC, 376–78, 415, 424

Eisenhower, Dwight D., 100–101; Asian policy of, 55; and civil religion, national-